W9-APD-845

Economics: A Contemporary Introduction

Fifth Edition

William A. McEachern

Professor of Economics

University of Connecticut

Prepared by

John Lunn

Hope College

South-Western College Publishing
Thomson Learning™

Australia • Canada • Denmark • Japan • Mexico • New Zealand • Philippines
Puerto Rico • Singapore • South Africa • Spain • United Kingdom • United States

Study Guide to accompany *Economics*, by William A. McEachern
Acquisitions Editor: Keri L. Witman
Developmental Editor: Dennis Hanseman
Marketing Manager: Lisa L. Lysne
Production Editor: Vicky True
Manufacturing Coordinator: Georgina Calderon
Cover Design: Tin Box Studio
Cover Illustrator: John Mattos
Production House: DPS Associates
Printer: Globus Printing, Inc.

Printed in the United States of America
1 2 3 4 5 02 01 00 99

For more information contact South-Western College Publishing, 5101 Madison Road,
Cincinnati, Ohio, 45227 or find us on the Internet at http://www.swcollege.com

For permission to use material from this text or product, contact us by
• **telephone: 1-800-730-2214**
• **fax: 1-800-730-2215**
• **web: http://www.thomsonrights.com**

ISBN: 0-538-88850-4

This book is printed on acid-free paper.

PREFACE

The purpose of this *Study Guide* is to provide a review of the materials in the textbook, exercises for you to practice using the analytical tools presented in the text, and an opportunity for you to check your understanding of the material. Each chapter in the *Study Guide* contains an introduction; an outline of the text chapter; a discussion of the chapter's topics; some extensions or examples of materials in the text in a section entitled "Lagniappe" (which is a French term used in Louisiana—it means "a little extra," something added for good measure); a list of key terms; review questions; and answers to all the questions.

You should always read the text before using the *Study Guide*. The discussion section presented in the *Study Guide* is not a substitute for the textbook. In fact, you will be unable to answer some of the questions in the *Study Guide* if you have not read the text. Work through the questions and answers carefully, making sure that you understand why the correct answers are correct. Note, too, that the answers to the discussion questions are suggestive rather than full and complete.

Thanks to my wife, Sheryl, and my children—Robert, David, and Shelley—for putting up with my grumbling when I had trouble coming up with just one more multiple-choice question. Thanks also to Robert and his wife, Amy, and Kristin Kotman and Joy Forgwe for their help in preparing the manuscript for publication.

John Lunn

CONTENTS

CHAPTER 1

The Art and Science of Economic Analysis

I. INTRODUCTION

This chapter presents an overview of economics and tells how economic analysis is performed. In particular, it introduces the concept of the economic problem and an important type of economic analysis: marginal analysis. There is also an appendix that discusses how graphs are used. Other tools of economic analysis are presented in the next chapter.

II. OUTLINE

1.   The Economic Problem. Because resources are scarce and human wants are unlimited, people cannot have everything they want. Economics is the study of how individuals choose to use their scarce resources in an attempt to satisfy their unlimited wants.

    1.1   Resources
        a.   Land (includes all natural resources). Payments to land are called *rent*.
        b.   Labor (physical and mental effort). Payments to labor are called *wages*.
        c.   Capital. Payments to capital are called *interest*.
            (1)   Physical capital (manufactured items used in the production of goods)
            (2)   Human capital (knowledge and skills people acquire to enhance their ability to produce)
        d.   Entrepreneurial ability (the talent of a person who tries to discover and exploit profitable activities). Payments for entrepreneurial ability are called *profit*.

    1.2   Goods and Services
        a.   Goods and services are produced to satisfy human wants.
        b.   Goods are tangible; services are intangible.
        c.   Both goods and services require scarce resources and are therefore themselves scarce.
        d.   Without scarcity there would be no economic problem.

    1.3   Economic Decision Makers
        a.   There are four types of decision makers in the economy: households, firms, governments, and the rest of the world.
        b.   Markets are the means by which buyers and sellers carry out exchanges.

    1.4   Microeconomics and Macroeconomics
        a.   Microeconomics is the study of how individual economic agents make decisions and how the choices of various decision makers are coordinated.
        b.   Macroeconomics is the study of the economy as a whole.

2.   The Art of Economic Analysis

   2.1   Rational Self-Interest
          a.   Economists assume that individuals act in their own best interests.
          b.   Economists also assume that individuals are rational, which means that people try to make
                the best choices possible under the circumstances.

   2.2   Economic Analysis Is Marginal Analysis
          a.   Marginal means "incremental" or "decremental."
          b.   An individual changes his or her behavior whenever the expected marginal benefit from
                doing so is greater than the expected marginal cost.

   2.3   Choice Requires Time and Information

   2.4   Normative versus Positive Analysis
          a.   A positive statement is one that can be verified by referring to the facts.
          b.   A normative statement is a statement representing someone's opinion or values; it cannot
                be proved or disproved.

3.   The Science of Economic Analysis

   3.1   The Role of Theory
          a.   A theory, or model, is a simplification of reality that focuses on only the most important
                features of a relationship.
          b.   Theory is needed to determine which facts are relevant to an analysis of a relationship.
          c.   Theory is also used to make predictions about the real world.

   3.2   The Scientific Method
          a.   Step One: Identify and define the relevant variables. (A variable is a quantity that can take
                on different possible values.)
          b.   Step Two: State the assumptions that specify the conditions under which the theory is to
                apply.
                (1)   *Ceteris paribus*: other things are held constant
                (2)   Behavioral assumption: a notion concerning individual behavior that is taken to be
                       true; for example, rational self-interest
          c.   Step Three: Formulate hypotheses about relations among the key variables.
          d.   Step Four: Test the theory.

   3.3   Economists Tell Stories

   3.4   *CASE STUDY:* A Yen for Vending Machines

   3.5   Predicting Average Behavior
          a.   Economic theories do not permit an economist to predict the behavior of individuals because
                any individual may behave in unpredictable ways.
          b.   The random behaviors of individuals tend to cancel each other, so the average behavior of
                a large group can be predicted.

3.6 Some Pitfalls of Faulty Economic Analysis
   a. Fallacy That Association Is Causation. It is a mistake in analysis to think that one event caused another simply because the first event preceded the second.
   b. Fallacy of Composition. It is erroneous to believe that what is true for the individual is true for the group.
   c. Mistake of Ignoring the Secondary Effects. Economic analysis should not ignore secondary effects, which develop slowly over time as people react to events.

3.7 If Economists Are So Smart, Why Aren't They Rich? The economics profession thrives because its models usually do a better job of explaining the real world than do alternative approaches.

3.8 *CASE STUDY:* College Major and Career Earnings

4. Appendix: Understanding Graphs. Graphs are a way of compressing information.

   4.1 Drawing Graphs. Graphs can express three types of relations between two variables:
      a. Positive (direct) relation: as one variable increases, the other variable increases.
      b. Negative (inverse) relation: as one variable increases, the other variable decreases.
      c. Independent relation: as one variable increases, the other remains constant; the variables are unrelated.

   4.2 The Slopes of Straight Lines. Slope is the change in the vertical distance between two points divided by the corresponding change in the horizontal distance between the points.

   4.3 The Slope, Units of Measurement, and Marginal Analysis
      a. The mathematical value of the slope depends on the units of measurement on the graph (e.g., the slope of a line relating price and output will be different if output is measured in feet than if it is measured in yards).
      b. The slope measures the marginal effects, so it is important in economic analysis.

   4.4 The Slopes of Curved Lines
      a. Slope of a curved line is different for each point on the curve.
      b. Slope of a curved line at a point is found by measuring the slope of a straight line tangent to the curve at the point.

   4.5 Curve Shifts. A curve can shift when a variable not measured on the horizontal or vertical axis changes.

III. DISCUSSION

The Economic Problem

   Two facts of life create the economic problem: scarce resources and unlimited human wants. Resources are combined to produce *goods* and *services*. Because resources are scarce, not all goods and services that people desire can be produced; that is, goods and services are also scarce. Consequently, individuals must make choices. Even though we cannot have everything we want, we can have some of the things we want.

Households, firms, governments, and the rest of the world are the four economic actors in the economy. Households act both as consumers who demand the goods and services produced and as resource owners who supply resources to firms and government. Everybody owns at least one productive resource: his or her own labor. Firms supply goods and services to consumers by hiring resources to produce them. The government provides some goods and services, such as national defense that tend not to be produced by private firms. The government also makes and enforces rules to be followed by other economic actors. The rest of the world includes foreign households, firms, and governments.

Buyers and sellers come together to carry out exchange in *markets*. Some markets—farmers' markets, for example—are physical places with specific geographic locations. Other markets are less concrete and consist of communications by individuals thousands of miles apart. For example, people can order books from a book club through the mail.

Economics is broken down into two parts: *microeconomics* and *macroeconomics*. Microeconomics concerns the economic behavior of individual decision makers, such as the consumer, the worker, and the manager of a firm. Macroeconomics examines the economic system as a whole and tries to explain unemployment, inflation, and economic growth.

The Art of Economic Analysis

Economists assume that people are motivated by self-interest. This means that they not only act selfishly, but that they also make choices that will make them better off, as they themselves define "better off." Religious or political zealots who risk their lives for a cause presumably do so because they believe they will be better off for doing so. Self-interest, by itself, does not allow us to make predictions or to explain human behavior adequately. However, when the assumption of rationality is added, we can begin to analyze and explain human behavior. By "rational" we mean consistent and reasonable. If we assume that people behave consistently, then we can predict how they will change their behavior when they face different economic environments.

It is very rare for people to have to make all-or-nothing decisions. Instead, decisions usually involve choices between the status quo and something else. One chooses among having apple pie for dessert, cake for dessert, or no dessert at all. A decision is made on the basis of a comparison of the extra (*marginal*) benefits and the extra (marginal) costs of the contemplated change. When marginal benefits exceed marginal costs, the individual makes the change.

Rational choice takes time and information. A choice can be a poor one if a decision maker lacks good information. The collection and assimilation of information take time and use up resources. Rational individuals collect information from a variety of sources as long as the expected marginal benefit of doing so exceeds the expected marginal cost.

Economists distinguish between positive economic statements and normative economic statements. *Positive economic statements* are associated with economic theory and involve facts or predictions that are testable. *Normative economic statements* involve value judgments and opinions. The statement "Tariffs on imported steel will increase employment in the U.S. steel industry" is an example of a positive statement. "Higher tariffs should be placed on imported steel" is an example of a normative statement.

The Science of Economic Analysis

An economy as large, diverse, and interrelated as the U.S. economy is too complex for any individual to understand. There is so much economic data that people cannot understand the reason for every transaction. A *theory* is used to reduce the complexity of an economic system to manageable limits. Consequently, a theory does not contain all relevant details and facts. A theory attempts to simplify economic reality by capturing the essential features of economic relations.

Economic analysis follows the scientific method, which can be broken down into four steps. First, the relevant *variables* must be identified and defined. Second, the assumptions that specify the conditions under which the theory applies must be identified. In economics, it is common to employ the assumption of *ceteris paribus*, which means "other things held constant." For example, when we say that a higher price for a good causes fewer units of the good to be sold, we hold income and tastes, among other things, constant. Third, hypotheses about the relations among variables are stated. These generally take the form of if-then statements. Fourth, the hypotheses are tested.

Some Pitfalls of Economic Thinking

It is easy to fall into several traps that lead to incorrect economic thinking. The *association-causation fallacy* is common. It is especially easy to fall into this trap when one event precedes another in time. It can even be the case that the second event caused the first event. For example, if one observed that many people at the race track were betting on a particular horse and then observed that that particular horse won the race, it would be erroneous to conclude that the horse won because many people bet on it. Rather, people expected the horse to win so they bet on the horse. Another common error is the *fallacy of composition*, which is the mistaken belief that what is true for the individual is also true for the group. One person can see a football game better by standing up, but if everyone stands nobody has a better view. Mistakes are also made when people ignore the *secondary effects* of an economic activity or policy.

Appendix: Understanding Graphs

If this is your first course in economics, read the appendix to this chapter in the textbook carefully. Economists often use *graphs* to represent relations. Graphs generally reflect a relation between two variables, such as price and quantity, money supply and interest rates, or wages and hours worked. An *independent variable* is one that has a causal effect on another variable. The other variable is called the *dependent variable* because its value depends on the value of the first variable.

A question that is often of interest in economics is whether one variable has a *positive*, or *direct*, effect on another variable or an *inverse*, or *negative*, effect. Exhibit 1 shows a line that represents a consumption function. The independent variable is income and the dependent variable is consumption expenditures. The graph represents the assumption that as a family's income increases, its consumption spending also increases. Hence, there is a direct, or positive, relation between a family's income and the amount the family spends.

Exhibit 1

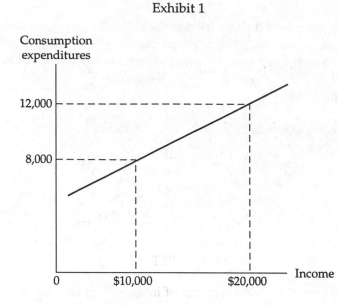

A negative, or inverse, relation is illustrated in Exhibit 2. Here the independent variable is hours of practice and the dependent variable is one's golf score. The more one practices, the lower the golf score will be.

Exhibit 2

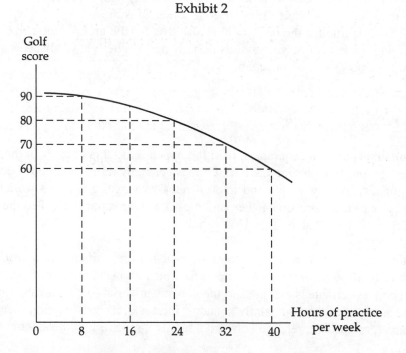

The *slope* of a line is the amount the vertical variable changes for a given increase in the horizontal variable. The slope of an upward-sloping line is positive; the slope of a downward-sloping line is negative. The slope of a straight line is constant, but the slope of a curved line changes at every point. To find the slope of a curved line at a point, draw a straight line *tangent* to the point. The slope of this line is the slope of the curved line at that point. Make sure that you understand the graphs that are used in the appendix in the textbook.

IV. LAGNIAPPE

The Consumption Function

The theory of the consumption function can be used to illustrate the scientific method as it is applied in economics. John Maynard Keynes developed the theory of the consumption function during the Great Depression. He identified two key variables—consumption spending and income—and hypothesized that people spend some percentage of any increase in income on goods and save the rest. Hence, consumption is a function of income. After World War II, many economists forecast a recession on the basis of the consumption function theory. They argued that incomes would fall after the war; this would lead to reduced consumption spending, which would reduce the incomes of even more people. However, the recession did not materialize. This caused some economists to reexamine the consumption function. Milton Friedman altered the theory by pointing out that people do not respond to temporary fluctuations in their incomes by altering consumption spending greatly. Instead, they make consumption spending decisions on the basis of their expected long-term average, or permanent, income. Once the theory was modified to include longer-term considerations, it was used more successfully in making predictions.

Question to Think About: Does the percentage of income spent on consumption goods vary with age?

Heroic Self-Interest

As stated before, the assumption of self-interest does not imply that people always behave in a selfish manner. Each person defines his or her own self-interest in a different way. Most of us probably would not consider actions that are likely to lead to our death as being in our self-interest. Yet it is possible for people to believe that. The ancient Greeks wrote of heroes who valued fame more than life and who were willing to die to gain this fame. In the story of the Trojan War, the gods had foretold that the first Greek who landed on Trojan soil would die. A young man named Protesilaos jumped ashore first so that his name would go down in history. The greatest Greek hero, Achilles, faced the option of going to Troy, where he would gain great fame and die, or staying at home, where he would live a long life and remain unknown. He chose to go to Troy. Evidently, he perceived it to be in his self-interest to gain fame rather than to die an unknown.

Question to Think About: Do you think all ancient Greeks would have made the same decision that Achilles made?

V. KEY TERMS

resources
economics
behavioral assumption
land
labor
capital
human capital
entrepreneurial ability
rent
wages
profit
interest
good
service
scarcity
market
product market
resource market
microeconomics
macroeconomics
rational self-interest
marginal

positive economic statement
normative economic statement
economic theory, or economic model
variable
other-things-constant assumption
hypothesis
association-causation fallacy
fallacy of composition
secondary effects
origin
horizontal axis
vertical axis
graph
time-series graph
functional relation
dependent variable
independent variable
positive, or direct, relation
negative, or inverse, relation
slope
tangent

VI. QUESTIONS

A. Completion

1. _____ is the study of how individuals use their _____ resources to satisfy their _____ wants.

2. The ultimate raw material associated with labor is _____.

3. There are two kinds of capital, _____ capital and _____ capital.

4. _____ includes management and organizational skills, combined with a willingness to take risks.

5. The entrepreneur is the _____ claimant.

6. An automobile is a _____; an airplane ride is a _____.

7. Exchange is carried out in _____.

8. A key behavioral assumption concerning human economic behavior is that of _____.

9. Economic choice usually involves a comparison of _____ benefits and costs.

10. A _____ is a simplification of economic reality that tries to capture the most important elements of the relation under consideration.

11. A _____ is a quantity that can take on different possible values.

12. _____ are conditional statements of the if-then variety.

13. A _____ economic statement represents an opinion.

14. Unintended consequences that develop slowly over time as people respond to circumstances are called _____ effects.

15. The relation between income and consumption is _____ because increases in income lead to increases in consumption.

B. True/False

_____ 1. The economic problem results from the fact that resources are scarce but human wants tend to be limitless.

_____ 2. A student's knowledge of computer programming is an example of human capital.

_____ 3. Profit goes to the owners of capital.

_____ 4. All goods are scarce but not all services are scarce.

_____ 5. Product markets refer to specific geographic locations.

_____ 6. Microeconomics is the study of the economy as a whole.

_____ 7. People who give to charity cannot be motivated by rational self-interest.

_____ 8. A decision to go to one college instead of another is an example of a marginal decision.

_____ 9. Time is a scarce resource.

_____ 10. Rational self-interest directs people to make any choice for which the total benefits exceed the total costs.

_____ 11. Good theories contain as many details as possible.

_____ 12. Assumptions are used to simplify theories by eliminating areas that are not expected to have important effects on the analysis.

_____ 13. A theory is not good if it cannot predict accurately all the time.

_____ 14. A positive statement is one that can be verified by reference to facts.

_____ 15. If one event follows another, then the first event necessarily caused the second event.

_____ 16. Policymakers generally pay close attention to both the primary and the secondary effects of policies.

_____ *17. Two variables are independent if increases in one leave the second unchanged.

_____ *18. The slope of a vertical line is zero.

C. Multiple Choice

1. Which of the following is an example of a scarce resource?
   a. coal
   b. water
   c. unskilled labor
   d. time
   e. All of the above.

2. Crude oil is considered which kind of resource?
   a. land
   b. labor
   c. physical capital
   d. human capital
   e. None of the above.

3. Since goods are scarce,
   a. we always have to pay money for the goods we get.
   b. we never can get what we want.
   c. everybody wants some of each good that exists.
   d. we must choose among them.
   e. a and d

4. Services differ from goods in that services
   a. do not always use scarce resources.
   b. do not always satisfy wants.
   c. often do not have a price.
   d. are intangible.
   e. are provided by the government.

5. Markets include
   a. shopping malls.
   b. arrangements by which buyers and sellers communicate their intentions.
   c. union hiring halls.
   d. All of the above.
   e. a and b only

---

*Throughout this study guide, asterisks next to question numbers indicate that the material is discussed in an appendix.

6. Which of the following decisions is not consistent with rational self-interest?
   a. giving money to charity
   b. choosing to work for the Peace Corps instead of for a large corporation
   c. buying a car without knowing everything about it
   d. becoming a bullfighter
   e. All are consistent with rational self-interest.

7. Economic choices are made by comparing
   a. total benefits and total costs.
   b. marginal benefits and marginal costs.
   c. average benefits and average costs.
   d. the behavior of rational people with that of irrational people.
   e. any of the above except d.

8. People are rational if they
   a. have perfect information about the future.
   b. know and understand philosophy.
   c. are selfish.
   d. make the best choices they can given their circumstances.
   e. None of the above.

9. If consumers must collect information to make rational decisions, then they should collect additional information as long as
   a. it helps them make good decisions.
   b. they learn something from the additional information.
   c. the marginal cost of the information is less than the expected marginal benefit from the information.
   d. there is anything they do not know about the good.
   e. All of the above.

10. A good theory is one that
    a. best replicates reality.
    b. uses the fewest assumptions.
    c. predicts more accurately than other theories.
    d. cannot be proven wrong.
    e. All of the above.

11. The validity of a theory is determined by
    a. testing the reasonableness of its assumptions.
    b. testing its predictions with evidence.
    c. making sure its variables are well defined.
    d. None of the above.
    e. All of the above.

12. *Ceteris paribus* means
    a. economic man.
    b. other things constant.
    c. the fallacy of composition.
    d. secondary effects.
    e. positive economics.

13. A positive statement is one that
    a. can be supported or rejected with reference to the facts.
    b. states how things ought to be.
    c. is true.
    d. cannot be refuted.
    e. all economists agree on.

14. Which of the following is an example of a normative statement?
    a. The rate of inflation is lower today than it was ten years ago.
    b. High interest rates cause lower economic growth.
    c. Since price controls cause shortages, the government should not use price controls to combat inflation.
    d. Per capita income is higher in the Soviet Union than in the United States.
    e. Tariffs result in higher prices to consumers.

15. Suppose that some individual decision makers in Los Angeles decide that removing the pollution control equipment on their cars will not have a noticeable effect on pollution in the area. Several months later pollution levels are higher than ever. The decision makers have fallen into
    a. ignoring the secondary effects.
    b. the fallacy that association is causation.
    c. the fallacy of composition.
    d. irrational self-interest.
    e. None of the above.

16. It has been found that minimum wage laws increase unemployment among teenagers. This is an example of
    a. ignoring the secondary effects.
    b. the fallacy that association is causation.
    c. the fallacy of composition.
    d. irrational self-interest.
    e. None of the above.

Exhibit 3

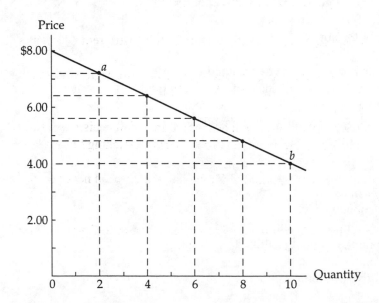

*17. In Exhibit 3, the relationship between price and quantity depicted by line *ab* is
   a. positive, with slope 0.4.
   b. positive, with slope –0.4.
   c. inverse, with slope –2.5.
   d. inverse, with slope –0.4.
   e. positive, with slope 2.5.

*18. The value of a dependent variable is determined by
   a. the value of the independent variable.
   b. the values of other dependent variables.
   c. the assumptions of the model.
   d. the reliability of the theory.
   e. b and d.

*19. A straight line is tangent to a curve at point *A*. If the slope of the straight line is +3, the slope of the curve at *A*
   a. is between 0 and +3.
   b. is equal to +3.
   c. is equal to –3.
   d. is more than +3.
   e. The slope cannot be determined without more information.

*20. If consumption is on the vertical axis and income is on the horizontal axis, a 45-degree line represents the
   a. expected relation between income and consumption.
   b. marginal benefit from another dollar of income.
   c. marginal cost of another dollar of income.
   d. best combination of income and consumption for a rational consumer.
   e. combination of points where consumption equals income.

D.   Discussion Questions

   1. Explain how scarcity and choice are related.

   2. How are human capital and entrepreneurial ability different from labor?

   3. The text says that a study of economic aggregates must begin with an understanding of individual choice. Why is this so?

   4. Explain the concept of rational decision making. Can decisions a student makes about what to take to college be said to involve rational decision-making? Explain.

   5. "People don't really act rationally. If they did, there would never be any mistakes." Evaluate this statement.

   6. The number of people volunteering to serve in the Peace Corps increased greatly during the late 1960s. Can you offer an explanation for this?

7. Sales of automobiles increased in December 1986 and fell in January 1987. The deductibility of sales taxes ended on December 31, 1986. Did the change in the tax laws affect sales of autos in December and January? Explain.

8. The text says that a company's decision to build a plant in Mexico can be an example of a marginal decision. Explain how such a large investment can be described as marginal.

9. People usually spend more time deciding which car to buy than they do choosing a brand of toothpaste. Can you offer an explanation for this observation?

10. Economic theory says that a rise in the price of a good will cause people to buy less of it. If the price of meat increases and John Doe buys more meat, has the theory been refuted? Explain.

11. How are economic theory and positive statements related?

12. Discuss the four steps of the scientific method.

13. How do predictions and forecasts differ?

14. If association is not the same as causation, then how can we determine when one variable affects another?

*15. Use the following information to answer the question below:

$x =$	0	2	4	6	8	10	12	14	16	18	20
$y =$	0	1	2	3	4	5	6	7	8	9	10

Exhibit 4

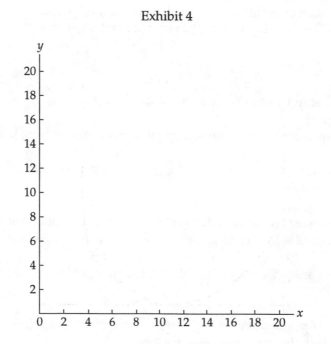

a. Graph the relation between x and y on Exhibit 4.
b. Is this a positive or a negative relation? How do you know?
c. What is the slope of the line?

*16. You are given the following information regarding the price of eggs and the quantity purchased.

Price:	$1.00	0.90	0.80	0.70	0.60	0.50	0.40
Quantity (dozens):	1	2	3	4	5	6	7

Exhibit 5

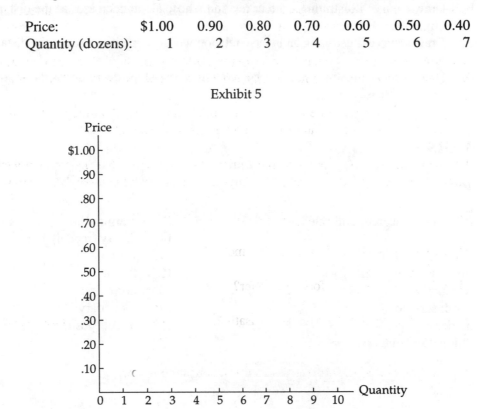

a. Graph the relation between price and quantity purchased on Exhibit 5.
b. What is the slope of the line?

*17. In Exhibit 6, what is the slope of the curve at point *a*? point *b*? point *c*? point *d*?

Exhibit 6

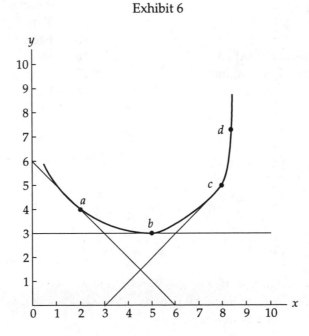

*18. a. Draw a curve whose slope increases with distance from the origin.
      b. Draw a curve illustrating a direct relation whose slope decreases as the distance from the origin increases.
      c. Draw a curve illustrating an inverse relation whose slope increases as the distance from the origin increases.
      d. Draw a curve illustrating an inverse relation whose slope decreases as the distance from the origin increases.

VII. ANSWERS

A. *Completion*

1. Economics; scarce; unlimited
2. time
3. human; physical
4. Entrepreneurial ability
5. residual
6. good; service
7. markets
8. rational self-interest
9. marginal
10. theory (model)
11. variable
12. Predictions
13. normative
14. secondary
15. direct (positive)

B. *True/False*

1. True
2. True
3. False
4. False
5. False
6. False
7. False
8. True
9. True
10. False. Decisions are based on marginal benefits and marginal costs.
11. False
12. True
13. False. A theory is good not because it predicts accurately all the time but because it predicts better than other theories.
14. True
15. False
16. False
17. True
18. False

C. *Multiple Choice*

1. e
2. a
3. d
4. d
5. d
6. e
7. b
8. d
9. c
10. c
11. b
12. b
13. a
14. c
15. c
16. a
17. d
18. a
19. b
20. e

D.   Discussion Questions

1. Scarcity implies that we cannot have everything that we want. Our resources are limited, so we must choose which of the many possible goods and services we will have. This applies to society as well as to any individual.

2. Human capital differs from labor in that human capital involves knowledge that people acquire to increase their *ability* to produce, whereas labor refers to the human time spent in production. Entrepreneurial ability is the special talent of bringing other resources together to produce goods in new and more profitable ways.

3. All choices are made by individuals. Consequently, to understand how the choices of many individuals affect the economy, it helps to know how the individual choices were made and how they interact to determine the aggregate performance.

4. Rational decision making involves comparing the status quo with the marginal benefits and marginal costs of alternative situations. The rational individual chooses so as to make himself or herself as well off as possible, given the constraints the individual faces. A college student cannot take everything to the dorm, so the student must choose which items to take. The things that are most likely to be used at college will go; those that are less likely to be used will not go. The larger the dorm room and the larger the vehicle taking the things, the more the student will take to college.

5. People do not know all possible effects of every decision. Therefore, people sometimes make mistakes. If individuals had better information, they would choose differently.

6. One explanation is that the military was drafting eligible young men in the late 1960s to fight in the Vietnam War. The Peace Corps was an alternative to the military, so many chose to join the Peace Corps.

7. Yes. People who were considering the purchase of a new car were spurred to act before the end of December to avoid the tax penalty. On the margin, it was more attractive to buy a new car in December 1986 than in January 1987.

8. A new plant increases the productive capacity of a firm. If the firm wants to increase capacity, it must either build a new plant or expand an existing plant. The decision is a marginal decision because it involves a change from the status quo rather than an all-or-nothing decision.

9. People make decisions on the basis of expected marginal benefits and expected marginal costs. Because the marginal costs of buying a new car are greater than those of buying a new tube of toothpaste, we expect people to inquire more about the expected benefits of the automobile.

10. No. Theory applies to people on average, not to specific individuals. There are many possible factors that could explain John Doe's behavior—he may have just quit being a vegetarian, he may have inherited a lot of money, or he may be getting ready to have a big dinner party.

11. The predictions of economic theory are positive statements, because they are capable of being tested and either upheld or refuted. Theory does not involve opinion or value judgments.

12. The first step is to identify and define the key economic variables. The second step is to state the assumptions, including behavioral assumptions, that specify the conditions under which the theory is to apply. Basically, this involves identifying the variables or conditions that would cause the theory not to predict as well as expected. The third step is to develop testable hypotheses about the relations among the variables. The last step is to test the theory.

13. Predictions are based on the implications of a theory and generally take the form of if-then statements. There is no expectation that the prediction will occur if the conditions are not met. A forecast is an educated guess that a certain event will actually occur.

14. One of the roles of theory is to identify likely causal relations. However, there will be occasions when we cannot ascertain causality.

15. a.

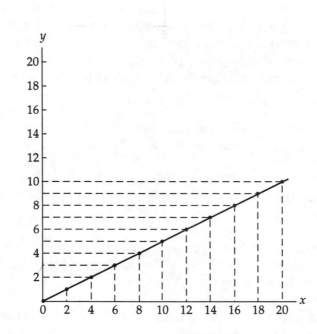

    b. The relation is positive because when x goes up, y goes up.
    c. 0.5

16. a.

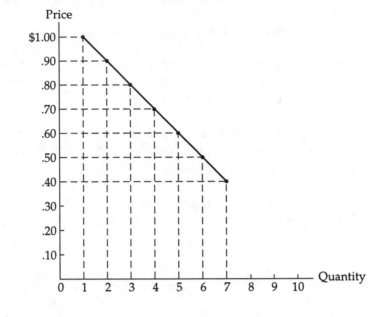

b. −.1

17. Slope at point *a*: −1; at point *b*: 0; at point *c*: 1; at point *d*: infinite

18.

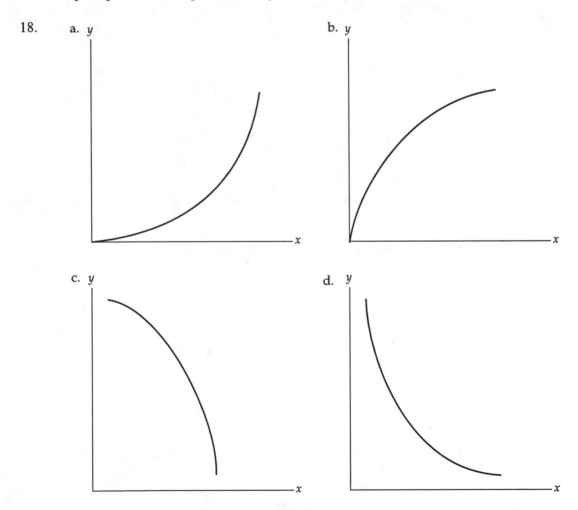

CHAPTER 2

Some Tools of Economic Analysis

I. INTRODUCTION

The previous chapter introduced the concept of scarcity. We saw that people must make choices because of scarcity. This chapter explores the idea of choice in more detail. The cost of a choice and the tools economists use to analyze cost are discussed. The chapter also examines some of the choices that any society must make.

II. OUTLINE

1. Choice and Opportunity Cost

  1.1 Opportunity Cost
    a. The opportunity cost of a choice is the benefit expected from the best alternative that is forgone.
    b. We do what we do because we have nothing better to do. If we had something better to do, we would do it.

  1.2 *CASE STUDY:* The Opportunity Cost of College

  1.3 Opportunity Cost Is Subjective
    a. Each individual must calculate the expected value of the best alternative for himself or herself.
    b. Calculating opportunity cost requires time and information.
    c. Time is the ultimate constraint.
    d. Opportunity cost may vary with circumstance.

  1.4 Sunk Cost and Choice
    a. A sunk cost is a cost that cannot be recovered no matter what you do.
    b. Sunk costs should be ignored in making economic decisions.

2. Specialization, Comparative Advantage, and Exchange

  2.1 The Law of Comparative Advantage. Combined output can increase when the individual with the lowest opportunity cost for producing a particular good specializes in producing that good.

  2.2 Absolute and Comparative Advantage
    a. A person has an absolute advantage when he or she can perform tasks with fewer resources than another person.
    b. A person has a comparative advantage when he or she can produce a given product at a lower opportunity cost than someone else.

     c.   Each person should specialize in the task for which he or she has a comparative advantage.

     d.   The law of comparative advantage applies to firms, regions, and nations as well as to individuals.

2.3   Specialization and Exchange

     a.   *Barter* is a system in which products are exchanged directly for other products.

     b.   Money is a medium of exchange because everyone is willing to accept it in exchange for goods and services. Money makes it easier to exchange goods and services.

     c.   Because of comparative advantage and specialization, people do not produce most of the things they want and must enter into exchange to acquire them.

2.4   Division of Labor and Gains from Specialization

     a.   Greater specialization can be achieved through division of labor: the separating of production into various tasks and the assigning of individuals to these separate tasks.

     b.   Division of labor is productive for several reasons:

          (1)   Tasks can be assigned according to preferences and abilities.

          (2)   As people perform the same tasks over and over, they become better at them.

          (3)   There is no time lost in moving from one task to another.

          (4)   Specialization of labor allows for the introduction of more sophisticated techniques.

2.5   *CASE STUDY:* Evidence of Specialization

3.   The Economy's Production Possibilities

3.1   Efficiency and the Production Possibilities Frontier

     a.   The production possibilities frontier (PPF) describes the possible combinations of two goods that can be produced when resources are used fully and efficiently.

     b.   Resources are used efficiently when they cannot be combined differently in any way that would increase the production of one good without decreasing the production of the other good.

3.2   Inefficient and Unattainable Production

     a.   Points inside the PPF represent combinations of the two goods that are produced inefficiently.

     b.   Points outside the PPF represent combinations of the two goods that cannot be attained, given society's resources and technology.

3.3   Shape of the Production Possibilities Frontier

     a.   The PPF slopes down because when resources are used fully and efficiently, more of one good can be produced only by producing less of the other good.

     b.   The PPF is bowed out when not all resources are equally productive in producing both goods.

     c.   The law of increasing opportunity cost applies to production of both goods: as additional units of one good are produced, more and more of the other good must be sacrificed.

3.4   What Can Shift the Production Possibilities Frontier?

     a.   Over time the PPF may shift out or in.

     b.   Shifts in the PPF will occur as a result of

       (1)   changes in resource availability;

       (2)   increases in the capital stock; and

       (3)   effects of technological change.

3.5   What We Can Learn from the PPF

    a.   The PPF demonstrates efficiency because it describes the efficient combinations of output that are possible.

    b.   The PPF demonstrates scarcity because there is a limit to what can be produced.

    c.   The downward slope of the PPF indicates opportunity cost.

    d.   The bowed shape of the PPF indicates the law of increasing opportunity cost.

    e.   The PPF illustrates the need to make choices.

    f.   Outward shifts in the PPF reflect economic growth.

3.6   Three Questions Each Economic System Must Answer

    a.   What goods and services will be produced?

    b.   How will goods and services be produced?

    c.   For whom will goods and services be produced?

    d.   These questions are interrelated, because what will be produced is often determined by the economic and social systems of the people for whom the goods are made.

4.   Economic Systems

4.1   Pure Market System

    a.   A pure market system is characterized by private ownership of resources.

    b.   Coordination of economic activity is accomplished by price signals in free markets.

    c.   Markets direct decisions concerning the three economic questions.

    d.   *Laissez faire* means letting people do as they choose without government intervention.

4.2   Pure Command Economy

    a.   A pure command economy is an economic system characterized by public ownership of resources.

    b.   Coordination is accomplished by central planning.

4.3   Mixed and Transitional Economies

    a.   No society is a pure capitalist or a pure command economy.

    b.   All societies mix elements of capitalism and the command economy, although the composition of the mix differs considerably.

4.4   Economies Based on Custom or Religion

III. DISCUSSION

Choice and Opportunity Cost

Everybody faces the problem of scarcity—even the very rich. Time is scarce for everyone, and any activity we engage in has an *opportunity cost* associated with it. Opportunity costs are subjective. For one student the opportunity cost of taking an economics course may be the course on Homer not taken, whereas the opportunity cost for another student may be the hours missed from work. Because the opportunity cost of any activity is the value of the best alternative choice that is forgone and different people have different alternative choices, opportunity costs differ for different people.

The concept of opportunity cost does not mean that the choice actually made will always be the best choice. After taking economics, a student may think that she made a mistake and should have taken Homer. Often, we do not know the true value of the forsaken alternative, so occasionally we make mistakes.

Calculating opportunity costs requires time and information. The time we spend collecting information could be spent doing other things; we do not always spend enough time collecting information and we make mistakes. Opportunity costs may also vary with circumstances. The opportunity cost of studying on a rainy day is less for most people than the opportunity cost of the same activity on a beautiful Saturday afternoon.

Specialization, Comparative Advantage, and Exchange

Dividing production in accordance with the *law of comparative advantage* leads to increased production. Since all people (or firms, regions, or countries) are not equally efficient in producing all goods and services, total output is greater when each individual specializes in producing the goods or services that she or he can produce relatively more efficiently.

The law of comparative advantage applies not only to people but also to all productive resources. Suppose a farmer has two acres of land. One acre can produce 1,000 bushels of wheat, or 800 bushels of corn, or some combination of both. The second acre can produce either 600 bushels of wheat or 200 bushels of corn. Although the first acre has an *absolute advantage* in producing both crops, it has a comparative advantage in producing corn. The opportunity cost of a bushel of corn on the first acre is 1.25 bushels of wheat. For the second acre, the opportunity cost of a bushel of corn is 3 bushels of wheat. The opportunity cost of corn is less for the first acre. What about wheat? The opportunity cost of a bushel of wheat on the first acre is 0.8 bushel of corn, and the opportunity cost for the second acre is 0.33 bushel of corn. The opportunity cost of wheat is less for the second acre than for the first, so the second acre of land has a comparative advantage in producing wheat.

In order to take advantage of comparative advantage, resources must specialize. *Specialization* implies that people do not produce most of the goods and services that they wish to consume. Instead, most people specialize, exchanging a single product or service for money and then exchanging money for the goods and services that they want to consume. This specialization is generally a part of the *division of labor*. Further, most people do not produce a single product by themselves. Instead, they perform a specialized task that helps produce a good or service. In some small commuter airlines, for example, the pilot may also sell tickets, but larger airlines divide tasks and assign different individuals to perform them. As a result, the total output can be larger than it would be without division of labor.

The Economy's Production Possibilities

The *production possibilities frontier* (PPF) describes the possible combinations of two goods that can be produced with maximum efficiency. Exhibit 1 presents a PPF for an economy that produces wheat and sweaters. The curve slopes down, which indicates that the only way to get more wheat is to produce fewer sweaters. At any point on the PPF, more of one good can be produced only by producing less of the other. This is what is meant by producing the goods efficiently. The PPF is also bowed out, which reflects the *law of increasing opportunity cost*. At point *a,* only sweaters are produced. If we want to produce 1,000 bushels of wheat, we see that we must give up fewer than 500 sweaters. To produce another 1,000 bushels of wheat, more than 500 sweaters must be sacrificed. Beginning at point *d,* 4,500 sweaters and 8,000 bushels of wheat, the production of sweaters must be curtailed by 2,000 units to increase wheat production by another 1,000 bushels. Between points *e* and *f*, an additional 2,500 sweaters must be sacrificed to produce yet another 1,000 bushels of wheat. In moving from point *a* to point *f*, each 1,000-bushel increase in wheat production requires sacrificing increasing numbers of sweaters. That is, the opportunity cost of wheat increases as more and more wheat is produced.

Exhibit 1

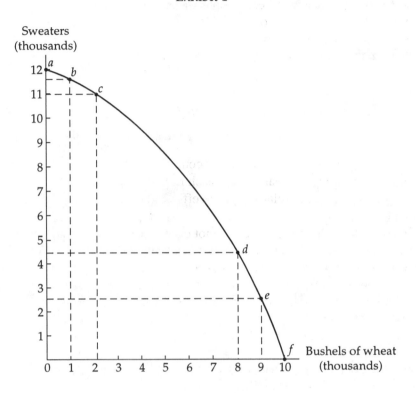

A production possibilities frontier is constructed for a given amount of resources and a given level of technology. If either the number of resources or the technology changes, the PPF shifts. The more capital a country produces in a year, the farther out the PPF shifts in future years. You should review Exhibit 2 in the text to make sure you understand these shifts.

Any society must answer three basic economic questions: What goods and services will be produced and in what quantities? How will the goods be produced? For whom will the goods be produced? Not all societies answer the three basic questions in the same manner. The two extreme types of arrangement are pure capitalism and the pure command economy. Under *pure capitalism*, all productive resources are privately owned. One's income depends on the resources one owns and the prices the resources command. The more income one has, the more "votes" one has in determining the type of goods that will be produced. Markets are used to coordinate the plans of the individual members of society, and changes in prices signal individuals to alter their behavior in certain predictable ways.

A *pure command economy* operates very differently from a capitalist economy. In a pure command economy, all productive resources are owned publicly (i.e., by the government). Decisions concerning what to produce and in what quantities are made by government officials. The economy is organized so that decisions are made at the top and carried out by the people lower in the pyramid.

No society on earth today has either a pure capitalist economy or a pure command economy. Instead, all societies use a mixture of government involvement and individual decision making. In some countries, such as the United States, most exchanges are carried out through markets and most productive resources are owned by individuals. In other countries, such as the People's Republic of China, most productive resources are owned by the government and many economic decisions are made by central planners. However, there is extensive government intervention in the economy of the United States and many examples of private ownership in the People's Republic of China.

IV. LAGNIAPPE

Advantages of the Division of Labor

Adam Smith, who is credited with recognizing the advantages of the division of labor, wrote:

The great increase of the quantity of work which, in consequence of the division of labor, the same number of people are capable of performing, is owing to three different circumstances; first to the increase of dexterity in every particular workman; secondly, to the saving of the time which is commonly lost in passing from one species of work to another; and lastly, to the invention of a great number of machines which facilitate and abridge labor, and enable one man to do the work of many. [Adam Smith, *The Wealth of Nations* (Chicago: The University of Chicago Press, 1976), p. 11. Originally published in 1776.]

Question to Think About: How do these three advantages of the division of labor coincide with the four reasons given in the text?

Ricardo and Comparative Advantage

David Ricardo (1772–1823) was the first to identify comparative advantage as the source of trade. As an example, he used the production of wine and cloth in England and Portugal. If England required 100 men per year to produce cloth and 120 men per year to produce wine, and it took only 90 men per year to produce the same amount of cloth in Portugal and 80 men per year to produce the same amount of wine, then Portugal had an absolute advantage in both. However, as Ricardo pointed out:

It would therefore be advantageous for her (Portugal) to export wine in exchange for cloth. This exchange might even take place notwithstanding that the commodity imported by Portugal could be produced there with less labor than in England. Though she could make the cloth with the labor of 90 men, she would import it from a country where it required the labor of 100 men to produce it, because it would be advantageous to her rather to employ her capital in the production of wine, for which she would obtain more cloth from England, than she could produce by diverting a portion of her capital from the cultivation of vines to the manufacture of cloth. [David Ricardo, *The Principles of Political Economy and Taxation* (London: A. M. Dent & Sons, 1973), p. 82. Originally published in 1821.]

Question to Think About: What is the opportunity cost of wine in Portugal? in England? What is the opportunity cost of cloth in England? in Portugal?

V. KEY TERMS

opportunity cost
sunk cost
law of comparative advantage
absolute advantage
comparative advantage
barter
division of labor
specialization of labor
production possibilities frontier (PPF)

efficiency
law of increasing opportunity cost
economic growth
economic system
pure market system
pure capitalism
pure command system
mixed system

VI. QUESTIONS

A. Completion

1. The _____ of any action is the expected benefit of the best alternative not chosen.

2. A cost that cannot be recovered no matter what you do is a _____ cost.

3. _____ is the ability to produce something with fewer resources than other producers.

4. _____ is the ability to produce something at a lower opportunity cost than other producers.

5. The _____ leads to greater output because it results in greater specialization of labor.

6. _____ is a system of exchange in which products are traded directly for other products.

7. Something that everyone is willing to accept in return for all goods and services is called a _____.

8. A society is producing on its _____ if it uses its resources fully and efficiently.

9. A bowed-out production possibilities frontier indicates that the cost of producing either good _____ as greater amounts of the good are produced.

10. Production is _____ if there is no way to rearrange resources that will allow more of one good to be produced without causing less of any other good to be produced.

11. Any economic system must decide what goods will be produced, for whom they will be produced, and _____.

12. Most societies are a mixture of _____ and _____.

13. The idea that people should be allowed to do as they choose without government interference is called _____.

14. In a command economy, resources are directed through _____.

B.   True/False

_____ 1.   The opportunity cost of an activity is the expected benefit from the best alternative that is forsaken.

_____ 2.   The price of something is usually the best measure of the opportunity cost of the activity.

_____ 3.   The opportunity cost of a given activity is usually the same for all people.

_____ 4.   Opportunity cost measures the cost of the alternative given up less the expected benefit from the opportunity chosen.

_____ 5.   Opportunity costs vary with circumstances.

_____ 6.   Opportunity costs tend to be constant over time.

_____ 7.   Comparative advantage is caused by absolute advantage.

_____ 8.   The law of comparative advantage calls for specializing in the task in which one has a comparative advantage.

_____ 9.   One function of money is to make it easier for exchange to take place.

_____ 10.   Barter decreases as an economy becomes more specialized.

_____ 11.   The division of labor allows the introduction of specialized machinery that makes workers more productive.

_____ 12.   A production possibilities frontier shifts out when society moves from inefficient to efficient production.

_____ 13.   A production possibilities frontier illustrates opportunity cost by sloping downward.

_____ 14.   The law of increasing opportunity cost generates a production possibilities frontier that bows outward.

_____ 15.   The PPF would not be bowed outward if the resources in an economy were all perfectly adaptable for the production of both goods.

_____ 16.   We would expect a society's PPF to shift out over time.

_____ 17.   If existing capital wears out faster than new capital is produced, the PPF will shift in over time.

_____ 18.   The answer to the question of how goods are to be distributed helps shape the incentives people have to produce.

_____ 19.   Under pure capitalism, market prices guide resources to their highest valued use.

_____ 20.   In a pure command economy, central planners decide how a good will be produced.

C.   Multiple Choice

1.   The opportunity cost of a vanilla ice cream cone is
   a.   a chocolate ice cream cone.
   b.   a piece of apple pie.
   c.   a hamburger.
   d.   a gallon of gasoline.
   e.   All of the above are possible.

2.   Which of the following is a true statement about opportunity costs?
   a.   The opportunity cost of an activity includes the expected benefit of the most attractive alternative passed up.
   b.   Opportunity cost implies that people are always pleased with the decisions they make.
   c.   Opportunity cost is an objective notion.
   d.   When making choices, people exhaustively calculate costs and benefits for all possible alternatives.
   e.   All of the above are true.

3.   For a toy store, the opportunity cost of closing for a day is likely to be greatest on
   a.   any given Wednesday.
   b.   any given day in February.
   c.   second Saturday of December.
   d.   the third Friday in June.
   e.   the Fourth of July.

4.   Opportunity costs are subjective because
   a.   they depend on circumstances, which may vary.
   b.   the best alternative may differ for different people.
   c.   they do not reflect money costs.
   d.   All of the above.
   e.   a and b only

5.   Sunk costs should be ignored in making economic choices because
   a.   they are usually trivial.
   b.   they are marginal costs so they are not as relevant as total costs.
   c.   they are not affected by the choice.
   d.   they are not monetary costs.
   e.   None of the above. They should not be ignored.

6. Fred and Samantha cook and clean. They have identical opportunity costs for cooking, but Samantha has an absolute advantage in cooking. We know, then, that
   a. Fred has an absolute advantage in cleaning.
   b. Fred has a comparative advantage in cleaning.
   c. Samantha has an absolute advantage in cleaning.
   d. Samantha has a comparative advantage in cleaning.
   e. None of the above. More information is needed.

7. A man has two sons, Robbie and David. Robbie can mow the lawn in 1 hour and wash the car in 50 minutes. David can mow the lawn in 40 minutes and wash the car in 30 minutes. Which statement below is true?
   a. David has an absolute advantage in both chores and a comparative advantage in mowing the lawn.
   b. David has an absolute advantage in both chores and a comparative advantage in washing cars.
   c. Robbie has an absolute advantage in both chores and a comparative advantage in mowing the lawn.
   d. Robbie has an absolute advantage in both chores and a comparative advantage in washing cars.
   e. Robbie has an absolute advantage in washing cars and David has an absolute advantage in mowing the lawn.

8. In the preceding example,
   a. Robbie should wash the car and David should mow the lawn.
   b. David should both mow the lawn and wash the car.
   c. David should wash the car and Robbie should mow the lawn.
   d. Robbie and David should share both jobs.
   e. We cannot tell who should do what chore without more information.

9. Specialization of labor implies that
   a. people must engage in exchange to acquire the goods they want.
   b. barter is an efficient way to carry out exchange.
   c. money is not a necessary part of the economy.
   d. the economy must be characterized by absolute advantage.
   e. output falls if labor is divided into too many specialized tasks.

10. Which of the following is a source of the increased productivity due to specialization of labor?
    a. People are assigned various tasks to perform so they will not get bored.
    b. Employees can be assigned tasks on the basis of the manager's preference and prejudices.
    c. People become better at a job the more they perform it.
    d. Workers can replace expensive machines in production.
    e. All of the above.

11. If the opportunity cost in the United States of 1 unit of wheat is 4 units of cloth, then
    a. the opportunity cost of wheat in England is more than 4 units of cloth.
    b. the opportunity cost of wheat in England is less than 4 units of cloth.
    c. the opportunity cost of 1 unit of cloth in the United States is $1/4$ unit of wheat.
    d. the United States has a comparative advantage in producing cloth.
    e. both a and d

12. If the United States has an absolute advantage in producing wheat and England has an absolute advantage in producing cloth, then
   a. neither country has a comparative advantage in either good.
   b. the United States has a comparative advantage in wheat and England has a comparative advantage in cloth.
   c. the United States should specialize in wheat and England should specialize in cloth.
   d. b and c
   e. None of the above. More information is needed.

13. Disadvantages of increased specialization include
   a. reduced standards of living.
   b. reduced contact with other people.
   c. increased job dissatisfaction.
   d. increased reliance on money.
   e. All of the above.

Exhibit 2

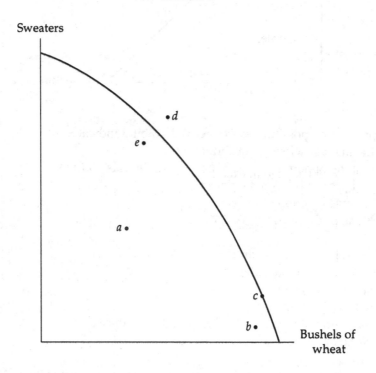

14. Which point in Exhibit 2 indicates where production is efficient?
   a. point *a*
   b. point *b*
   c. point *c*
   d. point *d*
   e. point *e*

15. Which point in Exhibit 2 cannot be attained?
    a. point *a*
    b. point *b*
    c. point *c*
    d. point *d*
    e. All points except *c* are unattainable.

Exhibit 3

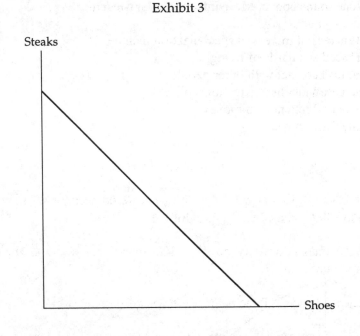

16. The production possibilities frontier in Exhibit 3 indicates
    a. the law of increasing opportunity cost.
    b. that the opportunity cost of producing shoes is constant.
    c. that production is not efficient.
    d. decreasing opportunity costs.
    e. None of the above.

17. Which of the following can cause the PPF to shift out?
    a. an increase in vacation time
    b. an increase in immigration
    c. a decrease in the retirement age
    d. migration of unskilled workers to other countries
    e. None of the above.

18. In a pure capitalist economy, productive resources are owned by
    a. the government.
    b. the people collectively.
    c. individuals.
    d. the rich.
    e. the army.

19. Which of the economic questions does not have to be solved in a primitive economy?
    a. What will be produced?
    b. How will goods be produced?
    c. For whom will goods be produced?
    d. both b and c
    e. They must all be solved.

20. In which country does the government own some resources?
    a. the United States
    b. France
    c. Cuba
    d. Canada
    e. All of the above.

D. Discussion Questions

1. How are opportunity cost and scarcity related?

2. The textbook says that we always do what we do because we have nothing better to do. Explain what this means.

3. Why are the opportunity costs of law school greater than the opportunity costs of undergraduate school?

4. The textbook says, "Time is the ultimate constraint." Explain why this is so.

5. If people always choose the alternative that provides the highest expected benefit, how can mistakes ever be made?

Use the information in Exhibit 4 about production of cloth and wheat in the United States and England to answer questions 6 and 7.

Exhibit 4

Output Produced per Day by One Worker

	England	United States
Wheat	3	10
Cloth	1	2

6. a. What is the opportunity cost of wheat in England? in the United States?
   b. Which country has a comparative advantage in the production of wheat? Which has a comparative advantage in the production of cloth?
   c. If the two countries trade, which will specialize in wheat and which in cloth? Which will export wheat and which will export cloth?

7. a. Which country has an absolute advantage in wheat and which in cloth?
   b. Why is trade based on comparative advantage rather than on absolute advantage?

8. What does money have to do with specialization and comparative advantage?

9. Explain how the division of labor increases productivity.

10. Under what conditions is it possible to increase production of one good without decreasing production of another good?

11. Suppose there are two resources used in an economy: labor and capital. Capital is relatively more useful in producing wheat, whereas labor is relatively more useful in producing cloth. Suppose the supply of capital falls by 10 percent and the supply of labor increases by 10 percent. How will the production possibilities frontier for wheat and cloth change?

12. What can we learn from the production possibilities frontier?

13. Suppose 10 percent of a country's capital stock wears out every year. What will happen to the PPF in future years if the country produces new capital each year equal to 20 percent of its capital stock at the beginning of the year? if it produces new capital equal to 5 percent of its beginning capital?

14. What are the three questions that all societies must answer and why must they be answered?

15. How are the three questions answered differently in a pure capitalist system and a pure command economy?

VII. ANSWERS

A. Completion

1.	opportunity cost	8.	production possibilities frontier
2.	sunk	9.	increases
3.	Absolute advantage	10.	efficient
4.	Comparative advantage	11.	how goods will be produced
5.	division of labor	12.	capitalism; a command economy
6.	Barter	13.	laissez faire
7.	medium of exchange	14.	central planning

B. True/False

1.	True	10.	True
2.	False. Calculations of opportunity cost must also include the time spent away from the most valued alternative.	11.	True
		12.	False
		13.	True
		14.	True
3.	False	15.	True
4.	False	16.	True
5.	True	17.	True
6.	False	18.	True
7.	False	19.	True
8.	True	20.	True
9.	True		

C. Multiple Choice

1.	e	6.	c	11.	c	16.	b
2.	a	7.	b	12.	d	17.	b
3.	c	8.	c	13.	c	18.	c
4.	e	9.	a	14.	c	19.	e
5.	c	10.	c	15.	d	20.	e

D. Discussion Questions

1. Scarcity implies that we must make choices since we cannot have everything that we want. Every choice involves an opportunity cost, so opportunity costs result from scarcity.

2. At any time we have many choices available to us. The alternative that we choose is the most preferred alternative. Consequently, there is no choice better than the one we choose—we have nothing better to do. If we had something better to do, we would do it.

3. Both law students and undergraduate students forgo earning a living while they are in school. The opportunity costs of law school are greater than those of undergraduate school, however, because undergraduate students are forgoing the relatively small salaries earned by workers with only high school diplomas, whereas law students are forgoing the salaries earned by college graduates.

4. Time is the ultimate constraint because consumption of goods and services takes time. One may have three cars but can only drive one at a time. A person can do only one thing at a time, so choices always have to be made.

5. People do not always have perfect information concerning alternatives. Information is scarce, and it takes time to collect accurate and complete information. Consequently, people sometimes make decisions that they later regret. At the time the decision is made, the person assumes it is a good decision, but events often do not turn out as expected; information can turn up later to prove a decision wrong.

6. a. Opportunity cost of wheat in England is $1/3$ unit of cloth; in the United States it is $1/5$ unit of cloth.
   b. The United States has a comparative advantage in the production of wheat, because the opportunity cost of producing wheat is lower in the United States. England has a comparative advantage in the production of cloth because the opportunity cost of producing cloth in England is 3 units of wheat compared with a cost of 5 units of wheat in the United States.
   c. The United States will specialize in wheat and England will specialize in cloth. The United States will export wheat and England will export cloth.

7. a. The United States has an absolute advantage in both wheat and cloth, because more of each good is produced by a worker in the United States.
   b. The cost of a good is measured not in terms of the hours of work required to produce it but rather in terms of opportunity cost (i.e., the amount of another good that must be given up to consume the first good). Basing trade on comparative advantage allows a country or producer with the lowest opportunity cost to specialize in producing a good.

8. Specialization results from comparative advantage. When people specialize, they tend to produce few of the things they consume and to consume few of the things they produce. They must rely on exchanging the goods they produce for the goods they want to consume. This would be difficult to do with a barter system, so money helps make exchange easier.

9. The division of labor allows people to work in their area of comparative advantage. By performing tasks over and over, people become better at performing them. There is also no time lost in workers' going from one task to another. Finally, the division of labor allows for the introduction of specialized machinery, which makes labor more productive.

10. We can produce more of one good without sacrificing production of another good when we are inside the PPF. If we can do so, we are either not using all available resources or not using them efficiently.

11. In the graph below, *AB* is the original PPF. The decrease in capital causes the production of wheat to fall more than the production of cloth, since capital is more efficient in producing wheat. The increase in labor causes the production of cloth to increase more than the production of wheat. The net effect is an increase in the production of cloth and a decrease in the production of wheat. *CD* is the new PPF.

Exhibit 5

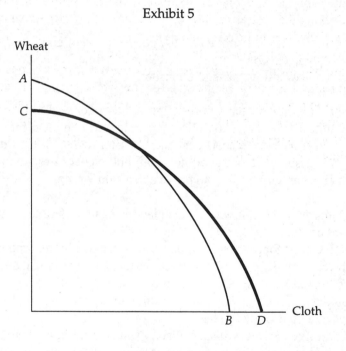

12. By showing the limits to productivity, the PPF illustrates the concept of scarcity and the need to make choices. It illustrates the concept of opportunity cost with its downward slope, and it illustrates increasing opportunity cost with its bowed-out shape. Finally, it illustrates the concept of efficiency, since there is at least one point on the PPF that is preferable to any point inside the PPF, and the concept of economic growth, since the entire PPF can shift away from the origin.

13. Annual production of new capital equal to 20 percent of the capital stock at the beginning of the year will cause the capital stock to increase by 10 percent in the future, because only 10 percent of the capital is consumed each year. The PPF will shift out the next year, indicating economic growth. A 5 percent yearly production of capital will cause the total capital stock to decrease by 5 percent in the future, because 10 percent of the capital stock is consumed each year. The PPF will shift in toward the origin.

14. Each society must decide what will be produced and in what quantities. People want goods and services, but they cannot have all they want because of scarcity. Hence, some criteria must be established to decide which goods will be produced. Different resource combinations can be used to produce a given good, so once a society decides what will be produced, it must also decide how goods will be produced. Finally, since everybody wants more than is available, society must decide who will get the goods that have been produced.

15. In a pure capitalist economy, individuals own the resources and decide how they will be used. Seeking the best places for their resources, they make their decisions on the basis of prices and changes in prices. Consumers decide what will be produced by demonstrating their willingness to pay for the goods. Entrepreneurs decide how the goods will be produced by making decisions designed to keep costs low. Goods are distributed based on incomes and the prices of the goods. The whole process is coordinated by people's responses to price changes. In a pure command economy, central planners decide what will be produced and how it will be produced. They also decide who gets what products. (The Marxist ideal is expressed by the axiom "From each according to his ability, to each according to his need.")

CHAPTER 3

The Market System

I. INTRODUCTION

The workhorses of economic analysis are the concepts of supply and demand. These tools are introduced in this chapter, although both tools will be developed much further in later chapters. Because the material in this chapter is a foundation for much of the course, be certain that you understand it and that you can use the tools developed here.

II. OUTLINE

1. Demand. Demand reflects the quantity of a good that people are both willing and able to buy at various prices, other things constant.

    1.1   The Law of Demand
        a.   The law of demand states that the quantity demanded of a good is inversely related to its price.
        b.   Demand differs from wants and needs.
        c.   The substitution effect of a price increase will be to encourage consumers to switch to other goods that are relatively cheaper.
        d.   A change in price also generates an income effect since the price change affects the buying power of consumer income, or real income.

    1.2   The Demand Schedule and Demand Curve
        a.   A demand schedule indicates the quantity of a commodity that consumers wish to buy at each possible price for a given period of time.
           (1)   Demand is a rate per period of time.
           (2)   Prices of other goods are held constant.
           (3)   A demand schedule looks at the effects of a relative price change.
        b.   A demand curve provides a graphical representation of the information in a demand schedule.
        c.   *Demand* refers to the entire demand schedule or demand curve.
        d.   *Quantity demanded* refers to an individual point on the demand curve.
        e.   A change in demand occurs when the entire demand schedule or demand curve shifts.
        f.   A change in quantity demanded occurs when the price of a good changes and one moves along the demand curve.
        g.   The market demand is the sum of the individual demands of all consumers in a market.

2. Changes in Demand

    2.1   Changes in Consumer Income
        a.   A change in income causes the entire demand curve to shift (i.e., causes a change in demand).
        b.   If the demand for a good increases as income increases, then the good is a normal good.
        c.   If the demand for a good decreases as income increases, then the good is an inferior good.

    2.2   Changes in the Prices of Related Goods
        a.   Two goods are substitutes if they are alternative ways of satisfying a particular want.
        b.   Two goods are complements if they are used in combination to satisfy a particular want.
        c.   If an increase in the price of one good causes the demand for a second good to increase, the two goods are substitutes.
        d.   If an increase in the price of one good causes the demand for a second good to decrease, the two goods are complements.

    2.3   Changes in Consumer Expectations
        a.   If consumers expect the price of a good to increase in the future, demand for the good will increase today.
        b.   If consumers expect an increase in future income, demand for goods will increase today.

    2.4   Changes in the Number or Composition of Consumers. The more people there are in the market, the greater the market demand.

    2.5   Changes in Consumer Tastes
        a.   Tastes are assumed to be relatively stable over time.
        b.   A change in demand cannot be attributed to a change in tastes before other possible reasons for the change are carefully considered.

3. Supply. The law of supply states that the quantity of product supplied in a given time period is usually directly related to its price, other things constant.

    3.1   The Supply Schedule and Supply Curve
        a.   A higher price makes producers more willing to offer more for sale because they are rewarded more for doing so.
        b.   A higher price enables producers to produce more because it allows them to cover the higher marginal costs that result as quantity produced increases, according to the law of increasing opportunity costs.
        c.   The market supply is the sum of the individual supplies of all suppliers in a market.

4. Changes in Supply

    4.1   Changes in Technology. A technological advance is reflected by a shift to the right in the market supply curve.

    4.2   Changes in the Prices of Relevant Resources. Lower resource costs lead to an increase in supply.

    4.3   Changes in the Prices of Alternative Goods. An increase in the price of an alternative good raises the opportunity cost of producing other goods that use the same resources.

4.4 Changes in Producer Expectations. If producers expect the price of a good to rise in the future, current supply could increase or decrease, depending on the type of good.

4.5 Changes in the Number of Producers
   a. An increase in the number of producers increases the market supply.
   b. A change in supply is a shift of the entire supply curve; a change in the quantity supplied is a movement along a supply curve when the price of a good changes.

5. Demand and Supply Create a Market

   5.1 Markets
       a. Markets coordinate the independent decisions of buyers and sellers.
       b. The transaction costs of an exchange are the costs of the time and the information required to complete the transaction.
       c. Markets reduce the transaction costs of exchange.
       d. Coordination takes place through markets by the operation of the "invisible hand" described by Adam Smith.

   5.2 Market Equilibrium
       a. The equilibrium price is the price at which quantity demanded equals quantity supplied.
       b. An excess quantity supplied, or surplus, exists when the quantity supplied exceeds the quantity demanded at prices above equilibrium.
       c. An excess quantity demanded, or shortage, exists when the quantity demanded exceeds the quantity supplied at prices below equilibrium.
       d. An equilibrium is achieved through the independent actions of thousands of buyers and sellers in the economy.
       e. Markets allocate a resource to its highest valued use.

6. Changes in Equilibrium Price and Quantity

   6.1 Impact of Changes in Demand. Any change in demand, holding supply constant, will change equilibrium price and quantity in the same direction as the changes in demand.

   6.2 Impact of Changes in Supply. A shift in the supply curve, holding demand constant, changes equilibrium quantity in the same direction but changes equilibrium price in the opposite direction.

   6.3 Simultaneous Changes in Demand and Supply
       a. When both curves shift simultaneously, the outcome depends on the nature of the shifts.
       b. If supply and demand both increase, the equilibrium quantity increases, but the effect on the equilibrium price depends on the size of the shift in demand relative to the size of the shift in supply. If both supply and demand decrease, the equilibrium quantity falls.
       c. If supply and demand shift in opposite directions, the equilibrium price rises with an increase in demand and falls with a decrease in demand. However, the effect on the equilibrium quantity depends on the size of the shift in demand relative to the size of the shift in supply.

   6.4 *CASE STUDY:* The Market for Professional Basketball

The Market System

7. Disequilibrium Prices

    7.1   Price Floors. Price floors, or minimum prices set by the government, tend to create surpluses.

    7.2   Price Ceilings. Price ceilings, or maximum prices set by the government, tend to create shortages.

    7.3   *CASE STUDY:* Toys Are Serious Business

III. DISCUSSION

Demand

    Demand is a relation that indicates the quantity of a commodity that consumers wish to buy at all possible prices during a given time period, other things constant. The *law of demand* states that the relationship between price and quantity demanded is an inverse relationship (i.e., fewer units are demanded at higher prices than at lower prices). Demand reflects consumers' willingness and ability to buy the commodity.

    The inverse relationship between price and quantity demanded refers to the real, or relative, price of the commodity. If the price of shoes increases 10 percent but all other prices also increase by 10 percent, then the relative price of shoes has not changed and quantity demanded will not change.

    A change in the price of a commodity has two effects on quantity demanded. The first is the *substitution effect*. If the price of one good increases while all other prices remain constant, then the good becomes more costly relative to other goods. Many consumers will respond by substituting a cheaper good for the now more expensive good, so the quantity demanded of the original good decreases. An increase in the price of one good encourages consumers to switch to other goods. The second effect—the *income effect*—affects consumers' ability to buy a good. If you have been buying 10 hamburgers a week at $1.00 per hamburger and the price increases to $1.25, then the $10.00 that used to buy 10 hamburgers can now buy only 8 hamburgers. The higher price reduces your *real income*, or purchasing power, which has the tendency to induce you to purchase fewer units of the good.

    The inverse relationship between price and quantity demanded can be shown by a demand schedule for any specific commodity. Exhibit 1 illustrates the quantities of gasoline demanded at various prices. Exhibit 2 provides the same information in the form of a *demand curve*. More units are demanded at lower prices, reflecting the law of demand. Several things are held constant: the prices of other goods and the incomes, expectations, and tastes of the consumers. A movement along the demand curve represents a *change in quantity demanded*. The market demand is found by adding up the demands of all consumers in the market.

Exhibit 1

The Demand Schedule for Gasoline

	Price per Gallon	Quantity Demanded (millions of gallons per week)
a	$1.25	8
b	1.00	10
c	0.90	12
d	0.80	14
e	0.70	16
f	0.60	20
g	0.50	25

Exhibit 2

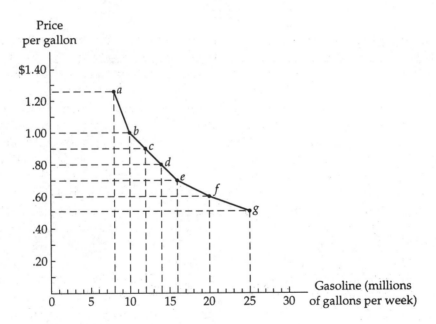

Changes in Demand

In the demand schedule and the demand curve in Exhibits 1 and 2, only the price of gasoline varied. However, demand can be affected by factors other than the price of the good being considered, such as consumer income, the prices of substitutes and complements, consumers' expectations, the number of consumers in the market, and consumer tastes. If any one of these factors changes, the entire demand schedule changes. That is, the demand curve shifts. When this occurs, there is a *change in demand*. (Be sure you understand how a change in demand differs from a change in quantity demanded.)

An increase in income increases demand for most products. Increasing demand means that the quantity demanded at every price increases. Exhibit 3 provides an example. When consumer income averages $20,000 a year, the demand schedule for gasoline is identical to that in Exhibit 1; this demand schedule is shown in the second column of Exhibit 3. When average income increases to $30,000 a year, the demand schedule changes. At each price, consumers demand a greater quantity of gasoline when income is greater. Exhibit 4 shows this change in demand by a shift in the demand curve from D to D'.

Exhibit 3

The Demand for Gasoline

| | | Quantity Demanded (millions of gallons per week) | |
	Price per Gallon	When Average Income Is $20,000	When Average Income Is $30,000
a	$1.25	8	10
b	1.00	10	12
c	.90	12	14
d	.80	14	16
e	.70	16	18
f	.60	20	22
g	.50	25	27

Exhibit 4

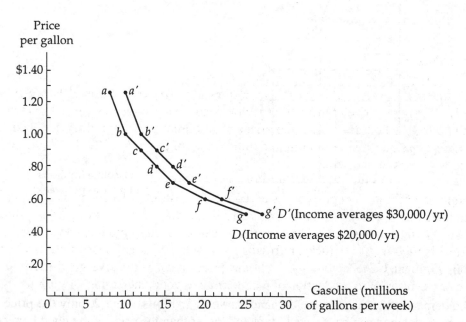

An increase in income may lead to a decrease in demand for some goods. Such goods are called *inferior goods*. People want fewer units of inferior goods when they have more income. Examples of such goods (at least for some consumers) are margarine, hamburger, bus travel, and inexpensive brands of many goods. People substitute a better product for the inferior good when they have more income. A good whose demand increases as income increases is called a *normal good*.

Any change in one of the other factors that affect demand (other than the price of the good itself) will cause a shift in the entire demand curve similar to the one shown in Exhibit 4. A change in the price of a substitute or complement will cause a change in demand. If an increase in the price of one good leads to an increase in demand for another good, the two goods are *substitutes*. If an increase in the price of one good leads to a decrease in demand for another good, the two goods are *complements*. If the goods are unrelated, a change in the price of one will have no effect on demand for the other.

Changes in consumer expectations about the future price of a good or future income can cause a shift in the current demand for the good. If price or income is expected to be higher in the future, current demand will increase. An increase in the number of consumers in the market will also cause an increase in market demand. A change in the composition of the population changes market demand. For example, demands change as population ages. Finally, a change in consumer tastes can cause a shift in demand. Again, make sure you understand the difference between a change in the quantity demanded and a change in demand. A change in quantity demanded is caused by a change in the price of the good itself; a change in demand is caused by a change in one of the other factors of demand.

Supply

The analysis of *supply* is similar to the analysis of demand. The law of supply states that the quantity of product supplied in a given time period is usually directly related to its price. An increase in quantity supplied is a result of producers' greater willingness and ability to supply more units at higher prices. Keep in mind the difference between demand and supply. The law of demand says there is an inverse relationship between price and quantity demanded, and the law of supply says there is a direct relationship between price and quantity supplied. Determination of the market supply is analogous to determination of market demand: all the supply schedules of the individual producers in a market are added up.

Changes in Supply

A change in the price of a good causes a *change in the quantity supplied*. However, other factors affect supply. A change in one of these other factors leads to a *change in supply*. The factors that affect supply include the state of technology, the prices of resources used to produce the good, the prices of alternative goods, producer expectations, and the number of producers. The last two have effects very similar to those discussed for demand.

An improvement in technology tends to reduce the costs of production; cheaper production costs generate an increase in supply. Similarly, a decrease in the price of a resource used to produce the good reduces costs and increases supply. Most resources can be used to produce more than one good. For example, steel is used in autos, trucks, refrigerators, and many other goods as well as in construction. These goods are called *alternative goods*. If the price of an alternative good increases, additional resources will be shifted into production of the alternative good, increasing its supply.

Demand and Supply Create a Market

Suppliers and demanders are brought together by markets. The *transaction costs* of exchange (the cost of time and information) are reduced by markets. A market is in *equilibrium* when the quantity demanded by consumers equals the quantity supplied by producers at a given price. Exhibits 5 and 6 illustrate a supply and demand schedule and supply and demand curves, respectively. The market is in equilibrium at a price of $0.80 per gallon because the quantity demanded equals the quantity supplied at that price. Any other price will generate either a shortage or a surplus. For example, if the price of a gallon of gasoline is $1.00, quantity demanded is 10 million gallons but quantity supplied is 20 million gallons, yielding a surplus of 10 million gallons. Any time the price is greater than the equilibrium price there will be a *surplus*. If the price is $0.60 per gallon, quantity demanded is 20 million gallons and quantity supplied is 10 million gallons; there is a shortage of 10 million gallons. Any time the price is below the equilibrium price there will be a *shortage*.

Exhibit 5

Market Supply and Demand for Gasoline

Price per Gallon	Quantity Demanded (millions of gallons per week)	Quantity Supplied (millions of gallons per week)
$1.25	8	28
1.00	10	20
0.90	12	16
0.80	14	14
0.70	16	12
0.60	20	10
0.50	25	6

Exhibit 6

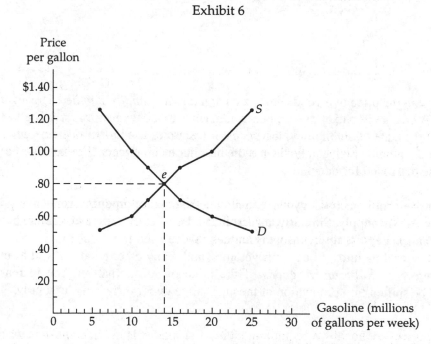

Changes in Equilibrium Price and Quantity

A market is in *equilibrium* when no economic agent in the market has any reason to alter his or her behavior. This is the case at the equilibrium price. That is, there is no reason for price to change unless either the supply or the demand changes. An increase in demand causes the demand curve to shift out, which generates a higher price and induces suppliers to increase the quantity supplied. What can cause demand to shift? Demand shifts when income, the price of a substitute or complement, consumer expectations, population, or consumer tastes change.

Exhibit 7 shows the effects of an increase in demand for gasoline. The demand curve shifts out to D', which causes the price to increase to $0.90 per gallon. The higher price encourages producers to increase the quantity supplied from 14 million gallons per week to 16 million gallons per week. That is, the new equilibrium price is $0.90 per gallon, and the new equilibrium quantity is 16 million gallons per week.

Exhibit 7

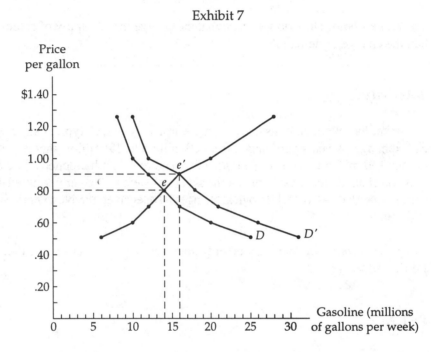

A change in supply has similar effects. An increase in supply shifts the *supply curve* down and out. Because of the increased supply, the price falls, which encourages consumers to buy more gasoline (i.e., quantity demanded increases).

It is possible for several factors to change at the same time; this generates shifts in both the demand curve and the supply curve. Review Exhibits 8 and 9 in the text to make sure that you understand the impact of simultaneous shifts in supply and demand.

Disequilibrium Prices

Actual prices are not always equilibrium prices. A market is in *disequilibrium* when the price does not equate quantity demanded and quantity supplied. In free markets, such disequilibria usually do not prevail for long periods of time. However, when the disequilibrium is due to the government's imposing either price ceilings or price floors, the disequilibrium can persist. When the government mandates a price floor above the equilibrium price, the result is a surplus. When the government mandates a price ceiling below the equilibrium price, the result is a shortage.

IV. LAGNIAPPE

The Market for Calculators

In the 1960s, engineering students did calculations using slide rules. Today slide rules have been replaced by handheld calculators. When such calculators first appeared on the market, their prices were fairly high (a minimum of $400) and their capabilities were fairly limited. During the 1970s, technological change increased the capabilities of calculators and reduced their production costs. Demand increased as calculators were designed to perform more functions, and quantity demanded increased as prices fell. Both supply and demand have increased, but the increase in supply has been much larger than the increase in demand.

Question to Think About: How do we know that the change in the supply of calculators has been much greater than the change in demand?

Stock Market Activity

The stock market has changed considerably in the last 15 years. A typical sales volume for the New York Stock Exchange 15 years ago ranged from 60 million to 85 million shares per day. Today it is not uncommon for 150 million shares to be traded in one day. What happened? The Securities and Exchange Commission changed its rules: high commission rates were no longer permitted. Consequently, rates fell and volume increased. Also, technological changes have enabled the New York Stock Exchange to handle larger volumes.

Question to Think About: Are there any other factors that may have caused the demand for stocks to increase in the last fifteen years?

V. KEY TERMS

demand	supply
law of demand	law of supply
relative price	supply curve
substitution effect	relevant resources
real income	market supply
income effect	alternative goods
demand curve	change in quantity supplied
market demand	change in supply
normal good	transaction costs
inferior good	surplus
substitutes	shortage
complements	equilibrium
tastes	disequilibrium
change in demand	price floor
change in quantity demanded	price ceiling

VI. QUESTIONS

A. Completion

1. Demand is a relation indicating the quantity of a commodity that consumers are _____ and _____ to purchase at various prices during a given time period, other things constant.

2. A price increase has two effects. The _____ effect means that a consumer switches to a relatively less expensive good; the _____ effect means that the consumer's purchasing power changes.

3. Bread is a _____ good if demand for it increases when income increases.

4. Two goods are _____ if an increase in the price of one causes the demand for the other to increase.

5. Consider a demand schedule. A change in the price of the good leads to a change in _____; a change in a relevant factor other than the price of the good leads to a change in _____.

6. Supply is a relationship between price and _____ during a given time period, other things constant.

7. An increase in price causes a(n) _____ in quantity supplied.

8. _____ are goods that are produced using the same resources.

9. A change in technology causes a change in _____.

10. The costs of time and information required for exchange are called _____.

11. If quantity demanded equals quantity supplied at a specific price, the market is in _____.

12. Government-imposed price floors tend to produce a _____.

13. A shortage exists when, for a given price, quantity demanded exceeds _____.

14. Price ceilings tend to produce _____.

B. True/False

_____ 1. Demand is the rate of desired and attainable purchase at each possible price, other things constant.

_____ 2. A demand schedule indicates what an individual desires.

_____ 3. Prices of all other goods are held constant for a given demand schedule.

_____ 4. An increase in the price of one good, other things constant, encourages consumers to switch to other goods.

_____ 5. A price increase results in a decrease in a consumer's real income.

_____ 6. The demand curve for a normal good slopes down, but the demand curve for an inferior good slopes up.

_____ 7. Movements along a demand curve represent changes in quantity demanded.

_____ 8. A change in income causes a change in quantity demanded.

_____ 9. Generally, economists assume that tastes change frequently and are the causes of changes in demand.

_____ 10. An increase in the price of a good provides an incentive to suppliers to switch resources from other goods and use them in producing more of the good with the higher price.

_____ 11. The market supply curve represents the sum of individual supply curves.

_____ 12. An increase in the price of a required resource shifts the supply curve of the good produced with it to the right.

_____ 13. Technological change causes an increase in quantity supplied.

_____ 14. Markets reduce the transaction costs of exchange.

_____ 15. If price is above the equilibrium price, there is an excess quantity supplied.

_____ 16. An increase in demand lowers the equilibrium price.

_____ 17. An increase in the price of a required resource will cause a change in quantity demanded of the good produced with it.

_____ 18. Disequilibrium can never exist if markets are allowed to operate without government intervention.

_____ 19. A price ceiling often leads to an excess quantity demanded.

C. Multiple Choice

1. Demand reflects the quantity that consumers
   a. want at alternative prices.
   b. need at alternative prices.
   c. are willing and able to buy at alternative prices.
   d. can buy at alternative prices.
   e. None of the above.

2. Which of the following is not held constant in defining the demand schedule?
   a. income
   b. prices of related goods
   c. tastes
   d. price of the good in question
   e. number of consumers

3. The substitution effect of a change in the price of good X is to
   a. increase the demand for good X if its price falls.
   b. decrease the demand for good X if its price rises.
   c. increase the quantity demanded of good X if its price rises.
   d. encourage consumers to substitute more of good X for other goods if X's price falls.
   e. encourage consumers to substitute other goods for good X if X's price falls.

4. A price change
   a. affects the consumer's ability to buy the good.
   b. affects the consumer's willingness to buy the good.
   c. changes the tastes of consumers.
   d. All of the above.
   e. a and b

5. The income effect of a price change will be greatest for which of the following goods?
   a. house
   b. automobile
   c. dinner at a restaurant
   d. gasoline
   e. The question cannot be answered without more information.

6. A movement along a demand curve can be caused by a change in
   a. income.
   b. the price of a substitute or complement.
   c. expectations about future prices.
   d. the price of the good in question.
   e. quantity supplied.

7. A change in quantity demanded is caused by a change in
   a. technology.
   b. income.
   c. the price of a related good.
   d. consumer tastes.
   e. quantity supplied.

8. Which of the following will cause an increase in the demand for an inferior good?
   a. an increase in income
   b. an increase in the price of a complement
   c. a drop in preferences for the good
   d. an increase in the number of consumers
   e. All of the above.

9. Supply indicates the quantity that producers
   a. are willing and able to offer for sale at a given price.
   b. can supply for a profit at a given price.
   c. will offer for sale if technical change takes place.
   d. All of the above.
   e. a and b only

10. Price and quantity supplied are usually directly related because
    a. higher prices mean that producers are rewarded more for production.
    b. the law of increasing opportunity cost applies.
    c. there is more prestige associated with producing a high-priced good.
    d. changes in technology lead to higher prices.
    e. a and b

11. Which of the following does not change supply?
    a. a change in price of the good in question
    b. a change in technology
    c. a change in producer expectations
    d. a change in the number of producers
    e. All of the above.

12. A movement along a supply curve is caused by
    a. a change in the number of consumers.
    b. a change in the number of producers.
    c. technological change.
    d. a change in supply.
    e. a change in quantity demanded.

13. If the price of an alternative good falls, but the price of good X remains the same,
    a. quantity supplied of good X will increase.
    b. quantity supplied of good X will decrease.
    c. quantity demanded of good X will decrease.
    d. supply of good X will decrease.
    e. supply of good X will increase.

14. The larger the market, the
    a. greater the transaction costs.
    b. greater the degree of specialization.
    c. less specialization there is.
    d. lower the price.
    e. more likely it is that producers will be large.

Exhibit 8

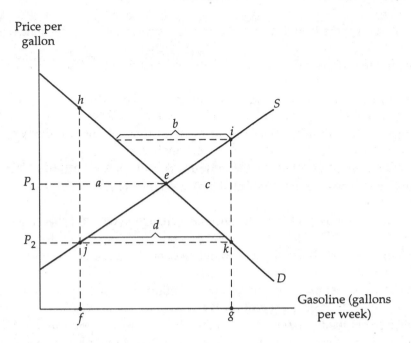

15. In Exhibit 8, equilibrium, shortage, and surplus are indicated by
    a. *e*, *d*, and *b*, respectively.
    b. *e*, *b*, and *d*, respectively.
    c. *e*, *a*, and *c*, respectively.
    d. *a*, *b*, and *d*, respectively.
    e. *c*, *d*, and *e*, respectively.

16. In Exhibit 8, if price is set by the government at P_2, the result is a
    a. surplus represented by *gf*.
    b. surplus represented by *gi*.
    c. shortage represented by *gf*.
    d. shortage represented by *jh*.
    e. shortage represented by *ke*.

17. An excess quantity demanded tends to
    a. put downward pressure on price.
    b. put upward pressure on price.
    c. cause demand to increase.
    d. cause supply to increase.
    e. b and d

18. A shift in the supply curve with demand held constant will cause
    a. equilibrium quantity to change in the same direction and equilibrium price to change in the opposite direction.
    b. equilibrium quantity to change in the opposite direction and equilibrium price to change in the same direction.
    c. both equilibrium quantity and equilibrium price to change in the same direction.
    d. both equilibrium quantity and equilibrium price to change in the opposite direction.
    e. changes that cannot be predicted without more information.

D. Discussion Questions

1. Explain why there is an inverse relationship between quantity demanded and price.

2. Explain the difference between a change in demand and a change in quantity demanded.

3. The correct answer to multiple choice question 7 is *a*. Why?

4. Explain the substitution effect and the income effect of a price change.

5. What would be the effect on the current price of coffee in this country if a period of unseasonably cold weather in Brazil destroyed a large portion of the coffee trees there?

6. Why are economists reluctant to attribute a change in demand to a change in taste?

7. Explain why there is usually a direct relationship between quantity supplied and price.

8. What is the effect on the supply of corn of an increase in the price of wheat?

9. A change in quantity demanded is caused by a change in price, and a change in quantity supplied is caused by a change in price. What causes the price to change?

10. In Exhibit 9, what are the results if the government sets the price of gasoline at $1.00 per gallon? What are the results if the price is set at $0.50 a gallon? How can these results be handled by the government?

Exhibit 9

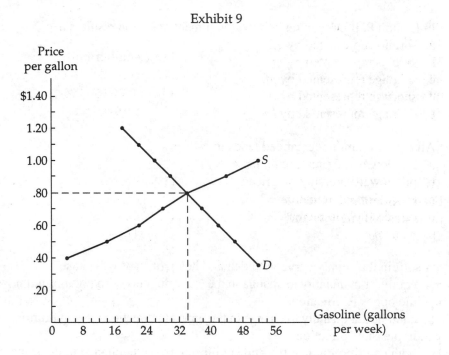

11. What are the effects on a market if demand increases and supply decreases?

12. Tickets for popular sporting events are often scalped at prices considerably above the prices printed on them. Using the concepts of supply and demand, explain why this happens. Why do those who produce the sporting events set such "low" prices for tickets when they know scalpers get much more?

13. In the mid-1970s no one had a personal computer at home. Today many people do. Using demand and supply curves, show the market for personal computers in the mid-1970s and today. Explain the difference between then and now.

14. Explain why disequilibrium can occur even in markets that are allowed to operate freely.

15. Offer a brief explanation for each of the following empirical observations:
    a. Americans began importing large quantities of Japanese autos in the 1970s.
    b. The price of medical care has increased substantially in recent years.
    c. A smaller proportion of the population smokes today than did so 20 years ago.
    d. Cable TV channels that show movies for a monthly fee have been losing viewers for the last couple of years.
    e. The number of people using the services of airlines has increased substantially over the last 15 years.

VII. ANSWERS

A. Completion

1. willing; able
2. substitution; income
3. normal
4. substitutes
5. quantity demanded; demand
6. quantity supplied
7. increase
8. Alternative goods
9. supply
10. transaction costs
11. equilibrium
12. surplus
13. quantity supplied
14. shortages

B. True/False

1. True
2. False. A demand schedule indicates willingness and ability to buy.
3. True
4. True
5. True
6. False
7. True
8. False
9. False
10. True
11. True
12. False
13. False
14. True
15. True
16. False
17. True. Supply of the good falls, raising the price and thus reducing the quantity demanded.
18. False
19. True

C. Multiple Choice

1.	c	6.	d	11.	a	16.	c
2.	d	7.	a	12.	a	17.	b
3.	d	8.	d	13.	e	18.	a
4.	e	9.	a	14.	b		
5.	a	10.	e	15.	a		

D. Discussion Questions

1. There is an inverse relationship between quantity demanded and price because people are willing and able to buy more at a lower price, other things constant. People are willing to buy more because of the substitution effect—they can substitute more of the lower-priced good for the higher-priced good. People also are able to buy more at a lower price because of the income effect—their real incomes have increased.

2. A change in quantity demanded occurs when there is a change in the price of the good. A change in demand occurs when there is a change in any factor that affects demand other than price. Changes in income, tastes, the prices of substitutes or complements, expectations about price and income in the future, and the number or composition of consumers in the market can all cause a change in demand. In these cases, the quantity demanded at each price changes, causing a change in the entire demand schedule, which shows up as a shift of the demand curve. A change in quantity demanded is a movement along the demand curve.

3. A change in quantity demanded is caused by a change in price. The change in price must be caused by a change in supply. Technology (answer *a*) is the only choice that causes supply to change.

4. When the price of one good goes up while the prices of all other goods remain constant, the good becomes relatively more costly. Consequently, some people consume less of the more costly good and more of other goods. This is the substitution effect. A price change also affects one's real income—that is, it causes an income effect. If real income increases, the consumer will want to buy more normal goods and fewer inferior goods; if real income decreases, the opposite will occur.

5. Unseasonably cold weather in Brazil would cause the current price of coffee in this country to rise because consumers would expect a shortage of coffee and thus a higher price in the future; this expectation would increase demand today. Further, suppliers would expect a higher price in the future; this expectation would induce them to remove some coffee from the market today and keep it to sell in the future. Hence, demand would increase and supply would decrease, so price would have to increase.

6. Tastes cannot be directly observed or measured. Hence, one can always attribute a change in demand to a change in taste and never be proven wrong. Because it is not observable, taste is not a good explanation of behavior. Since price and income changes can be observed, they are more useful as explanations of consumer behavior.

7. Producers are more willing and able to supply units at higher prices. They are more willing because the reward they earn by producing the product increases as price increases. They are also more able because higher prices allow them to pay the opportunity costs of resources used to produce the good. The law of increasing opportunity costs tells us that as production expands, opportunity costs increase. A higher price is required to cover these increased costs.

8. An increase in the price of wheat encourages producers to increase production of wheat, which takes resources. Some of these resources are likely to come from corn production, so the supply of corn will decrease.

9. A change in demand causes a change in price, which then causes a change in quantity supplied. A change in supply causes a change in price, which then causes a change in quantity demanded. So price changes whenever a factor other than price causes either demand or supply to change.

10. If the price is set at $1.00 per gallon, there is an excess quantity supplied; 52 gallons are supplied but only 26 gallons are demanded. Someone must purchase the extra 26 gallons (presumably the government). When the price is $0.50 per gallon, there is an excess quantity demanded, because 46 gallons are demanded but only 14 gallons are supplied. Some way must be found to ration these 14 gallons of gasoline among those who want it.

11. The price increases. The quantity purchased either increases or decreases, depending on whether the demand change or the supply change is greater.

12. Refer to the following exhibit. There are 60,000 tickets available, a number corresponding to the capacity of the stadium. $80 is the price that would clear the market, but the producers of the sporting event charge only $40. Hence, there is an excess demand for the tickets. Some who get the tickets would rather make a profit by selling them for the market-clearing price, $80, than go to the game, so they scalp their tickets. The people who set the price may set it low because they do not know what price is best or because it tends to be the best price on average.

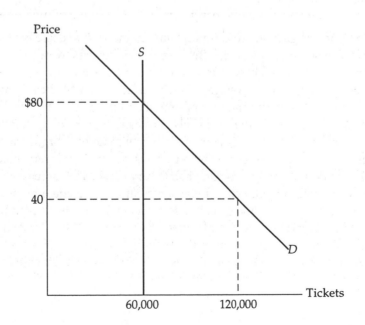

13. The following exhibit illustrates the answer to this question. Demand in the 1970s is indicated by *D*; supply is indicated by *S*. The supply curve intersects the vertical axis above the point where the demand curve intersects the vertical axis. This indicates that in the 1970s the cost of producing personal computers was too high given the demand. Because of technological changes, the supply curve has shifted out to *S′*. The demand curve has also shifted out, to *D′*, indicating increased demand. Demand has increased in part because of the increase in the availability of complementary goods such as computer games and software to make the personal computer useful in homes. The equilibrium price, $2,000, and quantity, 100,000, are indicated by point *e*.

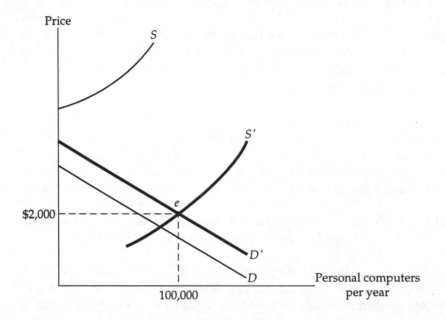

14. Disequilibrium exists whenever quantity demanded does not equal quantity supplied at the market price. If demand increases, there is an excess quantity demanded, which puts upward pressure on price. When price moves to the new equilibrium price, equilibrium is restored.

15. a. The price of gasoline rose significantly in the 1970s, decreasing the demand for cars that use a lot of gasoline. Because Japanese cars were more fuel efficient than American cars, imports of Japanese autos increased.

   b. Increased insurance coverage through Medicare and Medicaid programs has increased demand for medical care, thus raising the price. Second, technical changes have made medical treatment better, which also has caused greater expenditures on medical care.

   c. To explain the change in smoking habits, we can only argue that tastes are changing, since the relative price of cigarettes has not changed very much and increases in income do not change smoking habits very much. The increased awareness of the link between smoking and cancer has contributed to a change in tastes.

   d. The price of a substitute good has decreased—that is, the availability of video recorders and inexpensive movie rental outlets have decreased the demand for movie channels.

   e. With the deregulation of the airline industry, the price of air travel fell; this encouraged people to travel more by air. That is, there has been an increase in quantity demanded.

CHAPTER 4

Economic Decision Makers: Households, Firms, Governments, and the Rest of the World

I. INTRODUCTION

This chapter introduces the economic agents whose behavior we will analyze in the coming chapters. Of these, households are the most important because the demand for goods and services originates with households, and the resources used to produce goods and services are owned by households. Firms, governments, and the rest of the world are in some sense fictional characters—for example, there is no individual known as Government who makes decisions. Rather, people make decisions.

II. OUTLINE

1. The Household. The decisions of households are major factors in determining what is produced.

    1.1 The Evolution of the Household
         a. In earlier times, most households were farm families that were relatively self-reliant.
         b. Industrialization and urbanization altered the role of families in production.
         c. Since World War II married women have entered the labor force in significant numbers.
         d. Many two-income households demand more goods and services in product markets because they produce fewer goods and services at home.

    1.2 Households Maximize Utility
         a. Households are viewed as rational decision makers.
         b. Utility maximization is based on each household's subjective goals.

    1.3 Households as Resource Suppliers
         a. All resources are owned by households.
         b. Households can use resources to produce goods and services within the home.
         c. Households can supply their resources to firms or to governments.
         d. Labor is the most valuable resource owned by most households.
         e. Government gives some households transfer payments.
         f. Transfer payments include cash transfers and in-kind transfers.

    1.4 Households as Demanders of Goods and Services
         a. Households can allocate money in three ways: (1) personal consumption expenditures, (2) savings, and (3) taxes.
         b. Personal consumption is broken down into three categories: (1) durable goods, (2) nondurable goods, and (3) services.

2.   The Firm

    2.1   The Evolution of the Firm
        a.   Most production takes place outside the home because of the benefits of specialization and comparative advantage and because transaction costs make it too costly to use markets for every transaction.
        b.   During the cottage industry era, entrepreneurs arranged for production of goods and services and sold them to consumers. Production took place in the home.
        c.   During the Industrial Revolution, technological developments led to the organization of work in factories.
        d.   Firms are economic units formed by entrepreneurs to produce goods and services.
        e.   Firms seek to maximize profits.

    2.2   Why Does Household Production Still Exist?
        a.   Households produce at home when the opportunity cost of home production is less than the opportunity cost of using the market.
        b.   Some household production requires few specialized resources.
        c.   People can avoid taxes by relying on household production instead of on market purchases.
        d.   Household production reduces transaction costs in some cases.
        e.   Technological advances have made household production more efficient in some cases.

    2.3   *CASE STUDY:* The Electronic Cottage

    2.4   Kinds of Firms
        a.   A *sole proprietorship* is a single-owner firm.
           (1) Advantages
               (a)   Owner in complete control
               (b)   Easy to organize
           (2) Disadvantages
               (a)   Unlimited liability
               (b)   Difficult to raise money for construction and expansion
               (c)   Business generally ends at death of owner.
        b.   A *partnership* is two or more individuals working together in return for a share of the profit or loss.
           (1) Advantages
               (a)   Relatively easy to form
               (b)   Easier to raise startup funds
           (2) Disadvantages
               (a)   Decision making more difficult
               (b)   Each partner liable for the debts of the partnership
               (c)   Death or departure of one partner necessitates reorganization.
        c.   A *corporation* is a legal entity recognized by the state and treated as if it were an individual.
           (1) Advantages
               (a)   Easy to amass large sums of financing
               (b)   Liability for the firm's losses limited to the value of an owner's stock
           (2) Disadvantages
               (a)   Individual stockholder has little control over the firm's decisions.
               (b)   Corporate profits passed on to stockholders are taxed twice.

(3) The *S corporation* is a hybrid type of corporation.
   (a) The S corporation provides limited liability.
   (b) Corporate profits are taxed only once.
   (c) A firm must have no more than 35 stockholders to qualify as an S corporation.

2.5 Nonprofit Institutions

3. The Government

3.1 The Role of Government
   a. Government establishes and enforces the rules of the game: government protects private property and enforces contracts.
   b. Antitrust laws attempt to promote competition by preventing collusion.
   c. Government regulates natural monopolies.
   d. Government produces public goods.
   e. Government deals with problems associated with externalities.
   f. Government attempts to promote a more equal distribution of income.
   g. Government attempts to promote full employment, price stability, and economic growth.

3.2 Government's Structure and Objectives
   a. The United States has a federal system of government.
   b. It is difficult to define the objectives of the government. One useful theory is that elected officials are vote maximizers.
   c. Market exchange is based on voluntary exchange; public political choices may be enforced by the policing power of the government.
   d. Prices in the political system are not necessarily linked to costs.

3.3 Size and Growth of U.S. Government
   a. Government spending as a percentage of gross national product has increased from 10 percent in 1929 to 32 percent in 1998.
   b. The major source of growth has been federal outlays, particularly for Social Security and other transfer programs.

3.4 Sources of Government Revenue. Most of the government's revenue comes from income, sales, and property taxes.

3.5 Tax Principles and Tax Incidence
   a. Some think taxes should be based on the principle of ability to pay.
   b. Others think taxes should be based on the principle of benefits received.
   c. Tax incidence indicates who actually bears the burden of the tax.
   d. Important tax terms
      (1) *Marginal tax rate*: how much of each additional dollar of income must be paid in taxes
      (2) *Proportional taxes*: taxes for which the percentage of income paid is constant as income increases
      (3) *Progressive taxes*: taxes for which the percentage of income paid increases as income increases
      (4) *Regressive taxes*: taxes for which the percentage of income paid decreases as income increases

4.   The Rest of the World. The rest of the world consists of the households, firms, and governments of other countries. Some countries have formed economic alliances.

  4.1   International Trade
      a.   International trade occurs because the opportunity cost of producing specific goods differs across countries.
      b.   The volume of U.S. trade with the rest of the world has increased dramatically since 1970.
      c.   The merchandise trade balance equals the value of commodities exported minus the value of commodities imported.
      d.   A nation's balance of payments is the record of transactions between its residents and the residents of the rest of the world.

  4.2   Exchange Rates
      a.   *Foreign exchange* is the currency of another country that is used to carry out international transactions.
      b.   The exchange rate measures the price of one currency in terms of another.

  4.3   Trade Restrictions
      a.   Trade restrictions include the following:
          (1)   Tariffs, or taxes on imports and exports
          (2)   Quotas, or legal limits on the quantity of a commodity that can be imported or exported
          (3)   Other restrictions
      b.   Restrictions tend to benefit domestic producers and to harm consumers.

  4.4   *CASE STUDY:* Wheel of Fortune

5.   The Circular Flow Model. The circular flow model illustrates the interactions of the four types of economic decision makers.

  5.1   Flows between Households and Firms
      a.   Households supply resources to firms and purchase goods and services from firms.
      b.   Firms use resources obtained from households to produce goods and services and households use income received from firms to buy goods and services.

  5.2   Government-Related Flows
      a.   Governments purchase resources from households and convert these into public goods and services.
      b.   Governments finance their production by taxing households, firms, and the rest of the world, and by charging user fees for some services.
      c.   The net flows from households to governments equal taxes plus charges minus transfer payments.
      d.   The net flows from firms to governments equal taxes plus charges minus subsidies.

  5.3   Flows to and from the Rest of the World
      a.   The rest of the world both supplies resources to our resource markets and demands resources from our resource market.
      b.   The rest of the world demands goods and services from our markets and supplies goods and services to our markets.

III. DISCUSSION

The Household

Households are the most important economic agents because they are the ultimate demanders of goods and services and ultimate suppliers of all resources. Households make decisions about what goods and services to buy and what resources to sell so as to maximize *utility*. Utility is a subjective concept; activities that provide utility to one household may not be desirable to another.

Households receive income when they sell their resources to either firms or governments. The most important resource owned by most households is the labor services of family members. Labor earnings account for the majority of personal income in the United States. Most of the income received is spent on personal consumption of both durable and nondurable goods and services. The rest of the income is either saved or spent on taxes.

The Firm

A hundred years ago the majority of households produced most of what they consumed. Today, households purchase most of the goods and services they consume from firms. Increased specialization, fueled by technological change and increased industrialization, explains much of the change in household production and consumption. Firms developed to capture many of the gains from increased specialization.

Production still takes place within the home if the task requires very few specialized resources and is easy for households to perform. Generally, households will perform tasks whenever the opportunity cost of home production is less than the opportunity cost of purchasing the good or service in the marketplace.

Firms tend to specialize in certain tasks rather than produce everything. Entrepreneurs also specialize; an entrepreneur that is good at producing automobiles may not be good at finding oil. Firm size also tends to be limited because of the costs associated with coordinating the activities of more and more people. (Make sure you are familiar with the types of firms and their relative strengths and weaknesses.)

The Government

Not all goods are produced by households and firms. Voluntary exchange does not always produce all goods that society desires and does not always produce goods in an optimal manner. The government exists to handle situations that the market economy cannot handle adequately. One function of government is to promote an environment in which voluntary exchange can take place. That is, the government defines and enforces property rights so that theft and failure to fulfill contracts are limited.

The government also tries to limit the effects of *monopoly* in the economy. Some goods are produced in ways that make it most efficient for a single firm to supply the entire market. The government regulates such *natural monopolies* so that firms do not charge higher prices than necessary. Firms sometimes get together to try to raise prices above the competitive level; the government enacts antitrust laws designed to limit this behavior.

Another important role for the government is to provide public goods. A *public good* is a good that is available to everyone once it is produced. Private firms usually will not produce public goods in the quantities that society wishes or needs because people who have not paid for use of public goods can still consume them. The government, however, can produce public goods and force people to pay for them through taxes. One example of a public good is national defense.

The government intervenes in the economy to correct the problems associated with *externalities*, which are unpriced by-products of consumption or production. Reckless behavior caused by consuming too much beer, for example, and pollution caused by industrial production are examples of negative externalities; increased voting rates, a by-product of the consumption of education, is an example of a positive externality.

Finally, government also tries to promote equal distribution of income, full employment, price stability, and economic growth. A progressive tax system combined with *transfer payments* to the poor is used to promote the first goal; *fiscal* and *monetary policy* are used to promote the latter three goals.

The Rest of the World

People in the United States often trade with people in other countries. The rest of the world consists of all the other countries in the world. International trade occurs because the opportunity costs of producing specific goods differ across countries. A country exports goods for which its opportunity costs are relatively low. Even though international trade creates economic gains, most countries impose some sort of trade restrictions. These restrictions tend to benefit domestic producers at the expense of domestic consumers.

Trade with other countries involves using other currencies. If an American buys a sweater from an English firm, the sweater manufacturer expects to be paid in British pounds. *Foreign exchange*, the currency of other countries needed to carry out international transactions, can be bought and sold in foreign exchange markets. The *exchange rate* measures the price of one currency in terms of another. The *balance of payments* is the record of transactions between residents of one country and residents of the rest of the world.

The Circular Flow Model

The circular flow model illustrates the interactions of the four types of economic decision makers. Households are the ultimate demanders of goods and services. Households are also the ultimate suppliers of resources. The money paid to firms for goods and services is used by the firms to pay the resource owners for their resource services. Government also enters the picture by using resources to produce goods and services too. Government receipts can be taxes or user fees. Finally, households, firms, and governments of one country can interact with households, firms, and governments of other countries. Review Exhibit 4 in the textbook to make sure you understand the various flows.

IV. LAGNIAPPE

More on Households

We can see more clearly the role of households as suppliers of resources and buyers of goods by looking at the Jones family. Mr. Jones owns his own hardware store. Mrs. Jones works as an accountant for a corporation in the area. The family owns shares of stock in the company where Mrs. Jones works, and they own government bonds. The family is also renting out a house they own.

Mr. Jones's income is classified as proprietor's income. Mrs. Jones earns a salary. The dividends the couple receive from their shares of stock are another form of income, as is the interest from the government bonds. Finally, they receive rental income from the tenants who live in the house they own.

The Jones family earns money from the sale of the resources mentioned here. The family also purchases goods and services. Purchases of goods and services provide revenues for firms. The Joneses' taxes provide revenue to the government, which helps pay the salaries of government workers. Their savings also are used by others: government bonds help finance government activity, and the shares of stock help finance investments of the firm.

Question to Think About: How does government borrowing fit into the flow of expenditures and receipts discussed here?

Quasi-Public Goods

National defense is a public good because it is impossible to prevent nonpayers from receiving the benefits of the good once it is produced. Some goods do not have all the characteristics of a public good but are close enough so that the government generally provides them. For example, nonpayers can be excluded from receiving fire or police protection. But the high cost of determining whether someone who has just been mugged has paid for police protection makes it more efficient for government to provide police protection for all. Similarly, fire protection is provided for all even though it is possible not to serve nonpayers.

Question to Think About: On what other grounds besides those mentioned here might government-sponsored fire protection be extended to all citizens?

V. KEY TERMS

householder
utility
transfer payments
Industrial Revolution
firms
sole proprietorship
partnership
corporation
market failure
monopoly
natural monopoly
public good
externality
fiscal policy

monetary policy
ability-to-pay tax principle
benefits-received tax principle
tax incidence
proportional taxation
progressive taxation
marginal tax rate
regressive taxation
merchandise trade balance
balance of payments
foreign exchange
tariff
quota
circular flow model

VI. QUESTIONS

A. Completion

1.   Households are assumed to maximize their levels of satisfaction, or _____.

2.   Some households receive _____ from the government.

3.   Most personal income goes to _____.

4.   _____ are people who work for themselves.

5.   A cab ride is an example of a _____.

6.   The most common form of business is a _____.

7.   Stockholders are protected in the case of bankruptcy by the idea of _____.

8.   If a good is available to all once it is produced, it is a _____ good.

9.   _____ externalities convey unpriced benefits.

10.   The government's regulation of the money supply is called _____.

11.   _____ policy involves the government's taxing and spending powers.

12.   The percentage of income paid in taxes decreases as income increases under _____.

13.   Legal limits on the quantities of particular goods that can be imported are called _____.

14.   The _____ measures the price of one currency in terms of another.

15.   The merchandise trade balance is one component of a country's _____.

16. Households demand goods and services in the _____ and supply resources in the _____.

17. The _____ describes the interactions among the four types of economic decision makers.

18. Governments obtain receipts from _____ and _____.

B. True/False

_____ 1. The decisions made by households about consuming goods and services determine what is produced.

_____ 2. Utility maximization is based on an objective standard.

_____ 3. All resources are owned ultimately by households.

_____ 4. Rents and dividends make up about one-quarter of all personal income.

_____ 5. For most households, personal consumption expenditures use the largest share of personal income.

_____ 6. Farm families tend to be more self-sufficient than urban families.

_____ 7. Firms exist because of transaction costs.

_____ 8. Households with the highest opportunity cost of time tend to hire others to perform household tasks rather than engage in household production.

_____ 9. Partnerships offer limited liability.

_____ 10. The bulk of all business sales are made by corporations.

_____ 11. Market transactions generally reflect private benefits and costs as well as external benefits and costs.

_____ 12. A natural monopoly exists when one firm controls all of a natural resource.

_____ 13. Coercion is often a part of government involvement in the economy.

_____ 14. In comparison with other industrial countries, the proportion of government spending in GDP is greater in the United States.

_____ 15. Sales taxes provide the bulk of revenues to most states.

_____ 16. The gasoline tax is based on the principle of benefits received.

_____ 17. The marginal tax rate indicates how much of each additional dollar earned is paid in taxes.

_____ 18. Trade restrictions are imposed to benefit domestic consumers.

_____ 19. An increase in the dollar price of the yen is associated with a decrease in the yen price of the dollar.

_____ 20. It is impossible to run a deficit in all accounts in the balance of payments.

_____ 21. Demand and supply apply to product markets but not to resource markets.

C. Multiple Choice

1. Utility is
   a. a statement about who consumes a good or service.
   b. a measure of the usefulness of a good.
   c. the satisfaction received from consuming a good or service.
   d. the satisfaction received from making a decision.
   e. None of the above.

2. Which of the following could be produced either by individual households or by firms?
   a. lawn care
   b. cleaning services
   c. cooking
   d. child care
   e. All of the above.

3. The majority of personal income in the United States comes from
   a. labor earnings.
   b. ownership of land.
   c. ownership of capital.
   d. profits and dividends.
   e. the sum of b, c, and d.

4. The service sector has been growing rapidly in recent years because
   a. households are producing fewer of these services themselves.
   b. the opportunity cost of time for many households has increased.
   c. more married women are in the labor force.
   d. All of the above.
   e. None of the above.

5. Economists who have studied labor markets attribute the increase since World War II in the number of women who work outside the home to
   a. the high cost of living, which requires a family to have two incomes to maintain its standard of living.
   b. increasing demand for labor, which has raised wages and expanded job opportunities.
   c. inclusion of women under the Civil Rights Act.
   d. declines in the number of women who have children and delays in getting married.
   e. increasing college attendance by women relative to men.

6. Production by firms can be explained by
   a. increased specialization.
   b. increased specialization and comparative advantage.
   c. increased specialization and positive transaction costs.
   d. tax incentives.
   e. b and d.

7. Which of the following is most likely to be purchased from a firm rather than produced by the household?
   a. termite control
   b. child care
   c. washing the car
   d. painting the house
   e. putting in storm windows

8. Corporations account for the majority of sales in the economy because
   a. the corporation is the easiest form of business to begin.
   b. there are tax advantages for corporations that are not available to sole proprietorships or partnerships.
   c. corporations can more easily raise large sums for financing projects.
   d. owners have the greatest control over the decision making of the firm.
   e. a, b, and c

9. A natural monopoly evolves when
   a. there is only one firm in the industry.
   b. it is cheaper for one firm than for two or more firms to serve the market.
   c. the government establishes one firm as the only firm in a market.
   d. public goods are produced.
   e. firms successfully collude.

10. According to one theory of government behavior, elected officials attempt to maximize which of the following?
    a. utility
    b. votes
    c. the size of their administrative agencies
    d. profits
    e. tax revenues

11. Since World War II, federal government revenues have increasingly come from
    a. excise taxes.
    b. personal income taxes.
    c. corporate income taxes.
    d. payroll taxes.
    e. tariffs.

12. Which of the following sources of government revenue is based on the individual's ability to pay?
    a. the gasoline tax
    b. the toll on a government-owned bridge
    c. the progressive income tax
    d. the admission charge to a federal park
    e. All of the above.

13. In the absence of trade restrictions, exchange among countries
    a. is due to cultural differences.
    b. follows the law of comparative advantage.
    c. tends to harm consumers in less developed countries.
    d. benefits only those who are engaged in international trade.
    e. has declined in importance in the last 20 years.

14. The exchange rate of a foreign currency will tend to increase if
    a. demand for that country's goods increases.
    b. the value of the dollar also increases.
    c. the supply of the foreign currency in foreign exchange markets increases.
    d. people in that country increase their import buying.
    e. All of the above.

15. If a firm receives $100 million from selling its products, which portion of the $100 million must it give to resource owners?
    a. the portion that is interest
    b. the portion that is profit
    c. the portion that is the return on capital
    d. b and c
    e. The firm must give up the entire $100 million to resource owners.

16. If consumers buy $10 million worth of dolls from toy companies, the firms
    a. pay resource owners all of the $10 million except the amount that is profit.
    b. pay resource owners all of the $10 million except the amount that goes to stockholders.
    c. pay workers and suppliers of materials part of the $10 million. Profits, interest, and rent do not go to resource owners.
    d. pay the entire $10 million to resource owners.
    e. None of the above.

17. Owners of resources receive income from
    a. firms.
    b. governments.
    c. foreign firms and governments.
    d. All of the above.
    e. a and b only.

D. Discussion Questions

1. Firms often own resources—for example, many oil firms own oil wells. How, then, can the text say that all resources are owned by households?

2. Why is the household considered the most important actor in the economy?

3. Discuss the factors that have changed the household in the last hundred years. What effects have these changes had on the economy?

4. The text says that the rise of two-worker families reduces the advantages of specialized resources within the family. Explain.

5. Over the years, food prices at grocery stores have increased faster than the prices received by farmers. Can you offer a (partial) explanation for this?

6. Discuss the factors that determine whether tasks are performed by members of a household or by firms.

7. What are the weaknesses and strengths of the various forms of business? Why do corporations tend to be so much larger than sole proprietorships or partnerships?

8. Why does the government, rather than private firms, provide the judicial system?

9. What are public goods? Why does the government tend to produce public goods?

10. Why is it so difficult to determine the objectives of the government?

11. How does market exchange differ from exchange in political markets?

12. Discuss the two principles of taxation. Why are not all taxes collected on the basis of benefits received?

13. Why would a country impose trade restrictions if free trade is beneficial to the country?

14. What would be the effect of an increased demand in the United States for German goods?

15. During the 1980s, the amount of imports Americans purchased was greater than the amount of exports they sold. How was the deficit financed?

VII. ANSWERS

A. *Completion*

1. utility
2. transfer payments
3. personal consumption expenditures
4. Proprietors
5. service
6. sole proprietorship
7. limited liability
8. public
9. Positive
10. monetary policy
11. Fiscal
12. regressive taxation
13. quotas
14. exchange rate
15. balance of payments
16. product market; resource market
17. circular flow model
18. taxes; user fees

B. True/False

1.	True	12.	False
2.	False	13.	True
3.	True	14.	False
4.	False	15.	True
5.	True	16.	True
6.	True	17.	True
7.	True	18.	False
8.	True	19.	True
9.	False	20.	True
10.	True	21.	False
11.	False		

C. Multiple Choice

1.	c	6.	c	11.	d	16.	d
2.	e	7.	a	12.	c	17.	d
3.	a	8.	c	13.	b		
4.	d	9.	b	14.	a		
5.	b	10.	b	15.	e		

D. Discussion Questions

1. Firms are owned by individual stockholders, so ultimately all resources are owned by households.

2. Households are the ultimate demanders of goods and services, and they determine what will be produced by what they are willing and able to purchase. Households also ultimately supply all resources used in production.

3. Technological change increased farm productivity, and the Industrial Revolution created opportunities for employment off the farm. As people left farms and moved to cities, family size decreased and families undertook less home production of many goods and services. The increased demand for goods and services by households has been met by firms. The demand for such services increased as married women entered the labor force in larger numbers.

4. The higher opportunity cost of time for women who work outside the home implies that they will substitute market-produced goods for home-produced goods on many occasions. The reduced reliance on household production reduces the advantages of specialization in the home.

5. The increase in two-income families reduced the amount of "cooking from scratch" performed by households. Instead, families purchase foods that take less time to prepare. Such foods are already processed, at least to some degree, and this extra preparation by producers increases the price.

6. In general, a task will be performed by a household if the opportunity cost of home production is less than the opportunity cost of purchasing the good or service from a firm. The opportunity cost of home production depends on how specialized the required resources are and on the opportunity cost of time for the members of the family. A household may also perform certain tasks in order to have more control over the final products or to avoid taxes. In general, as the family income increases, more services will be bought rather than produced by members of the household.

7. Both sole proprietorships and partnerships are fairly easy to establish. The major weakness of each is the limited ability to raise financial capital for starting the company or increasing productive capacity. Owners and partners are also more exposed to risk in the case of lawsuits, and the death or departure of an owner can necessitate closing or reorganizing the firm. Corporations are more difficult to establish, but they provide limited liability and a much greater ability to raise financial capital (so they tend to be larger than other types of firms). However, corporate profits are often taxed twice, which is not true of the profits of sole proprietorships or partnerships.

8. Judicial services are not public goods, because it would be possible to exclude nonpayers from the system. However, society deems it inappropriate to rely on private firms to provide judicial services and charge people to use the system because that would put the poor at a disadvantage. A well-run judicial system provides external benefits to society, so providing judicial services is seen as a legitimate role for government.

9. Public goods are goods that nonpayers cannot be prevented from using once the goods are produced. Private firms are not likely to produce public goods because they cannot be assured of payment. The government provides such goods and requires people to pay for them by means of taxes.

10. Government is not a single entity—it includes the federal government, state governments, and local governments. Further, there are many agencies in the various branches of government. The legislative branch may have different objectives than the executive branch, and the agency heads may have different objectives yet. In addition, citizens disagree about what the objectives of the government should be.

11. Market exchange is voluntary and involves market prices. Exchange in political markets involves votes rather than dollars and often involves coercion, as in the case of the payment of taxes.

12. The two principles of taxation are the principle of ability to pay and the principle of benefits received. Proponents of the former argue that taxes should be based on one's ability to pay, that is, the rich should pay more than the poor. Proponents of the latter argue that taxes should be related to benefits received from the government. According to this principle, schools should be supported by parents rather than by all taxpayers. Not all taxes can be collected on the basis of benefits received, however, since the actual benefits received are often very difficult to measure. In some cases, people would have an incentive to lie about the benefits they received if it meant a lower tax bill. This would be especially true in the case of public goods. Further, any programs designed to help the poor could not be financed on a benefits-received principle—in such cases the people who receive the benefits are too poor to pay the taxes.

13.   Countries impose trade restrictions because domestic producers that face competition from cheaper imports lobby for protection.

14.   The German goods must be bought with German marks, so the demand for marks would increase. The increased demand for marks would cause the exchange rate to increase. More dollars would be needed to buy a given number of marks, so the dollar prices of the German good would increase.

15.   The deficit was financed by borrowing from foreigners.

CHAPTER 5

Introduction to Macroeconomics

I. INTRODUCTION

This chapter presents an overview of the field of macroeconomics. Macroeconomics is the study of the economy as a whole. Topics covered in this chapter include inflation, depression, unemployment, monetary policy, full employment, and stagflation.

II. OUTLINE

1. The National Economy. Macroeconomics is concerned with the overall performance of the economy. The *gross product* is the market value of final goods and services produced in a particular geographic region during a specific period of time.

 1.1 What's Special about the National Economy?
 a. There are great differences between the economies of different countries, so each must be treated as a separate entity.
 b. The focus of macroeconomics is the performance of the national and world economies.

 1.2 The Human Body and the Economy
 a. Money is the medium of exchange that facilitates the exchange of goods and services.
 b. Flows and stocks:
 (1) A flow variable measures an amount per unit of time.
 (2) A stock variable measures an amount at a particular point in time.
 c. Role of expectations. Expectations are often an important determinant of the performance of the economy and are often self-fulfilling.
 d. Differences of opinion. Economists may offer conflicting diagnoses of the problems of the economy and disagree on possible cures.

 1.3 Testing New Theories. It is very difficult to test new macroeconomic theories because there is no laboratory in which controlled experiments can be performed.

 1.4 Knowledge and Performance
 a. As long as the economy runs smoothly, we do not need to know how it operates.
 b. When the economy performs poorly, we need to know how it operates in order to repair it.
 c. Poor theories lead to poor decisions by policymakers.

2. Economic Fluctuations and Growth. The rise and fall of economic activity relative to the long-term growth trend of the economy are called *economic fluctuations*.

2.1 Economic Fluctuation Analysis
   a. A *recession* is any decline in the nation's total production lasting six months or more.
   b. A *depression* is a severe recession lasting more than a year.
   c. The economy generally has periods of expansion and periods of contraction, with total output increasing over the long run.

2.2 *CASE STUDY:* The Global Economy

2.3 Leading Economic Indicators. Certain activities called *leading economic indicators* tend to foreshadow turning points in the business cycle.

3. Aggregate Demand and Aggregate Supply

   3.1 Aggregate Output and the Price Level
      a. *Aggregate demand* is the relationship between the price level (an average of all prices in the economy) and total demand for goods and services produced in the economy.
      b. *Aggregate output* is the total quantity of all goods and services produced in an economy during a given time period.
      c. The *price level* is a composite measuring the prices on average of all goods.
      d. *Gross domestic product* (GDP), which is the market value of all goods and services in the United States in a year, is the most common measure of aggregate output.
      e. The price level can be measured by the consumer price index or the implicit price deflator.

   3.2 Aggregate Demand Curve
      a. The *aggregate demand curve* shows the relation between the price level and aggregate output demanded.
      b. As the price level falls, the aggregate quantity demanded increases.
         (1) People are able to buy more when the price level declines because their real wealth increases.
         (2) A drop in the U.S. price level means that U.S. goods are less expensive relative to foreign goods, so people buy more U.S. goods.

   3.3 Aggregate Supply Curve
      a. *Aggregate supply* is the relationship between the price level and aggregate output supplied in the economy, other things constant.
      b. The shape of the aggregate supply curve is a much debated topic.

   3.4 Equilibrium. The intersection of the aggregate demand and aggregate supply curves yields the equilibrium price level and aggregate output. Higher levels of aggregate output reflect higher levels of employment.

4. A Short History of the U.S. Economy

   4.1 The Great Depression and Before
      a. The economy was characterized by cycles of boom and depression.
      b. The Great Depression of the 1930s was the worst of these depressions.
      c. The cause of the Great Depression was a dramatic shift in aggregate demand as a result in part of grim expectations and the collapse of the banking system.

4.2 The Age of Keynes: After the Great Depression to the Early 1970s
   a. John Maynard Keynes argued that the economy might stay in a depression indefinitely.
   b. Keynes's recommendations focused on how to increase aggregate demand through fiscal policy and are called *demand-side policies*.
   c. The Employment Act of 1946 set a federal policy of maintaining "maximum employment, production, and purchasing power."
   d. In the 1960s, economists, using Keynes's model, believed they could fine-tune the economy.

4.3 The Great Stagflation: 1973–1980
   a. Keynesian policies did not work so well in the 1970s, when inflation was associated with economic stagnation.
   b. The problems in the 1970s tended to be associated with declining aggregate supply.

4.4 Experience Since 1980
   a. Supply-side economics emphasizes the importance of aggregate supply and economic incentives.
   b. During the 1980s output increased, unemployment declined, inflation fell and remained low, and the federal deficit increased.
   c. From 1992 to 1998, the American economy experienced growing prosperity, reduced unemployment, and low inflation.

4.5 *CASE STUDY:* A Half Century of Price Levels and Real GDP

III. DISCUSSION

The National Economy

An important measure of the performance of the national economy is the *gross domestic product:* the market value of final goods and services currently produced in the country. We focus on the national economy because there are few differences within a country with respect to economic activity; however, there are considerable differences between countries.

Money is a medium that circulates throughout the economy and facilitates the exchange of goods and services. At any given time there are a certain number of dollars in the economy. This amount of dollars is referred to as the money *stock*. But the average dollar is spent more than once in a year, so we can also speak of money as a *flow* variable. The distinction between stocks and flows is an important one in economics, and you should pay special attention whenever the distinction is made in the text.

Macroeconomics seems difficult to grasp at times. In part this difficulty is due to the key role of expectations. The expectations of economic agents are often self-fulfilling, which sometimes frustrates the efforts of policymakers to stabilize the economy. Another difficulty for students is that macroeconomists often seem to disagree on the problems facing the economy and on the solutions to the problems. Unfortunately, macroeconomic theories are difficult to test because controlled laboratory experiments are not feasible.

Economic Fluctuations and Growth

All industrial market economies experience fluctuating periods of expansion and contraction. Over the long run, economic output tends to increase, but it does not do so without fluctuations. Expansions tend to last longer than contractions, and the overall trend in the United States has been an increase in the standard of living. There are some similarities between various contractions and between various expansions, so economists have tried to look for signals that indicate when a turning point is coming. This process is still rather undeveloped.

Aggregate Demand and Aggregate Supply

The total demand for goods and services at various price levels, other things constant, is known as *aggregate demand*. The aggregate quantity demanded increases as the price level falls. The behavior of the aggregate demand curve is similar to that of a demand curve for a particular commodity, and the reason is similar. At a lower price level people are willing and able to buy more, so the quantity demanded of all goods and services increases. The aggregate quantity supplied at various price levels, other things constant, is known as *aggregate supply*. The shape of the *aggregate supply curve* is a source of debate among economists and will be discussed further in a later chapter. An upward-sloping curve indicates a positive relation between the price level and the quantity of aggregate output supplied. The equilibrium of the economy as a whole is determined by the intersection of the aggregate demand and the aggregate supply curves.

A Short History of the U.S. Economy

Before World War II, the economy was characterized by numerous fluctuations, and the government did not actively intervene to stabilize the economy except in a few rare circumstances. The worst *depression* occurred during the 1930s. In response to this economic event, John Maynard Keynes developed a theory that argued that depressions are not necessarily self-correcting, and that if left to itself, the economy might remain in a depression for a long period of time. To help restore economic expansion, he argued, the federal government should engage in deficit spending.

Between the end of the Great Depression and the inflation associated with the Vietnam War, Keynesian policies seemed to work well. However, when the aggregate supply shocks of the 1970s led to stagflation, Keynesian policies fell into disrepute. To stimulate aggregate supply, the Reagan administration attempted to increase incentives to work and invest by cutting income taxes. One result was large federal deficits through the 1980s. A combination of economic growth, reductions in government spending, and tax increases led to a budget surplus in 1998. Both unemployment and inflation were at low levels by post-war standards.

IV. LAGNIAPPE

Economic Fluctuations

Economists have long tried to understand economic fluctuations and predict turning points in them. There is still a long way to go. Theories have ranged from associating sunspot activity with economic fluctuations to hypothesizing that activities of entrepreneurs start upswings that ultimately end in recession.

Students may wonder if these economic fluctuations are regular. Since the economy is highly integrated, events that affect one industry often cause repercussions in many other industries. For example, the automobile industry is an important force in the economy. When auto sales are high, so are sales of steel, tires, rubber, and all other inputs used in auto production. Further, the communities where automobile plants are located do well, and people have a lot of money to spend, which benefits other businesses. When auto sales are down, however, the opposite happens, and a downturn in the auto industry causes a downturn in many other industries and communities. A cycle can develop because autos are durable goods. In difficult times people can postpone purchases of new cars. Eventually old cars wear out, however, and people buy new cars. This generates an upswing in auto sales and production.

Question to Think About: What are the repercussions of swings in housing activity?

Expectations After World War II

Economists and business people who believed that the end of World War II would cause a depression similar to the one that preceded the war were proven wrong. During the war, consumer durable goods either were not produced at all or were produced in very small amounts so that the materials that would otherwise go into them could be used to produce military equipment instead. As a result, by the end of the war the durable goods held by households were old and often in disrepair. After the war, the large demand for such products generated many jobs and the depression did not occur. Owners of businesses who believed a downturn was coming tended to be very cautious, failed to expand productive capacity, and were unprepared for the large demand for goods. Firms that expected a business upturn invested heavily and were prepared to meet the large demand. Such firms prospered and expanded in the immediate postwar years.

Question to Think About: Think of firms that expanded during the postwar years and some that did not. How are these firms doing today?

V.   KEY TERMS

economy

gross domestic product (GDP)

money

flow

stock

economic fluctuations

depression

recession

expansion

aggregate output

aggregate demand

price level

aggregate demand curve

aggregate supply curve

government budget deficit

demand-side economics

inflation

stagflation

supply-side economics

government debt

VI. QUESTIONS

A. Completion

1. The _____ is the market value of final goods and services produced in a geographic region in a certain period of time.

2. The focus of _____ is the performance of the national and world economy.

3. A _____ variable represents an amount of something at a particular point in time.

4. In economics, _____ can often be self-fulfilling.

5. A _____ is a decline in the nation's total output lasting at least six months.

6. Activities that tend to predict turning points in economic fluctuations are called _____ indicators.

7. Aggregate _____ consists of all final goods and services produced in the economy.

8. The _____ reflects the average prices of goods and services produced in the economy.

9. The most common measure of aggregate output is the _____.

10. The aggregate _____ curve slopes down.

11. The prevailing view before the Great Depression was that the economy was basically _____.

12. The Keynesian approach to promoting full employment focuses on ways to increase aggregate _____ and is often called _____-side economics.

13. _____ is a combination of economic contraction and inflation.

14. Advocates of _____-side economics emphasize the importance of economic incentives.

B. True/False

_____ 1. Macroeconomists tend to agree on how the economy works but disagree on what should be done when the economy performs poorly.

_____ 2. Each country answers the three economic questions in different ways.

_____ 3. Gross domestic product is a flow variable.

_____ 4. The expectations of economic agents are often self-fulfilling.

_____ 5. Economic fluctuations tend to affect just a few important sectors of the economy.

_____ 6. Over the long run, the total output of the economy tends to increase.

_____ 7. A recession is an increase in the unemployment rate.

_____ 8. The average expansion and the average contraction in the United States since the end of World War II have been about the same length.

_____ 9. Turning points in the economy are identified after the fact.

_____ 10. A change in the price level is a change in relative prices.

_____ 11. The GDP deflator tracks price changes of all items in the gross domestic product.

_____ 12. One reason the aggregate demand curve slopes down is that as the domestic price level falls, people buy more foreign goods.

_____ 13. An increase in the supply of resources causes the economy to move along the aggregate supply curve.

_____ 14. Higher levels of aggregate output are associated with higher levels of employment.

_____ 15. Prior to the 1930s most economists believed that recessions were self-correcting.

_____ 16. John Maynard Keynes argued that the economy was not always self-correcting.

_____ 17. The Council of Economic Advisers was established in 1932 by President Roosevelt.

_____ 18. An important part of demand-side economics is the idea that public policy should focus on the incentives people have to produce goods and services.

_____ 19. Stagflation is a combination of an economic contraction and inflation.

_____ 20. The goal of supply-side economics is to increase aggregate output while reducing the price level.

C. Multiple Choice

1. Which of the following would not be included in the gross domestic product?
   a. a meal at a restaurant
   b. an afternoon spent mowing your lawn
   c. tuition at a private college
   d. purchase of an airline ticket
   e. a trip to the car wash

2. Which of the following is a flow variable?
   a. the total deposits in all checking accounts today
   b. the total shares of all stocks outstanding
   c. a family's weekly income
   d. the number of people in the labor force
   e. the national debt

3. The first term is a flow and the second a stock in all but which one of the following pairs?
   a. income; wealth
   b. annual income tax collections; national debt
   c. a business's receipts; a business's capital stock
   d. a family's weekly spending; the amount in the family's checking account
   e. gross domestic product; the national spending in a year

4. It is difficult to test macroeconomic theories because
   a. economic theories are not testable.
   b. economic variables are impossible to measure.
   c. there is not enough agreement about which theories to test.
   d. the theories cannot be tested in laboratories or controlled settings.
   e. All of the above.

5. An expansion
   a. begins when the economy moves above its long-term growth trend.
   b. is the period between a trough and the subsequent peak.
   c. is usually followed by a recession of the same length.
   d. is the period six months before and six months after a peak.
   e. b and c only

6. Compared to those before World War II, recessions since the war have been
   a. shorter.
   b. less severe.
   c. more severe.
   d. more frequent.
   e. both a and b.

7. Which of the following is a leading economic indicator?
   a. gross domestic product
   b. unemployment
   c. the stock market
   d. the NBER
   e. All of the above.

8. A change in the price level is a change in
   a. the price of domestic goods relative to imported goods.
   b. the average price of all goods and services produced in the economy.
   c. the price of goods relative to services.
   d. All of the above.
   e. a and b only.

9. An increase in the cost of living
    a. increases aggregate demand.
    b. decreases aggregate supply.
    c. decreases the quantity demanded of aggregate output.
    d. decreases aggregate demand.
    e. increases the quantity demanded of aggregate output.

10. There is an inverse relationship between the price level and the quantity of output demanded, other things constant, because
    a. a reduction in the price level means that consumers can buy more goods and services with their savings.
    b. a reduction in the price level makes domestic goods relatively cheaper than foreign goods and causes an increase in consumption of domestic goods and services.
    c. a reduction in the price level decreases everyone's real wealth so people save less and buy more.
    d. the substitution effect of a lower price level is always greater than the income effect.
    e. a and b

11. The quantity of aggregate output producers supply
    a. rises when the price level rises faster than the cost of production.
    b. is independent of the price level.
    c. rises when wages increase.
    d. decreases when the price level increases.
    e. None of the above.

12. Greater output is associated with
    a. higher levels of employment.
    b. reduced unemployment.
    c. a higher price level.
    d. All of the above.
    e. a and b only

13. If there is a decrease in aggregate demand, the price level will tend to
    a. increase.
    b. remain unchanged.
    c. decrease.
    d. be unpredictable without more information.
    e. decrease in real terms.

14. The Great Depression can be viewed as a shift to the
    a. left of the aggregate supply curve.
    b. right of the aggregate supply curve.
    c. left of the aggregate demand curve.
    d. right of the aggregate demand curve.
    e. left of aggregate demand and a shift to the right of aggregate supply.

15. Prior to the Great Depression, government policy regarding economic fluctuations was to
    a. let the economy correct itself.
    b. raise taxes in a depression and cut taxes in a recession.
    c. follow demand-side economic policies.
    d. follow supply-side economic policies.
    e. increase government spending during a recession.

16. According to Keynes, aggregate demand is inherently unstable because
    a. the government is not able to fine-tune the economy.
    b. the investment decisions of business people are often destabilizing.
    c. taxes reduce the incentives people have to work and invest.
    d. the money supply is hard to control.
    e. All of the above.

17. An expansionary fiscal policy calls for
    a. a balanced federal budget.
    b. a federal budget deficit.
    c. a federal budget surplus.
    d. an increase in the money supply.
    e. None of the above.

18. The Keynesian approach to macroeconomics is to focus on
    a. increasing aggregate supply.
    b. increasing aggregate demand.
    c. keeping inflation relatively low.
    d. laissez-faire.
    e. None of the above.

19. Under the Employment Act of 1946, the federal government is responsible for encouraging
    a. full employment.
    b. maximum production.
    c. maximum purchasing power.
    d. maximum price levels.
    e. a, b, and c.

20. The purpose of the tax cuts in the 1980s was to
    a. increase the incentives for resource owners to supply their resources to productive activity.
    b. decrease the federal deficit.
    c. increase aggregate demand.
    d. decrease aggregate demand.
    e. control the money supply.

D. *Discussion Questions*

1. How is the U.S. national economy different from those of other nations?

2. Distinguish between a stock variable and a flow variable.

3. What role do expectations play in the economy?

4. Why is it difficult to test macroeconomic theories?

5. What are the characteristics of a recession?

6. Why is war associated with economic expansions?

7. How is an aggregate demand curve like a demand curve for a good? How is it different?

8. Explain why the aggregate demand curve slopes down.

9. Suppose the economy is initially in equilibrium. What are the effects on the economy of an increase in labor productivity?

10. What differences are there between the way economists after Keynes and economists prior to Keynes viewed the economy?

11. What differences are there between the way economists after Keynes and economists prior to Keynes viewed the economy?

12. What is stagflation? What policy did the government implement in the 1980s in an attempt to combat stagflation?

13. How does demand-side economics differ from supply-side economics?

14. Why has real GDP per capita increased in the United States from 1940 to 1998?

VII. ANSWERS

A. *Completion*

1. gross production
2. macroeconomics
3. stock
4. expectations
5. recession
6. leading economic
7. output
8. price level
9 gross domestic product
10. demand
11. self-correcting
12. demand; demand
13. Stagflation
14. supply

B. True/False

1. False
2. True
3. True
4. True
5. False
6. True
7. False
8. False. Expansions have been longer than contractions, on average.
9. True
10. False
11. True
12. False. People buy fewer foreign goods.
13. False. The aggregate supply curve shifts.
14. True
15. True
16. True
17. False
18. False
19. True
20. True

C. Multiple Choice

1. b
2. c
3. e
4. d
5. b
6. e
7. c
8. e
9. c
10. e
11. a
12. d
13. c
14. c
15. a
16. b
17. b
18. b
19. e
20. a

D. Discussion Questions

1. The U.S. national economy differs from those of other nations because the United States has a unique mix of economic resources, a unique cultural and political climate, its own monetary and banking system, and because it answers the three economic questions in its own ways.

2. A stock variable represents an amount of something at a particular time. Examples would include the stock of money in the economy on January 1, the number of cars licensed in the United States today, and the wealth of a family. A flow variable represents an amount per unit of time. Examples would include the number of cars produced in a week, the hours worked in a month, and the income of a family for a year.

3. Expectations often can be self-fulfilling. When consumers and business people are optimistic, jobs are plentiful and provide income for consumers that enables them to buy the goods that are produced. If everyone is pessimistic, then people are fearful to spend money or make investments.

4. There is no lab in which experiments can be performed. Comparisons across nations are tricky because each national economy is a unique blend of economic, cultural, and political conditions. The chance discovery is not very likely.

5. A recession is a decline in a nation's total output lasting at least six months. It is characterized by declining output and increasing unemployment.

6. Wars are characterized by increases in output of goods used by the military, such as planes and tanks; this means that economic activity increases in wartime.

7. The shape of the aggregate demand curve is like the shape of a demand curve for a good in that both slope down. Both also deal with a quantity and a price. However, the quantity for aggregate demand is the total quantity of goods and services produced. The price on a demand curve is a relative price, whereas the price on the aggregate demand curve is an average price for all goods.

8. The quantity of aggregate demand depends in part on household wealth; a reduction in the price level increases the amount of goods and services that can be purchased with a given amount of dollars. Another reason the aggregate demand curve slopes down is that a fall in the price level reduces the price of domestic goods relative to foreign goods; Americans then increase their purchases of U.S. goods and services.

9. Increased labor productivity means increased aggregate supply, represented by a shift to the right of the aggregate supply curve. The increase in aggregate output causes the price level to fall.

10. Prior to Keynes, economists believed the economy was basically self-correcting. This meant that they believed a recession would not persist and that counterforces would take effect that would bring the economy out of the recession. After Keynes, most economists believed that the economy could stay in recession for a long time and that the self-correcting tendencies of the economy acted too slowly or were too weak to be relied on.

11. The government takes a much more active role today in trying to stabilize the economy. The Employment Act of 1946 gave the responsibility for full employment and economic growth to the federal government. The Great Depression of the 1930s caused people to reconsider the laissez-faire attitude that prevailed prior to the war.

12. Stagflation is a combination of inflation and high unemployment. In the 1980s the government used tax cuts to try to encourage an increase in aggregate supply to combat stagflation.

13. Demand-side economics seeks to increase output by stimulating aggregate demand; supply-side economics attempts to stimulate aggregate supply. Hence, the former focuses on increasing government spending or stimulating business investments, and the latter focuses on tax cuts to increase the incentives for productive activity.

14. Real GDP per capita has increased because of increases in human capital and physical capital.

CHAPTER 6

U.S. Productivity and Growth

I. INTRODUCTION

Economic growth is essential if the standard of living of the population as a whole is to increase. Economists can identify factors that contribute to economic growth. It is much more difficult, however, to manipulate the determinants of growth in any systematic way. In this chapter we examine the sources of growth and recent trends in productivity.

II. OUTLINE

1. U.S. Productivity

 1.1 Growth and the Production Possibilities Frontier
 a. Economic growth is pictured as an outward shift of the production possibilities frontier.
 b. The economy can grow here because of
 (1) greater availability of resources;
 (2) improvements in the quality of resources; and
 (3) technological improvements.

 1.2 What Is Productivity?
 a. Productivity refers to how efficiently resources are employed.
 b. *Productivity* is defined as the ratio of a specific measure of output to a specific measure of input.

 1.3 Labor Productivity
 a. *Labor productivity* is the total output divided by total employment.
 b. Increases in capital lead to increases in labor productivity.

 1.4 The Per-Worker Production Function
 a. The *per-worker production function* shows the relation between capital per worker and output per worker.
 b. An increase in the amount of capital per worker leads to an increase in the amount of output per worker.
 c. Output per worker increases at a decreasing rate because of the law of diminishing marginal returns.
 d. An increase in capital causes a movement along the per-worker production function; a change in the quality of capital causes the function to shift.

1.5 Long-Term Productivity Growth
   a. U.S. labor productivity grew at an average annual rate of 2.1 percent from 1870 to 1998.
   b. Over long time periods, small differences in productivity growth rates generate large differences in the economy's ability to produce.

1.6 The Recent Slowdown in Productivity Growth. There has been a decline in the rate of growth of U.S. labor productivity in the last 25 years.

2. Why the Slowdown in Labor Productivity Growth?

2.1 Rate of Capital Formation. A slowdown in the growth rate of capital per worker may have contributed to the slowdown in labor productivity growth.

2.2 Changes in the Labor Force
   a. Younger workers tend to be less productive than more experienced workers. The decline in the average age of the labor force as more members of postwar generations entered the labor force could be a cause of the labor productivity slowdown.
   b. On net, the slowdown in productivity growth does not appear to be due to the change in workforce quality.

2.3 Changing Composition of Output. The changing composition of output has also been blamed, since service industries tend to be less capital intensive than manufacturing industries.

2.4 Budget Deficits. Although some analysts assert that federal deficits lead to massive borrowing, which "crowds out" private investment and thus limits investment in human capital, the link between federal deficits and labor productivity growth remains unclear.

3. Research and Development

3.1 Basic and Applied Research
   a. *Basic research* is the search for knowledge without concern for the commercial possibilities of the knowledge.
   b. *Applied research* is the application of scientific discoveries to the development of particular products.
   c. A technological breakthrough usually becomes embodied in new capital.

3.2 Expenditures for Research and Development. U.S. R&D expenditures as a percent of GDP is high compared with other countries.

3.3 *CASE STUDY:* Computers and Productivity Growth

3.4 International Productivity Comparisons. In comparison, U.S. productivity growth is lower than most other nations.

4. Other Issues of Technology and Growth

4.1 Industrial Policy
   a. *Industrial policy* refers to the idea that the government should encourage certain technologies and industries to gain an advantage over foreign competition.
   b. The government support comes in the form of subsidies, tax breaks, and regulations.

4.2 *CASE STUDY:* Picking Technological Winners

4.3 Does Technological Change Lead to Unemployment?
   a. Since technological change often reduces the number of workers needed to produce a given amount of output, some think it causes unemployment.
   b. Empirical evidence suggests that unemployment rates are lower in countries that have experienced a great deal of technological change.

4.4 Output per Capita
   a. The slowdown in economic growth experienced by the United States after 1973 also occurred in other developed countries.
   b. The U.S. decline was less than that in many other countries.

4.5 Do Economies Converge?
   a. The *convergence theory* argues that economies around the world will grow more alike over time.
   b. Differences in the quality of human capital across countries may prevent convergence.

III. DISCUSSION

U.S. Productivity

Productivity, which is a measure of how efficiently resources are used, is the ratio of a specific measure of output to a specific measure of input. *Labor productivity*, the most commonly used measure of productivity, is the ratio of GDP to total employment. The growth rate in labor productivity is used to measure changes in the economy's productive capability over time.

Labor productivity depends critically on the quantity and quality of capital for labor to use. This capital includes both physical and human capital. The *per-worker production function* depicts the relation between the amount of capital per worker and the output per worker in the economy. The more capital per worker, the more output per worker. The per-worker production function reflects the law of diminishing marginal returns, which implies that as capital per worker increases, the amount of the additional output produced gets smaller. An improvement in the quality of capital resulting from technological change causes the entire production function to change.

In the last 25 years, the growth rate of U.S. labor productivity has declined relative to its long-term trend. It is very difficult to determine the causes of this phenomenon, but there are probably several contributing factors. An important determinant of labor productivity is the amount of capital labor has to work with. If the rate of capital formation declines, it is likely that labor productivity will decline. There has been a slight decline in the U.S. capital–labor ratio, but it is unlikely that this decline is large enough to explain fully the decline in U.S. labor productivity growth.

The quality of labor is another important determinant of labor productivity. Younger, inexperienced workers tend to be less productive than their older counterparts. Beginning in the mid-1960s, the composition of the U.S. labor force shifted toward younger workers as members of the postwar generations entered the labor force. There has also been a decline in standardized test scores, which suggests that new entrants into the labor force are less qualified than in prior years, but the average level of education has increased.

The composition of U.S. output has changed as well, having moved toward service industries and away from manufacturing industries. Because service industries tend to be less capital intensive, labor productivity growth would tend to decline as an economy became more service oriented. Some argue that the budget deficits of the federal government also have contributed to the slowdown in productivity. Further, investment in public capital has declined.

Research and Development and Other Issues of Technology and Growth

Technological change is perhaps the most important source of productivity growth and economic growth. Most improvements in technology are the result of scientific research. *Basic research* is the search for knowledge without regard for the commercial applicability of the knowledge. *Applied research* is the attempt to find commercial applications for scientific knowledge. Often, technological change is embodied in new capital investment. Technological change frees resources for new uses. In particular, labor is often freed as a result of technological change.

Research and development spending of firms is one measure of efforts to improve the economy's productivity through technological change. Research and development expenditures in the United States fell during the 1970s; this suggests to many economists that the decline in productivity was due to the decline in research activity.

Given the importance of research and development, it is not surprising that the federal government often tries to stimulate research. Some argue the government should develop an industrial policy, which is a policy of using taxes, subsidies, or regulations to nurture the technologies and industries that are most likely to be important in the future. Others argue that the government is not likely to be good at picking winners and that the policy will become another example of pork barrel politics.

Another concern of some is that technological change may lead to unemployment. We all know of jobs that have been phased out as a result of the introduction of labor-saving capital. However, the jobs created in the industry that makes the capital may balance out those lost elsewhere. Further, empirical evidence suggests that overall unemployment is lower in countries that are technologically progressive than in countries that utilize less technology.

For several decades following World War II, the United States was the undisputed world leader in terms of production and technology. Since then, the U.S. dominance has disappeared. During 1948–1973, the U.S. annual growth rate in real GDP was about half that of other industrialized countries, such as Germany and Japan. Part of the reason for this was because the other countries started at lower levels of productivity after the war because of wartime destruction. In the 1980s the growth rates of real GDP per capita were more similar among industrialized countries. To some, this suggests that over time economies around the world have a tendency to converge. That is, growth in the rich countries will be slower than in the poorer countries until they become more alike. The examples of Germany and Japan after the war and of Korea in more recent years offer evidence to support this theory. But many poor countries show no signs of such growth. Differences in human capital across countries may account for the failure of countries to converge.

IV. LAGNIAPPE

Living and Dying by Industrial Policy

Japan used industrial policy for many years, and many attribute Japan's rise since World War II to this policy. Japan's Ministry of International Trade and Industry (MITI) has helped identify and support many industries and technologies that became important. Many argue that MITI has been crucial in Japan's success in areas such as electronics and computers. But not all of MITI's plans have succeeded. In the early 1980s MITI pushed Japanese firms to invest in producing memory (RAM) chips for computers. The U.S. Commerce Department also urged U.S. firms to focus attention on RAM chips. The Japanese firms did as MITI suggested, but most U.S. firms did not take the advice. Instead, U.S. firms focused on integrated circuits. Over the last eight to ten years, the integrated circuit market has been more lucrative than the RAM market. Consequently, the U.S. semiconductor industry strengthened relative to the Japanese industry, largely as a result of American success in integrated circuits.

Question to Think About: Would you have more confidence in the judgment of someone who invests his or her own funds or someone who invests taxpayers' money?

Productivity Growth and Different Types of Research and Development

Research and development activity is not homogeneous. Some R&D is directed toward basic research and some toward applied research. Another distinction can be made between research directed toward the development of new products and research directed toward improving production processes. It is likely, as Albert Link found, that R&D expenditures allocated to process innovations had a greater impact on productivity than R&D expenditures allocated to product innovations. (See Albert N. Link, "A Disaggregated Analysis of Industrial R&D," in *The Transfer and Utilization of Technical Knowledge.* Edited by Devendra Sahal. Lexington, MA: D. C. Heath, 1982.)

Question to Think About: Would the development of a new computer system be considered a product innovation or a process innovation?

V. KEY TERMS

productivity	applied research
labor productivity	industrial policy
per-worker production function	output per capita
basic research	convergence

VI. QUESTIONS

A. Completion

1. Total output divided by total input of a specific kind of resource indicates the _____ of that resource.

2. The resource most responsible for increasing labor productivity is _____.

3. The relation between the amount of capital per worker and the amount of labor per worker is known as the per-worker _____.

4. Output per worker increases at a _____ rate as capital per worker increases.

5. Over time, improvements in a country's standard of living result from more capital per worker and better _____ per worker.

6. Increases in capital intensity is called capital _____.

7. Some economists believe that changes in the _____ of the labor force have contributed to the decline in U.S. productivity growth.

8. There are more opportunities for technological change when producing goods than when producing _____.

9. Declining investment in _____ or infrastructure may serve as a drag on productivity growth.

10. According to Simon Kuznets, 90 percent of the increase in economic growth in developed market economies is attributable to improvements in the _____ of inputs.

11. _____ research seeks answers to specific questions or seeks to develop particular products.

12. Technological change impacts the economy by becoming _____ in capital.

13. The variations in R&D spending in the United States in the last 20 years are mostly due to changes in the share of R&D financed by _____.

14. The objective of _____ policy is to secure a leading role for American industry in the future.

15. The _____ theory argues that economies around the world grow more alike over time.

B.   True/False

_____ 1. Labor productivity is measured by the ratio of GDP to total employment.

_____ 2. As workers accumulate more human capital, their productivity increases.

_____ 3. Because the per-worker production function is characterized by diminishing marginal returns, a 10 percent increase in capital and a 10 percent increase in labor will lead to less than a 10 percent increase in output.

_____ 4. The level of technology is held constant along a per-worker production function.

_____ 5. Technological change is pictured by a movement along a per-worker production function.

_____ 6. The growth in U.S. productivity was negative during much of the 1970s.

_____ 7. Because younger workers tend to be more productive than older workers, one explanation for the decline in U.S. labor productivity growth is the increasing age of the workforce.

_____ 8. If productivity is inversely related to the quality of the air, then the slowdown in labor productivity does not imply a declining quality of life.

_____ 9. Capital formation is a major contributor to economic growth.

_____ 10. Technological change can free resources for new uses.

_____ 11. Basic research is the search for knowledge without regard to how the knowledge will be used.

_____ 12. About 50 percent of applied research is embodied in capital.

_____ 13. Research suggests that a dollar's worth of federally funded R&D contributes less to economic growth than a dollar's worth of company-supported R&D.

_____ 14. Most federal funding of R&D in the United States goes to support military research.

_____ 15. The drop in economic growth in the United States in the 1970s was larger than that in any of the other industrialized countries.

_____ 16. Proponents of industrial policy usually believe the market is the best allocator of scarce resources.

_____ 17. An increase in productivity would probably encourage greater unemployment.

_____ 18. According to the convergence theory, the rich get richer and the poor get poorer.

C. Multiple Choice

1. When an economy's labor productivity increases, the standard of living
   a. always rises.
   b. rises if employment growth exceeds population growth.
   c. rises if population growth exceeds employment growth.
   d. rises if population growth equals employment growth.
   e. falls.

2. Productivity is difficult to measure because
   a. it is difficult to account for changes in environmental quality.
   b. some activities are not counted in GDP.
   c. government output is difficult to measure.
   d. All of the above.
   e. a and b

3. With regard to the per-worker production function, diminishing marginal returns applies to
   a. labor.
   b. capital.
   c. labor per unit of capital.
   d. output.
   e. output per unit of labor.

4. If GDP per capita is $20,000 and 40 percent of the population is employed, then labor productivity is
   a. $8,000.
   b. $40,000.
   c. $50,000.
   d. $100,000.
   e. The question cannot be answered without more information.

5. All of the following have been suggested as causes of the slowdown in U.S. productivity growth except
   a. deregulation of many industries.
   b. reduced capital formation.
   c. changing composition of the labor force.
   d. reduced spending on R&D.
   e. changing composition of output.

6. A change in the composition of the labor force would contribute to a slowdown in productivity growth if
   a. the proportion of new workers was constant over time.
   b. the share of employment accounted for by new workers increased.
   c. the share of employment in service industries decreased.
   d. higher energy prices caused the substitution of capital for labor.
   e. None of the above.

7. Labor productivity can be increased most easily in which sector of the economy?
   a. government
   b. retailing
   c. education
   d. manufacturing
   e. All of the above.

8. Research and development expenditures financed by the U.S. federal government
   a. tend to be used for military research.
   b. tend to replace company-financed expenditures dollar for dollar.
   c. tend to increase economic growth more than an equal amount of company-financed expenditures.
   d. rose significantly as a percent of sales during the 1970s.
   e. a and b

9. Which of the following is likely to increase potential output?
    a. increasing the minimum wage
    b. eliminating job discrimination
    c. raising welfare payments
    d. raising unemployment benefits
    e. strengthening labor unions' control over entry into occupations

10. Which of the following is true regarding research and development?
    a. Technological breakthroughs are the direct result of success in basic research.
    b. Basic research has a larger immediate payoff than applied research.
    c. Basic research is likely to have a higher rate of return to society as a whole than applied research.
    d. Basic research is more likely to be embodied in capital than applied research.
    e. a, b, and c only

11. The average annual growth in labor productivity of each country below has been greater than the U.S. in the past.
    a. Canada
    b. France
    c. Germany
    d. Italy
    e. Japan

12. Industrial policy is a policy that
    a. encourages industrial development rather than agricultural development.
    b. the United States has followed since the end of World War II.
    c. encourages the development and growth of industries that the government thinks will be important industries in the future.
    d. b and c only
    e. None of the above.

13. Industrial policy has been advocated by
    a. Ronald Reagan.
    b. George Bush.
    c. Bill Clinton.
    d. Gene Grossman.
    e. All of the above.

14. Which of the following is a problem with industrial policy, according to its critics?
    a. The beneficiaries may share their expertise with foreign companies.
    b. The support from the government may be allocated on the basis of political influence rather than economic criteria.
    c. Government bureaucrats are less likely to know where to allocate funds than people in the business world.
    d. All of the above.
    e. None of the above.

15. Technological change
    a. can lead to structural unemployment in some industries.
    b. can lead to increases in production and employment by making products more affordable.
    c. has caused the natural rate of unemployment to increase 50 percent over the last 40 years.
    d. causes a larger reduction in employment in the long run than in the short run.
    e. a and b only

16. During the 1980s the growth rate in GDP per capita exceeded the growth rate in output per labor hour because
    a. employment grew faster than population.
    b. population grew faster than employment.
    c. the rate of technological change fell almost to zero.
    d. the quality of high school graduates increased substantially.
    e. None of the above.

17. The convergence theory states that
    a. economies around the world are getting less similar all the time.
    b. economies around the world are getting more alike all the time.
    c. the rich countries are getting more alike all the time.
    d. the gap between rich and poor within the United States is narrowing.
    e. the short-run growth rate converges on the long-run growth rate more rapidly in rich countries than in poor countries.

18. Which of the following is more likely to make the convergence theory correct?
    a. It is easier to copy new technology than to develop it.
    b. Technology is portable.
    c. The human capital needed to take advantage of new technology is very portable.
    d. All of the above.
    e. a and b only

D. Discussion Questions

1. What is productivity and how is it measured?

2. What factors determine the productivity of labor?

3. Explain how the law of diminishing marginal returns is related to the per-worker production function.

4. Distinguish between a movement along the per-worker production curve and a shift of the curve.

5. Suppose in 1980 one worker could produce 100 VCRs. How many VCRs can the worker produce in 1990 if the growth in labor productivity is 2 percent per year? 2.5 percent per year? 3 percent per year? What do these figures suggest about long-term growth?

6. What factors have been suggested as causes of the slowdown in U.S. labor productivity growth in the 1970s? Explain how each of these factors could contribute to the slowdown.

7. What role does technological change play in determining productivity growth?

8. Would you expect business firms to spend a greater proportion of their R&D expenditures on basic research or on applied research? Why?

9. What factors led to the slowdown in economic growth in the 1970s experienced by industrialized nations other than the United States?

10. How have the federal budget deficits affected productivity growth?

11. Why do economists believe that U.S. federally financed R&D has less impact on economic growth than company-financed expenditures?

12. What is meant by industrial policy?

13. Discuss the strengths and weaknesses of an industrial policy.

14. Does technological change lead to unemployment?

VII. ANSWERS

A. Completion

1.	productivity	9.	public services
2.	capital	10.	quality
3.	production function	11.	Applied
4.	diminishing (decreasing)	12.	embodied
5.	capital	13.	the federal government
6.	deepening	14.	industrial
7.	composition	15.	convergence
8.	services		

B. True/False

1.	True	10.	True
2.	True	11.	True
3.	False	12.	False
4.	True	13.	True
5.	False	14.	True
6.	False	15.	False
7.	False	16.	False
8.	True	17.	False
9.	True	18.	False

C. Multiple Choice

1.	b	7.	d	13.	c
2.	d	8.	a	14.	d
3.	b	9.	b	15.	e
4.	c	10.	e	16.	a
5.	a	11.	a	17.	b
6.	b	12.	c	18.	e

D. Discussion Questions

1. Productivity measures how effectively resources are employed. It is defined as the ratio of a specific measure of output to a specific measure of a particular input. Generally, total output divided by total input yields a measure of productivity.

2. The most important factor that determines the productivity of labor is the capital with which labor works. The more capital and the higher the quality of the capital, the more productive labor will be. This includes both physical capital (such as machines and tools) and human capital (such as formal education, formal training programs, and on-the-job training).

3. The per-worker production function relates the capital per worker to the output per worker. An increase in capital per worker means that capital is varying while labor is held constant. That is, capital is treated as a variable input and labor as a fixed input. The law of diminishing marginal returns applies to capital in this situation, so the additional output from additional units of capital (holding labor constant) will eventually diminish. Graphically, the curve relating capital per worker and output per worker is bowed.

4. An increase in the quantity of capital causes a movement along the per-worker production curve, since capital per worker is along the horizontal axis. An increase in the quality of capital arising from technological change causes the entire curve to shift.

5. One worker would produce 121.9 VCRs in 1990 at a growth rate of 2 percent per year, 128 at a growth rate of 2.5 percent, and 134.4 at a growth rate of 3 percent. The compounding of growth rates leads to large changes in labor productivity over even a short time period. (If the time period were 100 years, growth in labor productivity of 2 percent would yield 724.5 VCRs per worker in 2090; growth of 2.5 percent would yield 1,181.4 VCRs per worker in 2090.)

6. Five factors have been cited as sources of the slowdown in U.S. productivity growth. (1) The rate of capital formation fell. There is a direct relationship between the capital-labor ratio and labor productivity, so a decline in capital formation would lead to a decline in productivity growth. (2) The composition of the U.S. labor force changed. New workers are less productive than more experienced workers. Since the mid-1960s, the proportion of new workers in the workforce has increased, so the labor force is likely to be less

so there is less opportunity for labor productivity increases in the service industries. (5) Reduced spending on research and development has caused technological change to be less rapid.

7. Technological change encourages productivity growth because it permits the same output to be produced with fewer resources. Often the resource that is freed is labor. Consequently, less labor is used to produce the same output, so labor productivity increases.

8. Business firms are likely to spend more resources on applied research because the payoff with applied research is more certain and faster than it is with basic research.

9. Since all industrialized nations experienced a slowdown in the 1970s, it seems reasonable that the causes of the U.S. slowdown were not unique to the United States. In particular, all developed nations were affected by one likely determinant of the slowdown: higher energy prices. Similarly, Japan and the European developed nations experienced the kinds of changes in the composition of the labor force that affected the United States.

10. No one knows for sure. Government investment in public capital could actually increase productivity.

11. A large share of U.S. federally funded research has military objectives, which often have little or no effect on productivity in the rest of the economy.

12. Industrial policy refers to the government's picking certain industries and/or technologies as important for the future growth of the economy and supporting them with subsidies or tax breaks.

13. The idea of industrial policy relies on two phenomena. First, some technologies or industries have effects that spill over into other areas of the economy so that development of these industries will create benefits in a much larger section of the economy. Since firms in the key industries will not reap all the benefits from development of the industry, they will under-invest in research and in capital formation. The government can encourage more investment in both by subsidizing the industry. Second, the market often fails to allocate capital efficiently, so the government needs to help correct the situation.

    Opponents of industrial policy argue that those who run the businesses are more likely to know better where to allocate capital than government bureaucrats. The subsidies of the government are likely to be directed more by political than by economic considerations.

14. Technological change does cause some people to become unemployed—technological change means that more can be produced by fewer workers. However, employment increases in the industry producing the capital that embodies the technological change. Further, the technological change may lower costs sufficiently to stimulate sales and production so that unemployment does not develop. The increased productivity of labor increases the income of labor, which increases spending and production in other sectors of the economy. Consequently, technological change will tend to increase employment in the economy as a whole, especially over time.

CHAPTER 7

Unemployment and Inflation

I. INTRODUCTION

Inflation and unemployment are two of the most important problems with which policymakers have to grapple. Policymakers face a major dilemma in that policies designed to cure one of the problems often exacerbate the other. The causes of each phenomenon and their relationships are addressed in later chapters. In this chapter the two phenomena are described and defined.

II. OUTLINE

1. Unemployment. Unemployment has been linked to illness and crime. The real social costs of unemployment are the lost potential output and the economic and psychological damage to the unemployed and their families.

    1.1 Measuring Unemployment
        a. The adult population includes all persons 16 years or older, except those in prisons, mental institutions, or the military.
        b. The labor force consists of those in the adult population who are either working or looking for work.
        c. People are counted as unemployed if they have looked for work at least once in the previous four weeks.
        d. The unemployment rate equals the number of unemployed divided by the number in the labor force.
        e. Not all people who are not working are considered unemployed; for example, the following:
            (1) Full-time students
            (2) People who do not want to work
            (3) Retired people
            (4) Full-time homemakers
            (5) Discouraged workers: those who no longer seek employment because they have given up
        f. The *unemployment rate* is the number of unemployed divided by the labor force; it excludes military personnel from the labor force.
        g. The *labor force participation rate* is the number of people in the labor force divided by the adult population.

    1.2 Changes over Time in Unemployment Statistics
        a. The adult population changes slowly over time.
        b. The labor force participation rate can change more quickly than the adult population and has been increasing in the United States over the last 50 years.
        c. The unemployment rate is more volatile than the labor force participation rate. There has been an upward trend in the U.S. unemployment rate since 1950.

1.3   Unemployment in Various Groups
       a.   Unemployment rates tend to be higher for teenagers and blacks.
       b.   Unemployment rates of all groups tend to increase during recessions.

1.4   Duration of Unemployment
       a.   The duration of unemployment is not the same for all the unemployed.
       b.   Higher unemployment rates usually reflect both a larger number of unemployed and
             a greater average duration of unemployment.

1.5   Unemployment Differences across the Country. Some areas of the United States have much
       higher unemployment rates than others.

1.6   *CASE STUDY:* Poor King Coal

1.7   Types of Unemployment
       a.   A change in the unemployment rate can occur because of a change in the labor force
             or a change in the number of unemployed.
       b.   Four types of unemployment:
             (1)   Frictional unemployment
                   (a)   Frictional unemployment arises from the difficulty of matching labor
                         suppliers and labor demanders.
                   (b)   Frictional unemployment exists because information concerning job
                         vacancies and job candidates is costly to acquire and digest.
             (2)   Structural unemployment
                   (a)   Structural unemployment exists when the skills possessed by job seekers
                         do not match the skills demanded by employers or when job seekers do not
                         live in regions where the jobs are.
                   (b)   Structural unemployment arises from shifts in the demand and supply of
                         goods resulting from changes in consumer tastes, technological change, or
                         trade factors.
             (3)   Seasonal unemployment
                   (a)   Seasonal unemployment is unemployment that follows seasonal patterns.
                   (b)   Seasonal unemployment mirrors weather or holiday demand patterns; for
                         example, ski resorts close in the summer.
             (4)   Cyclical unemployment
                   (a)   Cyclical unemployment reflects the decline in aggregate output that occurs
                         during recessions.
                   (b)   Cyclical unemployment is caused by declines in aggregate demand.

1.8   The Meaning of Full Employment
       a.   Full employment does not mean zero unemployment.
       b.   There will always be some frictional, seasonal, and structural unemployment.

1.9   Unemployment Compensation
       a.   On losing their jobs, those who qualify can receive government unemployment
             benefits for up to six months, provided they are actively seeking employment.
       b.   Those who are unemployed because they quit their jobs or were fired for just cause,
             who are just entering the labor force, or who are reentering the labor force do not
             qualify for unemployment benefits.
       c.   The amount and availability of unemployment benefits can affect workers' incentives
             to find new employment and thus the level and average duration of unemployment.

1.10 International Comparisons of Unemployment
   a.   Not all countries calculate unemployment in the same way.
   b.   Cultural factors also affect the unemployment rates of other countries.

1.11 Problems with Official Unemployment Figures
   a.   Unemployment data ignore the problem of underemployment; people are counted as employed even when they work only part-time or are vastly overqualified for their jobs.
   b.   Since discouraged workers are not included, unemployment figures tend on net to understate the true rate of unemployment.

2.   Inflation. *Inflation* is a sustained and continuous increase in the average level of prices. *Hyperinflation* is extremely high inflation. *Deflation* is a sustained and continuous decrease in the average level of prices.

   2.1   *CASE STUDY:* Hyperinflation in Brazil

   2.2   Two Sources of Inflation
      a.   *Demand-pull inflation* is inflation arising from increases in aggregate demand.
      b.   *Cost-push inflation* is inflation arising from a decrease in aggregate supply.

   2.3   A Historical Look at Inflation and the Price Level
      a.   For much of U.S. history, the periods of inflation and the periods of deflation have about evened out.
      b.   Since the end of World War II, inflation has been more persistent, and the price level has risen steadily.

   2.4   Anticipated versus Unanticipated Inflation
      a.   Anticipated inflation poses fewer problems for the economy than unanticipated inflation.
      b.   Unanticipated increases in inflation tend to hurt those who lend money at fixed interest rates and those on fixed incomes.

   2.5   The Transaction Costs of Variable Inflation
      a.   Stable prices mean that people can be confident about the purchasing power of a dollar.
      b.   Inflation uncertainty increases the difficulty of making business decisions; this raises the cost of producing goods and lowers productivity.
      c.   Inflation diverts time and effort from productive concerns to finding ways to hedge against inflation.

   2.6   Inflation Obscures Relative Price Changes
      a.   Not all prices change at the same rate with inflation, so relative prices change.
      b.   Inflation makes it more difficult to determine relative price changes, which are important for efficiently allocating resources.

   2.7   International Comparisons of Inflation. Comparisons of inflation rates across countries must be made carefully because the quality of inflation statistics varies across countries.

   2.8   Inflation and Interest Rates
      a.   The *interest rate* is the amount of money earned for supplying the use of one dollar for one year.
      b.   The *nominal rate of interest* measures interest in terms of actual dollars paid.

    c.   The *real rate of interest* equals the nominal rate minus the inflation rate.

    d.   Lenders and borrowers must base decisions on the expected real rate of interest—the nominal rate minus expected inflation.

2.9   Why Is Inflation So Unpopular?

    a.   Inflation means higher expenditures but also higher incomes; however, many people do not recognize the link between prices and incomes.

    b.   Inflation affects everyone, whereas unemployment affects only a portion of the population.

    c.   Most tax laws do not distinguish between nominal and real income, so inflation affects taxes unfairly.

III. DISCUSSION

Unemployment

The *unemployment rate* is the figure used to measure the extent of unemployment in the economy. To calculate the unemployment rate, it is necessary first to calculate the number of people in the labor force. The *labor force* is composed of those noninstitutionalized adults (at least 16 years of age) who are working or who are looking for work. Hence, full-time students, full-time homemakers, retired people, young teenagers, and any who choose to be idle are not included in the labor force. To be classified as unemployed, one must be actively seeking employment; that is, one must have looked for work at least once in the previous four weeks. The *unemployment rate* represents the percentage of the labor force that is unemployed; it is the number of people who are looking for work divided by the number in the labor force.

There are several problems with the government's method of measuring the unemployment rate. First, it tends to understate the true extent of unemployment because *discouraged workers* are not included among the unemployed. Discouraged workers are those who have become so discouraged and frustrated in their search for work that they have quit looking for work. Since they no longer seek work actively, they are considered neither part of the labor force nor among the unemployed. Second, the unemployment rate does not take into consideration the underemployed: those who want to work full-time but can only find part-time jobs or those who are overqualified for their jobs. On the other hand, the unemployment rate includes people who are not very serious in their search for work and who would actually prefer to remain idle. Finally, the unemployment rate does not tell how long people have been unemployed.

The unemployment rate is the measure most commonly used to examine employment trends in the economy. However, another important measure is the *labor force participation rate*, which is the percentage of the adult population that is in the labor force. The labor force participation rate increases when a larger proportion of the adult population wants to work. It is possible for the total number of employed to increase at the same time that the unemployment rate increases if the labor force participation rate is also increasing.

The unemployment rate tends to rise during recessions and fall during expansions. Unemployment rates can also be calculated for various groups in the labor force. The overall unemployment rate may cover up some important differences among groups. For example, unemployment among teenagers usually is significantly greater than among adults, and unemployment among blacks generally is greater than among whites. Rates of the groups usually vary together.

People can be unemployed for many reasons. The majority of unemployed persons in the United States in 1989 were unemployed voluntarily (they had quit their jobs) or were just entering the labor force. If such people are unemployed for only a short period of time, the economy is functioning well. Of course, others are unemployed involuntarily, and unemployment causes more problems in these cases. The seriousness of unemployment is often related to the reason for unemployment. *Frictional unemployment* exists because it takes time for a person seeking work and an employer with a job opening to match up. The potential worker must find out about the job opening and determine whether the job is one that he or she would like and if the pay is satisfactory. The employer wants to know something about the background of the prospective jobholder: if the person is reliable, if the person has the needed skills, if the person has a reputation for being a troublemaker, and so forth. Collecting the necessary information takes time, and there will be some unemployment while all parties take the time to collect and assimilate information.

A second kind of unemployment is *structural unemployment*; it reflects the fact that the economy is not static but constantly changing. As a result of changes in tastes or income, consumers alter their buying patterns. Further, costs of production change as a result of technological change in some industries or changes in the prices of inputs that are important to some industries. The result of all these changes is that production of some goods expands and production of other goods contracts. As production of a good contracts, some people are laid off and become unemployed. If their skills are valuable in other industries in the region where they live, they usually can find new jobs relatively quickly. But if their skills are not wanted by the growing industries, they may be unemployed for a much longer period of time. In some cases, a person may have to be retrained and relocated in order to find a new job, or the person may be forced to accept a job at a wage that is significantly lower than his or her previous wage.

Seasonal unemployment is very straightforward. Some occupations depend a great deal on the weather; demand for labor is great when the weather is right but much smaller when the weather is inappropriate. Construction and agriculture are obvious examples. Other jobs are tied to specific times of the year. Extra hiring by department stores during the Christmas season, in hotels and restaurants in New Orleans during Mardi Gras, or in Louisville during Kentucky Derby week creates seasonal employment. The government adjusts unemployment rates to account for seasonal variations.

The final type of unemployment is called *cyclical unemployment* because it is related to fluctuations in the economy. During a recession, aggregate output falls and unemployment increases; during an expansion, aggregate output increases and unemployment decreases.

Although four types of unemployment have been defined, it is not always easy to determine which type is operating at any given time or what type of unemployment a specific individual is experiencing.

The stated goal of public policy is to promote full employment. Full employment does not mean zero unemployment, however, for that is an impossible goal in a dynamic economy. It is neither possible nor desirable to eliminate all frictional, seasonal, or structural unemployment. Government policy tends to focus on cyclical unemployment, although attempts have been made to alleviate the effects of structural unemployment by offering relocation and training programs to workers.

To reduce the cost of unemployment to the unemployed, the U.S. government operates an unemployment insurance system financed by a tax on employers. To qualify for unemployment benefits, one must have lost his or her job for certain reasons and must be actively seeking employment. New entrants and re-entrants into the labor force are not covered by government unemployment insurance; neither are those who quit their jobs or were fired for just cause. Unemployment benefits reduce the cost of unemployment; some believe that the more attractive the unemployment benefits, the longer recipients will remain unemployed, contributing to an increase in frictional unemployment.

Inflation is a sustained and continuous rise in the average level of prices; *deflation* is a sustained and continuous decline in the average level of prices. If inflation is due to an increase in aggregate demand, it is called *demand-pull inflation*; if it is due to a decrease in aggregate supply, it is called *cost-push inflation*. Throughout most of U.S. history, the periods of inflation and deflation about evened out. However, since the end of World War II, inflation has been more persistent, and the price level has increased an average of 3.9 percent per year.

When there is inflation, prices of all goods and services increase, on average, including the prices paid to owners of resources. This means that everyone's expenditures rise, but everyone's income rises too. If all prices increase by the same rate, then everyone's real income and expenditures are unchanged. But prices seldom go up at the same rate under inflation—some go up by more than the average rate of price increase, some go up by less, and some remain unchanged or even decrease. If a family's income remains unchanged while its expenditures increase, the family is worse off.

Economists distinguish between anticipated and unanticipated inflation. If people can correctly anticipate the inflation rate, then they can take inflation into account when entering into contracts. However, inflation cannot be anticipated correctly all of the time. When inflation is unanticipated, economic agents make decisions on the basis of poor information and thus make poor decisions. Those who are on fixed incomes or who have lent money at a fixed interest rate that is too low to compensate for inflation are hurt by unexpectedly high inflation; those who have borrowed money benefit.

In the real world, inflation does not cause all prices to rise exactly the same amount at exactly the same time. Instead, the price of wheat may increase by 5 percent one month, the price of autos may increase by 8 percent the next month, the price of gasoline may increase by 3 percent the next month, and so forth. Consequently, it is difficult to know whether a specific change in price is due to a change in demand or supply (and is thus a relative price change) or to inflation. Such uncertainty makes it difficult for economic decision makers to make correct decisions. The transaction costs of drawing up contracts increase, and individuals spend time and resources trying to find ways to hedge against the effects of inflation. Business executives spend time analyzing financial problems instead of production or distribution problems. These real costs associated with inflation cause a decline in productivity and a lower growth rate for the economy.

Unanticipated inflation can cause particular problems in credit markets. Families who bought homes in the early 1960s found that inflation caused the nominal value of their homes and their incomes to increase while their mortgage payments remained fixed. Such families were better off, but the institutions that lent money to the homebuyers were harmed. Eventually, financial institutions established variable mortgage rates to protect themselves against inflation. When inflation is anticipated, *nominal interest rates* merely adjust to reflect the expected inflation. The *real interest rate* equals the nominal interest rate less the inflation rate.

IV. LAGNIAPPE

"Farewell! Othello's occupation's gone."
Othello, Act III, Scene 3, Line 357

The words above, from Shakespeare's *Othello*, are the poignant words of a man who no longer has his work to occupy him. Like many others who have had to give up their occupation, Othello has a difficult time coping with the change.

What can be done when demand shifts or technological change causes some occupations to become obsolete? Society cannot lock into a set of job skills and a type of technology forever. Blacksmiths disappeared when the auto was invented, but a demand for auto mechanics was created. Railroad employment falls as airline and trucking employment increases.

Question to Think About: How is the specialization of labor related to structural unemployment?

Inflation versus a Price Increase

Inflation, the sustained and continuous increase in the average level of prices, must be distinguished from an increase in the price of a single good, no matter how important that good is in the economy. The increase in oil prices in the 1970s caused much disruption in the U.S. economy and caused many other prices to increase. However, an oil price increase may not have the sustained effect of causing prices to rise each year. Hence, a price increase is not the same thing as inflation. Further, if oil prices increase, the prices of some other goods must fall, *ceteris paribus*. Hence, we have relative price changes but not inflation.

Question to Think About: How much of the inflation in the 1970s was related to higher oil prices?

V. KEY TERMS

labor force	hyperinflation
unemployment rate	deflation
discouraged worker	disinflation
labor force participation rate	demand-pull inflation
frictional unemployment	cost-push inflation
structural unemployment	consumer price index (CPI)
seasonal unemployment	interest
cyclical unemployment	interest rate
full employment	nominal rate of interest
unemployment benefits	real rate of interest
underemployment	

VI. QUESTIONS

A. *Completion*

1. The _____ consists of those in the noninstitutional adult population who are working or are looking for work.

2. A _____ worker is one who has given up looking for employment.

3. The _____ equals the number in the labor force divided by the adult population.

4. A person entering the labor force for the first time contributes to _____ unemployment.

5. _____ unemployment refers to jobs lost because of shifts in buying patterns when consumer tastes change.

6. A recession leads to an increase in _____ unemployment.

7. _____ refers to jobs in which people are underutilized or working at tasks below their level of skill.

8. A country experiences _____ when there is a sustained and continuous decrease in the average level of prices.

9. Inflation that is due to an increase in aggregate demand is called _____ inflation; inflation that is due to a decrease in aggregate supply is called _____ inflation.

10. A change in the inflation rate that fools people is known as _____ inflation.

11. If all prices do not increase by the same percentage, then there are changes in _____ prices as well as in average prices.

12. _____ occurs when the inflation rate declines.

13. An increase in _____ inflation will cause nominal interest rates to increase.

14. The _____ interest rate is the rate earned after adjustment for inflation.

15. Because of inflation, a nominal capital _____ may actually be a loss in real terms.

B. True/False

_____ 1. The unemployment rate is the number of unemployed people divided by the number of people in the adult population.

_____ 2. Discouraged workers are included in the unemployment rate.

_____ 3. The labor force participation rate can change more quickly than the adult population.

_____ 4. In the United States there has been an upward trend in both the unemployment rate and the labor force participation rate since 1950.

_____ 5. Usually a rise in the unemployment rate results from both larger numbers of people being unemployed and a greater average duration of unemployment.

_____ 6. The teenage unemployment rate is greater than the unemployment rate of adult women.

_____ 7. Frictional unemployment may help increase the economy's level of efficiency.

_____ 8. Full employment means that everyone who wants a job has one.

_____ 9. The unemployment rate that corresponds to full employment is constant over time.

_____ 10. Unemployed people who receive unemployment benefits tend to search for employment less actively than those who do not receive unemployment benefits.

_____ 11. The price level falls both in times of deflation and in times of disinflation.

_____ 12. An increase in the price of oil represents inflation.

_____ 13. Before World War II, inflation was more common than deflation.

_____ 14. Inflation raises incomes as well as expenditures.

_____ 15. Anticipated inflation poses fewer problems for the economy than unanticipated inflation.

_____ 16. Inflation tends to increase the difficulty of making economic decisions.

_____ 17. Inflation figures for less developed countries are more reliable than inflation figures for the United States.

_____ 18. With inflation, the nominal rate of interest is greater than the real rate of interest.

_____ 19. An unexpected increase in the inflation rate causes the real rate of interest to decline, at least for a while.

_____ 20. An important difference between inflation and unemployment is that inflation tends to affect everyone, whereas unemployment affects only a fraction of the population.

C. Multiple Choice

1. If a large number of people take early retirement, which of the following will decrease?
   a. the noninstitutionalized adult population
   b. the labor force
   c. the number of unemployed
   d. the number of discouraged workers
   e. the unemployment rate

2. The unemployment rate declines when
   a. an unemployed person goes to prison.
   b. a high school student goes straight to college.
   c. a high school graduate joins the navy.
   d. a 14-year-old gets a job mowing lawns.
   e. a person moves from a part-time job to a full-time job.

3. The unemployment rate increases when
   a. the number of discouraged workers increases.
   b. the adult population increases.
   c. retired people live longer.
   d. aggregate demand increases.
   e. None of the above.

4. Of the U.S. adult population, the biggest group of people not working is
   a. the unemployed.
   b. discouraged workers.
   c. those who do not want to work.
   d. military personnel.
   e. None of the above.

5. Suppose the adult population is 180 million, and there are 60 million adults who are not in the labor force. If there are 115 million employed individuals, the unemployment rate is _____ and the labor force participation rate is _____.
   a. 4.3 percent; 66.7 percent
   b. 4.17 percent; 66.7 percent
   c. 8.3 percent; 75 percent
   d. 4.17 percent; 75 percent
   e. 4.3 percent; 63 percent

6. Which of the following is an accurate characterization of employment from 1950 to 1990 in the United States?
   a. The adult population increased slightly, the labor force participation rate increased significantly, and the unemployment rate increased somewhat.
   b. The adult population increased slightly, the labor force participation rate remained unchanged, and the unemployment rate increased significantly.
   c. The labor force participation rate for both men and women increased significantly, and the unemployment rate increased somewhat.
   d. The labor force participation rate fell, and the unemployment rate increased significantly.
   e. None of the above.

7. Which group in the United States has the highest unemployment rate?
   a. white males
   b. black males
   c. black teenagers
   d. white teenagers
   e. black females

8. A rise in the unemployment rate is usually due to
   a. an increase in the number of people unemployed.
   b. an increase in the average duration of unemployment.
   c. a decrease in the labor force.
   d. All of the above.
   e. a and b only.

9. Which of the following is an example of structural unemployment?
   a. an auto worker laid off because of increased imports
   b. a woman quitting her job to raise her children
   c. a clerk who had worked for an accounting firm who is laid off April 16
   d. a person quitting a job to look for a higher-paying job
   e. a college professor told she cannot teach summer school this year

10. Which of the following is an example of seasonal unemployment?
   a. an auto worker being laid off because of increased imports
   b. a woman quitting her job to raise her children
   c. a clerk who had worked for an accounting firm being laid off in late April
   d. a person quitting a job for a higher-paying job
   e. a college professor deciding not to teach summer school

11. An increase in unemployment benefits is likely to
   a. cause an increase in the unemployment rate.
   b. cause an increase in the number of unemployed.
   c. cause an increase in the average duration of unemployment.
   d. All of the above.
   e. b and c

12. An economy at full employment will still have some
   a. frictional unemployment.
   b. seasonal unemployment.
   c. structural unemployment.
   d. cyclical unemployment.
   e. a, b, and c only

13. For most of U.S. history, inflation has been associated with
   a. recessions.
   b. Democratic administrations.
   c. times of war.
   d. Republican administrations.
   e. periods of high taxation.

14. Inflation will increase when
   a. aggregate demand increases faster than aggregate supply.
   b. aggregate supply increases faster than aggregate demand.
   c. aggregate supply falls.
   d. aggregate demand falls.
   e. both a and c

15. Which of the following is likely to benefit from unanticipated higher inflation?
   a. a savings and loan institution
   b. a homeowner with a fixed-rate mortgage
   c. a retired person
   d. a holder of government bonds
   e. All of the above.

16. A major problem with inflation is
    a. that it raises people's expenditures without raising their incomes.
    b. that it makes it harder to determine changes in relative prices.
    c. that it raises the real interest rate.
    d. that it makes all homeowners worse off.
    e. the rising unemployment rate in the early stage of an inflationary period.

17. The term that describes a decline in the inflation rate from 8 percent to 3 percent is
    a. disinflation.
    b. deflation.
    c. reinflation.
    d. recessionary inflation.
    e. None of the above.

18. An increase in the expected inflation rate increases
    a. the real rate of interest.
    b. the nominal rate of interest.
    c. both the real and the nominal rates of interest.
    d. neither of the above, unless the increase in inflation is anticipated.
    e. the real rate of interest only if the inflation is unanticipated.

19. Inflation causes the economy's overall productivity to decrease because
    a. inflation makes everyone poorer.
    b. inflation hurts more people than it helps.
    c. inflation raises real interest rates.
    d. people spend more time and resources coping with the uncertainty created by the inflation.
    e. c and d

20. The inflation rate is 5 percent and you make a capital gain of $50 on a $1,000 investment. The tax rate is 30 percent. What is your real after-tax gain?
    a. $50
    b. $35
    c. −$15
    d. −$35
    e. The question cannot be answered without more information.

D. Discussion Questions

1. Use the information in Exhibit 1 concerning population and employment to answer the questions.

Exhibit 1

	1987	1992
Adult population	182,753,000	191,576,000
Employed persons	112,440,000	117,598,000
Unemployed persons	7,425,000	9,384,000

   a. What was the labor force participation rate in 1987? in 1992?
   b. What was the unemployment rate in 1987? in 1992?

2. Explain how the unemployment rate can increase even if the number of people employed is increasing.

3. How has the labor force participation rate changed over the last 40 years?

4. Suppose the unemployment rate is 10 percent and that the average duration of unemployment is 10 weeks. Each week 1 million workers become unemployed and another 1 million people find jobs.
   a. Suppose an additional 100,000 workers lose their jobs every week. What is the unemployment rate in the first week? What is the unemployment rate in the fifth week? What is the unemployment rate after ten weeks if 1.1 million people are able to find work that week?
   b. Suppose that the average duration of unemployment increases to 12 weeks. What is the new unemployment rate?

5. Describe the four types of unemployment. How do the four types differ in their effects on the economy and on the unemployed?

6. What is the purpose of unemployment insurance? What are the effects of unemployment insurance on unemployment rates?

7. What is meant by full employment? Why might it change over time?

8. What is the difference between demand-pull and cost-push inflation?

9. What is the difference between anticipated and unanticipated inflation? How do they differ in their effects on economic agents? Does inflation have no effects on the economy if it is anticipated? Explain.

10. How are inflation and relative price changes related?

11. What is the difference between disinflation and deflation?

12. Who is harmed by inflation? Who benefits? Explain.

13. During the early stages of unanticipated inflation, frictional unemployment often falls. Can you provide an explanation for this observation?

14. How are inflation rates and interest rates related?

15. Why do people dislike inflation?

VII. ANSWERS

A. Completion

1. labor force
2. discouraged
3. labor force participation rate
4. frictional
5. Structural
6. cyclical
7. Underemployment
8. deflation

9. demand-pull; cost-push
10. unanticipated
11. relative
12. Disinflation
13. anticipated
14. real
15. gain

B. True/False

1. False. The number of unemployed is divided by the number in the labor force.
2. False
3. True
4. True
5. True
6. True
7. True
8. False
9. False
10. True
11. False. The price level still increases in times of disinflation.

12. False. An increase in the price of oil is a relative price change and not an increase in all prices.
13. False
14. True
15. True
16. True
17. False
18. True
19. True
20. True

C. Multiple Choice

1.	b	6.	a	11.	d	16.	b
2.	a	7.	c	12.	e	17.	a
3.	e	8.	e	13.	c	18.	b
4.	c	9.	a	14.	e	19.	d
5.	b	10.	c	15.	b	20.	c

D. Discussion Questions

1. a. Labor force participation $= \dfrac{\text{Unemployed} + \text{employed}}{\text{Adult population}}$

    1987 $= 7{,}425{,}000 + 112{,}440{,}000/182{,}753{,}000$
    $= 65.58\%$

    1992 $= 9{,}384{,}000 = 117{,}598{,}000/191{,}576{,}000$
    $= 66.28\%$

   b. Unemployment rate $= \dfrac{\text{Unemployed}}{\text{Labor force}} = \dfrac{\text{Unemployed}}{\text{Unemployed} + \text{employed}}$

    1987 $= 7{,}425{,}000/119{,}865{,}000$
    $= 6.2\%$

    1992 $= 9{,}384{,}000/126{,}982{,}000$
    $= 7.4\%$

2. The unemployment rate is the number of unemployed divided by the labor force. The labor force is made up of the employed and the unemployed. If the labor force increases, both the number of employed and the number of unemployed can be increasing. If the latter increases faster, the unemployment rate can increase even while employment is increasing.

3. The labor force participation rate of women has increased by about 20 percentage points, whereas the participation rate of men has declined somewhat. The overall labor participation rate has increased.

4. a. Since there are 10 million unemployed and the unemployment rate is 10 percent, we know the total labor force is 100 million. When an additional 100,000 workers become unemployed, the unemployment rate increases to 10.1 percent (10,100,000/ 100,000,000). In the fifth week the total number unemployed is 10,500,000, so the unemployment rate is 10.5 percent. After the tenth week the total number unemployed is 11 million, so the unemployment rate is 11 percent.

   b. The total number unemployed at any one time is now 12 million, so the new unemployment rate is 12 percent.

5. Frictional unemployment is experienced by those who are unemployed because it takes time to find the right match between job seekers and employers with job openings. Structural unemployment is experienced by those who are unemployed because changes in buying patterns or the structure of production causes demand for their skills to fall, or because they do not live in the regions where jobs are available. Seasonal unemployment is experienced by those who are unemployed because their work is affected by the weather or takes place in certain periods of the year. Cyclical unemployment is experienced by those who are unemployed because the economy has entered a recessionary period.

   Frictional unemployment is necessary in a dynamic economy because it allows people to find the best alternatives; the economy becomes more efficient. Structural unemployment can have lasting negative effects, as the unemployed may be able to find work only by retraining or moving, both of which can be costly. Structural unemployment is a natural by-product of a dynamic economy, however. Seasonal unemployment can be anticipated. In addition, people in seasonal jobs (for example, construction work) often receive high wages while they are working, so the effects of seasonal unemployment are not as damaging on the unemployed as those of structural unemployment. Cyclical unemployment can have a great effect on the economy in terms of lost output. The effect on the unemployed depends on the length of the recession and the availability of unemployment benefits.

6. The purpose of unemployment insurance is to make it easier for workers who have lost their jobs to get by until they find new jobs or are recalled to work. One effect of unemployment insurance is to increase the level of unemployment and the average duration of unemployment, since unemployment benefits reduce the cost of unemployment.

7. Full employment refers to the situation when the economy is producing its potential output. There will still be some unemployment because the economy is dynamic—things are constantly changing. Hence, there will be seasonal, frictional, and structural unemployment. The unemployment rate associated with full employment may change over time as a result of institutional and demographic changes.

8. Demand-pull inflation refers to aggregate demand increasing faster than aggregate supply. Cost-push inflation refers to a situation in which aggregate supply is decreasing relative to aggregate demand. Increases in aggregate demand pull up the price level; decreases in aggregate supply cause resource prices to increase, which then pushes up the price level.

9. Inflation is anticipated when economic agents are able to predict the inflation rate correctly; unanticipated inflation occurs when the actual inflation rate is greater than people had predicted. People can take steps to offset the effects of inflation when it is anticipated, so the effects of anticipated inflation are less severe than those of unanticipated inflation. Inflation always has economic effects, however, unless everyone perfectly anticipates it and all prices increase at exactly the same rate at the same time.

10. Inflation makes it more difficult to tell whether an increase in price is due to the good becoming relatively more scarce or due to inflation. Hence, inflation raises the transaction costs of operating in the economy.

11. Deflation refers to a sustained period of falling prices; disinflation refers to a reduction in the inflation rate. That is, with disinflation there is still inflation.

12. Among the people harmed by inflation are those who hold dollars, since the purchasing power of the dollar decreases with inflation. People who have fixed incomes or who have signed contracts to receive payments of a fixed amount are also harmed. Among the people who benefit are those who have signed contracts to pay a fixed amount over time, such as homeowners.

13. People who make up the pool of the frictional unemployed are looking for the right jobs. One important characteristic of any job is the wage. People may be seeking a certain level of real wages, which they anticipate will result from a particular nominal wage, based on their expectations about inflation. Suppose they receive job offers at the desired nominal wages as inflation affects resource prices. With unanticipated inflation, the real wages are lower than people want, but they may not realize this. Hence they accept jobs and are no longer unemployed. But they might continue looking for jobs if they knew what the true inflation rate was.

14. The nominal interest rate is measured in terms of actual dollars paid. The real interest rate is the nominal interest rate minus the inflation rate. So an increase in the inflation rate causes nominal interest rates to increase. Since contracts often involve fixed interest rates, nominal interest rates will be determined by expected inflation rates. If the actual inflation rate differs from that expected, then real interest rates change until the borrowers and lenders alter their expectations.

15. Inflation affects everyone in some way. People see their expenses increasing and are unhappy, even though they may be receiving pay increases as well. Inflation makes it more difficult to make good economic decisions because it is difficult to distinguish between price changes that are due to inflation and price changes that signal changes in relative prices. People end up spending extra resources on gathering information and finding ways to hedge against the effects of inflation.

CHAPTER 8

Measuring Economic Aggregates and the Circular Flow of Income

I. INTRODUCTION

In order to diagnose what is right or wrong with the economy, one must be able to measure its health. The national income accounting system does this. This chapter discusses the calculation of the gross domestic product and some other important measures of economic performance. It is important for you to be very familiar with the terms and concepts introduced here.

II. OUTLINE

1. The Product of a Nation. Economic activity is measured as a flow. The national income accounting system summarizes economic activity in the United States.

   1.1 National Income Accounts
       a. Gross domestic product (GDP) measures the market value of all final goods and services produced by resources located in the United States.
       b. National income accounts use double-entry bookkeeping.
       c. There are two ways of measuring GDP: the expenditure approach and the income approach.
       d. To prevent double counting, GDP figures do not include sales of intermediate products, which are goods purchased for additional processing and resale. Purchases of goods produced in prior years are also excluded from current GDP.

   1.2 GDP Based on the Expenditure Approach
       a. Consumption, or personal consumption expenditures, refers to purchases of final goods and services by households during the year. It is the largest spending category.
       b. Investment, or gross private domestic investment, refers to spending during the year on output that is not used for present consumption.
          (1) Physical capital is the most important category of investment.
          (2) Investment also includes new residential construction and changes in inventories held by firms.
       c. Government purchases, or government consumption and gross investment, refer to spending for goods and services by all levels of government. Transfer payments are not included.
       d. For the U.S. economy, net exports refer to the value of U.S. goods and services purchased by foreigners minus the value of foreign goods and services purchased by Americans.
       e. The nation's aggregate expenditure, or GDP, is the sum of consumption, investment, government purchases, and net exports.

1.3 GDP Based on the Income Approach
   a. The income approach computes the aggregate income generated by production.
   b. Aggregate income equals the sum of all income earned by resource suppliers in the economy.
   c. To calculate GDP, we add the income earned, or value added, at each stage of production.
   d. Value added by a firm equals the firm's selling price minus the amount paid to other firms for materials.

2. The Circular Flow of Income and Expenditure. The circular flow illustrates how aggregate expenditure is equal to aggregate income.

   2.1 The Income Half of the Circular Flow
      a. Production generates income for the suppliers of resources to firms.
      b. GDP equals aggregate income
      c. Because of taxes, not all the aggregate income earned in the economy is available to households.
      d. *Disposable income* is the aggregate income plus transfer payments minus taxes.

   2.2 The Expenditure Half of the Circular Flow
      a. Disposable income flows to either consumption spending or saving.
      b. Financial markets link savers and borrowers.
      c. The primary borrowers are firms and government.
      d. Investment spending and government purchases are injections into the circular flow.
      e. Exports are an injection into the circular flow, and imports are a leakage from the flow.
      f. Aggregate expenditure equals aggregate income.

   2.3 Leakages Equal Injections. Leakages from the circular flow must equal injections into the circular flow.

   2.4 Planned Investment versus Actual Investment. National income accounting reflects actual investment, which includes planned investment plus unplanned changes in inventories.

3. Limitations of National Income Accounting

   3.1 Some Production Is Not Included in GDP
      a. GDP does not include household production because the products are not sold in markets.
      b. GDP does not include transactions for which there are no official records, such as those in the underground economy.
      c. Imputed income from certain activities outside of formal markets, such as a farm family's production of food for its own consumption, is included in GDP.

   3.2 Leisure, Quality, and Variety
      a. Leisure is not included in GDP.
      b. GDP does not measure improvements in the quality of products.

   3.3 *CASE STUDY:* Tracking an $8 Trillion Economy

3.4 Gross Domestic Product Ignores Depreciation
  a. GDP does not account for depreciation of the capital stock.
  b. Net domestic product equals GNP minus depreciation.

3.5 GDP Does Not Reflect All Costs. For example, costs to the environment are not included.

3.6 GDP and Economic Welfare. GDP measures dollar values of goods and services and does not distinguish among the social values of the goods and services produced.

4. Accounting for Price Changes. GDP is computed in current dollars. The real value of GDP must be used to compare GDP in different years.

  4.1 Price Indexes
    a. To compute price levels over time, we need a reference point from which to create index numbers.
    b. The prices of goods in a certain year are selected as a reference point; the year selected is the base year.
    c. Prices in other years are expressed in terms of the base year prices; the price index in the base year is always 100.
    d. A price index allows comparison between any two years.

  4.2 Consumer Price Index
    a. The CPI measures change over time in the cost of buying the "market basket" of goods and services purchased by a typical family.
    b. A price index can be calculated for different market baskets.

  4.3 Problems with the CPI
    a. The CPI neglects quality improvements.
    b. The CPI neglects buyer responses to changes in relative prices.
    c. The CPI has failed to keep up with the shift consumers have made toward discount outlets.

  4.4 The GDP Price Index
    a. Real GDP is output in a current year measured in base year prices.
    b. The GDP price index includes the prices of all domestically produced final goods and services.
    c. Nominal GDP divided by real GDP multiplied by 100 generates the GDP price index.

  4.5 Moving from Fixed Weights to Chain Weights
    a. Since relative prices change over time, distortions occur when a base year is used to compare with many years.
    b. The Bureau of Economic Analysis (BEA) moved from a fixed-weighted system to a chain-weighted system in early 1996.
    c. The chain-weighted real GDP index adjusts to price weights more or less continuously.

  4.6 *CASE STUDY:* Computer Prices and GDP Estimation

5. Appendix: National Income Accounts

5.1   National Income. National income measures income earned by resource suppliers; it equals Net National Product (NNP) plus government subsidies minus indirect business taxes.

5.2   Personal Income. Personal income (PI) measures all income received by individuals; it equals national income plus income received but not earned and minus income earned but not received.

5.3   Disposable Income. Disposable income (DI) measures the income available for households to spend; it equals personal income minus personal taxes and other government charges.

5.4   Summary of National Income Accounts. The components of the national income accounts are GDP, NDP, national income, PI, and DI.

5.5   Summary Income Statement of the Economy
       a.   National income represents the sum of all earnings from producing domestic product.
       b.   There are five components of national income:
             (1)   Employee compensation
             (2)   Proprietors' income
             (3)   Corporate profits
             (4)   Net interest
             (5)   Rental income of persons
       c.   The largest source of personal income is employee compensation.

III. DISCUSSION

The Product of a Nation

The federal government collects large quantities of data in order to measure the performance of the economy. The U.S. national income accounts, which have been devised by some of the top economists in the last 50 years, organize the data into a coherent framework. The government uses *gross domestic product* (GDP), which is the market value of all final goods and services produced by resources located in the United States, as its measure of product. GDP excludes income of Americans living in foreign countries and includes the income of foreigners living in the United States.

It is important to know what is and what is not included in gross domestic product. GDP includes *final goods and services* but does not include *intermediate goods and services*. Final goods and services are those that are sold to the ultimate user. Intermediate goods and services are those purchased for additional processing and resale. The classification of a good as a final good or an intermediate good depends on the identity of the buyer and the purpose of the purchase. A carburetor produced by General Motors and installed in one of its cars is an intermediate good; a carburetor sold to an individual who goes home and installs it herself is a final good.

Gross domestic product is a flow variable, so the calculation of GDP is for a particular period of time—generally a year. However, the government also makes quarterly calculations of GDP. GDP measures domestic production, so goods and services produced in the United States but exported to other countries are included; goods and services that are produced elsewhere and imported into the United States are deducted.

There are two ways to measure GDP. The *expenditure approach* measures GDP by adding up the *aggregate expenditure* on all final goods and services. There are four components of aggregate expenditure: *consumption, investment, government purchases*, and *net exports*. Consumption is the purchase of final goods and services by households; final goods include both durable goods and nondurable goods. Investment includes all spending on output that is not used for present consumption. Included in investment are the purchase of new plants and equipment by firms, changes in firms' *inventories*, and new residential construction. Government purchases include spending for goods and services by all levels of government but do not include transfer payments. This is because transfer payments do not involve the government purchase of goods and services. Net exports are exports minus imports and include expenditures on goods and services.

The second method of measuring GDP is the *income approach*. Income categories include wages, rent, interest, and profit. Production involves the use of inputs to produce the goods and services. Each input is owned by someone, and that person receives a payment for the use of the input. The total value of a good that is produced equals the total of payments made to input owners. Hence, if we measure the value of a good by its sale price, we will get the same figure as if we measure its value as the total of all payments to the owners of inputs used to produce the good.

Double counting is avoided by including only the market value of final goods and services or by calculating the *value added* at each stage of production. Value added is found by taking the selling price of the firm and subtracting the amount paid to other firms for materials. Hence, the value added reflects the amount paid to resource owners at that stage of production. By adding up the value added at each stage of production, we include the contribution of all resource owners to production.

The Circular Flow of Income and Expenditure

The circular flow model pictures the relationships among households, firms, the government, and the foreign sector, as well as the flow of aggregate expenditure and the flow of aggregate income that make up GDP. Make sure you understand the circular flow, illustrated in Exhibit 2 in the text. *Aggregate income* flows from firms to households, with a *leakage* of taxes and an *injection* of transfer payments. Households spend *disposable income* on consumption and saving. Savings flow into *financial markets*, where governments and firms come to borrow funds for government spending and investment spending. Consumption spending is combined with investment spending, government purchases, and net exports and flows back to firms. Net exports are either a net injection or a net leakage, depending on whether exports or imports are larger. Total leakages from the circular flow must equal total injections into the circular flow.

Since national income accounting uses double-entry bookkeeping, aggregate expenditure must equal aggregate income, and leakages must equal injections. However, double-entry bookkeeping does not imply that the plans of all people are always fulfilled or that the plans of all people mesh perfectly. In particular, GDP figures include *actual investment*, not *planned investment*. Unplanned changes in inventories can make actual investment different from planned investment. Potential differences between planned and actual investment is an important topic that is addressed more fully in a later chapter.

Limitations of National Income Accounting

As we mentioned earlier, it is important to know what is and what is not included in national income accounting. We have already seen that intermediate goods and services are not included, but other important categories are also not included. With some exceptions, GDP includes only products sold in formal markets, so it does not include household production. Child care, food preparation, lawn care, home maintenance, and the like, when produced by the members of a household, are not included in GDP. GDP measurements also exclude transactions in the *underground economy*, although this is not intentional. The government would like to include these transactions and tax the unreported income.

GDP also fails to reflect *depreciation* of capital goods. GDP ignores changes in the availability of leisure, changes in the quality of products, and changes in the availability of new products. It also fails to distinguish among types of goods, treating $100 spent on education the same as $100 spent on theft prevention. Further, it fails to include some important costs, especially costs to the environment from producing and consuming goods and services.

Accounting for Price Changes

Because national income accounts are based on *nominal values* (current dollars), it is difficult to make meaningful comparisons of the accounts over time. The government attempts to adjust for changes in GDP due to inflation so that it can measure changes in real GDP. To compare figures over time, an index number must be calculated as a reference point. Many types of price indexes can be calculated, but the government tends to use two: the *consumer price index* and the *GDP price index*.

The consumer price index identifies a "market basket" of goods and services consumed by a typical family in the base period. The cost of buying this basket of goods each year is determined, and changes in the cost reflect changes in the cost of living.

There are several problems with the CPI. First, it fails to account for changes in quality over time. Second, the prices of all goods do not go up by the same amount every year. Hence, even in inflationary times, relative prices are changing too. Consequently, buyers respond to relative price changes by altering the amount of the goods they purchase. The CPI presumes that the same quantities of each good are purchased each year and fails to consider buyer responses to changes in relative prices. Third, it neglects changes in consumer behavior such as the shift toward discount outlets.

Appendix A: A Closer Look at the National Income Accounts

The GDP price index keeps track of price changes for all production in the economy. The *GDP price index* is nominal GDP divided by real GDP. The real GDP is measured as a weighted sum of different goods and services produced in the economy. The important question is: What weights should be used? Recently, the BEA moved from a fixed-weighted system to a chain-weighted system. The weights change from year to year. The index of real GDP for 1995 is based on a geometric average of the prices for 1994 and 1995.

The appendix takes a closer look at some of the national income accounts. Exhibit 1 shows how disposable income is derived from GDP.

Exhibit 1

National Income Accounting 1996 (billions of dollars)

Consumer expenditures	$5,151.4	
Investment	1,117.0	
Net exports	-98.7	
Government purchases	<u>1,406.4</u>	
Gross domestic product		$7,576.1
Net factor income from rest of world	-8.9	
Gross national product	$7,567.1	
Less: Depreciation	<u>-845.5</u>	
Net national product		6,721.6
Plus: Subsidies	17.5	
Less: Indirect business taxes	<u>-617.9</u>	
National income		$6,164.2 *
Plus: Government transfers	1056.7	
Private business transfers	23.0	
Interest and dividend income	968.8	
Less: Corporate profits	-670.2	
Social insurance taxes	-403.3	
Other	<u>-689.7</u>	
Personal income		6,449.5
Less: Personal taxes and nontax		
payments	-863.8	
Disposable income		<u>$5,585.7</u>

*Includes items not shown separately

IV. LAGNIAPPE

GDP, Home Production, and Cross-Country Comparisons

Gross domestic product does not include household production, which can be an important source of production. This is especially true in less developed countries where formal markets are not well developed. Thus, home production as a percentage of total production in a country will be greater in less developed countries than in industrialized countries. When we compare the GDP of an industrialized country with that of a less developed country, the gap between the countries as measured by GDP is greater than it would be if we measured all production. Similarly, per capita income figures in less developed countries tend to understate the actual standard of living because they ignore home production.

Question to Think About: How could home production be measured in GDP figures?

Price Indexes and Quality

Price indexes tend to overstate the actual inflation rate because they ignore quality changes. Quality differences over time are often very significant. For example, in the early 1960s most television sets were black and white rather than color. Further, they used tubes that often burned out and had to be replaced. Today we have color TVs that are based on much more reliable technology. The quality of the color on television sets has also improved. Early color TVs required adjustments by professionals if they were moved from one location to another. Similar quality improvements have been made in shirts (we now have wash-and-wear shirts instead of shirts that need ironing), refrigerators, ovens, automobiles, and most other products. In addition, there are new products that did not exist in the 1960s: personal computers, video games, microwave ovens, and hand calculators, to name a few.

Question to Think About: Are there any products in existence today that did not exist in 1980?

V. KEY TERMS

expenditure approach to GDP	injection
income approach to GDP	planned investment
final goods and services	actual investment
intermediate goods and services	underground economy
double counting	depreciation
consumption	net domestic product
investment	nominal GDP
physical capital	real GDP
residential construction	base year
inventories	price index
government purchases	GDP price index
net exports	national income
aggregate expenditure	personal income
aggregate income	employee compensation
value added	proprietors' income
disposable income (DI)	corporate profits
net taxes (NT)	net interest
financial markets	rental income of persons
leakage	

VI. QUESTIONS

A. *Completion*

1. Only _____ goods and services are used in calculating gross domestic product.

2. Goods purchased for additional processing are _____ goods.

3. GDP can be calculated by either the _____ approach or the _____ approach.

4. An increase in firm _____ is counted as an investment in the national income accounts.

5. Disinvestment occurs when there is a net _____ on inventories during a year.

6. Aggregate _____ is equal to the sum of consumption spending, investment spending, government purchases, and net exports.

7. The _____ by a firm is the difference between the value of a product and the cost of intermediate products purchased from other firms.

8. In the flow of income and spending, total _____ (such as savings and taxes) must equal total _____ (such as transfer payments, investment, government purchases, and exports).

9. Financial markets channel funds from consumer _____ to be used for government purchases and _____ spending by firms.

10. The income available to households to spend or save is called _____.

11. _____ investment includes planned investment and unplanned inventory changes.

12. Market transactions that go unreported are part of the _____ economy.

13. GDP fails to account for the _____ of existing products and the changes in the _____ of new products.

14. The difference between gross domestic product and net domestic product is _____.

15. The manufactured capital stock is depreciated but the _____ capital stock is not.

16. The _____ GDP is based on prices that prevail at the time of the transaction.

17. Real GDP is found by deflating _____ GDP with a _____.

18. _____ investment rather than _____ investment is used in calculating GDP.

B.   *True/False*

_____ 1.   The national income accounts are based on a double-entry bookkeeping system.

_____ 2.   In the national income accounts, the total value of output produced must equal the total value of resource payments.

_____ 3.   All goods and services sold in a year are included in GDP.

_____ 4.   A sale of a used car in 1997 would be included in GDP in 1997.

_____ 5.   Consumption refers to purchases of final goods and services by households.

_____ 6.   Gross private domestic investment consists of spending during the year on current output that is not used in present consumption.

_____ 7.   Disinvestment occurs when there is a net increase in inventories.

_____ 8.   The value added at each stage of production represents income to resource suppliers at that stage.

_____ 9.   The market value of a good equals the sum of the value added at each stage of production.

_____ 10.   National income accounts always look at economic activity after the transaction has occurred.

_____ 11.   GDP fails to reflect changes in the availability of leisure time.

_____ 12.   Saving represents an injection into the circular flow.

_____ 13.   The sum of the leakages from the flow of income and spending must equal the sum of the injections into the flow.

_____ 14.   GDP is the same whether people do their own taxes or have accountants do their taxes.

_____ 15.   The government reduces GDP figures to reflect the costs associated with negative externalities.

_____ 16.   In calculating the GDP price index, the government includes all final goods and services produced in the economy.

_____ 17.   The consumer price index holds constant the bundle of commodities consumed over time.

_____ 18.   The CPI and the GDP price index differ only with respect to the goods and services included.

C. Multiple Choice

1. The total value of output is measured by
   a. the amount people pay for the output.
   b. the total amount paid at each stage of production.
   c. disposable income.
   d. GDP plus depreciation.
   e. the value added at the final stage of production.

2. Which of the following is included in GDP?
   a. purchase of a computer by General Motors
   b. sale of a car to IBM
   c. value of homeowner's time when mowing the lawn
   d. sale of U.S. wheat to Russia
   e. All of the above.

3. Which of the following is an example of a final good or service?
   a. steel purchased by General Motors
   b. milk purchased by a grocery store
   c. pickles purchased by McDonald's
   d. a truckload of tropical fish purchased by a pet store
   e. a new factory built by IBM

4. The difference between gross domestic product and net domestic product is
   a. investment spending.
   b. net exports.
   c. depreciation.
   d. the former uses the expenditure approach and the latter uses the income approach.
   e. saving.

5. The largest spending category is
   a. personal consumer expenditures.
   b. gross private domestic investment.
   c. government consumption and gross investment.
   d. imports.
   e. a and c are about the same size

6. Invisible is another term for
   a. inventories.
   b. services.
   c. indirect business taxes.
   d. depreciation.
   e. None of the above.

7. Which of the following would not be included in U.S. GDP?
   a. a waiter's cash tips that are not reported to the IRS
   b. cash payment made at a grocery store
   c. purchase of a new house
   d. payment of military salaries
   e. sale of an airline ticket by American Airlines for a flight from London to New York

8. In terms of the national income accounts, which of the following is an example of an investment?
   a. purchase of one hundred shares of IBM stock
   b. building of a new hospital by the government
   c. a farmer's purchase of a used tractor
   d. an increase in inventories during the year
   e. transfer of funds from a checking account to a savings account

9. Which of the following is not included in government purchases?
   a. The Pentagon's purchase of a new jet fighter
   b. The salary of the president
   c. An increase in Social Security benefits
   d. Purchase of office supplies by the Senate
   e. All are included in government purchases.

10. Suppose you pay $0.80 for a gallon of gasoline. Further, suppose the owner of the oil well received 20 cents per gallon, the oil refiner received $0.65 per gallon, and the gasoline wholesaler received $0.75 from the gas station. What is the contribution to GDP from the sale of the gasoline? What is the gasoline station's value added?
    a. $2.40; $0.80
    b. $0.80; $0.80
    c. $0.80; $0.05
    d. $0.80; $0.75
    e. $0.75; $0.75

11. GDP equals
    a. the market value of all final goods and services.
    b. the sum of all the income earned by resource suppliers in the economy.
    c. the sum of the value added at all stages of production.
    d. All of the above.
    e. b plus c.

12. Which of the following would increase GDP?
    a. A man repairs his car himself.
    b. A family sells its house.
    c. Ford buys a spark plug from an auto parts manufacturer rather than making it itself.
    d. A family takes its baby to day care rather than to the baby's grandmother for babysitting.
    e. All of the above increase GDP.

13. Saving is a leakage from the circular flow. Which of the following may be an injection financed by the flow of saving?
    a. investment spending
    b. government purchases of goods and services
    c. government transfer payments
    d. All of the above.
    e. a and b

14. Which of the following does not constitute a leakage?
    a. transfer payments
    b. taxes
    c. savings
    d. imports
    e. None of the above.

15. The U.S. nominal GDP was $3,777.2 billion in 1984 and $4,038.7 billion in 1985. The increase in GDP was due to
    a. an increase in the value of total production of the United States.
    b. inflation.
    c. an increase in government purchases.
    d. a reduction of import spending.
    e. All of the above. are possible explanations.

16. The CPI was 87.2 for 1983 and 91.0 for 1984 (1987 base year). What was the rate of inflation, calculated using the CPI?
    a. 4.3 percent
    b. 3.8 percent
    c. 178.2 percent
    d. 3.4 percent
    e. The question cannot be answered without more information.

17. The CPI and the GDP price index differ in that
    a. the CPI takes into consideration quality differences and the GDP price index does not.
    b. the GDP price index compares current prices to prices in a base year and the CPI does not.
    c. the CPI uses prices for a sample of consumption goods and services whereas the GDP price index uses prices of all final domestic production.
    d. the GDP price index holds the weight of each item's price constant over time whereas the CPI allows the weights to vary over time.
    e. c and d

18. GDP tends to grow as an economy becomes less rural and more urban, in part because
    a. people living in cities want more things than people on farms.
    b. people on farms tend to produce more of their own goods and services than people in cities.
    c. net exports tend to be greater in urban economies than in rural economies.
    d. farmers do not engage in investment spending.
    e. All of the above.

19. Which of the following is a problem with using GDP as a measure of economic welfare?
    a. GDP excludes environmental costs.
    b. GDP excludes the value of household production.
    c. GDP fails to distinguish among types of commodities.
    d. GDP fails to consider the value of leisure.
    e. All of the above.

20. The largest source of income is
    a. employee compensation.
    b. corporate profits.
    c. proprietors' income.
    d. government transfer payments.
    e. any of the above, depending on the year in question.

D. Discussion Questions

1. Discuss what is and what is not included in calculating GDP.

2. State whether each of the following transactions is a part of GDP and explain why.
   a. Profits made by an IBM plant in England
   b. Profits made by a Honda plant in Ohio

3. How do the expenditure and income approaches to calculating GDP differ? Why do they yield the same number for GDP?

4. How are changes in inventories handled in GDP accounts?

5. Why are welfare payments not included in government spending?

6. What is value added? How is value added related to the market value of the final good?

7. Suppose a firm sells its product for $10 and pays $6 for materials. If the cost of materials increases to $7 but the firm still sells its product for $10, what happens to GDP? What happens to the firms's value added? Explain.

8. Why do total leakages and total injections have to be equal?

9. Why does investment spending not equal saving in the circular flow?

10. Discuss the limitations of national income accounting.

11. Why does national income accounting ignore changes in leisure time and household production?

12. Fill in the blanks in Exhibit 2 on the following page.

Exhibit 2

Year	Basket of Goods (Nominal)	Basket of Goods (Real)	CPI	Inflation Rate
1988	$4,053.6	$4,294.1	94.4	
1989	4,277.7	_____	96.9	_____
1990	4,544.5	4,544.5	_____	_____
1991	_____	4,728.5	103.9	_____
1992	5,266.8	4,854.2	_____	_____
1993	_____	4,896.6	113.2	_____
1994	5,694.9	_____	117.8	_____
1995	_____	4,943.9	_____	2.9%

13. Why does the consumer price index exaggerate the inflation rate?

14. Per capita GDP is much higher in the United States than in China. Does this imply that U.S. consumers are that much better off than Chinese consumers? Explain.

15. Use the following information to answer the questions.

Consumer expenditures	$1,732.6
Depreciation	303.9
Government purchases	530.3
Government transfers	312.6
Indirect business taxes	230.3
Interest and dividend income	324.9
Investment	437.0
Net exports	32.1
Other income not received	200.9
Personal taxes and nontax payments	340.5
Private business transfers	12.1
Social insurance taxes	216.5
Net income from American resources abroad	5.7
Corporate profits	177.2

a. What is GDP?
b. What is NDP?
c. What is national income?
d. What is personal income?
e. What is disposable income?

VII. ANSWERS

A. Completion

1.	final	10.	disposable income
2.	intermediate	11.	Actual
3.	expenditure; income	12.	underground
4.	inventories	13.	quality; availability
5.	decrease	14.	depreciation
6.	expenditure	15.	natural
7.	value added	16.	nominal (or current-dollar)
8.	leakages; injections	17.	nominal; price index
9.	savings; investments	18.	Actual; planned

B. True/False

1. True
2. True
3. False. Only currently produced final goods and services are included.
4. False
5. True
6. True
7. False
8. True
9. True
10. True
11. True
12. False
13. True
14. False
15. False
16. True
17. True
18. False

C. Multiple Choice

1. a
2. d
3. e
4. c
5. a
6. b
7. a
8. d
9. c
10. c
11. d
12. d
13. d
14. a
15. e
16. a
17. c
18. b
19. e
20. a

D. Discussion Questions

1. GDP includes the total market value of all domestically produced final goods and services. It includes exports because they are produced here, but it does not include imports because they are not produced in the United States. It does not include intermediate goods because their value is included in the value of the final goods and services. With some exceptions, GDP does not include the value of production undertaken by households because such production does not involve market transactions. It also does not include transactions that take place in the underground economy, because they are not recorded.

2. a. No, because the plant is not located in the United States.
   b. Yes, because the plant is located in the United States.

3. The expenditure and income approaches differ in that they focus on different portions of the circular flow. The expenditure approach focuses on purchases made by different members of society; the income approach focuses on the income received by different resource owners. The two must be equal because the total expenditure on a good or service must exactly equal the sum of the incomes of all the resource owners who contributed resources to producing the good or service.

4. A net increase in inventories during the year adds to investment spending while a net decrease in inventories is subtracted from investment spending.

5. Government spending involves spending on goods and services. Welfare payments are a transfer payment, and so they are not included.

6. Value added is the difference at each stage of production between what the firm sells its product for and what the firm pays for the materials it purchased to make the product. The market value of the final good must equal the sum of the value added at each stage of production.

7. Since the price of the final good does not change, GDP does not change, but the firm's value added falls from $4 to $3. The higher income of owners of resources associated with the production of the product is exactly offset by the lower income received by resource owners associated with the firm. Value added at an earlier stage of production has increased.

8. Total leakages and total injections must be equal because any dollar given up by one member of society must go to another member of society. For example, taxes reduce disposable income but increase government revenues. Whether a dollar is spent by consumers or by the government, it contributes to GDP.

9. There are other injections and leakages besides investment spending and saving. The requirement is that total leakages and total injections be equal, or $S + (T - R) + M = I + G + X$. If saving and investment are not equal, the totals still can be equal because of the offsetting values of the other variables.

10. National income accounting has several limitations. GDP does not include most household production, which may often be an important source of production. GDP also misses unreported transactions. The national income accounts cannot account for changes over time in the availability of leisure, quality of products, and availability of new products. Further, GDP ignores some costs, such as the costs associated with pollution.

11. Presumably because both would be difficult to put dollar values on. The value a person places on leisure is subjective and difficult to measure. The value of household production could be included theoretically, but it would also be difficult to do practically. What activities would be included? Feeding the baby, getting dressed, and combing one's hair could all be done by hiring someone, yet these seem like unlikely candidates to include in GDP.

12.

Year	Basket of Goods (Nominal)	Basket of Goods (Real)	CPI	Inflation Rate
1988	$4,053.6	$4,294.1	94.4	
1989	4,277.7	**4,414.6**	96.9	**2.6%**
1990	4,544.5	4,544.5	**100.0**	**3.2%**
1991	**4,908.2**	4,728.5	103.9	**3.9%**
1992	5,266.8	4,854.2	**108.5**	**4.4%**
1993	**5,542.9**	4,896.6	113.2	**4.3%**
1994	5,694.9	**4,843.4**	117.8	**4.1%**
1995	**5,992.0**	4,943.9	**121.2**	2.9%

13. The CPI holds the weight of each price constant over time. When the price of a good increases relative to all other prices, people may respond by curtailing consumption of the good. Since the CPI operates as though consumption of the good were the same even though the relative price is higher, it overstates the weight of the good and overstates the inflation rate. It also fails to account for the introduction of new products, changes in quality, and changes in the quantity of leisure time.

14. China has a more rural economy than the United States, so household production is likely to be much more extensive in China than in the United States. Further, China is a centrally planned economy, so the goods produced do not always reflect consumers' desires, and prices tend to be set by government rather than by the interaction of supply and demand. In short, comparison between the GDPs of the two countries is very difficult to make.

15. a. GDP = $1,732.6 + 530.3 + 32.1 + 437 = $2,732.0
   b. NDP = $2,732.0 – 303.9 = $2,428.1
   c. National income = $2,428.1 + 5.7 – 230.3 = $2,203.5
   d. Personal income = $2,203.5 + 312.6 + 12.1 + 324.9 – 177.2 – 216.5 – 200.9 = 2,258.5
   e. Disposable income = $2,258.5 – 340.5 = $1,918.0

CHAPTER 9

Aggregate Expenditure: Consumption, Investment, Government Purchases, and Net Exports

I.   INTRODUCTION

We have already introduced aggregate demand and aggregate supply curves. Now we begin a closer look at aggregate demand. In particular, this chapter examines two important components of aggregate demand: consumption and investment. Both activities originate in the private sector of the economy. A third component of aggregate demand—net exports—is examined in the appendix. Aggregate supply will be discussed in future chapters.

II.   OUTLINE

1.   Consumption

    1.1   An Initial Look at Income and Consumption. Consumer spending and disposable income tend to move together over time.

    1.2   The Consumption Function
        a.   People decide how much to consume based on their disposable income, so consumption depends on disposable income.
        b.   The consumption function shows the relation between the amount spent on consumption and the level of income in the economy, other things constant.

    1.3   Marginal Propensities to Consume and to Save
        a.   The *marginal propensity to consume* (MPC) shows how much of an extra dollar received is spent on consumer goods, and it equals the change in consumption divided by the change in income.
        b.   The *marginal propensity to save* (MPS) equals the change in saving divided by the change in income.
        c.   The sum of the marginal propensity to consume and the marginal propensity to save must equal 1 because disposable income is either spent or saved.

    1.4   MPC, MPS, and the Slope of the Consumption and Saving Functions
        a.   The marginal propensity to consume equals the slope of the consumption function.
        b.   The marginal propensity to save equals the slope of the saving function.

    1.5   Nonincome Determinants of Consumption
        a.   The greater the level of their net wealth, the more willing households are to consume instead of save.
            (1)   Along a given consumption function, household net wealth is held constant.
            (2)   A change in net wealth causes the consumption function to shift; a change in income causes a movement along the consumption function.

b. An increase in the price level reduces consumption (the consumption function shifts down) and increases saving; a decrease in the price level increases consumption and decreases saving.

c. An increase in the interest rate promotes more saving and shifts the consumption function down; a decrease in the interest rate promotes less saving and shifts the consumption function up.

d. Changes in expectations also shift the consumption function.

(1) Expectations of higher income levels generate greater consumption prior to the actual change in income.

(2) Expectations of higher prices in the future also encourage people to increase current consumption spending.

1.6 *CASE STUDY:* The Life-Cycle Hypothesis

2. Investment. Investment consists of spending on construction of factories and equipment, construction of housing, and net increases in inventories. Investment does not consist of purchases of stocks, bonds, land, and so forth.

2.1 The Demand for Investment

a. Firms buy capital goods when the investment is expected to be more profitable than other possible uses of the funds.

b. The opportunity cost of funds is the market interest rate.

c. A firm will invest in capital stock when the expected rate of return exceeds the market rate of interest.

d. The demand for investment spending is inversely related to the interest rate.

2.2 From Micro to Macro

a. Just as a particular business's demand curve for investment slopes down, so does the market demand curve for investment.

b. The lower the interest rate, the greater the quantity of investment demanded, other things equal.

2.3 Planned Investment and the Economy's Level of Income

a. Investment is assumed to be autonomous; that is, it is assumed to be independent of the level of income.

b. In making decisions, investors look more at expected future profits than at current income levels.

c. The investment function, which relates planned investment to the current level of disposable income, is a horizontal line at the current level of investment demand.

2.4 Nonincome Determinants of Investment

a. The investment function shifts up when interest rates fall and shifts down when interest rates increase.

b. Business expectations of profit prospects greatly affect the level of investment spending.

2.5 *CASE STUDY:* Variability of Consumption and Investment

3. Government

   3.1 Government Purchase Function
      a. The government purchase function relates government purchases to the level of income in the economy.
      b. It is assumed that government purchases are autonomous, or independent of the level of income.

   3.2 Net Taxes. *Net taxes* are taxes minus transfer payments, and they are treated as autonomous.

4. Net Exports

   4.1 Net Exports and Income
      a. When disposable income increases, people spend more on all normal goods, including imports.
      b. There is a positive relationship between disposable income and imports.
      c. Exports are autonomous, since they depend on the income of foreigners.
      d. *Net exports* are exports minus imports, which decline as income increases.
      e. The analysis is simplified by assuming net exports are autonomous.

   4.2 Nonincome Determinants of Net Exports
      a. The net export function shows the relationship between net exports and the level of income, other things constant.
      b. Factors held constant include the following:
         (1) U.S. price level
         (2) Price levels in other countries
         (3) Interest rates in the United States and in other countries
         (4) Foreign income levels
         (5) Exchange rates between the dollar and foreign currencies
      c. A fall in the value of the dollar causes an increase in net exports, and a rise in the value of the dollar causes a fall in net exports.

5. Composition of Aggregate Expenditure.   Since 1950, consumption's share of aggregate spending has increased, and the share of spending by government goods and services has decreased.

6. Appendix: Variable Net Exports

   6.1 Net Exports and Income. Net exports are inversely related to U.S. income.

   6.2 Shifts in Net Exports. The net export function shifts up if the value of the dollar falls and shifts down if the value of the dollar increases.

III. DISCUSSION

Consumption

Consumption is a positive function of disposable income. The relationship between U.S. disposable income and consumption has been very stable, especially since World War II. The *consumption function* shows the relationship between the amount spent on consumption and the level of income, other things constant. Consumption spending increases as disposable income increases; that is, consumption spending and income are directly related. A graph of a consumption function is an upward-sloping line, as shown in Exhibit 3 in the text. Economists focus on what happens when disposable income changes. If disposable income increases, some of the additional income will be spent on consumption goods and some will be saved. The proportion of the additional income that is spent on consumption is called the *marginal propensity to consume* (MPC). That is, the marginal propensity to consume is the change in consumption spending divided by the change in income. Further, the change in income is the cause of the change in consumption spending. Similarly, the *marginal propensity to save* (MPS) is the change in saving divided by the change in disposable income.

Be sure that you understand Exhibits 4 and 5 in the text. Columns 1 and 3 in Exhibit 4 show levels of disposable income and consumption; columns 2 and 4 show the changes in disposable income and consumption. The MPC, then, is column 4 divided by column 2. In Exhibit 5, the MPC is measured by the slope of the consumption function, and the MPS is measured by the slope of the saving function. Since the only uses of additional income are consumption and saving, MPC + MPS = 1.

Consumption also depends on things other than income. In particular, consumption depends on net wealth, the price level, consumer expectations, and the interest rate. Net wealth is a stock, whereas income is a flow. That is, *net wealth* is the value of all the assets owned by a household less liabilities and debts owed to others. To increase net wealth, a household must either increase its saving or pay off debt. Since an important motive for saving is to increase one's wealth, the greater the wealth, the less the incentive to save and the more the household will spend on consumption. An increase in net wealth causes the consumption function to shift up; a reduction in net wealth causes the consumption function to shift down. Note that in either case the consumption function shifts because of a change in net wealth. A change in income has a different effect: it causes a movement *along* the consumption function.

An increase in the price level makes a household poorer because the purchasing power of the household's savings falls. As a result, the household will reduce consumption and increase saving, which generates a downward shift in the consumption function. A change in expectations will also shift the consumption function. Expectations of higher income in the future tend to encourage more consumption today, as do expectations of higher prices in the future. Finally, a change in the market rate of interest will cause the consumption function to shift. If the interest rate falls, savers are rewarded less and generally respond by saving less and consuming more. Keep in mind that a change in disposable income causes a movement along the consumption function, whereas changes in net wealth, in the price level, in expectations, or in the interest rate cause shifts in the consumption function.

Investment

Investment consists of spending on new factories and equipment, construction of housing, and net increases in inventories. Investment adds to the economy's stock of capital goods and is generally carried out by business firms. Firms engage in investment spending when they believe that the investment will be more profitable than other possible uses of their funds. This will be the case whenever the expected rate of return exceeds the opportunity cost of investing in capital, which is the market rate of interest. The demand for investment funds tends to be a negative function of the interest rate.

Investment spending tends to be related to businesses' expectations about future profits rather than to current income. Hence, investment tends to be independent of income, or *autonomous*. The autonomous investment function can be represented graphically as a horizontal line when disposable income is on the horizontal axis. An increase in the rate of interest will cause the investment function to shift down, and a decrease in the rate of interest will cause the investment function to shift up. A more optimistic business climate causes the investment function to shift up, and a less optimistic business climate causes the investment function to shift down.

Government

Governments purchase goods and services, borrow money, and collect taxes. Government purchases are assumed to be autonomous, that is, independent of the level of income. Net taxes (taxes – transfer payments) are also assumed to be autonomous.

Net Exports

Imports are consumer goods just like any other goods. When disposable income increases, Americans buy more of all goods, so spending on imports increases. Hence, imports are a positive function of disposable income. On the other hand, the level of exports is determined by spending in other countries, so exports are autonomous with respect to U.S. disposable income. Combining imports and exports yields net exports, which are inversely related to disposable income, other things constant. However, usually we will assume net exports are autonomous. Factors held constant along the net export function include domestic and foreign price levels, domestic and foreign interest rates, and the exchange rates between domestic and foreign currencies.

Composition of Aggregate Expenditure

The composition of aggregate expenditures has changed over the last 40 years. The government's share of it has fallen as defense spending has fallen, and consumption's share has increased.

Appendix: Variable Net Exports

Since imports are goods like those produced domestically, Americans buy more imports when their incomes increase. Similarly, foreigners buy more U.S. goods when their incomes increase. Imports of foreigners are U.S. exports, so U.S. exports depend on income levels in other countries rather than on U.S. income. Hence, U.S. exports are not a function of U.S. disposable income; that is, U.S. exports are autonomous. U.S. imports, though, are positively related to U.S. disposable income. Net exports are exports minus imports ($X - M$). Since exports are autonomous and imports are directly related to disposable income, net exports are inversely related to U.S. disposable income.

IV. LAGNIAPPE

Saving versus Hoarding

The link between saving and investment will be broken if savers actually hoard their money. If people do not place their funds in some type of financial intermediary and instead keep their funds at home, it is not possible for the funds to be invested. In such cases there will clearly be an imbalance between saving and investment. As long as people who save also want to receive interest on their funds, however, the link between saving and investment can exist.

Question to Think About: Why would anyone choose to hoard funds rather than place them in a financial intermediary?

Saving, Investing, and the Stock Market

Buying stocks and bonds is not considered investment. The stock market is related to investment activity in an important way, however. Firms often raise investment funds by selling shares of stock. Those who buy the shares are not investing. Instead, they are saving and providing the funds to the firm, which does invest by buying plants or equipment. If a person who buys newly issued shares of stock from a firm later sells the stock in the stock market, the firm receives no additional funds. The transaction involves only individuals, who interact through the stock market. The presence of the stock market does encourage investment activity. Firms would find it more difficult to attract funds if it were not possible to resell shares of stock. Since shareholders can sell their shares if they so desire, they are more willing to buy the initial offering of shares from the firm. The stock market is essentially a market for used shares, but this secondary market reduces firms' costs of raising investment funds.

Question to Think About: How is the bond market similar to the stock market?

V. KEY TERMS

consumption function	investment function
marginal propensity to consume (MPC)	autonomous
marginal propensity to save (MPS)	government purchase function
saving function	net export function
net wealth	

VI. QUESTIONS

A. Completion

1. Consumer _____ is the difference between disposable income and consumer spending.

2. The _____ shows a positive relationship between consumption spending and the level of income in the economy.

3. For a consumption function, the dependent variable is _____.

4. The fraction of additional income that is saved is indicated by the _____.

5. The sum of MPC and MPS is _____.

6. The slope of the consumption function equals the marginal propensity to _____.

7. _____ consists of the value of all the assets that a household owns minus any liabilities.

8. A change in the price level influences consumption by affecting the real value of _____.

9. Movement along the consumption function is caused by changes in _____.

10. The opportunity cost of investing in capital is the _____.

11. Investment spending is said to be _____ when it is independent of the level of income.

12. Investment depends primarily on business _____.

13. Government purchases are related to the level of income by the _____.

14. Government purchases do not include _____ payments.

B. True/False

_____ 1. The most important determinant of how much people spend on goods and services is their disposable income.

_____ 2. Consumption spending can never be greater than disposable income.

_____ 3. Since consumption spending increases with disposable income, saving must decrease with disposable income.

_____ 4. The entire consumption function shifts when income changes.

_____ 5. A decrease in the interest rate will shift the consumption function down.

_____ 6. Investment increases when new houses are built.

_____ 7. When a person buys shares of stock, he or she is saving and investing at the same time.

_____ 8. Investment spending tends to increase as interest rates fall.

_____ 9.   According to the textbook's simple model, investment spending is a positive function of disposable income.

_____ 10.   If firms become convinced a recession is imminent, they will increase investment spending.

_____ 11.   Consumption varies more than investment spending.

_____ 12.   Government purchases are autonomous.

_____ 13.   Spending on imports is a negative function of disposable income.

_____ 14.   Government purchases have declined as a share of total expenditures because of reductions in Social Security spending.

_____*15.   An increase in an economy's disposable income causes exports to increase.

_____*16.   If the value of the dollar falls, the net export function shifts upward.

C. Multiple Choice

1. The most important determinant of how much people spend is
    a. their tastes.
    b. tax policy.
    c. the inflation rate.
    d. the interest rate.
    e. how much they have available to spend.

2. The difference between disposable income and consumption is
    a. saving.
    b. taxes.
    c. net income.
    d. investment.
    e. consumption of consumer durables.

3. Disposable income is $2,000, $3,000, and $5,000 over a three-year period, and consumption is $2,000, $2,800, and $4,400 for the same three years. The marginal propensity to consume is
    a. 1.
    b. 0.933.
    c. 0.88.
    d. 0.80.
    e. different for each year.

---

*These questions are based on material developed in this chapter's Appendix.

4. In the previous question, saving in the first year is
   a. zero.
   b. $200.
   c. $600.
   d. $1,000.
   e. unknown. More information is needed.

5. (Refer to the information in question 3.) If consumption in the fourth year is $4,800, what is disposable income that year?
   a. $5,400
   b. $5,500
   c. $5,600
   d. $6,000
   e. The question cannot be answered without more information.

6. Which of the following is not held constant along a given consumption function?
   a. the price level
   b. the market rate of interest
   c. net wealth
   d. income
   e. expectations

7. Which of the following would cause a consumption function to shift up?
   a. a reduction in net wealth
   b. an increase in the price level
   c. a reduction in the interest rate
   d. expectations of lower future income
   e. None of the above.

8. Which of the following is an example of an investment?
   a. the manufacture of a lathe
   b. Chrysler's purchase of an American Motors factory
   c. an individual's purchase of 100 shares of stock in General Motors
   d. IBM's purchase of an existing office park in Houston
   e. All of the above.

9. A firm purchases capital goods as long as
   a. the expected rate of return exceeds the market rate of interest.
   b. the firm has funds available to invest.
   c. the firm is making a profit on all of its activities.
   d. the firm can borrow at the market rate of interest.
   e. None of the above.

10. According to the textbook's model of investment, which of the following affects the level of investment?
    a. disposable income
    b. the market rate of interest
    c. net wealth
    d. the inflation rate
    e. All of the above.

11. To say that investment spending is autonomous means that
    a. investment spending is not determined by the interest rate.
    b. investment spending is not determined by disposable income.
    c. investment spending has no effect on the economy.
    d. no one can determine what variables affect investment spending.
    e. the investment function coincides with the 45-degree line.

12. An increase in the interest rate leads to
    a. an increase in consumption spending.
    b. a decrease in investment spending.
    c. an increase in government spending.
    d. an increase in net exports.
    e. All of the above.

13. The most variable component of real GDP is
    a. consumption spending.
    b. investment spending.
    c. government spending.
    d. net taxes.
    e. None of the above.

14. Over the last four decades
    a. government purchases increased while all government outlays decreased.
    b. government purchases increased and all government outlays increased.
    c. government purchases decreased and all government outlays decreased.
    d. government purchases decreased while all government outlays increased.
    e. None of the above.

*15. Net exports are inversely related to the level of income because
    a. exports are inversely related to the level of income.
    b. imports are positively related to the level of income, exports are inversely related to the level of income, and the effect of exports is greater than the effect of imports.
    c. imports are positively related to the level of income and exports are autonomous.
    d. Americans buy fewer foreign goods and more U.S. goods at higher levels of income.
    e. None of the above.; net exports are autonomous.

*16. A rise in the value of a dollar will cause
    a. imports to increase.
    b. exports to decrease.
    c. net exports to decrease.
    d. All of the above.
    e. None of the above.

D. Discussion Questions

1. What is a consumption function? Describe the graph of a consumption function and explain its shape.

2. What is the marginal propensity to consume? to save? How are they related?

3. How is the marginal propensity to consume shown on a graph of the consumption function?

4. Explain how the following affect the consumption function:
   a. A decrease in net wealth
   b. An increase in the price level
   c. An expectation of lower prices in the future

5. Investment is not determined by income. Why not?

6. Why is there a negative relationship between the demand for investment funds and the interest rate?

7. Why does a reduction in the interest rate cause the investment function to shift up?

8. If total spending is consumption plus investment spending, how does an increase in the interest rate affect total spending?

9. Explain what would cause the government purchase function to increase. Will a change in Social Security spending affect government purchases?

*10. Explain why net exports are inversely related to the level of income.

*11. If total spending is $C + I + G + (X - M)$, how does an increase in domestic interest rates affect total spending? How would an increase in interest rates in foreign countries affect U.S. total spending?

VII. ANSWERS

A. *Completion*

1.	saving	8.	net wealth
2.	consumption function	9.	income
3.	consumption	10.	market interest rate
4.	marginal propensity to save	11.	autonomous
5.	1	12.	expectations
6.	consume	13.	government purchase function
7.	Net wealth	14.	transfer

B. *True/False*

1.	True	9.	False
2.	False	10.	False
3.	False	11.	False
4.	False	12.	True
5.	False	13.	False
6.	True	14.	False
7.	False	15.	False
8.	True	16.	True

---

*These questions are based on material developed in this chapter's Appendix.

C. Multiple Choice

1.	e	5.	b	9.	a	13.	b
2.	a	6.	d	10.	b	14.	d
3.	d	7.	c	11.	b	15.	c
4.	a	8.	a	12.	b	16.	d

D. Discussion Questions

1. The consumption function shows the relation between the amount spent on consumption goods and the level of income. The graph of a consumption function is an upward-sloping line because there is a positive relationship between consumption and income. That is, the greater one's income, the greater one's consumption spending, *ceteris paribus*. Disposable income is the major determinant of consumption. Where the consumption function intersects the 45-degree line, consumption and income are equal. To the left of this intersection, consumption exceeds income; to the right, income exceeds consumption.

2. The marginal propensity to consume is an expression of the proportion of additional income that is spent on consumption goods. The marginal propensity to save is an expression of the proportion of additional income that is saved. Households either consume or save, so the marginal propensity to consume and the marginal propensity to save must add up to 1.

3. The marginal propensity to consume is shown as the slope of the consumption function.

4. a. A decrease in net wealth causes the consumption function to shift down. People save to increase their net wealth, so a reduction in net wealth tends to encourage people to save more and consume less at every level of income.
    b. An increase in the price level makes the real value of a given amount of money fall, which tends to reduce the value of the savings people have accumulated. Consequently, people increase their saving and reduce consumption, and the consumption function shifts down.
    c. An expectation of lower prices in the future shifts the consumption function down. People put off spending today to spend more in the future if they expect prices to be lower in the future.

5. The investment decision depends on anticipated profits and opportunities and the market rate of interest rather than on current income.

6. Firms demand investment funds whenever the expected rate of return on an investment exceeds the market rate of interest. The lower the interest rate, the greater the number of investment projects that are profitable to undertake. Hence, the greater the demand for investment funds.

7. The investment function relates investment spending and disposable income. The investment function is autonomous, which means that disposable income has no effect on investment, and investment spending can be pictured as a horizontal line when disposable income is on the horizontal axis. Hence, the increased investment spending induced by a reduction in the interest rate is shown by an upward shift of the investment function.

8. An increase in the interest rate decreases total spending for two reasons. First, higher interest rates cause the quantity demanded of investment spending to decrease. Second, higher interest rates encourage people to save more and to spend less, reducing total spending.

9. Government purchases are autonomous, so an increase in government purchases would occur when government decides to buy more goods and services. No, transfer payments are not counted as a government purchase.

10. People buy more goods and services when their incomes increase. Because some of the goods and services they buy are made by foreign firms, rising levels of income induce greater import spending. Exports are determined by the income levels of foreigners rather than those of domestic residents. Hence, exports are autonomous. Net exports, which are exports minus imports, are inversely related to the level of income.

11. The answer is the same as for question 8, with the addition that the change in interest rates would also affect net export spending. The increase in interest rates reduces spending, which includes spending on imports. Hence, net exports would increase, offsetting to some extent the effects on consumption spending and investment spending. An increase in interest rates abroad would decrease net exports because foreigners would buy fewer U.S. exports.

CHAPTER 10

Aggregate Expenditure and Aggregate Demand

I. INTRODUCTION

In this chapter we derive the equilibrium level of aggregate output demanded for the economy. We focus on consumption and investment, although the government sector is included. The text treats net exports as autonomous; the appendix presents the situation when net exports are inversely related to income. The chapter introduces the multiplier, an important concept that you should be sure you understand. Aggregate supply is discussed in the next chapter.

II. OUTLINE

1. Aggregate Expenditure and Income

    1.1   The Components of Aggregate Expenditure
- a. Real GDP is GDP measured in terms of real goods and services produced.
- b. The economy will exhibit different levels of planned spending and saving for different levels of real GDP.
- c. There are two uses of disposable income: consumption and saving.
- d. There are three injections of spending into the circular flow: planned investment, government purchases, and net exports.
- e. Investment, government purchases, and net exports are treated as autonomous.
- f. The equilibrium quantity of aggregate demand occurs when planned aggregate expenditure equals real GDP.

    1.2   Quantity of Real GDP Demanded
- a. The income-expenditure model relates real GDP (that is, aggregate income or aggregate output) on the horizontal axis and aggregate expenditure on the vertical axis.
- b. The aggregate expenditure function shows the amount people plan to spend at each level of real GDP, holding the price level constant.
- c. The 45-degree line from the origin identifies all points where aggregate expenditure equals real GDP.
- d. Equilibrium is reached when aggregate expenditure equals aggregate output, which is where the aggregate expenditure function intersects the 45-degree line.

    1.3   When Output and Planned Spending Differ
- a. If planned spending and output are not equal, inventories change so that actual spending and output are equal.
- b. When planned spending is greater than output, there is an unintended drop in inventories and firms respond by increasing output.
- c. When planned spending is less than output, there is an unintended rise in inventories and firms respond by decreasing output.
- d. Equilibrium occurs when planned spending and output (or income) are equal. This occurs where the aggregate expenditure function crosses the 45-degree line.

e. For a given price level, there is only one quantity of output demanded at which income is equal to planned spending.

2. The Simple Spending Multiplier

    2.1 Effects of an Increase in Aggregate Expenditure
        a. A change in planned investment spending causes a proportionately larger shift in the equilibrium quantity of real GDP demanded in the same direction.
        b. An increase in investment generates higher incomes for some resource owners.
        c. Higher incomes generate increased consumption spending, which generates additional income for other resource owners. Saving also rises as income rises.
        d. The process stops when the entire change in investment spending drains from the circular flow as saving. Saving increases just enough to finance the increase in investment.
        e. If planned investment does not remain at the new, higher level, equilibrium spending will fall back to its initial level.
        f. The change in the equilibrium quantity of aggregate output demanded depends on how much the aggregate expenditure shifts and not on which spending component causes the shift.

    2.2 Simple Spending Multiplier
        a. The simple spending multiplier equals the number of times by which the change in real GDP demanded exceeds the change in planned investment spending.
        b. The change in the quantity of aggregate output demanded depends on how much the aggregate expenditure line shifts.

    2.3 Numerical Value of the Simple Spending Multiplier
        a. The expansion resulting from an increase in autonomous spending is limited by the leakage of income to saving.
        b. The smaller the portion of a change in income that is saved, the more that is spent in each round and the greater the multiplier.
        c. The simple multiplier equals the reciprocal of the marginal propensity to save.

    2.4 *CASE STUDY:* Hard Times in Connecticut

3. Deriving the Aggregate Demand Curve

    3.1 A Higher Price Level
        a. An increase in the price level makes consumers poorer, so they reduce consumption.
        b. A higher price level also reduces investment and net exports.
        c. If aggregate spending falls, the equilibrium quantity of aggregate output demanded falls.

    3.2 A Lower Price Level
        a. A decrease in the price level causes consumption, investment, and net exports to increase.
        b. The equilibrium quantity of aggregate output demanded is inversely related to the price level.
        c. The aggregate expenditure function shows how, for a given price level, consumption plus planned investment relates to the level of real GDP.
        d. The aggregate demand curve shows the quantity of real GDP demanded for various price levels.

3.3 The Multiplier and Shifts in Aggregate Demand
    a. An autonomous increase in planned spending shifts the aggregate expenditure function.
    b. For a given price level, the increase in planned spending increases the equilibrium quantity of aggregate output by an amount determined by the simple multiplier.
    c. The aggregate demand curve also shifts out as a result of the autonomous change in planned spending. At the prevailing price level, the size of the shift in the aggregate demand curve is determined by the simple multiplier.

3.4 *CASE STUDY:* Falling Consumption Triggers Japan's Recession

4. Appendix A: Variable Net Exports. Since imports are directly related to disposable income, it is more realistic to treat net exports as inversely related to the level of disposable income. Since net exports and income are inversely related, the addition of net exports reduces the slope of the aggregate expenditure function. The effect of net exports on equilibrium output demanded depends on the level of income where net exports equal zero.

4.1 Net Exports and the Spending Multiplier
    a. The marginal propensity to import (MPI) indicates the fraction of each additional dollar of income that is spent on imports.
    b. The multiplier equals $1/(MPS + MPI)$.
    c. The multiplier with net exports is lower than the simple domestic multiplier.

4.2 A Change in Autonomous Spending. An autonomous increase in net exports increases equilibrium output demanded; an autonomous decrease in net exports decreases equilibrium output demanded.

5. Appendix B: Algebra of Income and Expenditure

5.1 The Aggregate Expenditure Line
    a. The level of consumption when income is zero is called *autonomous consumption.*
    b. Increases in consumption that result when income increases are called *induced consumption.*

5.2 A More General Form of Income and Expenditure
    a. The consumption function, $C = a + b(Y - NT)$, is composed of autonomous consumption (a) and induced consumption, $b(Y - NT)$, where b is the marginal propensity to consume, Y is real income, and NT is net taxes.
    b. The investment function is autonomous and so is constant at the given level of investment, I.
    c. Government purchases, G, and autonomous net exports, $X - M$, are also added to the equation.
    d. Equilibrium is reached when income equals planned expenditure, or when $Y = C + I + G + X - M = a - bNT + bY + I + G + (X - M)$, which is equivalent to $Y = [1/(1 - b)](a - bNT + I + G + X - M)$.
    e. $(a - bNT + I + G + X - M)$ is autonomous spending (spending that occurs when income is zero) and $1/(1 - b)$ is the multiplier.

5.3 Introducing Variable Net Exports
    a. Exports are autonomous but imports are not, so net exports are $X - m(Y - NT)$, where m is the marginal propensity to import.
    b. Equilibrium is reached when $Y = a + b(Y - NT) + I + G + X - m(Y - NT)$, or $Y = [1/(1 - b + m)](a - bNT + I + G + X + mNT)$.

III. DISCUSSION

Aggregate Expenditure and Income

The *aggregate expenditure* at each level of income is the total planned spending, or, according to the chapter's model, the sum of consumption, planned investment spending, government purchases, and net exports. Real GDP is equal to the total output of the economy, which is also equal to the aggregate income generated by production. In equilibrium, aggregate expenditure must equal aggregate income.

It is important to note that aggregate income and planned aggregate expenditure are equal only if the economy is in equilibrium, whereas aggregate income and actual total expenditure are equal by definition. For the equilibrium condition to hold, planned consumption expenditures plus planned investment expenditures plus government purchases plus net exports must equal real GDP. When this happens, nobody has an incentive to change his or her actions or plans, and equilibrium is established. Even when we do not have equilibrium, actual total expenditure must equal real GDP because, as the circular flow model indicates, one individual's expenditure is another's income.

Exhibit 1 illustrates these concepts. In every row, actual total expenditure equals real GDP, but only in the sixth row does aggregate expenditure equal real GDP. Therefore, $10 trillion is the equilibrium level of real GDP demanded. At no other level of GDP does aggregate expenditure equal real GDP. For example, consider the second row, where real GDP is $6.0 trillion. Consumption is $4.8 trillion and saving is $0.2 trillion, but planned investment is $0.4 trillion. Planned aggregate expenditure is greater than real GDP. The economy is not producing enough output, so inventories are drawn down, generating an unanticipated inventory adjustment of $0.8 trillion. This yields an actual investment of –$0.4 trillion, not $0.4 trillion; this yields an actual total expenditure level of $6.0 trillion. This is not an equilibrium, since business planned on investing $0.4 trillion but actually disinvested $0.4 trillion. At real GDP of $10.0 trillion, there are no unintended inventory adjustments, so actual investment equals planned investment ($0.4 trillion). Finally, actual total expenditure equals real GDP and also equals (planned) aggregate expenditure. Hence, the equilibrium quantity of real GDP demanded is $10.0 trillion.

Exhibit 1
(trillions of dollars)

Real GDP (Y) (1)	Net Taxes (NT) (2)	Disposable Income Y – NT (3)	Consumption (C) (4)	Savings (S) (5)	Planned Investment I (6)	Gov't Purchases G (7)	Net Exports (X – M) (8)	Manual Aggregate Expenditure (9)	Unintended Inventory Adjustment (10)	Actual Investment (11)	Actual Total Expenditure (12)
$5.0	1.0	4.0	4.0	0	0.4	1.0	0.6	6.0	-0.4	-0.6	5.0
6.0	1.0	5.0	4.8	0.2	0.4	1.0	0.6	6.2	-0.8	-0.4	6.0
7.0	1.0	6.0	5.6	0.4	0.4	1.0	0.6	7.6	-0.6	-0.2	7.0
8.0	1.0	7.0	6.4	0.6	0.4	1.0	0.6	8.4	-0.4	0	8.0
9.0	1.0	8.0	7.2	0.8	0.4	1.0	0.6	9.2	-0.2	0.2	9.0
10.0	1.0	9.0	8.0	1.0	0.4	1.0	0.6	10.0	0	0.4	10.0
11.0	1.0	10.0	8.8	1.2	0.4	1.0	0.6	10.8	0.2	0.6	11.0
12.0	1.0	11.0	9.6	1.4	0.4	1.0	0.6	11.6	0.4	0.8	12.0

Exhibit 2 presents the information from Exhibit 1 graphically. The 45-degree line shows the points where real GDP equals aggregate expenditure.

Exhibit 2

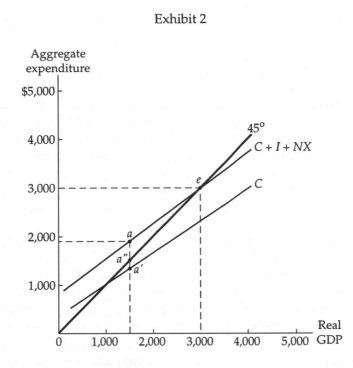

Point *e* is the equilibrium point, where real GDP and aggregate expenditure both equal $10.0 trillion. At real GDP of $5.0 trillion, point *a* indicates planned aggregate expenditure, *a′* indicates consumption, and *a″* indicates actual total expenditure. The distance between *a* and *a″* measures the unintended drop in investment of $0.4 trillion. The plans of consumers and business indicate a desire to purchase the amount at point *a*, but the economy actually spends the amount at point *a″*. As long as business responds to the unexpected decline in inventories by increasing production, the economy will expand and eventually arrive at the equilibrium real GDP demanded of $10.0 trillion (point *e*).

The Simple Spending Multiplier

Suppose we are at equilibrium in Exhibit 2. If businesses decide to change investment spending, then adjustments must be made by all participants in the economy until a new equilibrium is achieved. We can determine what these changes will be as long as we know the MPC. Suppose planned investment increases by $0.1 trillion, to $0.5 trillion. At the previous equilibrium level of real GDP demanded of $10.0 trillion, we have an excess demand for goods, since aggregate expenditure now equals $10.1 trillion instead of $10.0 trillion. There is an unintended reduction of inventories of $0.1 trillion. Those businesses that face excess demand for their output will increase production and hire more productive inputs. The payments to the productive inputs are income, which the input owners spend. That is, income increases by the amount of the extra payments to resource owners, and these individuals increase both consumption spending and saving. By how much do they increase consumption? Since the MPC is 0.8, consumption spending increases by $80 for every $100 in extra income.

This is not the end, though. The extra consumption spending provides income to those who produce and sell the extra consumption goods. The higher incomes of these individuals lead them to increase their own consumption spending, increasing income for other people, and another round of increased consumption spending and income occurs. Where does it end? It ends when the extra $0.1 trillion of investment spending increases income to the point where saving increases by $0.1 trillion. Since the MPS is 0.2, every extra $100 of income generates an extra $20 of saving. For saving to increase by $0.1 trillion, income must increase by $0.5 trillion. That is, real GDP must increase from $10.0 trillion to $10.5 trillion for saving to increase from $1.0 trillion to $1.1 trillion.

Exhibit 3 illustrates these changes. The $C + I + NX$ curve is the same as in Exhibit 2, and point e is the original equilibrium. The increase in planned investment spending causes the $C + I + NX$ curve to shift up to $C + I' + NX$. The distance from e to f is $100. The extra investment spending is income to others and generates increased consumption spending, as described. The new equilibrium is e', where real GDP and aggregate expenditure are equal at $3,500.

Exhibit 3

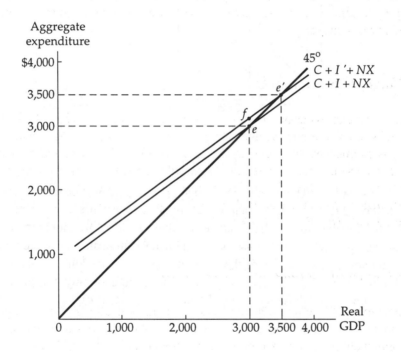

The *multiplier* is a number that indicates the number of times by which the change in the quantity of real GDP demanded exceeds the change in planned investment spending. In the previous case, the multiplier is equal to 5, since real GDP increased by $0.5 trillion after planned investment spending increased by $0.1 trillion. There is a relation between the multiplier and the MPS, as the previous discussion suggests. Since income must increase enough to allow saving to increase by an amount equal to the increase in planned investment, the multiplier equals 1/MPS. In the previous case, the multiplier equals 1/0.2 = 5. Further, MPS = 1 − MPC, so the multiplier also equals 1/(1 − MPC). The multiplier can also be used to calculate the change in real GDP demanded that follows a decrease in planned investment spending or autonomous changes in consumption spending and saving.

Deriving the Aggregate Demand Curve

In the last chapter we saw how changes in the price level shift the consumption function: increases in the price level lower the consumption function, and decreases in the price level raise the consumption function. The aggregate demand curve illustrates the relationship between the price level and real GDP demanded. Exhibit 4 in the textbook derives the aggregate demand curve. Changes in the price level cause the consumption function, the investment function, and net exports to shift, which causes the aggregate expenditure function to shift. Hence, there is a different equilibrium level of real GDP demanded for each price level. The aggregate demand curve is found by relating the equilibrium level of real GDP demanded with the appropriate price level. Be sure that you understand how the aggregate demand curve is derived.

Autonomous changes in consumption, investment, government purchases, or net exports induce shifts in the aggregate demand curve. An increase in planned investment spending shifts the aggregate expenditure curve upward, which generates a new, higher real GDP demanded. Since the increase in planned investment does not imply a change in the price level, the higher real GDP demanded is associated with the same price level as before. That is, as a result of the increase in planned investment spending, the aggregate demand curve shifts to the right by an amount equal to the multiplier times the change in planned investment spending.

Appendix A: Variable Net Exports

The text treats net exports as autonomous, but spending on imports actually is directly related to the level of income. When disposable income increases, consumption spending increases, and part of this increased spending is on imports. Since exports are autonomous, an increase in disposable income causes increased imports and decreased net exports. In this model, with net exports inversely related to the level of income, the new aggregate expenditure function is flatter than the domestic function. Further, the multiplier is lower, since imports increase with income and imports are a leakage from the circular flow. The new multiplier equals 1/(MPS + MPM), where MPM equals the marginal propensity to import.

Appendix B: Algebra of Income and Expenditure

The aggregate expenditure function can be derived algebraically. The consumption function has two components: an autonomous component (that is, consumption that occurs when income equals zero) and an induced component (that is, consumption that depends on the level of income). Hence, we have

$C = a + b(Y - NT)$, where a is the autonomous component and b is the marginal propensity to consume. Investment spending is autonomous, so it is constant at level I. Government purchases are also autonomous, so they are constant at level G. When net exports are treated as autonomous, net exports are constant at level $X - M$. Since $Y = C + I + G + (X - M)$, we can substitute the individual functions into this equation and get:

$$Y = a + bY - bNT + I + G + (X - M)$$

$$Y = [1/(1 - b)](a - bNT + I + G + X - M)$$

When exports vary with the level of income, we substitute $m(Y - NT)$ for M, where m is the marginal propensity to import. The equilibrium level of real GDP can be found as above:

$$Y = a - bNT + I + G + X + mNT + (b - m)Y$$

or

$$Y = [1/(1 - b + m)](a + I + G + X + mNT)$$

The term $(a - b\ NT + I + G + X + mNT)$ represents autonomous spending and $1/(1 - b + m)$ is the multiplier.

IV. LAGNIAPPE

On Autonomous and Induced Spending

The relationship between aggregate expenditure and real GDP is not a simple one, but it is extremely important. There are two kinds of spending: autonomous and induced. *Autonomous spending* is any spending that is independent of the level of income. In our model autonomous spending includes investment spending, government purchases, export spending (and sometimes net exports), and a component of consumption spending. In the income-expenditure model the consumption function intercepts the vertical axis above the origin. This means that real GDP equals zero, yet expenditures on consumption are positive. This amount of consumption spending is autonomous spending. (If $C = a + bY$, the autonomous portion is a.)

Induced spending is spending that occurs because of changes in the level of income. When there is a "marginal propensity to . . . ," there is induced spending. Changes in income cause changes in spending. When autonomous spending increases, income increases. But the increase in income (real GDP) causes changes in induced spending. So the relationship between spending and income is complex.

Question to Think About: Is saving autonomous or induced?

Multipliers and Public Works

The principles behind the multiplier are at work in many situations. If Honda builds a factory in a community, many jobs are created and spending in the area increases. The effects are more than just the immediate effects of building the plant and hiring people to work in the plant. The higher incomes of the people who work there increase their spending, which causes the incomes of others to increase, thus increasing their spending. The multiplier is at work.

It is also possible for multiplier effects to be exaggerated. Suppose a local sports team threatens to move unless it gets a better deal with respect to renting the local stadium. Newspapers are likely to report that the "economic impact" of the loss of the team would be fairly large. The impact would include the loss of salaries by those who work for the team and at the stadium on game days. It would also include the loss of dollars spent at the game on tickets, merchandise, and concessions. A multiplier is estimated and a total loss to the city is calculated. But this analysis would probably exaggerate the influence of the team on the local economy. Attending a sporting event can be thought of as entertainment. If the team were not in the area, people would do something else: go to a movie, eat dinner at a restaurant, go to the zoo, or any number of other things. If most of the money spent at the game would have been spent in the local area anyway, the economic impact of the team is reduced.

Question to Think About: If many people who attended the games traveled a long distance, would the multiplier associated with the team be higher or lower?

V. KEY TERMS

aggregate expenditure line   simple spending multiplier
income-expenditure model   marginal propensity to import (MPM)

VI. QUESTIONS

A. *Completion*

1. GDP measured in terms of goods and services is known as _____ GDP.

2. Disposable income is real GDP less _____.

3. Households have two possible uses for disposable income: _____ and _____.

4. The diagram that relates aggregate expenditures and aggregate income is called the _____ model.

5. For a given price level, the total planned spending at each level of income is shown by the _____.

6. If net exports and government purchases are zero, the difference between the aggregate expenditure function and the consumption function is _____.

7. An unintended inventory reduction occurs when _____ investment exceeds _____ investment.

8. In equilibrium, planned spending exactly equals the amount produced and exactly equals _____ spending.

9. For a given price level, there is only one quantity of output demanded for which _____ spending equals income.

10. The _____ relates an autonomous change in spending to the resulting change in equilibrium real GDP demanded.

11. The larger the marginal propensity to save, the _____ the multiplier.

12. An increase in planned saving at each level of income causes a decrease in _____ consumption.

13. A decrease in the price level increases _____ spending.

14. The aggregate expenditure function and the aggregate demand curve look at _____ from different perspectives.

*15. When import spending is directly related to income, the multiplier is _____.

B. True/False

_____ 1. In the model without government, households either consume their incomes or save part of them.

_____ 2. The consumption function relates consumption spending to the price level.

_____ 3. The difference between the 45-degree line and the consumption function measures planned investment.

_____ 4. When planned spending and output are not equal, there is an unintended change in inventories.

_____ 5. Actual investment equals planned investment plus unintended changes in inventories.

_____ 6. Unintended changes in inventories are signals to producers to change their rates of production.

_____ 7. In the income-expenditure model, planned investment always equals actual investment.

_____ 8. Consumption plus actual investment plus government purchases plus net exports always equals real GDP.

_____ 9. There are many quantities of output demanded at which income equals planned spending for a given price level.

_____ 10. The marginal propensity to consume equals total consumption spending divided by total income.

_____ 11. MPC = 1 – MPS.

_____ 12. An increase in autonomous investment of $100 will increase equilibrium real GDP demanded by $100.

_____ 13. If the multiplier is 3, equilibrium real GDP demanded will fall by $3,000 if planned investment falls by $1,000.

_____ 14. The multiplier increases if the MPS increases.

_____ 15. A decrease in the price level causes consumption spending to increase but causes net exports to decrease.

_____ 16. An increase in the price level increases equilibrium real GDP demanded.

_____ 17. The simple multiplier overstates the real-world multiplier.

_____ *18. An increase in exports leads to a higher equilibrium real GDP demanded.

_____ *19. The marginal propensity to import is usually less than zero.

_____ *20. The multiplier is lower when net exports are included than when they are not included.

C. *Multiple Choice*

1. Planned aggregate expenditures include
   a. consumption.
   b. actual investment.
   c. net exports.
   d. All of the above.
   e. a and c only.

2. In the income-expenditure model described in the textbook,
   a. consumption, saving, and investment increase with income.
   b. consumption, saving, and investment spending are autonomous.
   c. saving and investment are autonomous.
   d. saving is autonomous.
   e. consumption and saving increase as income increases.

3. The distance between the 45-degree line and the consumption function at each income level measures
   a. saving.
   b. taxes.
   c. net income.
   d. investment.
   e. consumption on consumer durable goods.

Exhibit 4

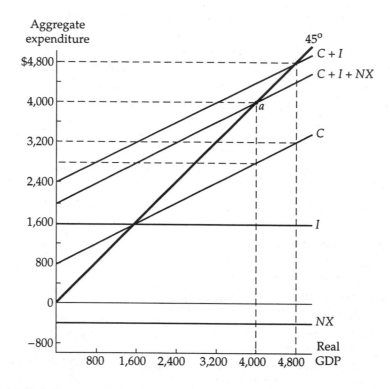

4. In Exhibit 4, the equilibrium level of consumption is
   a. $800.
   b. $1,600.
   c. $2,800.
   d. $4,000.
   e. The answer cannot be determined without more information.

5. In Exhibit 4, saving at the equilibrium level of real GDP equals
   a. $0.
   b. $400.
   c. $800.
   d. $1,000.
   e. $1,200.

6. In Exhibit 4, if the economy is at point *a*,
   a. aggregate expenditure is greater than real GDP.
   b. inventories will tend to grow, forcing producers to decrease their rate of production.
   c. inventories will tend to decrease, forcing producers to increase their rate of production.
   d. real GDP will increase.
   e. actual investment equals planned investment.

7. In Exhibit 4, the marginal propensity to consume is
   a. 0.5.
   b. 0.6.
   c. 0.7.
   d. 0.75.
   e. 0.9.

8. In Exhibit 4, if net exports increased by $400, the new equilibrium level of real GDP equals
   a. $3,200.
   b. $4,000.
   c. $4,400.
   d. $4,800.
   e. $6,000.

9. In Exhibit 4, the value of the multiplier is
   a. 0.
   b. 1.
   c. 2.
   d. 4.
   e. 5.

10. Actual investment always equals
    a. planned investment.
    b. consumption.
    c. consumption minus saving.
    d. unplanned inventory changes.
    e. None of the above.

11. In an economy in equilibrium,
    a. production of the equilibrium quantity of aggregate output demanded generates enough income to purchase that output.
    b. aggregate expenditure equals real GDP.
    c. planned injection equals leakages.
    d. unintended inventory changes equal zero.
    e. All of the above.

12. If the marginal propensity to consume is 0.7 and income falls by $500, saving falls by
    a. $150.
    b. $200.
    c. $350.
    d. $70.
    e. None of the above. Saving will increase.

13. If the MPC is 0.9, the simple multiplier is
    a. 1.
    b. 1.11.
    c. 5.
    d. 9.
    e. 10.

14. Suppose the equilibrium real GDP demanded is $2,500 and the MPC is 0.75. If planned investment falls by $250, equilibrium real GDP demanded will
    a. remain unchanged.
    b. fall by $250.
    c. fall by $1,000.
    d. fall by $750.
    e. The answer cannot be determined without more information.

Aggregate Expenditure and Aggregate Demand

15. An increase in planned investment increases equilibrium real GDP demanded by an amount larger than the change in planned investment. The increase in income stops when
    a. the increase in real income doubles the increase in investment spending.
    b. the marginal propensity to consume falls to zero.
    c. the inflation rate increases.
    d. the multiplier becomes 1.
    e. saving increases by the same amount as planned investment.

16. An increase in the price level _____ the equilibrium quantity of aggregate output demanded by _____.
    a. reduces; lowering the aggregate expenditure function
    b. increases; increasing the aggregate expenditure function
    c. reduces; lowering the saving function
    d. reduces; lowering the marginal propensity to consume
    e. increases; reducing the marginal propensity to save

17. The aggregate demand curve slopes down
    a. because the aggregate expenditure function shifts down as the price level falls.
    b. because the aggregate expenditure function shifts up as the price level falls.
    c. because people are willing to save less as the price level falls.
    d. All of the above.
    e. b and c

*18. When net exports are variable, a decrease in exports leads to
    a. a reduction in real GDP demanded.
    b. a reduction in imports.
    c. a reduction in consumption spending.
    d. a reduction in aggregate expenditure.
    e. All of the above.

*19. An economy that opens up trade with other countries and has variable exports will experience
    a. a flatter consumption function.
    b. a flatter aggregate expenditure function.
    c. a steeper saving function.
    d. All of the above.
    e. None of the above.

*20. Refer back to Exhibit 4. Suppose the net exports function had a vertical intercept of $400 and equaled –$400 at real GDP of $4,000. The new equilibrium level of real GDP and the new multiplier would be
    a. $4,800 and 3.
    b. $4,000 and 2.
    c. $4,000 and 1.48.
    d. $3,600 and 1.48.
    e. $3,600 and 1.7.

D. Discussion Questions

Use the following table to answer questions 1 through 3.

Exhibit 5

Real GDP	Consumption	Saving	Planned Investment	Unintended Inventory Adjustment	Actual Investment
$5,000	$4,900	$100	$1,000	_____	_____
5,500	5,250	250	1,000	_____	_____
6,000	5,600	400	1,000	_____	_____
6,500	_____	_____	1,000	_____	_____
7,000	_____	_____	1,000	_____	_____
7,500	_____	_____	1,000	_____	_____
8,000	_____	_____	1,000	_____	_____
8,500	_____	_____	1,000	_____	_____
9,000	_____	_____	1,000	_____	_____
9,500	_____	_____	1,000	_____	_____
10,000	_____	_____	1,000	_____	_____

1. a. Fill in the blanks in the table.
    b. What is the equilibrium aggregate output demanded? How do you know?
    c. Graph the 45-degree line, the consumption function, and the aggregate expenditure function. Show the equilibrium point on the graph.
    d. Suppose real GDP is initially $10,000. Explain how the equilibrium real GDP demanded is attained.
    e. What is the MPC? the MPS? the multiplier?

2. In Exhibit 5, if net exports are –$300, what is the new equilibrium level of real GDP? What is saving?

3. Suppose the economy represented in Exhibit 5 is in equilibrium, but then planned investment falls to $800. What is the new equilibrium quantity of aggregate output demanded?

4. Suppose the economy represented in Exhibit 5 is in equilibrium; let the government purchases increase from 0 to $500. What is the new equilibrium quantity of aggregate output demanded?

5. What role do unintended inventory changes play when an economy moves to an equilibrium position?

6. How are the marginal propensity to consume, the marginal propensity to save, and the simple multiplier related to each other?

7. What would happen if the marginal propensity to consume were greater than 1?

8. "Savings can be greater or less than investment spending in equilibrium." Do you agree or disagree? Why?

9.   If the multiplier is 4 and society wants income to increase by $8 billion, does it matter whether investment increases or net exports increase?

10.   A decrease in the price level causes aggregate spending to increase. Why?

11.   How is an aggregate demand curve derived? What would cause the aggregate demand curve to shift to the right?

12.   What happens to the aggregate demand curve if the MPC falls?

13.   Let $C = \$1,000 + 0.75(Y - NT)$, $I = \$2,000$, and $G = NT = \$1,000$.
   a.   Find the equilibrium aggregate expenditure.
   b.   What is the level of consumption spending at equilibrium? of saving?
   c.   What is the value of the multiplier?

*14.   Given the information in question 13, suppose a country starts trading and net exports are $1,000. What is the new equilibrium level of real GDP?

*15.   In the previous situation, if $M = .25Y$ and autonomous exports are $1,000, what is the new equilibrium level of real GDP?

*16.   U.S. exports are the imports of other countries. Suppose the demand function for the rest of the world is $0.1Y^*$, where Y^* equals income of all countries except the United States. If the MPM of the rest of the world increases to .2, what happens to the U.S. multiplier? Explain.

VII. ANSWERS

A.   *Completion*

1.	real	6.	planned investments	11.	smaller
2.	net taxes	7.	planned; actual	12.	autonomous
3.	consumption; saving	8.	actual	13.	aggregate
4.	income-expenditure	9.	planned	14.	real GDP
5.	aggregate expenditure function	10.	multiplier	15.	smaller

B.   *True/False*

1.	True	10.	False
2.	False. It relates consumption spending to the level of income for a given price level	11.	True
		12.	False
		13.	True
3.	False	14.	False
4.	True	15.	False
5.	True	16.	False
6.	True	17.	True
7.	False	18.	True
8.	True	19.	False
9.	False	20.	True

---

*These questions refer to material developed in this chapter's Appendix.

C. Multiple Choice

1.	e	6.	e	11.	e	16.	a
2.	e	7.	a	12.	a	17.	e
3.	a	8.	d	13.	e	18.	e
4.	c	9.	c	14.	c	19.	b
5.	e	10.	e	15.	e	20.	c

D. Discussion Questions

1. a.

Real GDP	Consumption	Saving	Planned Investment	Unintended Inventory Adjustment	Actual Investment
$5,000	$4,900	$100	$1,000	-$900	$100
5,500	5,250	250	1,000	-700	250
6,000	5,600	400	1,000	-600	400
6,500	5,950	550	1,000	-450	550
7,000	6,300	700	1,000	-300	700
7,500	6,650	850	1,000	-150	850
8,000	7,000	1,000	1,000	0	1,000
8,500	7,350	1,150	1,000	150	1,150
9,000	7,700	1,300	1,000	300	1,300
9,500	8,050	1,450	1,000	450	1,450
10,000	8,400	1,600	1,000	600	1,600

   b. The equilibrium aggregate output demanded is $8,000. At that level, aggregate expenditure equals $8,000, which is also the real GDP.

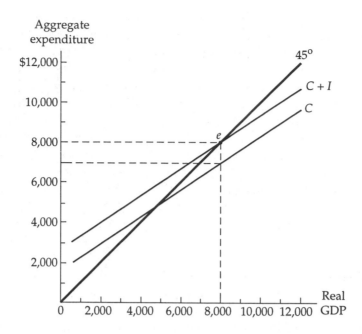

d. At real GDP of $10,000, aggregate expenditure equals $9,400, which is less than real GDP. Therefore, actual output exceeds aggregate expenditure by $600, and firms experience an unintended increase in their inventories. The firms respond by cutting back output, which means that resource owners see their incomes fall. When resource owners receive less, they spend less, which causes output to fall further. This process stops when aggregate expenditure exactly equals real GDP, so there are no unintended inventory adjustments.

e. The MPC is 350/500 = 0.7.
The MPS is 150/500 = 0.3.
The multiplier is 1/MPS = 1/0.3 = 3.33.

2. $7,000; $700.

3. To find the change in the equilibrium quantity of output demanded, we first multiply the change in planned investment spending by the multiplier: (–$200)(3.33) = – $666.67. This figure is the change in real GDP, so the new equilibrium is $8,000 – 666.67 = $7,333.33. At this real GDP, consumption spending is $6,533.33 and saving (and planned investment) is $800.

4. Multiply the change in government purchases ($500) by the multiplier (3.33). The new real GDP is $8,000 plus $1,665 or $9,665.

5. When the economy is not in equilibrium, planned spending either exceeds or falls short of output. When this happens, business inventories either decrease or increase. The unintended change in inventories is a signal to businesses that their output rate is incorrect. If inventories are falling, then the output rate is too low and output should increase. As businesses increase production, the economy moves closer to equilibrium. When there is no unintended change in inventories, businesses know they are producing the correct quantity, and they will not make any other production changes. At this point the economy is in equilibrium.

6. Because any change in income must be either spent or saved, the marginal propensity to save and the marginal propensity to consume must total 1. The multiplier indicates how a change in autonomous spending leads to a larger change in equilibrium real GDP demanded. It is related to the MPC and the MPS because a change in spending leads to a change in income for resource owners; this induces them to change their levels of both consumption and saving. The extent of the change is given by the MPC and MPS. The change in spending generates another change in income, which induces still more changes in consumption and saving. The process stops when planned saving equals planned investment. Hence, saving must change enough to bring planned saving and planned investment back to equality. The MPS tells us how much saving changes with a change in income, so we can use the MPS to find out how much income must change to generate the correct amount of saving. Income must change by 1/MPS, so the multiplier equals 1/MPS. Further, since MPS + MPC = 1, the multiplier must also equal 1/(1 − MPC).

7. An MPC greater than 1 would indicate that an increase in income leads to a greater increase in consumption spending. Such a situation cannot last for long, as the extra consumption must be financed somehow. The only sources of financing are savings and borrowing. For the economy as a whole, borrowing would have to be from foreigners. An MPC greater than 1 is unstable and cannot persist.

8. Injections equal leakages. In this model, saving and net taxes are leakages, and investment, government purchases, and net exports are injections. So, $S + NT = I + G + (X − M)$. Saving equals investment only if government spending plus net exports equals net taxes.

9. No. The multiplier effect will be the same as long as autonomous spending increases, regardless of the source of the autonomous spending.

10. The lower price level increases consumption because people perceive that their wealth has increased. This shifts the consumption function up. The lower price level also makes U.S. goods cheaper relative to foreign goods, so exports will increase, imports decrease, and net exports increase. Finally, the lower price level also causes investment spending to increase. Since all components of aggregate spending increase, aggregate spending also increases.

11. The aggregate expenditure function generates an equilibrium real GDP demanded for a given price level. If the price level changes, people change their consumption and saving because the change in price level changes the real value of their net wealth. The aggregate demand curve is derived by tracing out the equilibrium real GDPs demanded with their respective price levels. The aggregate demand curve will shift to the right if planned investment increases or autonomous consumption increases.

12. A fall in the MPC means that both the consumption function and the aggregate expenditure function are flatter, and both rotate down. Equilibrium real GDP demanded falls as a result, so the real GDP associated with the prevailing price level falls. This is also true for any other price level, so the aggregate demand curve shifts to the left.

Aggregate Expenditure and Aggregate Demand   **171**

13. a. $Y = C + I + G = \$1,000 + 0.75(Y - 1,000) + \$2,000 + \$1,000$
   $Y - 0.75Y = \$4,000 - 750 = 3,250$
   $Y = \$3,250/0.25 = \$13,000$

   b. $C = \$1,000 + 0.75(\$12,000 - 1,000)$
   $= \$1,000 + 0.75(12,000)$
   $= \$1,000 + \$9,000 = \$10,000$
   $S = (Y - NT) - C = \$12,000 - \$10,000 = \$2,000$

   c. Multiplier $= 1/(1 - MPS) = 1/0.25 = 4$

14. Autonomous spending is $4,250, so $Y = \$4,250 \times (1/.25) = \$17,000$.

15. The new multiplier is $1/(MPS + MPI) = 1/(0.25 + 0.25) = 1/0.5 = 2$. Autonomous expenditures are $4,250, so $Y = \$4,250 \times 2 = \$8,500$.

16. Nothing. The change in import spending in the rest of the world would show up in the United States as changes in exports, which is a type of autonomous spending because they are independent of U.S. income levels.

CHAPTER 11

Aggregate Supply

I. INTRODUCTION

The previous two chapters introduced the concept of aggregate expenditure and derived an aggregate demand curve. In this chapter we examine the concept of aggregate supply. When aggregate supply and aggregate demand are combined, we can determine the equilibrium level of prices and output in the economy. The following chapters begin to examine how government policy affects the equilibrium level of prices and output.

II. OUTLINE

1. Aggregate Supply in the Short Run. The aggregate supply curve relates the price level to the quantity of aggregate output firms are willing and able to supply, other things constant. The supply of resources in the economy, the state of technology, and the set of formal and informal institutions that undergirds the economy are held constant along an aggregate supply curve.

   1.1 Labor Supply and Aggregate Supply
      a. The higher the nominal wage, other things constant, the greater the quantity of labor supplied.
      b. The *nominal wage* is the wage measured in terms of current dollars.
      c. The *real wage* is the wage measured in terms of goods and services; it equals the nominal wage divided by the price level.
      d. Labor agreements are based on expectations about the future price level and are negotiated in terms of nominal wages.

   1.2 Potential Output and the Natural Rate of Unemployment
      a. The economy's *potential output* is the level of output that exists if the actual price level equals the expected price level.
      b. Potential output is the economy's maximum sustainable output level, given the supply of resources and the state of technology.
      c. Potential output is also called the *natural rate of output*, the *high-employment level of output*, and the *full-employment level of output*.
      d. Not all resources are employed at the potential level of output, since a dynamic economy requires some frictional, structural, and seasonal unemployment to function smoothly.
      e. The *natural rate of unemployment* is the rate of unemployment that occurs when the economy is producing its potential output.
      f. When the actual price level turns out as expected, the economy produces its potential output.

   1.3 Actual Price Level Higher Than Expected
      a. In the short run, when the price level increases, the prices of firms' products increase, on average, while some resource costs remain fixed by contract in the short run. Profits will increase if output expands.

173

b. When the actual price level exceeds the expected price level on which long-term contracts are based, firms find it profitable to expand production.

c. At such times, the economy's output is greater than its potential output.

d. The economy can produce more than its potential output for only a short period of time because resources must be used more intensively than is optimal.

1.4 Why Costs Rise When Output Exceeds Potential

a. The increased output creates increased demand for resources, which generates higher prices for the resources.

b. Higher resource prices lead to higher marginal costs of production.

c. Since the costs of some resources are contractually fixed in the short run, the marginal cost of production rises less than the marginal revenue generated from the higher price level.

d. Therefore, profit-maximizing firms increase the quantity supplied.

1.5 The Price Level, Real Wages, and Labor Supply

a. In the short run, workers may increase the quantity of labor supplied even though their real wage falls as the actual price level rises.

b. Workers may do this because
   (1) they are fulfilling their contracts.
   (2) firms are operating as described by the efficiency wage theory, which argues that firms keep wages above the market-clearing level in order to have an abundant worker pool from which to hire.

1.6 Actual Price Level Lower Than Expected

a. If the price level decreases, production is less profitable, because the product prices fall while some resource prices remain constant in the short run.

b. When nominal wages are fixed by contract, a lower-than-expected price level means that workers' real wages increase.

c. Firms lay off some workers because wage contracts usually do not specify both the wage rate and a guaranteed number of hours worked; actual output falls below potential output.

d. Marginal costs decline as output declines because the prices of some resources fall as firms lay off less productive resources.

1.7 The Short-Run Aggregate Supply Curve

a. There is a positive relationship between the price level and the quantity of aggregate output supplied in the short run.

b. The short-run aggregate supply curve is drawn for a particular contract period, based on a given expected price level.

c. The slope of the short-run aggregate supply curve depends on how quickly marginal production costs rise as aggregate output expands. The more quickly marginal costs rise, the steeper the short-run aggregate supply curve.

2. From the Short Run to the Long Run

2.1 Actual Price Level Higher Than Expected

a. The difference between the actual output in the short run and potential output is called the *expansionary gap*. Unemployment is below the natural rate.

b. In the long run, all resource suppliers adjust their contracts in response to the higher actual prices.

c.   As resource suppliers negotiate higher resource prices, the short-run aggregate supply curve shifts back to intersect the aggregate demand curve at the potential output.

d.   In long-run equilibrium,
   (1)   the actual price level equals the expected price level.
   (2)   the quantity supplied equals the potential output.
   (3)   the quantity supplied equals the quantity demanded.

e.   Actual output can exceed potential output in the short run but not in the long run.

2.2   Actual Price Level Lower Than Expected
   a.   In the short run, actual output falls short of potential output by an amount called the *contractionary gap*. Unemployment exceeds the natural rate.
   b.   The short-run aggregate supply curve shifts outward when resource owners adjust in the long run to the lower actual price level. Nominal resource payments fall or at least rise more slowly than output prices.
   c.   The length of the adjustment process depends on downward flexibility in product and resource prices. The more inflexible the wages and prices, the longer the contractionary gap persists.

2.3   Tracing Potential Output
   a.   The long-run aggregate supply curve is vertical at the economy's potential output.
   b.   The potential output is consistent with any price level in the long run; it depends only on the supply of resources and level of technology.

2.4   Evidence on Aggregate Supply
   a.   Nominal wages do not change as quickly in a downward direction as they do in an upward direction. Therefore, unemployment may remain above the natural rate for prolonged periods.
   b.   The *efficiency wage theory* argues that firms do not lower wages in times of unemployment because they use a relatively high wage to encourage greater productivity.
   c.   Nominal wages may also be sticky downward as a result of factors such as long-term wage contracts, minimum wage laws, workers' psychological resistance to wage cuts, and the like.
   d.   Nominal wages need not decline to close a contractionary gap but must rise more slowly than prices.

2.5   *CASE STUDY:* Output Gaps and Wage Flexibility

3.   Changes in Aggregate Supply

3.1   Increases in Aggregate Supply
   a.   Potential output changes as the quantity and quality of resources change.
   b.   Technological change can also change the potential output.
   c.   Long-term improvements in the economy's ability to produce generate shifts to the right in both the short-run aggregate supply curve and the long-run aggregate supply curve.
   d.   *Beneficial supply shocks* are unexpected events that increase aggregate supply. For a given aggregate demand curve, output rises and the price level falls.

3.2   Decreases in Aggregate Supply
   a.   *Adverse supply shocks* are unexpected events that reduce aggregate supply, often only temporarily.
   b.   Stagflation can occur when an adverse supply shock reduces output and raises prices.

3.3   *CASE STUDY:* Why Is Unemployment So High in Europe?

III. DISCUSSION

Aggregate Supply in the Short Run

Workers and other resource owners make decisions concerning how much of their resources to supply for a particular time period on the basis of expected *real wages* or prices. But wages and prices are always stated in dollar terms (i.e., as *nominal wages* and prices). Often nominal resource prices, including wages paid to labor, are set for a given time period by explicit or implicit contracts. If the actual price level differs from the expected price level on which the contracts are based, resource owners will not receive the real return that they expected. If the actual price level is greater than expected, the real wage falls as the nominal wage remains constant; the opposite occurs if the actual price level is less than expected.

Some resource prices adjust more quickly than others. Some workers may agree to 12-month contracts, others may agree to 6-month contracts, and still others may not agree to contracts at all. Similarly, one electric utility may agree to long-term contracts with coal suppliers; others may rely on spot markets. Prices set by contracts tend to be more stable than those set in spot markets. Consequently, when the actual price level exceeds the expected price level, some resource prices adjust quickly while others remain constant for a while. Production costs rise more slowly than product prices, on average, because of the stability of some resource prices.

If a firm's product price increases at the same rate as the average level of prices, expanding output increases the firm's profit because the extra cost of producing an additional unit of output rises more slowly than the extra revenue received from an additional unit of output. Hence, the firm has an incentive to increase production in the short run when the actual price level rises above the expected price level reflected in long-term contracts. When the actual price level falls below the expected price level, costs do not fall as quickly as product prices. Again, the relative stability of some resource prices is the reason costs do not change at the same rate as the price level. Firms respond to the lower profitability by curtailing production and laying off some resources.

We have seen that firms increase output when the price level is higher than had been expected and decrease output when the price level is lower than had been expected. What happens when the actual price level equals the expected price level reflected in long-term contracts? When expectations about prices prove correct, economic agents have no reason to change their actions. If all households and firms find their expectations about prices are correct, then the output decisions of firms and the resource-supply and consumption decisions of households are correct. There are no surprises, and the economic actors will continue doing the same thing until something fundamental changes, such as tastes or technology. Since all resource owners and all firms continue doing what they have been doing, output remains constant until a fundamental change occurs. Hence, the output level in this situation is the natural level of output. This output level is often called the *potential output*, or the full-employment level of output. The unemployment rate that prevails when the potential output is being produced is called the *natural rate of unemployment.*

Because firms expand production when the actual price level exceeds the expected price level, actual output exceeds potential output and the actual rate of unemployment is less than the natural rate of unemployment. Such a situation cannot last for a long time because higher prices mean that some resource owners are earning less in real terms than they expected. These resource owners will try to negotiate higher payments at their next opportunity, which will increase production costs, reduce profits, and encourage firms to reduce output. This process will stop when actual output again equals potential output. Similarly, when the actual price level is less than expected, firms' profitability falls, so they reduce output below potential output and unemployment rises above the natural rate. When they can renegotiate resource prices to reflect the actual state of the economy, then their resource costs will adjust to reflect the lower actual price level, they will again increase production, and aggregate output will equal potential output.

The changes in output that result when actual prices differ from the expected prices reflected in long-term contracts are short-run changes. Once the economic actors learn the true state of the economy and have time to adjust their behavior, output becomes equal to potential output. In the *short run*, there is a positive relationship between the price level and the quantity of aggregate output supplied. At prices greater than expected prices, actual output exceeds potential output; at prices lower than expected prices, actual output falls below potential output. The short-run aggregate supply curve slopes upward and is defined for a given contract period, reflecting a given expected price level. If expectations about prices change, the short-run aggregate supply curve shifts.

From the Short Run to the Long Run

The short-run aggregate supply curve is relevant only as long as some resource prices remain fixed. As these resource prices respond in the long run to new situations, the short-run aggregate supply curve shifts. As a result, the economy returns to the potential output and the natural rate of unemployment. In Exhibit 1, potential output is $5 trillion and the expected price level is 100.

Exhibit 1

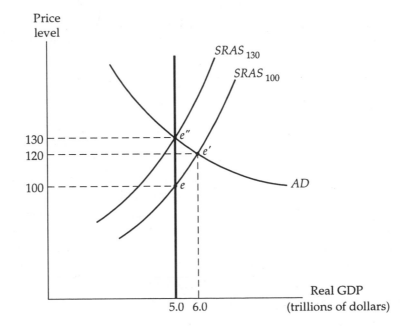

Suppose the short-run aggregate supply curve is $SRAS_{100'}$, which intersects the aggregate demand curve (AD) at e′. Hence, actual output is $6.0 trillion, and there is an *expansionary gap* of $6.0 − 5.0 = $1.0 trillion. The actual price level is 120, which is greater than the expected price level of 100. The output, $6.0 trillion, cannot be sustained for long because it exceeds the potential output. Nothing fundamental to the economy has changed; instead, output has increased because people's expectations have not been realized. Economic actors negotiate higher resource prices in the long run, firms curtail production, and the short-run aggregate supply curve shifts to the left, to $SRAS_{130}$. New long-term contracts reflect the expected price level of 130. The new long-run equilibrium is at e″, with output of $5.0 trillion and an actual price level of 130. A similar adjustment process occurs when the actual price level is lower than expected, only in that case the short-run aggregate supply curve shifts to the right as a result of the pressures created by a *contractionary gap*.

Whenever the economy is in long-run equilibrium—that is, whenever the actual price level equals the expected price level reflected in long-term contracts—the real GDP is equal to the potential output. That is, the long-run aggregate supply curve is vertical at the potential output. This potential GDP is consistent with any price level as long as all resource prices adjust to the actual price level.

Potential output depends on the supply of resources in the economy, the state of technology, and the institutional structure of the economic system. The long-run supply curve is vertical at the potential output. The location of the short-run aggregate supply curve depends on the expected price level.

Changes in Aggregate Supply

Potential output is determined by real factors in the economy—factors such as the quantity and quality of the resources available to the economy and the state of technology. Potential output will change only when one of these factors changes. An increase in the labor force, the discovery of new sources of raw materials, an increase in education levels of the population, and technological change are events that can cause potential output to increase. Both the long-run and the short-run aggregate supply curves will shift when potential output changes. The short-run aggregate supply curve can also shift without a change in potential output. The short-run aggregate supply curve shifts in response to *supply shocks*— unexpected events that affect the supply of a resource, often only temporarily. For example, a severe hailstorm may reduce the supply of wheat, thus affecting the supply of bread in the economy. This type of supply shock does not reduce the economy's output permanently, because wheat production can return to normal levels the next year.

IV. LAGNIAPPE

Contracts and Price Stickiness

The existence of a contract, even a long-term contract, does not imply that prices are fixed for the length of the contract. Often prices are not stated in long-term contracts; instead, formulas based on inflation and other relevant conditions are used to determine prices at future dates. It is not uncommon for the parties to a contract to renegotiate the terms of the contract before it has expired. Examples of this are fairly common in professional sports, especially when a rookie turns out to be a star. The owners of the team often increase the player's salary even though they are under no contractual obligation to do so. Even so, prices determined by contracts are not as flexible in the short run as prices determined in spot markets. As long as the firm hires resources and pays resource prices that differ in their flexibility, the firm's costs will not change at the same rate as the price level changes.

Question to Think About: Why would firms want long-term contracts for some resources but not for others?

Downward Stickiness of Price

You may wonder why wages would be stickier downward than upward. Presumably, if workers were interested in their real wage and they knew that prices had fallen, they would accept a lower nominal wage to keep working. However, workers may not realize that the price level has fallen. If they agreed to lower nominal wages when the price level was lower, firms might try to fool workers and fake a curtailment in production to induce workers to accept lower nominal wages. Workers would probably be skeptical of the need to accept a lower wage given this type of opportunistic behavior on the part of employers. Further, if a contract were involved, the workers might not have to accept a lower wage; in addition, workers would be free to go elsewhere if higher wages were offered by other firms. In such cases, wages would be more flexible in an upward direction than in a downward direction.

Question to Think About: How would you determine whether the firm you worked for was doing poorly because of mismanagement or because of a weak economy?

V.   KEY TERMS

nominal wage
real wage
potential output
natural rate of unemployment
short run
efficiency wage theory
short-run aggregate supply curve (SRAS)
short-run equilibrium
expansionary gap

long run
long run equilibrium
contractionary gap
long-run aggregate supply (LRAS) curve
coordination failure
supply shocks
beneficial supply shocks
adverse supply shocks

VI. QUESTIONS

A.   Completion

1.   The supply of resources to producers is held constant along a(n) _____ supply curve.

2.   The _____ wage is measured in terms of current dollars.

3.   The nominal wage is difficult to change during the short run because relationships between resource owners and firms are governed by _____ contracts and _____ contracts.

4.   The economy's _____ is the level of output that would prevail if the price expectations of all economic agents were met.

5.   The unemployment rate that prevails when the economy is producing its potential output is the _____ rate of unemployment.

6. In the _____ , expectations about the price level may differ from the actual price level.

7. When the actual price level rises above the expected price level in the short run, _____ increase at a lower rate than the price level, and profits increase if output expands.

8. If the actual output exceeds the economy's potential output in the short run there is a(n) _____.

9. The _____ argues that employers keep wages above the market-clearing wage to make workers compete to keep their jobs.

10. Layoffs often occur when there is a(n) _____ gap.

11. Contractionary gaps result from a _____ failure.

12. The _____ aggregate supply curve slopes upward, and the _____ aggregate supply curve is vertical.

13. _____ affect the short-run aggregate supply curve but do not affect the long-run aggregate supply curve.

14. The combination of reduced output and a higher price level is known as _____.

15. The idea that the natural rate of unemployment depends on its recent history is known as _____.

B. True/False

_____ 1. The short-run aggregate supply curve slopes up for the same reasons that the supply curves for individual goods slope up.

_____ 2. The nominal wage is determined by factors from the past, and the real wage is based on expectations about the future.

_____ 3. Explicit contracts determine real wages; implicit contracts determine nominal wages.

_____ 4. The potential output of the economy is its maximum sustainable output level, given the supply of resources and the level of technology.

_____ 5. When the economy is producing its potential output, all resources in the economy are employed.

_____ 6. If actual prices are greater than expected prices reflected in long-term contracts, firms find it profitable to expand production beyond the economy's potential output.

_____ 7. Production costs tend to rise when actual output exceeds potential output.

_____ 8. When actual prices are lower than expected prices reflected in long-term contracts, the unemployment rate tends to rise above the natural rate of unemployment.

_____ 9. The short run is the period during which some resource prices are set by agreement.

_____ 10. The short-run aggregate supply curve is drawn for a contract period reflecting a given expected price level.

_____ 11. Actual output cannot exceed potential output in the long run.

_____ 12. The long-run aggregate supply curve slopes upward.

_____ 13. The economy's potential output is consistent with any actual price level.

_____ 14. In the long-run, a reduction in aggregate demand causes potential output to decrease.

_____ 15. Technological change can lead to a higher level of potential output.

_____ 16. Supply shocks can lead to temporary changes in the price level.

_____ 17. Adverse supply shocks cause only the short-run aggregate supply curve to shift; beneficial supply shocks cause only the long-run aggregate supply curve to shift.

_____ 18. Unemployment rates increased throughout the 1980s in Europe and in the United States.

C. Multiple Choice

1. If all prices increase by 10 percent, then in the long run
   a. nominal wages increase by 10 percent and real wages are constant.
   b. nominal wages are constant and real wages increase by 10 percent.
   c. nominal wages are constant and real wages decrease by 10 percent.
   d. nominal wages and real wages are equal.
   e. None of the above.

2. If the price level is higher than expected, firms tend to increase production in the short run because
   a. real wages are also increasing.
   b. the costs of producing a unit of a good are falling.
   c. the extra revenue from an additional unit of output rises relative to the extra cost of producing an additional unit.
   d. the real wage rises relative to the nominal wage.
   e. All of the above.

3. Nominal wages tend to be relatively constant in the short run
   a. for workers with explicit contracts but not for those with implicit contracts.
   b. because of the existence of explicit and implicit contracts.
   c. because real wages tend to be constant in the short run.
   d. except when actual prices differ from expected prices.
   e. None of the above.

4. Potential output is
   a. the maximum level of output that is sustainable.
   b. the level of output when actual prices equal expected prices.
   c. the level of output that exists when there are no surprises about the price level.
   d. All of the above.
   e. b and c

5. The natural rate of unemployment
   a. is zero.
   b. depends on the price level.
   c. occurs when the economy is producing its potential output.
   d. exists when there is no frictional unemployment.
   e. is always lower than the actual rate of unemployment.

6. If the actual price level equals the expected price level reflected in long-term contracts,
   a. potential output will exceed actual output.
   b. unemployment will be less than the natural rate of unemployment.
   c. firms will reduce production in order to lower nominal wages.
   d. firms will increase production in order to lower real wages.
   e. None of the above.

7. When the actual price level exceeds the expected price level reflected in long-term contracts,
   a. firms find it profitable to expand production beyond the economy's potential output.
   b. firms cut back production because the higher prices make extra production too costly.
   c. firms cut back production because they believe that prices will be even higher in the future and profits will be greater in the future.
   d. firms cut back production because costs rise relative to the price of the product.
   e. None of the above.

8. Which of the following is true when actual output exceeds potential output?
   a. In the short run, the costs of production stay constant because of explicit and implicit costs.
   b. Labor costs tend to increase even though there are contracts because of overtime or the hiring of those who had been structurally unemployed.
   c. Labor costs increase because workers tend to break their labor contracts and refuse to work unless they get paid more.
   d. Overall production costs tend to remain constant. Labor costs tend to rise but the costs of other resources tend to fall, and the two effects offset each other.
   e. Overall production costs tend to remain constant and the economy quickly returns to its potential output.

9. The short-run aggregate supply curve
   a. slopes upward.
   b. is drawn for a contract period reflecting a given expected price level.
   c. intersects the long-run aggregate supply curve at the potential output.
   d. reflects the relationship between the actual price level and the quantity of aggregate output producers are willing and able to supply.
   e. All of the above.

10. If short-run actual output exceeds potential output,
    a. there is pressure to increase productive capacity so that potential output can increase.
    b. there is a contractionary gap that closes as actual output and potential output become equal.
    c. there is an expansionary gap that is reduced as potential output increases.
    d. there is upward pressure on the actual price level.
    e. None of the above.

11. Actual output can exceed potential output because
    a. the natural rate of unemployment can be reduced.
    b. resources can work harder than usual for a short period of time.
    c. technological change can increase actual output.
    d. people work more for a higher real wage.
    e. None of the above. Actual output cannot exceed potential output.

12. If the contractionary gap is $0.4 trillion, then the
    a. natural rate of unemployment increases.
    b. natural rate of unemployment decreases.
    c. unemployment rate exceeds the natural rate of unemployment.
    d. unemployment rate is less than the natural rate of unemployment.
    e. unemployment rate equals the natural rate of unemployment.

13. The efficiency wage theory argues that firms attract a sufficient number of highly qualified workers by
    a. advertising heavily.
    b. offering wages equal to the equilibrium level of wages.
    c. offering wages higher than the wages necessary to attract enough workers.
    d. offering payment as a function of output instead of a wage rate.
    e. None of the above.

14. At long-run equilibrium,
    a. the actual price level equals the expected price level reflected in long-term contracts.
    b. short-run aggregate output equals long-run aggregate output.
    c. the quantity of aggregate output demanded equals the quantity of aggregate output supplied.
    d. the quantity demanded of any resource equals the quantity supplied of the resource.
    e. All of the above.

15. A contractionary gap lasts longer when
    a. potential output equals the long-run aggregate supply curve.
    b. wages and prices are not flexible.
    c. aggregate demand is increasing.
    d. the long-run aggregate supply curve is vertical.
    e. All of the above.

16. Which of the following will be observed if nominal wages are stickier downward than upward?
    a. The long-run aggregate supply curve will slope upward instead of being vertical.
    b. Real wages will increase over time as the economy moves closer to its potential output.
    c. The short-run aggregate supply curve will become more vertical.
    d. The economy will return rapidly to its potential output from a period of high unemployment.
    e. An unemployment rate that is higher than the natural rate of unemployment will persist longer than a rate that is lower than the natural rate of unemployment.

17. Wages could be sticky downward because of
    a. minimum wage laws.
    b. the efficiency wage theory.
    c. long-term contracts.
    d. the presence of powerful labor unions.
    e. All of the above.

18. Which of the following would cause the potential output level to decrease?
    a. a winter that is more severe than usual
    b. an increase in the amount of unskilled labor
    c. technological change that destroys an industry
    d. a decline in the labor force
    e. a decline in the actual unemployment rate

19. Potential output will increase if
    a. aggregate demand increases.
    b. inflation is reduced.
    c. supply shocks are avoided.
    d. immigration increases.
    e. All of the above.

20. Hysteresis implies that
    a. there is no natural rate of unemployment.
    b. the actual unemployment rate eventually becomes the natural rate of unemployment.
    c. the natural rate of unemployment eventually becomes the actual rate of unemployment.
    d. the longer the actual unemployment rate remains above the natural rate of unemployment, the more the natural rate itself will increase.
    e. None of the above.

D. Discussion Questions

1. What can cause aggregate supply to increase?

2. What is the difference between the nominal wage and the real wage? What happens to the real wage when the actual price level is below the expected price level reflected in long-term contracts?

3. What is the potential output of the economy? How is the potential output determined? How are the potential output and the natural rate of unemployment related?

4. Suppose that a firm is making zero profits and that labor prices, which are set by a contract, account for 25 percent of the firm's costs. Now suppose average prices increase by 10 percent. What happens to the firm's profits?

5. Given the information in question 4, explain what will happen to the firm's profits in the long run.

6. Why do firms tend to expand output when the actual price level exceeds the expected price level reflected in long-term contracts?

7. Why do production costs rise when actual output exceeds potential output?

8. Why are workers willing to work the same number of hours when their real wage falls because of inflation?

9. Explain the derivation of a short-run aggregate supply curve.

10. What determines the slope of the short-run aggregate supply curve?

11. Suppose the actual price level is below the expected price level reflected in long-term contracts. Using a graph, illustrate the short-run and long-run adjustments that would occur.

12. What is the shape of the long-run aggregate supply curve? Why does it have this shape?

13. If the labor force grows over time, what happens to real GDP? Explain. What happens to the price level? Explain.

14. What are supply shocks? How do they affect the short-run aggregate supply curve? the long-run aggregate supply curve?

15. What is hysteresis and how does it apply to unemployment? What can cause the effect?

VII. ANSWERS

A. Completion

1. aggregate
2. nominal
3. explicit; implicit
4. potential output
5. natural
6. short run
7. costs
8. expansionary gap
9. efficiency wage theory
10. contractionary
11. coordination
12. short-run; long-run
13. Temporary supply shocks
14. stagflation
15. hysteresis

B. True/False

1. False
2. False
3. False
4. True
5. False
6. True
7. True
8. True
9. True
10. True
11. True
12. False
13. True
14. False
15. True
16. True
17. False
18. False

C. Multiple Choice

1. a
2. c
3. b
4. d
5. c
6. e
7. a
8. b
9. e
10. d
11. b
12. c
13. c
14. e
15. b
16. b
17. e
18. d
19. d
20. b

D. Discussion Questions

1. Aggregate supply would increase if the supply of resources increased, technology improved, or the economic institutions provided better incentives to produce more. (Remember, an increase in the price level causes an increase in the quantity of aggregate supply in the short run.)

2. The nominal wage is the wage measured in dollars; the real wage is measured in terms of the goods and services it will buy. The real wage increases as the actual price level falls below the expected price level, since the prices of some goods and services fall, allowing consumers to buy more with the same nominal wage.

3. The potential output of an economy is the maximum output that can be sustained for a long period of time. It will be produced if economic agents experience no surprises. This situation occurs when the actual price level equals the expected price level reflected in long-term contracts, so nobody makes incorrect decisions and all resource markets are cleared. The potential output is defined for a given level of technology and supply of resources. The natural rate of unemployment is the unemployment rate that prevails if the economy is producing its potential output.

4. If prices increase by 10 percent, total revenues increase by 10 percent, assuming the rate of sales stays constant. Total costs increase by less than 10 percent because the price of labor is fixed. Hence, profits increase, and the firm is willing to increase its rate of output.

5. In the long run, wages will increase by 10 percent and the firm's profits will return to zero.

6. The answer to question 4 illustrates what happens when the actual price level is greater than expected. Some costs are stable in the short run, so production costs rise less than the actual price level. Hence, the extra revenue from an additional unit of output rises above the extra cost of producing an additional unit, and expanding output generates higher profits. The firm expands output to obtain the higher profits.

7. Costs increase when output exceeds potential output because the increased demand for resources drives up any resource prices that are not set by contract. Furthermore, the firm must offer higher nominal wages to get new workers to come to work or pay overtime wages to get current workers to work more hours.

8. They may be merely fulfilling their contractual obligations, or they may have been receiving an above-market wage rate. The latter would be true if the firm paid higher wages in order to attract a large pool of good workers.

9. A short-run aggregate supply curve is drawn for a given expected price level in a given contract period. If the actual price level equals the expected price level, actual output equals the potential output. If actual prices exceed expected prices, firms expand production. The higher prices do not mean all prices increase. Some resource prices are fixed for a while by contract. Consequently, revenues increase more than costs increase, and it is profitable to expand production. The opposite occurs when prices fall, so the short-run aggregate supply curve slopes upward.

10. The slope of the short-run aggregate supply curve depends on how quickly the cost of additional production rises as aggregate output increases. The faster the costs rise, the steeper the short-run aggregate supply curve.

11. If actual prices are below expected prices, there is a contractionary gap. In the following graph, potential output is $5.0 trillion and the expected price level is 120, but the actual price level is 112. Therefore, the short-run equilibrium is at e, where $SRAS_{120}$ intersects the aggregate demand curve. The contractionary gap is $5.0 - 4.2 = $0.8 trillion. The contractionary gap exists because some resource prices are locked in by contract and product prices are lower than expected, which implies that profits are lower than the firm expected. The firm responds by reducing output, so aggregate output is less than potential output. In time the explicit and implicit contracts come to an end, and labor and management renegotiate the nominal wage in light of lower actual prices. Nominal wages fall, or at least rise more slowly than the price level. The real wage falls to the level consistent with potential output, firms return production to normal levels, and the short-run

aggregate supply curve shifts out. The new equilibrium is achieved when the new short-run aggregate supply curve, $SRAS_{100}$, intersects the aggregate demand curve at e'. The economy is now producing its potential output, and the expected price level and the actual price level both equal 100.

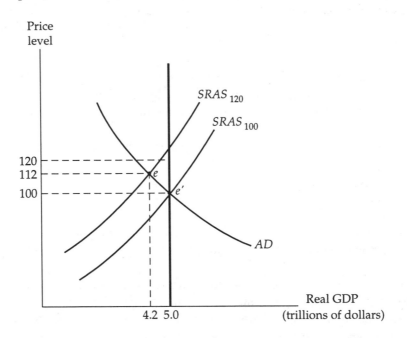

12. The long-run aggregate supply curve is vertical at the level of potential output. The potential output is determined by the level of technology and the amounts of resources available for production. Resource owners determine how much to supply to the market on the basis of expected real resource prices. Regardless of the overall price level, these expected real resource prices will be attained once all markets clear. Consequently, the potential output does not depend on the actual price level; that is, in the long run, the economy will produce its potential output, so the long-run aggregate supply curve is vertical.

13. Real GDP will increase over time as the labor force increases because potential output increases. We cannot be certain about what will happen to the price level, because an increase in the labor force is likely to be associated with an increase in aggregate demand. For a given aggregate demand curve, the price level would fall.

14. Supply shocks are unexpected events that (often temporarily) affect aggregate supply. A temporary shock, such as a drought, causes the short-run aggregate supply curve to shift to the left but does not affect the long-run aggregate supply curve. Temporary supply shocks do not affect the economy's potential output. Supply shocks with more permanent effects, such as a prolonged drop in oil prices or a technological breakthrough, also generate changes in the long-run aggregate supply curve and in potential output.

15. Hysteresis means that the natural rate of unemployment depends in part on the recent history of unemployment. So the longer the actual rate of unemployment exceeds the natural rate of unemployment, the more the natural rate itself will increase. The result can happen if the unemployed lose valuable skills, reducing their ability to find a job. The work ethic can diminish.

CHAPTER 12

Fiscal Policy

I. INTRODUCTION

This chapter examines how the government sector affects the output of the economy. The government affects output through government purchases, taxes, and transfer payments. An appendix derives the various multipliers discussed in this chapter. In the next few chapters we will examine the use and effects of money on the economy.

II. OUTLINE

1. Theory of Fiscal Policy. The government affects the circular flow of income by collecting taxes, purchasing goods and services, and making transfer payments. Fiscal policy involves the use of government purchases, transfer payments, and taxes to influence aggregate output, employment, and the price level. The tools of fiscal policy include automatic stabilizers and discretionary fiscal policy.

   1.1 Changes in Government Purchases
      a. An increase in government purchases, other things constant, increases equilibrium real GDP directly and by means of the multiplier.
      b. The multiplier for any change in autonomous government purchases (with taxes held constant) is the same as that for a change in investment spending: $1/(1 - MPC)$.

   1.2 Changes in Net Taxes
      a. A change in net taxes also affects the equilibrium quantity of real GDP demanded but in a less direct manner than does a change in government purchases.
      b. A reduction in net taxes increases disposable income, which generates an increase in consumption spending.
      c. A reduction in net taxes causes the consumption function to shift up by the same amount.
      d. The effect of a change in autonomous net taxes on equilibrium quantity of real GDP demanded is the shift in the consumption function times the simple tax multiplier. That is, the change in Y = change in net taxes × $[- MPC/(1 - MPC)]$.
      e. The total effect of changes in government purchases and autonomous taxes equals the sum of their individual effects.
      f. The absolute value of the multiplier is greater for a given change in government purchases than for an equal change in autonomous net taxes because the change in government purchases affects aggregate spending directly whereas changes in autonomous net taxes do not.

2.   Including Aggregate Supply

    2.1   Discretionary Fiscal Policy in Response to a Contractionary Gap
        a.   Expansionary fiscal policy can be used to stimulate aggregate demand to move the economy to its potential GDP.
        b.   An increase in government purchases or transfer payments or a reduction in taxes shifts the aggregate expenditure function.
        c.   The increased output generally is accompanied by rising prices.

    2.2   Discretionary Fiscal Policy in Response to an Expansionary Gap
        a.   Fiscal policy can be used to reduce aggregate demand when there is an expansionary gap.
        b.   The chosen policy may be to increase taxes, to reduce government expenditures, to reduce transfer payments, or to use some combination of the three.
        c.   With just the right reduction in aggregate demand, output falls to the potential output level and the price level drops to the expected price level.

    2.3   The Multiplier and the Time Horizon
        a.   The short-run aggregate supply curve slopes upward, so changes in the price level reduce the effect on output of any shift in aggregate demand. The short-run multiplier therefore is smaller than the multiplier when the price level is constant.
        b.   If the economy is at its potential output, the long-run spending multiplier is zero.

3.   The Evolution of Fiscal Policy

    3.1   The Great Depression and World War II
        a.   The classical economists thought a prolonged depression was not impossible.
        b.   The Great Depression led some economists to doubt the self-correcting power of the economy.
        c.   The positive effects on output and employment of increased government spending during World War II provided evidence of the possible effectiveness of fiscal policy.
        d.   The passage of the Employment Act of 1946 gave the federal government responsibility for full employment and price stability.
        e.   After the Great Depression and World War II, policymakers gave up trying to achieve the goal of annual balanced budgets.

    3.2   Automatic Stabilizers
        a.   *Automatic stabilizers* smooth fluctuations in disposable income over the business cycle, maintaining aggregate expenditure in recessionary periods and restraining aggregate expenditure in expansionary periods.
        b.   Examples of automatic stabilizers include the progressive income tax, unemployment insurance, and welfare benefits.
        c.   *Discretionary fiscal policy* is the conscious manipulation of taxes and government spending to achieve macroeconomic stability.

    3.3   From the Golden Age to Stagflation
        a.   President Kennedy expanded the scope of fiscal policy to promote long-term economic growth during the 1960s.
        b.   The stagflation of the 1970s created concerns that demand-management policies were insufficient to keep the economy at potential output with stable prices.

3.4 Fiscal Policy and the Natural Rate of Unemployment
   a. Fiscal policy cannot reduce the rate of unemployment below its natural level in the long run.
   b. Demand-management attempts to increase real GDP beyond potential output in the long run only lead to inflation.

3.5 Lags in Fiscal Policy
   a. It takes time to implement fiscal policy; this may hamper its effectiveness.
   b. Sometimes a change in fiscal policy actually causes harm because time lags cause the policy change to take effect after economic conditions have already changed—when the policy change is no longer appropriate.

3.6 Discretionary Policy and Permanent Income
   a. *Permanent income* is the income households expect to receive on average over the long term.
   b. To the extent that households base consumption decisions on permanent income, short-term manipulation of tax rates will have little effect if people believe the changes are temporary.

3.7 Feedback Effects of Fiscal Policy on Aggregate Supply. Fiscal policy may adversely affect individual work incentives, thus reducing aggregate supply.

3.8 U.S. Budget Deficits of the 1980s and 1990s
   a. In the early 1980s, a large tax cut, designed to stimulate aggregate supply, and a major increase in military spending provided a sizable fiscal stimulus to the economy.
   b. Despite improvements in labor productivity, real GDP did not grow enough to offset the budget impact of lower tax rates and increased government purchases.
   c. The size of the federal budget deficits increased substantially, reducing the government's ability to use discretionary fiscal policy as a tool for economic stabilization.

3.9 *CASE STUDY:* The Supply-Side Experiment

3.10 *CASE STUDY:* Discretionary Policy and Presidential Elections

3.11 Balancing the Federal Budget

4. Appendix: The Algebra of Demand-Side Equilibrium

   4.1 Net-Tax Multiplier
      a. The consumption function when autonomous net taxes are included is $C = a + b(Y - NT)$.
      b. When the consumption function is substituted into the aggregate expenditure function, we get $Y = a + b(Y - NT) + I + G + (X - M)$.
      c. Solving for Y yields: $Y = [1/(1 - b)](a - bNT + I + G + X - M)$.
      d. The autonomous net tax multiplier is $-b/(1 - b)$.

   4.2 The Multiplier When Both G and NT Change. When autonomous net taxes and government purchases increase by the same amount, the multiplier is 1.

   4.3 The Multiplier with a Proportional Income Tax
      a. If the tax rate is t, disposable income is $Y - Yt = Y(1 - t)$.
      b. The multiplier is $1/[1 - b(1 - t)]$.

4.4 Including Variable Net Exports
    a.   The spending multiplier for a model with a proportional income tax and a foreign sector (MPM equals m) is $1/[(1 - b + m) + t(b - m)]$.
    b.   The multiplier decreases with a lower marginal propensity to consume, a higher marginal propensity to import, or a higher income tax rate.

III. DISCUSSION

Theory of Fiscal Policy

Government affects national income in several ways. By taxing households, government reduces their disposable income. This in turn reduces the consumption component of aggregate expenditure. Some of the taxes are used to finance transfer payments, which partially offset the effect of the taxes on disposable income. Government purchases of goods and services are an injection into the circular flow, which directly raises aggregate expenditure. *Fiscal policy* refers to the ways government can affect income through changes in purchases, transfer payments, and/or taxes.

The equilibrium quantity of GDP demanded occurs when total spending consumption (C) plus investment (I) plus net exports ($X - M$) plus government purchases (G) equals GDP. A change in government purchases financed through borrowing has the same effects as a change in investment spending and has the same multiplier: $1/(1 - MPC)$. Like an increase in investment, an increase in government purchases increases the incomes of those from whom the purchases are made, which causes them to increase their spending by an amount equal to the change in income times the MPC. The increased spending in the first round leads to higher incomes for some in the second round, inducing additional spending, and so forth.

Government spending need not be financed through borrowing. Taxes are another important source of financing for government spending. Further, government transfer payments affect disposable income. *Net taxes* are taxes minus transfer payments and are assumed to be autonomous. The effect on national income of autonomous net taxes is similar, but not identical, to the effect of a decrease in government purchases or a decrease in investment spending. For a given increase in autonomous net taxes, autonomous consumption falls by an amount equal to the tax increase times the marginal propensity to consume.

If consumption spending had been $10,000 and the MPC is 0.8, a tax increase of $2,000 reduces autonomous consumption by $2,000 \times 0.80 = $1,600. That is, consumption spending falls to $8,400. The total effect of the tax increase is even greater, however. The reduction in autonomous consumption spending generates multiplier effects as the reduced spending reduces incomes. The reduction in equilibrium GDP demanded equals the change in autonomous consumption times $1/(1 - MPC)$, or $1,600 \times 1/0.2 = $8,000. Putting the two effects together, we find that the multiplier for a change in autonomous net taxes is $-MPC/(1 - MPC)$. In our example this equals $-0.8/0.2 = -4$. In other words, a $2,000 increase in autonomous net taxes generates an $8,000 reduction in equilibrium quantity of GDP demanded.

Since the multiplier for a change in autonomous net taxes differs from the multiplier for government purchases, a neutral fiscal policy change (in which an increase in purchases is financed by an equal increase in autonomous net taxes) will generate a change in equilibrium GDP demanded. Suppose government purchases increase by $1,000 and autonomous net taxes increase by $1,000. Note that an increase in government purchases of $1,000 causes aggregate expenditure to increase in the first round by $1,000, whereas an increase in taxes of $1,000 causes consumption spending, and thus aggregate expenditure, to fall in the first round by less than $1,000. This is because some of the taxes come out of saving. Thus, the overall impact on aggregate expenditure of the increase in government purchases is greater than the impact of the tax. The total change in equilibrium output demanded equals $1,000 × 1/(1 − MPC), which is the effect of the change in government purchases, plus $1,000 × − MPC/(1 − MPC), which is the effect of the change in taxes. Using an MPC of 0.8, we obtain the total change of $1,000(1/0.2) − $1,000(0.8/0.2) = $5,000 − $4,000 = $1,000. That is, equilibrium real GDP demanded increases by the amount of the increase in government purchases when the purchases are financed by an equal increase in autonomous net taxes.

Including Aggregate Supply

The use of discretionary fiscal policy to correct a contractionary gap is illustrated in Exhibit 1. Potential output is $5 trillion but actual income is $4.5 trillion, determined by the intersection of AD and $SRAS_{110}$. The question is, how can the contractionary gap between $4.5 trillion and $5.0 trillion be removed? A glance at Exhibit 1 suggests two possibilities: an increase in short-run aggregate supply (a shift to $SRAS'$) through natural adjustments in resource markets or an increase in aggregate demand (a shift to AD') through government intervention. (The first approach was discussed in the last chapter.) It may take a long time to accomplish an increase in aggregate supply since it depends on a drop in wages and other resource prices. As we have seen in previous chapters, prices tend to be sticky in the downward direction. Aggregate demand will increase if consumption spending increases, investment spending increases, net exports increase, or government purchases increase. With the tools discussed so far, the government can increase government purchases or it can increase consumption spending by reducing net taxes (that is, by reducing taxes or increasing transfer payments). Thus, the government can remove the contractionary gap by employing discretionary fiscal policy.

Exhibit 1

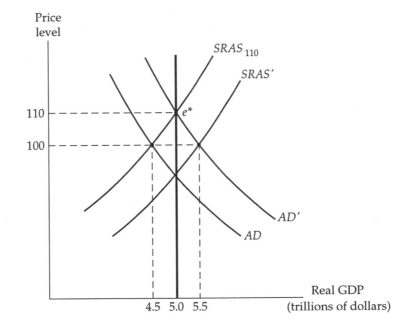

If the government increases spending to remove the contractionary gap, aggregate demand shifts out to AD'. At the current price level of 100, the quantity of GDP demanded increases to $5.5 trillion, which exceeds potential output. There is an excess quantity demanded, and prices increase, which generates a shift along AD' until the equilibrium is reached at e^*. The fiscal policy has been accompanied by a price increase, but it has eliminated the contractionary gap. (A review of Exhibit 4 in your textbook will help you understand fiscal policy and expansionary gaps.)

It is important to note that the effects of fiscal policy may differ in the long run and the short run. Since the short-run aggregate supply curve slopes upward, shifts of aggregate demand caused by changes in fiscal policy cause both output and price changes. That is, a stimulating fiscal policy increases output but also increases the price level, which reduces the quantity of output demanded. Consequently, the multiplier in the short run is smaller than the multiplier calculated when the price level was assumed constant. Further, the potential output of the economy is determined by real forces such as technology and the supply of resources, and fiscal policy cannot be used to stimulate the economy into a sustained level of output that exceeds potential output.

The Evolution of Fiscal Policy

Prior to the Great Depression, the government did not make use of *discretionary fiscal policy*, which involves conscious decisions to change government spending or taxation to affect the macroeconomy. Instead, the government sought to balance the budget each year. From the publication of Keynes's *General Theory* until the early 1970s, many economists believed that discretionary fiscal policy could be used to fine-tune the economy so as to maintain economic growth and relatively stable prices. The rising inflation rate that began in the late 1960s proved difficult to control with fiscal policy, however, and some problems associated with lags in implementing fiscal policy came to be more widely recognized. It became clear that fiscal policy often has less impact even in the short run because people make decisions on the basis of their *permanent incomes* and not their current incomes alone. Further, it came to be recognized that fiscal policy may affect aggregate supply by affecting the incentives people have to work.

Appendix: The Algebra of Demand-Side Fiscal Policy

The appendix to this chapter provides formal algebraic derivations of the multipliers. The equilibrium condition is expressed by the equation

$$Y = C + I + G + (X - M)$$

I, $(X - M)$, and G are not functions of income; they are autonomous. Consumption is a function of disposable income, so

$$C = a + b(Y - NT)$$

where a equals autonomous consumption spending, b equals the marginal propensity to consume, and NT equals net taxes.

The effects of changes in autonomous net taxes can be calculated. The total change in equilibrium GDP demanded caused by a change in autonomous net taxes is

$$Y' - Y = [(a - bNT' + I + G + (X - M))/(1 - b)] - [(a - bNT + I + G + (X - M))/(1 - b)] = [-b/(1 - b)](NT' - NT)$$

Thus, the autonomous net tax multiplier is $-b/(1 - b)$, or $-MPC/(1 - MPC)$. We can combine the effects of a change in government purchases and a change in autonomous net taxes. If government purchases increase by G'' and autonomous net taxes increase by NT'', then the total effect is

$$Y' - Y = [1/(1 - b)]G'' + [-b/(1 - b)]NT'' = (G'' - bNT'')/(1 - b)$$

If $G'' = NT''$, the expression simplifies to $(1 - b)/(1 - b) = 1$. In other words, the *balanced budget multiplier* is 1.

If the government taxes income at rate t, income (Y) must be replaced in the consumption function by disposable income (DI). $DI = Y(1 - t)$, so $C = a + bY(1 - t)$. Equilibrium GDP demanded is then

$$Y = a + bY(1 - t) + I + G + (X - M)$$
$$Y - bY(1 - t) = a + I + G + (X - M)$$
$$Y[1 - b(1 - t)] = a + I + G + (X - M)$$
$$Y = (a + I + G + (X - M))/1 - b(1 - t)]$$

A \$1 change in a, I, $(X - M)$, or G would cause Y to change by

$$\$1/[1 - b(1 - t)]$$

which is the autonomous spending multiplier with a proportional income tax.

Next, variable net exports are included. Exports (X) are autonomous, but imports depend on income, so $M = mY$, where m is the marginal propensity to import. Equilibrium output demanded now equals

$$Y = a + bY(1 - t) + I + G + X - mY(1 - t) = (a + I + G + X)/[1 - b + m + t(b - m)]$$

The introduction of m makes the denominator larger, so the multiplier is smaller.

IV. LAGNIAPPE

Fine-Tuning

Policymakers in the early 1960s were highly optimistic about the government's ability to fine-tune the economy to maintain full employment and stable prices. Some even believed that the government could effect frequent minor adjustments to government spending or tax rates in order to keep the economy on the full-employment path. Several factors make it unlikely that fine-tuning will be effective. First, there is a time lag between when a change occurs in the economy and when that change is observed. For example, a recession is defined as a decline in real GDP for two consecutive quarters. That means that at least six months must pass before the problem is recognized. Second, it takes time to initiate fiscal policy, since both tax changes and expenditure changes must be approved by Congress. This often takes a year or two. Third, Congress is also susceptible to pressure from interest groups that want specific changes in either taxes or spending. Fourth, it takes time for a change in fiscal policy to take effect. When all the time lags are combined, it is likely that by the time a specific change in fiscal policy occurs, the problem it was designed to control will have disappeared and new problems will have developed.

Question to Think About: Can you think of any way to reduce some of these lags?

An important assumption in President Reagan's economic policy was that government spending and taxing activities affect incentives to work, invest, and save. The text discussed a proportional income tax, but in fact the U.S. income tax system has been progressive. Reagan and his supporters argued that high marginal tax rates discourage work and investing. If so, aggregate supply is affected by the government policies on taxes. Hence, the president pushed for reductions in the tax rates and in the extent of their progressivity. In its 1987 Annual Report, the president's Council of Economic Advisers stated, "An efficient tax system entails low and unvarying marginal tax rates that have minimal effects on private investment and consumption choices." High marginal tax rates encourage tax avoidance activities that generally do not enhance the productivity of the economy.

Question to Think About: What taxes (other than the personal income tax) might affect investment and consumption choices?

V. KEY TERMS

automatic stabilizers

discretionary fiscal policy

simple tax multiplier

classical economists

permanent income

political business cycles

proportional income tax

VI. QUESTIONS

A. *Completion*

1. _____ involves the various ways government can influence GDP through changes in purchases, taxes, and transfer payments.

2. _____ government purchases do not vary with the level of real GDP.

3. Autonomous net taxes are taxes minus _____.

4. An increase in government purchases _____ through the economy, raising real GDP.

5. Government _____ affect aggregate demand directly; _____ and _____ affect aggregate demand indirectly.

6. The government purchases multiplier is _____ than the multiplier associated with changes in transfer payments.

7. An increase in autonomous net taxes causes the _____ function to shift down.

8. To close a contractionary gap, the government can increase _____.

9. An increase in taxes may be an appropriate policy response in the face of a(n) _____ gap.

10. The long-run multiplier when the economy is producing its potential output is _____.

11. _____ are changes in government purchases, transfer payments, or taxes that do not require discretionary actions on the part of the government.

12. Deliberate efforts to promote full employment through changes in government purchases, transfer payments, or taxes involve _____.

13. The _____ associated with implementing discretionary fiscal policy often hamper the policy's effectiveness.

14. People tend to be less responsive to changes in _____ income than to changes in _____ income.

15. The theory that incumbent presidents use expansionary policies to stimulate the economy is the theory of _____.

B. True/False

_____ 1. Discretionary fiscal policy involves ways the government can influence the economy's income through changes in the banking system.

_____ 2. Net taxes must always be greater than or equal to zero.

_____ 3. An increase in autonomous net taxes, other things constant, reduces the equilibrium level of real GDP demanded.

_____ 4. Transfer payments affect the equilibrium level of real GDP demanded indirectly, whereas taxes affect it directly.

_____ 5. The multiplier for a change in autonomous government purchases is the same as the multiplier for a change in autonomous investment spending.

_____ 6. If the multiplier for a change in autonomous government purchases is 4, the multiplier for a change in autonomous net taxes is 3.

_____ 7. An increase in autonomous net taxes of $1 million will cause both consumption spending and the equilibrium level of real GDP demanded to fall by $1 million.

_____ 8. An increase in government purchases of $1 billion has a bigger effect on real GDP than an increase in transfer payments of $1 billion.

_____ 9. If the aggregate supply curve slopes upward, an increase in autonomous spending will generate a smaller increase in aggregate expenditure than is implied by the autonomous spending multiplier.

_____ 10. The government can increase aggregate expenditure without a price increase by using fiscal policy.

_____ 11. If society is producing its potential GDP, the spending multiplier in the long run is zero.

_____ 12. Discretionary fiscal policy is implemented only after government officials make a conscious choice to change government spending or taxes.

_____ 13. Lags reduce the effectiveness of fiscal policy as a tool of economic stabilization.

_____ 14. Discretionary fiscal policy is used by policymakers to influence aggregate supply.

_____ 15. Temporary tax cuts provide more stimulus to the economy than permanent tax cuts.

_____ 16. The huge federal deficits of the 1980s crowded out private investment spending.

_____ 17. Political business cycle theory argues that the business cycle is the same length as the term of office of the president of the United States.

_____ *18. The higher the proportional tax rate, the less households have to spend and the lower the equilibrium level of real GDP demanded.

_____ *19. A proportional income tax increases the autonomous spending multiplier.

_____ *20. A decrease in the marginal propensity to import will cause the spending multiplier to increase.

C.   Multiple Choice

1.   Which of the following is expected to increase equilibrium GDP demanded?
    a.   increases in government purchases of goods
    b.   a reduction in taxes
    c.   increases in net exports
    d.   increases in transfer payments
    e.   All of the above.

2.   Which of the following is assumed to be autonomous?
    a.   consumption spending
    b.   saving
    c.   government spending
    d.   All of the above.
    e.   b and c only

---

* These questions refer to material developed in this chapter's Appendix.

3. Taxes and transfer payments affect aggregate spending
   a. directly.
   b. by changing disposable income.
   c. by affecting interest rates because the government has to borrow whenever taxes do not equal transfer payments.
   d. All of the above.
   e. None of the above. They do not affect aggregate spending.

4. Which of the following has the same effects on equilibrium GDP demanded as a $1,000 increase in government purchases?
   a. a $1,000 increase in transfer payments
   b. a $1,000 decrease in autonomous net taxes
   c. a $1,000 increase in exports
   d. a $1,000 decrease in investment spending
   e. All of the above.

5. Suppose that government purchases increase by $1 million and that business investment spending falls at the same time by $1 million. If the MPC is 0.8, the change in aggregate expenditure will be
   a. −$1 million.
   b. zero.
   c. $1 million.
   d. $4 million.
   e. $5 million.

6. An increase in autonomous net taxes causes
   a. the slope of the consumption function to change.
   b. government spending to increase.
   c. the aggregate expenditure curve to shift down.
   d. equilibrium real GDP demanded to increase.
   e. None of the above.

7. If the MPC is 0.9, the absolute value of the autonomous net taxes multiplier is
   a. 0.
   b. 1.
   c. 1.11.
   d. 9.
   e. 10.

8. If the MPC = 0.8, which of the following would cause the biggest change in real GDP?
   a. a $200 million increase in government purchases
   b. a $250 million increase in transfer payments
   c. a $1 billion increase in government purchases and a $1 billion increase in net taxes
   d. All of the above.
   e. a and b only

9. If the economy is experiencing a contractionary gap, it might be appropriate for the government to use fiscal policy to
   a. stimulate aggregate supply.
   b. stimulate aggregate demand.
   c. reduce aggregate supply.
   d. reduce aggregate demand.
   e. a and b

10. Because the aggregate supply curve slopes upward, expansionary fiscal policy tends to be accompanied by
    a. falling prices.
    b. rising prices.
    c. stable prices.
    d. any of the above.
    e. increased investment spending.

11. The economy is producing its potential output and the government increases transfer payments. As a result,
    a. unemployment falls in the short run and in the long run.
    b. prices increase in the short run and in the long run, but output remains constant.
    c. output increases in the short run, but falls back to its original level in the long run.
    d. there are no effects, since changes in transfer payments do not affect the macroeconomy.
    e. None of the above.

12. Prior to the Great Depression, the goal of fiscal policy was
    a. to maintain full employment.
    b. to maintain stable prices.
    c. to encourage economic growth.
    d. to balance the budget.
    e. All of the above.

13. Keynes's main disagreement with classical economics involved
    a. the definition of unemployment.
    b. his emphasis on the importance of supply-side economics.
    c. whether prices and wages were flexible enough to ensure full employment.
    d. the reliance of classical economists on automatic stabilizers.
    e. both b and c only.

14. Which of the following is not an example of an automatic stabilizer?
    a. a temporary increase in the income tax rate
    b. an unemployment compensation program
    c. a progressive income tax
    d. a proportional income tax
    e. welfare programs

15. One result of automatic stabilizers is that
    a. disposable income varies less during economic fluctuations than does GDP.
    b. disposable income grows faster over time.
    c. tax receipts increase during recessions and decrease during expansions.
    d. net taxes vary inversely with real GDP.
    e. None of the above.

16. Which of the following makes discretionary fiscal policy less effective?
    a. lags in discretionary fiscal policy
    b. the fact that individuals make decisions based on permanent income instead of current income
    c. the fact that fiscal policy may affect aggregate supply as well as aggregate demand
    d. the fact that the aggregate supply curve slopes upward
    e. All of the above.

17. If people base decisions on their permanent income,
    a. spending multipliers are larger.
    b. the multiplier associated with changes in autonomous net taxes is larger.
    c. consumption is less responsive to temporary changes in income than to permanent changes.
    d. All of the above.
    e. a and b only

18. According to the theory of political business cycles,
    a. presidents use contractionary discretionary policies to hold down inflation during an election year.
    b. presidents use expansionary discretionary policies to stimulate the economy during an election year.
    c. Republican presidents try to hold down inflation whereas Democratic presidents try to stimulate the economy during election years.
    d. the only goal of an incumbent president is to be reelected.
    e. both c and d

*19. Which of the following will make the autonomous spending multiplier smaller?
    a. a decrease in autonomous net taxes
    b. a decrease in the income tax rate
    c. an increase in the marginal propensity to consume
    d. an increase in autonomous net taxes
    e. an increase in the income tax rate

*20. If the current equilibrium GDP demanded is $100 billion, the MPC is 0.8, the marginal propensity to import is 0.1, the income tax rate is 0.2, and there is a $10 billion increase in government purchases, what is the change in equilibrium GDP demanded?
    a. $17.9 billion
    b. $35.7 billion
    c. $10.0 billion
    d. $22.7 billion
    e. $33.3 billion

D. Discussion Questions

1. In discussion question 1 in the chapter titled *Aggregate Expenditure and Aggregate Demand* equilibrium output demanded was $8,000. Suppose government spending amounts to $1,000. Using the information from that chapter, calculate the new equilibrium level of output demanded. Are planned saving and planned investment still equal? Why or why not?

2. Using the information from the chapter titled *Aggregate Expenditure and Aggregate Demand (Chapter 10)*, calculate what the level of equilibrium output demanded would be if the government purchases were financed by autonomous net taxes of $1,000. Explain.

---

* These questions refer to material developed in this chapter's Appendix.

3. Why is an increase in output that is generated by stimulative fiscal policy accompanied by rising prices? Use a graph to illustrate your answer.

4. How does aggregate supply affect the multiplier?

5. Can discretionary fiscal policy be used to increase potential output? Explain.

6. How do automatic stabilizers differ from discretionary fiscal policy tools?

7. In what ways can fiscal policy affect aggregate supply?

8. Explain the factors that make it difficult for the government to fine-tune the economy by using fiscal policy.

9. Explain how the federal budget was balanced in 1998.

*10. How does a proportional income tax affect the spending multiplier?

*11. The slope of the consumption function without an income tax is b. What is the slope of the consumption function if the proportional tax rate is t?

*12. If $I = \$1,500$, $G = \$2,500$, $(X - M) = -\$500$, $b = 0.7$, $a = \$500$, and $t = 0.25$, what is the equilibrium quantity of real GDP demanded?

*13. In question 12, suppose the income tax rate falls to 20 percent but autonomous net taxes increase by $500. What is the new equilibrium quantity of real GDP demanded?

*14. In question 12, if the MPI is 0.1 and exports are $2,000, what is the new equilibrium quantity of real GDP demanded?

VII. ANSWERS

A. Completion

1. Fiscal policy
2. Autonomous
3. transfer payments
4. multiplies
5. purchases; taxes; transfer payments
6. greater
7. consumption
8. governmental purchases (or transfer payments)
9. expansionary
10. zero
11. Automatic stabilizers
12. discretionary fiscal policy
13. lags
14. current; permanent
15. political business cycles

---

* These questions refer to material developed in this chapter's Appendix.

B. True/False

1. False	6. True	11. True	16. False
2. False	7. False	12. True	17. False
3. True	8. True	13. True	18. True
4. False	9. True	14. False	19. False
5. True	10. False	15. False	20. True

C. Multiple Choice

1. e	6. c	11. c	16. e
2. c	7. d	12. d	17. c
3. b	8. d	13. c	18. b
4. c	9. b	14. a	19. e
5. b	10. b	15. a	20. d

D. Discussion Questions

1. In discussion question 1 in the chapter titled *Aggregate Expenditure and Aggregate Demand*, the MPC was 0.7, so the government purchases multiplier is 3.33. The change in equilibrium output demanded that is due to government purchases is $1,000 \times 3.33 =$ $3,333, which raises equilibrium output demanded to $11,333. Consumption spending increases by $2,333 ($3,333 \times 0.7$), and saving increases by $1,000 ($3,333 \times 0.3$). Planned saving is now $2,000 and no longer equals planned investment of $1,000. Instead, saving now equals planned investment plus government purchases. Since $Y = C + I + G$ and $Y = C + S4$, it must be true that $S = I + G$.

2. The equilibrium before the government purchases and changes in autonomous net taxes was $8,000, of which $7,000 was consumption spending and $1,000 was investment spending. Government purchases are $1,000, but disposable income falls by $1,000 because of the increase in autonomous net taxes. Therefore, consumption spending falls to $6,300 and saving falls to $700. Real GDP equals $8,000, but aggregate expenditure equals $8,300 ($C = \$6,300$, planned investment $= \$1,000$, and $G = \$1,000$). Inventories are being drawn down because actual investment is less than planned investment, so production increases. When real GDP equals $9,000, disposable income equals $8,000, C equals $7,000, $I = \$1,000$, $G = \$1,000$, and $S = \$1,000$. Hence, aggregate expenditure equals real GDP, and $9,000 is the new equilibrium real GDP demanded.

3. The short-run aggregate supply curve slopes upward and is drawn for a given expected price level. Fiscal policy can eliminate a contractionary gap by shifting the aggregate demand curve to the right. Because the short-run aggregate supply curve slopes upward, there is an excess quantity demanded at the current price level after aggregate demand shifts. The excess quantity demanded causes prices to increase. See Exhibit 1 in the discussion section of this chapter for the graphical analysis.

4. A positively sloped aggregate supply curve reduces the multiplier because some of the changes in spending and income cause prices to change; this dampens the multiplier effects.

5. Potential output is determined by the level of technology and the supply of resources. Fiscal policy does not tend to affect these determinants, so fiscal policy cannot be used to increase potential output.

6. Automatic stabilizers are government programs already in place that smooth fluctuations in disposable income over the business cycle so that consumption spending does not vary as much as GDP. In this way, the effects of changes in GDP are reduced. In contrast, discretionary fiscal policy involves intentional manipulation of government spending and taxes. It requires that legislation be passed, which often is a time-consuming process.

7. Since fiscal policy involves government spending and taxes, fiscal policy may affect the incentives people have to work and invest. An increase in the tax rate decreases the cost of leisure activity, which may induce people to work less and consume more leisure. An increase in transfer payments raises the opportunity cost of work, which suggests that some will work less. In either case, aggregate supply is affected.

8. Time lags associated with observing that a disequilibrium exists and with passing legislation to implement policies hamper the effectiveness of fiscal policy. Further, changes in fiscal policy may affect the incentives of economic actors, which may affect aggregate supply. To the extent that households base consumption decisions on permanent income, changes in current income have little impact on spending.

9. Taxes were raised and government spending was constrained, thus reducing the deficit. The growing economy provided additional tax revenues that eliminated the deficit.

10. An income tax reduces disposable income; changes in consumption and saving are related to changes in disposable income. The change in disposable income equals the change in income times $(1 - t)$, where t is the tax rate. The change in consumption spending equals the change in disposable income times the MPC. Putting the two effects together yields the change in consumption spending, which equals the change in income times $(1 - t)$ times the MPC. The multiplier without an income tax is $1/(1 - \text{MPC})$; with an income tax it is equal to $1/[1 - \text{MPC}(1 - t)]$. That is, the value of the multiplier with an income tax is less than the value of the multiplier without an income tax.

11. A proportional income tax means that income (Y) must be replaced by disposable income (DI) in the consumption function. $\text{DI} = (1 - t)Y$, so the consumption function becomes $C = a + b(1 - t)Y$, and the slope is $b(1 - t)$. Since t is less than 1, the slope with an income tax is less than the slope without an income tax.

12. $Y = [a + I + (X - M) + G]/[1 - b(1 - t)]$
$= [\$500 + \$1,500 - \$500 + \$2,500]/[1 - 0.7(1 - 0.25)]$
$= \$4,000/0.475 = \$8,421$

13. $Y = [\$500 - 0.7(\$500) + \$1,500 - \$500 + \$2,500]/[1 - 0.7(1 - 0.2)]$
$= \$3,650/0.44 = \$8,295.45$

14. $Y = (\$500 + \$1,000 + \$2,500 + \$2,000)/[1 - 0.7 + 0.1 + 0.25(0.7 - 0.1)]$
$= \$6,000/0.55 = \$10,909$

CHAPTER 13

Money and the Financial System

I. INTRODUCTION

The subject of this chapter is money. The chapter defines many new terms and presents a historical overview of the development of money and a description of the U.S. monetary system. The chapter also describes how the U.S. monetary system works and how money is created. The role of monetary policy will be discussed in the following chapter.

II. OUTLINE

1. The Evolution of Money

    1.1   Barter and the Double Coincidence of Wants
        a.   *Barter* involves the trading of one commodity directly for another.
        b.   Barter requires a *double coincidence of wants*, which occurs when one trader is willing to exchange a product for what another trader is selling.
        c.   The more specialized the economy, the more difficult it is to rely on barter.

    1.2   Earliest Money and Its Functions
        a.   Money serves three important functions:
            (1)   Medium of exchange. Whatever serves as money must be generally accepted in return for goods and services.
            (2)   Unit of account. Prices of all goods are defined in terms of the commodity that serves as money.
            (3)   Store of value. Money retains its purchasing power over time.
        b.   Any commodity that is widely accepted in payment for goods and services is *money*.

    1.3   Problems with Commodity Money
        a.   The quality of the commodity that serves as money may be difficult to maintain.
        b.   Commodity money tends to be bulky.
        c.   Commodity money may not be easily divided into smaller units.
        d.   *Gresham's Law* states that "bad money drives out good money"—that is, people trade away inferior commodity money and hoard better commodity money. The quality of the commodity money in circulation therefore declines, reducing its acceptability.
        e.   The opportunity cost of commodity money is often high because the commodity used has other uses.
        f.   The value of the commodity depends on supply and demand of the commodity, which may vary unpredictably.
        g.   The best money is durable, portable, divisible, and of uniform quality, and has a low opportunity cost, but its supply can be controlled.

    1.4   Coins
        a.   Both the quality and quantity of precious metals are difficult to determine.
        b.   Coinage developed to control the quantity and quality of silver and gold used as money.

    c.   The power to coin money came to be associated with sovereigns.

    d.   When the face value of a coin is greater than the cost of the coinage, the minting of coins can generate government revenue, which is referred to as *seigniorage*.

    e.   Token money is money whose face value exceeds the value of the commodity from which it was made.

1.5   Money and Banking

    a.   People began to leave their gold in the safes of local goldsmiths.

    b.   Depositors began writing instructions to goldsmiths to pay people instead of getting their gold from the goldsmiths and paying their debts themselves. This process led to the first checking accounts.

    c.   The goldsmiths began making loans by creating accounts against which borrowers could write checks, thereby creating money.

    d.   This system was a type of fractional reserve banking system because the claims against the bank, or total deposits, exceeded the bank's gold and other reserves.

1.6   Paper Money

    a.   *Bank notes* were pieces of paper promising that the bearer would receive a specific amount of gold when the paper was presented to the bank.

    b.   *Fiduciary money* is notes backed by gold or other valuable commodities.

    c.   *Fiat money* does not have any commodity backing it. It is declared legal tender by the government, so creditors must accept it in payment for debts.

1.7   The Value of Money

    a.   People accept fiat money because they believe others will accept it.

    b.   The value of money is reflected in its purchasing power.

    c.   The value of a dollar (relative to a base year) is found by dividing 100 by the price index for the year.

1.8   When Money Performs Poorly

    a.   A well-balanced money system can increase an economy's performance.

    b.   Too much money in the economy generates inflation, which makes it more difficult to use money as a store of wealth, a medium of exchange, or a standard of value. If the currency becomes so inflated that it is no longer accepted as payment, people resort to barter.

    c.   If the official currency is scarce or fails to serve as a medium of exchange, some other form of money may evolve to facilitate exchange.

1.9   *CASE STUDY:* When the Monetary System Breaks Down

2.   Financial Institutions in the United States

2.1   Commercial Banks and Thrifts

    a.   Financial institutions serve as intermediaries between savers and borrowers.

    b.   Depository institutions obtain funds primarily by accepting deposits from the public.

       (1)   Commercial banks were established to make loans primarily to businesses.

       (2)   Thrift institutions were established to make loans to households.

    c.   Other financial intermediaries obtain funds by collecting premiums or by borrowing.

2.2   Development of the Dual Banking System. The United States has a system consisting of both state banks and national banks.

2.3 Birth of the Federal Reserve System
   a. Because of a series of bank failures, the government established the Federal Reserve System (the Fed) in 1914 as the U.S. central bank and monetary authority.
   b. All national banks were required to become members of the Fed.

2.4 Powers of the Federal Reserve System
   a. The authority to issue bank notes was taken away from national banks and turned over to the Federal Reserve System.
   b. The Federal Reserve can also buy and sell government securities, extend loans to member banks, clear checks, and establish levels of required reserves equal to some percentage of member banks' deposits.

2.5 Banking during the Great Depression
   a. Many banks failed because the Fed failed to perform properly.
   b. The Fed should have extended more loans to banks experiencing short-term shortages of funds.
   c. The Fed contributed to the deterioration of the economy by failing to stabilize the banking system.

2.6 Roosevelt's Reforms
   a. The Federal Reserve Board became the Board of Governors, with newly centralized authority to set monetary policy.
   b. The Federal Open Market Committee, consisting of the seven members of the Board of Governors plus the presidents of five reserve banks, was established to consolidate decisions about the purchase and sale of government securities by the Fed.
   c. The Board of Governors could control the money supply by its power to vary the percentage of deposits member banks were required to hold as reserves, to set discount rates, and to buy and sell government securities.
   d. The Federal Deposit Insurance Corporation (FDIC) and the Federal Savings and Loan Insurance Corporation (FSLIC) were established to insure deposits held in member banks and savings and loans.
   e. Commercial banks were forbidden to buy and sell corporate stocks and bonds.
   f. The Fed has six objectives: high employment, economic growth, price stability, stability in interest rates, stability in financial markets, and stability in foreign exchange markets.

2.7 From the Great Depression to Deregulation
   a. The Fed set interest-rate ceilings, which reduced interest-rate competition for deposits among depository institutions.
   b. When inflation surged in the 1970s, depositors left depository institutions as interest rates offered by other financial institutions rose above the rates the Fed permitted depository institutions to pay depositors.
   c. Depository institutions often had to support outstanding loans by borrowing at higher interest rates than they earned on their loans.

2.8 Bank Deregulation
   a. Banks and thrifts were given greater control over their operations, and interest-rate ceilings were eventually eliminated.
   b. Many states reduced regulation of state-chartered savings and loan associations.
   c. The thrifts were able to make high-risk loans, knowing that the FSLIC protected depositors.
   d. Many thrifts failed in the 1980s.

2.9   Bailing Out the Thrifts
       a.   The collapse of so many thrifts prompted Congress in August of 1989 to approve a
             huge financial bailout for the industry.
       b.   Under the new law, the FSLIC was abolished, thrift deposits were insured by the
             FDIC, and thrifts were put under the supervision of the U.S. Treasury. New
             regulations were established to dictate the types of investments thrifts could make.

2.10   Commercial Banks Were Also Failing. Commercial banks experienced difficulties similar
       to those of the thrifts in the late 1980s and early 1990s.

2.11   The Structure of U.S. Banking
       a.   The United States has more banks than any other country, and U.S. bank assets are
             more evenly distributed across banks.
       b.   Restrictions on interstate banking create inefficiencies.
       c.   Two developments allow banks to get around these restrictions:
             (1)   A bank holding company is a corporation that may own several banks.
             (2)   Banks have merged to create a greater volume of transactions and thus reduce
                    operating costs per customer.

2.12   *CASE STUDY:* Banking Troubles in Japan

III. DISCUSSION

Because this chapter focuses on the historical development of the U.S. monetary system and
introduces many new terms, this discussion section will review the terms introduced in the chapter.

Barter is trading one commodity directly for another. A major problem with barter is that it
requires a *double coincidence of wants* on the part of the traders. That is, each party in the exchange must
be willing to exchange his or her product for what the other is willing to sell. Barter becomes more
difficult as the number of goods increases and as the economy becomes more complex and specialized.

Money makes exchange easier. If one good becomes generally accepted in return for all other goods,
it begins to function as money. To be considered money, a good must serve three functions: (1) it must act as
a *medium of exchange*—it must be generally accepted in exchange for other goods and services; (2) it must
serve as a *unit of account*—prices of all other goods must be defined in terms of money; and (3) it must be a
store of value—it must hold its value over time. Whatever good serves these three functions is money.

Commodity money is a good or commodity, such as corn or gold, that also serves as money. There
are problems with using most commodities as money: Many commodities deteriorate over time; in
addition, they tend to be bulky, to vary in quality, and to change value with changes in supply and
demand. According to *Gresham's Law*, when commodities differ in quality, bad money drives out good.
That is, people tend to trade away the inferior money and hoard the best, so the quality of the commodity
in circulation declines; this reduces its usefulness as a medium of exchange.

Over time, metals came to be used instead of other commodities for money. But precious metals
could be debased with cheaper metals, so people had to determine both the quantity and the quality of
the precious metals. Coinage was developed to handle the problem of quality control. Governments took
over coinage, often earning *seigniorage*: revenues arising from the difference between the face value of
a coin and the cost of coinage. Coins whose value exceeded their metallic value were called *token money*.

The 17th century saw the development of a *fractional reserve banking system*, in which a bank
kept reserves to back up only a fraction of the deposits placed in the bank. Banks created money by

making loans through the creation of new deposits on which borrowers could write checks, even though the reserves were not there to back up the deposits. *Bank notes* are pieces of paper that promise that the bearer will receive a specific amount of gold when the paper is presented to the bank. Such notes are a type of *fiduciary money*. *Fiat money* is notes that are not redeemable in gold or other valuable metals. Fiat money is declared to be *legal tender* by the government that issues it, which means that it must be accepted for payment of debts. Most paper money throughout the world, including U.S. currency, is fiat money.

People accept fiat money because they have confidence in its value or in the government that issued it. If people lose confidence in fiat money, other commodities are used for money on the black market, or barter is used. When this happens, the economy is working inefficiently. A smoothly functioning monetary system is essential to a modern industrial society.

Financial intermediaries are institutions that link savers and borrowers by accepting funds from savers and lending these funds to borrowers. *Commercial banks* and *thrift institutions* are two examples of *depository institutions*: financial intermediaries that acquire funds by accepting deposits from the public. A *demand deposit* is an account that a depositor can draw from at any time by writing a check. In this country, banks have been chartered both by states and by the national government, which means that the United States has a dual banking system.

Today the Board of Governors of the *Federal Reserve System* is responsible for controlling the U.S. money supply. The Fed requires banks to hold a certain percentage of their deposits in the form of reserves. The Fed also influences the money supply by *open market operations*—the buying and selling of government securities. It also lends money to member banks and charges an interest rate called the *discount rate*. For a long time, the Fed set maximum interest rates that banks could pay on deposits. The deregulation of depository institutions in the 1980s was a response to their insolvency problems, which had been caused by the inflation of the 1970s. Regulation of thrifts has resumed, however, as a result of the failure of many thrifts in the 1980s and the financial bailout approved by Congress.

IV. LAGNIAPPE

When Money Loses Its Value

There have been instances in history when a country's money supply increased so fast that the inflation rate became astronomical. One of the best examples was the hyperinflation in Germany after World War I. The inflation rate was so great that workers demanded to be paid several times a day and would give their pay to family members so that they could buy products before the prices increased again. Prior to World War I, the value of all home mortgages in Germany was 40 million marks. During the height of the hyperinflation in the early 1920s, 40 million marks could buy a postcard.

Question to Think About: How could relative prices be determined in such a situation?

The Euro

On January 1, 1999, most of the members of the European Union fixed their exchange rates with respect to each other and created a new European money—the euro. At first the euro is an accounting money only. Currency will be introduced between January 1 and June 30, 2002, at which time the German mark, French franc, and other national currencies will be withdrawn from circulation. There is a European central bank headquartered in Frankfort, Germany. Many Germans have been very confident in the German mark and are not anxious to exchange it for this new money.

Question to Think About: What impact will the euro have on the worldwide use of the American dollar?

V. KEY TERMS

double coincidence of wants
money
medium of exchange
commodity money
unit of account
store of value
Gresham's Law
seigniorage
token money
fractional reserve banking system
bank notes
fiat money

legal tender
financial intermediaries
depository institutions
commercial banks
demand deposits
thrift institutions (thrifts)
Federal Reserve System
reserves
open-market operations
money market mutual fund
bank holding company

VI. QUESTIONS

A. *Completion*

1. Barter requires a _____.

2. Anything that people generally accept in payment for goods and services is _____.

3. If prices of all goods are expressed in terms of a commodity used as money, then the commodity becomes a _____.

4. Money serves as a _____ when it retains purchasing power over time.

5. The expression "bad money drives out good" is known as _____.

6. Coins whose face value exceeds their metallic value are _____ money.

7. Revenue earned from coinage is known as _____.

8. Reserves as a proportion of total claims against total deposits is the _____.

9. _____ money is not backed by anything of intrinsic value.

10. The rate at which money is exchanged for goods and services is the _____ of money.

11. _____ were developed to make loans primarily to businesses rather than to households.

12. When member banks borrow from a Federal Reserve bank, they pay the _____.

13. The Fed engages in _____ operations when it buys and sells U.S. government securities.

14. The United States has more banks than other countries because of government restrictions on _____.

15. The nation's major banks are all owned by _____.

B. *True/False*

_____ 1. Increased specialization made the barter system more costly.

_____ 2. There is no common measure of value in a barter economy.

_____ 3. Money allows the sale of one good to be separate from the purchase of another.

_____ 4. To serve as money, a good must be durable.

_____ 5. Gresham's Law says that good money drives out bad money.

_____ 6. Before coinage was fully developed, one problem with metallic money was that the quality of the metal had to be determined at each exchange.

_____ 7. Seigniorage is earned when the face value of a coin exceeds the cost of minting the coin.

_____ 8. U.S. coins now in circulation are examples of token money.

_____ 9. The total claims against a bank cannot exceed the bank's reserves under a fractional reserve banking system.

_____ 10. Bank notes are a type of fiduciary money.

_____ 11. Fiat money is money backed by gold.

_____ 12. Federal Reserve notes are backed by gold.

_____ 13. The value of money is measured by its purchasing power.

_____ 14. An insurance company is an example of a depository institution.

_____ 15. The United States no longer has a dual banking system.

_____ 16. The Fed is empowered to set reserve requirements for banks.

_____ 17. Federal Reserve banks can fail if they do not have enough reserves.

_____ 18. Bank holding companies are used to circumvent federal laws against interstate branch banking.

_____ 19. During the inflation of the 1970s, ceilings on interest rates resulted in depositors' withdrawing deposits from commercial banks and thrifts.

_____ 20. Federal deposit insurance encourages managers of thrifts and banks to engage in risky loans.

C.   Multiple Choice

1.   Which of the following is a problem of barter?
   a.   negotiating numerous exchange rates among commodities
   b.   achieving a double coincidence of wants
   c.   seigniorage
   d.   a and b
   e.   None of the above.

2.   Money is
   a.   anything that is generally accepted as payment for goods and services.
   b.   something that the government of a nation has always made and controlled.
   c.   gold and other precious metals.
   d.   something that is backed by a commodity that has intrinsic value.
   e.   All of the above.

3.   Which of the following is not a function of money?
   a.   medium of exchange
   b.   creator of seigniorage
   c.   store of value
   d.   unit of account
   e.   b and c

4.   Which of the following commodities would work best as a store of value?
   a.   pebbles
   b.   milk
   c.   gold
   d.   corn
   e.   cattle

5.   For a commodity to serve as money and be a store of value, it must
   a.   be easily divided up.
   b.   have value as a commodity.
   c.   maintain its purchasing power.
   d.   be easily reproduced.
   e.   be declared legal tender by the government.

6.   One problem with using commodity money is
   a.   the commodity's homogeneity.
   b.   the value of the commodity depends on its supply and demand.
   c.   good money drives out bad money.
   d.   the commodity tends to lack intrinsic value.
   e.   the difficulty of achieving a double coincidence of wants.

7. Which of the following was **not** a means of maintaining the value and quality of gold or silver coins?
   a. stamping the coins
   b. making sure the metal in the coin was worth more than its face value
   c. putting borders on the coins
   d. making counterfeiting illegal
   e. None of the above.

8. Debasement of a currency could be accomplished by
   a. printing more paper money.
   b. adding base metals to coins.
   c. shaving small amounts of metal off a coin.
   d. clipping small amounts of metal off the edges of a coin.
   e. All of the above.

9. Early banks created money by
   a. loaning out reserves to people.
   b. coining money.
   c. creating fiduciary money.
   d. creating deposits against which borrowers could write checks.
   e. issuing commodity money.

10. Bank notes differ from checks in that checks
    a. are written against thrifts and bank notes against banks.
    b. are backed by gold and notes are not.
    c. are created by banks and notes by the government.
    d. can be redeemed only by the individual to whom they are directed, whereas notes can be redeemed by anyone who holds them.
    e. are legal tender and notes are not.

11. Fiat money derives its status as money from
    a. the gold that backs it.
    b. the power of the government.
    c. its intrinsic value.
    d. being redeemable for commodity money.
    e. All of the above are possible.

12. The value of money falls when
    a. the price level rises.
    b. the price level falls.
    c. it can be exchanged for more goods.
    d. interest rates fall.
    e. None of the above. The value of money is constant.

13. When there is too little money in an economy, people often resort to
    a. strict price controls.
    b. barter.
    c. demanding more frequent payment for labor.
    d. frequent price changes.
    e. All of the above.

14. The dual banking system refers to
    a. a time when states owned some banks and citizens owned other banks.
    b. a time when banks and thrifts competed for deposits.
    c. the current deregulated system, in which banks compete with other financial intermediaries such as brokerage houses and insurance companies.
    d. a system that only existed prior to the formation of the Fed, in which some banks were chartered by states and some by the federal government.
    e. a system that still is in existence, in which some banks are chartered by states and others are chartered by the federal government.

15. The Federal Reserve System has the power to
    a. issue bank notes.
    b. buy and sell government securities.
    c. extend loans to member banks.
    d. set reserve requirements of member banks.
    e. All of the above.

16. The interest rate the Fed charges on loans made to member banks is the
    a. reserve ratio.
    b. reserve rate.
    c. discount rate.
    d. bank rate.
    e. prime rate.

17. During the Great Depression, the Fed
    a. prevented the depression from being worse by solving the banking crisis.
    b. extended too many loans to member banks, which got them into further trouble.
    c. initiated discretionary fiscal policy that made the depression worse.
    d. failed to act as a lender of last resort to member banks, causing many of them to fail.
    e. purchased securities in order to prevent a collapse of the securities markets.

18. As a result of legislation passed during the Great Depression,
    a. the Fed set reserve requirements of 100 percent.
    b. commercial banks were forbidden to buy and sell corporate securities.
    c. interest rate ceilings were set.
    d. All of the above.
    d. b and c

19. Commercial banks and thrifts faced difficult times in the 1970s because of
    a. deflation.
    b. high interest rates on borrowed funds relative to interest rates on mortgages.
    c. excessive competition between banks and thrifts.
    d. deregulation of financial markets.
    e. a, b, and c.

20. The financial bailout of the thrift industry passed by Congress in 1989
    a. deregulated the thrift industry too.
    b. established the FSLIC to insure deposits in thrifts.
    c. required that thrifts hold at least 70 percent of their assets in mortgages.
    d. required that thrifts hold at least 40 percent of their assets in junk bonds.
    e. made it more difficult for commercial banks to acquire thrifts.

D. Discussion Questions

1. a. Suppose there are two goods, A and B, and the price of A in terms of B is 1A = 2B. What is the price of B in terms of A? How many different relative prices are there?
   b. A third good, C, is added, and 1A = 4C. What is the price of B in terms of C? How many different price ratios are there, and what are they?
   c. A fourth good, D, is added, and 1A = 8D. What is the price of D in terms of C? How many different price ratios are there?

2. Discuss the advantages of money over barter.

3. What are the three functions of money, and why are they important?

4. State whether each of the following would be a good or bad commodity to use as money and discuss why.
   a. beads
   b. tobacco
   c. cattle
   d. boulders
   e. cigarettes

5. How did coinage help solve the quality control problems associated with using precious metals as money?

6. Are coins that are currently minted in the United States milled around the edges to prevent clipping? Why or why not?

7. Describe a fractional reserve banking system.

8. Are all forms of paper money fiat money? Explain.

9. Why do people accept fiat money? What might cause people to stop accepting fiat money?

10. What determines the value of fiat money?

11. What happens if there is too much money in the economy? What happens if there is not enough money in the economy?

12. Wars are often associated with inflation. Based on what you have learned so far, offer an explanation for this observation.

13. Why was the Federal Reserve System created? What are its powers under current banking law?

14. Explain why the text describes banking prior to the 1970s as a "quiet life."

15. Discuss the factors that led to deregulation of U.S. financial markets in the 1980s.

VII. ANSWERS

A. Completion

1. double coincidence of wants	6. token	11. Commercial banks
2. money	7. seigniorage	12. discount rate
3. unit of account	8. reserve ratio	13. open-market
4. store of value	9. Fiat	14. branches
5. Gresham's Law	10. purchasing power	15. bank holding companies

B. True/False

1. True	7. True	15. False
2. True	8. True	16. True
3. True	9. False	17. False
4. True; otherwise money would not serve as a store of value.	10. False	18. True
	11. False	19. True
	12. False	20. True
5. False	13. True	
6. True	14. False	

C. Multiple Choice

1. d	6. b	11. b	16. c
2. a	7. b	12. a	17. d
3. b	8. e	13. b	18. e
4. c	9. d	14. e	19. b
5. c	10. d	15. e	20. c

D. Discussion Questions

1. a. $1B = 0.5A$; there is one relative price.
    b. Since $1B = 0.5A$ and $0.5A = 2C$, $1B = 2C$; there are three price ratios: P_A/P_B is one ratio; P_A/P_C is a second; and P_B/P_C is a third. (The reciprocals are not different price ratios.)
    c. Since $1A = 4C$ and $1A = 8D$, $8D = 4C$, or $1D = 0.5C$, there are ten price ratios.

2. Barter requires a double coincidence of wants, which is difficult to achieve in highly specialized economies. The more goods there are, the more difficult it is to obtain a double coincidence of wants and the more exchange rates there are to negotiate. Money permits the separation of the decision to sell one good from the decision to buy another and permits more efficient exchange.

3. Money functions as a medium of exchange, a unit of account, and a store of value. As a medium of exchange, money facilitates exchange by separating the purchase of one commodity from the sale of another commodity. As a unit of account, money eliminates the need to establish exchange rates between all possible pairs of commodities. As a store of value, money permits people to hold their wealth in a convenient form.

4.   None of the items would be very good choices for money. The values of beads, tobacco, cattle, and cigarettes can vary widely as they are determined by the interaction of the supply and demand for each. Boulders would not be divisible, so paying for small items would be difficult. All the items listed have been used for money at some time in history, however.

5.   The quality of precious metals is hard to determine because of the possibility of adding cheaper metals. The government took over coinage to control the quality. There were still problems, however, because people scraped small amounts of the metal off coins to make extra money. The milling of the edges and the stamping of coins helped to reduce this problem.

6.   No. The value of the metal in the coins is too low to make clipping profitable. The coins are fiat money and not commodity money.

7.   A fractional reserve system is one in which banks do not keep enough reserves on hand to cover all possible withdrawals. Deposits and withdrawals tend to balance out, so a steady pool of funds remains available for lending. Banks make loans by creating demand deposits for borrowers and use their reserves to cover the relatively small portion of the demand deposits that is withdrawn. Bankers know that not all deposits will be withdrawn at any given time, so they can make the loans safely.

8.   No. Fiat money is money because the government says it is money. Paper money could be backed by commodities such as gold, in which case it would not be fiat money.

9.   Fiat money is accepted because the government declares it to be legal tender and because other people readily accept it. People would stop accepting fiat money if the value of the money fell substantially because of inflation or if they lost confidence in the government backing the money.

10. The value of fiat money is determined by its purchasing power—the rate at which it can be exchanged for goods and services. This rate is determined by the quantity of money that has been placed in circulation relative to the quantity of goods and services produced. When more money is created and the goods and services produced by the economy have not increased, the prices of the goods and services increase, which means that the value of money falls.

11. Too much money is associated with inflation, which makes it more costly to use markets. In this situation, it is difficult to determine whether a price change results from inflation or is only a relative price change. Under these conditions money fails to serve as a standard of value or a store of wealth. Economic actors expend resources trying to determine the source of a change in a price and to protect themselves from the effects of inflation. The economy becomes less productive. When there is too little money, people have a hard time making transactions that require money. Hence, they will either find an alternative to money, such as the money of another country or some commodity that serves as money, or they will engage in barter more frequently.

12. During wars, governments purchase many more goods and services than they do during peacetime. Because of the additional revenues required for the war effort, governments often use their power to coin and to print money to increase the amount of money in the economy; this leads to inflation.

13. The Federal Reserve System was created to stabilize the country's financial system. For many years the banking system experienced bank failures during recessions. The Fed is empowered to control the money supply by buying and selling government securities, by setting reserve requirements for member banks, and by being a lender of last resort to member banks.

14. Prior to the 1970s, banks were strictly regulated; they had little freedom and experienced little competition. Interest rate ceilings prevented depository institutions from competing for deposits by offering higher interest rates. Depository institutions also could not buy or sell corporate securities, and commercial banks generally did not compete for borrowers with thrifts.

15. Inflation and higher interest rates at other financial institutions caused depository institutions to lose deposits in the 1970s. As banks and thrifts lost deposits, they had to support their outstanding low-interest loans by borrowing at higher market interest rates. Thrifts were hardest hit because of the long-term nature of their loans. Further, new savings instruments such as money market funds were created and provided competition for deposits. Deregulation helped commercial banks and thrifts compete on a more equal footing with other financial institutions.

CHAPTER 14

Banking and the Money Supply

I. INTRODUCTION

In this chapter we examine how the Federal Reserve System controls the nation's money supply. The chapter covers the role of depository institutions as well as the types of deposits they hold. The following chapter examines the effect of money on the economy.

II. OUTLINE

1. Banks, Their Deposits, and the Money Supply

    1.1   Banks Are Financial Intermediaries
        a.   Banks serve as financial intermediaries by bringing borrowers and savers together.
        b.   The market for loans is characterized by asymmetric information—borrowers know their credit history better than the lenders.
        c.   Banks specialize in assessing information about prospective borrowers.
        d.   Banks minimize risk to each individual saver through diversification.

    1.2   The Narrow Definition of Money: M1
        a.   A deposit is a *liability* to the bank because the bank must promise to repay the depositor.
        b.   *Checkable deposits* are deposits against which checks can be written. They include demand deposits, NOW accounts, credit union share draft accounts, and the like.
        c.   Monetary aggregates are various measures of the money supply.
        d.   The narrowest definition of the money supply is *M1*, which consists of currency held by the nonbank public, checkable deposits, and travelers checks.
        e.   Checks are not legal tender, but they are so widely accepted as a medium of exchange that checkable deposits are considered part of the money supply.
        f.   Federal Reserve notes are liabilities of the Federal Reserve banks and provide the primary currency in the U. S. economy. The other component of currency is coins.

    1.3   *CASE STUDY:* Tracking the Supernote

    1.4   Broader Monetary Aggregates
        a.   Some other assets perform the standard-of-value and store-of-wealth functions of money.
        b.   The most important of these assets are:
            (1)   *Savings deposits* (or *passbook savings accounts*): deposits that earn interest but do not have a specific maturity
            (2)   *Time deposits*: deposits that earn a fixed amount of interest if held for a specified period of time

    (3) *Money market mutual fund accounts*: shares representing claims on a portfolio of short-term interest-earning assets

  c. The definition of money is often broadened to include some of these assets.

  d. Monetary aggregates are measures of money used by the Federal Reserve.

    (1) *M2* is M1 plus savings deposits, small-denomination time deposits, and money market mutual fund balances.

    (2) *M3* is M2 plus large-denomination time deposits.

  e. Credit cards are <u>not</u> money.

2. How Banks Work

2.1 Starting a Bank

a. To start a bank, the founders must have a charter from the U.S. Comptroller of the Currency in the case of a national bank or the state banking authority in the case of a state bank.

b. The owners invest funds in the bank in exchange for shares of stock in the bank. The value of that stock is the *owners' equity*, or net worth of the bank.

c. *Assets* are physical property and financial claims owned by the bank.

d. Assets must equal liabilities plus net worth.

e. *Liabilities* are claims on the bank by nonowners (for example, checkable deposits).

2.2 Reserve Accounts

a. *Reserves* are cash held in the bank's vault or deposits held at the Fed. They do not earn interest.

b. The *required reserve ratio* is set by the Fed and determines what fraction of deposits must be held as reserves.

c. *Required reserves* are the dollar amount the Fed requires banks to hold in reserve. Reserves must equal total deposits times the required reserve ratio.

d. *Excess reserves* are reserves in excess of required reserves and can be used to make loans or purchase interest-bearing assets.

2.3 Liquidity Versus Profitability

a. A bank must be prepared to satisfy depositors' demands for funds.

b. A bank loses reserves whenever a depositor demands cash or writes a check that is deposited in another bank.

c. Liquidity is the ease with which an asset can be converted to cash without a significant loss of value.

d. A bank wants to maintain sufficient liquidity to meet unexpected demands on its reserves or to make loans to valued customers.

e. A bank also wants to earn profits, which are generated by earning interest on loans and other assets.

f. Since the assets earning the highest interest rates tend to be the least liquid, the two objectives of liquidity and profitability are often at odds.

g. Banks can borrow in the federal funds market to meet temporary reserve deficiencies.

3. How Banks Create Money

3.1 Creating Money Through Excess Reserves

a. The Fed can create excess reserves by buying government securities on the open market, lending reserves to depository institutions through the discount window, or lowering the required reserve ratio.

b. Banks create money by loaning out excess reserves.

c. A bank makes a loan by creating a checkable deposit, which is money.

      d.   When the borrower writes a check that is deposited in another bank, the excess reserves of that bank are increased. That bank can lend the excess reserves out, creating more money.

      e.   An individual bank cannot lend out more than its excess reserves because borrowers usually spend the amount borrowed.

      f.   When a bank lends its excess reserves, the reserves do not leave the banking system. Thus the system can expand checkable deposits by a multiple of the initial increase in excess reserves.

3.2   Summary of Rounds

      a.   The banking system increases the money supply by a multiple of new reserves.

      b.   When a check clears, the reserves of one bank fall, but the drop in reserves is offset by an increase in the reserves of another bank.

      c.   Deposit expansion stops when the increase in required reserves resulting from the new deposits matches the initial increase in excess reserves.

      d.   The Fed could buy securities from a dealer instead of a bank, but the dealer would deposit the check into a bank and excess reserves would be created.

3.3   Excess Reserves, Reserve Requirements, and Money Expansion

      a.   Money creation requires the injection of excess reserves into the banking system.

      b.   Once additional excess reserves enter the system, the total possible expansion of the money supply equals the new excess reserves times the money multiplier.

      c.   The simple money multiplier equals $1/r$, where r is the required reserve ratio. It indicates the maximum possible expansion of the money supply from a given injection of excess reserves.

3.4   Limitations on Money Expansion

      a.   The money multiplier is reduced when people take cash out of the system or when banks hold excess reserves.

      b.   The Fed can make excess reserves available to banks, but cannot make banks extend loans or make people borrow.

3.5   Multiple Contraction of the Money Supply. A sale of government securities by the Fed has the opposite effect from a purchase of government securities by the Fed.

4.   Fed Tools of Monetary Control

4.1   Open-Market Operations. The Fed carries out open-market operations when it buys and sells government bonds in the open market. This process was described in the last section.

4.2   The Discount Rate

      a.   The discount rate is another tool of monetary policy.

      b.   A lower discount rate encourages more loans and expands the money supply.

      c.   A higher discount rate tends to decrease the money supply.

4.3   Reserve Requirements

      a.   Reserve requirements are regulations regarding the minimum amount of reserves banks must hold against deposits.

      b.   Reserve requirements influence how much money the banking system can create.

4.4   The Fed Is a Money Machine
   a.   Most of the Fed's assets are U.S. government bonds, which earn interest for the Fed.
   b.   Most of the Fed's liabilities are Federal Reserve notes, which pay no interest.
   c.   The Fed makes money on the interest received.
   d.   The Fed also "makes" money by supplying the economy with Federal Reserve notes.

4.5   *CASE STUDY:* Banking on the Net

III. DISCUSSION

Banks, Their Deposits, and the Money Supply

Savers and borrowers are not the same people. Most people who save want access to their funds. Thus, they do not want to lend their money directly to other people or firms. Instead, savers place their deposits in banks and other depository institutions; these institutions lend the funds out to borrowers and retain reserves to meet the withdrawal demands of their depositors. Banks serve as financial intermediaries, and the matching of savers and borrowers is called *intermediation*. This matching is an important function of banks. Banks specialize in making loans, so they develop expertise in evaluating loan applicants and monitoring contracts. This expertise makes it possible for banks to economize on the transaction and enforcement costs associated with loan agreements. Further, they are able to reduce the risk to individual savers by diversifying their loan portfolios.

From a macroeconomic standpoint, the importance of banks stems from their role in the creation of money. Deposits are *liabilities* to banks because they represent a promise to repay the depositor. Loans issued by the banks are *assets* because they represent the borrower's promise to repay funds to the bank. *Checkable deposits* are deposits against which checks can be written; the bank must be prepared to honor these liabilities. Checkable deposits are considered part of the money supply because checks are widely accepted as a medium of exchange. There are other assets that are very liquid, so they serve all the functions of money except that of a medium of exchange. The narrowest definition of the money supply, M1, encompasses currency held by the nonbank public, checkable deposits, and travelers checks. Broader definitions also include these other assets.

How Banks Work

Banks are businesses, and their stockholders expect them to earn profits like other businesses. Although banks earn income by charging fees for checking and savings accounts, check-cashing services, safe deposit boxes, and travelers checks, the biggest source of bank profits is the interest earned on loans and other assets. As stated earlier, banks bring together savers and borrowers. This suggests that we can examine banks from the perspective of their sources of funds and their uses of funds.

In general terms, banks have three sources of funds: deposits, borrowing, and owners' equity. Deposits include checkable deposits, savings deposits, and time deposits. Borrowing includes borrowing from the Fed or in the federal funds market. Owners' equity, or *net worth*, refers initially to the investment by the founders of the bank. Over time, it is measured as the difference between the assets of the bank and the liabilities of the bank. Deposits and borrowings are liabilities of the bank.

Bankers use double-entry bookkeeping. Threfore, the sum of assets must be equal in value to the sum of liabilities and owners' equity. Assets tend to be created or purchased as the bank uses the funds it has raised. A bank has numerous uses for its funds; these uses include purchasing buildings and furnishings, making loans, purchasing government securities, purchasing stock in the Fed if the bank is a member bank, making deposits with the Fed, and maintaining cash on hand.

This discussion of bank assets and liabilities illustrates the fact that one person's assets are another's liabilities. Checkable deposits are assets to the depositor but liabilities to the bank; the bank's deposits at the Fed are assets to the bank and liabilities to the Fed. Further, loans made by the bank are assets to the bank and liabilities to the borrowers.

Exhibit 1 shows a *balance sheet* for a new bank that has not yet accepted deposits or extended loans. The right-hand side lists liabilities and net worth, which at this stage includes the amount of $2,000,000 raised by the initial investors. The assets side includes $1,400,000 for buildings and furnishings; $500,000 in stock in the Federal Reserve bank; and $100,000 in cash. At this point the bank has nothing to generate a profit and has only $100,000 to work with. It can use the $100,000 in cash to buy government securities and earn a return, but the investors could have done this directly. To generate profits, the bank must attract deposits and create loans that generate returns greater than those the investors could earn in the capital markets.

Exhibit 1

Assets		*Liabilities and Net Worth*	
Buildings and furnishings	$1,400,000	Net worth	$2,000,000
Stock in Fed	500,000		
Cash	100,000		
Total	$2,000,000	Total	$2,000,000

The fundamental trade-off between *liquidity* and profitability is illustrated in Exhibit 2. The bank has received checkable deposits of $3,000,000. The bank has placed $300,000 of the funds on deposit with the Fed and has kept $2,700,000 in cash. The bank must always be ready to convert checkable deposits to cash whenever depositors write checks against their checkable deposits. Since the bank knows that not all deposits will be demanded at once, it does not need to keep cash on hand to cover the entire $3,000,000 in checkable deposits. Neither the cash on hand nor the deposits in the Fed earn interest, so the bank must find other uses for at least some of these funds in order to make a profit. The more funds that are used in profit-making activities, the fewer funds the bank has available to cover checks written against the checkable deposits. On one hand, the bank wants to keep funds available in the event that checks are written against checkable deposits; on the other hand, the bank wants to use the funds in profit-making activities. The more the bank leans toward making profits, the less liquid it is; the more liquid the bank, the lower its profitability.

Exhibit 2

Assets		Liabilities and Net Worth	
Buildings and furnishings	$1,400,000	Checkable deposits	$3,000,000
Stock in Fed	500,000	Net worth	2,000,000
Deposits at Fed	300,000		
Cash	$2,800,000		
Total	$5,000,000	Total	$5,000,000

The bank generates profits by using its funds to make loans and investments. Loans vary in duration, risk, and size, and the interest earned will depend on these factors. Interest rates tend to be greater the longer the loan period and the riskier the borrower. Hence, to enhance profitability, the bank may want to generate many long-term loans to risky individuals and firms. The bank still must be concerned about liquidity, however, and a portfolio of loans that are all long term will reduce the bank's liquidity considerably. Further, high-risk loans will have a higher default rate, which the bank will not want either. Thus, the bank will attempt to structure its assets to generate profitability but in ways that do not decrease liquidity or increase risk beyond acceptable levels. Keep in mind, too, that the bank can borrow from the Fed or in the federal funds market if it runs short of cash to cover checks written against checkable deposits.

The Federal Reserve requires banks to keep a portion of their deposits as reserves. The balance sheet in Exhibit 2 shows that the bank has $3,100,000 in reserves, since reserves include cash held in the bank's vault ($2,800,000) and the bank's deposits with the Fed ($300,000). If the *required reserve ratio* is 20 percent, then the *required reserves* are $600,000 ($3,000,000 × 0.2) and *excess reserves* are $2,500,000. The bank can lend up to $2,500,000 to individuals or businesses. If actual reserves fall below $600,000, the bank will have to call in some loans or borrow from either the Fed or the federal funds market.

Checkable deposits are part of the money supply, but what about the cash held in the bank's vault? It is not part of the money supply, and neither are the deposits the bank holds at the Fed. The money supply as measured by *M1* (a *monetary aggregate*) includes currency in the hands of the nonbank public, deposits in checkable accounts, and travelers checks. Money is not created when depositors deposit currency in their checking accounts. When this happens, money in the form of currency is merely converted into money in the form of checkable deposits. The same is true when a depositor removes cash from a checkable deposit: money in the form of a checkable deposit is converted into currency. But banks can create money because they are able to lend money.

How Banks Create Money

In our discussion of Exhibit 2, we noted that the bank can use $2,500,000 to make investments or to extend loans. Suppose it loans $1,000,000 to a business. The loan creates an asset for the bank—the business's promissory note—and creates a new liability—the business's checkable deposits of $1,000,000. Exhibit 3 shows the bank's balance sheet after it makes the loan to the business. Total checkable deposits are now $4,000,000, so required reserves equal $800,000 and excess reserves are $2,300,000.

Chapter 14

Exhibit 3

Assets		Liabilities and Net Worth	
Buildings and furnishings	$1,400,000	Checkable deposits	$4,000,000
Stock in Fed	500,000	Net worth	2,000,000
Deposits at Fed	300,000		
Cash	$2,800,000		
Loan	1,000,000		
Total	$6,000,000	Total	$6,000,000

What has happened to the money supply as a result of the loan? The newly created checkable deposits are part of the money supply, so the money supply has increased by $1,000,000. By creating checkable deposits for the business that borrowed funds, the bank created an additional amount of money equal to the amount of the loan. The bank did not merely alter the form of the money; it actually increased the quantity of money in the economy. The business can spend the $1,000,000 just as it could if it had created the checkable deposit by depositing its own $1,000,000 in cash in the bank.

Suppose the business spends the loan on equipment. It pays for the equipment by writing a check for $1,000,000, and the supplier deposits the check in another bank. Once the check has cleared, the first bank's checkable deposits fall back to $3,000,000, its required reserves fall to $600,000, its total reserves fall to $2,100,000, and its excess reserves fall to $1,500,000. Now the maximum loan the bank can make is $1,500,000. Exhibit 4 shows changes in the balance sheet of the bank that received the $1,000,000 deposit. Its checkable deposits have increased by $1,000,000, and its deposits at the Fed have increased by $1,000,000. If the bank had zero excess reserves before, it now has $800,000 in excess reserves and $200,000 in additional required reserves. This means that the bank can loan up to $800,000. If it does so, checkable deposits and therefore the money supply will increase by $800,000. If the $800,000 ends up in a third bank, then that bank can extend additional loans up to $640,000. This process can continue as long as deposits in a bank generate excess reserves for the bank.

Exhibit 4

Assets		Liabilities and Net Worth	
Deposits in Fed	+$1,000,000	Checkable deposits	+$1,000,000

The money-creating ability of banks is limited by the quantity of excess reserves in the banking system. If the banking system receives an increase in excess reserves of $1,000,000, the money supply can increase by $1,000,000 times the *money multiplier*. The *simple money multiplier* is $1/r$, where r is the required reserve ratio; that is, the simple money multiplier is the reciprocal of the required reserve ratio. In our example, the money multiplier is $1/0.20 = 5$. That is, the money supply can increase by $5,000,000 when the banking system receives an injection of $1,000,000 in excess reserves.

Fed Tools of Monetary Control

The Fed controls the nation's money supply through its ability to control the quantity of excess reserves. The Fed can increase excess reserves by lowering the reserve requirement or by purchasing government securities from banks or the public. It can also encourage additional bank lending by lowering the discount rate; this allows banks to hold fewer excess reserves and borrow from the Fed at more favorable terms when they experience temporary shortages of required reserves. The Fed relies primarily on the buying and selling of government securities to control the money supply.

IV. LAGNIAPPE

Liability Management and the Profitability–Liquidity Trade-Off

In the past, banks operated very conservatively and worked hard at maintaining liquidity. Liquidity was achieved by stocking up on such liquid assets as short-term government securities. Beginning in the 1960s, banks altered their behavior and began relying increasingly on liabilities to maintain liquidity rather than on assets. Banks would take on short-term liabilities, such as loans in the federal funds market or repurchase agreements, to maintain liquidity, which allowed them to earn higher interest on their reserves by using them to extend longer-term loans. As inflation and interest rates increased, banks did not want to be holding only short-term government securities— the opportunity costs of doing so were too great. Instead, they extended loans that generated higher interest payments and handled short-term liquidity problems by borrowing in the federal funds market or by entering the negotiable CD market.

Question to Think About: Does the change in banking behavior imply that deposits in banks are not as safe today as they were 30 years ago?

Cash, Excess Reserves, and Money Creation

Banks generally cannot create money to the extent implied by the simple money multiplier for two reasons. First, people usually carry some money in the form of currency. When a bank makes a loan and creates checkable deposits for a borrower and the borrower writes a check against the checkable deposits, the recipient of the check may not deposit the entire amount in his or her checking account. Instead, the recipient may hold some of the amount in cash and deposit the rest. Consequently, the deposit in the second bank is less than the check written against the checkable deposits in the first bank, and there has been a loss of reserves to the banking system. Second, banks generally do not loan out all of their excess reserves. Instead, they often hold a fraction of their excess reserves to protect against an unexpected demand for reserves.

Question to Think About: What factors are likely to affect a bank's decision concerning the amount of excess reserves to maintain?

V. KEY TERMS

asymmetric information
checkable deposits
monetary aggregates
M1
savings deposits
time deposits
M2
liquidity

M3
net worth
balance sheet
asset
liability
required reserve ratio
required reserves
excess reserves

federal funds market
federal funds rate
money multiplier
simple money multiplier
open-market operations
discount rate
open-market purchase
open-market sale

VI. QUESTIONS

A. Completion

1. The market for loanable funds is characterized by _____ because lenders do not know the reliability of borrowers as well as borrowers know themselves.

2. Banks serve as financial _____ when they bring savers and borrowers together.

3. Money consists primarily of _____.

4. M1 is made up of _____, _____, and _____.

5. Time deposits are not considered money because they do not function as a _____.

6. The proportion of deposits that must be held in reserve by banks is called the _____.

7. The two conflicting objectives of a bank are _____ and _____.

8. _____ are required for monetary expansion to occur.

9. A customer's deposit is a _____ to a depository institution.

10. _____ measures the ease with which any asset can be converted into the medium of exchange without a significant loss of value.

11. A bank can borrow the excess reserves of another bank in the _____ market.

12. A depository institution's deposits at the Fed are _____ to the Fed and _____ to the depository institution.

13. The maximum amount that an individual depository institution can loan out equals the amount of its _____.

14. The _____ equals the reciprocal of the required reserve ratio.

15. Borrowing from the Fed is cheaper when the Fed lowers the _____ rate.

B. True/False

_____ 1. Banks specialize in information so they know more about the reliability of a potential borrower than the borrower knows.

_____ 2. Finance companies get part of their funds from depositors.

_____ 3. Banks reduce the risk to each individual saver by choosing a diversified portfolio of assets.

_____ 4. Checkable deposits are liabilities and time deposits are assets to depository institutions.

_____ 5. Both checks and currency are legal tender.

_____ 6. The most liquid asset is currency.

_____ 7. Money market mutual fund accounts are part of M2.

_____ 8. The two sides of the balance sheet must always be equal.

_____ 9. A deposit by a customer increases the bank's assets and net worth.

_____ 10. A bank can only loan out its required reserves.

_____ 11. The greater the required reserve ratio, other things constant, the greater the excess reserves.

_____ 12. Banks can meet an unexpected demand for reserves by selling some short-term assets.

_____ 13. Generally speaking, the more liquid the bank, the more profitable the bank.

_____ 14. The Fed puts reserves into the banking system when it sells government securities.

_____ 15. Banks create money by converting IOUs into checkable deposits.

_____ 16. A flow of excess reserves into the banking system can generate an increase in the money supply of no more than the increase in excess reserves.

_____ 17. When a check clears, the reserves of the entire banking system are reduced.

_____ 18. The smaller the required reserve ratio, other things constant, the larger the simple money multiplier.

_____ 19. The actual money multiplier tends to be larger than the simple money multiplier.

_____ 20. The Fed often buys and sells securities issued by foreign governments.

C. Multiple Choice

1. Which of the following would lead to a problem of asymmetric information?
   a. A borrower will have a difficult time repaying a loan if she loses her job.
   b. A borrower defaulted on a loan two years ago.
   c. A borrower does not know which bank is offering the lowest interest rates.
   d. A borrower knows he will soon be out of work and does not tell the bank.
   e. All of the above.

2. Which of the following are important functions of depository institutions?
   a. serving as intermediaries
   b. reducing risk to individual savers by holding diversified portfolios of assets
   c. specializing in making loans so that the costs of evaluating alternative loan applicants are reduced
   d. All of the above.
   e. a and b

3. According to the narrowest definition, money includes
   a. legal tender only.
   b. currency and coins held by the nonbank public only.
   c. currency and coins held by the nonbank public, checkable deposits, and credit card balances.
   d. currency and coins held by the nonbank public, checkable deposits, and travelers checks.
   e. checkable deposits only.

4. Federal Reserve notes are IOUs of the Fed and can be exchanged for
   a. gold.
   b. government securities.
   c. other Federal Reserve notes.
   d. silver.
   e. None of the above.

5. Which of the following assets is the most liquid?
   a. time deposits
   b. checkable deposits
   c. nonnegotiable certificates of deposit
   d. land
   e. savings accounts

6. The amount of money in the economy (defined as M1) increases when
   a. an individual cashes a check written by a business.
   b. an individual purchases clothes with a credit card.
   c. an individual switches funds from a savings account to a checking account.
   d. a bank buys a piece of furniture by writing a check.
   e. All of the above.

7. Which of the following is not included in M2?
   a. large-denomination time deposits
   b. money market mutual funds
   c. checking accounts
   d. currency held by the nonbank public
   e. a and b

8. Among a bank's liabilities is
   a. its net worth.
   b. the cash held by the bank.
   c. checkable deposits.
   d. its stock in the Fed.
   e. its deposits at the Fed.

9. Legal reserves include
   a. a bank's deposits at the Fed.
   b. a bank's government securities.
   c. stock in the Fed.
   d. business loans.
   e. a, b, and c.

10. A bank's required reserves will increase and its excess reserves fall when
    a. the required reserve ratio is increased.
    b. a customer makes a deposit in a checking account.
    c. a customer repays a loan.
    d. the bank sells a government security to the Fed.
    e. a borrower defaults on a loan.

11. A bank manager can increase the bank's liquidity by
    a. increasing its reserves.
    b. buying short-term government securities with the funds provided when a mortgage is paid off.
    c. borrowing in the federal funds market.
    d. buying a new computer system.
    e. a, b, and c.

12. Among the liabilities of the Federal Reserve System are
    a. Federal Reserve notes.
    b. deposits of the U.S. Treasury.
    c. deposits of banks.
    d. deposits of thrifts.
    e. All of the above.

13. The Fed can decrease bank reserves by
    a. lowering the discount rate.
    b. lowering the required reserve ratio.
    c. selling government securities.
    d. destroying old Federal Reserve notes.
    e. None of the above.

14. The supernote is
    a. the largest denomination of American currency.
    b. a reference to the Fed's ability to produce money.
    c. a $100 bill made by the Fed but used in Europe.
    d. a counterfeit $100 bill of high quality.
    e. None of the above.

15. When a person deposits a check drawn on another bank into a checking account, the
    a. reserves of the entire banking system increase.
    b. reserves of the bank where the deposit is made are unchanged.
    c. money supply decreases.
    d. reserves of the entire banking system are unchanged, but the reserves of the bank in which the deposit is made increase and reserves of the other bank decrease.
    e. money supply increases.

16. The money-creating ability of the banking system will be less than indicated by the simple money multiplier when
    a. interest rates are high.
    b. banks decide to hold excess reserves.
    c. people hold a portion of their money in the form of currency.
    d. All of the above.
    e. b and c

17. The maximum amount that an individual bank can loan out is the
    a. value of its excess reserves times the money multiplier.
    b. sum of its excess reserves and its vault cash.
    c. value of its excess reserves times the reserve ratio.
    d. sum of the checkable deposits and time deposits held by the bank.
    e. value of its excess reserves.

18. The reserves of the entire banking system will fall when
    a. an individual pulls cash out of a checking account.
    b. an individual deposits a check drawn on another bank.
    c. the Fed burns old, worn-out Federal Reserve notes.
    d. the Fed increases the required reserve ratio.
    e. All of the above.

19. A bank can replenish reserves by
    a. extending more loans at a higher rate of interest.
    b. recalling outstanding loans.
    c. increasing its vault cash by drawing down its deposits at the Fed.
    d. repaying loans to the Fed.
    e. None of the above.

20. The Fed can pursue a tight monetary policy by
    a. selling government securities.
    b. raising the discount rate.
    c. raising the reserve requirement.
    d. All of the above.
    e. None of the above.

Banking and the Money Supply

D. Discussion Questions

1. Explain how banks are financial intermediaries.

2. Explain why "d" is the correct answer to multiple choice Question 1 and why choices "a" through "c" are incorrect.

3. Explain how a checkable deposit can be both an asset and a liability.

4. What is the difference between money and other assets that are similar to money?

5. What are the differences among the various monetary aggregates?

6. Discuss the competing objectives of a bank: liquidity and profitability.

7. The text states that the Fed is both literally and figuratively a money machine. Explain why this is true.

8. Suppose three banks have zero excess reserves. Show how each bank's balance sheet changes as a result of the following transactions. (Assume that the banks always carry zero excess reserves and that the reserve ratio is 0.2.)
   a. Mr. Smith deposits $1,000 in his checking account in Bank A. Mrs. Jones then borrows all she can from the bank.
   b. Mrs. Jones uses her loan to buy furniture from the Acme Furniture Co., which deposits the check from Mrs. Jones into Bank B.
   c. Ms. Anderson borrows all she can from Bank B and buys a used car from the Fly-by-Night Auto Co., which deposits the check from Ms. Anderson in Bank C.
   d. Bank C buys a government security from the Fed with all of its excess reserves.

9. By how much does the money supply change as a result of the transactions described in Question 8? If Bank C had also made a loan instead of buying the government security and the process had continued, what is the maximum amount of money the banking system could have created?

10. What are reserves? What are excess reserves? Explain how the Fed can affect the quantity of excess reserves in the banking system.

11. Explain why an individual bank can increase the money supply by the amount of its excess reserves, whereas the banking system as a whole can increase the money supply by a multiple of its excess reserves.

12. Explain how the money multiplier can actually be smaller than the reciprocal of the reserve ratio.

13. Explain why the Fed can be more confident of its ability to contract the money supply than of its ability to expand the money supply through credit expansion.

14. How can the Fed affect the money supply by using the discount rate?

VII. ANSWERS

A. Completion

1. asymmetric information
2. intermediaries
3. checkable deposits
4. checkable deposits, currency held by the nonbank public, travelers checks
5. medium of exchange
6. required reserve ratio
7. liquidity; profitablilty
8. Excess reserves
9. liability
10. Liquidity
11. federal funds
12. liabilities; assets
13. excess reserves
14. simple money multiplier
15. discount

B. True/False

1. False
2. False
3. True
4. False
5. False
6. True
7. True
8. True
9. False
10. False
11. False
12. True
13. False
14. False. Reserves fall when the Fed sells government securities
15. True
16. False
17. False
18. True
19. False
20. True

C. Multiple Choice

1. d
2. d
3. d
4. c
5. b
6. c
7. a
8. c
9. a
10. a
11. e
12. e
13. c
14. d
15. d
16. e
17. e
18. a
19. b
20. d

D. Discussion Questions

1. Banks bring together two sides of the market—those who want to save and those who want to borrow. Then they act as a go-between, or a financial intermediary.

2. The idea of asymmetric information is that information held by one party to a transaction is not held by the other party. Answer "d" describes a situation in which the borrower knows something the bank cannot know unless the borrower provides the information. Answers "a" and "b" describe situations in which information is known by both parties or can be known with a normal credit check. The situation in answer "c" does not involve asymmetric information since the borrower can obtain the information by contacting a number of banks.

3. A checkable deposit is a liability to the bank because the bank must pay out the funds if a check is drawn on the account. It is an asset to the depositor because he or she can draw on the account at any time.

4. Some financial assets have some, but not all, of the characteristics of money. In particular, they are like money except that they do not serve as a medium of exchange. These assets are less liquid than currency and checkable deposits.

5. M1 includes checkable deposits, currency held by the nonbank public, and travelers checks. The other monetary aggregates include other financial assets. M2 includes M1 plus savings deposits, small-denomination time deposits, and money market mutual funds. M3 includes M2 plus large-denomination time deposits.

6. A bank is a business designed to make profits. To make profits, banks must use reserves in profit-making ways, such as purchasing securities or other assets and extending loans that earn interest. Loans and assets that earn high interest tend not to be very liquid, however. Banks must also be prepared to satisfy depositors' requests for funds. If a bank does not do so, it could fail. The more the bank tries to be liquid, the lower its profits. The more the bank strives for profits, the less liquid it is and the greater the possibility of bank failure.

7. The Fed provides the economy with Federal Reserve notes, which are part of the money supply; that is, it literally creates paper money. The Fed also earns interest with its assets but pays no interest on its liabilities, so the Fed makes a profit, which is turned over to the U.S. Treasury. This creates money in the figurative sense.

8. a. Bank A:

Assets		Liabilities and Net Worth	
Deposits at Fed	+$1,000	Checkable Deposits	+$1,800
Loan	+ 800		
	+$1,800		

b. Bank A:

Assets		Liabilities and Net Worth	
Deposits at Fed	+$ 200	Checkable Deposits	+$1,000
Loan	+ 800		
	+$1,000		

Bank B:

Assets		Liabilities and Net Worth	
Deposits at Fed	+$800	Checkable Deposits	+$800

c. Bank B:

Assets		Liabilities and Net Worth	
Deposits at Fed	+$160	Checkable Deposits	+$800
Loan	+ 640		
	+$800		

Bank C:

Assets		Liabilities and Net Worth	
Deposits at Fed	+ $640	Checkable Deposits	+ $640

d. Bank C:	Assets		Liabilities and Net Worth	
Deposits at Fed	+$128		Checkable Deposits	+$640
Loan	+ 512			
	+$640			

9. The money supply increased by $800 in part a of Question 8 and by $640 in part c of Question 8, a total increase of $1,440. The maximum amount of money that could have been created is the product of the initial increase in excess reserves and the simple money multiplier, or

$$\$800 \times (1/r) = \$800 \times (1/0.02) = \$800 \times 5 = \$4,000.$$

10. Reserves are made up of the cash a bank holds in its vault and the bank's deposits in the Fed. Excess reserves are reserves in excess of the quantity required by the Fed. The Fed can affect the quantity of excess reserves by buying or selling government securities. If it sells government securities to banks, for example, the banks pay for them with reserves, so they have fewer reserves. The Fed can also change the required reserve ratio, which directly affects required reserves and excess reserves. It can also change the discount rate. The lower the discount rate, the cheaper it is for banks to borrow reserves in case they find themselves with no excess reserves and the more likely they are to lend a greater proportion of the reserves they have on hand.

11. An individual bank can increase the money supply only by the amount of its excess reserves because it can make loans only with its excess reserves. The bank must operate on the assumption that a borrower will spend a loan and the check will be deposited in another bank, in which case the first bank has no more excess reserves to use in creating money. On the other hand, a check written on one bank and deposited in another stays within the banking system as a whole. That is, the excess reserves of the entire banking system can support a greater expansion of money because the reserves are never lost to the banking system.

12. The money multiplier is smaller than $1/r$ when people hold some of their loans in the form of currency and when banks decide to hold more reserves than required by the Fed.

13. The Fed can be certain that it can successfully restrict credit by pursuing a tighter credit policy since banks must hold required reserves in the amount dictated by the Fed. The Fed cannot force banks to lend out excess reserves, however, so when the Fed wishes to pursue an expansionary policy it cannot be certain that the banks will lend the excess reserves to borrowers.

14. Banks can borrow from the Fed if their excess reserves are depleted, and they pay the Fed an interest rate equal to the discount rate. If the discount rate is low, banks can loan more of their excess reserves because they can borrow cheaply if their reserves fall below the required level. Higher discount rates increase the cost of allowing reserves to fall below the required level. Therefore, banks are more likely to lend more of their excess reserves when the discount rate is low than when the discount rate is high.

CHAPTER 15

Monetary Theory and Policy

I.   INTRODUCTION

In the previous two chapters, we examined the functions of money, how the banking system creates money, and how the Fed controls the money supply. In this chapter, we turn to a discussion of monetary theory and monetary policy. We examine the effects of changes in the money supply on the economy and then discuss the possible policies the government can pursue in trying to achieve full employment and stable prices. Other macroeconomic policy issues are addressed in the following two chapters.

II.   OUTLINE

1.   Money and the Economy: The Indirect Channel. Money and income are not the same thing. Money is a stock variable and is measured at a particular point in time. Income is a flow variable and is measured over a period of time. The demand for money is a demand for cash balances in the form of checking accounts, currency, or travelers checks to carry out transactions. The demand for money is a demand for a stock—a desire to hold some amount of money. The phrase *demand for money* does *not* refer to a desire for more income or wealth.

   1.1   The Demand for Money
      a.   Money allows people to carry out their transactions more easily.
      b.   The demand for money is affected by:
         (1)   The number of transactions to be financed over a given period
         (2)   The average selling price of each unit of output
      c.   People hold money to finance both anticipated and unanticipated exchanges.
      d.   Money is also a store of wealth, and people demand money in order to store purchasing power for future expenditures.
      e.   People can store their purchasing power in the form of money or in the form of some other financial asset.
      f.   Money's advantage as a store of wealth derives from its liquidity.
      g.   The opportunity cost of holding money is the interest that is forgone when money is not placed in assets that earn more interest.

   1.2   Money Demand and Interest Rates
      a.   The lower the interest rate, the lower the opportunity cost of holding money, so the larger the fraction of wealth people hold as money.
      b.   The quantity of money demanded varies inversely with the real interest rate, other things constant.
      c.   The money demand curve shows the quantity of money demanded at alternative interest rates.
      d.   The price level and the level of real GDP are held constant along a money demand curve. An increase in the level of prices or real GDP shifts the money demand curve to the right.

1.3   Supply of Money and the Equilibrium Interest Rate
   a.   For the most part, the Fed determines the supply of money.
   b.   The money supply curve is vertical if we make the simplifying assumption that the quantity supplied is independent of the interest rate.
   c.   The intersection of the money demand curve and the money supply curve determines the equilibrium interest rate.
   d.   When demand for money is held constant, increases in the money supply lower interest rates and decreases in the money supply raise interest rates.

2.   Money and Aggregate Demand

   2.1   Interest Rates and Planned Investment
      a.   Investment spending is the component of aggregate demand that is most affected by changes in interest rates.
      b.   Monetary policy affects interest rates, which affects the level of planned investment.
      c.   An increase in the money supply lowers interest rates, which induces increased investment spending and increased aggregate demand.
      d.   As long as investment is sensitive to changes in the interest rate and the interest rate is sensitive to changes in the money supply, changes in the money supply can alter planned investment.

   2.2   Adding Aggregate Supply
      a.   An increase in the money supply causes aggregate demand to increase.
      b.   Because the aggregate supply curve slopes upward, an increase in the money supply that leads to an increase in aggregate demand also generates a higher price level.
      c.   The steeper the aggregate supply curve for a given shift in aggregate demand, the smaller the increase in real GDP and the larger the increase in the price level.
      d.   The Fed can attempt to close a contractionary gap with an expansionary monetary policy.

   2.3   Fiscal Policy with Money
      a.   In the short run, an increase in government spending leads to an increase in both the level of real output and the price level.
      b.   An increase in either real output or the price level leads to an increase in the demand for money.
      c.   An increase in the demand for money, when the supply of money is held constant, leads to higher interest rates, which cause a reduction in investment spending and dampen the effect of fiscal policy on real output.
      d.   Consequently, the simple spending multiplier overstates the increase in real output generated by any given fiscal stimulus.

3.   Money and the Economy: The Direct Channel.
   a.   In the direct channel, money is seen as an asset that can be a store of value and can be similar to other financial real assets.
   b.   An increase in the money supply makes the quantity supplied exceed the quantity demanded at the initial interest rate, so people try to reduce their holdings of money.
   c.   When people attempt to reduce their monetary holdings, they increase their demand for all types of assets, real and financial, which directly increases aggregate demand.

3.1 The Equation of Exchange
   a. The *equation of exchange* is $M \times V = P \times Y$, where M is the money supply, V is the velocity of money, P is the price level, and Y is real GDP.
   b. The *velocity of money* is the average number of times per year each dollar is used to purchase final goods and services.
   c. The equation of exchange is an identity, not a theory.

3.2 The Quantity Theory of Money
   a. Monetarists argue that the velocity of money changes very little in the short run, and any changes that do occur are predictable. Thus, the equation of exchange can be used to predict the effects of changes in the money supply on nominal income, $P \times Y$.
   b. If the velocity of money is stable, then changes in the money supply must lead to proportional changes in nominal income.
   c. Whether a change in the money supply leads to a change in real output or a change in the price level depends on the shape of the aggregate supply curve.
   d. In the long run, changes in the money supply lead to changes in the price level only. The economy's potential output is not influenced by changes in the money supply.
   e. Monetarists caution that there are time lags of variable and uncertain length in the process. Consequently, monetary policy is a poor tool for changing nominal income.

3.3 *CASE STUDY:* The Money Supply and Inflation

3.4 What Determines the Velocity of Money?
   a. Customs and conventions of commerce, such as the use of credit cards
   b. The frequency with which people are paid
   c. The effectiveness of money as a store of wealth

3.5 How Stable Is Velocity?
   a. From 1915 to 1947, velocity of M1 fluctuated greatly, with a downward trend.
   b. Velocity of M1 was more stable from 1947 to 1979, but with an upward trend.
   c. Since 1979, velocity of M1 has been more erratic, making the equation of exchange a less reliable predictor of the effects of a change in M1 on nominal GDP.
   d. The velocity of M2 has been more stable than the velocity of M1.

4. Money Supply versus Interest Rate Targets. According to the indirect channel, monetary policy affects the economy via its effect on interest rates. The monetarist view is that monetary policy has a direct effect on aggregate demand. Thus, there is much debate over whether monetary authorities should target interest rates or the stock of money.

4.1 Contrasting Policies
   a. If there is a change in the demand for money, monetary authorities can either do nothing, thereby keeping the money stock constant and letting the interest rate change, or they can try to keep the interest rate constant by changing the money supply.
   b. Monetary authorities cannot keep both the money stock and the interest rate constant.
   c. Interest rate fluctuations can be undesirable if they create similar fluctuations in investment. However, changes in the money supply designed to stabilize interest rates tend to reinforce fluctuations in economic activity, adding instability to the economy.

4.2 Targets until 1982
  a. Between the end of World War II and October 1979, the Fed tried to stabilize interest rates.
  b. In October 1979, the Fed announced it would de-emphasize targeting interest rates and focus more on targets for monetary growth.
  c. In October 1982, the Fed announced it would pay attention to both interest rates and money growth.

4.3 Targets after 1982
  a. The rapid pace of financial innovations and deregulation make it difficult to measure the money supply.
  b. In recent years, the Fed has used short-term interest rates as the instrument of monetary policy.
  c. The Fed tracks a variety of indicators of inflationary pressure.

4.4 *CASE STUDY:* The World of Finance

5. Conclusion. The model that focuses on the indirect channel sees money supply changes as primarily affecting aggregate demand through changes in interest rates. Monetarists see changes in the money supply as more directly affecting prices and output.

III. DISCUSSION

Monetary theory is concerned with the effects of the quantity of money on the economy's price level and the level of real output. There is considerable debate among economists concerning what these effects are. One difficulty in determining the effects is that *monetary policy* changes and fiscal policy changes often occur at the same time, so it is difficult to sort out the effects of one from those of the other. This chapter describes two views of how money affects the economy: an indirect channel and a direct channel.

Money and the Economy: The Indirect Channel

A person's demand for money is not the same as the person's desire for a greater income. When economists speak of a demand for money, they are referring to the desire to hold a particular amount of money, either in checking accounts or as cash. That is, the *demand for money* is a demand to hold a stock of money at a particular time. Since money is used to facilitate exchange of goods and services and people engage in exchange on a regular basis, people hold money balances. The demand for money is greater the greater the number of transactions (as measured by real GDP) and the higher the average price at which each good is sold, that is, the greater nominal GDP.

Money also competes with other financial assets as a store of wealth. Compared with other financial assets, money has one major advantage and one major disadvantage. Money's advantage is its liquidity—it can be directly exchanged for goods and services. Its disadvantage is that it earns either no interest or substantially less interest than other financial assets. The opportunity cost of holding money is the additional interest that could have been earned by using the money to buy alternative interest-bearing financial assets. Consequently, the cost of holding money increases with the real interest rate, and we expect the demand for money to vary inversely with the real interest rate, other things constant. That is, the demand curve for money slopes downward when real interest rates are on the vertical axis.

The supply of money in the economy is determined primarily by the Fed, so we make the simplifying assumption that the quantity of money supplied is constant no matter what the interest rate is. Hence, the supply curve for money is a vertical line at whatever quantity of money the Fed has determined. Exhibit 1 illustrates the money market. The demand for money slopes down, as mentioned, and the supply curve for money is perfectly inelastic. Suppose that the supply of money is indicated initially by supply curve S. The intersection of the two curves determines the equilibrium interest rate, 10 percent. An increase in the supply of money shifts the supply curve to S' and generates a lower equilibrium interest rate, 6 percent; an increase in the demand for money generates a higher interest rate.

Exhibit 1

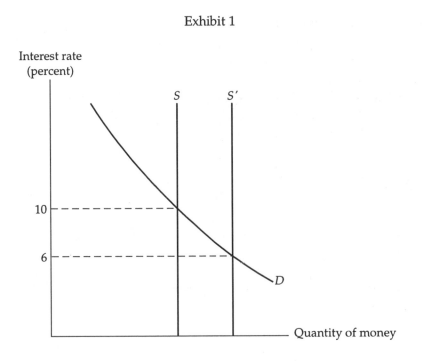

Money and Aggregate Demand

If money is to affect aggregate demand, it must do so by affecting one of several things: consumption spending, investment spending, government spending, or net exports. As we have just seen, changes in the supply of money cause changes in interest rates. In the model that uses the indirect channel, then, monetary policy affects aggregate demand indirectly by influencing the market rate of interest, which affects the level of planned investment.

Suppose the Fed wants to pursue a tight monetary policy and reduce the supply of money. The Fed can reduce the money supply by raising the discount rate, selling government securities, or raising the required reserve ratio. Regardless of which method is used, the money supply curve shifts to the left and the market rate increases. In Exhibit 2, the higher interest rate causes a movement along the demand curve for investment and the level of investment falls. The top half of Exhibit 3 shows how in this situation the $C + I + G + NX$ curve (where NX refers to net exports) shifts down to $C + I' + G + NX$, generating a lower level of real GDP demanded. As a result, aggregate demand shifts to the left, as shown in the lower half of Exhibit 3.

Exhibit 2

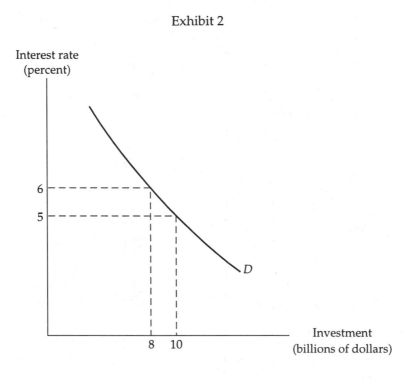

Exhibit 3

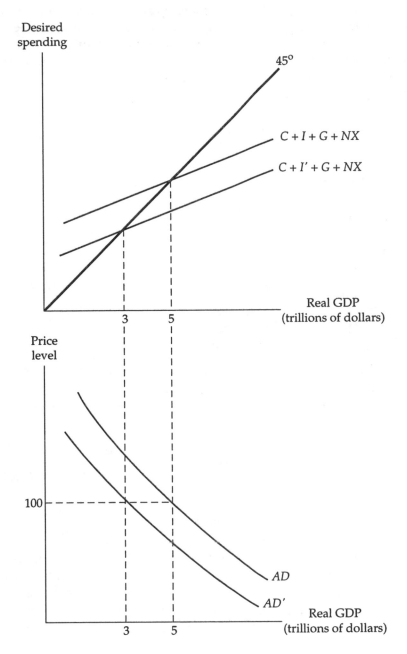

The shifts in the curves in Exhibit 3 are not the end of the story. The aggregate supply curve slopes upward, so the ultimate effects of a change in the money supply are partially determined by the shape of the aggregate supply curve. Exhibit 4 shows the bottom part of Exhibit 3 with a short-run aggregate supply curve added. At the original price level, 100, there is an excess supply after the aggregate demand curve shifts from *AD* to *AD'*. The excess supply causes prices to fall until equilibrium is reached at price level 90 and real GDP of $4 trillion. Thus, the reduction of the money supply has generated a reduced level of GDP and a lower price level.

Exhibit 4

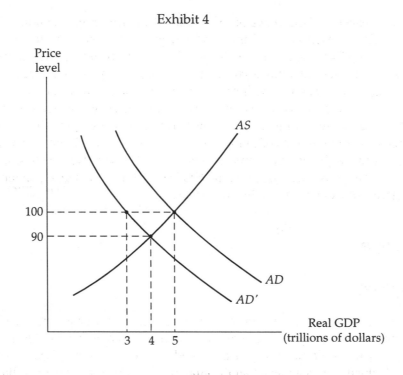

Money and the Economy: The Direct Channel

Monetarists believe money affects aggregate demand directly as well as indirectly. They use the *equation of exchange* to analyze the effects of changes in the money supply. Monetarists argue that an increase in the money supply leaves individuals with larger money balances than they desire. Individuals reduce their money balances by increasing their spending on all goods, not just other financial assets. The increased spending on all goods has a direct effect on aggregate demand.

The equation of exchange is a tautology—that is, it is true by definition. Nominal income equals real output, Y, times the price level, P. Since money is used in exchange, nominal income must be equal to the quantity of money in the economy, M, multiplied by the average number of times per year money changes hands to purchase final goods and services, V. Hence, $M \times V = P \times Y$. The average number of times money changes hands in a year, V, is called the *velocity of money*. The *quantity theory of money* states that velocity is predictable and stable. Consequently $M = (P \times Y)/V$, and changes in the money supply cause predictable changes in nominal income. Whether the change in nominal income is due to changes in the price level or to changes in real output depends on the shape of the aggregate supply curve. In the short run, the aggregate supply curve slopes upward, so an increase in aggregate demand induced by an increase in the supply of money leads to increased real output and higher prices. In the long run, the aggregate supply curve is vertical, and an increase in aggregate demand leads only to an increase in the price level.

Chapter 15

Those who focus on the indirect channel do not accept the monetarist belief that velocity is stable. Instead, they believe that velocity varies with the interest rate. According to this view, an increase in the interest rate increases the opportunity cost of holding money, so the quantity of money held falls and the velocity of money rises. To the extent that a change in interest rates affects velocity, changes in the money supply are offset by changes in velocity.

Money Supply versus Interest Rate Targets

Given the differences in their views of the effects of money on the economy, it should not be surprising that the policy prescriptions of those who focus on the indirect channel differ from the prescriptions of those who focus on the direct channel. Those who believe that monetary policy affects the economy by affecting interest rates argue that monetary policy should focus on interest rates. Monetarists believe that money has a more direct effect on nominal income, so they argue that monetary authorities should focus more on money supply targets. For most of the postwar period, monetary authorities have focused on interest rate targets rather than on monetary growth rate targets. In recent years there have been large movements of funds into and out of the United States in response to interest rate differentials between the United States and other countries. These flows affect the exchange rate and the level of imports and exports. Consequently, the Fed has been forced to give greater consideration to the international effects of its monetary policy decisions.

IV. LAGNIAPPE

Money and Inflation

Suppose you wake up tomorrow and have twice as much money as you have today. Are you wealthier? It depends. Suppose that everyone else has twice as much money as before. Then you, along with everyone else, try to spend most of your new funds on goods and services. But the fact that the money supply has doubled does not mean that the amount of goods and services available has doubled. As everyone tries to increase spending on goods and services, prices of the goods and services will be driven up. Ultimately, prices will double, total spending will double, and money balances held by individuals will double. Real GDP will not change, however, and neither will the real value of the money held by the individuals. Consequently, the doubling of the money stock will lead to a doubling of prices and no change in real output. That is, increases in the money supply tend to lead only to increases in the price level.

Question to Think About: Is this relationship between money and the price level likely to be a long-run or a short-run relationship?

The Money Supply, Interest Rates, and Inflation

Monetarists argue that the Fed should not make nominal interest rates the targets of its monetary policy. The initial effect of an expansionary monetary policy is to lower interest rates. This occurs because the Fed generally expands the money supply by buying government bonds. The increased demand for bonds leads to higher prices for bonds, which implies lower interest rates on the government bonds. Suppose that the Fed has been pursuing an expansionary monetary policy that has generated inflation. Investors are interested in their real return, so the nominal interest rate must increase to cover the inflation rate plus the desired real rate of interest. If the Fed is targeting interest rates, the higher nominal interest rates cause the Fed to increase the money supply further to bring interest rates back down. The Fed can be successful in this attempt only in the short run. Over time the increased money supply causes additional inflation, which in turn raises nominal interest rates and generates another round of bond sales to bring nominal interest rates back down. Hence, the Fed may be prone to pursue inflationary policies if it targets nominal interest rates.

Question to Think About: What would happen if the Fed tried to target real interest rates?

V. KEY TERMS

demand for money
equation of exchange

velocity of money
quantity theory of money

VI. QUESTIONS

A. *Completion*

1. Monetary _____ is concerned with the effect of the quantity of money on the economy's price level and on the level of real output.

2. The _____ is a desire to hold a particular amount of money.

3. The demand for money is related to the volume of _____ in the economy.

4. The advantage of money as a store of wealth is its _____.

5. The demand for money varies inversely with the _____, other things constant.

6. A vertical supply curve of money indicates that the quantity of money supplied is _____ of the market rate of interest.

7. According to the indirect channel view, monetary policy affects aggregate demand indirectly through its effect on _____.

8. An increase in the money supply increases aggregate expenditures by increasing _____ spending.

9. For a given shift in the aggregate demand curve, the steeper the short-run aggregate supply curve, the _____ the increases in the price level.

10. An increase in government purchases increases money demand, which causes _____ to increase and the quantity of investment spending to fall.

11. The _____ of money measures the average number of times per year each dollar is used to purchase final goods and services.

12. One aspect of _____ is the view that changes in the money supply directly affect aggregate demand.

13. According to the _____ of money, the velocity of money is stable or at least predictable.

14. $M \times V = P \times Y$ is the _____.

15. Monetary policy can focus on keeping either _____ or interest rates stable.

B. True/False

_____ 1. People demand money because more money is the same as more income.

_____ 2. Most people demand all the money they can get their hands on.

_____ 3. The demand for money is greater if the volume of exchange is greater.

_____ 4. The desire to carry cash in case of car trouble is an example of the demand for money.

_____ 5. The demand for money varies directly with the interest rate, other things constant.

_____ 6. The supply curve of money is horizontal at the market rate of interest.

_____ 7. Decreases in the supply of money raise the interest rate.

_____ 8. A drop in the interest rate tends to increase investment spending.

_____ 9. According to those who focus on the indirect channel of money, an increase in the money supply does not have a direct effect on aggregate demand.

_____ 10. The flatter the aggregate supply curve, the greater the effect on real GDP of an increase in the money supply.

_____ 11. Any fiscal policy designed to reduce aggregate demand will be tempered by monetary effects.

_____ 12. According to monetarists, an increase in the supply of money leads to an increase in the demand for financial assets but not to a direct increase in the demand for goods and services.

_____ 13. The equation of exchange holds only when velocity is a constant.

_____ 14. Monetarists claim that the velocity of money changes little in the short run.

_____ 15. Monetarists claim that changes in the money supply cause changes in real GDP in the long run.

_____ 16. The velocity of money is greater the more often people get paid.

_____ 17. In the indirect channel framework, changes in velocity offset changes in the money stock.

_____ 18. Monetarists argue that the Fed should set monetary policy to maintain interest rates at a certain level.

_____ 19. Through most of the postwar era, the Fed has used money supply targets rather than interest rate targets.

_____ 20. The Fed can use monetary policy to stabilize the money supply and interest rates simultaneously.

C. *Multiple Choice*

1. An important distinction between money and income is that
   a. money is only one component of income.
   b. money is a measure of wealth whereas income is a source of wealth.
   c. money is a flow variable whereas income is a stock variable.
   d. money is a stock variable whereas income is a flow variable.
   e. there is no important distinction.

2. People demand money
   a. by selling their labor to get money.
   b. by holding money despite the opportunity cost of doing so.
   c. because money increases their wealth.
   d. All of the above.
   e. a and b

3. Other things constant, the quantity of money demanded is greater
   a. the lower the interest rate.
   b. the higher the interest rate.
   c. the greater the opportunity cost of money.
   d. the lower the price level.
   e. during a recession.

4. Like other assets, money is demanded for the flow of services it provides. Its most important service is
   a. protection against inflation.
   b. the interest income it provides.
   c. insurance against theft.
   d. its liquidity.
   e. None of the above.

5. The quantity of money demanded
   a. varies directly with the interest rate.
   b. varies inversely with the interest rate.
   c. is constant no matter what the interest rate is.
   d. is indicated by a vertical line.
   e. None of the above.

6. The supply of money
    a. is inversely related to the interest rate.
    b. is directly related to the interest rate.
    c. varies with the demand for money.
    d. is determined primarily by commercial banks.
    e. is determined primarily by the Fed and can be assumed to be constant no matter what the interest rate is.

7. An increase in the money supply
    a. generates an increase in the quantity of money demanded.
    b. generates a lower interest rate.
    c. increases the level of planned investment.
    d. leads to a higher level of nominal GDP.
    e. All of the above.

8. According to the indirect channel, a decrease in the money supply would
    a. increase aggregate demand.
    b. reduce aggregate demand because the quantity of money demanded would fall.
    c. generate a reduction in government spending, which would cause aggregate demand to fall.
    d. reduce aggregate demand because interest rates would increase and planned investment would fall.
    e. cause a reduction in aggregate supply.

9. One reason the aggregate demand curve slopes downward is that decreases in the price level generate
    a. decreases in the money supply.
    b. increases in the transactions demand for money.
    c. increases in the money supply.
    d. decreases in the transactions demand for money.
    e. decreases in investment spending.

10. The behavior of money demand in the economy causes the effects of fiscal policy to be
    a. enhanced.
    b. completely neutralized.
    c. diminished.
    d. uncertain.
    e. None of the above. Money demand makes no difference.

11. One reason the aggregate demand curve slopes downward is
    a. the inverse relationship between the demand for money and the price level.
    b. the volatility of velocity.
    c. that higher price levels lead to an increase in the money supply.
    d. that higher price levels lead to higher interest rates, which result in less planned investment.
    e. that higher price levels lead to increases in the supply of loanable funds.

12. According to monetarists, a decrease in the money supply
   a. decreases interest rates.
   b. has no effect on interest rates but causes aggregate demand to fall.
   c. has a direct impact on aggregate demand and an indirect impact caused by rising interest rates and falling investment.
   d. has effects on aggregate demand that are opposite those predicted by those who focus on the indirect channel.
   e. None of the above.

13. According to monetarists, an increase in the money supply
   a. increases the interest rate.
   b. decreases aggregate demand.
   c. increases aggregate demand directly.
   d. increases aggregate demand only indirectly.
   e. has no effect on aggregate demand or on the interest rate.

14. The equation of exchange is expressed as
   a. $M \times Y = P \times V$.
   b. $M \times V = P \times Y$.
   c. $R \times P = V \times V$.
   d. $M = V/P \times Y$.
   e. None of the above.

15. Which of the following is not an identity?
   a. MPG = miles driven/gallons of gasoline used
   b. $Y = C + I + G + NX$
   c. $M = P \times Y/V$, where V = a constant
   d. $M \times V = P \times Y$
   e. All are identities.

16. The quantity theory of money states that
   a. the equation of exchange is true.
   b. the money supply is directly related to the interest rate.
   c. the velocity of money is stable or at least predictable.
   d. the aggregate supply curve slopes upward.
   e. All of the above.

17. The velocity of money is
   a. lower the better money serves as a store of wealth.
   b. highly variable, according to monetarists.
   c. lower the more often people get paid.
   d. constant over long periods of time.
   e. greater the greater the quantity of money balances held by the public.

18. According to those who focus on the indirect channel, the velocity of money is
   a. lower the greater the interest rate.
   b. constant over long periods of time.
   c. very predictable.
   d. greater the greater the interest rate.
   e. b and c.

19. Suppose $M = \$1,000$, $V = 5$, and $P \times Y = \$5,000$ initially. If the money supply doubled, then nominal income would be _____, according to the monetarist view.
    a. $5,000
    b. $7,000
    c. $7,500
    d. $10,000
    e. $15,000

20. Monetary authorities can
    a. keep the money supply constant.
    b. keep interest rates constant.
    c. do either a or b but not both simultaneously.
    d. do both a and b simultaneously.
    e. None of the above.

D. Discussion Questions

1. "If people want to be rich they will demand all the money they can." Is this statement true or false? Briefly explain.

2. What is meant by the demand for money? Which way does the demand for money curve slope? Why?

3. Money serves as both a medium of exchange and a store of value. What competes with money in these roles?

4. What can cause the demand curve for money to shift to the left? What can cause a movement along the demand curve for money?

5. What can cause the supply curve for money to shift to the right?

6. Use the indirect channel perspective to explain how monetary policy affects aggregate demand.

7. Why does the aggregate demand curve slope downward?

8. Suppose the economy is in long-run equilibrium. What would be the short-run and the long-run effects of an increase in the money supply?

9. What would be the short-run and long-run effects of a decrease in government purchases?

10. How do monetarists differ from those who focus on the indirect channel in their views of how a change in the money supply affects aggregate demand?

11. If nominal GDP is $10 billion and the velocity of money is 4, what is the quantity of money in the economy?

12. How do monetarists turn the equation of exchange from an identity into a theory?

13. Because the equation of exchange is an identity, why do those who focus on the indirect channel of money *not* agree with monetarists that increases in the money supply directly affect aggregate demand?

14. The velocity of M1 is less stable than the velocity of M2. Can you offer an explanation?

15. Explain why the Fed can attempt to target either changes in the money supply or changes in interest rates, but not both.

VII. ANSWERS

A. *Completion*

1.	theory	6.	independent	11.	velocity
2.	demand for money	7.	interest rates	12.	monetarism
3.	transactions	8.	investment	13.	quantity theory
4.	liquidity	9.	greater	14.	equation of exchange
5.	interest rate	10.	the interest rate	15.	the money stock

B. *True/False*

1.	False	7.	True	13.	False. The equation of exchange always holds.	16.	True
2.	False	8.	True			17.	True
3.	True	9.	True			18.	False
4.	True	10.	True	14.	True	19.	False
5.	False	11.	True	15.	False	20.	False
6.	False	12.	False				

C. *Multiple Choice*

1.	d	6.	e	11.	d	16.	c
2.	b	7.	e	12.	c	17.	a
3.	a	8.	d	13.	c	18.	d
4.	d	9.	d	14.	b	19.	d
5.	b	10.	c	15.	c	20.	c

D. Discussion Questions

1. False. The demand for money refers to the demand to hold money balances in order to make transactions. It is not a demand for wealth. Since most forms of money do not provide an income, people do not want all of their wealth tied up in money. Instead, they want assets that will provide a return.

2. The demand for money refers to people's desire to hold money balances at a given time. The opportunity cost of holding money is the additional interest that could have been earned if the money had been used to purchase alternative interest-bearing financial assets. The demand curve for money shows the quantity of money demanded at various interest rates, other things constant. It slopes down because at lower interest rates people forgo less interest if they hold their wealth in the form of money. Therefore, they hold more money and buy fewer alternative interest-bearing financial assets.

3. Nothing competes with money as a medium of exchange, since a medium of exchange is money. Other financial assets compete with money as a store of value and usually also provide a return in the form of interest.

4. The demand curve for money will shift to the left if the price level falls or if the level of real GDP falls. A change in interest rates causes a movement along the demand curve for money.

5. The supply curve of money will shift to the right if the Fed increases the money supply by buying government bonds, lowering the required reserve ratio, or lowering the discount rate.

6. Because the demand curve for money slopes down, a change in the money supply causes the interest rate to change. The change in the interest rate causes investment spending to change, and investment spending is one component of aggregate expenditure. The equilibrium quantity of real GDP demanded at the prevailing price level changes by the change in investment times the spending multiplier, causing a corresponding shift in aggregate demand.

7. The aggregate demand curve slopes down for three reasons. First, an increase in the price level lowers the real value of dollar-denominated assets, which in turn lowers individuals' wealth and consumption spending and the quantity of aggregate output they demand. Second, as the price level increases, domestic products become more costly relative to foreign products, so exports decrease and imports increase. The drop in net exports causes a reduction in the quantity of aggregate output demanded. Third, money is demanded to finance transactions. An increase in the price level increases the average dollar cost of each transaction. More money is needed to finance transactions, so the demand for money increases, which drives the interest rates higher. The higher interest rates cause investment spending to fall, which means the quantity of aggregate output demanded decreases.

8. You can see the effects of an increase in the money supply by referring to the graph. Point e is the original equilibrium. The increase in the money supply causes the aggregate demand curve to shift to the right as falling interest rates stimulate investment spending. The new short-run equilibrium is at e', and there is an increase in both real output and the price level. The rate of output exceeds the potential output of the economy, however, and the actual price level is greater than the expected price level. Once people learn the new situation, the short-run aggregate supply curve shifts to $SRAS^{105}$, and the new long-run equilibrium is at $e*$.

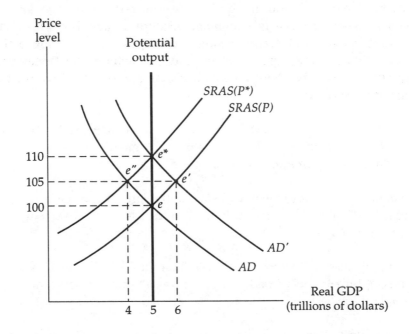

9. Refer again to the graph, starting at $e*$. A reduction in government purchases shifts the aggregate demand curve from AD' to AD, and the new short-run equilibrium is at e''. Unemployment increases, real output falls below the economy's potential output, and the actual price level is less than the expected price level. Once people realize the new situation, the short-run aggregate supply curve shifts to $SRAS^{100}$, and e is again the long-run equilibrium.

10. Those who focus on an indirect channel believe that a change in the money supply affects aggregate demand only indirectly by affecting interest rates, which affect investment spending. Monetarists believe that when people try to change the amount of money they hold, they change their purchases of all assets and not just their purchases of financial assets. Hence, according to this view, a change in the supply of money also has a direct effect on aggregate demand.

11. $M \times V = P \times Y$. If $P \times Y = \$10$ billion and $V = 4$, then $M = (P \times Y)/V = \$10$ billion$/4 = \$2.5$ billion.

12. Monetarists assume that velocity is constant or at least very predictable, so the equation of exchange becomes the quantity theory of money. This theory states that increases in the money supply lead to predictable increases in nominal GDP.

13. Monetarists convert the equation of exchange from an identity to a theory by assuming that velocity is constant or at least predictable. Those who focus on the indirect channel believe that changes in the money supply will be offset by changes in velocity. If they are correct, then changes in the money supply will not directly affect aggregate demand.

14. Changes in government regulations and innovations in financial markets may be responsible for the differences in velocity. What were formerly near moneys may now be more like money and may need to be included in our definition of money.

15. The demand curve for money slopes downward; the supply curve of money is vertical. A shift in the demand curve for money will cause interest rates to change. The only way the Fed can keep interest rates stable is to change the money supply. That is, it cannot keep both the money supply and interest rates stable in the face of a shift in demand for money.

CHAPTER 16

The Policy Debate: Active or Passive?

I. INTRODUCTION

In the previous chapters, we examined how fiscal policy and monetary policy affect the level of output and the inflation rate. The effectiveness of either policy in stabilizing the economy is a topic that is hotly debated among economists. This chapter discusses the views of both those who advocate active government intervention in the economy and those who advocate a passive role for government. The role of expectations in neutralizing government stabilization policies is also discussed.

II. OUTLINE

1. Active Policy versus Passive Policy. Proponents of the passive approach argue that the private economy is basically self-correcting; proponents of the active approach do not agree.

   1.1 Closing a Contractionary Gap
   - a. The passive approach is to allow natural market forces to shift the short-run aggregate supply curve outward and bring the economy to its potential output.
   - b. According to the passive approach, wages and prices are flexible enough to correct short-run surpluses or shortages fairly quickly; the active approach stresses that wages and prices are less flexible, especially in the downward direction.
   - c. The longer it takes for the economy to move naturally to its potential output, the more costly the passive approach.
   - d. The activist approach is to speed the return to potential output by increasing aggregate demand through changes in fiscal policy, monetary policy, or a combination of the two.
   - e. One cost of an activist approach is an increase in the price level.

   1.2 Closing an Expansionary Gap
   - a. According to the passive approach, natural market forces will prompt firms and workers to renegotiate higher nominal wage agreements, increasing production costs and shifting the short-run aggregate supply curve until the expansionary gap is eliminated. The price level will rise.
   - b. According to the active approach, the economy can return to its potential output without inflation if aggregate demand is reduced.

   1.3 Problems with Active Policy
   - a. It is difficult to identify the economy's potential output.
   - b. In order to pursue an active policy, policymakers must
     - (1) be able to predict what would happen if they did nothing;
     - (2) have access to the tools necessary to achieve the desired result in a timely manner;
     - (3) be able to forecast the effects of their policy on the economy's key performance measures;

(4)   obtain cooperation of the separate government bodies that implement fiscal policy and monetary policy;

(5)   implement the appropriate policy; and

(6)   deal with a variety of lags.

1.4   The Problem of Lags

a.   Recognition lag: it takes time to recognize that the economy is not at its potential output.

b.   Decision-making lag: it takes time for policymakers to decide on the correct actions to take.

c.   Implementation lag: it takes time to carry out a change in policy, especially when it is a fiscal policy.

d.   Effectiveness lag: it takes time for the policy to have an impact on the economy.

1.5   Review of Policy Perspectives

a.   An active approach emphasizes that there is a high cost associated with a noninterventionist policy, particularly when unemployment is high. Prolonged unemployment may cause potential GDP to fall.

b.   A passive approach emphasizes that the uncertainties in the economy and the lags associated with policy changes often cause harm, so nonactivists want to allow the natural forces in the economy to work.

1.6   *CASE STUDY:* Active Versus Passive Presidential Candidates

2.   Role of Expectations. People's expectations influence the short-run aggregate supply curve and therefore the effects of a particular policy. The *rational expectations* school of thought argues that people form expectations on the basis of all relevant information, including information about the likely future actions of policymakers.

2.1   Monetary Policy and Expectations

a.   A greater-than-expected increase in the money supply can cause a short-run increase in output and employment if economic actors are surprised by the monetary authorities' policies.

b.   The long-run effect of unanticipated changes in monetary policy is an increase in the price level with no change in output.

c.   The time inconsistency problem arises when policymakers have an incentive to announce one policy, hoping to affect expectations, but then pursue another policy after expectations have been formed.

2.2   Anticipating Monetary Policy

a.   When people have been caught by surprise by policymakers in the past, they are less likely to believe them in the future.

b.   If people do not believe policymakers and policymakers pursue their stated policies, then the result may be a relatively large short-run gap between actual and potential GDP.

c.   People form expectations on the basis of what they believe policymakers will do and not on the basis of what policymakers say they will do.

d.   The rational expectations school believes that government discretionary policies have no short-run or long-run effect on output or employment if the policies are fully and correctly anticipated.

2.3 Policy Credibility
  a. If policymakers think of their reputations as valuable resources, they are less likely to seek short-term reductions in unemployment that generate greater inflation in the long run.
  b. Policy is more likely to be stable over time if policymakers take a long-run view of their duties.

2.4 *CASE STUDY:* Central Bank Independence and Price Stability

3. Policy Rules versus Discretion

  3.1 Rationale for Rules
    a. Monetarists believe that stability in the money supply growth rate is better for the economy than any discretionary monetary policy.
    b. Monetarists often advocate the use of monetary rules, which are rules that specify the relationship between a policy instrument and policy objectives.
    c. Monetarists argue that in the long run excessive monetary growth generates inflation.

  3.2 Rules and Rational Expectations
    a. Followers of the rational expectations school advocate rules because they believe the public on average predicts the behavior of policymakers with reasonable accuracy.
    b. Discretionary policy tends to be ineffective when anticipated correctly by the public. It affects only the price level.
    c. Economists in this school advocate a fixed rule because it makes it easier for economic actors to predict the future state of the economy, thus reducing departures from potential output.

4. The Phillips Curve. The Phillips curve represents a trade-off faced by policymakers between unemployment and inflation. According to the Phillips curve, lower employment comes at the cost of higher inflation. The stagflation of the 1970s caused economists to reexamine the concept that policymakers face a stable, long-run trade-off between inflation and employment.

  4.1 The Short-Run Phillips Curve
    a. The short-run aggregate supply curve reflects an inverse relationship between the inflation rate and the level of unemployment.
    b. If the inflation rate, and therefore the price level, is lower than expected, the actual unemployment rate tends to be greater than the natural rate of unemployment.
    c. If the inflation rate, and therefore the price level, is higher than expected, the actual unemployment rate tends to be lower than the natural rate of unemployment.
    d. The intersections of alternative aggregate demand curves with a given short-run aggregate supply curve determine inflation-unemployment combinations along a short-run Phillips curve. The short-run aggregate supply curve, and therefore the short-run Phillips curve, is based on a given expected inflation rate.

  4.2 The Long-Run Phillips Curve
    a. Monetary or fiscal policy that is unexpected affects only the price level in the long run.
    b. The long-run Phillips curve is a vertical line at the natural rate of unemployment; policymakers only choose from among alternative inflation rates.

4.3 The Natural Rate Hypothesis
   a. The *natural rate hypothesis* contends that the economy tends toward the natural rate of unemployment in the long run.
   b. The natural rate of unemployment is independent of the stimulus to aggregate demand provided by policymakers.
   c. The natural rate hypothesis implies that a policy of low inflation is optimal.

4.4 Evidence of the Phillips Curve
   a. Evidence from the 1960s tends to be consistent with the Phillips curve.
   b. A trade-off was less apparent in the 1970s.
   c. It appears the Phillips curve is about where it was in the 1960s.

III. DISCUSSION

Active Policy versus Passive Policy

The federal government is very much concerned with economic policy questions. The Employment Act of 1946 makes the federal government responsible for maintaining full employment. Even without such a law, politicians would be interested in economic policy. Incumbents find it easier to be reelected when the economy is functioning well than when inflation is high and rising or unemployment rates are high. Thus, the question of interest is which policy is the best policy. Unfortunately for policymakers, the answer to the question remains unclear, and the topic is hotly debated among economists.

Some economists advocate an *active* role for the federal government. An active policy is one in which policymakers make use of discretionary stabilization policies to keep the economy running at or near potential output while maintaining relatively stable prices. Discretionary fiscal and monetary policies tend to focus on shifting the aggregate demand curve to achieve full employment. An expansionary monetary policy is used to stimulate spending when real GDP is below potential, and a restrictive monetary policy is used to reduce spending when the economy is overheated. Fiscal policy can also be used to stimulate or reduce aggregate demand. Advocates of an active policy tend to argue that the private economy is basically unstable and private spending cannot be counted on to maintain aggregate demand at the full employment level. According to this view, by implementing the correct discretionary policies the government can stabilize the economy around potential output.

Other economists disagree and advocate a *passive* role for the government. They believe the private economy is inherently stable and self-correcting. Deviations from potential GDP tend to be short-lived because self-correcting market forces push the economy toward its potential output. Since the economy is basically stable, there is no need for discretionary stabilization policy. In fact, according to this view, government stabilization policies are inherently destabilizing because there are various time lags between the recognition of a problem, the selection and implementation of a policy to correct it, and the impact of a policy change on the economy. During the time lags, the economy's self-correcting mechanisms return the economy to its full employment level. Consequently, when the discretionary policy takes effect, it may generate a new problem, because the problem it was designed to alleviate has already corrected itself.

Role of Expectations

Individuals make economic decisions on the basis of their experiences; the information they have about prices, inflation, and the like; and their expectations, which are based on information about future economic conditions. This information comes from many sources. For example, a possible change in government tax policy is discussed and debated in public for a considerable time before it is implemented. Money supply figures are published regularly, as are unemployment rates and numerous other measures of economic activity.

By affecting short-run aggregate supply, the expectations of economic actors play a crucial role in determining whether a particular discretionary policy will be effective. The *rational expectations* school of thought holds that people form expectations on the basis of all relevant information, including information about how government stabilization policy operates and is implemented. Consequently, if policymakers attempt to stimulate the economy by increasing the rate of growth of the money supply and people correctly anticipate that the Fed is going to do this, then the monetary growth will not have any short-run effect on output. Instead, the only effect will be a long-run increase in the inflation rate.

Exhibit 1

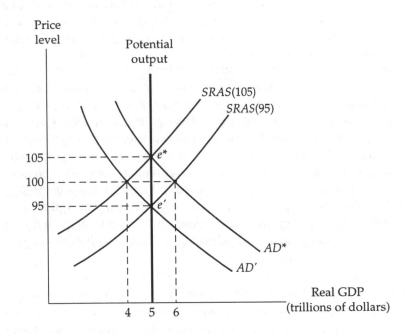

Exhibit 1 illustrates the views of the rational expectations school. Potential output is $5 trillion, and the current equilibrium is at *e**. Suppose the Fed announces a restrictive monetary policy in an effort to reduce the price level to 95, and it initially pursues the restrictive monetary policy. Aggregate demand shifts to *AD′*, real GDP falls to $4 trillion, and the price level falls to 100. Once the public perceives the new conditions and adjusts its decisions about supplying resources in the light of its new information, the short-run aggregate supply curve shifts to $SRAS^{95}$, and the new long-run equilibrium is at *e′*. Suppose, however, that the Fed abandons its restrictive monetary policy before the public adjusts its price expectations to 95. If the public is unaware of this change, aggregate demand returns to *AD** at the same time that the short-run aggregate supply curve shifts to $SRAS^{95}$, and real GDP increases to $6 trillion. The public gets caught by surprise. Eventually, people will realize the true state of the economy, and the short-run aggregate supply will shift back to $SRAS^{105}$.

By failing to implement its announced policy, the Fed loses its credibility with the public. If the Fed now announces a restrictive monetary policy to combat inflation, the public will be less likely to believe the announcement. Consequently, people will not change their price expectations, and the short-run aggregate supply curve will not shift. The Fed would have to pursue its restrictive monetary policy for a longer period of time to convince the public that it was serious. During this time, however, real GDP would be below potential output, and unemployment would be above the natural rate of unemployment.

Policy Rules versus Discretion

Since advocates of a passive policy believe the government's use of discretionary policy tends to destabilize the economy, they advocate the use of monetary policy rules. A monetary policy rule specifies the relationship between a policy instrument and a policy objective. Monetarists tend to support rules on the grounds that the government cannot effectively control the economy because it is so complex and the lags involved in discretionary policies are too long and variable. Those who favor this rational expectations approach advocate rules because they believe the public is sophisticated enough in forming its expectations that discretionary policy tends to affect only the level of prices. By making policy on the basis of a rule, the Fed makes it possible for the public to formulate expectations about the future with greater certainty and permits the economy to achieve the natural rate of output.

The Phillips Curve

The *Phillips curve* is a graphical representation of a trade-off between inflation and unemployment. The trade-off shown by a Phillips curve is between low unemployment rates and low inflation rates. That is, if the government wants to lower the unemployment rate, it must be willing to accept a higher inflation rate. Exhibit 2 illustrates two possible Phillips curves. During the 1960s, policymakers acted on the belief that there was a stable, long-run trade-off between inflation and unemployment for the economy. As inflation became a greater problem in the late 1960s and early 1970s, however, this view became suspect. Critics of an active policy argued that the trade-off is a short-run, not a long-run, phenomenon. According to this view, the government may be able to trade greater inflation for lower unemployment in the short run. Once the public realizes the true state of the economy, however, unemployment will return to its natural rate. In Exhibit 2, the natural rate of unemployment is 6 percent. Suppose the economy is at point *a*. The government can temporarily reduce unemployment by creating inflation; in that case, the economy moves to point *b*. Once the public perceives the new economic situation, people adjust their expectations, and the economy returns to the natural rate of unemployment (point *c*). Now the natural rate of unemployment is associated with a higher inflation rate, and there is a new short-run Phillips curve. The long-run Phillips curve is vertical at the natural rate of unemployment.

Exhibit 2

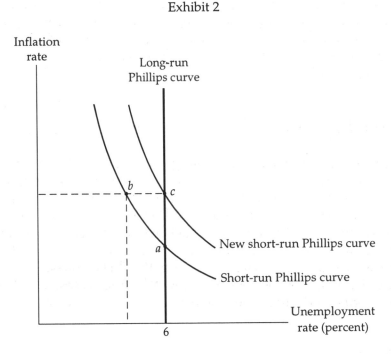

IV. LAGNIAPPE

Leading Economic Indicators and Stabilization Policy

An important lag mentioned in the text is the *recognition lag*, which is the time needed to determine that a problem has developed in the economy. Economists have developed a number of leading economic indicators to try to identify turning points in economic activity. If we knew that a recession was coming in the near future, it might be possible to take corrective actions that would reduce the severity of the recession. Unfortunately, the leading indicators are not accurate enough to form the basis of monetary and fiscal policy. Although the leading indicators often predict turning points in the economy, they err on too many occasions. That is, leading indicators sometimes fail to reveal turning points and sometimes predict turning points that do not materialize.

Question to Think About: What degree of accuracy would you require of leading economic indicators before allowing them to be used in setting stabilization policy?

Is the Market Self-Correcting?

As we have seen in this and several other chapters, there is considerable debate among economists about whether the market is self-correcting. Those who believe it is not self-correcting often use the Great Depression of the 1930s as evidence. Those who believe the market is self-correcting argue that the severity of the depression was increased by government attempts to stabilize the economy. They also argue that the economy has proven to be basically self-correcting throughout most of the postwar period.

A possible synthesis of the two views has been suggested by Axel Leijonhufvud. He argues that the economy is self-correcting most of the time. People and firms use buffers to protect against unexpected layoffs or business downturns. Buffers include savings, inventories, and insurance. If a shock to the economy is much greater than usual, however, then the buffers may get used up. When this happens, the economy's ability to correct itself is weakened considerably, and the recessionary state can persist for a long time—as it did during the Great Depression when the Fed cut the money stock by a third.

Question to Think About: Were the oil shocks of the 1970s enough to cause people to use up the kinds of buffers discussed by Leijonhufvud?

V. KEY TERMS

recognition lag
decision-making lag
implementation lag
effectiveness lag
rational expectations
time inconsistency problem

cold turkey
Phillips curve
short-run Phillips curve
long-run Phillips curve
natural rate hypothesis

VI. QUESTIONS

A. *Completion*

1. A(n) _____ approach emphasizes the vigorous use of discretionary policies.

2. According to the active approach, economic fluctuations are due to instabilities in the _____ sector.

3. Those who advocate a(n) _____ approach consider the private sector to be relatively stable.

4. The _____ approach to a contractionary gap or an expansionary gap is to allow natural market forces to close the gap.

5. Because it takes time to identify a problem, policymakers face a _____ lag.

6. The time needed to carry out a change in policy is called the _____ lag.

7. The time needed for a policy to have an impact on the economy is called the _____ lag.

8. The school of thought that argues that people form expectations on the basis of all relevant information is known as _____.

9. The _____ problem occurs when policymakers have an incentive to announce one policy but then pursue another policy.

10. The Fed will be more _____ if it consistently pursues the policies it says it will pursue.

11. A _____ specifies the relation that ties monetary policy instruments to policy objectives.

12. Many monetarists advocate that the Fed follow a _____ monetary policy.

13. A _____ illustrates a trade-off between unemployment and inflation.

14. The long-run Phillips curve is _____ at the natural rate of unemployment.

15. The _____ rate of unemployment is the unemployment rate consistent with the economy's potential level of output.

B. True/False

_____ 1. According to the active approach, wage reductions take a long time to work through the economy.

_____ 2. An active approach emphasizes the use of monetary policy; a passive approach emphasizes the use of fiscal policy.

_____ 3. In order to pursue an appropriate active policy, policymakers must be able to forecast what aggregate demand would be without government intervention.

_____ 4. The implementation lag associated with fiscal policy tends to be longer than the implementation lag associated with monetary policy.

_____ 5. According to those who advocate a passive approach, the lags associated with discretionary policies cause such policies to destabilize the economy.

_____ 6. According to the rational expectations school of thought, short-run aggregate supply is affected by the macroeconomic course policymakers are expected to pursue.

_____ 7. Members of the rational expectations school tend to favor active discretionary policy on the part of the government.

_____ 8. According to the rational expectations school, the best policy for government policymakers is to keep the public surprised continually.

_____ 9. The rational expectations school believes that an expansionary monetary policy has no effect on output or employment if the policy is fully and correctly anticipated.

_____ 10. One solution to the time inconsistency problem is to allow policymakers no discretion.

_____ 11. One cost to the Fed of implementing unanticipated changes in monetary policy is a loss of credibility.

_____ 12. A monetary rule always represents a passive form of monetary policy.

_____ 13. Milton Friedman argues that the precise rate of growth decided on is more important than the fact that a rate of growth of the money supply is established.

_____ 14. Monetarists advocate the use of rules because of ignorance on the part of policymakers.

_____ 15. A rule that links money supply growth to interest rates is an active rule.

_____ 16. Followers of the rational expectations school believe that the public's behavior neutralizes discretionary policy.

_____ 17. A high unemployment rate will be associated with a high inflation rate, according to the short-run Phillips curve.

_____ 18. Countries with high rates of growth of money supply also have high inflation rates.

_____ 19. The long-run Phillips curve is a vertical line that corresponds to the economy's potential GDP.

_____ 20. The natural rate of unemployment is determined by the short-run Phillips curve.

C. Multiple Choice

1. According to the active approach,
   a. prices and wages are not very flexible, especially downward.
   b. wage reductions in the face of unemployment tend to take a long time.
   c. the private economy is inherently unstable.
   d. discretionary policy can make the economy more stable.
   e. All of the above.

2. A comparison of the active approach and the passive approach stabilization policy reveals that
   a. the cost of the passive approach is greater.
   b. the active approach is more concerned with problems of inflation than is the passive approach.
   c. the active approach relies on monetary policy whereas the passive approach relies on fiscal policy.
   d. the passive approach is more concerned with the inflexibility of wages and prices than is the active approach.
   e. the passive approach relies on the self-correcting tendencies of the economy more than the active approach does.

3. On December 7, 1992, then President-elect Clinton convened an economic summit in Little Rock, Arkansas. This activity was a signal that the Clinton administration would pursue a(n)
   a. monetarist policy.
   b. rational expectations approach to policy.
   c. active policy.
   d. passive policy.
   e. inflationary policy.

4. Increasing government spending to stimulate the economy is an example of
   a. a passive policy.
   b. an attempt to increase potential output.
   c. an active policy.
   d. a policy consistent with the rational expectations school.
   e. None of the above.

5. To pursue an active policy, policymakers must
   a. be able to forecast what aggregate demand and aggregate supply would be without government action.
   b. have automatic stabilizers in place.
   c. control fiscal policy but allow the Fed to do whatever it wants.
   d. be concerned primarily with getting the president reelected.
   e. None of the above.

6. The lag in the time it takes to identify a problem in the macroeconomy is known as the
   a. recognition lag.
   b. decision-making lag.
   c. implementation lag.
   d. effectiveness lag.
   e. registration lag.

7. Those who advocate a passive policy argue that lags imply that an active approach should not be used because
   a. policymakers do not know what should be done to correct the existing problem.
   b. the active policy will delay the moment when the economy begins moving back to potential output.
   c. the active policy imposes additional fluctuations in the price level and the output level.
   d. the potential output level of the economy shifts frequently.
   e. All of the above.

8. The effect of stabilization policy depends on what the public expects the government to do because
   a. the public tends to be irrational.
   b. the short-run aggregate supply curve is based on price expectations.
   c. the long-run aggregate supply curve is vertical.
   d. the public knows that the government will select the correct stabilization policy.
   e. the government employs such a large portion of the labor force.

9. Followers of the rational expectations school believe that
   a. the government does not have enough information to pursue a reasonable stabilization policy.
   b. the public anticipates the policies the government will implement and the effects of the policies on output and prices.
   c. the government establishes a stabilization policy by anticipating how the public will react to the policy and the effects of the public's actions on the implementation of the policy.
   d. b and c
   e. None of the above.

10. Which of the following represents the time inconsistency problem?
    a. The lags associated with discretionary policy sometimes cause the discretionary policy to take effect after market forces have adjusted and eliminated the original problem.
    b. Leading economic indicators do not perfectly predict upturns or downturns in the economy.
    c. Policies that have certain effects in the short run may be ineffective in the long run.
    d. Elected officials may announce a policy to reduce inflation but not stick with the policy out of fear of losing the next election.
    e. Discretionary policy is ineffective in altering the natural rate of unemployment.

11. The Fed will have a difficult time getting its policy to be effective if
    a. the economy is in a recession.
    b. it is pursuing a contractionary policy.
    c. policymakers take a long-run view of their duties.
    d. monetary policymakers have lost credibility.
    e. All of the above.

12. If the public forms expectations rationally, then any correctly anticipated discretionary policy will
    a. affect short-run output and prices but have no long-run effect.
    b. affect output in the short run but have no effect on short-run prices.
    c. affect prices in the short run but not in the long run.
    d. be effective more quickly than if the public formed no expectations.
    e. have no effects on output or employment.

13. Many monetarists advocate
    a. that the Fed pursue an active stabilization policy.
    b. fine-tuning the economy.
    c. a monetary rule that fixes the rate of growth of the money supply.
    d. a monetary rule that pegs interest rates to a certain nominal rate.
    e. a monetary rule that pegs interest rates to a certain real rate.

14. If monetary policy is fully anticipated by workers and firms,
    a. it will be effective more quickly.
    b. it will have no effect on output.
    c. it will have no effect on the price level.
    d. the economy moves along the short-run Phillips curve.
    e. None of the above.

15. One who believes the economy is very complex and that economic aggregates interact in obscure ways likely will advocate
    a. an active fiscal policy.
    b. an active monetary policy.
    c. a passive policy.
    d. policies to push the Phillips curve out.
    e. both a and b only.

Exhibit 3

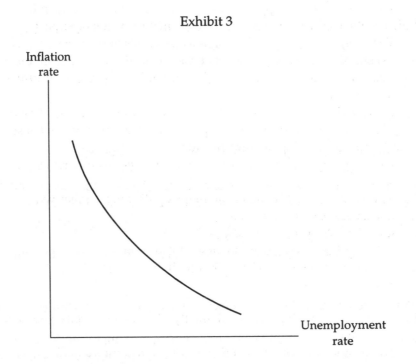

16. What is the name of the relationship shown in Exhibit 3?
    a. the natural rate hypothesis
    b. the Phillips curve
    c. monetarism
    d. rational expectations
    e. the aggregate demand curve

17. The relationship illustrated in Exhibit 3 shows that
    a. lower inflation brings about lower employment.
    b. lower inflation brings about higher unemployment.
    c. inflation and unemployment are directly related.
    d. inflation and unemployment have the same causes.
    e. inflation is a short-run phenomenon.

18. The short-run Phillips curve can be derived if
    a. the short-run aggregate supply curve slopes upward.
    b. the short-run aggregate supply curve is vertical.
    c. the short-run aggregate demand curve is horizontal.
    d. we are discussing the long run.
    e. None of the above.

The Policy Debate: Active or Passive?

19. According to the natural rate hypothesis,
    a. the long-run Phillips curve is vertical at the natural rate of unemployment.
    b. the long-run Phillips curve is vertical at the natural rate of inflation.
    c. the natural rate of unemployment is 4 percent.
    d. the unemployment rate is inversely related to the inflation rate.
    e. c and d.

20. The trade-off between inflation and unemployment expressed by a short-run Phillips curve is more likely to exist when
    a. shifts in aggregate supply are large.
    b. shifts in aggregate supply dominate shifts in aggregate demand.
    c. shifts in aggregate demand dominate shifts in aggregate supply.
    d. neither aggregate demand nor aggregate supply is shifting.
    e. monetary policy is used instead of fiscal policy.

D. Discussion Questions

1. Explain how an active policy differs from a passive policy.

2. Suppose the economy is operating at a real GDP greater than its potential output and the price level is greater than the expected price level. What would an active policy to correct the problem be?

3. What would happen if a passive approach were taken to address the situation described in Question 2?

4. Explain the lags associated with discretionary policy and the problems they cause.

5. What problems are caused by following the passive approach if the economy is not self-correcting? What problems are caused by following the active approach if the passive approach is needed?

6. Explain the rational expectations theory. Does the theory imply that the public never makes mistakes? Explain.

7. What is the time inconsistency problem? What factors contribute to the problem?

8. The text discusses the role of expectations in the context of monetary policy. Discuss the relationship between expectations and fiscal policy. Assume that the government's stated goal is to reduce the deficit.

9. Explain why credibility is hard to develop but easy to undermine and how credibility is relevant to stabilization policy.

10. What is a policy rule and what is the purpose of such a rule?

11. Suppose the relationship between unemployment and inflation actually is as depicted by a downward-sloping Phillips curve. What implications does this have for the conduct of stabilization policy?

12. What is the natural rate hypothesis?

13. How do the weak version and the strong version of the natural rate hypothesis differ?

14. Explain how the short-run Phillips curve, the long-run Phillips curve, the short-run aggregate supply curve, the long-run aggregate supply curve, and the natural rate hypothesis are all related. How do active and passive views of these concepts differ?

VII. ANSWERS

A. Completion

1. active
2. private
3. passive
4. passive
5. recognition
6. implementation
7. effectiveness
8. the school of rational expectations

9. time inconsistency
10. credible
11. monetary rule
12. fixed-growth-rate
13. short-run Phillips curve
14. vertical
15. natural

B. True/False

1. True
2. False
3. True
4. True
5. True
6. True
7. False
8. False
9. True
10. True
11. True

12. False. Some monetary rules may be relatively active.
13. False
14. True
15. True
16. True
17. False
18. True
19. True
20. False

C. Multiple Choice

1.	e	6.	a	11.	d	16.	b
2.	e	7.	c	12.	e	17.	b
3.	c	8.	b	13.	c	18.	a
4.	c	9.	b	14.	b	19.	a
5.	a	10.	d	15.	c	20.	c

D. Discussion Questions

1. According to the passive policy approach, the private economy is relatively stable and natural market forces will rapidly correct any deviations from potential output. An active approach states that the private economy is basically unstable and that wages and prices are inflexible enough that deviations from potential output can persist for long periods of time. Consequently, the latter claims that it is important for the government to implement discretionary monetary and fiscal policy in order to maintain economic stability.

2. An active policy would reduce aggregate demand by using either fiscal policy, monetary policy, or both. The use of fiscal policy could involve a reduction in government spending or a tax increase. The goal of monetary policy would be to reduce the money supply and increase interest rates, which would reduce investment spending.

3. Firms and workers would negotiate higher wage agreements, which would increase production costs and shift the short-run aggregate supply curve to the left. Output would fall to the potential output and prices would be higher.

4. There are four lags associated with discretionary policy. The recognition lag is the time it takes to recognize that an economic problem exists. The decision-making lag is the time it takes to decide what policy to use. The implementation lag is the time it takes to put the selected policy into action. The effectiveness lag is the time it takes for the policy to affect the economy once it is implemented. The problem created by these lags is that natural market forces may already be in operation by the time a discretionary policy takes effect. Consequently, the problem the discretionary policy was created to solve may no longer exist, and the discretionary policy may generate new problems.

5. If the economy is not self-correcting and a passive approach is adopted, then the economy will persist in disequilibrium indefinitely. With a contractionary gap, the cost will be lost output and higher unemployment in each period. With an expansionary gap, the cost is ongoing inflation. On the other hand, if an active policy is pursued when a passive policy is called for, then the economy is likely to experience wider swings in the expansion–contraction cycle. For example, if the economy is in a recession and the government pursues expansionary policies, there is a lag before they take effect. If the economy is already moving out of the recession when the expansionary policies take effect, then the economy may overheat, causing greater inflationary pressures than would have occurred normally.

6. Rational expectations theory assumes that people learn from observation how the economy functions and how government policymakers respond to various economic problems. People then take actions based on their expectations about the future state of the economy and the likely policy responses. The theory does not imply that the public never makes a mistake. It does imply that the public will not continually be surprised by policymakers.

7. The time inconsistency problem refers to the situation in which policymakers have an incentive to announce one policy in the hope that people will adjust their expectations in a certain way and then pursue a different policy. The various lags associated with discretionary policy and the desire of politicians to get reelected contribute to the problem.

8. In the graph, the economy is initially at point *e*. If the government decides that it is going to reduce the deficit, it must either reduce government spending or increase taxes, either of

which reduces consumption spending. In either case, aggregate demand falls to AD'. For AD' to be consistent with potential output of $5 trillion, the price level must fall to 95. For this to happen, the public must expect lower prices and cause the short-run aggregate supply curve to shift to $SRAS^{95}$. The new equilibrium would be e'.

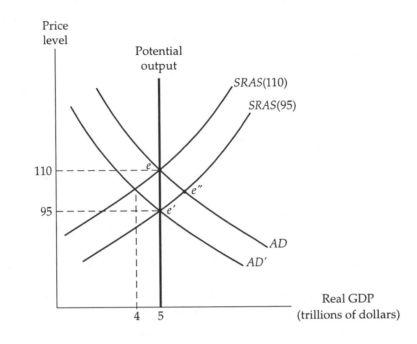

If the public believes the government policy will take effect but the government fails to implement its policy, the economy moves to e''. Eventually, the public adjusts to the actual economic conditions; the short-run aggregate supply curve returns to its original position, and the economy is in equilibrium at e. The next time the government announces a policy of deficit reduction, the public is less likely to believe that it will actually be implemented. Consequently, the short-run aggregate supply curve does not shift. If the aggregate demand curve does shift to AD', output is reduced to $4 trillion and unemployment rises. To return the economy to potential output, the government must maintain its policy for a long time until natural forces adjust or allow deficit spending to increase again.

9.   If previous policymakers have often failed to follow through on their stated policies, the public is unlikely to believe the policy statements of future policymakers. Consequently, the new policymakers must be persistent in their selected policies. It will take time for the public to believe and trust them. Further, it will take only a few cases of inconsistent behavior for the policymakers to lose their credibility. The success of stabilization policy depends on the public's view of policymakers' credibility because the public's expectations determine the behavior of the short-run aggregate supply curve.

10. A policy rule is the opposite of discretionary behavior. It establishes a specified policy response to specific economic conditions, or even fixes policy on a permanent basis. The purpose of such rules is to reduce discretionary behavior on the part of policymakers on the assumption that such discretionary policies are actually destabilizing.

11. If the relationship depicted by the Phillips curve does exist, then policymakers can choose the combination of unemployment and inflation that they think is optimal for the economy and use an active discretionary policy to achieve that combination.

12. The natural rate hypothesis states that in the long run the economy tends toward the rate of unemployment that is consistent with the economy's potential output. Hence, attempts to reduce the unemployment rate below the natural rate through increases in aggregate demand must fail in the long run.

13. Both versions of the natural rate hypothesis argue that there is not a long-run trade-off between inflation and unemployment. The weak version admits there is a trade-off in the short run, whereas the strong version argues that the short-run reductions in unemployment from a given increase in inflation get smaller over time as people learn what policymakers are doing.

14. The intersections of various aggregate demand curves with a given short-run aggregate supply curve can generate a short-run Phillips curve; movement along a long-run aggregate supply curve generates different inflation-unemployment combinations along a long-run Phillips curve. The short-run aggregate supply curve slopes upward, whereas the long-run aggregate supply curve is vertical at the economy's potential output. The shapes of both the short-run aggregate supply curve and the short-run Phillips curve result from the public's being misinformed about the true inflation rate. The natural rate hypothesis states that in the long run the economy moves to the natural rate of unemployment, which is the rate of unemployment that would prevail if the economy operated at its potential output. Hence, the long-run Phillips curve is vertical at the natural rate of unemployment.

Advocates of a passive approach believe that the transition from the short run to the long run occurs fairly quickly; advocates of an active approach believe that it takes a long time for the market to achieve potential output on its own. Hence, advocates of an active approach urge the use of discretionary policy to maintain the economy at its potential output.

CHAPTER 17

Federal Budgets and Public Policy

I.   INTRODUCTION

The federal budget deficit has been an important topic of public policy debates in recent years. In this chapter, we examine the government budget process and how the deficits have grown in recent years. The chapter also discusses the effects of the national debt and examines some of the policy prescriptions that have been offered.

II.   OUTLINE

1.   The Federal Budget Process. The government budget is a plan for government expenditures and revenues for a specified period. The U.S. federal government's fiscal year runs from October 1 to September 30.

   1.1   The Presidential Role in the Budget Process
      a.   The president was not involved in the federal budget process prior to 1921.
      b.   The Budget and Accounting Act of 1921 changed the budget procedure to include the president.
      c.   The act created the Office of Management and Budget (OMB) to help the president develop budget proposals.
      d.   The Employment Act of 1946 created the Council of Economic Advisers to assist the president in formulating fiscal policy.
      e.   Now the president presents a budget proposal to Congress in January of each year.

   1.2   The Congressional Role in the Budget Process
      a.   Expenditure decisions often are made in two stages: authorization and appropriations.
      b.   Congress passes a budget resolution, which presents an overall strategy that is supposed to establish the framework within which committees make spending and revenue decisions.
      c.   The difference between expenditures and revenues is one measure of the budget's fiscal impact, because a rising deficit is expected to stimulate aggregate demand and a rising surplus is expected to dampen aggregate demand.

   1.3   Problems with the Budget Process
      a.   Congress passes continuing resolutions instead of making budget decisions.
      b.   Overlapping committee authority: several committees have authority over most budget sections.
      c.   The lengthy budget process hampers fiscal policy: budget preparations begin more than a year and a half before the budget goes into effect.
      d.   Much of the budget is difficult to control; about three-fourths of the budget is in categories determined by existing law.

e. The minute detail in the budget reduces the executive branch's ability to respond to changing economic conditions.

1.4 Suggested Budget Reforms
   a. Convert the annual budget into a biennial budget.
   b. Consolidate authorization and appropriation.
   c. Simplify the budget by concentrating on major groupings and eliminating line items.

2. Federal Budget Deficits

   2.1 Rationale for Deficits
      a. Some outlays are for investments that should be financed over time. However, a capital budget is not part of the federal budget process.
      b. Before the Great Depression, only wars generated federal budget deficits.
      c. Keynes developed a rationale for deficits to stimulate the economy in recessions.

   2.2 Budget Philosophies and Deficits
      a. Annually balanced budget
         (1) The budget should be balanced every year.
         (2) This view prevailed prior to World War II.
      b. Cyclically balanced budget
         (1) The government should run deficits during recessions and surpluses during expansions.
         (2) The budget should be balanced over the business cycle.
      c. Functional finance
         (1) Use the budget to ensure that the economy produces at its potential output and do not worry about balancing the budget.
         (2) It appears that this approach has been used in the United States since World War II.

   2.3 Deficits in the 1980s
      a. U.S. federal budget deficits increased substantially in the 1980s.
      b. The government cut taxes but did not cut spending.
      c. The recession in the early 1980s also created larger deficits.

   2.4 Why Did Deficits Persist So Long? Public choice theory suggests that politicians seeking reelection have a tendency to pass expenditure bills but not tax bills.

   2.5 The Relationship between Deficits and Other Aggregate Variables
      a. There is no necessary relationship between deficits and various measures of economic performance such as the price level, interest rates, or real output.
      b. A deficit resulting from automatic stabilizers is associated with lower levels of prices and real output, which reduce the demand for money. The effect on the interest rate will depend on the size of the decrease in the demand for money relative to the increase in the supply of government securities sold to finance the deficit.
      c. A deficit resulting from discretionary fiscal policy is associated with higher levels of prices, real output, and interest rates.

2.6　Crowding Out and Crowding In
   a.　Crowding out occurs when government borrowing causes interest rates to increase so that private business investment declines.
   b.　The extent of crowding out is a matter of debate.
   c.　In some situations, government borrowing could stimulate investment, which is called crowding in.

2.7　The Twin Deficits
   a.　In part as a result of relatively high U.S. interest rates, the U.S. balance of trade has been in deficit throughout the 1980s; this means foreigners have accumulated dollars.
   b.　Foreigners have purchased U.S. assets, including government securities; this process helped fund the federal budget deficit.

2.8　The Miraculous Budget Surplus. The federal budget was in surplus in 1998.
   a.　Taxes were increased in 1990 and 1993.
   b.　The rate of growth of federal spending fell after 1990.

2.9　*CASE STUDY*: Reforming Social Security

3.　The National Debt. Whereas the federal deficit is a flow variable, the national debt is a stock variable that measures the net accumulation of past deficits. The total debt includes U.S. Treasury securities purchased by various federal agencies, which is debt the federal government owes to itself. Generally, debt figures exclude debt held by government agencies and focus on debt held by the public.

3.1　The National Debt since World War II
   a.　In nominal terms, the U.S. national debt increased slowly from the end of World War II until 1974 and then increased very rapidly.
   b.　In real terms, the U.S. national debt decreased from the end of World War II until 1974 and then increased.

3.2　An International Perspective on National Debt. In terms of the level of its debt as a percentage of GDP, the United States is about in the middle of all industrial countries.

3.3　Interest on the Debt. Gross interest payments are determined by the size of the national debt and the interest rate on the debt.

3.4　Who Bears the Burden of the Debt?
   a.　To the extent Americans hold the debt, it is not a burden on future generations.
   b.　Foreign Ownership of Debt
      (1)　The inflow of credit from abroad keeps interest rates lower than they would be otherwise.
      (2)　The increased reliance on foreigners increases the burden of the debt to future generations because future debt service payments no longer stay in the United States.

3.5　Crowding Out and Capital Formation
   a.　Crowding out leads to reduced domestic investment and net exports because of higher interest rates and appreciation of the dollar.
   b.　The long-run effect of crowding out is to reduce total investment as well as the portion of investment funded by domestic residents.

c. The opportunity cost of crowding out depends on the use to which the government puts the funds it invests.

d. If the government uses the funds to make capital investments that are productive, then there may be no harmful effects on the economy's capital formation from crowding out.

3.6 *CASE STUDY:* An Intergenerational View of Deficits and Debt

III. DISCUSSION

The Federal Budget Process

Until this century, Congress handled the federal budget process, and the president was not involved. However, a number of measures have increased the president's role in the budget process, which has become very complex. In recent years, many have come to believe that it is out of control. As evidence these observers cite the increasing tendency of Congress to pass continuing resolutions instead of making specific budget decisions.

There are numerous problems with the current budget process. Several congressional committees have jurisdiction over the same budget items, so decisions require extensive committee deliberations. The budget process is very lengthy, and this makes fiscal policy less effective as a discretionary tool. Also, as noted, Congress has often relied on continuing resolutions that keep the government functioning but do not address the existing budget problems. The budget is very detailed and gives the executive branch little leeway in specifics while burdening the Congress with the detail. Finally, much of the budget is difficult to control because the expenditures are set by previous legislation.

Critics of the current budget process have offered suggestions for its reform. So that Congress spends less time on the budget, some have suggested adopting two-year budgets instead of annual budgets. However, this would limit the budget's usefulness as a tool of fiscal policy. Another suggestion is to combine the authorization and appropriation stages of the budget process. A third reform is to simplify the budget document by having Congress consider only major budget headings and leave specifics to the relevant government agencies.

Federal Budget Deficits

U.S. federal budget deficits, although they have turned to surpluses in recent years, have become a hotly debated topic. For much of the time since the publication of Keynes's *General Theory*, the U.S. government has attempted to use fiscal policy as a counter cyclical discretionary tool. Prior to Keynes, the government attempted to balance the budget annually. Those who advocate a cyclically balanced budget would use fiscal policy to counter recessions and temper expansions. Such an approach allows deficit spending during recessions and has the government accumulate a surplus in expansions. The goal is to balance the budget over the business cycle instead of every single year. It appears the U.S. government has actually followed a philosophy of functional finance, in which fiscal policy is used to keep the economy at or close to its potential output.

Some critics of the recent budget deficits argue that deficits are associated with inflation or rising interest rates. Neither economic theory nor empirical evidence supports a consistent link between government deficits and other aggregate variables, however. The relationship varies depending on whether a rising deficit is due to automatic stabilizers or discretionary fiscal policy. A surprise to many was how quickly the large deficits in the early 1990s turned into a surplus by 1998.

The National Debt

A federal budget deficit adds to the national debt. In nominal terms, the U.S. national debt grew slowly between 1946 and 1974, after which it grew at a more accelerated rate. When national debt figures are deflated to account for inflation or taken as a percentage of GDP, a different picture emerges. The national debt in real terms and as a percentage of GDP declined from the end of World War II to 1974 and has increased since 1974. The national debt is not something that is necessarily worrisome. Families undertake debt for many reasons. A family that borrows to buy a house or to finance a college education is not considered foolish or spendthrift; a family that borrows extensively for dinners out and vacations is. Similarly, government borrowing may be worthwhile if the funds are spent on assets that enhance the productivity of the economy over many years, such as roads and education.

The national debt creates current expenditures for the government: interest payments. The importance of interest payments in the budget increased when inflation drove interest rates to record levels in the 1970s. But the interest payments actually paid to people overstate their importance in the budget. Since interest payments are income to the recipients, income taxes are paid on the payments. Seigniorage also makes net interest payments less than gross interest payments.

Deficits occur when current government expenditures exceed current tax receipts. As a result, the national debt increases, generating interest payments in future years. Thus, the national debt imposes burdens on future generations. Is this a problem? Again, there is debate concerning the answer. If government borrowing is used to finance the purchase of government investment goods, then the future productivity of the economy is enhanced, and the debt does not impose a burden on future generations. This is true even when government borrowing *crowds out* private investment, as long as the productivity of the government investment equals or exceeds the productivity of the private investment.

The U.S. national debt has been financed, in part, by the purchase of government securities by foreigners. As a result, U.S. interest rates have not increased as much as they would have otherwise. Increased foreign participation may increase the burden of the debt on future generations, however, since the future debt service payments will be paid to foreigners.

IV. LAGNIAPPE

Crowding Out and Foreign Capital

Crowding out of private investment occurs when government borrowing increases interest rates, reducing private sector borrowing for investment spending. Have the U.S. deficits in recent years caused such crowding out? Probably not. World financial markets are interrelated. A slight rise in the interest rate in the United States, other things constant, leads to an increase in foreign purchases of U.S. government securities. That is, the deficit has increased the amount of the national debt held by foreigners.

Question to Think About: What problems might be associated with foreigners' owning so many government securities?

Deficits and Inflation

Exhibit 1 presents figures on the size of the U.S. federal budget deficit and U.S. inflation rates from 1960 through 1999. Through the 1960s and 1970s, there was some evidence of a positive relationship between deficits and inflation. In the 1980s, however, deficits rose to record levels and inflation fell from record levels. As the text points out, deficits and surpluses are not systematically related to other aggregate variables.

Exhibit 1

Federal Deficits and Inflation Rates

Fiscal Year	Federal Surplus (+) or Deficit (−) ($ billions)	Federal Deficit/GDP (percent)	Inflation Rate (percent)
1961	−3.3	0.6	0.7
1962	−7.1	1.2	1.2
1963	−4.8	0.8	1.6
1964	−5.9	0.9	1.2
1965	−1.4	0.2	1.9
1966	−3.7	0.5	3.4
1967	−8.6	1.1	3.0
1968	−25.2	2.8	4.7
1969	+3.2	n/a	6.1
1970	−2.8	0.3	5.5
1971	−23.0	2.1	3.4
1972	−23.4	1.9	3.4
1973	−14.9	1.1	8.8
1974	−6.1	0.4	12.2
1975	−53.2	3.4	7.0
1976	−73.7	4.2	4.8
1977	−53.7	2.7	6.8
1978	−59.2	2.7	9.0
1979	−40.2	1.6	13.3
1980	−73.8	2.7	12.4
1981	−79.0	2.6	8.9
1982	−128.0	4.1	3.8
1983	−207.8	6.3	3.8
1984	−185.4	5.0	3.9
1985	−212.3	5.4	3.8
1986	−221.2	5.3	1.1
1987	−149.8	3.4	4.4
1988	−155.2	3.2	4.4
1989	−152.5	2.9	4.6
1990	−221.2	3.9	5.4
1991	−269.4	4.6	4.2
1992	−290.4	4.7	3.0
1993	−255.0	3.9	3.0
1994	−203.1	3.1	2.6
1995	−163.9	2.3	2.8
1996	−107.5	1.4	3.0
1997	−21.9	0.0	2.3
1998	69.2	0.8	1.6

Source: Economic Report of the President, February 1999.

Question to Think About: Are the deficits likely to lead to higher inflation rates in the future?

V. KEY TERMS

federal budget
budget resolution
continuing resolutions
entitlement programs
annually balanced budget

cyclically balanced budget
functional finance
crowding out
crowding in
national debt

VI. QUESTIONS

A. *Completion*

1. The government _____ is a plan for government expenditures and revenues for a specified period, usually a year.

2. The Budget and Accounting Act of 1921 created the _____ to help the president develop budget proposals.

3. The Council of Economic Advisers was created by the _____ of 1946.

4. A _____ resolution sets the framework that guides spending and revenue decisions for the new budget.

5. A rising _____ is expected to stimulate aggregate demand.

6. For the federal government, the _____ begins October 1.

7. In recent years, Congress has passed _____ resolutions when budget decisions have not been made by the start of a new fiscal year.

8. The budget philosophy called _____ does not attempt to balance the budget over any specific period of time.

9. A _____ budget calls for budget deficits during recessions and budget surpluses during expansions.

10. The view before the Great Depression was that budget deficits were _____.

11. _____ occurs when government borrowing replaces private borrowing for investment.

12. The ability of government deficits to stimulate private investments is called _____.

13. The _____ is the net accumulation of past federal budget deficits.

14. Unlike the budgets of private firms, the U.S. federal budget does not include a _____ budget.

15. _____ refers to government investments in roads, bridges, airports, and the like.

B. True/False

_____ 1. During the 19th century and the early part of the 20th century, the president had little power over the U.S. federal budget.

_____ 2. In January of each year, Congress presents a budget proposal to the president for approval.

_____ 3. Today authorization and appropriations are handled at the same time in the U.S. federal budget process.

_____ 4. The current U.S. federal budget process is a lengthy one that hampers fiscal policy.

_____ 5. The heads of U.S. government agencies have a lot of discretion in the allocation of funds within their departments.

_____ 6. The U.S. federal budget treats capital expenditures differently from current expenditures.

_____ 7. An annually balanced budget calls for spending reductions in recessions and spending increases during expansions.

_____ 8. U.S. federal budget deficits increased with the tax cuts of the early 1980s even though federal spending fell sharply.

_____ 9. Federal budget deficits have a consistently positive relation to inflation.

_____ 10. Crowding out occurs when government borrowing raises interest rates, thereby reducing private investment spending or net exports.

_____ 11. Crowding in refers to the situation when foreigners buy many of the bonds sold by the government to finance the deficit.

_____ 12. The federal budget surplus is a flow variable, and the national debt is a stock variable.

_____ 13. Although the U.S. national debt has grown larger in recent years, it has actually grown smaller as a percentage of GDP.

_____ 14. The United States has a higher deficit-to-GDP ratio and a higher debt-to-GDP ratio than any other country except Italy.

_____ 15. GDP must grow in real terms in order for the national debt as a percentage of GDP to decline.

_____ 16. Some of the interest payments made by the U.S. federal government on its debt actually return to the U.S. Treasury.

_____ 17. If crowding out occurs, then deficit spending must reduce the economy's long-run productive capacity.

_____ 18. Increased borrowing by the federal government that leads to higher interest rates usually also leads to a reduction in net exports.

C.   Multiple Choice

1.   The portion of the federal budget that is spent directly on goods and services is approximately
   a.   one-fifth.
   b.   one-fourth.
   c.   one-third.
   d.   one-half.
   e.   two-thirds.

2.   The president's role in the U.S. federal budget process is to
   a.   authorize the budget expenditures.
   b.   appropriate the money for the budget expenditures.
   c.   alter taxes to bring the budget into balance.
   d.   develop the budget resolution to cover the budget process.
   e.   None of the above.

3.   The budget has a congressional gestation period of approximately
   a.   six weeks.
   b.   three months.
   c.   six months.
   d.   nine months.
   e.   one year.

4.   Which of the following is a problem with the U.S. federal budget process?
   a.   Congressional committees have overlapping authority.
   b.   The budget process is a lengthy procedure.
   c.   The budget is too detailed.
   d.   The budget timetable tends to be ignored by Congress.
   e.   All of the above.

5.   An advantage of a biennial budget is that
   a.   it makes discretionary fiscal policy more effective.
   b.   it would force Congress to stop using continuing resolutions.
   c.   it would reduce the proportion of time spent by Congress on budgetary considerations.
   d.   it would prevent the use of better long-range economic forecasts.
   e.   None of the above.

6. Prior to the Great Depression, budget deficits were usually associated with
   a. recessions.
   b. depressions.
   c. war.
   d. All of the above.
   e. None of the above.

7. The U.S. federal budget deficits of the 1980s were caused by
   a. the Reagan administration's efforts to stimulate the economy by using deficit financing.
   b. increases in military spending.
   c. tax cuts.
   d. b and c.
   e. None of the above.

8. A budget philosophy that advocates running a deficit during recessions and a surplus during expansionary periods is known as
   a. an annually balanced budget.
   b. a cyclically balanced budget.
   c. functional finance.
   d. a structural budget.
   e. a biennial budget.

9. The relationships between deficits and either inflation or unemployment are best described as
   a. positive.
   b. negative.
   c. positive for inflation and negative for unemployment.
   d. inconsistent.
   e. positive for inflation and nonexistent for unemployment.

10. Crowding out of private investment is more likely
    a. the more elastic is the savings curve.
    b. the more foreigners are willing to buy U.S. securities.
    c. the greater the increase in the interest rate due to government borrowing.
    d. the deeper the economy is in a recession.
    e. All of the above.

11. The impact on U.S. interest rates of the increasing size of the U.S. federal deficits in the 1980s was dampened by
    a. expansionary monetary policy.
    b. falling inflation.
    c. increased foreign purchases of U.S. government securities.
    d. rising military expenditures.
    e. income tax cuts.

12. If the budget were balanced next year, the national debt would
    a. stay the same.
    b. increase.
    c. decrease.
    d. drop to zero.
    e. either stay the same or increase, but more information is needed to determine which.

13. If the federal government used conventional accounting practices, the deficit would
    a. be larger.
    b. be the same size.
    c. be smaller.
    d. be larger, but the net debt would be smaller.
    e. Any of the above is possible.

14. Net interest payments are smaller than gross interest payments because
    a. interest payments are tax deductible.
    b. the Fed pays a higher interest rate than the Treasury.
    c. the primary purpose of the Fed is to reduce the burden of the national debt.
    d. those who receive interest payments must pay taxes on them.
    e. b and d

15. The potential long-run effect of crowding out is
    a. a reduction in the spending multiplier.
    b. a reduction in the growth rate of the capital stock.
    c. to harm the economy's long-run productive capability.
    d. a reduction in the real interest rate.
    e. b and c.

16. U.S. government deficits can lead to reductions in U.S. net exports because
    a. the deficit is created by the government's buying goods that would otherwise be sold to foreigners.
    b. the borrowing increases interest rates, which causes the dollar to appreciate.
    c. the borrowing increases interest rates, which causes the dollar to depreciate.
    d. the borrowing increases interest rates, which causes investment spending to fall, causing net exports to fall.
    e. None of the above. The deficit has no effect on net exports.

17. Which of the following would reduce national debt as conventionally measured?
    a. selling Yellowstone National Park to private investors and using the proceeds to pay off government bonds
    b. canceling government job training programs and making employers pay for the programs
    c. reducing spending on highways
    d. All of the above.
    e. None of the above.

D. Discussion Questions

1. Describe the current U.S. federal budget process.

2. What problems are associated with the U.S. federal budget process? What solutions have been offered to these problems?

3. Which of the following government expenditures would likely enhance future productivity and why?
   a. spending to expand the interstate highway system
   b. an increase in farm subsidies
   c. an increase in government loans for education
   d. payments to construct a new missile system
   e. payments to dredge the Mississippi River

4. How does a cyclically balanced budget differ from functional finance?

5. What factors contributed to the large U.S. federal deficits in the 1980s?

6. What budget deficit reduction laws have been enacted recently? Have they been successful?

7. Why does the United States tend to have budget deficits? Why didn't the country often have deficits before World War II?

8. Is it accurate to state that deficits are a cause of inflation? Why or why not?

9. How are automatic stabilizers related to deficits?

10. Distinguish between crowding out and crowding in.

11. Describe what has happened to the U.S. national debt since the end of World War II.

12. Could the federal government increase the surplus and save on future taxes by selling off some federal assets, such as national parks? Explain.

13. Why are net interest payments lower than gross interest payments on the U.S. national debt?

14. Why is crowding out not necessarily harmful to the economy's long-run productive capability?

VII. ANSWERS

A. *Completion*

1.	budget	9.	cyclical balance
2.	Office of Management and Budget	10.	immoral
3.	Employment Act	11.	Crowding out
4.	budget	12.	crowding in
5.	deficit	13.	national debt
6.	fiscal year	14.	capital
7.	continuing	15.	Public capital
8.	functional finance		

B. True/False

1. True
2. False
3. False
4. True
5. False
6. False
7. True
8. False
9. False
10. True

11. False
12. True
13. False. The national debt has grown as a percentage of GDP since 1980.
14. False
15. False. Nominal GDP must grow faster than nominal debt.
16. True
17. False
18. True

C. Multiple Choice

1. c
2. e
3. d
4. e
5. c
6. c

7. d
8. b
9. d
10. c
11. c
12. a

13. c
14. d
15. e
16. b
17. d

D. Discussion Questions

1. The president initiates the budget process by submitting a budget to Congress in January. The budget reflects the president's spending proposals for the coming fiscal year. Congress then develops an overall budget strategy, which is expressed in a budget resolution, and establishes a timetable for making budget decisions. Various congressional committees and subcommittees assess the budget and recommend authorization of the budget items that come under their jurisdictions. Congress approves the entire budget. Once the president has accepted the budget, Congress then has to pass appropriations bills in order for spending to actually take place. If the budget process is not complete by October 1, Congress passes continuing resolutions to allow agencies to spend at the rate of the previous year's budget until a new budget is approved.

2. The overlapping authority of congressional committees makes it difficult to arrive at final budget figures. Further, the process takes so much time that it is difficult to use fiscal policy for stabilization purposes. Often the budget process breaks down, and Congress relies on continuing resolutions instead of making budget decisions by the October 1 deadline. Many believe the budget is too detailed. Finally, many of the items in the budget, such as entitlement programs, are beyond Congress's control. Suggested reforms include using a biennial budget instead of an annual budget, combining the authorization and appropriations stages of the process, and having Congress consider a broad budget plan, leaving it to the relevant government departments to work out budget details.

3. Expansion of the interstate highway system would probably enhance future productivity because the system is important to the country's transportation system. Similarly, increasing loans to college students and dredging the Mississippi would likely enhance future productivity—the former by increasing the productivity of the recipients of the loans and the latter by enhancing the Mississippi as a route for shipping. Increasing farm subsidies would not increase future productivity, as it would encourage current consumption. The impact of a new missile system is more complex. The missiles would not have the same effect on future productivity as the roads or loans but would be part of the national defense system, for which the federal government is responsible. Note that there is no guarantee that any of these items would in fact enhance future productivity. If the funds used would have been more productive in the private sector, the future productivity of the economy could be harmed rather than enhanced.

4. A cyclically balanced budget would allow deficits during recessions and surpluses during expansions, such that the budget would be balanced over the length of the business cycle. Functional finance strives to operate the economy at its potential output rather than to balance the federal budget.

5. The deficit grew as a result of tax cuts, increased government spending, and a recession.

6. The Budget Enforcement Act of 1990 was passed as a deficit reduction act, and a tax increase was enacted in 1993. In recent years, the deficit has fallen but is expected to increase again by the end of the decade.

7. The public choice model suggests that deficits occur because politicians seeking reelection have a greater incentive to pass expenditure bills than tax bills. Some believe that prior to the Great Depression, deficits were considered immoral, so the government did not generate deficits. According to this view, Keynes's work showed that deficits could be useful in stabilizing the economy, so the national aversion to deficit spending faded.

8. Deficits do not cause inflation; they can be associated with rising inflation, disinflation, or falling prices. Deficits often rise automatically when aggregate demand falls and moves the economy into recession, which is usually a time when prices are falling or disinflation occurs. Alternatively, discretionary fiscal policy to increase aggregate demand leads to higher prices as the deficit is rising.

9. Automatic stabilizers are programs that increase the deficit during recessions and decrease the deficit during expansions. For example, during a recession unemployment increases, decreasing tax revenues and increasing government spending on unemployment benefits. During an expansion, the opposite occurs.

10. Crowding out occurs when government borrowing drives up interest rates and reduces private investment. Crowding in occurs when government borrowing stimulates the economy, which encourages private investment.

11. The national debt has increased since the end of World War II, especially since 1974. When measured in constant dollars, however, the national debt as a percentage of GDP declined between 1945 and 1974 and increased after 1974.

12. No. The durable assets of the federal government are part of the financial strength of the government. Selling them might reduce the deficit and the national debt as currently measured but would not generate savings to the government.

13. Interest payments received by individuals are treated as income and are subject to taxation. Thus, a portion of the interest payments made by the government will return to the government as taxes. Further, some of the interest payments are paid to the Fed, which returns the bulk of the interest it receives to the U.S. Treasury.

14. It is true that the private investment that is crowded out by government borrowing would have increased the future productive capability of the economy. Federal government spending may also increase the future productive capability of the economy, however. Only if the private investment crowded out would have been more productive than the investment made by the government will crowding out be harmful to the future productive capability of the economy.

CHAPTER 18

Elasticity of Demand and Supply

I. INTRODUCTION

We know that demand curves generally slope downward and supply curves generally slope upward. Sometimes we need more information about demand and supply to be able to analyze a particular market. In this chapter, the concept of elasticity is introduced and explained. Elasticity is a very important concept in economics, so make sure that you understand the material in this chapter.

II. OUTLINE

1. Price Elasticity of Demand. Price elasticity of demand is a measure of the responsiveness of quantity demanded to a change in price.

    1.1   Calculating Price Elasticity of Demand
        a.   *Price elasticity of demand* equals the percentage change in quantity demanded divided by the percentage change in price.
        b.   Price elasticity is always a negative number.
        c.   Elasticity expresses a relationship between relative amounts, not absolute amounts.
        d.   The price elasticity formula is:

$$E_D = \frac{q_D{}' - q_D}{(q_D{}' + q_D)} \div \frac{p' - p}{(p' + p)}$$

    1.2   Categories of Price Elasticity of Demand
        a.   Inelastic: price elasticity has a value between 0 and -1.0 since the percentage change in quantity demanded is less than the percentage change in price.
        b.   Unit elastic: price elasticity has a value equal to -1.0 since the percentage change in quantity demanded equals the percentage change in price.
        c.   Elastic: price elasticity has a value more negative than -1.0 since the percentage change in quantity demanded is greater than the percentage change in price.

    1.3   Elasticity and Total Revenue
        a.   Total revenue is the revenue the firm receives from selling its products; it equals price times the quantity sold.
        b.   Total revenue increases if price increases and demand is inelastic, or if price decreases and demand is elastic.
        c.   Total revenue decreases if price increases and demand is elastic, or if price decreases and demand is inelastic.
        d.   Total revenue is unchanged by a price change if demand is unit elastic.

1.4 Price Elasticity and the Linear Demand Curve
   a. Along a linear demand curve, consumers are more responsive to price changes when the price is relatively high than when the price is relatively low.
   b. Demand becomes less elastic as one moves down along a linear demand curve.
   c. Demand is unit elastic at the midpoint of a downward-sloping linear demand curve.
   d. Demand is elastic above the midpoint of a downward-sloping linear demand curve.
   e. Demand is inelastic below the midpoint of a downward-sloping linear demand curve.
   f. Along a downward-sloping linear demand curve, total revenue increases as the price is reduced until the midpoint is reached and then decreases as price falls further.

1.5 Constant-Elasticity Demand Curves
   a. A horizontal demand curve has an elasticity value of minus infinity and represents perfectly elastic demand.
   b. A vertical demand curve has an elasticity value of zero and represents perfectly inelastic demand.
   c. Demand curves can also be unit elastic at all points.

2. Determinants of the Price Elasticity of Demand

2.1 Availability of Substitutes
   a. The more close substitutes for the good there are available, the more elastic the demand.
   b. The number and closeness of substitutes depend on how the good is defined.
   c. The more narrow the definition of a good, the more substitutes there are and the more elastic the demand.

2.2 Proportion of the Consumer's Budget Spent on a Good. The more important an item is as a percentage of a consumer's budget, the more elastic the demand.

2.3 A Matter of Time. Elasticity is greater the longer the time period involved.

2.4 Elasticity Estimates

2.5 *CASE STUDY*: Deterring Young Smokers

3. Price Elasticity of Supply
   a. *Price elasticity of supply* is a measure of the responsiveness of quantity supplied to a change in price.
   b. The price elasticity of supply is:

$$E_S = \frac{q'_s - q_s}{(q'_s + q_s)} \div \frac{p' - p}{(p' + p)}$$

3.1 Categories of Supply Elasticity
   a. Supply is elastic if the supply elasticity has a value greater than 1.0.
   b. Supply is inelastic if the supply elasticity has a value less than 1.0.
   c. Supply is of unitary elasticity if the supply elasticity equals 1.0.
   d. A horizontal supply curve represents a supply that is perfectly elastic.
   e. A vertical supply curve represents a supply that is perfectly inelastic.
   f. A linear supply curve that emanates from the origin is of unitary elasticity.

3.2   Determinants of Supply Elasticity
  a.   Elasticity of supply depends on how cost changes as output increases. The more rapidly marginal cost rises as output expands, other things constant, the more inelastic the supply.
  b.   Supply is more elastic the longer the time period involved.

4.   Other Elasticity Measures

  4.1   Income Elasticity of Demand
    a.   *Income elasticity of demand* is a measure of how demand changes in response to a change in income, prices held constant; it measures the percentage change in quantity demanded divided by the percentage change in income.
    b.   Inferior goods have a negative income elasticity of demand.
    c.   Normal goods have a positive income elasticity of demand.
    d.   Demand is income inelastic if the value of the elasticity is between zero and 1.0 and elastic if the value is greater than 1.0. Goods that are income inelastic are sometimes called *necessities*; those that are income elastic are sometimes called *luxuries*.

  4.2   *CASE STUDY:* The Market for Food and "The Farm Problem"
    a.   The demand for most farm products is price-inelastic.
    b.   Because demand is inelastic, fluctuations in output caused by weather or other factors generate relatively large changes in prices (and therefore in farm income).
    c.   The problem is compounded in the long run by the fact that demand for food also tends to be income inelastic, leading to generally declining real farm income as the economy grows over time.

  4.3   Cross-Price Elasticity of Demand
    a.   *Cross-price elasticity of demand* is the percentage change in quantity demanded of one good divided by the percentage change in the price of another good; it measures the responsiveness of demand for one good to changes in the price of another good.
    b.   Two goods are *substitutes* if the cross-price elasticity of demand is positive.
    c.   Two goods are *complements* if the cross-price elasticity of demand is negative.

III. DISCUSSION

Price Elasticity of Demand

If the price of a good decreases, we expect the quantity demanded to increase because a demand curve slopes downward. Government officials, consumers, and business managers are often very much concerned about how much quantity demanded changes—that is, how responsive quantity demanded is to a change in price. Economists have developed a tool to help answer these questions: the concept of *price elasticity of demand*. Exhibit 1 illustrates this concept. The exhibit shows two demand curves: D_1 and D_2. At a price of $1.00, the demand curves intersect and the quantities demanded of each good are equal at 100 units each. If the price falls to $0.90, quantity demanded of good 1 increases to 105 units (demand curve D_1) and quantity demanded of good 2 increases to 150 units (demand curve D). Obviously, the quantity demanded of good 1 is much less responsive to the $0.10 change in price than is the quantity demanded of good 2. Economists say that demand curve D_2 is more *elastic* than demand curve D_1.

Exhibit 1

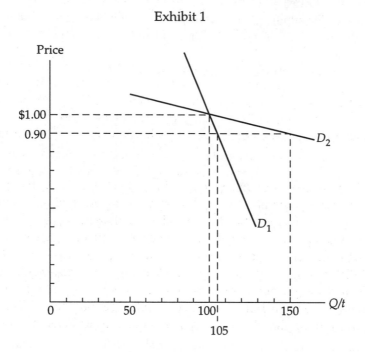

We can calculate the value of the price elasticity for each demand curve. The formula for price elasticity of demand is:

$$E_d = \frac{q'_d - q_d}{(q_d' + q_d)} \div \frac{p' - p}{(p' + p)}$$

In Exhibit 1, the price elasticity of D_1 is:

$$\frac{100 - 105}{(100 + 105)} \div \frac{1.00 - 0.90}{(1.00 + 0.90)} = \frac{-5}{205} \div \frac{0.10}{1.9} = -0.46$$

The price elasticity of D_2 is:

$$\frac{100 - 150}{(100 + 150)} \div \frac{1.00 - 0.90}{(1.00 + 0.90)} = \frac{-50}{250} \div \frac{0.10}{1.90} = -3.8$$

The price change is the same for both, but the quantity response is much greater for D_2 than for D_1. The result is that D_2 at a price of \$1 is more elastic than D_1 at the same price.

Price elasticity of demand is a concept important to producers because it tells them what will happen to *total revenue* if price changes. In Exhibit 1, the total revenue at a price of $1 is the same on both D_1 and D_2: $1 × 100 = $100. At a price of $0.90, total revenue on D_1 is 0.90 × 105 = $94.50 and total revenue on D_2 is 0.90 × 150 = $135. The lower price caused total revenue on D_1 to fall and total revenue on D_2 to increase. Note that for this change in price, D_1 represents an *inelastic* demand and D_2 an *elastic* demand. When demand is elastic, a given percentage change in price leads to a larger percentage change in quantity demanded. Hence, when demand is elastic, a price reduction will generate so many more sales that total revenue will increase. On the other hand, if demand is inelastic, a lower price generates a smaller percentage increase in quantity, so total revenue falls.

In Exhibit 1, D_1 is steeper than D_2. Since we know that D_1 is inelastic and D_2 is elastic, it is tempting to think that a steep demand curve always represents inelastic demand and a flatter demand curve always represents elastic demand. This conclusion is false, however. Exhibit 2 illustrates why. The demand curve in panel *a* is steeper than the one in panel *b*, even though they represent the same demand for milk and the same value for price elasticity. The panels represent demand in terms of different units of measure: panel *a* shows gallons of milk demanded per time period, and panel *b* shows eight-ounce glasses demanded per time period. The difference in the slopes of the curves is due to the different scales on the horizontal axes. (With *intersecting* curves on the same graph, it is correct that the flatter demand curve represents the more elastic demand.)

Exhibit 2

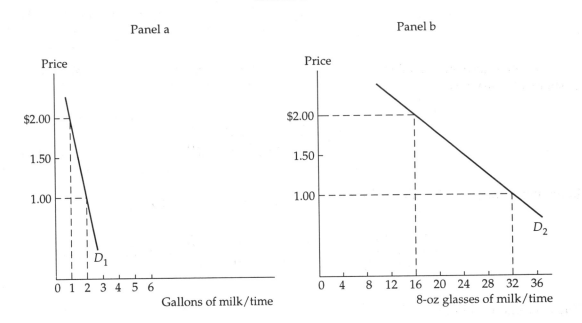

Although we cannot always use the slope of a demand curve to determine elasticity in general, there are some cases when we can use it. In the case of a downward-sloping *linear demand curve*, we know that elasticity falls as we move down the demand curve. Demand is of *unitary elasticity* at the midpoint of the demand curve, elastic above the midpoint, and inelastic below the midpoint. (Review Exhibit 2 in the text.) We also know that a horizontal demand curve is *perfectly elastic*; that is, it has an elasticity value of minus infinity everywhere. This means that any increase at all in price will cause sales to fall to zero. A vertical demand curve is *perfectly inelastic* ($E_D = 0$), which means that the same quantity is demanded regardless of the price. Finally, for a demand curve that is unit elastic at all points, total revenue is the same at every point on the demand curve.

Determinants of the Price Elasticity of Demand

What characteristics of a product cause demand to be elastic or inelastic? The most important determinant of demand elasticity is the number and closeness of substitutes. If the price of a good increases and consumers believe the good is unique, then sales will not decrease by very much. If there are many other products that consumers believe are close substitutes for the good, then consumers will switch and sales will decrease sharply.

The way goods are defined affects the number and closeness of substitutes and thus the value of elasticity. The demand for gasoline is less elastic than the demand for Exxon gasoline. If all gas stations increase prices by 10 percent, studies have shown that people will reduce their purchases by less than 10 percent. If Exxon raises its price by 10 percent while all other gasoline sellers maintain the old prices, however, many Exxon consumers will switch to other brands. Note that the number and closeness of substitutes determine consumer behavior in this case. Among the substitutes for gasoline are public transportation, walking, bicycle riding, carpooling, and staying at home. All of these are also substitutes for Exxon gasoline. In addition, Shell, Mobil, Phillips, and all other brands of gasoline are very close substitutes for Exxon gasoline.

Another determinant of price elasticity of demand is the proportion of the consumer's budget spent on the good. If expenditures on a good constitute a fairly large proportion of a consumer's budget, then a price change will have a large effect on the consumer's real income. In the case of a price increase, real income falls, and the consumer is forced to cut back expenditures on the good. A 10 percent increase in the price of an automobile has a bigger impact on the budget than a 10 percent increase in the price of salt. Demand for automobiles thus tends to be more elastic than demand for salt.

The third determinant of demand elasticity, time, is also related to the number and closeness of substitutes. A sudden increase in the price of electricity may induce consumers to make sure lights are off in empty rooms and to run air conditioners at 78 degrees instead of 72 degrees. As time passes, consumers may add insulation to their houses and replace electric stoves with gas stoves. It is easier (less costly) to substitute away from electricity the longer the time period, so demand becomes more elastic.

Price Elasticity of Supply

We can also measure the responsiveness of quantity supplied to a change in price. The *price elasticity of supply* is calculated the same way as price elasticity of demand, except quantity supplied is used instead of quantity demanded. The terminology is similar, too. If the value of supply elasticity is greater than 1.0, supply is elastic; if the value is less than 1.0, supply is inelastic; and if the value equals 1.0, supply is of unitary elasticity. A vertical supply curve has a supply elasticity of zero and represents a perfectly inelastic supply; a horizontal supply curve has a supply elasticity equal to infinity and represents a perfectly elastic supply.

The elasticity of supply depends on how production costs change with output, a topic that will be examined further in later chapters. The more slowly marginal cost rises as output expands, the more elastic supply will be. A second determinant is time. The longer the time allowed for adjustment, the more elastic the supply. An increase in price will encourage existing producers to expand production and new producers to enter the market. But it takes time to build new factories and increase purchases of material inputs.

Other Elasticity Measures

There are two other useful measures of elasticity: income elasticity of demand and cross-price elasticity of demand. The *income elasticity of demand* is defined as the percentage change in quantity demanded divided by the percentage change in income. Demand for some goods falls as income increases. These goods are called *inferior goods* and they have a negative income elasticity of demand. *Normal goods* are those with a positive income elasticity of demand, which means that demand for such goods increases as income increases. Normal goods can be divided into goods that are income elastic and those that are income inelastic.

The *cross-price elasticity of demand* measures the percentage change in quantity demanded of one good divided by the percentage change in price of another good. An increase in the price of McDonald's hamburgers generates an increase in the sales of Burger King hamburgers. A positive value of cross-price elasticity of demand indicates that two goods are substitutes, and the larger the value, the more consumers consider the two goods to be close substitutes. Some pairs of goods are complements because consumption of one often involves consumption of the other. Some familiar complements are cereal and milk, gasoline and tires, and hamburgers and hamburger buns. An increase in the price of hamburger encourages people to buy less hamburger. If they buy less hamburger, they also buy fewer hamburger buns. Complements have negative values of cross-price elasticity.

IV. LAGNIAPPE

Time, Elasticity, and Nuclear Power

In the 1970s, the Organization of Petroleum Exporting Countries (OPEC) increased the price of oil by curtailing production. Oil prices rose rapidly, but consumption did not fall by as large a percentage. This indicated an inelastic demand. Electricity prices rose as a result of higher oil prices. Many people feared that the increased scarcity of oil would lead to a scarcity of electricity, which would limit economic growth. One response to the problem was to increase the construction of nuclear power plants. The long-run demand for oil and electricity turned out to be more elastic than had been thought, however, and people conserved more energy than had been expected. Further, new sources of oil were discovered, which helped bring about lower oil prices.

Question to Think About: Has the decline in oil prices that started in January 1986 generated a return to the energy consumption patterns of the 1960s?

Are Children Inferior Goods?

An inferior good is one that people consume less of as their incomes increase. Economists have long noted that family size tends to decline as income increases. That is, wealthier people tend to have fewer children. It appears, then, that children are inferior goods.

Question to Think About: What are the implications of the relationship between income and family size for developing countries that currently have very high rates of population growth?

V. KEY TERMS

price elasticity of demand	unit-elastic demand (supply)
price elasticity formula	constant-elasticity demand curve
inelastic demand	price elasticity of supply
elastic demand	perfectly elastic supply curve
total revenue	perfectly inelastic supply curve
linear demand curve	unit-elastic supply curve
perfectly elastic demand (supply) curve	Income elasticity of demand
perfectly inelastic demand (supply) curve	cross-price elasticity of demand

VI. QUESTIONS

A. Completion

1. Elasticity is another word for _____.

2. If a 1-percent decrease in price leads to a 3-percent increase in quantity demanded, demand is _____.

3. A perfectly inelastic demand curve is _____.

4. A perfectly inelastic demand curve has an elasticity value of _____.

5. Demand is more price elastic the greater the number of _____.

6. If total revenue stays the same after a price increase, demand is _____.

7. The more _____ a good is defined the fewer substitutes it has.

8. The price elasticity of demand is greater the _____ the time period.

9. The elasticity of supply is _____ the longer the period of adjustment.

10. The ability of firms to alter quantity supplied in response to price changes varies across _____.

11. A good that is income inelastic is a _____.

12. Goods with an income elasticity greater than one are sometimes called _____.

13. A good with a negative income elasticity of demand is an _____ good

14. If the cross-price elasticity of demand between two goods is positive, then the goods are _____.

15. Two goods are complements if the cross-price elasticity of demand is _____.

B. *True/False*

_____ 1. The price elasticity of demand equals the change in quantity demanded divided by the change in price.

_____ 2. The greater the slope, the greater the elasticity of demand.

_____ 3. A demand curve with a price elasticity of –2 is more elastic than one with an elasticity of –1.

_____ 4. Price elasticity of demand does not depend on the unit of measurement used.

_____ 5. If demand for a good is price elastic, the producer can increase total revenue by lowering the price of the good.

_____ 6. Along a downward-sloping linear demand curve, higher prices are associated with a less elastic demand.

_____ 7. Total revenue is the same at all points, regardless of price, along a unit-elastic demand curve.

_____ 8. Total revenue is at a maximum when the price elasticity of demand is –1.0.

_____ 9. A perfectly inelastic demand curve has a slope of infinity.

_____ 10. If supply is perfectly inelastic, then an increase in price will generate less total revenue.

_____ 11. Demand is more price elastic the closer are the available substitutes.

_____ 12. The larger the price elasticity of demand, the smaller the price elasticity of supply.

_____ 13. The demand for personal computers is more price elastic than the demand for paper clips.

_____ 14. The demand for food is more price elastic than the demand for steak.

_____ 15. Demand becomes more inelastic as time passes.

_____ 16. The most important determinant of elasticity of supply is the price of related goods.

_____ 17. The longer the period of time for adjustment, the greater the elasticity of supply.

_____ 18. The value of income elasticity of demand must be positive.

_____ 19. The income elasticity of demand for food is greater than 1.0.

_____ 20. If two goods have a cross-price elasticity of demand equal to zero, the two goods are substitutes.

C.   Multiple Choice

1. Price elasticity of demand is defined as the
    a.   change in quantity demanded divided by the change in price.
    b.   change in price divided by the change in quantity demanded.
    c.   percentage change in price divided by the percentage change in quantity demanded.
    d.   percentage change in quantity demanded divided by the percentage change in price.
    e.   percentage change in demand divided by the percentage change in supply.

2. Which of the following is true of the relationship between slope and elasticity?
    a.   They are the same thing.
    b.   They are unrelated.
    c.   The slope affects elasticity along with the existing price and quantity demanded.
    d.   The slope is the inverse of elasticity of demand.
    e.   None of the above.

3. If demand is price elastic, then
    a.   the numerical value of price elasticity is between zero and –1.0.
    b.   a price increase will generate an increase in total revenue.
    c.   the demand curve is horizontal.
    d.   total revenue is at a maximum.
    e.   total revenue will increase if the price falls.

4. If demand is price elastic and price decreases, then
    a.   the extra revenues from the extra units sold are exactly offset by the loss in revenues as a result of the lower price.
    b.   the extra revenues from the extra units sold exceed the loss in revenues from the lower price.
    c.   the extra revenues from the extra units sold are less than the loss in revenues from the lower price.
    d.   more information is necessary to determine what happens to total revenue.
    e.   the firm sells more units but at a loss.

5. If a demand curve has an elasticity of demand of –1.0 everywhere, then a 40 percent change in price will
    a.   cause a 40 percent increase in total revenues.
    b.   cause a 40 percent decrease in total revenues.
    c.   cause quantity demanded to be constant.
    d.   not cause a change in total revenue.
    e.   None of the above.

6. Price elasticity of demand is greater
    a.   the more unique the product.
    b.   the lower the price.
    c.   the greater the availability of close substitutes.
    d.   the fewer close substitutes that are available.
    e.   a and d

Exhibit 3

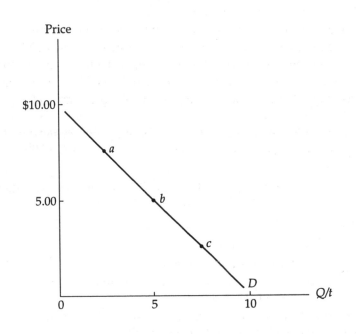

7. Demand for the good in Exhibit 3 is
    a.   more elastic at point *a* than at point *b*.
    b.   more elastic at point *c* than at point *b*.
    c.   of unitary elasticity at point *a*.
    d.   of unitary elasticity everywhere.
    e.   perfectly elastic.

Exhibit 4

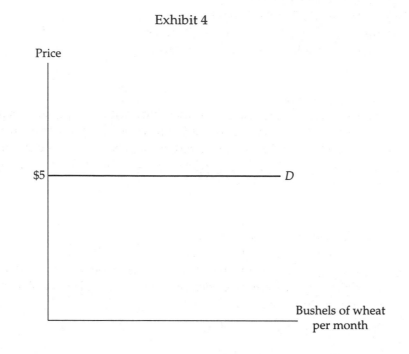

8. The demand curve in Exhibit 4
   a. is perfectly elastic.
   b. is perfectly inelastic.
   c. has a price elasticity value of minus infinity.
   d. has a price elasticity value of zero.
   e. a and c

9. If a firm faced the demand curve in Exhibit 4 and it raised its price,
   a. its revenues would increase.
   b. its revenues would remain constant.
   c. the quantity sold would remain constant.
   d. the quantity sold would fall to zero.
   e. None of the above.

10. When expenditures on a certain good make up a large proportion of your budget,
    a. demand is price elastic because an increase in price has a large effect on your ability to buy the good.
    b. demand is price elastic because an increase in price has a large effect on your willingness to buy the good.
    c. demand is price inelastic because the good is very important to you.
    d. demand is price inelastic because the good must have a few close substitutes.
    e. None of the above.

11. Price elasticity of demand increases over time because
    a. price increases over time.
    b. goods make up a large proportion of one's budget over time.
    c. the prices of other goods change over time.
    d. the ability to substitute away from higher-priced goods increases over time.
    e. supply elasticity increases over time.

12. Salt has a low elasticity of demand because
    a. it has few close substitutes.
    b. it is a small fraction of a consumer's budget.
    c. it is a luxury.
    d. both a and b
    e. None of the above. Salt has a high elasticity of demand.

13. Which of the following statements is correct?
    a. A vertical demand curve is perfectly inelastic, but a vertical supply curve is perfectly elastic.
    b. A vertical demand curve is perfectly elastic, but a vertical supply curve is perfectly inelastic.
    c. Both a vertical demand curve and a vertical supply curve are perfectly inelastic.
    d. A horizontal demand curve is perfectly elastic, but a horizontal supply curve is perfectly inelastic.
    e. a and d

14. Which of the following statements is correct?
    a. Total revenue falls if price goes up and supply is inelastic.
    b. Supply is more elastic the longer the time period under consideration.
    c. Supply is more elastic over time because producers are able to adjust their production plans and techniques more easily.
    d. Elasticity of supply does not depend on time.
    e. b and c

15. As time increases
    a. demand becomes more elastic and supply becomes less elastic.
    b. demand becomes less elastic and supply becomes more inelastic.
    c. both demand and supply become more elastic.
    d. both demand and supply become less elastic.
    e. demand becomes more elastic but elasticity of supply is unaffected.

16. Suppose demand increases with rising income, but by a smaller percentage than the increase in income. In this case,
    a. the income elasticity of demand is negative.
    b. the income elasticity of demand is between zero and 1.0.
    c. the income elasticity of demand is greater than 1.0
    d. the good is income elastic
    e. c and d.

17. If the income elasticity of demand is very high, we expect the price elasticity of demand to be
    a. elastic.
    b. inelastic.
    c. of unitary elasticity.
    d. perfectly elastic.
    e. perfectly inelastic.

18. The cross-price elasticity of demand indicates
    a. whether two goods are substitutes or complements.
    b. whether two goods are income elastic.
    c. whether demand for the goods is inelastic.
    d. whether the two goods are produced by the same seller.
    e. None of the above.

Elasticity of Demand and Supply

19. A product has a large negative cross-price elasticity with several other products. We would expect the product's price elasticity of demand to be
    a. elastic.
    b. inelastic.
    c. of unitary elasticity.
    d. perfectly elastic.
    e. perfectly inelastic.

20. If the elasticity of demand for a good X is -0.01, the cross-price elasticity of demand between X and Y is
    a. positive and large
    b. positive and small
    c. negative and large
    d. negative and small
    e. We can't tell without more information.

D. Discussion Questions

Exhibit 5

1.

Price	Quantity Demanded	Total Revenue	Price Elasticity
$20	0.5	_____	_____
18	1.5	_____	_____
16	2.5	_____	_____
14	4.0	_____	_____
12	6.0	_____	_____
10	8.0	_____	_____
8	11.0	_____	_____
6	15.0	_____	_____
4	20.0	_____	_____
2	26.0	_____	_____

a. Calculate the values of price elasticity of demand using the information in Exhibit 5. Fill in the two columns on the right side of the table.
b. For which prices is demand elastic? Inelastic?
c. If price decreases from $12 to $10, how much of the increased revenue is due to selling more units?
d. What is the change in total revenue as a result of the lower price of units previously sold at $12?
e. Calculate the combined effect of the above changes on total revenue.
f. Calculate the change in revenue from increased sales, the change in revenue from the decreased price of units previously sold at a higher price, and the combined effect of these changes on total revenue when the price changes from $4 to $2.

2. How are slope and elasticity related?

3. Suppose you attend a meeting at work to discuss whether to change the price of your product. You think demand is elastic, but a colleague thinks it is inelastic. Does it matter whether demand is elastic or not? Explain. Is it possible that you are both right? Explain.

4. Label as *a* the point in Exhibit 6 where demand is unit elastic. Indicate where the demand curve is elastic and where it is inelastic.

Exhibit 6

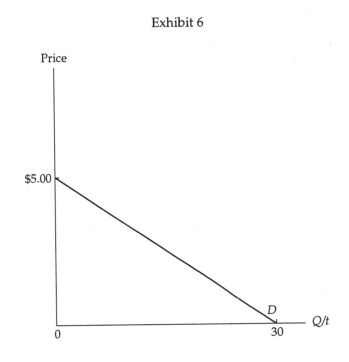

5. Explain why price elasticity of demand is greater for goods with a large number of close substitutes than it is for goods with fewer substitutes.

6. Indicate for each pair of goods which good has the more elastic price demand and why.
   a. automobile; gasoline
   b. electricity; amusement park admission
   c. blue jeans; a pair of pants

7. Explain why demand is more elastic in the long run than in the short run.

8. Explain why supply is more elastic in the long run.

9. Explain why the ability of firms to alter quantity supplied in response to price changes differs across industries.

10. Can a good be an inferior good for all levels of income? Explain.

11. If the demand curve for a good is vertical, what can we conclude about the income elasticity of the good?

Elasticity of Demand and Supply

12. Suppose that demand for good A is unit elastic everywhere along the demand curve and that you spend all your income on good A and good B. What can we conclude about the cross-price elasticity of goods A and B?

13. Explain why the correct answer to multiple choice Question 19 is *a*.

14. Explain why the correct answer to multiple choice Question 20 is *e*. What do you think the cross-price elasticity of demand will equal?

VII. ANSWERS

A. *Completion*

1.	responsiveness	9.	greater
2.	elastic	10.	industries
3.	vertical	11.	necessity
4.	zero	12.	luxuries
5.	substitutes	13.	inferior
6.	unit elastic	14.	substitutes
7.	broadly	15.	negative
8.	longer		

B. *True/False*

1.	False. Price elasticity of demand measures percentage changes, not simply changes in quantity.	11.	True
		12.	False. There is no fixed relationship between price elasticity of demand and price elasticity of supply.
2.	False. Elasticity and slope are not the same thing.	13.	True
3.	True	14.	False
4.	True	15.	False
5.	True	16.	False
6.	False	17.	True
7.	True	18.	False
8.	True	19.	False
9.	True	20.	False. They are unrelated.
10.	False. Total revenue will rise.		

C. *Multiple Choice*

1.	d	6.	c	11.	d	16.	b
2.	c	7.	a	12.	d	17.	a
3.	e	8.	e	13.	c	18.	a
4.	b	9.	d	14.	e	19.	a
5.	d	10.	a	15.	c	20.	e

Discussion Questions

1. a.

Price	Quantity Demanded	Total Revenue	Price Elasticity
$20	0.5	$10	_____
18	1.5	27	9.50
16	2.5	40	4.25
14	4	56	3.46
12	6	72	2.60
10	8	80	1.57
8	11	88	1.42
6	15	90	1.08
4	20	80	0.71
2	26	52	0.39

b. Demand is elastic at prices between $20 and $6. Demand is inelastic for prices below $6.

c. At $10, two more units are sold, and the extra revenue that comes from selling more units is $20.

d. The seller could have sold six units at $12 each, for $72. Now these six units are sold at $10 each, for a total of $60. Thus, total revenue declines by $12.

e. The increase in total revenue from selling more units (part c) is $20. The decrease in total revenue resulting from the lower price on units previously sold at $12 (part d) is $12. The combined effect on total revenue is $20 – 12 = $8. That is, when price falls from $12 to $10, total revenue increases by $8, from $72 to $80.

f. When the price drops from $4 to $2, the seller can sell six additional units at $2 each, for an increase in revenue of $12. The decrease in total revenue resulting from the price decrease on units previously sold at $4 is $40. The total effect is $12 – 40, or a decrease in total revenue of $28.

2. The slope influences the elasticity of demand but not in a systematic way that can be stated as a rule. If price and quantity are held constant and slope increases, elasticity of demand also increases. But linear demand curves have a constant slope, and elasticity of demand varies along the demand curve, whereas a unitary elastic demand curve has a constant elasticity of demand but slope differs along the demand curve.

3. Yes, it matters whether demand is elastic or not. If you raise prices, total revenue will increase if demand is inelastic but decrease if demand is elastic. It is possible for demand to be inelastic in the short run but elastic when a longer time period is considered.

4.

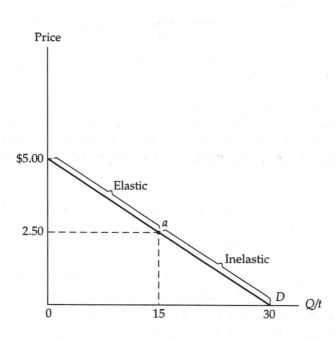

5.   If a good has many close substitutes, it is easy for consumers to respond to a price increase by switching to one of the substitutes.

6.   a.   Demand for an automobile is more elastic because it takes up a larger proportion of a consumer's budget.
     b.   Demand for amusement park admission is more elastic because there are more substitutes for it (i.e., other recreational activities) than for electricity.
     c.   Demand for blue jeans is more elastic because they are a more narrowly defined good than a pair of pants. Anything that is a substitute for a pair of pants is also a substitute for blue jeans, and other types of pants are also substitutes for blue jeans.

7.   Demand is more elastic in the long run than in the short run because people have more options open to them in the long run. Anything that can be done to respond to a change in price in the short run can also be done in the long run. But more adjustments can be made in the long run than in the short run.

8.   Producers are better able to adjust to changes in relative prices. Firms need time to alter the amounts of fixed inputs they use.

9.   The ability to adjust production capacity varies across industries. For example, it takes much longer to build a new automobile assembly plant than a new fast-food restaurant.

10. No. Consumption of an inferior good falls as income rises, and increases as income falls. If a consumer consumes zero units at zero income, the consumer cannot decrease consumption as income increases. All goods are normal goods at low levels of income.

Chapter 18

11. Income elasticity must be negative. As was pointed out in the chapter titled "The Market System," the substitution effect of a price increase is to consume less of the good. However, a vertical demand curve means that the same number of units is consumed at each price. Hence, the income effect must be negative and the good must be an inferior good, so the decrease in real income associated with a price increase has an impact opposite to that of the substitution effect.

12. Unit elastic means that your total expenditures on good A are the same regardless of its price. If you always spend the same amount on good A, your expenditure on good B is also constant. Thus, a change in the price of good A, other things constant, will not lead to a change in the quantity of good B purchased, and the cross-price elasticity of demand is zero.

13. If a product has a large, negative cross-price elasticity of demand with several products, then the product has several close substitutes. Hence, one would expect its price elasticity of demand to be relatively elastic.

14. We don't know if X and Y are substitutes or complements. If they are substitutes, the cross-price elasticity of demand will be positive but close to zero. If they are complements, the cross-price elasticity of demand will be negative but close to zero because the quantity of X will not change much. Hence, the value of the cross-price elasticity of demand is close to zero.

CHAPTER 19

Consumer Choice and Demand

I. INTRODUCTION

This chapter provides a closer look at consumer choice by introducing the concept of utility analysis. We will derive a downward-sloping demand curve by using numerical measures of utility. An alternative approach, indifference curve analysis, is presented in an appendix.

II. OUTLINE

1. Utility Analysis. *Utility* is the term economists use to describe the sense of pleasure or satisfaction that consumers receive from consuming goods and services. Utility is a subjective concept.

   1.1 Tastes and Preferences
      a. The utility a consumer derives from consuming a particular good depends on the consumer's tastes and preferences.
      b. Economists assume tastes are given and are relatively stable.

   1.2 The Law of Diminishing Marginal Utility
      a. *Total utility* is the total satisfaction received from consumption of a good, and *marginal utility* is the extra satisfaction received from consuming one more unit of the good.
      b. The *law of diminishing marginal utility* states that the more of a good that is consumed per time period, other things constant, the smaller the increase in total utility received from each additional unit consumed.

2. Measuring Utility

   2.1 Units of Utility
      a. *Units of utility* are imaginary numbers that allow us to assign relative weights to the utility derived from consumption.
      b. Each individual has a unique subjective utility scale.

   2.2 Utility Maximization in a World without Scarcity
      a. A consumer's objective is to maximize total utility.
      b. When the price of a good is zero, utility is maximized by consuming more of the good as long as the marginal utility from consuming an additional unit is positive.

   2.3 Utility Maximization in a World of Scarcity
      a. Consumer equilibrium occurs when the budget is completely exhausted and there is no way to increase utility by reallocating the budget.
      b. To maximize utility, consumers must take into consideration their relative preferences for goods, the prices of the goods, and their incomes.

2.4 The Utility-Maximizing Conditions
   a. Utility is maximized when the budget is completely exhausted and the last dollar spent on each good yields the same marginal utility, or when $MU_X/p_X = MU_Y/p_Y$ for the last unit of each good purchased.
   b. In equilibrium, higher-priced goods must yield more marginal utility than lower-priced goods.

2.5 *CASE STUDY*: Water, Water, Everywhere

2.6 The Law of Demand and Marginal Utility
   a. Consumer equilibrium is found for a set of prices, preferences, and income, which provides one point on an individual's demand curve.
   b. The price of the good under consideration is changed and the new equilibrium is found, other things constant. This provides a second point on the demand curve.
   c. The process continues for different prices until a demand curve is derived.

2.7 Consumer Surplus
   a. Along the demand curve, the price of a good measures the dollar value to the consumer of the marginal utility derived from the last unit consumed.
   b. Consumer surplus measures the difference between the value of total utility received from consuming a good and the total expenditure on the good, or between the maximum amount you were willing to pay and what you actually paid.
   c. Along a typical downward-sloping demand curve, consumer surplus increases as the price of a good falls.

2.8 Market Demand and Consumer Surplus
   a. The *market demand curve* is the horizontal sum of the individual demand curves for all consumers in the market.
   b. Consumer surplus applies to the market demand curve as well as to individual demand curves.
   c. Market consumer surplus is indicated by the area whose lower boundary is the prevailing price and whose upper boundary is the demand curve.

2.9 *CASE STUDY:* The Marginal Value of Free Medical Care

3. The Role of Time in Demand. Consumption takes time. The cost of consumption has two components: the money price of a good and the time price of a good. The time price of consumption differs across individuals because individuals have different opportunity costs of time.

4. Appendix: Indifference Curves and Utility Maximization

4.1 Consumer Preferences
   a. *Indifference curves* show all combinations of two goods that provide a consumer with the same total satisfaction, or total utility.
   b. The *marginal rate of substitution*, MRS, indicates the maximum amount of one good a consumer is willing to give up in order to get one more unit of another good while maintaining the same level of total utility.

c. The marginal rate of substitution equals the slope of an indifference curve.
d. Each curve in an indifference map represents a different level of utility. Curves further from the origin reflect higher levels of total utility.
e. Properties of indifference curves:
   (1) Indifference curves reflect a constant level of utility; that is, the consumer is indifferent among consumption combinations along an indifference curve.
   (2) Indifference curves slope down.
   (3) Because of the law of diminishing marginal rate of substitution, indifference curves are bowed in toward the origin.
   (4) Higher indifference curves represent higher levels of utility.
   (5) Indifference curves do not interesect.

4.2 The Budget Line
   a. The *budget line* reflects the income of the consumer and prices of the goods, indicating all combinations of the two goods that the consumer can purchase.
   b. The slope of the budget line equals minus the price of the good on the horizontal axis divided by the price of the good on the vertical axis.

4.3 Consumer Equilibrium at the Tangency
   a. The consumer wants to select a combination of goods on an indifference curve as far from the origin as possible but must stay on or within the budget line.
   b. Equilibrium occurs when the consumption bundle selected is on an indifference curve that is tangent to the budget line.
   c. At equilibrium the MRS equals minus the ratio of the prices of the two goods.
   d. The MRS also equals minus the marginal utility of the good on the horizontal axis divided by the marginal utility of the good on the vertical axis. That is, in equilibrium $MU_X/MU_Y = -p_X/p_Y$ or $MU_X/p_X = MU_Y/p_Y$.

4.4 Effects of a Change in Price
   a. A change in price of one good, other things constant, causes the slope of the budget line to change.
   b. The demand curve can be derived by changing the price of the good and finding the new equilibrium.

4.5 Income and Substitution Effects
   a. The impact of a change in price can be divided into an income effect and a substitution effect.
   b. The substitution effect always results in a change in quantity demanded in the opposite direction of the change in price. It is measured by movement along the same indifference curve on which equilibrium occurred before the price change to a point where the MRS equals the new price ratio.
   c. The income effect is positive for normal goods and negative for inferior goods. It is measured as the distance between the point on the original indifference curve indicating the substitution effect to the point indicating the new equilibrium.
   d. The total effect of a price change is the sum of the substitution effect and the income effect.

III. DISCUSSION

Utility Analysis

If a consumer has a choice between buying an apple for $0.50 or an orange for $0.50 and chooses the apple, then we presume that the consumer expects to receive more enjoyment from the apple than from the orange. We call this enjoyment *utility* and state that the consumer expects to receive more utility from the apple than from the orange. If the consumer assigns a value of 5 to the utility received from the orange, then a value greater than 5, say 7, is assigned to the apple. If the consumer also buys the orange, *total utility* is 12 (7 + 5), and the *marginal utility* of the orange is 5 units of utility.

Utility is subjective. We cannot compare the utility one consumer receives from consuming an apple with the utility received by a different consumer. Utility depends on the tastes and preferences of the consumer.

The basic principle of utility analysis is the *law of diminishing marginal utility*. This law states that marginal utility eventually decreases with each additional unit of the good consumed, other things constant. Since marginal utility is the increase in total utility from consuming one more unit, total utility increases as more units are consumed but at a decreasing rate. Keep in mind that the law of diminishing marginal utility refers to a particular period of time. You may not want another piece of cake right now if you have just eaten three pieces, but you may want another piece tomorrow.

Measuring Utility

Economists assume that people attempt to maximize their total utility. In a world without scarcity, this would mean that consumers could increase utility by consuming additional units of a good as long as marginal utility was positive. In the real world—a world with scarcity—the more a person consumes of one product, the less he or she is able to consume of other products. The consumer will consume more units of a good as long as the extra utility per dollar obtained from each additional unit is greater than the utility given up by consuming less of other products.

A consumer maximizes utility by consuming goods so that the marginal utility, MU, of the last dollar spent on each good is the same. If there are three goods—coffee, hamburgers, and pizza—then utility is maximized when the consumer's budget is completely exhausted and, for the last unit purchased of each good,

$$\frac{MU_c}{p_c} = \frac{MU_h}{p_h} = \frac{M_p}{p_p}$$

If people maximize utility and the law of diminishing marginal utility applies, then their demand curves for goods slope down. Exhibit 1 presents a utility schedule for a consumer's purchases of food and clothing. If the consumer has an income of $20, the price of a unit of food is $3, and the price of a unit of clothing is $2, utility is maximized by consuming 4 units of food and 4 units of clothing:

$$\frac{MU_f}{P_f} = \frac{9}{3} = 3 = \frac{6}{2} = \frac{MU_c}{P_c}$$

Exhibit 1

Units of Food/Period	Total Utility	Marginal Utility	$\dfrac{MU_F}{P_F}$	Units of Clothes/Period	Total Utility	Marginal Utility	$\dfrac{MU_C}{P_C}$
0	0	—	—	0	0	—	—
1	25	25	8.33	1	20	20	10
2	41	16	5.33	2	34	14	7
3	53	12	4	3	44	10	5
4	62	9	3	4	50	6	3
5	68	6	2	5	54	4	2
6	72	4	1.33	6	57	3	1.5

Suppose the price of food increases to $4. The consumer cannot continue to buy 4 units of each good because that would take $24 and the consumer has only $20. We also know that the consumer is no longer in equilibrium because

$$\frac{MU_f}{p_f} = \frac{9}{4} = 2.25 < 3 = \frac{6}{2} = \frac{MU_c}{p_c}$$

To return to equilibrium, either MU_F must increase or MU_C must fall. But MU_C will decrease only if the consumer buys more clothing. Obviously, the consumer cannot do this; spending already must be reduced by $4. Hence, the consumer must reduce the number of units of food that are purchased. By cutting back to 3 units of food, the consumer returns to equilibrium.

$$\frac{MU_f}{p_f} = \frac{12}{4} = 3 = \frac{MU_c}{p_c}$$

The demand curve for food is shown in Exhibit 2. Point a shows the amount of food purchased at $4, and b shows the amount at $3. The demand curve slopes down.

Exhibit 2

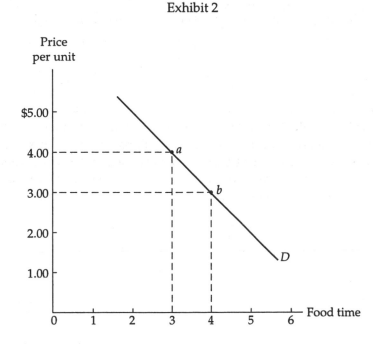

Consumer Choice and Demand

In the previous discussion, the total utility from consuming food fell as a result of the higher price for food. The consumer received 53 units of utility from spending $12 on food when $p_F = \$4$ per unit, and 62 units of utility when $p_F = \$3$ per unit. That is, the higher price for food made the consumer worse off.

Consumer surplus is the difference between the value of the total utility received from consuming a good and the total expenditure on the good. Along the demand curve, the value of the marginal utility from consuming an additional unit is the price of that unit. The law of diminishing marginal utility implies that the value of the first unit exceeds the value of the second, which exceeds the value of the third, and so on. If the consumer buys 5 units at $2, then the consumer values the fifth unit at $2. However, we know that the consumer values units 1 through 4 at more than $2. Since the consumer pays $2 for each of the 5 units, he or she receives more value than was paid for (i.e., he or she receives consumer surplus).

The market demand curve is obtained by adding up the quantities demanded by each consumer for a specific price. If Alvin will buy 5 units of a good at $2, Fred 3 units, and Sophie 6 units, then the total quantity demanded at $2 is 14 units. (Review Exhibit 7 in the text to make sure you understand the process of deriving a market demand curve.) Similarly, total consumer surplus equals the sum of individual consumer surpluses. At a price of $2, for example, consumer surplus is represented by the area below the demand curve and above a price of $2.

The Role of Time in Demand

It takes time to fix and eat a meal, to go to a movie, or to play a round of golf. That is, consump-tion involves time. The time price of consumption affects consumer decisions just as the money price does. The money price of a good is usually the same for all buyers, but the time price differs because different people have different opportunity costs of time.

Appendix: Indifference Curves

The appendix to the chapter explains an alternative approach to analyzing consumer behavior: indifference curves. Since consumer choice is essentially a subjective decision, it is useful to have a tool that does not rely on measuring utility. An *indifference curve* shows all the combinations of two goods that yield the same total satisfaction or total utility to a consumer.

Suppose a consumer consumes 8 donuts and 6 cups of coffee per day. This combination of coffee and donuts yields some level of satisfaction to the consumer. Now ask the consumer, "What is the maximum number of donuts you are willing to give up to get one more cup of coffee?" Suppose the individual is willing to give up 2 donuts. Then the consumer is indifferent between a combination of 8 donuts and 6 cups of coffee and a combination of 6 donuts and 7 cups of coffee. Someone is indifferent between two combinations when he or she does not care which combination is consumed. Further, the individual's *marginal rate of substitution* (MRS) of coffee for donuts equals 2 because he or she is willing to give up 2 donuts for 1 cup of coffee.

Other combinations of coffee and donuts that yield the same total satisfaction can be found in a similar fashion by posing the same question, "What is the maximum number of donuts you are willing to give up to get one more cup of coffee?" The *law of diminishing marginal rate of substitution* indicates that the consumer will respond with a number less than 2 when he or she is already consuming 7 cups of coffee. Assume the response is 1.5. That is, the consumer is indifferent between the following combinations of coffee and donuts: 8 donuts and 6 cups of coffee; 6 donuts and 7 cups of coffee; or 4.5 donuts and 8 cups of coffee.

Exhibit 3 presents an *indifference map*. Indifference curve I_2 shows the three combinations mentioned earlier (points *a*, *b*, and *c*, respectively) as well as other combinations that yield the same total satisfaction to the consumer. The consumer is indifferent between points on the same indifference curve. Further, the consumer prefers any point on indifference curve I_2 to any point on indifference curve I_1 and prefers any point on I_3 to any point on either I_2 or I_1. The consumer wants to be on the indifference curve that is the farthest from the origin because it represents a higher level of total utility.

Exhibit 3

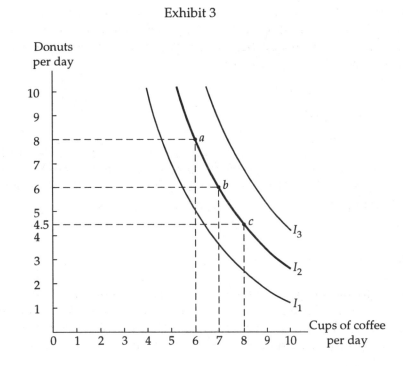

Earlier in the chapter, we saw that consumers maximize utility subject to their budget constraints. In indifference curve analysis, the budget constraint is represented by a *budget line*. Suppose the consumer has $6 a day to spend on donuts and coffee. The price of a donut is $0.50 and the price of a cup of coffee is $1. The consumer can buy 12 donuts or 6 cups of coffee, or a combination of the two. Exhibit 4 shows the consumer's budget line. The vertical intercept is 12 (Income/p_D) and the horizontal intercept is 6 (Income/p_C). The slope of the budget line is –2; this slope indicates the rate at which the consumer can trade donuts for coffee and is found by calculating $-p_C/p_D$. The consumer must be either on the budget line or closer to the origin; he or she cannot consume a combination of coffee and donuts that lies outside the area defined by the budget line.

Exhibit 4

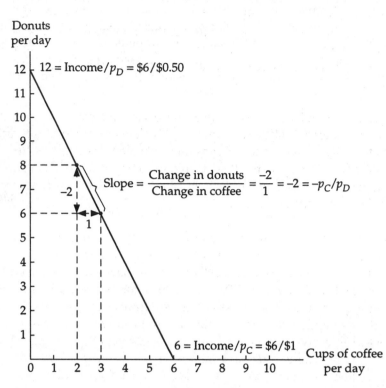

A consumer maximizes satisfaction (or utility) by consuming a combination of the two goods that lies on the indifference curve farthest from the origin but also touching the budget line. Exhibit 5 illustrates.

Exhibit 5

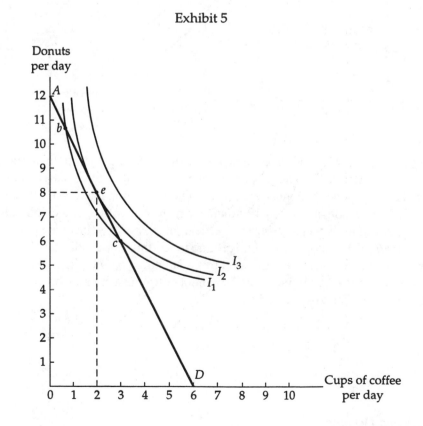

The budget line is line *AD*. The consumer can be on indifference curve I_1 or I_2, but not on I_3. I_2 is farther from the origin, so it is preferred over I_1. Point *e*, where curve I_2 is tangent to the budget line, represents the combination of coffee and donuts that maximizes the consumer's utility, given the prices and the consumer's income. At *e*, MRS = $-p_C/p_D$. That is, the rate at which the consumer is willing to exchange donuts for coffee equals the rate at which the market will allow the consumer to exchange donuts for coffee.

Make sure you understand the effects of price changes and income changes on the budget line and how to use indifference curve analysis to show why a demand curve slopes down. We can use indifference curves to analyze many types of consumer behavior. Examine the use of food stamps to subsidize food consumption. Food stamps allow recipients to buy more food than they could otherwise. Food stamps are supposed to be used to buy food and cannot be used to purchase most nonfood items, including cigarettes and alcoholic beverages.

Exhibit 6 illustrates the effects of the use of food stamps on food consumption. Originally, the consumer's budget line is *AB*, and utility is maximized at point *e* (F_1 units of food and N_1 units of nonfood). Suppose the government gives the consumer a cash grant equal to the dollar equivalent of *ef* units of food. The budget line shifts out to *CD*, and the consumer's new equilibrium is *e′*; the consumer can now consume more of both food and nonfood items. However, the government does not want the recipient to increase consumption of nonfood items and so switches from a cash grant to food stamps. That is, the recipient now receives food stamps that will allow the purchase of an additional *ef* units of food only. The new budget line is *AgD*, since the food stamps cannot be used to increase nonfood consumption above *A* (the maximum amount of nonfood items that could be purchased without food stamps). The recipient's new equilibrium is still *e′*, which allows increased consumption of both food and nonfood items. The food stamps are equivalent to a cash grant as long as the new equilibrium with a cash grant lies on the line segment *gD*.

Exhibit 6

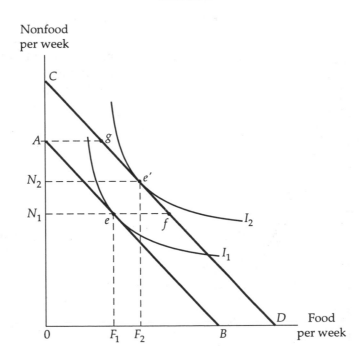

IV. LAGNIAPPE

Consumer Surplus and Sellers' Tactics

As the term implies, *consumer surplus* is the surplus value the consumer receives but does not pay for. It indicates that a consumer would be willing to pay more than he or she actually has to pay. Sellers would like to find a way to capture some of the consumer surplus for themselves. Some amusement parks charge a fee to enter the park plus a charge for each ride. The entry fee is an attempt to capture part of the consumer surplus. Similarly, some restaurants are for members only. A price is charged to join the club, and a separate price is charged for each meal. The membership fee is an attempt to capture part of the consumer surplus.

Question to Think About: Why do firms *not* use pricing tactics that allow them to capture all the consumer surplus?

Children and Time

In the last chapter, we discussed whether children are inferior goods. In this chapter, we can see part of the explanation for the tendency for higher-income families to have fewer children. Children involve time, and the opportunity cost of time is greater when income is higher. Consequently, wealthier people tend to have fewer children. Further, wealthier people will spend more on time-saving goods to help raise their children: nannies, tutors, boarding schools, and the like.

Question to Think About: Is the total cost of a child (time plus money cost) likely to be greater or smaller for a wealthy couple than for other people?

V. KEY TERMS

tastes

total utility

marginal utility

law of diminishing marginal utility

consumer equilibrium

marginal valuation

consumer surplus

indifference curve

marginal rate of substitution (MRS)

law of diminishing marginal rate of

    substitution

indifference map

VI. QUESTIONS

A. Completion

1. _____ is the term used to describe the satisfaction derived from consuming goods.

2. _____ measures the satisfaction from eating three hamburgers; _____ measures the satisfaction from eating the third hamburger.

3. According to the _____, the greater the rate of consumption of a good during a given time period, other things constant, the smaller the increase in total utility received from each additional unit consumed.

4. A consumer wishes to maximize _____ utility.

5. A consumer's utility is _____ when the last dollar spent on each good consumed yields the same utility, and the consumer's budget is completely exhausted.

6. Consumer _____ is achieved when the budget is exhausted and the last dollar spent on each good yields the same utility.

7. The maximum price a consumer is willing to pay for another unit of a good measures the consumer's _____ of the good.

8. The difference between the value of the total utility a consumer receives from consuming a given quantity of a good and the consumer's total expenditure on the good is called _____.

9. The market demand curve is the _____ summation of the individual demand curves for all the consumers in the market.

10. The _____ price of a good is the same for all consumers, but the _____ price of the good differs among individuals.

11. The _____ of time is greater the greater the wage a person receives.

*12. A consumer is _____ between any two points on an indifference curve.

*13. A person's utility function can be expressed graphically as an indifference _____.

*14. The _____ indicates the maximum amount of one good the consumer will give up to get an additional unit of another good while maintaining the same level of total utility.

*15. The budget line is also known as the _____ frontier.

B. True/False

_____ 1. Utility analysis provides an explanation of how consumer tastes are formed.

_____ 2. Economists assume tastes are given and never change.

_____ 3. The law of diminishing marginal utility says that total utility declines as more units of a good are consumed during a given time period.

---

* These questions refer to material developed in this chapter's Appendix.

_____ 4. Economists are working on ways to measure utility objectively.

_____ 5. At a price of zero, a consumer will maximize utility by consuming additional units of the good as long as marginal utility is positive.

_____ 6. In consumer equilibrium, the total utility received from each good consumed is the same.

_____ 7. A bundle of goods maximizes utility if any change permitted by the consumer's budget leads to lower utility.

_____ 8. If two goods have the same price, then a consumer's equilibrium implies that the marginal utility from consuming the last unit of each good is the same.

_____ 9. If a consumer is allocating income to goods A and B, and if, for the last units consumed, $MU_A/p_A > MU_B/p_B$, the consumer should consume either more A or less B.

_____ 10. Along the demand curve, price measures the value of the marginal utility derived from the last unit of consumption.

_____ 11. The height of a demand curve measures total utility.

_____ 12. At a price of zero, consumer surplus equals the value of the total utility obtained from consuming the good.

_____ 13. The market demand curve is the vertical sum of the individual demand curves of all consumers on the market.

_____ 14. Consumer surplus applies to individual demand curves but not to market demand curves.

_____ 15. The money price of a good tends to be greater for wealthier people.

_____ *16. Indifference curves have the same shape as production possibility frontiers.

_____ *17. As one moves down an indifference curve, the slope decreases.

_____ *18. Indifference curves can intersect once.

_____ *19. We can derive a downward-sloping demand curve using marginal utility analysis but not using indifference curve analysis.

_____ *20. An increase in the price of a good causes the consumer's real income to decrease.

_____

* These questions refer to material developed in this chapter's Appendix.

C. Multiple Choice

1. If marginal utility is positive but diminishes as more units of a good are consumed, then total utility is
   a. increasing at a constant rate.
   b. increasing at a decreasing rate.
   c. constant.
   d. decreasing at a constant rate.
   e. decreasing at a decreasing rate.

2. Which of the following statements is true?
   a. Diminishing marginal utility is a feature of all consumption.
   b. Marginal utility can never be negative.
   c. The rate at which marginal utility falls is the same for all consumers.
   d. The law of diminishing marginal utility applies to food items only.
   e. a, b, and c

3. If total utility is decreasing, then marginal utility is
   a. positive but decreasing.
   b. negative.
   c. zero.
   d. equal to total utility.
   e. None of the above.

4. Units of utility can be used
   a. to compare the satisfaction an individual receives from different goods.
   b. to compare the marginal utility an individual receives from additional units of the same good.
   c. to compare the utility received by different consumers.
   d. All of the above.
   e. a and b

5. If the price of all goods is zero, then a utility-maximizing consumer will
   a. consume all available units of the goods.
   b. consume the same number of units of all goods.
   c. consume additional units of each good as long as the good's marginal utility is positive.
   d. consume additional units of all goods as long as total utility is positive.
   e. behave consistently with the law of demand.

Use the following information to answer questions 6 through 8. $p_X = \$5$, $p_Y = \$10$, and the consumer's income equals $50. The consumer is in equilibrium when consuming 6 units of X and 2 units of Y.

6. If p_X increases to $8, then equilibrium will be restored when the consumer
    a. raises p_Y to $16.
    b. increases income to $80.
    c. decreases consumption of X.
    d. increases consumption of X.
    e. decreases the marginal utility of X.

7. At the original consumer equilibrium,
    a. the total utility from X must be greater than the total utility from Y.
    b. the marginal utility of the sixth unit of X equals the marginal utility of the second unit of Y.
    c. consumer surplus must be greater for X than for Y.
    d. the marginal utility of the sixth unit of X is half of the marginal utility of the second unit of Y.
    e. there is not enough information to compare either marginal or total utility.

8. If the price of X increases to $10, the new equilibrium will be characterized by
    a. an increase in consumption of Y.
    b. the purchase of an equal amount of X and Y by the consumer.
    c. a reduction in the marginal utility of X.
    d. the marginal utility of X being equal to the marginal utility of Y.
    e. a change in tastes.

9. Consumer equilibrium is reached when the consumer's budget is completely exhausted and
    a. the total utility for all goods is the same.
    b. the marginal utility for the last unit consumed of each good is the same.
    c. total utility divided by price is the same for the last unit consumed of each good.
    d. marginal utility divided by price is the same for the last unit consumed of each good.
    e. None of the above.

10. Suppose a consumer allocates income to goods X and Y. If $MU_X = 8$, $p_X = \$4$, $p_Y = \$120$, and the consumer is in equilibrium, then $MU_Y =$
    a. 16.
    b. 60.
    c. 120.
    d. 240.
    e. The question cannot be answered without more information.

11. As price falls and consumption increases, consumer surplus
    a. increases.
    b. decreases.
    c. remains constant.
    d. a, b, and c are all possible
    e. a if demand is elastic, but b if it is inelastic

Exhibit 7

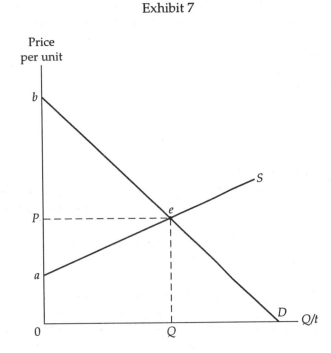

12. In Exhibit 7, consumer surplus at market equilibrium is measured by the area
    a. 0*be*.
    b. *abe*.
    c. *Pbe*.
    d. *Pea*.
    e. 0*aeQ*.

13. In Exhibit 7, the consumer surplus of the last unit equals
    a. the distance *eQ*.
    b. the distance *ae*.
    c. the distance *aP*.
    d. zero.
    e. The answer cannot be determined without more information.

14. A market demand curve is found by
    a. adding the price each person is willing to pay for a certain quantity demanded.
    b. adding the quantity demanded by each person at each price.
    c. adding the consumer surplus of each person.
    d. horizontally adding the marginal utilities of each person.
    e. None of the above.

15. Suppose there are two goods that provide the same service. Which of the following statements is true?
    a. The good with the higher time price will tend to have the lower money price.
    b. The good with the higher money price will tend to have the higher time price.
    c. There is probably no relationship between time price and money price.
    d. People will decide which one to buy on the basis of money price only.
    e. Wealthy people will tend to buy the good with the higher time price.

Exhibit 8

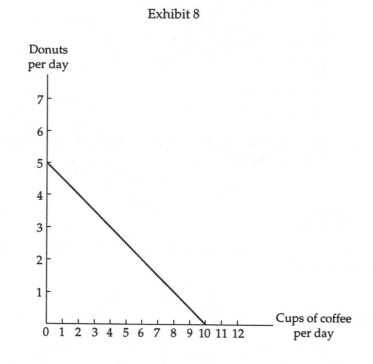

*16. In Exhibit 8, what are the prices of coffee and donuts, and what is the slope of the budget line? Income is $5 per day.
   a. $p_C = \$0.50$, $p_D = \$0.25$, slope $= -2$
   b. $p_C = \$0.50$, $p_D = \$1$, slope $= -2$
   c. $p_C = \$0.50$, $p_D = \$1$, slope $= -1/2$
   d. $p_C = \$1$, $p_D = \$0.50$, slope $= -1/2$
   e. $p_C = \$1$, $p_D = \$0.50$, slope $= -2$

*17. The law of diminishing marginal rate of substitution implies that indifference curves
   a. cannot intersect.
   b. are bowed in to the origin.
   c. are linear.
   d. slope downward.
   e. All of the above.

*18. Suppose the maximum rate at which a consumer is willing to give up gasoline for an additional movie is 3 when the consumer is in equilibrium. Which of the following are possible prices for gasoline (p_G) and movies (p_M)?
   a. $p_G = \$0.90$, $p_M = \$2.70$
   b. $p_G = \$3.00$, $p_M = \$1.00$
   c. $p_G = \$0.90$, $p_M = \$0.30$
   d. $p_G = \$0.25$, $p_M = \$1.00$
   e. More information is necessary to answer the question.

---

* These questions refer to material developed in this chapter's Appendix.

*19. Consider two goods, X and Y. Assuming the price of X falls,
   a. the substitution effect will cause fewer units of Y to be purchased, whereas the income effect will encourage the purchase of more units of Y.
   b. both the substitution effect and the income effect cause more X to be purchased, and the consumption of Y will be constant.
   c. both the substitution effect and the income effect cause less Y to be purchased.
   d. more Y will be purchased only if the income effect is smaller than the substitution effect.
   e. None of the above. The substitution and income effects only affect X and have no bearing on the consumption of Y.

D. Discussion Questions

1. State the law of diminishing marginal utility. What does this law have to do with explaining consumer behavior?

Use Exhibit 9 to answer questions 2 through 4.

Exhibit 9

Units of Steak (1)	Total Utility (2)	Marginal Utility (3)	$\frac{MU}{P_1}$ (4)	$\frac{MU}{P_2}$ (5)	$\frac{MU}{P_3}$ (6)	Units of Shirts (7)	Total Utility (8)	Marginal Utility (9)	$\frac{MU}{P_4}$ (10)	$\frac{MU}{P_5}$ (11)
0	0	—	—	—	—	0	0	—	—	—
1	150	—	—	—	—	1	200	—	—	—
2	290	—	—	—	—	2	350	—	—	—
3	390	—	—	—	—	3	480	—	—	—
4	470	—	—	—	—	4	580	—	—	—
5	530	—	—	—	—	5	660	—	—	—
6	580	—	—	—	—	6	700	—	—	—

2. a. Let the price of steak (P_1) equal $6 and the price of shirts (P_4) equal $10. Complete columns (3), (4), (9), and (10).
   b. If the consumer's income is $70, how many steaks and shirts will he or she buy per time period?
   c. Suppose the price of steaks increases to $10. Complete column (5). How many steaks does the consumer buy now? how many shirts?
   d. Why does the consumer's consumption of steak fall?
   e. Suppose the price of steaks falls to $5. Complete column (6). How many steaks does the consumer buy now?
   f. Draw the demand curve for steak.

---

* These questions refer to material developed in this chapter's Appendix.

3. a. Let the price of shirts fall to $8. Complete column (11). How many shirts does the consumer buy now? Assume the price of steaks is $6.
    b. Draw the demand curve for shirts.

4. Suppose all the numbers in columns (2) and (8) are divided by 10. Will any of your responses to questions 2 and 3 change? Why or why not?

5. Without graphs, explain how a demand curve can be derived using utility theory.

6. Explain why higher-priced goods must provide more utility than lower-priced goods in equilibrium.

7. What is consumer surplus? How is consumer surplus related to the law of diminishing marginal utility?

Exhibit 10

Price per Game	Quantity Demanded
$8	1
7	2
6	4
5	6
4	8
3	11
2	15
1	20

8. Exhibit 10 shows your demand schedule for golf games.
    a. If the price of a game is $4, how many golf games will you play a month?
    b. Suppose the golf course charges $10 to be a member and $4 per game played. How many golf games per month will you play in that case?
    c. Suppose the golf course charges $6 for the first four games per month and $4 for all other games played. How many will you play?
    d. What are your total expenditures on golf for a month under the three pricing arrangements?
    e. What is your consumer surplus under each of these arrangements?

Exhibit 11

| | Quantity Demanded | | | |
Price	Art	Bill	Carla	Market
$10	1	0	0	_____
9	2	0	1	_____
8	3	0	3	_____
7	4	1	6	_____
6	5	2	9	_____
5	6	3	15	_____
4	7	4	22	_____
3	8	5	30	_____
2	9	6	40	_____
1	10	8	50	_____

9. Exhibit 11 shows individual demand schedules for three people.
   a. Fill in the blanks to determine the market demand.
   b. Draw all four demand curves on Exhibit 12.
   c. Shade in the total consumer surplus when the price is $6.

Exhibit 12

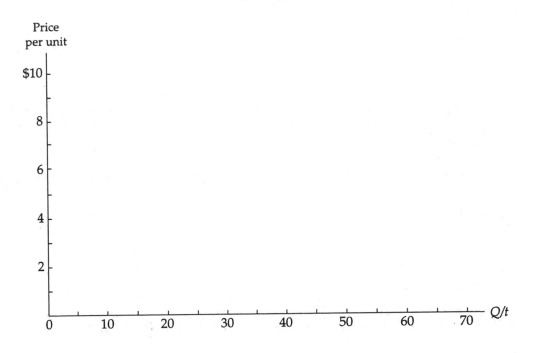

10. Everybody has the same number of hours in a day, so how can the time price of consumption differ from person to person?

*11. What does the slope of an indifference curve measure?

*12. Using indifference curves, show that a consumer will buy less food at a higher price for food. (*Hint*: Put food on the horizontal axis.)

*13. Using indifference curves, show the income and substitution effects of a price increase.

*14. If a consumer is in equilibrium and then income increases, the new equilibrium will involve the same marginal rate of substitution. Why? Will the marginal utilities of the goods also be the same? Explain.

VII. ANSWERS

A.   *Completion*

1. Utility	9. horizontal
2. Total utility; marginal utility	10. money; time
3. law of diminishing marginal utility	11. opportunity cost
4. total	12. indifferent
5. maximized	13. map
6. equilibrium	14. marginal rate of substitution
7. marginal valuation	15. consumption possibilities
8. consumer surplus	

B.   *True/False*

1. False	11. False
2. False	12. True
3. False. Total utility increases but at a decreasing rate.	13. False. It is the horizontal sum.
4. False	14. False
5. True	15. False
6. False	16. False
7. True	17. True
8. True	18. False
9. True	19. False
10. True	20. True

---

* These questions refer to material developed in this chapter's Appendix.

C. Multiple Choice

1.	b	12.	c
2.	a	13.	d
3.	b	14.	b
4.	e	15.	a. If one good had both a higher time price and a higher money price, everyone would buy the other good.
5.	c		
6.	c		
7.	d		
8.	d	16.	c
9.	d	17.	b
10.	d	18.	a
11.	a	19.	a

D. Discussion Questions

1. The law of diminishing marginal utility states that the greater the rate of consumption of a particular good during a given time period, other things constant, the smaller the increase in total utility received from each additional unit consumed. This law helps explain why demand curves slope down. If additional units of a good provide smaller increases in utility, then a consumer will not pay as much per unit for additional units as he or she was willing to pay for previous units.

2. a.

Units of Steak (1)	Total Utility (2)	Marginal Utility (3)	$\frac{MU}{P_1}$ (4)	$\frac{MU}{P_2}$ (5)	$\frac{MU}{P_3}$ (6)	Units of Shirts (7)	Total Utility (8)	Marginal Utility (9)	$\frac{MU}{P_4}$ (10)	$\frac{MU}{P_5}$ (11)
0	0	—	—	—	0	0	—	—	—	
1	150	150	25	15	30	1	200	200	20	25
2	290	140	23.33	14	28	2	350	150	15	18.75
3	390	100	16.67	10	20	3	480	130	13	16.25
4	470	80	13.33	8	16	4	580	100	10	12.50
5	530	60	10	6	12	5	660	80	8	10
6	580	50	8.33	5	10	6	700	40	4	5

b. Five steaks and four shirts

c. Three steaks and four shirts

d. At the higher price for steak, $MU/p = 6$ for the fifth steak, which is less than MU/p for the fourth shirt. The consumer cannot continue buying five shirts since that would take $90 and income is only $70. To return to equilibrium, the consumer needs to increase the utility per dollar spent on steak. This is accomplished by buying fewer steaks since the marginal utility of the third steak is greater than the marginal utility of the fifth steak. At three steaks, $MU/p = 10$, which is the same as that for the fourth shirt, and the entire $70 is used up.

e. Six steaks

f.

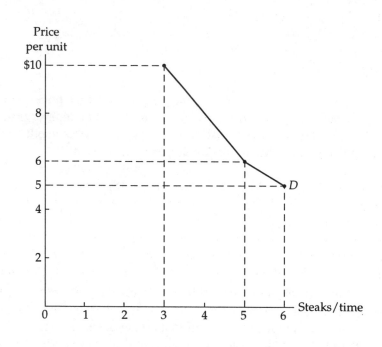

3. a. Five shirts

    b.

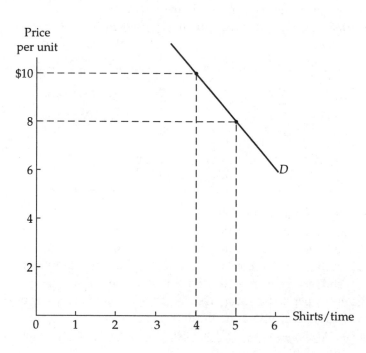

4. No. Since all the numbers on the table are divided by the same amount, 10, the ratios will not be changed by the change in scale of utility.

5. In a consumer equilibrium, the marginal utility of the last dollar spent on each good is the same. If we take one good, X, then some number of units are consumed at the existing

price. If the price of X increases, the consumer is no longer in equilibrium because $MU/_p$ of X has fallen. To get back to an equilibrium condition, the consumer must reduce consumption of X because of the law of diminishing marginal utility. Since MU falls as consumption increases, reducing consumption will yield a higher marginal utility. The reduced consumption of X generates a higher MU of X, raising $MU/_p$.

6. In equilibrium, the marginal utility per dollar spent is the same for each good—$MU_X/p_X = MU_X/p_Y$. If the price of X is less than the price of Y, then the marginal utility of X must also be less than the marginal utility of Y. That is, for a consumer to buy the more costly good, it must provide more utility than lower-priced goods.

7. Consumer surplus is the difference between the value of the total utility received from consuming a good and the total expenditures for the good. Along the demand curve, the per-unit price paid for the good equals the value of the marginal utility of the last unit purchased. But this is also the price paid for all the units purchased. We know that the marginal utility of the previous units exceeds the marginal utility of the last unit consumed because of the law of diminishing marginal utility. Hence, the consumer receives more value than the per-unit price paid on all units except the last unit. This extra value is consumer surplus.

8. a. Eight golf games
   b. Eight games. The total value of utility is still greater than total expenditure.
   c. Eight games
   d. $32; $42; $40
   e. $8 + $7 + (2 × $6) + (2 × $5) + (2 × $4) = $45 = value of total utility. Consumer surplus under the arrangement in part a is $45 – $32 = $13; under the arrangement in part b, it is $45 – $42 = $3; and under the arrangement in part c, it is $45 – 40 = $5.

9. a.

| | Quantity Demanded | | | |
Price	Art	Bill	Carla	Market
$10	1	0	0	1
9	2	0	1	3
8	3	0	3	6
7	4	1	6	11
6	5	2	9	16
5	6	3	15	24
4	7	4	22	33
3	8	5	30	43
2	9	6	40	55
1	10	8	50	68

b. and c.

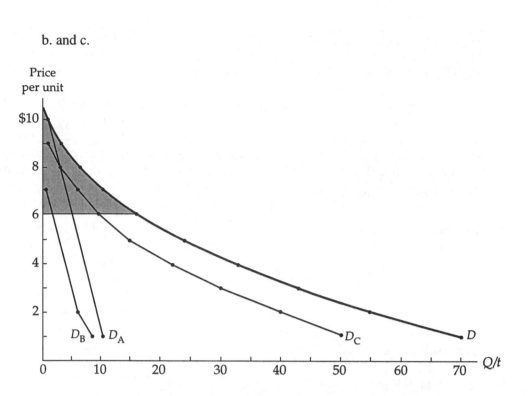

10. The value of time differs for different people because different people have different opportunity costs of time. The greater the opportunity cost, the more valuable the time and the more people look for time-saving products.

11. The slope equals the marginal rate of substitution, which measures the maximum rate at which a consumer is willing to exchange one good for an additional unit of another good while maintaining the same level of satisfaction. It represents the consumer's subjective valuation of one good in terms of the other good.

12. In the following graph, the original budget line is *AB* and the original equilibrium is *e*. A higher price for food shifts the budget line to *AC*. The consumer cannot reach equilibrium at *e* any longer; the new equilibrium is *e′*. Consumption of food falls from F_1 to F_2.

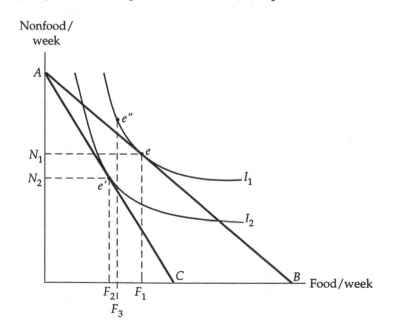

13. The substitution effect is found by finding the point where a line with the same slope as AC would be tangent to I_1. In the graph in answer 12, this is point e'', associated with F_3. The substitution effect is $F_1 - F_3$ and the income effect is $F_3 - F_2$.

14. The marginal rate of substitution does not change because the prices of the two goods do not change. At the new equilibrium, the marginal rate of substitution equals the ratio of the prices. Since the prices did not change, MRS does not change. The marginal utility of each good does change, though, because of the law of diminishing marginal utility. More of both goods are consumed at the higher income, so marginal utility falls for both goods. In fact, the marginal utilities fall proportionately because the ratio of the marginal utilities is the same at the new equilibrium as at the old. (Recall that in equilibrium MRS = p_X/p_Y = MU_X/MU_Y.)

CHAPTER 20

Production and Cost in the Firm

I.   INTRODUCTION

In this chapter, we turn our attention to the supply side of markets. Firms produce goods and services by combining various resource inputs and then selling the finished goods to consumers or other firms. Production involves technical processes and physical relationships; for example, steel is produced by using iron ore, coal, and other materials. Costs are related to production because all resources have opportunity costs. The costs of production are then related to supply curves. The analysis in this chapter applies to all firms. The next three chapters consider additional features to show how certain types of firms behave.

II.   OUTLINE

1.   Cost and Profit

    1.1   Explicit and Implicit Costs
        a.   Whether a resource is owned by the firm or hired in resource markets, the use of the resource involves an opportunity cost.
        b.   *Explicit costs* are actual cash payments for resources purchased in resource markets.
        c.   *Implicit costs* are opportunity costs to the firm of using resources owned by the firm or provided by the firm's owners.

    1.2   Alternative Measures of Profit
        a.   *Accounting profit* is total revenue minus explicit costs.
        b.   *Economic profit* is total revenue minus explicit and implicit costs.
        c.   *Normal profit* is the profit required to induce the firm's owners to employ their resources in the firm.

2.   Production in the Short Run

    2.1   Fixed and Variable Resources
        a.   *Variable resources* are inputs that can be quickly varied to increase or decrease the rate of production.
        b.   *Fixed resources* are resources that cannot be varied in the short run.
        c.   The *short run* is a period of time during which at least one resource is fixed.
        d.   The *long run* is a period of time during which all resources can be varied.

    2.2   The Law of Diminishing Marginal Returns
        a.   The *total product* is the total output of goods or services produced by the firm.
        b.   The *marginal product* is the amount by which total product (output) increases with each additional unit of a resource, all other resources constant.
        c.   Increasing marginal returns: Marginal product often increases with the first units hired because of increased specialization among units of the resource.

d. The law of diminishing marginal returns: As additional quantities of a variable resource are combined with a given amount of a fixed resource, a point is eventually reached when the additional units of the variable resource yield a smaller and smaller marginal physical product.

e. The law of diminishing marginal returns is the most important feature of firm production in the short run.

2.3 The Total and Marginal Product Curves
a. The total product curve increases at an increasing rate when marginal returns are increasing.
b. The total product curve increases at a decreasing rate when marginal returns are decreasing but still positive.
c. The total product curve decreases when marginal returns are negative.

3. Costs in the Short Run. *Fixed costs* are costs that must be paid even if no output is produced. They do not vary as output changes. *Variable costs* vary directly with changes in output. They equal $0 when output is zero.

3.1 Total Cost and Marginal Cost in the Short Run
a. There are three types of total cost:
(1) Total fixed cost (TFC)
(2) Total variable cost (TVC)
(3) Total cost (TC) = $TFC + TVC$
b. *Marginal cost* is the change in total cost that occurs as output changes by one unit. It equals the slope of the TC curve at each level of output.
c. Marginal cost is the key to decision making in the short run.
d. Changes in marginal cost reflect changes in marginal product of the variable input.
e. Marginal cost falls when the marginal product of the variable resource increases and rises when the marginal product of the variable resource declines (i.e., when diminishing marginal returns set in).

3.2 Average Cost in the Short Run
a. There are three types of average cost:
(1) Average total cost (ATC) = $TC/q = AFC + AVC$
(2) Average variable cost (AVC) = TVC/q
(3) Average fixed cost (AFC) = TFC/q, where q = level of output
b. The U-shaped form of the average variable cost curve and the average total cost curve is determined by the shape of the marginal cost curve.

3.3 The Relationship between Marginal Cost and Average Cost
a. If marginal cost lies below average cost, it pulls average cost down; if marginal cost lies above average cost, it pulls average cost up.
b. The marginal cost curve intersects both the average variable cost curve and the average total cost curve from below, where the average curves are at a minimum.

3.4 Summary of Short-Run Cost Curves
a. The level of the firm's fixed cost, the price of variable resources, and the law of diminishing marginal returns determine the shapes of all the short-run cost curves.
b. The shapes of the average variable cost and average total cost curves are determined by marginal cost, which is determined by the shape of the variable resource's marginal product curve.

4. Costs in the Long Run

    4.1   The Long-Run Average Cost Curve
        a.   The long-run average cost curve is the "envelope curve," or planning curve, made up of the segments of short-run average total cost curves for various sizes of plant that represent the lowest cost per unit for each output level.
        b.   Each short-run cost curve is tangent to the planning curve.

    4.2   Economies of Scale
        a.   Economies of scale exist when long-run average cost declines as plant size increases.
        b.   Economies of scale can result from increased opportunities for specialization.

    4.3   Diseconomies of Scale
        a.   Diseconomies of scale exist when long-run average cost rises as plant size increases.
        b.   Diseconomies arise as a result of:
            (1)   The information problems associated with a large bureaucracy
            (2)   The firm's lack of control over some resources
        c.   The *minimum efficient scale* is the lowest rate of output at which the firm can take full advantage of economies of scale.

    4.4   *CASE STUDY:* At the Movies

    4.5   Economies and Diseconomies of Scale at the Firm Level. To this point, the text discussion on economies of scale has referred mainly to a particular plant rather than to a firm.

    4.6   *CASE STUDY:* Billions and Billions of Burgers
        a.   McDonald's experiences economies of scale at the firm level.
        b.   Standardized menus and operating procedures, centralized management training programs, and advertising lead to economies of scale.

5. Appendix: A Closer Look at Production and Costs

    5.1   The Production Function and Efficiency
        a.   The production function identifies the maximum quantity of a particular good or service that can be produced per time period by various combinations of resources for a given level of technology.
        b.   It is assumed that the firm produces the maximum possible output given the combination of resources employed; that is, it is assumed that production is *technologically efficient*.
        c.   Firms that maximize profits will be efficient.

    5.2   Isoquants
        a.   An *isoquant* is a curve that shows all the technologically efficient combinations of two resources that can produce a certain amount of output.
        b.   Properties of isoquants
            (1)   Isoquants farther from the origin represent higher output levels.
            (2)   Isoquants slope down and to the right as long as both resources have a positive marginal physical product.
            (3)   Isoquants do not intersect.
            (4)   Isoquants are usually convex to the origin.

      c.   The slope of an isoquant is the marginal rate of technical substitution (*MRTS*) and equals (minus) the ratio of the marginal physical products of two resources. The *MRTS* indicates the rate at which one resource can be substituted for the other resource while the same level of output is maintained.

5.3   Isocost Lines
      a.   An *isocost line* identifies all combinations of two resources that can be purchased for a given total cost.
      b.   The slope of an isocost line equals minus the price of the resource on the horizontal axis divided by the price of the resource on the vertical axis.
      c.   A firm is not limited to a particular isocost line the way a consumer is limited to a budget line.

5.4   The Choice of Input Combinations
      a.   The efficient (and profit-maximizing) combination of resources for a given total cost is found at the point of tangency between an isoquant and the isocost line.
      b.   At an efficient combination, *MRTS* = ratio of resource prices.

5.5   The Expansion Path
      a.   The *expansion path* traces least-cost combinations of two resources that produce various quantities of output, holding prices of resources constant.
      b.   The expansion path is closely linked to the firm's long-run average cost curve.
      c.   Changes in relative prices of resources cause the firm's expansion path to change.

III. DISCUSSION

Cost and Profit

Resources used by firms to produce goods and services can be classified in several ways. One classification distinguishes between resources that are hired or purchased by the firm and those that are owned by the firm (or by the firm's owners). Both types of resources have opportunity costs, but they are treated differently by accountants. The actual cash payments for resources purchased in resource markets are called *explicit costs* and are treated as costs by both economists and accountants. The opportunity costs for resources owned by the firm or provided by the firm's owners are called *implicit costs* and generally are not treated as costs by accountants.

Accounting profits and *economic profits* differ in their treatment of implicit costs. Accounting profit equals total revenue minus explicit costs; economic profit equals accounting profit minus implicit costs. When a firm makes zero economic profit, it is said to be making a *normal profit* because all relevant opportunity costs are exactly covered. A firm will go out of business if it cannot cover all relevant opportunity costs.

Production in the Short Run

Another system of classifying inputs distinguishes between fixed and variable resources. A *fixed resource* is one that cannot be varied in the short run. The *short run* is defined as the period for which at least one resource is fixed. A *variable resource* is one that is easily varied. In the *long run*, all inputs are variable resources.

In the short run, the most important feature of production is the *law of diminishing marginal returns*. Remember, in the short run at least one resource is fixed. To increase output in the short run, the firm must change one or more of its variable inputs. As larger amounts of a variable resource are combined with the fixed resource, output increases. The extra output produced when an additional unit of a variable resource is combined with a fixed resource is called the *marginal product* of that variable resource. The law of diminishing returns states that eventually marginal physical product will get smaller as additional units of the variable resource are combined with the fixed resource. Make sure you understand Exhibit 3 in the text, and especially make sure that you know where diminishing returns begin.

Costs in the Short Run

In the short run, we distinguish between fixed and variable costs. *Fixed costs* are obligations that exist even if the firm is not producing any output and that do not change as output increases. *Variable costs* are zero when output is zero and increase as output increases. *Total cost* is the sum of fixed and variable costs. An important type of cost is *marginal cost*, which is the change in total cost that results when output changes by one unit. Marginal cost is the key to decision making by the firm in the short run since the firm can alter variable and total costs by changing output.

Exhibit 1

Land	Labor	Total Product (Bushels of wheat)	Marginal Product	FC	VC	TC	AVC	ATC	MC
5	0	0		$5000		5000	-	-	-
5	1	100	100	5000	1000	6000	10.00	60.00	10.00
5	2	400	300	5000	2000	7000	5.00	17.50	3.33
5	3	1000	600	5000	3000	8000	3.00	8.00	1.67
5	4	1500	500	5000	4000	9000	2.67	6.00	2.00
5	5	1900	400	5000	5000	10000	2.64	5.38	2.50
5	6	2200	300	5000	6000	11000	2.72	5.00	3.33
5	7	2400	200	5000	7000	12000	2.92	5.00	5.00
5	8	2500	100	5000	8000	13000	3.20	5.20	10.00

Exhibit 1 illustrates the connection between short-run production and short-run costs. Land is fixed at 5 units, and costs $1,000 per unit, so total fixed costs are $5,000. A unit of labor also costs $1,000. Marginal product increases at first, but diminishing marginal returns begin with the fourth worker. Variable costs equal $1,000 times the number of workers hired. Total costs equal total fixed costs plus total variable costs. To calculate average variable costs, we take variable costs and divide by total output (not by the number of workers). So, at 1,000 bushels of wheat, average variable costs are $3,000/1,000 bushels of wheat = $3. Marginal cost is found by taking the change in variable costs and dividing by the change in total product. With the fourth worker, additional costs are $1,000 and additional output is 500 units, so marginal cost is $2. Note that marginal costs decline while marginal returns are increasing, but increase when marginal returns decline.

Exhibit 5 in the text illustrates total and marginal cost curves, and Exhibit 7 illustrates average and marginal cost curves. The shape of each curve (except the curves for fixed costs) reflects the law of diminishing marginal returns. When marginal cost increases, total cost increases at an increasing rate. Since average costs are found by dividing total cost by output, average costs also owe their shape to the law of diminishing returns.

Costs in the Long Run

In the long run, there are neither fixed resources nor fixed costs. The long run is a planning period during which all inputs can be varied, a new firm can be started, or a firm can go out of business. In the long run, the firm can determine the best method of production for every possible rate of output and select the scale of plant that is best for the desired rate of output. Hence, the long-run planning curve is the envelope of the least-cost segments of the short-run average cost curves for each output level. Review Exhibits 8 and 9 in the text to be sure that you understand the derivation of the planning curve.

The *long-run average cost curve* (or planning curve) tends to be U-shaped. As output expands, the firm is able to use more specialized equipment and workers; this enables it to produce more output at a lower per-unit cost. Eventually, however, the firm may become so large that it becomes unwieldy to run. Per-unit costs may now increase as the firm experiences *diseconomies of scale*. Many studies have found a large range of output for which average costs are constant as output increases; at such levels of output there are neither *economies of scale* nor diseconomies of scale.

Appendix: A Closer Look at Production and Costs

There are many ways to produce the same good. Automobiles can be produced by hand, using very little capital equipment, or they can be produced by very capital-intensive methods. Further, the amount of steel can be varied by substituting aluminum or even plastic for some auto parts. A *production function* identifies the maximum quantity of a good that can be produced by various combinations of resources. Note that less of one resource and more of another resource can be used to produce the same total quantity of output. Make sure you understand the production function given in Exhibit 11 in the text. Remember, the numbers in each row show how output changes when one resource is fixed.

Tools similar to those developed in the appendix to the previous chapter can be used to analyze production. An *isoquant* is a curve defined by points that indicate various combinations of two inputs that yield the same quantity of output. The farther an isoquant is from the origin, the greater the output. Isoquants slope downward, are bowed in to the origin, and cannot intersect. The slope of an isoquant indicates the *marginal rate of technical substitution* of one resource for the other and also equals the negative of the ratio of the marginal physical products of the resources.

An *isocost line* is similar to a consumer's budget line. It identifies all combinations of two resources the firm can buy for a given total cost. Its slope is minus the ratio of the prices of the resources.

Although the firm's equilibrium is similar to the consumer equilibrium described in the last chapter, there are some important differences. The consumer wants to maximize utility, but the firm wants to maximize profits, not output. Hence, the firm has no desire to get to the isoquant farthest from the origin. Instead, the firm wants to minimize the cost of producing a given amount of output. Alternatively, we can say the firm seeks to maximize output for a given total cost. Both approaches yield the same solution: a tangency between an isoquant and an isocost line. Review Exhibit 14 in the text to be sure you understand these concepts.

A firm may decide to expand production. Presumably, it does so because it believes profits can be greater if it produces a higher rate of output. If prices of resources do not change, the isocost line shifts out to a parallel position and a new point of tangency with a different isoquant curve is established. This point of tangency represents the firm's new minimum total cost to produce the higher rate of output. The line connecting all such tangencies is the *expansion path*. If the price of a resource changes, then the slope of the isocost line changes. The firm will alter its use of resources to use more of the relatively cheaper resource and less of the relatively expensive resource.

IV. LAGNIAPPE

Be Careful with the Terms

Several new terms have been introduced in this chapter, and it is easy to make mistakes by using the terms incorrectly or carelessly. For example, it is easy to associate fixed resources with fixed costs. Although fixed inputs often generate fixed costs, there is not a one-to-one correspondence between them. For example, coaches at both the college and professional levels are often given multiyear contracts. The coach is not a fixed resource, though, as demonstrated by the fact that coaches are often fired before their contracts have expired. The team owners are still obligated to pay the coach's salary for the length of the contract, however. Hence, the coach's salary is a fixed cost.

The boundary between the short run and the long run is also fuzzy. Generally, the short run is defined as the period of time in which at least one resource is fixed, and the long run is the period of time in which all resources are variable. But the time it takes to alter all resources depends on economic factors, too. A factory can be built slowly for less money or faster for more money by having construction crews work around the clock.

Question to Think About: What factors might encourage a firm to build a new plant very quickly but at a high cost?

Adam Smith on Specialization of Labor

An important source of economies of scale is the productivity that results from increased specialization of labor. Adam Smith pointed this out in 1776:

> To take an example, therefore, from a very trifling manufacture; but one in which the division of labour has been very often taken notice of, the trade of the pinmaker; a workman not educated to this business (which the division of labour has rendered a distinct trade), nor acquainted with the use of the machinery employed in it . . . could scarce . . . make one pin in a day, and certainly could not make twenty. But in the way in which this business is now carried on . . . it is divided into a number of branches, of which the greater part are . . . peculiar trades. One man draws out the wire, another straights it, a third cuts it, a fourth points it, a fifth grinds it at the top for receiving the head; to make the head requires two or three distinct operations; to put it on is a peculiar business, to whiten the pins is another; it is even a trade by itself to put them into the paper; and the important business of making a pin, is, in this manner divided into about eighteen distinct operations. . . . I have seen a small manufactory of this kind where ten men only were employed, and where some of them consequently performed two or three distinct operations. But though they were very poor, and therefore but indifferently accommodated with the necessary machinery, they could, when they exerted themselves, make among them about twelve pounds of pins in a day. There are in a pound upwards of four thousand pins of a middling size. Those ten persons, therefore, could make among them upwards of forty-eight thousand pins in a day. Each person . . . might be considered as making four thousand eight hundred pins in a day. But if they had all wrought separately and independently . . . they certainly could not each of them have made twenty, perhaps not one pin in a day; that is, certainly, not . . . what they are at present capable of performing, in consequence of a proper division and combination of their different operations. [Adam Smith, *The Wealth of Nations*. Edited by Edwin Cannan. (Chicago: University of Chicago Press, 1976), 8–9.]

Question to Think About: What limits the advantages of specialization of labor?

V. KEY TERMS

explicit cost
implicit cost
accounting profit
economic profit
normal profit
variable resource
fixed resource
short run
long run
total product
marginal product
increasing marginal returns
law of diminishing marginal returns
fixed cost

variable cost
total cost
marginal cost
average variable cost
average total cost
long-run average cost curve
economies of scale
diseconomies of scale
minimum efficient scale
technologically efficient
marginal rate of technical substitution (MRTS)
isocost line
expansion path

VI. QUESTIONS

A. Completion

1. The opportunity costs to the firm of using resources owned by the firm are _____ costs.

2. Economic profit equals _____ minus _____.

3. If economic profits are zero, _____ profits equal accounting profits.

4. All resources can be varied by the firm in the _____.

5. The amount by which total product increases with each additional unit of the variable resource that is combined with a fixed resource is called _____.

6. The _____ is the most important feature of production in the short run.

7. Costs that do not change when output changes are called _____ costs.

8. _____ is the change in total cost as output increases by one unit.

9. Average fixed costs _____ with output.

10. The _____ curve always intersects both the _____ curve and the _____ curve at their minimum points.

11. If the long-run average cost curve slopes downward, then _____ are being realized.

12. The lowest rate of output at which economies of scale are achieved fully is the _____.

*13. The slope of an isoquant measures the _____.

*14. The slope of an isocost line measures the _____ prices of the inputs.

*15. The line connecting least-cost combinations of inputs (holding input prices constant) for several output levels is the _____.

B. True/False

_____ 1. Implicit costs are opportunity costs, but explicit costs are not.

_____ 2. The difference between accounting profit and economic profit is in the treatment of implicit costs.

_____ 3. A normal profit is zero.

_____ 4. The short run is the time period during which at least one resource is fixed.

_____ 5. Marginal product can decrease but can never become negative.

_____ 6. Production in the short run tends to be characterized by diminishing marginal returns at first and increasing marginal returns later.

_____ 7. The marginal product curve reaches its peak at the same quantity of the variable input as the total physical product curve.

_____ 8. At a zero rate of output, total cost equals fixed cost in the short run.

_____ 9. Fixed costs increase as marginal cost increases.

_____ 10. Marginal cost can be derived from the total variable cost curve but not from the total cost curve.

_____ 11. Marginal cost decreases when there are increasing marginal returns and increases when there are diminishing marginal returns.

_____ 12. In the short run, the key to economic decision making is marginal cost.

_____ 13. The shapes of the short-run variable cost and total cost curves are determined by the increasing and decreasing returns to the variable inputs.

_____ 14. The long-run average cost curve is the envelope of the minimum points on the short-run average total cost curves.

---

* These questions refer to material developed in this chapter's Appendix.

_____ 15. The shape of the long-run average cost curve is determined by the law of diminishing returns.

_____ 16. Average costs are minimized at the minimum efficient scale.

_____ 17. Many firms operate on the upward-sloping portion of their long-run average cost curves.

_____ *18. Any point on an isoquant is technologically efficient.

_____ *19. Isoquants differ from indifference curves in that isoquants can intersect.

_____ *20. A change in the relative prices of resources generates a new expansion path.

C. Multiple Choice

1. The difference between explicit costs and implicit costs is that
   a. implicit costs are opportunity costs and explicit costs are not.
   b. explicit costs are associated with variable resources and implicit costs with fixed resources.
   c. explicit costs are short-run costs and implicit costs are long-run costs.
   d. explicit costs are associated with resources hired by the firm and implicit costs with resources owned by the firm or provided by the firm's owners.
   e. b and c

2. If accounting profit is $45,000 and economic profit is $20,000, then
   a. normal profit is $20,000.
   b. explicit costs are $25,000.
   c. implicit costs are $25,000.
   d. fixed costs are $25,000.
   e. the firm is not maximizing profit.

3. In Question 2, if the owner paid himself a salary of $25,000, then
   a. normal profit would be zero.
   b. implicit costs would increase by $25,000.
   c. economic profit would still be $20,000.
   d. economic profit would equal normal profit.
   e. accounting profit would fall to zero.

_____

* These questions refer to material developed in this chapter's Appendix.

Exhibit 2

Acres of Land	Workers	Bushels of Corn
5	0	0
5	1	200
5	2	500
5	3	900
5	4	1,200
5	5	1,400

4. In Exhibit 2, diminishing marginal returns begin with worker number
   a. 1.
   b. 2.
   c. 3.
   d. 4.
   e. 5.

5. If the marginal product of the eighth worker is zero, then
   a. diminishing marginal returns begin with the eighth worker.
   b. total product is at a maximum when eight workers are hired.
   c. the marginal product of the ninth worker is positive.
   d. diseconomies of scale are beginning.
   e. total product will begin increasing at a decreasing rate.

6. When marginal product begins to decline,
   a. additional units of the variable input are unproductive.
   b. total product begins to decline, too.
   c. average product begins to decline.
   d. total product increases at a decreasing rate.
   e. both b and c.

7. In the short run, total cost is expected eventually to
   a. increase at a decreasing rate.
   b. increase at an increasing rate.
   c. increase at a constant rate.
   d. decrease.
   e. be constant.

8. When the firm experiences increasing marginal returns,
   a. marginal costs are increasing.
   b. marginal costs are decreasing.
   c. marginal costs are constant.
   d. total costs are decreasing.
   e. The question cannot be answered without more information.

9. The minimum point of the average total cost curve is
   a. at the same rate of output as the minimum of the average variable cost curve.
   b. to the left of the minimum of the average variable cost curve.
   c. to the right of the minimum of the average variable cost curve.
   d. below the minimum point of the average variable cost curve.
   e. a and d.

10. If marginal cost is less than average total cost but is rising, then
    a. average total cost is rising.
    b. average total cost is constant.
    c. average total cost is falling.
    d. average total cost is at a minimum.
    e. total cost is at a minimum.

11. If the long-run average cost curve is a horizontal line, then
    a. there are economies of scale at all rates of output.
    b. every plant size has the same minimum average cost.
    c. total costs increase at a constant rate.
    d. All of the above.
    e. b and c.

12. Every point on a long-run average cost curve
    a. represents the least-cost way of producing that level of output.
    b. involves a tangency between the short-run average cost curve and the long-run average cost curve.
    c. represents a different plant size.
    d. All of the above.
    e. a and b only

13. One factor that gives rise to economies of scale is
    a. diminishing marginal returns.
    b. increased specialization of labor.
    c. information problems.
    d. many fixed inputs.
    e. None of the above.

14. In the long run, if 1,000 units are produced at a cost of $8,000 and 1,200 units at a cost of $9,200, then in this output range there are
    a. diseconomies of scale
    b. economies of scale.
    c. increasing marginal returns.
    d. diminishing marginal returns.
    e. decreasing marginal costs.

15. Which of the following statements is true?
    a. Most large firms produce where there are diseconomies of scale.
    b. The minimum efficient scale is the rate of output where diminishing marginal returns begin.
    c. Long-run average cost curves must be U-shaped.
    d. The minimum efficient scale occurs at the rate of output that takes advantage of all economies of scale.
    e. c and d

*16. Which of the following is held constant in a production function?
  a. tastes
  b. labor
  c. capital
  d. technology
  e. b, c, and d

*17. Profit maximization implies that firms
  a. maximize output.
  b. produce efficiently.
  c. minimize costs of production of a given output.
  d. All of the above.
  e. b and c

*18. Along a particular isoquant,
  a. the amount of output is constant.
  b. the amount of labor is constant.
  c. the amount of capital is constant.
  d. the marginal physical product of each resource is constant.
  e. total cost is constant.

*19. If a firm selects a combination of capital and labor that minimizes costs of producing a given output level, then
  a. $MPP_L/MPP_C = w/r$.
  b. $MRTS = w/r$.
  c. $MRTS = MPP_L MPP C$.
  d. All of the above.
  e. a and b.

*20. Along an expansion path,
  a. prices of resources are constant.
  b. the scale of the plant is constant.
  c. output decreases if there are diseconomies of scale.
  d. output increases at a constant rate.
  e. None of the above.

D. Discussion Questions

1. In a meeting about whether to store inventory in a company-owned warehouse or rent a warehouse, a colleague says, "We should use our own warehouse and save the cost of renting one." Do you agree or disagree? Explain.

* These questions refer to material developed in this chapter's Appendix.

2. Suppose you own your own business and have the following costs:

Salaries	$30,000
Materials	15,000
Electricity	2,000
Phones	2,000
Rent	12,000

You use your own car instead of renting a similar make for $4,000 a year, and you could earn $20,000 working for someone else. Total revenue is $80,000.
   a. What is your accounting profit?
   b. What is your economic profit?
   c. What is your normal profit?
   d. Should you stay in business?

3. Explain why true/false question 3 is false.

4. Why would anyone stay in business if they earned zero economic profit?

Use Exhibit 3 to answer questions 5 and 6.

Exhibit 3

Acres of Land (1)	Workers (2)	Bushels of Wheat (3)	Marginal Product (4)	Total Fixed Cost (5)	Total Variable Cost (6)	Total Cost (7)	Marginal Cost (8)	AVC (10)	ATC (11)
3	0	0	___	___	___	___	___	___	___
3	1	50	___	___	___	___	___	___	___
3	2	125	___	___	___	___	___	___	___
3	3	225	___	___	___	___	___	___	___
3	4	315	___	___	___	___	___	___	___
3	5	385	___	___	___	___	___	___	___
3	6	445	___	___	___	___	___	___	___
3	7	490	___	___	___	___	___	___	___
3	8	520	___	___	___	___	___	___	___
3	9	540	___	___	___	___	___	___	___
3	10	550	___	___	___	___	___	___	___

5. a. Complete column (4).
   b. Where do diminishing marginal returns begin?
   c. Draw the total product curve and the marginal product curve.

6. Suppose land rents for $500 an acre and workers receive $100 per time period.
   a. Complete the remaining columns in the table.
   b. Draw the total cost curves on one graph and the average cost curves and marginal cost curves on another.
   c. At what output rate does marginal cost begin to rise? How many workers are associated with this rate of output?

7. According to the text, the shapes of the short-run average variable cost curve, the short-run average total cost curve, and the marginal cost curve are determined by the increasing and decreasing returns of the variable inputs. Explain why this is so.

Refer to Exhibit 4 to answer questions 9 and 10.

Exhibit 4

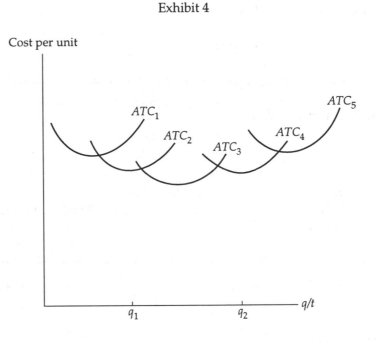

8. There are five short-run average total cost curves in Exhibit 3. Indicate what the long-run average cost curve associated with these short-run curves looks like. Which size plant should be built if the firm wants to produce q_1 units? q_2 units?

9. Indicate where the firm experiences economies of scale and diseconomies of scale. What is the minimum efficient scale?

10. Explain what causes economies of scale.

11. Can economies of scale and diminishing marginal returns apply to the same firm? Explain.

Use the production function for wheat shown in Exhibit 5 in answering question 12.

Exhibit 5

Number of Acres Cultivated per Year	Tons of Fertilizer per Year					
	1	2	3	4	5	6
1	90	135	170	200	225	245
2	135	200	245	285	315	340
3	170	245	300	340	375	405
4	200	285	340	390	430	465
5	225	315	375	430	480	510
6	245	340	405	460	510	550

*12.   a.   Draw isoquants for 200, 225, 245, and 340 bushels of wheat.

           b.   Does the production function display the law of diminishing marginal returns? How do you know?

           c.   Suppose that the farmer wants to produce 200 bushels of wheat, land costs $200 an acre, and fertilizer is $200 per ton. Add the isocost line to your graph. How many tons of fertilizer would the farmer buy and how much land would she use? What are the total costs of production?

           d.   What does the expansion path look like? How much fertilizer and land would the farmer use to produce 400 bushels of wheat? 500 bushels?

*13.   If $MRTS_{LC} > -w/r$, is the firm maximizing profits? Explain. What should the firm do?

*14.   How are the expansion path and the long-run average cost curve related?

VII. ANSWERS

A.   Completion

1.   implicit
2.   accounting profit; implicit costs (or, total revenue; explicit and implicit costs)
3.   normal
4.   long run
5.   the marginal product
6.   law of diminishing marginal returns
7.   fixed

8.   Marginal cost
9.   decrease
10.   marginal cost; average variable cost; average total cost
11.   economies of scale
12.   minimum efficient scale
13.   marginal rate of technical substitution
14.   relative
15.   expansion path

---

* These questions refer to material developed in this chapter's Appendix.

B. True/False

1.	False	11.	True
2.	True	12.	True
3.	False	13.	True
4.	True	14.	False. It is the envelope of the portion of each short-run average total cost curve that represents the lowest cost per unit for each output level.
5.	False		
6.	False. Diminishing marginal returns typically follow increasing marginal returns.		
7.	False	15.	False
8.	True	16.	True
9.	False	17.	False
10.	False. Total costs include total variable costs, so marginal cost can be derived from either one.	18.	True
		19.	False
		20.	True

C. Multiple Choice

1.	d	6.	d	11.	e	16.	d
2.	c	7.	b	12.	d	17.	e
3.	c	8.	b	13.	b	18.	a
4.	d	9.	c	14.	b	19.	d
5.	b	10.	c	15.	d	20.	a

D. Discussion Questions

1. You should disagree with your colleague's reasoning. The company-owned warehouse could be rented to another company for a fee. If the inventory is stored there, the firm bears the opportunity cost of the forgone rental payments. If the explicit cost of renting a different warehouse is greater than the implicit cost of using the company-owned warehouse (i.e., the forgone rental payments), the company-owned warehouse should be used.

2. a. Accounting profit = $80,000 – $61,000 = $19,000
   b. Economic profit = $19,000 – $24,000 = –$5,000
   c. Normal profit = $4,000 + $20,000 = $24,000
   d. You should not remain in business if you want to maximize your wealth.

3. A normal profit is the accounting profit when zero economic profits are made. That is, normal profits equal the implicit costs.

4. Zero economic profit occurs when the firm covers all relevant opportunity costs, including the opportunity cost of the owner's capital investment and time. Thus, the firm is making a normal profit when it makes zero economic profits. The owners of the firm are doing as well as they would do in their next best alternatives.

5. a.

Acres of Land (1)	Workers (2)	Bushels of Wheat (3)	Marginal Product (4)	Total Fixed Cost (5)	Total Variable Cost (6)	Total Cost (7)	Marginal Cost (8)	AFC (9)	AVC (10)	ATC (11)
3	0	0	____	$1,500	$0	$1,500	____	____	____	____
3	1	50	50	1,500	100	1,600	$2.00	$30.00	$2.00	$32.00
3	2	125	75	1,500	200	1,700	1.33	12.00	1.60	13.60
3	3	225	100	1,500	300	1,800	1.00	6.67	1.33	8.00
3	4	315	90	1,500	400	1,900	1.11	4.76	1.27	6.03
3	5	385	70	1,500	500	2,000	1.43	3.90	1.30	5.20
3	6	445	60	1,500	600	2,100	1.67	3.37	1.35	4.72
3	7	490	45	1,500	700	2,200	2.22	3.06	1.43	4.49
3	8	520	30	1,500	800	2,300	3.33	2.88	1.54	4.42
3	9	540	20	1,500	900	2,400	5.00	2.78	1.67	4.45
3	10	550	10	1,500	1,000	2,500	10.00	2.73	1.82	4.55

b. Diminishing marginal returns begin with the fourth worker.

c.

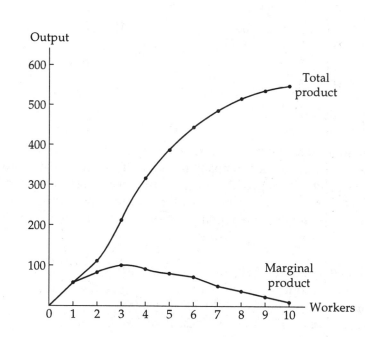

6. a. See the table in the answer to part a of question 5. *Note:* For columns 8 through 10, you should have used output and not the number of workers. For example, marginal cost equals the change in cost divided by the change in output. The first figure in column 8 is $2.00 because the change in total costs is $100 ($1,600 – $1,500) and the change in output is 50 (50 – 0).

b.

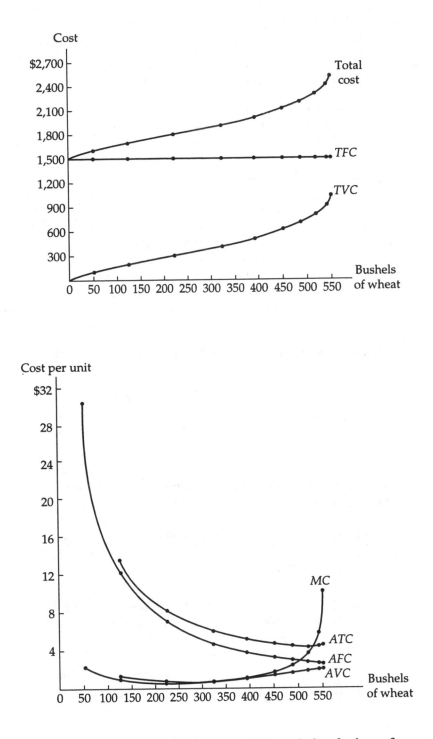

c. Marginal cost begins to rise at output of 315 bushels of wheat; four workers are associated with this rate of output.

7. When returns are increasing and extra workers are hired, additions to output increase (i.e., the marginal physical product increases). The addition to cost is the same for each worker hired, however. Therefore, the marginal cost of output must be falling. When returns are diminishing, each additional worker generates smaller increases in output. Since costs increase by the same amount for each worker and output increases are getting smaller, marginal costs must be increasing. The shape of the marginal cost curve determines the

shape of the total variable cost curve and the total cost curve since marginal cost is the additional cost of producing an additional unit of output. Thus, marginal cost also determines the shape of the average variable cost curve and the average total cost curve.

8.

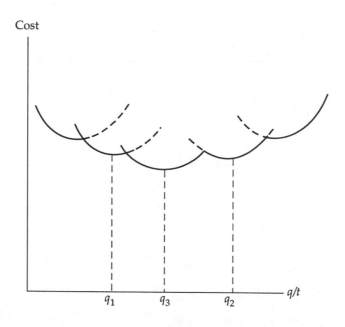

The long-run average cost curve is the solid line shown here. The firm should build a plant of size 2 if it wants to produce q_1 units; it should build a plant of size 4 if it wants to produce q_2 units.

9. Economies of scale prevail up to an output rate of q_3 units; diseconomies of scale exist for output rates greater than q_3. The minimum efficient scale is plant size 3, as q_3 is associated with the lowest of all ATC curves.

10. Economies of scale are due to the use of more specialized machines and the greater specialization of labor that is possible in larger plants. As a result, output increases at a faster rate than costs increase.

11. Yes. Economies of scale is a long-run phenomenon; diminishing marginal returns is a short-run phenomenon. They are unrelated, so the same firm could experience both.

12. a.

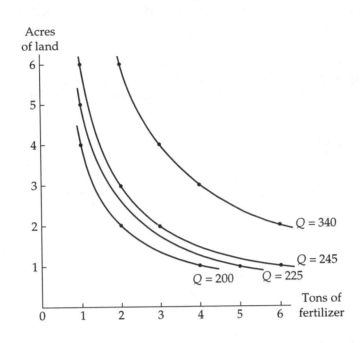

b. Yes, the production function does illustrate the law of diminishing marginal returns because changes in output get smaller along every row and along every column.

c. Under these conditions, the farmer would buy 2 tons of fertilizer and use 2 acres of land. Total costs = $400 + $400 = $800.

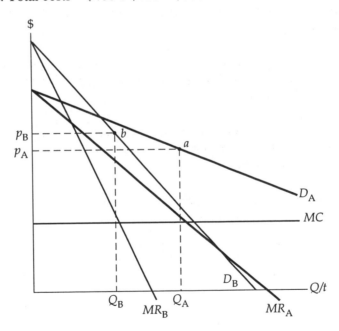

d. The expansion path is a line through the origin that connects 2 tons and 2 acres, 3 tons and 3 acres, and so forth. The farmer would use 4 tons of fertilizer and 4 acres of land to produce 400 bushels of wheat, and 5 tons of fertilizer and 5 acres of land to produce 500 bushels.

13. No, the firm is not producing in the least costly way. It can adjust its input mix (i.e., its employment of labor relative to capital) in a way that will produce the output at a lower cost. The firm should increase its use of labor relative to capital, lowering $MRTS$ until $MRTS = -w/r$.

14. The expansion path shows the lowest-cost combination of inputs for each rate of output. The long-run average cost curve also shows the lowest average cost for each output level. Hence, every point on an expansion path coincides with a point on the long-run average cost curve.

CHAPTER 21

Perfect Competition

I. INTRODUCTION

This chapter introduces the model of perfect competition. The model of perfect competition is an abstraction from reality since it does not describe many actual industries. Even so, it is useful because it allows us to focus on the essential question of how firms adjust the quantity they produce when prices change. That is, what lies behind the firm and industry supply curves? The perfect competition model is also an important benchmark for evaluating the efficiency of other market structures.

II. OUTLINE

1. An Introduction to Perfect Competition. The decisions a firm faces depend on the structure of the market in which it operates. *Market structure* describes the main features of the market: number of firms, type of product, ease of entry, and the like.

    1.1   Perfectly Competitive Market Structure
        a.   Assumptions of the model of perfect competition:
            (1)   There are many buyers and sellers.
            (2)   All firms produce a homogeneous product.
            (3)   All participants in the market are fully informed about prices, the availability of inputs and outputs, and production processes.
            (4)   Firms and all resources are freely mobile.
        b.   Firms are price takers—they have no control over price.
        c.   Firms can vary only the amount of the product they offer for sale.

    1.2   Demand under Perfect Competition
        a.   The demand curve for the output of an individual firm is horizontal at the market price.
        b.   There is no price competition among firms—all are price takers.

2. Short-Run Profit Maximization. Economists assume the firm's goal is to maximize economic profit. Since the firm cannot affect price, the question of how to maximize profit becomes a question of which rate of output to produce.

    2.1   Total Revenue minus Total Cost
        a.   The firm can find an output level that maximizes profit by calculating the difference between total revenue and total cost for each possible output level.
        b.   The profit-maximizing level of output is the point at which total revenue exceeds total cost by the greatest amount.

2.2 Marginal Cost Equals Marginal Revenue in Equilibrium
   a. *Marginal revenue* is the extra revenue a firm receives from selling one more unit of output.
   b. In perfect competition, marginal revenue equals price.
   c. If marginal revenue exceeds marginal cost, the firm will expand output.
   d. If marginal revenue is less than marginal cost, the firm will contract output.
   e. The *golden rule of profit maximization* is that the firm should produce all units of output for which marginal revenue exceeds marginal cost and none for which marginal cost exceeds marginal revenue.

2.3 Economic Profit in the Short Run
   a. Marginal revenue also equals *average revenue* for a perfectly competitive firm.
   b. Profit per unit of output is found by comparing average revenue and average cost at the profit-maximizing rate of output.
   c. Total profit equals average profit multiplied by output. It is indicated by the vertical distance between the total revenue and total cost curves.

3. Minimizing Short-Run Losses. It is possible for the market price to be so low that no level of output will yield a profit. Faced with losses at all levels of output, a firm can either continue to produce at a loss or shut down.

3.1 Fixed Cost and Minimizing Losses
   a. If a firm shuts down, its losses will equal its fixed costs.
   b. The firm's losses will be less if there is a rate of output where revenues cover all variable costs and some of the fixed costs.
   c. If the total cost curve lies above the total revenue curve at all output rates, losses are minimized where the vertical distance between the curves is minimized.

3.2 Marginal Cost Equals Marginal Revenue
   a. The firm should consider expanding the rate of output as long as marginal revenue exceeds marginal cost.
   b. If price is greater than average variable cost at this rate of output, the firm should produce.

3.3 Shutting Down in the Short Run
   a. If price falls below the lowest point on the average variable cost curve, the firm should shut down.
   b. By shutting down, the firm limits its losses to its fixed costs.

3.4 The Firm and Industry Short-Run Supply Curves
   a. As price changes, a firm varies its output to equate marginal revenue and marginal cost as long as the price allows the firm to cover its average variable costs.
   b. The firm's *short-run supply curve* is the portion of its marginal cost curve that is equal to or that rises above the minimum of the average variable cost curve.
   c. The *industry supply curve* is the horizontal sum of the supply curves of all firms in the industry.
   d. A perfectly competitive firm selects the short-run output that maximizes profit or minimizes loss. Sometimes minimizing loss implies the firm shuts down.

3.5 *CASE STUDY:* Auction Markets

4. Perfect Competition in the Long Run. Short-run economic profits attract new entrants, and losses encourage firms to leave. In the long run, the entry and exit of firms eliminate economic profits and losses.

   4.1 Zero Economic Profit in the Long Run
      a. The industry is in long-run equilibrium when firms make zero economic profit.
      b. Each firm adjusts its scale of operations until average cost is minimized.

   4.2 The Long-Run Adjustment to a Change in Demand
      a. Effects of an increase in demand: existing firms make profits as the price rises and new firms enter, which increases short-run supply in the industry and lowers price until profits return to the normal level.
      b. Effects of a decrease in demand: existing firms suffer losses as the price falls and some firms leave the industry, which decreases short-run supply in the industry and raises price until remaining firms are earning a normal profit.

5. The Long-Run Industry Supply Curve

   5.1 Constant-Cost Industries
      a. In constant-cost industries, cost curves do not change as firms enter or leave the industry.
      b. The long-run industry supply curve is horizontal, or perfectly elastic, for such industries.

   5.2 Increasing-Cost Industries
      a. In increasing-cost industries, production costs increase for all firms as new firms enter the industry.
      b. The long-run industry supply curve slopes upward because higher production costs mean that firms require a higher price to earn a normal profit.

   5.3 Decreasing-Cost Industries
      a. In decreasing-cost industries, average costs fall as industry output expands.
      b. The long-run industry supply curve slopes downward because lower production costs mean that firms earn a profit at a lower price.

6. Perfect Competition and Efficiency

   6.1 Productive Efficiency
      a. Output is produced using the least-cost combination of inputs.
      b. The entry and exit of firms in perfect competition ensures that firms produce at the minimum point of the long-run average cost curve in the long run.

   6.2 Allocative Efficiency
      a. The goods produced are those most preferred by consumers.
      b. Allocative efficiency is achieved when price equals the marginal cost of the last unit sold, which occurs at equilibrium in perfect competition.

   6.3 What's So Perfect about Perfect Competition?
      a. Market exchange usually benefits both consumers and producers.
      b. Consumers gain because they receive consumer surplus whenever they would be willing to pay more than the market price for some units of the good consumed.

c. Producers also gain because they receive producer surplus when the amount they receive for their output exceeds the minimum amount required to supply the good.

d. In the short run, *producer surplus* is the total revenue received minus total variable costs for producing the good.

e. The combination of consumer surplus and producer surplus shows the gains from voluntary exchange.

f. Producer surplus is not the same as profit

g. There is no producer surplus in perfectly competitive industries in the long run except possibly in increasing-cost industries.

6.4 *CASE STUDY:* Experimental Economics

7. Conclusion

a. Many buyers and sellers are necessary in a perfectly competitive market to prevent any individual buyer or seller from influencing price.

b. Firms must produce a homogeneous product so consumers care only about price.

c. All market participants must have full information so only one price prevails.

d. Free entry and exit must be ensured so that the long-run equilibrium condition of zero profits is achieved.

III. DISCUSSION

An Introduction to Perfect Competition

The model of *perfect competition* is characterized by two important features: first, firms are *price takers*, and second, firms make zero economic profits in the long run. The perfect competition model rests on four assumptions. (1) There are many buyers and sellers, which means that no single buyer or seller can affect price. (2) All firms produce a homogeneous product, which implies that customers care only about the price charged by one seller or another. (3) All market participants have access to all relevant information, so no consumer mistakenly pays a price higher than the market price and no firm mistakenly pays more for resources than other firms pay. (4) Firms and resources are free to enter or leave the industry at will. The last assumption ensures that firms will make only a normal profit in the long run. New firms enter the industry as long as firms in the industry are making economic profits. Perfectly competitive firms are price takers, that is, they face a horizontal demand curve at the market price.

Short-Run Profit Maximization

We assume that firms seek to maximize profits. Under perfect competition, the firm has no control over price. The only thing the firm can decide is the level of output it will produce. There are two ways the firm can determine the profit-maximizing output. Fortunately, they both yield the same output level. The first method is for the firm to calculate total revenue and total cost for every possible output and then choose to produce the output for which the difference between total revenue and total cost is the greatest. Review Exhibits 2 and 3 in the text to make sure you understand this method.

The second method of finding the profit-maximizing output is to expand output as long as *marginal revenue* exceeds marginal cost and stop expanding output before marginal cost exceeds marginal revenue. If the marginal revenue from producing one more unit is greater than the marginal cost of the unit, the firm's profits will increase if it produces that unit. On the other hand, if marginal cost is greater than marginal revenue, the extra unit should not be produced, because it will raise costs by more than it increases revenues. The firm will maximize profits by producing at the level of output where marginal revenue equals marginal cost.

Minimizing Short-Run Losses

If the price is too low to allow a firm to make a profit at any output, it will try to make its losses as small as possible. The firm has two decisions to make in this situation. First, the firm must decide whether to produce or not. By shutting down, the firm limits its losses to its fixed costs. However, if there is an output level for which total revenue exceeds total variable costs, then the firm should produce at that output level. If total revenue exceeds total variable costs, then the variable costs of producing the output are covered. There is then some revenue left over to apply to fixed costs, and the firm is better off producing.

The firm faces a second decision if it decides to produce: it must choose the output level that minimizes losses. The way the firm finds this output level is similar to what it does when it is making a profit. It either finds the output that minimizes the difference between total cost and total revenue or it finds the output level where marginal revenue equals marginal cost. Again, either approach yields the same solution.

We know the firm produces the level of output where marginal revenue equals marginal cost. For a perfectly competitive firm, marginal revenue equals the price of the good. That is, since the firm's price is constant, the extra revenue from selling one more unit will be the price received. The firm's short-run supply curve, then, is the portion of its marginal cost curve that is at or above the minimum point of its average variable cost curve. In Exhibit 6 in the text, the short-run supply curve begins at point 2 and includes all of the marginal cost curve above point 2. The industry supply curve is found by adding up the quantities produced by each firm at each price. (Note that this is similar to the way the industry demand curve was determined from the individual demand curves.)

Exhibit 1

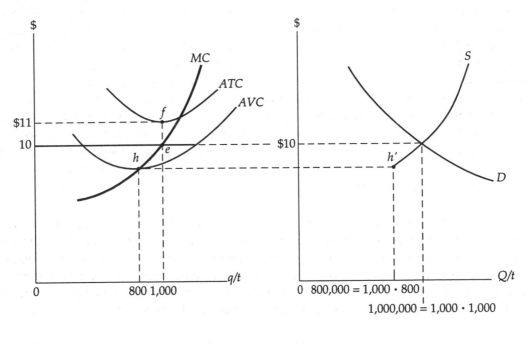

– a –   – b –

Exhibit 1 illustrates a short-run equilibrium. The right-hand panel shows the industry supply and demand curves. The market price is $10 and output is 1,000,000. The left-hand side shows the situation of an individual firm in this industry. Its demand curve is horizontal at $10. The firm's supply curve begins at point h, where the firm produces 800 units. We assume that all firms are identical and that there are 1,000 firms in the industry. Hence, the industry supply curve begins at h', with an output of 800,000. The firm is producing 1,000 units because that is where $MR = MC$. The firm loses $1,000, which is less than it would lose by shutting down since the price is above the minimum point on the AVC curve.

Perfect Competition in the Long Run

Over time, firms can enter or leave an industry. If firms are making economic profits, new firms will enter the industry. This will continue until economic profits are zero. If firms are losing money, some firms will leave. Again, this will continue until economic profits are zero. With zero economic profits, or a normal profit, firms have no incentive either to leave or to enter the industry. Long-run equilibrium under perfect competition is characterized by zero economic profits. Exhibit 9 in the text illustrates a long-run equilibrium.

Suppose an industry is initially in long-run equilibrium, and then demand increases. The increase in demand causes prices to increase, and firms already in the industry begin earning economic profits. Over time, new firms enter the industry. These firms must hire labor, raw materials, and other inputs to produce the good. If these inputs are already employed elsewhere, the new firms may have to bid up prices in order to hire them. Thus, costs for these firms will be higher than costs were for the original firms. However, costs for existing firms also increase as a result of the entry of new firms. This is because firms already in the industry will have to match the higher prices the entering firms paid for inputs or lose their supplies of these inputs. The new long-run equilibrium price must be high enough to cover the higher costs, so the new equilibrium will be established at a higher price than the original equilibrium. Exhibit 12 in the text illustrates this process. Such an industry is known as an *increasing-cost industry*, and its long-run supply curve slopes upward.

The Long-Run Industry Supply Curve

In some cases, entering firms may be able to pay the same for inputs as the firms that are already in the industry. Then the new firms' costs will be the same as those of the existing firms, and the new equilibrium price will be the same as the original equilibrium price. The long-run supply curve of a *constant-cost industry* is horizontal. In theory, a *decreasing-cost industry* is also possible. For such an industry, the long-run supply curve slopes downward if costs of production fall as industry output expands.

Perfect Competition and Efficiency

Perfect competition is efficient. In the long run, firms are at the minimum points on their long-run average cost curves, so goods cannot be produced at a lower cost. This implies that resources are not being wasted and *productive efficiency* is being achieved. *Allocative efficiency* also is achieved by perfectly competitive industries when the goods consumers want most are actually produced. The value of a good is measured by its price; marginal cost measures the value of the resources used to produce an extra unit of the good. If $p = MC$, the value of the resources used in producing the good equals their value in producing their next best alternative. When this occurs, consumers will not be any better off if either more or less of the good is produced. At equilibrium under perfect competition, $p = MC$.

Exchange is usually beneficial to both consumers and producers. Consumers receive consumer surplus, which was defined and illustrated in the preceding chapter. *Producer surplus* is a parallel concept. An upward-sloping supply curve implies that the firm is willing to supply more units for higher prices. The producer is also willing to supply some units at a lower price, however. Hence, the producer is receiving more revenues from supplying some units than would be required to get the producer to supply the units. This difference is producer surplus. It is calculated by subtracting total variable cost from total revenue. Graphically, producer surplus is the area above the firm's (or industry's) supply curve and below the market price.

IV. LAGNIAPPE

Profits over Time

The model of perfect competition assumes that additional firms enter an industry when existing firms in the industry are making economic profits. By entering an industry, new firms cause economic profits in the industry to decline. The economic function of profits is to direct entrepreneurs to use resources as society wants them to be used. But the process eliminates the profits that attracted the new firms.

If firms in the real world behaved as described by our model, we should observe a tendency for profits of all firms to gravitate toward the national average. In fact, studies have found that firms making high profits one year tend to have profit rates closer to the average several years later. We do not expect this process to produce zero profits for all firms for several reasons. First, accounting profits and not economic profits are measured. Second, the risk borne by firms differs across industries. Finally, the economy is constantly changing, causing demand and costs to shift.

Question to Think About: What would happen if new firms could not enter an industry?

Resource Mobility and Profits

Resources tend to move from unprofitable to profitable ventures. Sometimes we can see this process at work by looking at the movement of people. In the 1970s, high oil prices encouraged many people to move to oil states such as Louisiana, Texas, and Alaska. In the 1980s, oil prices fell sharply, and people moved away from these areas. Both Dallas and Houston experienced very high vacancy rates in office space. It was even difficult to find a U-Haul truck in these states.

Question to Think About: What factors would cause labor not to be perfectly mobile?

V. KEY TERMS

market structure
perfect competition
price taker
marginal revenue
golden rule of profit maximization
average revenue
short-run industry supply curve
short-run firm supply curve

long-run industry supply curve
constant-cost industry
increasing-cost industry
decreasing-cost industry
productive efficiency
allocative efficiency
producer surplus

VI. QUESTIONS

A. Completion

1. Market _____ describes the important features of a market, such as the number of firms in the market.

2. When the product of one firm is identical to the product of other firms in the market, the product is said to be _____ .

3. Resources are freely _____ if firms can enter and exit an industry easily.

4. A firm is a _____ if it faces a horizontal demand curve for its product.

5. Under perfect competition, price always equals _____ and _____.

6. As long as price at least covers variable costs, a profit-maximizing firm produces where _____ equals _____.

7. If marginal cost exceeds marginal revenue, the firm should _____ its output level.

8. The short-run supply curve of a perfectly competitive firm is the portion of its _____ curve that lies above the minimum point of its _____ curve.

9. Long-run equilibrium in perfect competition is characterized by _____ economic profits.

10. In long-run equilibrium in perfect competition, each firm produces at the _____ of the long-run average cost curve.

11. A _____ -cost industry can decrease output and not see resource prices fall.

12. If new firms entering an industry have higher production costs than existing firms, the industry is a(n) _____-cost industry.

13. _____ efficiency is achieved when firms produce the goods society values the most.

14. Allocative efficiency occurs when firms produce at the rate of output where _____ equals _____.

15. If the amount producers receive for their output is greater than the minimum amount they require to produce the output, then producers receive _____.

B. True/False

_____ 1. The decisions a firm makes depend on the structure of the market in which it operates.

_____ 2. Under perfect competition, each firm has only to decide how much of a good to produce.

_____ 3. The product of one producer is identical to the products of all other producers in the market under perfect competition.

_____ 4. Under perfect competition, a firm will not advertise its product.

_____ 5. Perfectly competitive firms try to change the profit-maximizing price.

_____ 6. Firms compete vigorously with each other under perfect competition.

_____ 7. The slope of the perfectly competitive firm's total revenue curve is the price of the good.

_____ 8. For a firm in a perfectly competitive industry, marginal revenue equals the market price.

_____ 9. Firms maximize profits by producing where total revenue equals total cost.

_____ 10. In the short run, perfectly competitive firms can make economic profits or losses.

_____ 11. In the short run, a firm should never have to lose more than its fixed costs.

_____ 12. If price is greater than average variable cost for some range of output, the firm should produce in the short run.

_____ 13. The firm's marginal cost curve is also its short-run supply curve.

_____ 14. If the market demand curve and the market supply curve intersect at a price of $5, the minimum point of the AVC curve must be below $5.

_____ 15. In the long run, perfectly competitive firms can make economic profits.

_____ 16. In long-run equilibrium, the competitive firm produces at the minimum point of its long-run average cost curve.

_____ 17. A decrease in market demand causes some competitive firms to leave the industry in the long run.

_____ 18. The industry long-run supply curve always slopes upward.

_____ 19. Where there is productive efficiency there must also be allocative efficiency.

_____ 20. Producer surplus is positive only when economic profits are positive.

C. Multiple Choice

1. Which of the following is not a feature of perfectly competitive markets?
   a. differentiated products
   b. many buyers
   c. many sellers
   d. fully informed participants in the market
   e. resource mobility

2. A price taker is a firm that
   a. faces a downward-sloping demand curve.
   b. faces a perfectly elastic demand curve.
   c. is large relative to other firms in the market.
   d. has only limited control over price.
   e. None of the above.

3. Firms that seek to maximize profits will
   a. never experience losses.
   b. choose the level of output where total revenue equals total cost.
   c. choose the level of output where the difference between marginal revenue and marginal cost is the greatest.
   d. choose the level of output where the difference between price and marginal cost is the greatest.
   e. choose the level of output where the difference between total revenue and total cost is the greatest.

4. Marginal revenue in perfect competition equals
   a. marginal cost at every rate of output.
   b. price.
   c. the change in total revenue from producing one more unit.
   d. b and c.
   e. a and c.

Exhibit 2

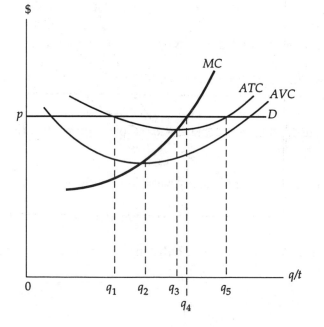

5. In Exhibit 2, the profit-maximizing firm will produce how many units?
   a. q_1
   b. q_2
   c. q_3
   d. q_4
   e. q_5

6. In Exhibit 2, if price increases, profits
   a. increase.
   b. decrease.
   c. remain constant.
   d. We cannot tell without knowing what happens to costs.
   e. We cannot tell without knowing what the market demand curve looks like.

7. Profits in the short run are
   a. overstated because fixed costs are not included.
   b. equal to the difference between marginal revenue and marginal cost times the number of units sold.
   c. equal to the difference between price and average total cost times the number of units sold.
   d. only normal profits and not economic profits.
   e. accounting profits only.

8. The firm should shut down in the short run if price falls below the minimum point of
   a. marginal cost.
   b. marginal revenue.
   c. average total costs.
   d. fixed costs.
   e. average variable cost.

Exhibit 3

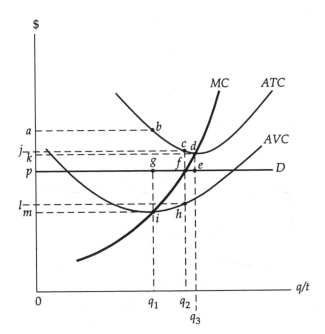

9. In Exhibit 3, losses at equilibrium are equal to area
   a. *abgp.*
   b. *kdep.*
   c. *jcfp.*
   d. *pfhl.*
   e. *pgim.*

10. In Exhibit 3, if price falls to *m*, the firm's losses will
    a. exceed total fixed costs.
    b. be less than total fixed costs.
    c. equal total fixed costs.
    d. equal *migp.*
    e. The question cannot be answered without more information.

Exhibit 4

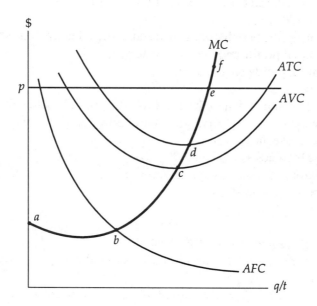

11. In Exhibit 4, the perfectly competitive firm's short-run supply curve is
    a. *abcdef.*
    b. *bcdef.*
    c. *cdef.*
    d. the marginal cost curve.
    e. *bcde.*

12. If perfectly competitive firms are making economic profits, then
    a. wages will always be bid up until the profits are gone.
    b. the firms must be superior and will continue to make profits.
    c. new firms will enter the industry.
    d. they are not equating marginal revenue and marginal cost.
    e. None of the above.

13. Suppose a constant-cost, perfectly competitive industry is in long-run equilibrium, and then demand increases. Eventually, a new long-run equilibrium is reached. Output for a firm originally in the industry
    a. initially increases and then returns to its original level.
    b. initially increases and remains at its higher level.
    c. initially increases and then decreases to a higher level than it was at originally.
    d. initially increases some and then increases more later.
    e. stays the same throughout.

14. A decrease in demand causes the long-run equilibrium price to fall. One result is
    a. a reduction in long-run profits.
    b. reduced profits for firms entering the industry.
    c. reduced prices for some resource owners.
    d. an increase in the minimum efficient scale.
    e. None of the above.

15. In an increasing-cost, perfectly competitive industry,
    a. the long-run supply curve slopes upward.
    b. new entrants bid up the price of resources used in the industry.
    c. economic profits are zero in long-run equilibrium.
    d. existing firms' costs increase as output increases.
    e. All of the above.

16. Along a long-run industry supply curve in perfect competition,
    a. economic profits are zero.
    b. economic profits can be positive, negative, or zero.
    c. the number of firms in the industry is constant.
    d. normal profit is zero.
    e. None of the above.

17. Productive efficiency is achieved when
    a. firms produce at the lowest possible marginal cost.
    b. $p = MC$.
    c. firms produce at the minimum point of their long-run average cost curves.
    d. firms produce the goods consumers want.
    e. economic profits are being made.

18. Allocative efficiency is achieved when
    a. firms produce at the lowest possible cost.
    b. economic profits are being made.
    c. $p = MC$.
    d. marginal cost is at a minimum.
    e. a and b

19. Producer surplus is greater in the short run than in the long run because
    a. there are no profits in the long run.
    b. there is never any producer surplus in the long run.
    c. the short-run supply curve is more inelastic than the long-run supply curve.
    d. a and b
    e. None of the above.

20. Producer surplus is zero
    a. when the long-run supply curve is elastic.
    b. when economic profits are zero.
    c. when all workers receive the same wage rate.
    d. when a constant-cost industry is in long-run equilibrium.
    e. None of the above.

D. Discussion Questions

1. Perfectly competitive firms are called price takers. What does this mean? Why are they price takers?

2. Show that price equals both marginal revenue and average revenue for a perfectly competitive firm.

Exhibit 5

Price	Quantity	Total Revenue	Total Cost	Marginal Cost	Marginal Revenue	Average Variable Cost	Average Total Cost	Economic Profit
$4.00	0	____	$10.00	____	____	____	____	____
4.00	1	____	14.20	____	____	____	____	____
4.00	2	____	17.80	____	____	____	____	____
4.00	3	____	20.60	____	____	____	____	____
4.00	4	____	23.10	____	____	____	____	____
4.00	5	____	25.70	____	____	____	____	____
4.00	6	____	28.50	____	____	____	____	____
4.00	7	____	31.50	____	____	____	____	____
4.00	8	____	34.70	____	____	____	____	____
4.00	9	____	38.10	____	____	____	____	____
4.00	10	____	41.70	____	____	____	____	____
4.00	11	____	45.50	____	____	____	____	____
4.00	12	____	49.50	____	____	____	____	____
4.00	13	____	53.70	____	____	____	____	____
4.00	14	____	58.20	____	____	____	____	____
4.00	15	____	63.20	____	____	____	____	____

3. a. Fill in the blanks in Exhibit 5.
   b. At what level of output are profits maximized? Explain two methods of determining this level of output. What is the firm's profit?
   c. Is this level of output a long-run equilibrium? How do you know?
   d. Suppose price increases to $4.50. How many units will the firm produce? What will its profit be?
   e. How far would price have to fall before the firm would shut down?
   f. What adjustments will the industry make in the long run?

4. Suppose there are 1,000 firms in the industry of the firm described in the previous question.
   a. Draw the industry supply curve in the right-hand grid of Exhibit 6. Add a demand curve that intersects the supply curve at the correct place.
   b. Draw the relevant curves for the firm in the left-hand grid.
   c. Indicate the firm's profits or losses.

Exhibit 6

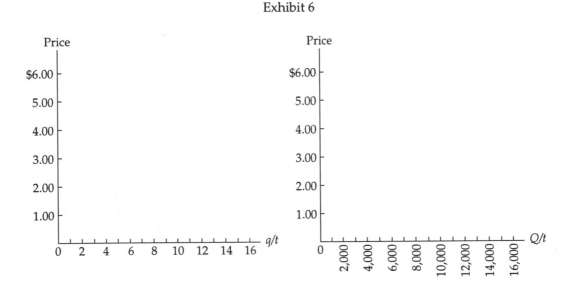

5. What is the golden rule of profit maximization? Explain why the rule maximizes profits.

6. Why does a firm ever produce when it is losing money?

7. Why is economic profit zero all along a long-run supply curve in perfect competition?

8. Explain what determines the shape of an industry long-run supply curve.

9. Why are profits so important in the perfect competition model when they are always zero in the long run?

10. What is productive efficiency? How does perfect competition guarantee productive efficiency?

11. What is allocative efficiency? How does perfect competition guarantee allocative efficiency?

12. Under perfect competition, the marginal cost of supplying the good exactly equals the marginal benefit of the good to consumers. Further, firms earn zero profits in the long run. Does this mean that market exchange provides no benefits to participants? Explain.

VII. ANSWERS

A. Completion

1. structure
2. homogeneous
3. mobile
4. price taker
5. marginal revenue; average revenue
6. marginal revenue; marginal cost
7. decrease
8. marginal cost; average variable cost
9. zero
10. minimum
11. constant
12. increasing
13. Allocative
14. price; marginal cost
15. producer surplus

B. True/False

1. True
2. True
3. True
4. True
5. False. They have to take whatever market price prevails.
6. False. The output decisions of one firm have no effect on the other firms.
7. True
8. True
9. False
10. True
11. True. The firm can always limit losses to its fixed costs by shutting down
12. True
13. False. The firm's short-run supply curve is only that portion of the MC curve that is at or above the minimum point of the average variable cost curve.
14. True. The supply curve of a firm is the portion of its marginal cost curve that lies above the minimum point of the average variable cost curve. The market supply curve is the horizontal summation of the supply curves of all the firms in the industry.
15. False
16. True
17. True
18. False. The statement is true only for increasing-cost industries.
19. False
20. False

C. Multiple Choice

1. a	6. a	11. c	16. a
2. b	7. c	12. c	17. c
3. e	8. e	13. a	18. c
4. d	9. c	14. c	19. c
5. d	10. c	15. e	20. d

D. Discussion Questions

1. Perfectly competitive firms are called price takers because they have no individual control over price. A firm can sell as many units as it wants at the market price. In perfect competition, there are so many firms that any changes in output a firm makes will not affect the market price. In addition, the goods produced by such firms are homogeneous, so buyers do not care which seller they buy from—they only care about getting the best price. (We assume the consumers know what the market price is.)

2. Total revenue equals price times quantity ($p \times q$). Marginal revenue equals the change in total revenue from selling one more unit. Since price does not change, total revenue increases by the price when one more unit is sold. Average revenue equals total revenue divided by quantity, or $pq/q = p$.

3. a.

Price	Quantity	Total Revenue	Total Cost	Marginal Cost	Marginal Revenue	Average Variable Cost	Average Total Cost	Economic Profit
$4.00	0	____	$10.00	____	____	____	____	−$10.00
4.00	1	$4.00	14.20	$4.20	$4.00	$4.20	$14.20	−10.20
4.00	2	8.00	17.80	3.60	4.00	3.90	8.90	−9.80
4.00	3	12.00	20.60	2.80	4.00	3.53	6.87	−8.60
4.00	4	16.00	23.10	2.50	4.00	3.28	5.78	−7.10
4.00	5	20.00	25.70	2.60	4.00	3.14	5.14	−5.70
4.00	6	24.00	28.50	2.80	4.00	3.08	4.75	−4.50
4.00	7	28.00	31.50	3.00	4.00	3.07	4.50	−3.50
4.00	8	32.00	34.70	3.20	4.00	3.09	4.34	−2.70
4.00	9	36.00	38.10	3.40	4.00	3.12	4.23	−2.10
4.00	10	40.00	41.70	3.60	4.00	3.17	4.17	−1.70
4.00	11	44.00	45.50	3.80	4.00	3.23	4.14	−1.50
4.00	12	48.00	49.50	4.00	4.00	3.29	4.13	−1.50
4.00	13	52.00	53.70	4.20	4.00	3.36	4.13	−1.70
4.00	14	56.00	58.20	4.50	4.00	3.44	4.16	−2.20
4.00	15	60.00	63.20	5.00	4.00	3.55	4.21	−3.20

b. Profits are maximized at 12 units of output. Calculating the difference between total revenue and total cost is one method of determining this output; this method yields a minimum loss of $1.50. Also, $MR = MC$ at 12 units of output. The firm's profit is −$1.50.
c. No, this level of output is not a long-run equilibrium because the firm is losing money.
d. The firm will produce 14 units and make a profit of $4.80.
e. Price would have to fall below $3.07, which is the minimum of average variable cost.
f. In the long run, some firms will leave the industry.

4.

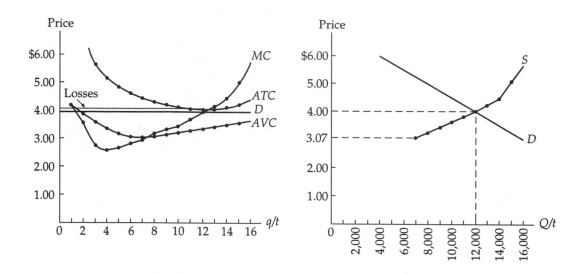

5. The golden rule of profit maximization is that the firm should expand output as long as marginal revenue exceeds marginal cost and should stop expanding output when marginal cost exceeds marginal revenue. In other words, it should produce at the output level where marginal cost equals marginal revenue. This maximizes profits because the firm will increase profits by producing an additional unit whenever marginal revenue is greater than marginal cost. When this happens, revenues increase more than costs when the extra unit is produced. If marginal cost is greater than marginal revenue, reducing output by one unit will cause costs to fall more than revenues, again increasing the profits. If the firm expands whenever $MR > MC$ and contracts whenever $MR < MC$, then it will produce when $MR = MC$.

6. In the short run, the firm has to pay its fixed costs whether it produces or not. It will produce any time its losses, when it produces, are less than its fixed costs. This will be the case whenever price is above average variable cost at some level of output.

7. The long-run supply curve applies when all firms have made all adjustments they wish to make. Hence, every point on a long-run supply curve is a long-run equilibrium, which is characterized by zero economic profits.

8. New firms entering an industry must obtain the necessary resources in order to produce the goods. If they can hire the resources for the same prices that existing firms pay, industry costs remain constant and the long-run supply curve is horizontal. If they have to bid up the prices of resources, their costs rise. However, the costs to existing firms also rise in that case. The new long-run equilibrium price is thus higher than the old one, and the long-run supply curve slopes upward. If production costs fall as industry output expands, the long-run supply curve slopes downward.

9. Profits (or losses) induce entrepreneurs to move resources from one area to another. If profits can be made in a market, entrepreneurs will enter the market to capture some of these profits. These actions result in a reduction of profits until all firms receive zero economic profits.

10. Productive efficiency is using the least-cost combination of inputs to produce a good. That is, with productive efficiency, inputs are not wasted. In the long run under perfect competition, firms produce at the minimum point of their long-run average cost curve, so they are efficient.

11. Allocative efficiency is the production of goods that consumers want. The price of a good reflects the value consumers attach to the last unit they consume. The marginal cost of the last unit measures the value of the resources used to produce the good in their best alternative use. When $p = MC$, the marginal cost of producing the last unit of output exactly equals the marginal benefit consumers receive from that unit. The right amount of the good is produced when $p = MC$. Under perfect competition, firms are in equilibrium when price equals marginal cost.

12. No, because consumers usually receive some consumer surplus and producers usually receive producer surplus. This will be true if demand curves slope down and supply curves slope up.

CHAPTER 22

Monopoly

I. INTRODUCTION

This chapter analyzes monopoly. Like the model of perfect competition, the model of monopoly is a tool used to analyze markets, not a descriptive model of real-world firms. Pure monopoly is very rare, just as perfect competition is very rare. The next chapter examines two intermediate market structures: monopolistic competition and oligopoly.

II. OUTLINE

1.   Barriers to Entry. *Barriers to entry* are restrictions on the entry of new firms into an industry.

      1.1   Legal Restrictions. The government can make it illegal for another firm to enter a market.
          a.   *Patents* award the developers of new products the exclusive rights to production for 20 years.
          b.   Patent laws are designed to be incentives for inventors to allocate resources to developing inventions.
          c.   The government also restricts entry into some areas by licenses and other restrictions.

      1.2   Economies of Scale
          a.   A monopoly can emerge when a firm experiences declining average costs over the entire range of output demanded by consumers.
          b.   When this occurs, the firm is said to be a *natural monopoly*.

      1.3   Control of Essential Resources
          a.   A firm that controls the supply of a nonreproducible resource critical to production can restrict entry.
          b.   Over time, technological change tends to break down barriers to entry.

      1.4   *CASE STUDY:* Are Diamonds Forever?

2.   Revenue for the Monopolist

      2.1   Revenue Schedule
          a.   The demand curve for a monopolist is identical to the market demand curve, so the monopolist faces a downward-sloping demand curve.
          b.   The demand curve is also the monopolist's average revenue curve.

      2.2   Revenue Curves
          a.   A monopolist's marginal revenue curve lies below the demand curve.
          b.   Total revenue is maximized when marginal revenue equals zero.
          c.   When marginal revenue is positive, demand is price elastic; when marginal revenue is negative, demand is price inelastic.

3.   The Firm's Costs and Profit Maximization

    3.1   Profit Maximization
        a.   The monopolist can find the rate of output for which the difference between total revenue and total cost is the greatest. If economic profit is possible, that output will maximize profit.
        b.   Alternatively, the monopolist can expand output as long as marginal revenue exceeds marginal cost but stop before marginal cost exceeds marginal revenue.
        c.   Monopolies always produce on the elastic portion of the demand curve.

    3.2   Short-Run Losses and the Shutdown Decision
        a.   The monopolist will continue to produce at a loss if marginal cost equals marginal revenue where price exceeds average variable cost but is below average total cost.
        b.   A monopoly will shut down if revenue fails to cover variable costs at all output levels.
        c.   Since the monopolist produces where $MR = MC$, but MR does not equal price, the marginal cost curve does not show the relation between price and quantity supplied.
        d.   Since there is not a unique relationship between price and output, the monopolist does not have a supply curve.

    3.3   Long-Run Profit Maximization
        a.   Because there are barriers to entry into a monopoly industry, economic profits can persist in the long run.
        b.   A monopolist seeks to find the scale of the firm that maximizes profit.
        c.   If a monopolist that is suffering losses cannot eliminate the losses in the long run, the firm will leave the industry.

4.   Monopoly and the Allocation of Resources

    4.1   Price and Output under Perfect Competition
        a.   Price equals marginal cost at equilibrium under perfect competition.
        b.   At equilibrium, the marginal cost to society of producing the final unit of output equals the marginal benefit consumers assign to that unit.

    4.2   Price and Output under Monopoly
        a.   At equilibrium, marginal revenue equals marginal cost for a monopoly, but price exceeds marginal revenue.
        b.   Therefore, price exceeds marginal cost, and consumers value an additional unit of output at more than the marginal cost to society of producing the unit of output.

    4.3   Allocative and Distributive Effects
        a.   As long as it does not have significant economies of scale, a monopolist produces a smaller rate of output and charges a higher price than a firm under perfect competition.
        b.   Monopoly profits are a transfer from consumers to the monopolist of what would be consumer surplus under perfect competition.
        c.   The welfare loss, or *deadweight loss*, of a monopoly is measured by the lost consumer surplus that is not transferred to anyone else.

5.   Problems Estimating the Welfare Cost of Monopoly

  5.1   Why the Welfare Loss of Monopoly Might Be Lower
    a.   If a monopolist experiences significant economies of scale, the price under monopoly could be lower than under competition.
    b.   Fear of potential rivals: high profits might attract new entrants, which would reduce future profits, so the monopolist does not raise price as much as it could.
    c.   Fear of public intervention: high profits and a high price might result in the government's stepping in and taxing profits or setting prices.

  5.2   Why the Welfare Loss of Monopoly Might Be Higher
    a.   A monopolist could grow lazy and fail to minimize the costs of production or be generally lacking in innovation. However, the market for corporate control limits these tendencies.
    b.   Monopolists may expend resources to obtain and maintain the monopoly. This is called *rent seeking*.

  5.3   *CASE STUDY:* The Mail Monopoly?

6.   Models of Price Discrimination

  6.1   Conditions for Price Discrimination
    a.   A producer must face a downward-sloping demand curve.
    b.   There must be at least two identifiable classes of customers with different elasticities of demand.
    c.   The monopolist must be able to distinguish easily between customers in the two groups.
    d.   The monopolist must be able to prevent buyers who face the lower price from reselling to buyers who face the higher price.

  6.2   Examples of Price Discrimination
    a.   Airlines and telephone utilities charge businesses higher prices than they charge house-holds.
    b.   Many businesses give price discounts to students or senior citizens.

  6.3   A Model of Price Discrimination
    a.   For each class of customer the monopolist sets a rate of output at which marginal revenue equals marginal cost.
    b.   The group with the more price elastic demand will face the lower price.

  6.4   Perfect Price Discrimination: The Monopolist's Dream
    a.   *Perfect price discrimination* involves charging a different price for each unit of output sold.
    b.   If monopolists could price discriminate perfectly, all the consumer surplus under perfect competition would be transferred to the monopolist in the form of profits.
    c.   Perfect price discrimination would result in allocative efficiency and there would be no deadweight loss.

III. DISCUSSION

Barriers to Entry

A *monopoly* is the sole seller of a good that has no close substitutes. Monopolists often earn economic profits. We saw in the previous chapter that profits usually attract new firms to enter the market. A monopoly must prevent such entry from taking place. Factors that prevent new firms from profitably entering are called *barriers to entry*.

There are three types of barriers to entry. First, the government can create legal barriers that restrict other firms from entering the industry. *Patents* are an example of a legal barrier, although patents are justified on the grounds that they create incentives for firms to spend time and resources on inventive activity. In other cases, the government may restrict entry to only those firms or individuals with a certain type of license and then limit the number of licenses. Second, production may be characterized by significant economies of scale. In such cases, a single firm can attain lower average costs by expanding production and underpricing other firms. The result is called a *natural monopoly*. The third type of barrier to entry is control of an essential resource.

Revenue for the Monopolist

The demand curve faced by a monopolist is the market demand curve because there are no other firms in the industry. All the differences between monopoly and perfect competition derive from the facts that the monopolist faces a downward-sloping demand curve and the entry of new firms is restricted. Since the demand curve slopes downward, the monopolist must lower price to sell additional units of output. This implies that the monopolist's marginal revenue curve lies below its demand curve. Recall that for a competitive firm, the demand curve is also the marginal revenue curve. Exhibit 1 shows a demand schedule and other revenue schedules for a monopolist.

Exhibit 1

Price	Quantity Demanded	Total Revenue	Average Revenue	Marginal Revenue
$5.00	10	$50.00	$5.00	$5.00
4.80	20	96.00	4.80	4.60
4.60	30	138.00	4.60	4.20
4.40	40	176.00	4.40	3.80
4.20	50	210.00	4.20	3.40
4.00	60	240.00	4.00	3.00
3.80	70	266.00	3.80	2.60
3.60	80	288.00	3.60	2.20
3.40	90	306.00	3.40	1.80
3.20	100	320.00	3.20	1.40

Average revenue equals $TR/q = pq/q = p$, so price is always the same as average revenue. The key difference between monopoly and perfect competition is that marginal revenue does not equal price.

Suppose a firm is selling 50 units a week at $4.20 per unit. Its total revenue is $210.00. If it lowers price to $4.00, the firm can sell an additional 10 units and obtain an additional $40.00 from those units. However, this is not the only effect of the price reduction. The 50 units that the firm used to sell at $4.20 now sell for $4.00 each. Instead of receiving $210.00 for the 50 units, the firm now receives $200.00— $10.00 less than before. Thus, the price decrease has two effects. The sale of additional units increases revenues, but the lower price reduces the revenue from those units that formerly were sold at the higher price. The change in total revenues from selling the additional 10 units is the sum of the two effects: $40.00 + (–$10.00) = $30.00. Marginal revenue is $3.00, which is less than the price of $4.00. Hence, the marginal revenue curve lies below the demand curve.

The Firm's Costs and Profit Maximization

The golden rule of profit maximization is the same for the monopolist as it is for the perfectly competitive firm: find the rate of output for which marginal revenue equals marginal cost. In the case of perfect competition, this rule implies that the firm sets price equal to marginal cost. This is not true for the monopolist because price is greater than marginal revenue. Hence, in equilibrium, the monopolist's price is greater than its marginal cost. Make sure that you understand Exhibits 4, 5, and 6 in the textbook as well as the discussion that accompanies those exhibits.

Monopolists do not always make positive profits, and may face the decision of whether to produce at a loss or to shut down in the short run. The procedure for deciding is identical to that used by a competitive firm. If there is no price that is greater than average variable cost, the firm should shut down and minimize its losses by limiting them to the amount of the fixed costs. The firm should produce if there is some rate of output at which all variable costs and some fixed costs are covered.

We saw in the last chapter that when competitive firms make profits in the short run, new firms enter the industry in the long run until all firms make zero profits. In monopoly, new firms are prevented from entering the industry, so the distinction between the long run and the short run is not as clear. Still, all resources can vary in the long run, so the monopolist will alter the scale of the firm so as to maximize profits.

Monopoly and the Allocation of Resources

Unless it experiences significant economies of scale, an industry that is a monopoly produces a smaller rate of output and charges a higher price than an industry under perfect competition. The restricted output and higher price imply that consumer surplus is smaller under monopoly than it is under perfect competition. Some of the consumer surplus is transferred to the monopolist in the form of profits, and some is lost to society. This loss is known as the *deadweight loss* of monopoly. Under perfect competition, price equals marginal cost; under monopoly, price exceeds marginal cost. Consequently, the allocation of resources is different when production is carried on in a perfectly competitive industry than it is when production is carried on in a monopoly.

Problems Estimating the Welfare Cost of Monopoly

The actual social cost of monopoly may be larger or smaller than the deadweight loss of monopoly described. A monopolist may not charge the short-run profit-maximizing price for fear that the large economic profits it would earn would attract new entrants or would attract the attention of government officials. To the extent this is true, the deadweight loss of monopoly is smaller than that indicated in Exhibit 8 in the text. On the other hand, monopolies may not minimize the cost of production and may spend resources to obtain or maintain the monopoly. When either of these situations occurs, the true social cost of monopoly is greater than that indicated by Exhibit 7.

Models of Price Discrimination

Monopolists can often increase profits by practicing *price discrimination*: charging different prices to different customers or charging the same consumer different prices for different units of the same good. To price discriminate, a firm must face a downward-sloping demand curve, must have at least two different groups of customers with different elasticities of demand, must be able to identify members of the different groups easily, and must be able to prevent resale of its products between members of the groups.

To maximize profits by price discriminating, the monopolist equates marginal revenue for each group of customers with the marginal cost of supplying the good. The group with the more price inelastic demand will pay the higher price.

In the best of all worlds, a monopolist could practice perfect price discrimination: it could charge a different price for each unit of the good sold. In this way, every dollar of consumer surplus would be converted to profit for the monopolist. However, no monopolist is able to perfectly price discriminate because the necessary information about individual demand schedules is impossible to obtain.

IV. LAGNIAPPE

Barriers to Entry and Time

Barriers to entry often last for a relatively short time. In the United States, patents have a legal life of 20 years. In most European countries, firms must renew patents annually and pay a substantial fee to renew. Studies have found that the average duration of a European patent is closer to 7 years than 20. That is, firms often do not find it profitable to renew the patent after 7 years because the patent has lost its value. A patent loses its value when new discoveries make the patented product or process obsolete or less unique.

Another barrier to entry—control of a key resource—also tends to be weakened over time. Few resources are in such limited supply that one firm can capture all of the supplies. Even when this does occur, other firms are likely to search for alternative sources of the resource or for other resources that can be used as substitutes. For example, over time, discoveries of bauxite reduced Alcoa's control of bauxite. Similarly, at one time U.S. Steel controlled most of the high-quality iron ore reserves in the country. Depletion of those reserves, combined with new discoveries of rich iron ore reserves elsewhere in the world, have broken down this barrier to entry.

In contrast, economies of scale can have long-lasting effects, as they are based on technical considerations and not on economic behavior. Government restrictions can also be long lasting, although the protected firms may have to spend resources (that is, engage in *rent seeking*) to maintain their privileged position.

Question to Think About: How could a firm that experiences significant economies of scale ever lose its monopoly position?

Price Elasticity and Price Discrimination

We learned from the text that a monopolist that price discriminates charges a higher price to the group of customers with the less elastic demand. Price elasticity of demand is determined by the number and closeness of substitutes. Hence, the monopolist is charging the group with fewer alternatives a higher price. If the firm tried to charge the higher price to the group with the more elastic demand, people would switch to substitutes.

The relationship between substitutes and price discrimination can be seen by examining prices set by local phone companies and by local electric utilities. Most electric utilities charge a higher rate to residential customers than to industrial customers. To some extent, this difference reflects lower costs of servicing industrial customers. However, it also reflects the fact that industrial customers have more substitutes for the utility's electricity than residential customers have. Residential customers have very few options other than conservation if electricity rates increase; industrial users can often generate their own electricity.

Most phone companies charge business users a higher rate than they charge residential users. Again, the rate differential is due to the availability of substitutes. Residential users can always use pay phones or a neighbor's phone if rates go up—or they can do without a phone. Businesses cannot do without a phone as easily. It's not good for a business's image if prospective customers must call a neighboring establishment to do business! Consequently, business demand for phone service is more inelastic.

Question to Think About: What are other examples of price discrimination? How do elasticities of demand and the availability of substitutes relate to the different prices in such examples?

V.   KEY TERMS

barrier to entry   deadweight loss
patent   rent seeking
innovation   price discrimination
price searcher   perfectly discriminating monopolist

VI. QUESTIONS

A. Completion

1. To have a monopoly, it is necessary to prevent new firms from profitably entering the market, which requires some kind of _____

2. To encourage innovation, the government awards _____ that grant exclusive rights to produce a product for 20 years.

3. State _____ are required in order to provide some types of services, such as haircuts and legal assistance.

4. When there are significant economies of scale over the full range of market demand, the result is a _____ monopoly.

5. The demand curve for a monopoly is the _____ demand curve.

6. The marginal revenue curve for a monopoly that does not perfectly discriminate lies _____ the demand curve.

7. Marginal revenue is negative when the demand curve is _____.

8. A monopoly maximizes profits by producing where _____ equals marginal cost.

9. A monopoly produces on the _____ portion of the demand curve.

10. A monopoly does not have a _____ curve.

11. Because there are _____, a monopoly can earn long-run economic profits.

12. When a monopoly restricts output and raises prices, it creates a _____ loss to society.

13. Firms engage in _____ activity when they lobby politicians for economic transfers.

14. Monopolies practice _____ when they charge different prices to different groups of customers.

15. There is no deadweight loss if a monopolist is able to engage in _____ price discrimination.

B. True/False

_____ 1. A barrier to entry is something that prevents new firms from profitably entering an industry.

_____ 2. Local utilities usually are monopolies because they control essential resources.

_____ 3. Technological change sometimes helps break down barriers to entry.

_____ 4. A major difference between a monopolistic firm and a competitive firm is that the monopolist faces a downward-sloping demand curve, whereas a competitive firm faces a horizontal demand curve.

_____ 5. Under monopoly, price is greater than average revenue but lower than marginal revenue.

_____ 6. The monopolist's demand curve is also its average revenue curve.

_____ 7. Unless it price discriminates perfectly, the monopolist's marginal revenue curve lies below its demand curve because the demand curve slopes down.

_____ 8. Marginal revenue is positive whenever the price elasticity of demand is less than one.

_____ 9. A monopolist maximizes profit by selecting the rate of output where price equals marginal cost.

_____ 10. The supply curve of a monopoly is less elastic than the supply curve of a perfectly competitive industry.

_____ 11. All monopolists make an economic profit.

_____ 12. Most monopolists try to charge the highest price possible.

_____ 13. The more elastic the demand curve a monopoly faces, the higher the price it charges.

_____ 14. Monopoly profits represent a transfer from consumers to the monopolist producer.

_____ 15. The deadweight loss of monopoly is measured by the monopolist's economic profit.

_____ 16. Monopolists may not charge the monopoly price if they fear government intervention.

_____ 17. The welfare loss of monopoly is greater, the more rent seeking that occurs.

_____ 18. To be able to price discriminate, a monopolist must be able to prevent resale of its product between customers.

_____ 19. The group with the more elastic demand faces the higher price when price discrimination occurs.

_____ 20. Perfect price discrimination is inefficient because profits are so great.

C. Multiple Choice

1. In states where the government runs liquor stores, the monopoly results from
    a. economies of scale relative to the market demand.
    b. control of an essential resource.
    c. patents.
    d. legal restrictions.
    e. None of the above.

2. If a small town has only one grocery store, the grocer has a monopoly as a result of
    a. economies of scale relative to the market demand.
    b. control of an essential resource.
    c. licenses.
    d. legal restrictions.
    e. None of the above.

3. For a monopolist that does not price discriminate perfectly, marginal revenue is less than price because
    a. the firm must lower price on all units to sell additional units.
    b. the firm faces a downward-sloping demand curve.
    c. average revenue is less than price.
    d. marginal cost is less than price.
    e. a and b

4. Total revenue for a monopolist is at a maximum when
    a. marginal revenue equals marginal cost.
    b. price equals marginal revenue.
    c. price equals marginal cost.
    d. marginal revenue equals zero.
    e. marginal revenue equals average revenue.

5. If a monopoly lowers price to sell additional units, its revenues increase if
    a. the number of units sold is greater than the drop in price.
    b. the percentage increase in units sold is greater than the percentage decrease in price.
    c. the monopolist faces no close substitutes.
    d. it is losing money at its current rate of output.
    e. average revenue is above marginal cost.

6. A monopolist always produces
    a. where price is at a maximum.
    b. where total revenue is at a maximum.
    c. on the elastic portion of the demand curve.
    d. on the unitary elastic portion of the demand curve.
    e. on the inelastic portion of the demand curve.

Exhibit 2

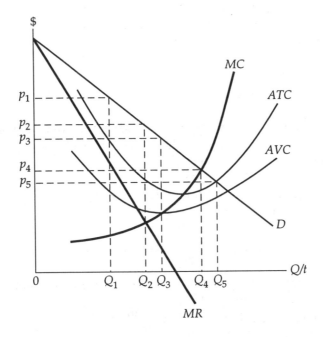

7. A monopolist will maximize profits at which rate of output in Exhibit 2?
   a. Q_1
   b. Q_2
   c. Q_3
   d. Q_4
   e. Q_5

8. In Exhibit 2, what will the profit-maximizing rate of output be if fixed costs increase?
   a. Q_1
   b. Q_2
   c. Q_3
   d. Q_4
   e. The question cannot be answered without more information.

Monopoly   **391**

Exhibit 3

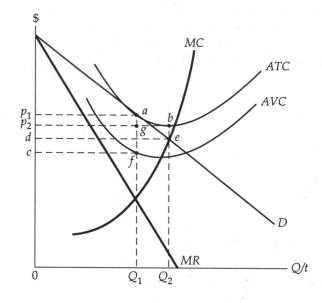

9. In Exhibit 3, the monopolist's economic profits are
   a. the area p_1agp_2.
   b. the area p_1afc.
   c. the area p_2bed.
   d. zero.
   e. Profits cannot be determined without more information.

10. In Exhibit 3, a monopoly that price discriminates perfectly will
    a. produce Q_1 units.
    b. produce Q_2 units.
    c. make zero profits.
    d. charge p_1 to some customers and p_2 to other customers.
    e. The question cannot be answered without more information.

11. In Exhibit 3, what could cause the *ATC* curve to shift down to the *AVC* curve without affecting the *MC* curve?
    a. a change in the price of the good
    b. a change in the price of labor
    c. a reduction of fixed costs by 50 percent
    d. elimination of fixed costs
    e. None of the above.

12. The fundamental difference between a monopoly and a firm in perfect competition is that a monopoly
    a. is large.
    b. can make more profits.
    c. can price discriminate.
    d. faces a downward-sloping demand curve.
    e. tries to maximize profits.

13. In the long run, a monopolist will
     a. expand the size of the firm until it makes zero profits.
     b. adjust the scale of the firm to maximize profits.
     c. go out of business if it makes zero profits.
     d. charge a higher price than in the short run.
     e. b and d

Exhibit 4

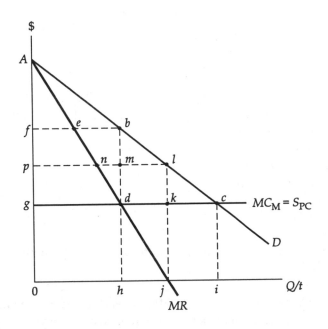

14. Consider Exhibit 4. What is the price-output combination if the industry is perfectly competitive? if it is a monopoly that does not price discriminate?
     a. Perfect competition: quantity $= j$, price $= p$
         Monopoly: quantity $= h$, price $= f$
     b. Perfect competition: quantity $= j$, price $= g$
         Monopoly: quantity $= j$, price $= p$
     c. Perfect competition: quantity $= i$, price $= g$
         Monopoly: quantity $= j$, price $= p$
     d. Perfect competition: quantity $= i$, price $= g$
         Monopoly: quantity $= h$, price $= f$
     e. None of the above.

15. The monopoly in Exhibit 4 does not price discriminate. What is its deadweight loss?
     a. *lkc*
     b. *bml*
     c. *bdc*
     d. *djl*
     e. *fbdg*

16. In Exhibit 4, what are the profits of a monopolist that is able to price discriminate perfectly?
    a. *fbdg*
    b. *Acg*
    c. *fbcg*
    d. *fbdg + lkc*
    e. *Adg*

17. In Exhibit 4, what are the deadweight losses if the firm price discriminates perfectly?
    a. *fdbg*
    b. *Abf*
    c. *Acg*
    d. *bdc*
    e. zero

18. Which of the following could make actual deadweight losses different from what is indicated by a typical graphical analysis?
    a. fear of potential rivals
    b. fear of public intervention
    c. failure to minimize costs
    d. rent-seeking activity
    e. All of the above.

19. Which of the following is not a requirement for price discrimination?
    a. monopoly power
    b. economies of scale
    c. different groups of customers with different elasticities of demand
    d. ability to easily identify members of different customer groups
    e. ability to keep the members of different customer groups separate

20. A price-discriminating monopolist charges the highest price to
    a. the group with the largest demand.
    b. the group with the most elastic demand.
    c. the group with the least elastic demand.
    d. the group with demand that is of unitary elasticity.
    e. the oldest group.

D.   Discussion Questions

1. Indicate the source of the monopoly in each of the following cases:
    a. U.S. Post Office
    b. Local phone company
    c. State-owned liquor store
    d. The National Football League
    e. Taxi company in a major city
    f. Local cable TV company
    g. Madonna
    h. OPEC

2. Explain what a natural monopoly is.

3. Discuss the types of barriers to entry, and explain whether each type is likely to provide long-term monopoly power.

Use the information in Exhibit 5 about a monopoly to answer question 4.

Exhibit 5

Price	Qty	TR	MR	AR	TVC	TC	AVC	ATC	MC
$12.00	0	—	—	—	——	$5.00	—	—	—
11.00	1	—	—	—	$13.00		—	—	—
10.00	2	—	—	—	16.00		—	—	—
9.00	3	—	—	—	20.00		—	—	—
8.00	4	—	—	—	25.00		—	—	—
7.00	5	—	—	—	31.00		—	—	—
6.00	6	—	—	—	38.00		—	—	—
5.00	7	—	—	—	46.00		—	—	—
4.00	8	—	—	—	56.00		—	—	—
3.00	9	—	—	—	68.00		—	—	—
2.00	10	—	—	—	82.00		—	—	—
1.00	11	—	—	—	99.00		—	—	—

4. a. Fill in the blanks in the table.
   b. Draw the demand curve, marginal revenue curve, average variable cost curve, average total cost curve, and marginal cost curve on the graph in Exhibit 6.

Exhibit 6

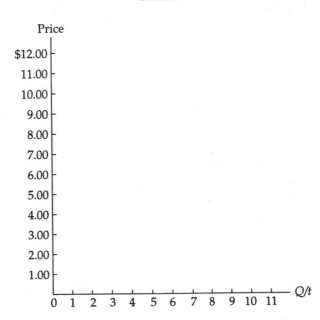

c.   What are the profit-maximizing rates of output and price? Indicate your answer on the graph.
d.   What is the profit for the monopolist?
e.   Suppose variable costs increase by $2 at every rate of output. What are the new profit-maximizing rates of output and price? What are the profits now?
f.   Assume variable costs are as indicated in Exhibit 5 and that fixed costs increase by $2. What are the new profit-maximizing rates of output and price? What are the new profits?

5.   If there are no rivals for a monopolist's product, how can it ever lose money?

6.   Explain why a monopoly does not have a supply curve.

7.   What are the allocative and distributive differences between monopoly and perfect competition? What causes these differences?

8.   Exhibit 7 in the text illustrates the welfare loss of monopoly. Discuss the factors that could make the actual welfare loss of monopoly either greater or less than the amount *bmc* shown in that exhibit.

9.   "If it engages in rent-seeking activity, a monopolist's economic profits may actually be zero." Is this statement true or false? Why?

10.   Most cases of price discrimination involve services rather than goods. Can you offer an explanation for this observation?

11.   Why does a price-discriminating monopolist charge a higher price to the customers with the most inelastic demand?

12.   Indicate in Exhibit 7 the price charged and output supplied to submarket A and submarket B by a price-discriminating monopolist.

Exhibit 7

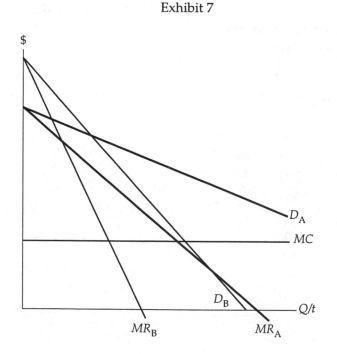

Chapter 22

13. What is perfect price discrimination? What is the deadweight loss associated with perfect price discrimination?

14. Explain why the answer to true/false question 20 is false.

15. If perfect price discrimination is so profitable, why do firms not engage in it more?

VII. ANSWERS

A. Completion

1. barrier to entry
2. patents
3. licenses
4. natural
5. market
6. below
7. inelastic
8. marginal revenue
9. elastic
10. supply
11. barriers to entry
12. deadweight (or welfare)
13. rent-seeking
14. price discrimination
15. perfect

B. True/False

1. True
2. False
3. True
4. True
5. False
6. True
7. True
8. False
9. False
10. False. A monopolist does not have a supply curve.
11. False
12. False
13. False
14. True
15. False
16. True
17. True
18. True
19. False
20. False

C. Multiple Choice

1. d
2. a
3. e
4. d
5. b
6. c
7. b
8. b
9. d
10. b
11. d
12. d
13. b
14. d
15. c
16. b
17. e
18. e
19. b
20. c

D. Discussion Questions

1. a. Legal restrictions
    b. Economies of scale
    c. Legal restrictions
    d. Control of essential resources
    e. Legal restrictions
    f. Natural monopoly
    g. Control of an essential resource (her talent)
    h. Control of an essential resource

2. A natural monopoly exists when economies of scale generate declining average costs over the entire range of market demand. In such situations, there is room for only one producer in the market.

3. Barriers to entry include legal restrictions (such as patents and licenses), economies of scale, and control of essential resources. Economies of scale are likely to provide long-term monopoly power, although sometimes technological change produces new products that are close substitutes for the product supplied by monopoly. Control of essential resources often diminishes over time because new sources are found or technological change develops substitutes. Patents expire after 20 years, but license requirements by the government can be long lasting.

4. a.

Price	Qty	TR	MR	AR	TVC	TC	AVC	ATC	MC
$12	0	$0	—	—		$5	—	—	—
11	1	11	$11	$11	$13	18	$13.00	$18.00	$13
10	2	20	9	10	16	21	8.00	10.50	3
9	3	27	7	9	20	25	6.67	8.33	4
8	4	32	5	8	25	30	6.25	7.50	5
7	5	35	3	7	31	36	6.20	7.20	6
6	6	36	1	6	38	43	6.33	7.17	7
5	7	35	−1	5	46	51	6.57	7.29	8
4	8	32	−3	4	56	61	7.00	7.63	10
3	9	27	−5	3	68	73	7.56	8.11	12
2	10	20	−7	2	82	87	8.20	8.70	14
1	11	11	−9	1	99	104	9.00	9.45	17

b.

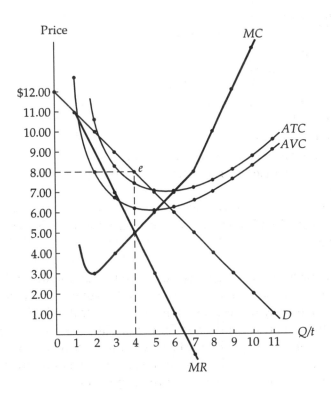

c. $Q = 4$, $p = \$8$; see point e on the graph.
d. The monopolist's profit is $2.
e. $Q = 3$, $p = \$9$; profits = 0.
f. $Q = 4$, $p = \$8$; profits = 0.

5. A monopolist will lose money whenever the costs of production exceed the revenues from sales. This happens whenever average costs are above the demand curve at all points. Having a monopoly is no guarantee of making economic or even normal profits.

6. A supply curve expresses a direct relationship between price and quantity supplied. A monopolist chooses its output level by equating marginal revenue and marginal cost and then finds price on the demand curve. A change in demand generates a new marginal revenue curve, which must be used to find the profit-maximizing output level, and then again price is found on the demand curve. There is not a direct relationship between price and quantity supplied. In fact, depending on how demand shifts, it is possible for a new price to be associated with the old quantity supplied.

7. Unless it experiences substantial economies of scale, a monopolist produces fewer units of output and charges a higher price than does a firm under perfect competition; output is less than the allocatively efficient level. There is also a transfer of consumer surplus from consumers to the monopolist producer in the form of profits and a loss of consumer surplus that nobody captures and that results from the higher prices and the restricted output associated with monopoly.

8. The actual welfare loss of a monopoly may be less when the firm has substantial economies of scale or when it does not charge the full monopoly price because of the fear of potential rivals or government intervention. In this case, the monopolist is willing to sacrifice some current profits for continuing long-run profits. The actual welfare loss may be greater if the

monopolist becomes lazy because it faces no competition. In this case, the monopolist fails to produce in the least costly manner. Another factor that may cause welfare losses to be higher is rent-seeking activity.

9. True. The profits available to a monopoly are the rewards from successfully lobbying and being awarded the monopoly. A firm might be willing to spend up to the value of the monopoly profits, so the successful firm could find that it has actually earned zero profits when it considers the resources it spent in obtaining the monopoly.

10. In order to price discriminate, a monopolist must be able to prevent the customers who pay a low price from reselling to the customers who pay a high price. Goods are sometimes easy to resell, but services cannot be resold.

11. Customers with elastic demand will reduce consumption more than those with inelastic demand for a given price increase. Therefore, the monopolist will charge the group with the more inelastic demand the higher price.

12.

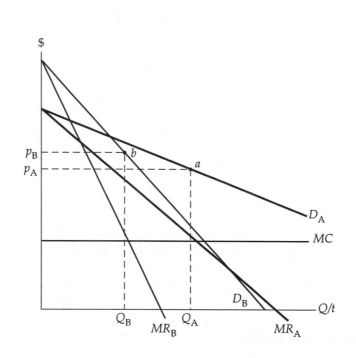

13. Perfect price discrimination occurs when a monopolist charges a different price for every unit sold. There is no deadweight loss in such situations because all consumer surplus is transferred to the monopolist in the form of monopoly profits.

14. Deadweight loss has to do with reduced output to raise price and not with whether the firm makes profits or not. A monopoly engaged in perfect price discrimination produces as many units as would be produced under perfect competition, so there is no deadweight loss.

15. Firms do not engage in more perfect price discrimination because they lack the information about the demand curves of each customer. Further, many firms find it very difficult to prevent resale of their products by those who buy units at a low price.

Chapter 22

CHAPTER 23

Monopolistic Competition and Oligopoly

I. INTRODUCTION

Two models of markets are introduced in this chapter: monopolistic competition and oligopoly. Both are intended to describe real-world market structures more closely than do the polar models of perfect competition and monopoly. Monopolistic competition is similar to perfect competition in that both are characterized by many firms, each of which is too small to affect the decisions of rivals. Monopolistic competition differs from perfect competition in that in the former, firms produce differentiated products, whereas in the latter, firms produce homogeneous products. Oligopoly (few sellers) is closer to monopoly (one seller) in that the firms tend to be large and to have considerable influence over price.

II. OUTLINE

1. Monopolistic Competition

   1.1 Characteristics of Monopolistic Competition
       a. There are a large number of producers.
       b. Producers offer products that differ slightly, so each firm faces a downward-sloping demand curve; each firm has some control over the price it charges.
       c. Each firm is too small to have any significant impact on other firms; each firm acts independently.
       d. Firms can enter or leave the market with relative ease.

   1.2 Product Differentiation. Producers differentiate their products in four ways:
       a. Physical characteristics of goods
       b. The number and variety of locations where the product is available
       c. Services accompanying the product
       d. Product image

   1.3 Short-Run Profit Maximization or Loss Minimization
       a. Because of product differentiation, the firm faces a downward-sloping demand curve. The firm's demand curve will be more elastic the greater the number of competing firms and the less differentiated the firm's product.
       b. If the firm can at least cover its variable cost, it produces at the rate of output where $MR = MC$.
       c. The firm seeks to maximize profits and may earn profits in the short run.
       d. The firm will minimize losses in the short run by shutting down if $p < AVC$ at all output levels.

   1.4 Zero Economic Profit in the Long Run
       a. Since there are no barriers to entry or exit, firms make a normal profit in the long run.
       b. Monopolistic competition is similar to perfect competition in this way.

1.5 *CASE STUDY:* Fast Forward

1.6 Monopolistic Competition and Perfect Competition Compared
   a. In monopolistic competition, a firm does not produce at the minimum of the average total cost curve.
   b. In monopolistic competition, a firm produces where price exceeds marginal cost; under perfect competition, price equals marginal cost.
   c. Firms under monopolistic competition may spend resources on advertising or other methods of differentiating their products; perfectly competitive firms need not do so.

2. An Introduction to Oligopoly. This type of market includes only a few sellers, which implies that the firms are interdependent.

   2.1 Varieties of Oligopoly
      a. Some oligopolistic industries produce a homogeneous product; others produce differentiated products.
      b. The interdependence of firms makes it difficult to analyze the behavior of a firm in an oligopolistic industry.
      c. Each firm knows that any change in its own policies will affect its rivals and probably cause a reaction by the rivals.
      d. Some type of barrier to entry usually is associated with oligopoly.

   2.2 *CASE STUDY:* The Unfriendly Skies

   2.3 Economies of Scale. Many oligopolies are characterized by extreme economies of scale that make entry difficult.

   2.4 High Cost of Entry. High start-up costs and the need for costly promotional efforts may discourage entry into a market by causing production costs to be higher than they would be otherwise.

3. Models of Oligopoly. Because of the interdependence of firms in this type of market, there is no single model.

   3.1 Collusion
      a. A *cartel* is a group of firms that agree to coordinate production and pricing decisions to maximize joint profits.
      b. Firms in a cartel want to replicate the monopoly price-output decision.
      c. The joint profit-maximizing rate of output is determined by equating the marginal cost of production for the cartel and the market's marginal revenue.
      d. The cartel then must allocate output among the firms.
      e. It is difficult to maintain a cartel under certain conditions:
          • If there are significant differences in costs of production among firms
          • If the number of firms is large
          • If output is differentiated across firms
          • If entry barriers to the industry are low
          • If cheating on the agreement becomes widespread
      f. The fundamental problem of a cartel is to prevent cheating by the members.
      g. A cartel cannot survive if new entry into the industry is easy.

3.2 Price Leadership
   a. *Price leader* is a firm that sets prices for the rest of the industry.
   b. Price leadership is a type of informal, or tacit, collusion.

3.3 Game Theory
   a. *Game theory* examines oligopolistic behavior as a series of strategic moves and counter-moves among rivals.
   b. Game theory focuses on the players' incentives to cooperate or compete.
   c. There are several strategies that can be considered in game theory.

3.4 The Kinked Demand Curve
   a. The kinked demand curve model explains price rigidity in oligopolies.
   b. The model assumes that a firm expects that if it raises its price its rivals will not match the increase, but if it lowers its price its rivals will follow.
   c. Given this assumption, the oligopolist faces a demand curve that is kinked at the current price, more elastic at higher prices, and less elastic at lower prices.
   d. The marginal revenue curve has a gap at the current output, so small shifts in marginal costs will not change the profit-maximizing price or output.
   e. An assessment of the kinked demand curve model:
      • The theory fails to provide an explanation of how the equilibrium price and quantity are initially determined.
      • Empirical evidence refutes the model's predictions concerning price stability in oligopoly.

3.5 Summary of Oligopoly Models. Each model was developed to explain certain phenomena observable in oligopolistic markets.

3.6 Comparison of Oligopoly and Perfect Competition
   a. Prices are usually higher under oligopoly.
   b. Profits are usually higher in the long run under oligopoly because of barriers to entry.

III. DISCUSSION

Monopolistic Competition

The key characteristic of *monopolistic competition* is product differentiation. Under perfect competition, all firms produce an identical, homogeneous product, but the product produced by a monopolistically competitive firm differs slightly from the products of other firms in the industry. As an example, consider milk sold in retail stores; assume the milk is identical in all stores. If the retail market is perfectly competitive, then store A cannot raise its price above the price charged by all other retail stores. If it did it would lose all its sales to the other stores. However, if the retail market is characterized by monopolistic competition, store A can raise price by a small amount and lose some, but not all, of its sales.

Why would anyone pay more at store A? Consumers would willingly pay a higher price at store A if the store were closer to their homes so they spent less time and money on travel, or if its checkout person were quicker, or if it were open all night. Hence, convenience stores are able to charge higher prices than some other retail outlets because consumers view their products as slightly different (in this case because of the convenience that accompanies the product). Note, though, that the convenience store might lose all sales if it tried to raise price by too much.

The short-run price and output combination of a firm under monopolistic competition is found as it is under monopoly. Each firm faces a downward-sloping demand curve, which implies that its marginal revenue curve slopes down and lies below the demand curve. The firm chooses its output rate (assuming the demand curve lies above average variable cost at some point) by finding the rate of output for which $MR = MC$. Exhibit 1 illustrates the situation of a firm in monopolistic competition that is making positive profits. In the long run, new firms that are attracted by the profits enter the industry, drawing customers away from existing firms and reducing the demand facing each firm. Long-run equilibrium is achieved when firms make zero profits, just as in perfect competition.

Exhibit 1

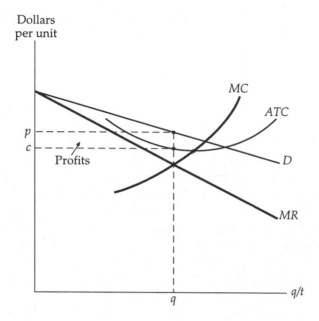

The difference between the long-run equilibrium condition of the firm in perfect competition and that of the firm in monopolistic competition is illustrated in Exhibit 2. Both panels show that the long-run equilibrium is characterized by a tangency between the firm's demand curve and the average total cost curve. The perfectly competitive firm's demand curve is horizontal, so the tangency occurs at the minimum point of the average total cost curve; the firm in monopolistic competition faces a downward-sloping demand curve, so the tangency occurs to the left of the minimum point of the average total cost curve. Hence, the firm in monopolistic competition is not producing at the lowest point on its average total cost curve. If we compared a perfectly competitive industry and a monopolistically competitive industry, we would find that there were more firms in the monopolistically competitive industry and each firm produced a smaller rate of output. That is, monopolistic competition is characterized by excess capacity. Some economists argue that this excess capacity is wasteful, but others argue that the excess capacity is not wasteful because it is associated with increased choice for consumers.

Exhibit 2

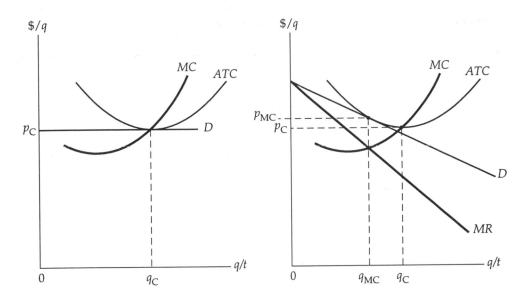

An Introduction to Oligopoly

The key characteristic of *oligopoly* is the interdependence of firms in such an industry. Since oligopoly is a market dominated by a few large firms, each firm recognizes that its price-output decisions affect the other firms and that the other firms are likely to respond to changes in their rivals' behavior. Thus, each firm must take into consideration the likely responses of its rivals. (Note that only in oligopoly does a firm have rivals. In perfect competition and in monopolistic competition, firms can behave as if their actions had no effect on other firms. There is no interdependent behavior.) Consequently, it is very difficult to develop a model of oligopoly markets, for the firms can respond to each other in a variety of ways. There are many models of oligopoly, and the text examines five of the better-known models.

Models of Oligopoly

A monopoly is able to earn above-normal profits by restricting output and raising price above the perfectly competitive price. A group of firms can increase profits by cooperating and agreeing to restrict output and to raise prices. Such cooperative behavior on the part of firms is called *collusion*. The firms maximize joint profits by determining the industry marginal revenue curve, horizontally summing all the firms' marginal cost curves, and setting the aggregated marginal cost equal to marginal revenue. The problem then is to assign output quotas to each firm, since each would like to sell more at the higher price. Firms in *cartels* have an incentive to cheat (either to sell some extra units secretly or to sell units at a price lower than the cartel price, or both). Cheating can cause prices to fall. Collusion is illegal in the United States. Firms may try to avoid collusion by following a *price leader*, a single firm that establishes a price that the other firms follow. If the price set is the monopoly price, the incentive to cheat is still strong.

Game theory provides several other models of oligopoly. Firms establish strategies in the face of interdependence. Moves and countermoves are planned by rival firms. The problem with game theory is that once a strategy is decided upon by a firm, it ceases to be optimal if other firms realize what the strategy is.

Exhibit 3

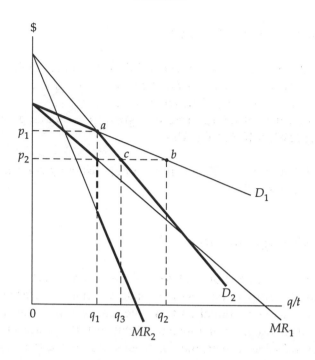

The *kinked demand curve* model was developed to explain alleged price stability in oligopoly. Exhibit 3 illustrates the derivation of the kinked demand curve. Suppose the current price is p_1 and the firm produces q_1 units per month (point a). The firm is considering whether to lower price to p_2. If it lowers the price to p_2 and all other firms continue to charge p_1, then the firm will move to point b, and its sales will increase from q_1 to q_2. However, if its rivals match its price cut, the firm will move to point c and sell q_3 units. The distance between q_2 and q_3 represents sales that now go to the other firms. Connecting points a and b generates demand curve D_1, and connecting points a and c yields demand curve D_2. Demand curve D_1 is more elastic than D_2.

The behavioral assumption used in this model is that the firm's rivals will match price cuts but not price increases. That is, demand curve D_2 applies in the case of price cuts, and D_1 applies in the case of price increases. Consequently, the demand curve is kinked at point a. The kink on the demand curve generates a gap in the marginal revenue curve at output q_1. This implies that marginal costs can shift by a considerable amount and still cross the gap in marginal revenue at output rate q_1. Hence, price is rigid at price p_1 even if costs fluctuate within the limits of the gap in the marginal revenue curve.

Since there is not a single model of oligopoly, comparisons of oligopoly and perfect competition are difficult. In general, price, costs associated with product differentiation, and long-run profit tend to be higher in oligopoly than in perfect competition.

IV. LAGNIAPPE

Monopolistic Competition and College

U.S. colleges and universities can be seen as "firms" in a monopolistically competitive industry. Each produces a similar product (education), but the products are not identical. A college can raise price (tuition) without losing all of its students. The product differs by location (students tend to attend colleges relatively close to home), extent of services (prestige, good sports teams, partying, contacts), quality, and image (Harvard's image differs from UCLA's).

Question to Think About: As "firms" in a monopolistically competitive industry, are colleges characterized by excess capacity?

Cheating on Collusive Agreements

Collusive agreements are often difficult to establish and maintain, because it is profitable to cheat. Suppose you are head of a corporation that has made a collusive agreement to set the price of your product at $40, which is above marginal cost. A potential customer wants to buy 10,000 units of the product at $34 each, which also is greater than marginal cost. If you accept, your profits will be greater than if you do not get the sale. Further, the customer informs you that another firm that is in on the collusive agreement has offered to sell the product at $36 per unit. You have to decide whether the customer is telling you the truth and whether to cheat on the agreement yourself. Collusion is profitable, but cheating on the agreement can be even more profitable.

Question to Think About: Would you be more willing to cheat if the order were large than if it were small? How would you determine if other firms were cheating on the agreement?

V. KEY TERMS

monopolistic competition	game theory
excess capacity	duopoly
oligopoly	strategy
collusion	payoff matrix
cartel	kinked demand curve
price leader	

VI. QUESTIONS

A. Completion

1. _____ is an industry made up of many relatively small firms producing goods that are relatively close substitutes.

2. A firm in monopolistic competition makes output and price decisions _____ of other firms.

3. A firm in monopolistic competition is not a price _____.

4. For a firm in monopolistic competition that can at least cover its variable costs, marginal cost equals _____ in equilibrium.

5. Firms in monopolistic competition make _____ economic profits in the long run.

6. Monopolistic competition is characterized by _____; that is, firms produce to the left of the minimum point on the average total cost curve.

7. The key characteristic of monopolistic competition is _____; the key characteristic of oligopoly is the _____ of firms.

8. In oligopoly, a change in policies by one firm will produce a _____ from its rivals.

9. A _____ is a group of firms that agree to coordinate production and pricing decisions.

10. The fundamental problem of a cartel is _____.

11. Price leadership is a type of _____ collusion.

12. _____ examines oligopolistic behavior as a series of strategic decisions.

13. Alleged price rigidity in oligopoly is explained by the _____ model.

14. When firms agree to restrict output and raise price, they are involved in _____.

15. Regardless of market structure, profit maximization encourages firms to produce the rate of output where _____ equals _____.

B. True/False

_____ 1. Monopolistic competition is similar to perfect competition as firms in both market structures produce homogeneous products.

_____ 2. Because monopolistically competitive firms are small and numerous, they act as price takers.

_____ 3. Product differentiation implies that the firm's demand curve slopes down.

_____ 4. Product differentiation refers to differences in the physical properties of goods.

_____ 5. The monopolistically competitive firm that can cover its variable costs produces at the rate of output at which marginal cost equals price.

_____ 6. Firms in monopolistic competition behave like monopolists when it comes to setting price and output.

_____ 7. The difference in the long-run equilibrium for perfect competition and the long-run equilibrium in monopolistic competition is due to differences in the shapes of the demand curves faced by the firms.

_____ 8. Long-run equilibrium under monopolistic competition is characterized by excess capacity.

_____ 9. Long-run equilibrium under monopolistic competition is characterized by positive economic profits.

_____ 10. Oligopoly differs from other market structures in that each firm has to be concerned with reactions to its decisions from the other firms in the industry.

_____ 11. Oligopolies tend to be industries in which production is characterized by substantial economies of scale.

_____ 12. Firms in oligopolistic industries that produce homogeneous products tend to be more interdependent than firms in oligopolistic industries that produce differentiated products.

_____ 13. The biggest problem facing cartels is how to prevent cheating.

_____ 14. Cartels often practice price leadership.

_____ 15. Game theory is used to analyze the behavior of firms that cooperate but not firms that compete.

_____ 16. A firm faces a kinked demand curve when its rivals follow neither a price increase nor a price decrease.

_____ 17. A kinked demand curve causes kinked marginal revenue curves.

_____ 18. The kinked demand curve was developed to explain price rigidity in oligopolies.

C. Multiple Choice

1. Which of the following is not a characteristic of monopolistic competition?
   a. many firms
   b. product differentiation
   c. excess capacity
   d. a downward-sloping demand curve
   e. interdependence

2. Product differentiation is an important characteristic of monopolistic competition because
   a. most products are differentiated.
   b. it generates downward-sloping demand curves for firms.
   c. it results in firms' producing at too high a level of output.
   d. it generates the long-run equilibrium condition of zero profits.
   e. None of the above.

3. Which of the following is a way in which sellers can differentiate their products?
   a. color
   b. location
   c. hours of operation
   d. provision of extra services
   e. All of the above.

4. Monopolistic competition is like perfect competition except that
   a. firms in monopolistic competition can make long-run profits.
   b. there are substantial economies of scale with monopolistic competition.
   c. firms are large in monopolistic competition.
   d. firms in monopolistic competition face downward-sloping demand curves.
   e. both b and c

Exhibit 4

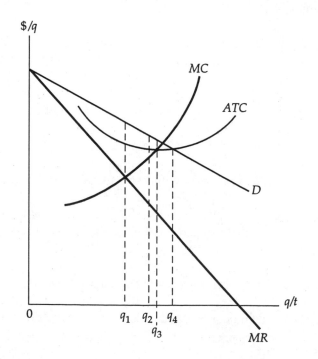

5. In Exhibit 4, the profit-maximizing output rate is
    a. $q1$.
    b. $q2$.
    c. $q3$.
    d. $q4$.
    e. zero.

6. The monopolistically competitive firm in Exhibit 4 is in
    a. short-run equilibrium, making positive economic profits.
    b. short-run equilibrium, experiencing economic losses.
    c. long-run equilibrium, making zero economic profits.
    d. long-run equilibrium, making positive economic profits.
    e. neither short-run nor long-run equilibrium.

7. Long-run equilibrium under monopolistic competition is
    a. similar to that in perfect competition in that the firms produce at the minimum point of their average cost curves.
    b. similar to that in monopoly in that profits are being made.
    c. similar to that in oligopoly in that anything can happen.
    d. similar to that in perfect competition in that firms make zero economic profits.
    e. similar to that in perfect competition in that price equals marginal cost.

8. Which of the following is true of monopolistic competition in long-run equilibrium?
    a. $p = MR$ and $p = MC$
    b. $p > ATC$ and $MR = MC$
    c. $p = ATC$ and $MR = MC$
    d. $p = ATC$ and $p = MC$
    e. $p > ATC$ and $p > MR$

9. Under monopolistic competition, there is excess capacity because
    a. firms are wasteful.
    b. there are not enough firms.
    c. there are substantial economies of scale.
    d. the firm's demand curve slopes down, and the firm makes zero economic profits in long-run equilibrium.
    e. firms may want to produce more in the future if demand increases.

10. Which of the following statements about a firm in long-run equilibrium is true?
    a. $p > AR$ under monopolistic competition and $p = ATC$ under perfect competition.
    b. $p = MC$ under both, but price under monopolistic competition is higher than it is under perfect competition.
    c. $p > MC$ under monopolistic competition and $p = MC$ under perfect competition.
    d. $p = MC = ATC$ under perfect competition but $p < MC = ATC$ under monopolistic competition.
    e. a and b

11. Interdependence means that
    a. firms face the same demand curve.
    b. firms are considering merging.
    c. firms depend on each other for business.
    d. the actions of one firm affect other firms.
    e. All of the above.

12. Which of the following is a source of oligopoly?
    a. economies of scale
    b. control over an essential resource
    c. product differentiation
    d. inelastic demand curves
    e. a and b

13. Firms in a cartel increase profits by
    a. working together to produce a better profit.
    b. jointly restricting output to raise price.
    c. setting up joint advertising campaigns.
    d. working to make their demand curves more elastic.
    e. working to make themselves less interdependent.

14. Which of the following makes it easier to reach a collusive agreement?
    a. few firms in the industry
    b. different costs among the firms
    c. product differentiation
    d. frequent shifts in demand
    e. None of the above.

15. Which of the following statements is true of the oligopolist that can cover its variable costs and is in equilibrium?
    a. $p = MC = ATC$
    b. $p > MC$
    c. $p > MR$ and $p = MC$
    d. $p < MC$ and $MR = MC$
    e. a is true, but only in the long run

16. According to game theory,
    a. oligopolist firms always avoid the worst outcome.
    b. outcomes can be volatile.
    c. oligopolistic firms collude.
    d. price wars are the normal outcome in oligopolies.
    e. oligopolistic firms merge.

17. A kinked demand curve with the shape discussed in the text is generated when the firm
     a.   believes all competing firms will match a price reduction but not match a price increase.
     b.   believes all competing firms will match a price increase but not match a price decrease.
     c.   believes it can change price without any response from competing firms.
     d.   is colluding with all competing firms.
     e.   is a price leader.

Exhibit 5

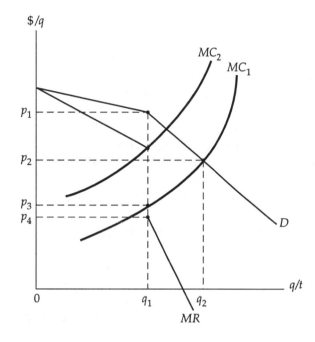

18. In Exhibit 5, if MC_1 is the relevant marginal cost curve, the firm
     a.   produces at q_1 and charges a price of p_3.
     b.   produces at q_2 and charges a price of p_2.
     c.   produces at q_1 and charges a price of p_2.
     d.   produces at q_1 and charges a price of p_1.
     e.   produces at q_1 and charges a price of p_4.

19. In Exhibit 5, if costs increase to MC_2, the firm
    a. keeps output constant and raises prices.
    b. decreases output and raises prices.
    c. continues to produce q_1 and charges price p_1.
    d. decreases production but continues to charge price p_1.
    e. may do anything. The exhibit does not provide enough information to determine what will happen.

20. Under oligopoly,
    a. price is always higher than under perfect competition.
    b. price is always higher than under monopolistic competition.
    c. price can be higher or lower than under perfect competition.
    d. both a and b only.
    e. None of the above.

D. Discussion Questions

1. Explain why product differentiation leads to differences between monopolistic competition and perfect competition.

2. Explain why the answer to true/false Question 4 is false.

3. How is monopolistic competition like monopoly? How is it different?

4. What is excess capacity? Why are firms characterized by excess capacity under monopolistic competition?

5. Is excess capacity necessarily wasteful?

6. How is oligopoly like monopoly? How is it different?

7. Explain why it is difficult to analyze the behavior of a firm under oligopoly.

8. Explain how oligopoly is the only market structure characterized by rivalry among firms.

9. Explain how collusion can be profitable. Explain how cheating on a collusive agreement can be profitable.

10. If collusion is profitable, why don't all firms collude?

11. Contrast perfect competition and oligopoly.

12. Describe game theory.

13. How does the kinked demand curve model explain price rigidity?

14. What are the problems with the kinked demand curve model?

VII. ANSWERS

A. Completion

1. Monopolistic competition
2. independently
3. taker
4. marginal revenue
5. zero
6. excess capacity
7. product differentiation; interdependence
8. reaction
9. cartel
10. cheating
11. tacit
12. Game theory
13. kinked demand curve
14. collusion
15. marginal revenue; marginal cost

B. True/False

1. False
2. False
3. True
4. False
5. False. $MR = MC$.
6. True
7. True
8. True
9. False
10. True
11. True
12. True
13. True
14. False. Cartels are formal agreements to work together; price leadership is an informal, or tacit, collusive tactic. Cartels are illegal in the United States.
15. False
16. False
17. False. Marginal revenue curves have a gap at the output where the demand curve is kinked.
18. True

C. Multiple Choice

1. e
2. b
3. e
4. d
5. a
6. a
7. d
8. c
9. d
10. c
11. d
12. e
13. b
14. a
15. b
16. b
17. a
18. d
19. c
20. c

D. Discussion Questions

1. Product differentiation implies that each firm can raise its price a little without losing all its customers. That is, the firm faces a downward-sloping demand curve. All the differences between perfect competition and monopolistic competition are due to the downward-sloping demand curve. A downward-sloping demand curve implies that the marginal revenue curve lies below the demand curve (under perfect competition, the demand curve and the marginal revenue curve are equal). Thus, when the firm sets $MR = MC$, $p > MC$. Since the demand curve slopes down, the zero-profit long-run equilibrium condition implies that the average total cost curve is tangent to the demand curve to the left of the minimum point of the average total cost curve. That is, there is excess capacity.

2. Product differentiation can occur even if the products are physically identical. Products can differ by location, by services, or by image. In other words, physical differences are only one way to differentiate products.

3. Monopolistic competition is like monopoly in that firms face downward-sloping demand curves and, in equilibrium, $p > MC$. The two market structures differ in that free entry under monopolistic competition leads to zero economic profits in the long run. The products offered by a monopoly have no close substitutes, whereas the products of the firms under monopolistic competition are close, but not perfect, substitutes. A monopoly can earn positive economic profits in the long run.

4. Excess capacity occurs when a firm could lower its average total costs by expanding production (i.e., the firm produces to the left of the minimum of its average total cost curve). Firms are characterized by excess capacity under monopolistic competition because the long-run equilibrium condition of zero economic profits implies that the firm produces at the rate of output where the demand curve is tangent to the average total cost curve. Since the demand curve slopes down, this must be to the left of the minimum of the average total cost curve.

5. Excess capacity is not necessarily wasteful, because consumers value product variety and excess capacity is a necessary result of product differentiation.

6. Oligopoly and monopoly are alike in that firms under both market structures tend to be large, there is some sort of barrier to entry, and firms have considerable influence on price. They differ in that firms under oligopoly are interdependent; each must consider possible reactions of the other firms to any change it makes in price or output.

7. Interdependence among firms makes it difficult to analyze the behavior of a firm under oligopoly. Since firms can react in many ways, each firm may make plans and adjustments in many ways. There is no single type of behavior.

8. The choices of output levels made by a firm under perfect competition have no effect on any other firms in the industry. Firms make decisions independently of one another. The same is true for monopolistic competition—decisions are made independently. Under monopoly, a firm has no rivals. Only under oligopoly are firms interdependent and take into consideration how rivals may respond to changes they make in price-output policies.

9.   Collusion can be profitable because the colluding firms stop trying to compete, agree to restrict output, and raise prices to the level a monopoly would charge. That is, firms collectively act as if they were a monopoly. A collusive agreement sets $p > MC$ and $p > ATC$, so that firms maximize their joint profits. Since $p > MC$, an individual firm can increase its profits by selling additional units as long as the price received exceeds the marginal cost of the units. Each firm faces this temptation to cheat. If firms do cheat, prices will tend to fall and the collusive agreement will fall apart.

10.   Collusion can be profitable, but it is often not feasible. In many industries there are too many firms for collusion to be practical. In addition, if firms collude, raise prices, and make economic profits, new firms may enter the industry. It is also more difficult to collude when costs differ greatly and when the products are differentiated. Finally, collusion is illegal in the United States, which deters some firms from trying to collude.

11.   Perfect competition and oligopoly differ in several ways. Perfect competition is characterized by many firms; in oligopoly there are only a few firms. Firms under perfect competition face horizontal demand curves; oligopolists face downward-sloping demand curves with slopes that depend upon the reactions of other firms in the industry. Firms under perfect competition make decisions independently of each other; oligopolists are interdependent. In long-run equilibrium under perfect competition, $p = MC$ and the firm produces at the minimum of its average total cost curve. Under oligopoly, $p > MC$ and a firm may or may not produce at the minimum of its average total cost curve. Some oligopolists also have the added costs of product differentiation. Finally, oligopolists are likely to earn above-normal profits; competitive firms earn zero profits in long-run equilibrium.

12.   Game theory examines oligopolistic behavior as a series of strategic moves among rivals. A strategy reflects a player's operational plan and the payoff matrix lists the profits that each of the rivals can expect based on the strategy each firm adopts.

13.   Because the demand curve is kinked at the current output, there is a gap in the marginal revenue curve at the current output. This means that marginal costs can shift up or down and still intersect the marginal revenue curve at the current output. This implies that price will not change unless there is a very large change in costs.

14.   The model of the kinked demand curve does not explain how the original equilibrium price and quantity are determined. Also, there is empirical evidence that oligopolistic prices are no more rigid than prices in other market structures.

CHAPTER 24

Resource Markets

I. INTRODUCTION

Up to this point, we have focused on product markets—the markets for goods and services. We now change our emphasis and begin to analyze resource markets—the markets for such resources as labor, land, and capital. The material in this chapter applies to all resources. In the next chapter, we will examine labor markets in more detail.

II. OUTLINE

1. The Once-Over

    1.1 Resource Demand. Additional units of a resource will be demanded as long as the extra revenue generated exceeds the extra cost.

    1.2 Resource Supply. Resource owners will supply additional units as long as doing so increases their utility.

2. The Demand and Supply of Resources. In product markets, households are demanders and firms are suppliers; in resource markets, households are suppliers and firms are demanders. The supply and demand for resources depend on the willingness and ability of buyers and sellers to participate in the market.

    2.1 The Market Demand for Resources
        a. Firms demand resources because those resources are needed to make the good or service the firm produces.
        b. The demand for a resource is a derived demand—it is derived from the value of the final product.
        c. The demand curve for a resource slopes downward because as the price of a resource falls, producers are more willing and more able to employ the resource.
            (1) As the price of a resource declines, other things constant, the firm is more willing to use the resource, since it is cheaper relative to other resources than it used to be.
            (2) At a lower price, the producer can hire more resources for the same total cost, so its ability to buy more has increased.

    2.2 The Market Supply for Resources
        a. The supply curve of a resource slopes upward because resource owners are more willing and able to supply the resource at a higher price.
        b. The owner of a resource is more willing to supply it at a higher price, other things constant, because the higher price increases his or her real income.
        c. The owner is more able to supply the resource at a higher price, because the higher price enables the owner to incur the higher costs of supplying more of the resource.

2.3 Temporary and Permanent Resource Price Differences
   a. We expect the prices paid for identical resources to tend toward equality over time, regardless of the market to which the resource is being supplied.
   b. Sometimes resource prices are not the same because the resource market is in a transitory state of disequilibrium but is moving toward equilibrium.
   c. There can be permanent differences in resources; these do not induce a reallocation of resources.
   d. Permanent resource price differences occur when
      (1) resources are immobile;
      (2) there are differences in resource quality;
      (3) the training requirements of resources differ;
      (4) nonmonetary rewards of jobs differ.

2.4 Opportunity Cost and Economic Rent
   a. The minimum amount the owner of a resource must receive to supply the resource for a particular use is the *opportunity cost* of the resource.
   b. *Economic rent* is the amount the resource owner receives above the opportunity cost.
   c. When supply is perfectly inelastic, all earnings are economic rent.
   d. When supply is perfectly elastic, all earnings are opportunity costs.
   e. When the supply curve slopes upward, resource owners collect both opportunity costs and economic rent.

3. A Closer Look at Resource Demand

3.1 The Firm's Demand for a Resource. The law of diminishing marginal returns states that the marginal physical product declines as more of a variable resource is combined with a given quantity of other resources.

3.2 Marginal Revenue Product
   a. The marginal revenue product (*MRP*) of labor is the amount by which total revenue increases as a result of hiring one more worker. It depends on
      (1) the amount of additional output produced—the marginal physical product of labor; and
      (2) the price of the output.
   b. For the perfectly competitive firm, *MRP* equals the price times the marginal physical product of labor.
   c. For a firm with market power, *MRP* equals the change in total revenue that results from hiring an additional unit of labor. As more of a resource is hired, *MRP* declines both because of diminishing marginal physical product and because the selling price of the good must fall if the firm is to sell additional units.

3.3 Marginal Resource Cost
   a. The marginal resource cost (*MRC*) is the change in total cost that results from hiring one more unit of a resource.
   b. If a firm is a price taker in the resource market, *MRC* equals the price of the input.
   c. A profit-maximizing firm employs each resource up to the point where its marginal resource cost equals its marginal revenue product.
   d. The firm's marginal revenue product curve is viewed as its demand curve for that resource when the firm hires resources in a competitive market.
   e. The profit-maximizing level of output can be found by either this method or finding where $MR = MC$.

3.4   Shifts in the Demand for Resources. The demand for resources will shift when
      a.   there are changes in the quantities or qualities of other resources used;
      b.   there is a change in technology or training; or
      c.   demand for the final product changes.

3.5   *CASE STUDY:* The Derived Demand for Architects

3.6   Optimal Use of More Than One Resource
      a.   To maximize profits, the firm should employ resources so that the last dollar spent on each resource gives one dollar's worth of marginal revenue product.

$$\frac{MRP_L}{MRC_L} = \frac{MRP_K}{MRCSUB}K = 1$$

      b.   For labor (L) and capital (K), the above condition is equivalent to

3.7   *CASE STUDY:* The McMinimum Wage

4.   Distribution of U. S. Resource Earnings. Wages and salaries represent the largest share of U.S. national income. Labor's share of total income has increased also.

III. DISCUSSION

The Demand and Supply of Resources

Firms require resources to produce goods and services. Households own the resources. A firm will hire quantities of various resources to maximize profits, and households will supply resources so as to maximize utility. The demand for a resource is a *derived demand*; it is derived from the value of the final product.

The demand curve for a resource slopes downward. Resources can be combined in different amounts to produce a product. If the price of one resource falls, other things constant, the firm will hire more of that resource. At a lower price, the firm is able to hire more of the resource.

The supply curve of a resource slopes upward. At a higher price, other things constant, the owner is willing and able to supply more because of the extra real income he or she receives.

Other things equal, resource owners will supply their resources to the firm offering the highest price. Consequently, in theory, identical resources tend to receive the same price in all markets. Differences in prices induce resource owners to move their resources to the higher-paying uses.

In the real world, however, we often observe that similar resources do not receive the same price. In some cases, the inequality of resource prices indicates that the resource market is in disequilibrium. Things are often changing in product and resource markets, and changes generate temporary differences in resource prices. Over time, the prices will move back toward equality. In other cases, differences in resource prices can persist, even in a market in equilibrium. It may be that the resources are not mobile, so they cannot move to higher-paying firms; the resources may differ in quality of training; or the nonmonetary aspects of jobs may differ.

Economic rent is a concept students often find confusing, but it need not be. The opportunity cost of a resource is the minimum amount a resource owner must receive to supply a resource to a particular use. Any earnings above opportunity costs are called economic rent. Review Exhibit 3 in the text to be sure you understand the relationships among supply, opportunity costs, and economic rent.

A Closer Look at Resource Demand

A firm can increase output by hiring more resources. Suppose we focus on one resource, say labor. We know that because of the law of diminishing marginal returns, output eventually increases by smaller amounts as additional workers are hired. The firm sells the extra output produced by an additional worker at the market price. The additional revenue received is the *marginal revenue product* of labor. If the firm is a competitive firm, or price taker, in the output market, it can sell as many units of the final good as it wants without affecting the market price. The firm's marginal revenue product (MRP) falls as additional workers are hired because of the law of diminishing marginal returns. If the firm is not a competitive firm—if it is a price searcher in the output market—then it can sell additional units of output only by lowering the price of the output. The MRP of such a firm falls for two reasons: (1) the law of diminishing marginal returns and (2) the fact that the firm must lower price on all units sold in order to sell more units of its product. You should compare Exhibits 4 and 5 in the text carefully to be sure you understand these differences between the two types of firms.

When the firm buys labor in a competitive market, its marginal revenue product curve for labor is also its demand curve for labor. The additional revenue gained from hiring an additional worker is the most that the firm is willing to pay for the additional worker. The extra cost to the firm of hiring an additional worker is called the *marginal resource cost* (MRC) of labor. If the firm is a *price taker* in resource markets, MRC equals the market wage for labor. For such firms, the supply curve of labor is perfectly elastic. The firm maximizes profits by hiring workers up to the level where marginal resource cost equals marginal revenue product ($MRC = MRP$).

We have seen that the demand curve for labor is also the firm's MRP curve in a competitive labor market and that MRP depends on the price of the good produced and the marginal physical product of labor. Anything that causes either the price of the final product or the marginal physical product of labor to change will cause the demand curve for labor to shift. In Exhibit 1, the firm's demand curve for labor (D_1) intersects the firm's supply curve at 10 units of labor. Assume that the marginal physical product of the tenth worker is 2 units of output per day, the product price is $10, and the daily wage is $20. MRP is $20 when 10 workers are hired; point *a* represents the equilibrium. If the price of the firm's product increases to $15, then the marginal revenue product of the tenth worker increases to $30 ($15 × 2). The demand curve for labor shifts up to D_2 and passes through point *b*. Now $MRP > MRC$, and the firm will hire more workers.

Exhibit 1

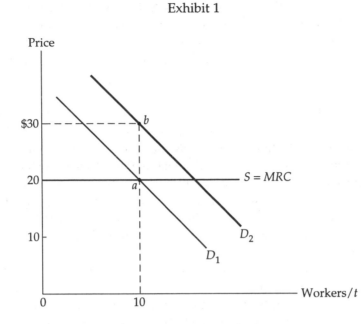

The demand curve for labor could also shift from D_1 to D_2 if the price of the product stayed at $10 but labor became more productive. Suppose the firm purchases more units of other inputs. If these other inputs and labor are complements, the marginal physical product of labor will increase. Say the marginal physical product of the tenth worker increases to 3 units of output. Now $MRP = \$10 \times 3 = \$30$, and demand shifts to D_2. The productivity of labor could also increase if technological improvements occurred or if labor received additional training. In both cases, labor is more productive and therefore more valuable.

Distribution of U. S. Resource Earnings

About three-fourths of national income is made up of wages and salaries. In recent decades, the proportion of national income going to proprietors' income has fallen.

IV. LAGNIAPPE

Optimal Resource Use

Firms can combine resources in many different ways. The technique they use depends on the prices of resources. Firms combine resources in a way that conserves the more costly resources. In Louisiana, rice farmers use a lot of capital equipment and relatively little labor; in Thailand, rice farmers use relatively more labor. The reason is that labor is much cheaper in Thailand than it is in the United States. Electric utilities produce electricity using water power in the Pacific Northwest and coal in Ohio. The output of wheat per acre is greater in Great Britain than it is in the United States. Because good farmland is scarce in Great Britain, British farmers use relatively more of other inputs on an acre and produce more wheat on the acre than do U.S. farmers.

Question to Think About: What changes did firms make as a result of the decline in prices of computers over the last decade?

Sole Proprietorships

The text notes that labor's share of total income has grown mostly because sole proprietorships have declined in number. Sole proprietorships declined steadily for years but have increased slightly in recent years. Technological change in information and communication have made sole proprietorships relatively more favorable. Immigrants tend to be self-employed more than native born workers too.

Question to Think About: Is self-employment more likely in large cities or in small towns?

V.   KEY TERMS

derived demand
economic rent
marginal revenue product
marginal resource cost

VI.   QUESTIONS

A.   Completion

1.   Households _____ resources and _____ products; firms _____ products and _____ resources.

2.   The firm's demand for resources arises from the demand for the good produced with them, so the demand for resources is a _____ demand.

3.   Wage differentials for similar workers that encourage workers to relocate are called _____ differentials.

4.   Wage differentials for similar workers that do not trigger a shift of resources to other uses are called _____ differentials.

5.   The minimum price necessary to get a resource owner to supply his or her resource is its _____.

6.   The amount of earnings above the opportunity cost of a resource is called _____.

7.   All earnings are opportunity costs when the resource's supply curve is _____.

8. When the supply curve is vertical, _____ determines the equilibrium price.

9. A profit-maximizing firm will hire an additional worker if the wage is less than labor's _____.

10. The marginal revenue product in perfect competition is also called the _____ of the marginal product.

11. The competitive firm's demand curve for labor slopes downward because of the _____.

12. The additional cost of buying an additional unit of a resource is its _____.

13. A reduction in the price of one resource will lead to an increase in demand for another resource if the resources are _____.

14. The marginal revenue product curve can be thought of as the firm's _____ for the resource.

15. The additional cost of hiring one more unit of labor is the _____ of labor.

B. True/False

_____ 1. In deciding between two jobs, a worker always chooses the higher-paying job.

_____ 2. A firm has a demand for a resource because of the resource's ability to produce goods and services.

_____ 3. As the price of a resource falls, other things constant, producers are more willing and more able to employ that resource.

_____ 4. As the price of a resource increases, other things constant, resource owners are willing to supply more of the resource but not necessarily more able to do so.

_____ 5. Resource markets operate so that the price of a homogeneous resource tends toward equality across markets over time, *ceteris paribus*.

_____ 6. If wages are not the same for identical labor, then this indicates a temporary resource price differential.

_____ 7. Resource price differences can reflect differences in the nonmonetary aspects of similar jobs.

_____ 8. Both temporary resource price differentials and permanent resource price differentials spur movement of resources away from lower-priced uses toward higher-priced uses.

_____ 9. The opportunity cost of a resource equals its economic rent.

_____ 10. How resource returns are divided between economic rent and opportunity costs depends on the shape of the supply curve.

_____ 11. When the supply of a resource is perfectly inelastic, demand determines the equilibrium price.

_____ 12. The demand curve for a resource slopes downward because of the law of diminishing marginal returns.

_____ 13. If the price of the good produced with labor increases, the marginal revenue product of labor increases.

_____ 14. For price-taking firms in the resource market, the price paid for each unit of a resource equals its marginal resource cost.

_____ 15. A profit-maximizing firm employs each resource up to the point where its marginal resource cost equals its marginal revenue product.

_____ 16. A firm with market power in its product market faces an upward-sloping supply curve for a resource.

_____ 17. If demand for a final product increases, demand for inputs used to produce the good also increases.

_____ 18. The proportion of income from corporate profits has risen over the last 30 years.

C. Multiple Choice

1. We assume that in the market for resources,
    a. firms seek to maximize profits and resource owners seek to maximize utility.
    b. firms seek to maximize profits and resource owners seek to maximize income.
    c. firms and resource owners seek to maximize utility.
    d. firms seek to minimize costs and resource owners seek to maximize income.
    e. None of the above.

2. In assuming that profit maximization motivates firms, we assume that the firms
    a. choose the most efficient production process.
    b. choose the least costly combination of resources.
    c. restrict output to increase profits.
    d. All of the above.
    e. a and b only

3. The perfectly competitive firm's demand curve for a resource slopes downward because
   a. the demand curve for the final product slopes down.
   b. there are fewer resources available at lower prices.
   c. there are diseconomies of scale.
   d. firms will substitute away from a resource if its price increases.
   e. firms are willing to use more of a resource at a higher price.

4. Which of the following is assumed constant along a demand curve for an input?
   a. technology
   b. quantity of other inputs used by the firm
   c. prices of other inputs used by the firm
   d. price of the product produced by the firm
   e. All of the above.

5. Which of the following is likely to happen if salaries of schoolteachers increase, other things constant?
   a. Some teacher's aides become teachers.
   b. Some part-time teachers become full-time teachers.
   c. Some people in other occupations switch to teaching.
   d. Enrollments in education courses in colleges increase.
   e. All of the above.

6. The example in Question 5 is an illustration of what happens when
   a. people are greedy.
   b. workers differ in productivity.
   c. there are temporary resource price differentials for labor.
   d. there are permanent resource price differentials for labor.
   e. jobs differ in attractiveness.

7. If two identical workers earn different salaries, then
   a. one worker must have more training than another.
   b. one worker must be more skillful than another.
   c. the nonmonetary aspects of their jobs may differ.
   d. the market may not be in equilibrium.
   e. c and d

8. The division of resource earnings between opportunity costs and economic rent depends on
   a. the demand for the resource.
   b. nonmonetary aspects of the job.
   c. the resource owner's elasticity of supply.
   d. the elasticity of supply of the good produced.
   e. a and c.

Exhibit 2

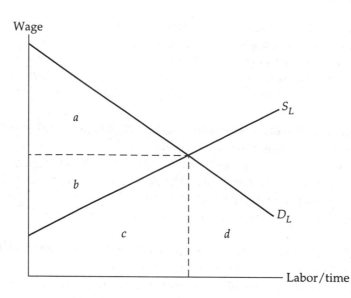

9. In Exhibit 2, at equilibrium, opportunity costs are represented by area _____ and
    economic rent by area _____.
    a. *a*; *b*
    b. *b*; *c*
    c. *b*; *d*
    d. *c*; *a*
    e. *c*; *b*

10. In Exhibit 2, if the supply curve became more elastic but still intersected the demand curve
    at the same point,
    a. opportunity costs would increase.
    b. opportunity costs would decrease.
    c. economic rent would increase.
    d. consumer surplus would increase.
    e. None of the above.

11. The marginal revenue product of a resource depends on
    a. the price of the resource.
    b. the supply of the resource.
    c. the price of the firm's output.
    d. the marginal physical product of the resource.
    e. c and d.

12. For a price taker in the output market, the marginal revenue product curve slopes down
    because
    a. the demand curve for the final product slopes down.
    b. marginal revenue curves slope down.
    c. of diminishing marginal returns.
    d. the marginal resource cost slopes down.
    e. a and b

13. Labor and capital are used to produce automobiles. An increase in the demand for labor can be due to
    a. an increase in the wage rate.
    b. an increase in the demand for automobiles.
    c. an increase in the productivity of labor.
    d. All of the above.
    e. b and c only.

14. An increase in the amount of capital used by a firm will
    a. make all labor at that firm more productive.
    b. increase the demand for labor that is a substitute for the capital.
    c. increase the demand for labor that is a complement to the capital.
    d. have no effect on labor usage.
    e. decrease the productivity of all labor employed by the firm.

15. A technological improvement that increases the marginal productivity of a resource will
    a. cause an increase in the demand for that resource.
    b. cause a decrease in the quantity demanded of that resource.
    c. cause an increase in the supply of that resource.
    d. lead to a lower wage.
    e. lead to less economic rent for owners of that resource.

16. To maximize profit, a firm should employ resources so that
    a. the ratio of labor to capital equals 1.00.
    b. the marginal revenue product of labor equals the marginal revenue product of capital.
    c. the last dollar spent on each resource yields one dollar's worth of marginal revenue product.
    d. the marginal product of all resources equals one.
    e. None of the above.

17. A profit-maximizing firm employs labor and capital to the point that
    a. $MRP_L/MRC_L = MRP_K/MRC_K = 0$
    b. $MRP_L/MRP_K = 1$
    c. $MRC_L/MRC_K = 1$
    d. $MRP_L/MRC_L = MRP_K/MRC_K = 0$
    e. both b and c only.

18. In the United States,
    a. proprietors' share of income has risen in this century.
    b. corporate profits account for about one-fourth of society's income.
    c. interest and rent each account for about 20 percent of society's income.
    d. labor's share of total income has grown in this century.
    e. the largest share of income belongs to labor, but this share has declined in this century.

D. Discussion Questions

1. What does it mean to say that the demand for a resource is a derived demand?

2. Why does the supply curve of a resource slope upward?

3. Why do we expect that the prices paid for identical resources of production will tend toward equality across markets over time?

4. How do temporary resource price differentials and permanent resource price differentials differ in their effects on labor markets?

5. Would you expect to find a greater permanent price differential in the price of coal or in the wages of clerks across firms? Explain.

6. Would you expect garbage truck drivers to receive the same wage as delivery truck drivers? Explain.

7. Suppose the labor supply schedule is as shown in Exhibit 3, and the market wage is $70 per day. What are the opportunity costs and economic rent of each worker hired?

Exhibit 3

Salary/Day	Workers
$50	1
55	2
60	3
65	4
70	5
75	6

8. Why does the division of resource earnings between economic rent and opportunity costs depend on the resource owner's elasticity of supply?

9. a. Fill in the blanks in Exhibit 4.

Exhibit 4

Units of Labor	Total Physical Product	Marginal Physical Product	Product Price	Marginal Revenue Product
0	0	_____	$5	_____
1	20	_____	5	_____
2	38	_____	5	_____
3	54	_____	5	_____
4	68	_____	5	_____
5	80	_____	5	_____
6	90	_____	5	_____
7	98	_____	5	_____
8	104	_____	5	_____

   b. If the firm is a resource price taker, how many workers does it hire at a market wage of $60?
   c. Suppose product price falls to $3. How many workers are hired?

10. What can cause the demand for a resource to shift?

11. Why do workers in the United States earn more, on average, than workers in Mexico?

12. Why do stores in suburban shopping centers provide free parking, whereas stores in downtown areas of cities do not?

13. Suppose a firm is hiring workers and capital so that $(MRP_L/MRC_L) = (MRP_K/MRC_K) = 2$. Is the firm maximizing profits? If not, what should the firm do?

VII. ANSWERS

A. Completion

1. supply; demand; supply; demand
2. derived
3. temporary resource price
4. permanent
5. opportunity cost
6. economic rent
7. horizontal (perfectly elastic)
8. demand
9. marginal revenue product
10. value
11. law of diminishing marginal returns
12. marginal resource cost
13. complements
14. demand curve
15. marginal resource cost

B. True/False

1. False
2. True
3. True
4. False
5. True
6. False
7. True
8. False
9. False
10. True
11. True
12. True
13. True
14. True
15. True
16. False
17. True
18. False

C. Multiple Choice

1. a
2. e
3. d
4. e
5. e
6. c
7. e. Note that if either a or b is true, the workers are not identical.
8. c
9. e
10. a
11. e
12. c
13. e
14. c
15. a
16. c
17. d
18. d

D. Discussion Questions

1. Firms do not demand resources for the same reasons consumers demand goods and services. The firm values resources because the resources produce the goods and services that the firm sells. The value of a resource to the firm is derived from the value of the product the resource helps produce.

2. Resource owners are more willing and more able to supply a good as price increases, other things constant. They are more willing because the higher price means they will be able to buy more goods and services. They are more able because they can supply resources that have higher opportunity costs when the price is higher.

3. A resource owner who was receiving a lower price than those working for a different firm or industry in jobs with the same nonmonetary benefits will move to the higher-paying area. This process will continue until all identical resources receive the same price.

4. Temporary resource price differentials for labor encourage those receiving the lower wages to move to occupations or locations where wages are better. Permanent resource price differentials do not induce workers to change jobs.

5. The wages of clerks are likely to vary more. Nonmonetary differences may generate wage differences for clerks, but coal owners will not be concerned about nonmonetary factors.

6. No. Working on a garbage truck is more unpleasant than driving a delivery truck. Drivers will demand more pay to work on the garbage truck.

7.

Worker	Opportunity Costs	Economic Rent
1	$50	$20
2	55	15
3	60	10
4	65	5
5	70	0

Note that the sixth worker is not hired if the market wage is $70 per day.

8. If supply is perfectly elastic, the resource can earn as much in its best alternative use as in its current use. Any reduction in earnings in the current use will induce the resource to go elsewhere, so there is no economic rent. When supply is perfectly inelastic, the resource has no other use, so its opportunity costs are zero. Thus, the proportion of resource earnings that is opportunity costs is greater the more elastic the supply of the resource.

9. a.

Units of Labor	Total Physical Product	Marginal Physical Product	Product Price	Marginal Revenue Product
0	0	___	$5	___
1	20	20	5	$100
2	38	18	5	90
3	54	16	5	80
4	68	14	5	70
5	80	12	5	60
6	90	10	5	50
7	98	8	5	40
8	104	6	5	30

   b. five workers
   c. one worker

10. The demand for a resource is determined by its marginal revenue product, which depends on the price of the good produced and the productivity of the resource. Anything that causes the product price to change or the resource's productivity to change will cause the resource's demand curve to shift.

11. Workers in the United States are more productive, on average, than workers in Mexico. This is so for at least two reasons. First, U.S. workers tend to have more capital to work with and, second, U.S. workers tend to be better educated and trained.

12. Land is more expensive in downtown areas than it is in suburbs, so suburban shopping centers can better afford to provide free parking.

13. No, the firm is not maximizing profits. It should employ resources so that the last dollar spent on each resource yields one dollar's worth of marginal revenue product. It should hire both more labor and more capital until $(MRP_L/MRC_L) = (MRP_C/MRC_C) = 1$.

CHAPTER 25

Labor Markets and Labor Unions

I. INTRODUCTION

The previous chapter examined resource markets in general. This chapter focuses attention on labor markets. The chapter derives the individual worker's labor supply curve and the market supply curve. Wage determination and factors causing wage differences are also examined. An examination of labor unions follows.

II. OUTLINE

1. Labor Supply. Each worker has a labor supply curve for each possible use of his or her labor. The individual worker's supply curves for each use of labor depend on the opportunity costs of his or her time in other activities.

    1.1 Labor Supply and Utility Maximization
        a. There are two sources of utility that are of interest in discussions of labor supply:
            (1) Consumption of goods and services
            (2) Leisure activities
        b. There are three uses of time:
            (1) Market work: selling time in labor markets for money
            (2) Nonmarket work: producing goods and services for oneself or acquiring skills and education
            (3) Leisure
        c. Work can be a source of disutility.
        d. The *net utility of work* (the utility of the consumption that work makes possible less the disutility of the work itself) makes work an attractive use of time.
        e. Utility maximization: consumers attempt to allocate time so that the expected marginal utility of the last unit of time spent in each activity is identical.
        f. Some implications of the model of time allocation are the following:
            (1) Individuals use nonmarket work to produce those goods they can provide more cheaply than the market can.
            (2) The higher the expected earnings for a high school graduate, the greater the opportunity cost of college.

    1.2 Wages and Individual Labor Supply
        a. Substitution and income effects of a wage increase
            (1) Substitution effect: the consumer supplies more time to market work.
            (2) Income effect: the consumer supplies more time to leisure and less time to market work.

b. Backward-bending labor supply curve: eventually the income effect outweighs the substitution effect.

1.3 Nonwage Determinants of Labor Supply
   a. The greater the other sources of income, the less market work one will perform.
   b. The better the amenities of the job, the more likely one is to perform market work.
   c. The more a job provides experience that will increase future income, the more likely one is to perform market work.
   d. The more a job accords with one's tastes, the more likely one is to perform market work.

1.4 *CASE STUDY:* Winner-Take-All Labor Markets

2. Unions and Collective Bargaining

2.1 Kinds of Unions
   a. The first unions in the United States were *craft unions*—unions made up of workers in particular crafts, such as carpenters or masons.
   b. The American Federation of Labor (1886) was an organization made up of craft unions whose focus was on economic issues.
   c. An industrial union includes all unskilled, semi-skilled, and skilled workers in an industry.
   d. The Congress of Industrial Organizations was a national organization of unions in mass-production industries such as automobiles and steel.

2.2 Collective Bargaining
   a. Collective bargaining: union and management negotiate a mutually acceptable contract.
   b. Mediation and arbitration
      (1) *With mediation*, an impartial observer (mediator) listens to both sides and makes suggestions for resolving differences.
      (2) With *binding arbitration*, an arbitrator is appointed and empowered to issue a decision that both sides must accept.

2.3 The Strike. A union withholds labor from the firm.

3. Union Wages and Employment

3.1 Inclusive, or Industrial, Unions
   a. The union negotiates a wage above the equilibrium wage.
   b. Excess supply of labor results.
   c. This model characterizes strong industrial unions.
   d. Wage gains come at the cost of lower total employment than would prevail without a union.
   e. Nonunion wages tend to fall as the supply of labor in the nonunion sector increases.

3.2 Exclusive, or Craft, Unions
   a. The union shifts the supply curve to the left.
   b. The restricted supply pushes wages up.
   c. This model characterizes craft unions, assuming they can restrict membership and force all employers in the market to hire only union members.

3.3 Increasing Demand for Union Labor
   a. Unions can increase demand for labor by appealing to consumers to buy union-made products.
   b. Unions can increase demand for labor by restricting the supply of products that compete with union-made products.
   c. The demand for labor is increased if unions generate increased productivity.
   d. *Featherbedding* is the practice of requiring producers to hire more union workers than they need.

3.4. Recent Trends in Union Membership
   a. Union membership as a percentage of the U.S. work force has declined over the last 45 years.
   b. The decline is due in part to structural changes in the economy that have arisen because the service sector is less unionized than the industrial sector.
   c. The United States has a lower level of union participation than other industrialized nations.

3.5 *CASE STUDY:* Hardball at Caterpillar

III. DISCUSSION

Labor Supply

It is a basic axiom of economics that people seek to maximize utility. An earlier chapter discussed utility maximization as it relates to the consumption of goods and services. But consumption takes time. A television or a stereo provides very little utility to a person who has no time to use it. Leisure time is time spent relaxing, sleeping, and consuming goods and services. Leisure is considered to be a normal good and is subject to the law of diminishing marginal utility.

There are three ways to spend time: in market work, nonmarket work, or leisure. *Market work* involves time spent working for money. *Nonmarket work* may be as laborious as market work but does not involve monetary payments. Time not spent in one form of work or another is considered *leisure*. Of the three types of activities, only leisure is assumed to provide utility directly. Market work provides income that is used to purchase goods and services that provide utility, but market work itself generally does not provide utility. Nonmarket work also does not provide utility directly but is often necessary in order to receive utility from goods. Cooking a meal may not provide utility but eating it does. The net utility of market work is the utility of the consumption made possible through work minus the disutility of the work itself. Rational consumers maximize utility by allocating their time so that the expected marginal utility of the last unit of time spent in each activity is identical. (Compare this to the rule concerning utility maximization and consumption of goods derived in the chapter titled *Consumer Choice and Demand*.)

What happens when someone's wage rate increases? That person may substitute more market work for nonmarket work, because the opportunity cost of nonmarket work has increased. Instead of repairing the car, the person may take it to a mechanic and work longer at the office. The person may also decide to spend more time on leisure activities—for example, eating out more.

An increase in the wage rate has two opposing effects on an individual worker. On one hand, the higher wage raises the opportunity cost of both nonmarket work and leisure, so the person will want to supply more hours to market work. This is called the *substitution effect* of a wage increase. On the other hand, a higher wage rate increases the individual's income. As income increases, the person will most likely want to consume more leisure. To do so, the worker must devote fewer hours to market work or to nonmarket work. The income effect of a higher wage rate is to reduce the number of hours supplied to market work. Typically, the substitution effect is stronger at relatively low wage rates, but eventually the income effect dominates. Once the income effect dominates, a higher wage rate leads to a smaller quantity of market labor supplied, and the individual's labor supply curve bends backward, as shown in Exhibit 1 in the text. The market supply curve is derived from the individual supply curves. (You should also review Exhibit 2 in the text.)

The previous chapter discussed the demand factors that generate wage differentials. This chapter discusses wage differentials that relate to the supply of labor. People have different tastes. Jobs that are boring or repugnant to one person might appeal to another. Even so, some occupations are so universally disliked that employers must compensate employees in those jobs with higher wages. In some cases, the undesirability of a job may arise from the risk associated with it. Occupations with a higher probability of causing a worker's injury or death tend to be characterized by higher wages.

Individual differences also account for differences in wages. Some jobs require considerable training and education. During the training period, the person's income is less than it would be if the person worked at another job and gave up the training. For people to give up income during the training years, they must receive higher salaries later. People also differ with respect to ability. Sometimes people have to move in order to find a better wage. Geographic differences in wages encourage people to migrate. Individual wages can also differ because of racial or gender discrimination. Finally, labor union members usually earn more than similar nonunion workers.

Unions and Collective Bargaining

A labor union is a group of workers who join together to improve their terms of employment. A craft union is made up of workers with a particular skill, such as plumbers or carpenters. An industrial union includes all workers (unskilled, semiskilled and skilled) in an industry, such as all autoworkers.

A union represents the workers in a firm or industry in negotiations with management on wages and other issues. Most of the time, the two sides reach an agreement through *collective bargaining*. If the two sides are unable to reach an agreement, however, the union can *strike*. The goal of a strike is to withhold labor from the firm so the firm is not able to produce and sell its products. In some cases, negotiations must be resolved through *mediation*, in which a *mediator*, an impartial observer, attempts to bring about a compromise. In other cases, *binding arbitration* is used. Under binding arbitration, the two sides agree to be bound by the decisions of the arbitrator.

Union Wages and Employment

Clearly, an important objective of unions is to raise the wages of their members. There are three ways to raise wages above the market wage. First, the union can negotiate a higher wage and let the firm hire as many workers as it wishes at that wage. (Review Exhibit 4 in the text.) For the entire industry, the higher wage reduces the quantity of labor demanded and increases the quantity supplied, generating an excess supply of labor. The union must find some way to allocate jobs among its members.

Second, unions can raise wages by restricting supply. To do this, a union must be able to restrict membership and prevent employers from hiring nonunion workers. If the union is successful, the supply curve of labor shifts to the left and wages increase. (See Exhibit 5 in the text.) There is not an excess supply of labor as there was in the first case, but this is because the union has restricted entry into the union. There are fewer people employed than there would be otherwise.

The final method of raising wages involves increasing the demand for union workers. This can involve advertising union-made goods, restricting imports from abroad, or *featherbedding*. Some economists argue that union workers are more productive than nonunion workers, so their higher wages merely reflect these differences in productivity. This increased productivity may come from workers' greater confidence and security because the union is monitoring the employer's treatment of workers, handling of pension funds, and the like.

The 1970s saw an increase in public employee unions but a decline in traditional union strongholds in the United States. U.S. unions are finding it more difficult to increase wages and prevent competition by nonunion workers because of structural changes in the economy and increased competition from imports.

IV. LAGNIAPPE

Time, Wage Rates, and Labor Supply

The theory developed in the first part of the chapter explains why an individual's labor supply curve bends backward. Some may question the assertion that the substitution effect dominates at lower wage rates and the income effect at higher wage rates. One reason this may be the case is that the worker may be substituting market work for nonmarket work rather than for leisure. As the wage rate increases, additional time spent in market work need not come out of leisure. In fact, it is possible for both leisure and market work to increase as the individual reduces nonmarket work. Eventually, though, leisure time may be affected. One cannot work all 24 hours of every day, and it is impossible for an individual's labor supply curve to continually slope upward.

There is evidence for a backward-bending supply curve. Employers' practice of offering time-and-a-half pay for overtime work is consistent with a backward-bending labor supply curve, since the firm is greatly increasing the opportunity cost of nonmarket work and of leisure in order to induce employees to work more hours. The observation that the length of the work week has decreased as incomes have increased also supports the theory.

Question to Think About: Can you think of any evidence to contradict the notion of a backward-bending labor supply curve?

Unions, Environmentalists, and NAFTA

The textbook points out that a method now used by unions to promote their interests is to team up with other organizations. A good example of this is the opposition to the North American Free Trade Agreement (NAFTA). This agreement reduced barriers to trade and capital mobility among Canada, Mexico, and the United States. Union leaders believe the agreement will precipitate a decline in employment of union members in the United States as some plants and factories move to Mexico because of the lower Mexican wages. Environmentalists argue that firms will move productive facilities to Mexico to avoid tougher environmental laws in the United States. The cooperation between union members and environmentalists in opposing NAFTA was a surprise to many of those involved in the negotiations. The arguments of the unions may seem self-serving to some, but by teaming up with environmentalist arguments, the unions can appear less self-interested.

Question to Think About: What position would you expect union leaders to take in domestic disputes involving the loss of jobs to protect the environment?

V.   KEY TERMS

market work   craft union
nonmarket work   industrial union
leisure   collective bargaining
substitution effect of a wage rate increase   mediator
income effect of a wage increase   binding arbitration
backward-bending supply curve of labor   strike
labor union   featherbedding

VI. QUESTIONS

A. Completion

1. Any time not spent in market work is spent in _____ or
   _____.

2. Economists treat time spent working as a source of _____.

3. A rational individual will allocate time so that the expected marginal utility of the last hour of leisure equals the expected net marginal utility of the last hour of _____, which equals the expected net marginal utility of the last hour of _____.

4. The _____ effect of a higher wage encourages a person to work fewer hours.

5. The _____ effect of a higher wage encourages a person to work more hours.

6. An individual's labor supply curve begins bending backward when the _____ effect dominates the _____ effect.

7. Because the individual must be present to provide labor, _____ of the job are important determinants of labor supply.

8. A job that provides more valuable job experience, other things constant, tends to pay _____ wages.

9. Jobs associated with a higher probability of injury are _____ and have higher wages, other things constant.

10. Imperfect labor _____ leads to different wages across regions.

11. The American Federation of Labor was made up of _____ unions and the Congress of Industrial Organizations of _____ unions.

12. Labor and management negotiate a mutually acceptable contract through _____.

13. A _____ tries to resolve differences between labor and management by listening to both sides and making suggestions about how each side could adjust its position.

14. _____ is a method of solving union-management problems whereby a third party listens to both sides and comes to a decision, and both sides are committed to abiding by the decision.

15. A _____ is a union's attempt to withhold labor from the firm.

16. _____ is an attempt to force employers to hire more union workers than they would prefer.

B. True/False

_____ 1. Each individual has only one labor supply curve.

_____ 2. Market work does not provide utility, but nonmarket work and leisure do provide utility.

_____ 3. A rational individual maximizes utility by maximizing leisure time.

_____ 4. Doing homework is a type of nonmarket work.

_____ 5. People who maximize utility use nonmarket work to provide goods and services they can produce more cheaply than the market can.

_____ 6. A higher market wage increases a person's opportunity cost of repairing his or her own car.

_____ 7. The substitution effect of a higher market wage is to work less because the worker can substitute more goods and services for work.

_____ 8. If leisure were an inferior good, the income effect and substitution effect of an increase in the market wage would be the same.

_____ 9. People who are wealthy are willing to supply more hours of market work than people who are not wealthy, other things constant.

_____ 10. Owning labor is different from owning other resources, such as land, because an individual must be present to provide labor.

_____ 11. The supply of labor to a particular job will be greater the more attractive the amenities of the job.

_____ 12. Economists assume that tastes for work are homogeneous across workers.

_____ 13. The market supply curve for labor must bend backward.

_____ 14. Occupations that include frequent periods of unemployment pay lower wages than other occupations, other things constant.

_____ 15. Labor migration reduces wage differentials.

_____ 16. Other things constant, jobs with low status pay less than jobs with higher status.

_____ 17. Collective bargaining agreements can include all aspects of employment.

_____ 18. An arbitrator has more authority to bring labor negotiations to a close than a mediator.

_____ 19. A strike imposes great costs on employers but few costs on the union membership.

_____ 20. Most labor negotiations in the United States end in strikes.

_____ 21. Craft unions typically try to raise wages by increasing the demand for their services.

_____ 22. A union can obtain higher wages for its members only by accepting reduced employment.

C. Multiple Choice

1. The primary sources of utility are
   a. the consumption of goods and services.
   b. leisure.
   c. nonmarket work.
   d. All of the above.
   e. a and b.

2. Leisure is a
   a. normal good.
   b. inferior good.
   c. a normal good for people who do not engage in market work and an inferior good for everyone else.
   d. a normal good for people who do not engage in nonmarket work and an inferior good for everyone else.
   e. None of the above. It is not treated as a good at all.

3. The difference between market work and nonmarket work is that
   a. market work is not enjoyable and nonmarket work is.
   b. one receives money for market work but not for nonmarket work.
   c. one obtains utility from nonmarket work but not from market work.
   d. nonmarket work is done only when one is unemployed.
   e. b and c.

4. Market work is an attractive use of time because
   a. it provides utility.
   b. it provides meaning to life.
   c. it enables one to avoid nonmarket work that has more disutility than market work.
   d. it permits one to buy goods and services, that provide utility.
   e. None of the above. It is not an attractive use of time.

5. Rational consumers
   a. balance their time among market work, nonmarket work, and leisure in order to maximize utility.
   b. divide their time so that the expected net marginal utility of the last hour spent on nonmarket work equals the expected marginal utility of the last hour of leisure, which equals the expected net marginal utility of the last hour spent on market work.
   c. attempt to maximize utility by allocating time so that the expected marginal utility of the last unit of time spent in each activity is identical.
   d. All of the above.
   e. b and d.

6. Which of the following is an example of a leisure activity?
   a. going to college
   b. repairing the car
   c. doing dishes
   d. mowing the lawn
   e. None of the above.

7. Which of the following is a possible response to a reduction in the wage rate?
   a. go to college
   b. go fishing more often
   c. work fewer hours
   d. paint the house
   e. All of the above.

8. An individual's labor supply curve bends backward because
   a. leisure is a normal good.
   b. of a progressive income tax.
   c. people are basically lazy.
   d. market work is an inferior good.
   e. nonmarket work is a normal good.

9. Suppose an individual's labor supply curve is vertical at 40 hours a week. We know that
   a. the substitution effect and income effect offset each other at this number of hours.
   b. the income effect is always zero.
   c. the substitution effect is always zero.
   d. leisure is an inferior good.
   e. the substitution effect always dominates the income effect.

10. Which of the following would cause a person's labor supply to decrease?
    a. The person gets a new supervisor, who allows more personal freedom at work.
    b. The person's best friend gets a job at the company.
    c. The workplace is air-conditioned.
    d. The individual wins a lottery.
    e. None of the above.

11. Most law clerks to Supreme Court justices receive lower wages than they could get in other work. The reason people take these jobs is
    a. they cannot get better jobs.
    b. they have better sources of additional income and wealth.
    c. the value of the job experience increases expected future earnings.
    d. because they desire to live in Washington, D.C.
    e. None of the above.

12. The market supply curve of labor need not bend backward because
    a. different individuals have different opportunity costs and different tastes for work.
    b. some people do not have backward-bending labor supply curves.
    c. women are working more now.
    d. there are laws against job discrimination.
    e. the market supply curve has nothing to do with the labor supply curves of individuals.

13. Wage differentials are due to
    a. differences in risk among jobs.
    b. differences in amenities among jobs.
    c. differences in training.
    d. differences in ability.
    e. All of the above.

14. Factors that help narrow wage differentials include
    a. labor migration.
    b. differences in ability.
    c. differences in risk.
    d. immigration quotas.
    e. a and b.

15. Construction workers on skyscrapers receive higher wages the higher up they work. This wage differential is due to the greater risk with the higher jobs. The wage premium for risk is narrowed by
    a. monopsony power of the employers.
    b. labor migration.
    c. the extra status workers receive for showing the courage to work at the jobs.
    d. sorting by workers so that those less adverse to risk tend to take the riskier jobs.
    e. None of the above.

16. The United Auto Workers is an example of
    a. a craft union.
    b. an industrial union.
    c. a closed shop.
    d. a union that endorses the right to work.
    e. None of the above.

17. An impartial observer who attempts to resolve differences between union and management but cannot impose a settlement is a(n)
    a. arbitrator.
    b. mediator.
    c. member of the National Labor Relations Board.
    d. judge.
    e. None of the above.

18. Collective bargaining can focus on which of the following issues?
    a. wages
    b. working conditions
    c. pension plans
    d. layoff procedures
    e. All of the above.

19. Which of the following would aid unions in a strike?
    a. unemployment benefits for strikers
    b. prohibiting picketing at the plant site
    c. police protection for nonstriking workers
    d. large inventories of the good produced by the firm
    e. a and d

Labor Markets and Labor Unions

20. A strike is costly to both sides, but
    a. each side must act as if it could endure a strike rather than give in to the other side.
    b. each side must want a strike for it to occur.
    c. generally a strike hurts the firm more than it does union members.
    d. generally a strike hurts union members more than it does the firm.
    e. None of the above.

21. Which of the following would not increase the wage rate of union workers?
    a. negotiating a wage that was 20 percent above the market wage
    b. establishing high membership fees to join the union
    c. toughening standards for getting a license or a union card
    d. increasing immigration quotas
    e. repealing right-to-work laws

22. If a union negotiates a wage above the competitive wage, employment tends to fall. The reduction in employment will be greater the more
    a. elastic the supply curve of labor.
    b. inelastic the supply curve of labor.
    c. elastic the demand curve for labor.
    d. inelastic the demand curve for labor.
    e. The question cannot be answered without more information.

23. Increased wages can accompany increased employment among union workers if
    a. wages for nonunion workers decline.
    b. the union makes it more difficult for people to join the union.
    c. union labor's productivity increases.
    d. demand for the final product falls.
    e. the union is negotiating with a monopolist producer.

24. U.S. union membership has declined in recent years because
    a. the government has made it more difficult for public employees to join unions.
    b. many union workers have retired in recent years.
    c. yellow-dog contracts are legal again.
    d. the economy has changed and now includes more high-tech industries, and unions have not been successful at organizing high-tech workers.
    e. All of the above.

D. Discussion Questions

1. What is the price of an hour of leisure? An hour of nonmarket work?

2. What does it mean to say that leisure is a normal good?

3. If work provides disutility, why do people ever engage in either market work or nonmarket work?

4. "Some people live to work and others work to live." What does this mean in light of the analysis presented in this chapter?

5. Since it costs about $7 to change the oil in your own car and about $15 to have a garage change the oil, you are being irrational if you do not change the oil yourself. Is the statement true or false? Why?

6. Explain the substitution and income effects of a wage decrease.

7. Bill earns $378 a week at $9 an hour, and $410 a week at $10 an hour. Which is greater for Bill in this range of wages, the substitution effect or the income effect?

8. Why does the individual's labor supply curve bend backward?

9. A new lawyer has one job offer from a law firm and another job offer to work as a clerk for a judge. The latter pays $10,000 less than the former. Why would anyone accept the latter offer?

10. Why doesn't the market supply curve for labor bend backward?

11. Explain why differences in taste help narrow wage differences.

12. Why are wages for a given occupation not the same in all parts of the country?

13. Distinguish between craft unions and industrial unions.

14. Distinguish between mediation and arbitration.

15. Other things equal, a strike is less costly to schoolteachers than to airline pilots. Explain why.

16. Explain how industrial unions tend to raise wages. Use a graph to illustrate why this approach to increasing wages generates an excess supply of labor. Explain why unemployed workers do not offer to work for less money.

17. Many states have wage laws that require any government job to pay union wage rates whether or not union labor is hired. Who would favor such a law? What are its effects?

18. Explain how being in unions might increase workers' productivity.

VII. ANSWERS

A. *Completion*

1. nonmarket work; leisure
2. disutility
3. market work; nonmarket work
4. income
5. substitution
6. income; substitution
7. nonmonetary factors
8. lower
9. riskier
10. mobility
11. craft; industrial
12. collective bargaining
13. mediator
14. Binding arbitration
15. strike
16. Featherbedding

B. *True/False*

1. False. Each person has as many supply curves as there are labor markets.
2. False
3. False
4. True
5. True
6. True
7. False
8. True
9. False
10. True
11. True
12. False
13. False
14. False
15. True
16. False
17. True
18. True
19. False
20. False
21. False
22. False. Increased labor demand generates higher wages and higher employment.

C. *Multiple Choice*

1. e
2. a
3. b
4. d
5. d
6. e
7. e
8. a
9. a
10. d
11. c
12. a
13. e
14. a
15. d
16. b
17. b
18. e
19. a
20. a
21. d
22. c
23. c
24. d

D. Discussion Questions

1. The price of both is the same—it is the income one could earn in an hour of market work.

2. Leisure is a good, so people want to consume more of it. People typically are willing and able to consume more leisure as their incomes increase, which makes leisure a normal good by definition.

3. People engage in market work to earn money to buy goods and services, which provide utility. People engage in nonmarket work to produce some goods and services rather than buying them in the marketplace. In either case, it is the goods and services that become available through work that ultimately provide utility to people.

4. The first part of the statement contradicts the analysis of this chapter, for it is saying that some people like to work a lot—that is, they obtain utility directly from work. The second type of people mentioned in the statement conforms to the analysis used in this chapter.

5. False. It takes time to change the oil, and your opportunity cost of time and the disutility of doing it yourself may be greater than the $8 difference in monetary price.

6. If wages decrease, the opportunity cost of leisure and of nonmarket work both decrease. Consequently, people substitute more leisure and/or nonmarket work for market work. The substitution effect of a wage decrease is that the worker devotes fewer hours to market work. The lower wage also lowers one's income. Since leisure is a normal good, less time will be spent in leisure activities at a lower wage rate. The income effect of a wage decrease is that the worker provides more hours to market work. Because the two effects are in conflict, we cannot say for sure how the individual will respond to the wage decrease.

7. The income effect is larger. Bill works 42 hours a week at $9 an hour and 41 hours a week at $10 an hour—that is, at a higher income Bill works fewer hours.

8. The substitution effect of a higher wage is to work more, and the income effect is to work less. At lower wage rates, the substitution effect dominates, and the labor supply curve slopes up. The income effect eventually dominates at higher wages, however, so fewer hours are worked and the labor supply curve bends backward.

9. The clerkship provides experience that will increase the lawyer's market value in future years. A lawyer who thinks the value of this experience is more than $10,000 will accept the clerkship.

10. The market supply curve is the horizontal sum of individual labor supply curves. As wages increase, some people's labor supply curves bend backward, but those of others do not. In addition, at higher wages some people may just be entering the labor market; individuals in other labor markets may switch over if the wage rises enough. All these new entrants keep the market labor supply curve sloping upward.

11. Some people dislike physical labor and like office work. If everyone were like this, work involving physical labor would pay more and office work less. But some people dislike working at a desk all day and prefer physical labor. Since those who like physical labor tend to seek that type of work and those who like office work tend to seek office jobs, wage differentials are not as wide as they would be if all workers were alike and everyone wanted to do some kinds of work and no one wanted to do other kinds.

12. Wage rates can differ geographically. If people in the lower wage areas migrate to the higher wage areas, then wages will equalize. But if not enough people are willing and able to relocate, wage differences can persist.

13. Craft unions are unions that include people who perform a specific task or craft. Examples would be plumbers, carpenters, and other construction trades. Industrial unions organize workers of all types and skills that work in a particular industry. Examples would include the United Auto Workers and the United Steel Workers.

14. In both mediation and arbitration, an outside party enters the negotiations. A mediator has no power to force an agreement; rather, a mediator offers suggestions that may help the two sides reach an agreement. An arbitrator has the power to force compromises and bring about an agreement.

15. People on strike lose their incomes for the time period they are on strike. For many union workers, the lost wages are gone forever. This would be the case for airline pilots. Teachers, however, usually end up teaching the same number of days, so their annual income would not fall as a result of the strike.

16. Industrial unions tend to negotiate a wage above the market wage. The firm can then hire as many workers as it wants at the negotiated wage. The following graph illustrates the situation. At a negotiated wage of W^*, firms want to hire fewer workers ($L_3 < L_1$), but more workers are willing to work in this market ($L_2 > L_1$). Consequently, there is an excess supply of labor of $L_2 - L_3$. Because the wage was agreed to collectively by the firm and the union members, the firm cannot hire anyone for less than W^*, nor can individual workers offer to work for less.

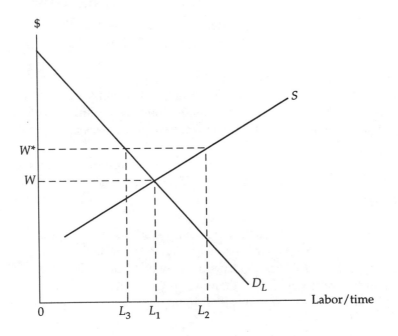

17. Union workers would favor such a law. If the government must pay union wage rates, it may decide to hire union workers. This increases the demand for union workers and helps keep union wage rates above the competitive level.

18. Conflict between workers and management can reduce worker productivity. Workers may also be less productive if they worry about whether the employer is handling such benefits as pension plans properly. If a union reduces these conflicts and worries, the workers may become more productive.

CHAPTER 26

Capital, Interest, and Corporate Finance

I.   INTRODUCTION

In the previous few chapters, we examined the demand for resources in general as well as the way wages and the return to labor are determined. In this chapter, we examine the returns to capital and returns to other resource owners.

II.   OUTLINE

1.   The Role of Time in Consumption and Production

1.1   Production, Saving, and Time
   a.   Production takes time.
   b.   Producers must rely on savings to survive during the time that production is going on—when the product is not yet completed and ready to consume or sell.
   c.   Producers must rely on savings in order to invest in capital.
   d.   Production with money and financial markets:
      (1)   Because of the existence of financial markets that transfer money between savers and borrowers, a producer does not have to rely on his or her own savings.
      (2)   Money is not a resource but is demanded because it can be used to purchase productive resources.

1.2   Consumption, Saving, and Time
   a.   Present consumption is valued more than future consumption.
   b.   Households must be rewarded if they are to save.
   c.   Interest is the reward offered to forgo present consumption.
   d.   The quantity of loanable funds supplied is greater at higher interest rates, other things constant.

1.3   Optimal Investment
   a.   In a perfectly competitive output market, the marginal revenue product of capital equals the marginal physical product of capital multiplied by the price of the good purchased.
   b.   If capital is expected to last indefinitely, operating expenses are negligible, and output prices are expected to remain constant in the future, the marginal rate of return on investment is equal to the marginal revenue product of capital divided by its marginal resource cost.
   c.   A producer will buy capital equipment up to the point where the marginal rate of return on investment equals the market rate of interest.
   d.   The firm's demand curve for investment slopes downward and is the same as its marginal rate of return on investment curve.
   e.   The market demand curve for investment also slopes downward.

f. The analysis used to determine the optimal investment is the same whether the firm must borrow funds for the investment or already has the funds from past profits.

1.4 The Market for Loanable Funds
   a. The demand curve for loanable funds slopes downward.
   b. The supply curve for loans slopes upward.
   c. The intersection of the supply and demand curves determines the quantity of loans and the interest rate.

1.5 Why Interest Rates Differ
   a. There are many interest rates in the economy.
   b. Several factors cause interest rates to differ.
      (1) Interest rates are higher the greater the risk of default.
      (2) The longer the duration of the loan, the greater the risk of higher-than-expected inflation and the higher the interest rate.
      (3) The larger the loan, the lower the cost of administering it relative to the total cost of the loan; thus, the interest rate may be lower for larger loans.
   c. Differences in the tax treatment of different types of loans affect the interest rate.

1.6 *CASE STUDY:* The Value of a Good Idea—Intellectual Property

2. Present Value and Discounting

   2.1 Present Value of Payment One Year Hence
      a. The value today of a sum of money payable in the future is the sum's *present value*.
      b. The present value discounts a payment to be received in one year by dividing it by 1.0 plus the relevant interest rate; $PV = M/(1 + i)$.
      c. The present value of a sum falls as the interest rate increases.

   2.2 Present Value for Payments in Later Years
      a. $PV = M/(1 + i)^t$, where M equals the dollars received t years from now and i is the interest rate.
      b. The present value of a given amount of money falls the further into the future the amount is to be paid.

   2.3 Present Value of an Income Stream. The present value of an income stream equals the sum of the discounted stream of payments.

   2.4 Present Value of an Annuity
      a. An *annuity* is a given sum of money paid each year for a specified number of years.
      b. The present value of an infinite annuity, or perpetuity, is $PV = A/i$, where A is the amount received each year.

   2.5 *CASE STUDY:* The Million-Dollar Lottery

3. Corporate Finance. Corporations acquire funds for investment in three ways: by selling stock, by retaining some profit, and by borrowing.

3.1 Corporate Stock and Retained Earnings
   a. Corporations float new stock issues to raise money for working capital and to buy new plants and equipment.
   b. A share of stock represents a claim on a share of the firm's earnings and assets.
   c. Shareholders often receive dividends out of the corporation's after-tax profits.
   d. Retained earnings are reinvested profits, which allow the firm to finance expansion.

3.2 Corporate Bonds
   a. A *bond* is a promise to pay the holder a fixed sum of money at a specified maturity date plus an annual interest payment, or coupon.
   b. The payment stream for bonds is more predictable than that for stocks.

3.3 Securities Exchanges
   a. Holders of stocks or bonds (securities) can sell them on security exchanges.
   b. The New York Stock Exchange is the largest security exchange in the world.
   c. Securities markets allocate funds more readily to successful firms than to firms in financial difficulty.

4. Corporate Ownership and Control. An entrepreneur organizes an enterprise and assumes the risk of operation.

4.1 Managerial Behavior in Large Corporations
   a. The ownership of large corporations is distributed among many stockholders.
   b. No single stockholder has the incentive or ability to control the manager.
   c. Some economists wonder whether firms perform differently when operated by professional managers rather than owner-entrepreneurs.
   d. Managers may promote their own goals rather than those of the stockholders.

4.2 Constraints on Managerial Discretion
   a. Competition in the marketplace forces managers to maximize profits in order to survive.
   b. A manager's compensation is often tied to the performance of the firm.
   c. Dissatisfied stockholders can sell their shares. If enough do this, the price of the stock falls, making it easier for corporate raiders to take over the firm.
   d. Many shares of stock are now purchased by institutional investors such as mutual funds. These large institutional investors often exercise greater control over managers.

III. DISCUSSION

The Role of Time in Consumption and Production

All economic activity takes place over time. For example, it takes time to travel to a restaurant, to order, to wait for a meal, to eat the meal, to pay the bill, and to return home. Time affects the decisions of both consumers and producers. Consider a banana. Today it may be ripe and very appealing. In a week, it will turn brown and mushy. Time has changed the banana. A consumer prefers today's banana to the same banana a week from now. In a week, the consumer may be sick and unable to eat the banana, or next week's banana may not actually be as good as today's. Present consumption is valued more than future consumption. In other words, consumers have a *positive rate of time preference*.

Without additional compensation, consumers are not willing to give up consumption of a specific good today in return for consumption of an identical good a year from now. People must receive a reward to postpone consumption. The *interest rate* is the amount of the reward offered to savers. Suppose the interest rate is 8 percent. Then an individual who saves $100 reduces current consumption by $100. A year later, the individual has $108 and is able to consume $108 worth of goods at that time. If the interest rate is 12 percent instead of 8 percent, then the individual can consume $112 worth of goods in the future. The opportunity cost of $100 of current consumption is $108 of future consumption when the interest rate is 8 percent and $112 when the interest rate is 12 percent. The cost of current consumption is greater the higher the interest rate, other things constant, so the quantity of savings supplied increases as interest rates increase.

Production cannot take place without savings. There are at least two reasons for this. First, production takes time, which implies that there is a lag between the time the decision to produce a good is made and the time it is made and consumed or sold. Meanwhile, the owners of the resources used to produce the good must live. In order to purchase inputs and pay labor costs, the producer needs money. The producer either must have previously saved money or must borrow it from others who have saved.

Second, production generally involves *capital goods*—goods that are used to produce other goods and services. Capital goods are made from resources that could have been used to produce consumption goods. Thus, if more capital goods are produced, fewer consumption goods are made in the present. Capital goods enable producers to produce more in the future than could be produced without the capital goods.

Producers can borrow money in the market for loans to finance production and can purchase capital goods in the marketplace. The firm's demand for capital goods is like the demand for any productive resource. In a perfectly competitive output market, the marginal revenue product of capital is found by multiplying the price of the good produced by the marginal physical product of capital. The firm's demand curve for capital slopes down because the law of diminishing marginal returns applies to capital just as it does to labor. The opportunity cost of the money used to purchase the capital equipment is measured by the interest rate, i. The purchaser will want to earn at least i. In the simple model presented in the text, the *marginal rate of return on investment* equals the marginal revenue product of capital divided by its marginal resource cost. As long as the marginal rate of return on investment exceeds the market interest rate, the firm is better off buying the capital equipment than placing its money in savings. The optimal amount of capital is determined at the point where the marginal rate of return on investment equals the market interest rate. This is true also if the firm must borrow the money, since the interest rate still measures the opportunity cost of the funds.

The market rate of interest is found by bringing the *demand for loanable funds* and the *supply of loanable funds* together. The interest rate is a price, and it is determined by the interaction of demand and supply just like other prices. An increase in the demand for loans leads to a higher interest rate, and an increase in the supply of loans leads to a lower interest rate.

There are actually many interest rates in the economy. Interest rates differ depending on several factors: risk, the duration of the loan, the cost of administering the loan, and how the loan is treated with regard to taxes.

Present Value and Discounting

If we wish to compare monetary values in different time periods, or income flows of various lengths, we must adjust money figures to account for the effect of time. The *present value* of a sum to be received in the future is the value of that sum today. How much is that $100 you expect to get from your grandmother a year from now worth today? The answer depends on the interest rate. Let the interest rate be 8 percent. Put $92.59 in a savings account at 8 percent interest and it will grow to $100 in a year. Hence, the present value of $100 a year from now at 8 percent is $92.59. ($92.59 × 1.08 = $100.) The present value of $100 a year from now is found by dividing $100 by 1 plus the interest rate:

$$\frac{100}{(1+0.08)} = \frac{\$100}{1.08}$$

We can also calculate the present value of $100 at 10 percent interest ($90.91) or at 5 percent interest ($95.24). The present value of $100 a year from now falls as the interest rate rises.

Present value also falls as the time period increases. The present value of $100 today at 8 percent interest is $100; its present value a year from now is $92.59; its present value two years from now is $85.73. The present value of M dollars t years from now is $M/(1 + i)^t$.

Corporate Finance

The industrial revolution created both capital-intensive, large-scale production and the need for large sums of money to purchase equipment. The corporation evolved in response to these requirements and is a legal creation of the state. A corporation can own property, incur debt, and earn profits. Shareholders own a portion of the firm. A corporation acquires funds for investment in three ways: by selling shares, by borrowing, and by retaining a portion of the firm's profits.

Corporations issue new stock to raise funds. Each share of stock represents a share of the company's profits and assets. Another source of funds is debt. Corporations raise funds by issuing *bonds*, which are basically IOUs. People who buy bonds are loaning the company money. They expect the principal to be paid back at a specified date in the future and to earn annual interest payments. The third method of acquiring funds for investment is to take part of the firm's profits and reinvest them in the firm rather than return them to the stockholders as dividend payments.

People are less likely to buy shares of stock if they cannot get rid of them later if they decide to do so. *Security exchanges* are places where stocks and/or bonds can be bought and sold. Sales of stock on stock exchanges involve stocks already held by the public rather than new issues of stock; a security exchange is like a market for used shares of stocks and bonds. There is a link between stocks sold on exchanges and new issues of stocks or bonds, however. The price of a share of stock on an exchange depends on the profitability of the company. If a firm does poorly in the market, its stock price usually falls. If such a company wants to issue new stock, it will get a relatively low price for each share and have a more difficult time raising funds. On the other hand, a profitable firm is able to acquire funds more easily and get a better price on its new issue of shares or a lower interest rate on its new issue of bonds. So even though they do not deal in new issues, security exchanges affect the prices a firm can get on its newly issued stocks and bonds.

In the modern corporation, most managers are not the owners of the firm, which means they do not receive the residual. This suggests that managers of large corporations may have an incentive to shirk and may not always be acting in the best interests of stockholders. Stockholders want management to maximize the profits of the firm, but managers may want to divert profits to increase their own utility.

Economists have identified several constraints on the behavior of managers. Firms whose managers do not generate sufficient profits will go out of business. Managers who want to move up to larger corporations must be successful where they are in order to be promoted to better positions. The manager's compensation package often includes bonuses tied to the performance of the firm. Stockholders can vote out the current management team and replace it with another group, or corporate raiders may buy up enough shares to replace managers of firms believed to be poorly run. There is considerable debate today over the effectiveness of the market for corporate control in controlling the behavior of management.

Corporate Ownership and Control

In the modern corporation, most managers are not the owners of the firm, which means they do not receive the residual. This suggests that managers of large corporations may have an incentive to shirk and may not always be acting in the best interests of stockholders. Stockholders want management to maximize the profits of the firm, but managers may want to divert profits to increase their own utility.

Economists have identified several constraints on the behavior of managers. Firms whose managers do not generate sufficient profits will go out of business. Managers who want to move up to larger corporations must be successful where they are in order to be promoted to better positions. The manager's compensation package often includes bonuses tied to the performance of the firm. Stockholders can vote out the current management team and replace it with another group, or corporate raiders may buy up enough shares to replace managers of firms believed to be poorly run. There is considerable debate today over the effectiveness of the market for corporate control in controlling the behavior of management.

IV. LAGNIAPPE

Additional Thoughts on Time

A little reflection can demonstrate the importance of time in investment and production decisions. The acquisition of human capital takes time—including the time you are spending in college. I am writing this in April, but the book will not be in print until next fall. Salespeople on commission often have lags of several months from the time of the sale until they receive their commission check, especially if the firm has to bill the client first. Magazine editors make plans for the Christmas issue in April. People who build their own homes have to either obtain short-term financing or sell their current house and rent while the new home is being built. Finally, farmers are entrepreneurs who know about the importance of time.

Question to Think About: Is saving necessary for all the examples above?

The concern over the separation of ownership and control in large corporations goes back at least to a book written by A. A. Berle and G. C. Means in 1933, *The Modern Corporation and Private Property*. It has been a persistent theme in economics ever since. However, recent research questions the need to be concerned and suggests that stockholdings by managers and corporate directors do reduce the problem considerably. Harold Demsetz and Kenneth Lehn ("The Structure of Corporate Ownership: Causes and Consequences," *Journal of Political Economy* 93(6), 1985) found no relationship between variations in stockholder concentration and profits, and Demsetz ("The Structure of Ownership and the Theory of the Firm," *Journal of Law and Economics* 26, 1983) found share ownership by directors and managers to be substantial, even in most Fortune 500 firms.

Question to Think About: Why do people buy stock in large companies if they have no control over the firm?

V.   KEY TERMS

positive rate of time preference	annuity
interest rate	initial public offering (IPO)
marginal rate of return on investment	stock
loanable funds market	dividends
supply of loanable funds	retained earnings
demand for loanable funds	bond
term structure of interest rates	entrepreneur
present value	portfolio
discounting	separation of ownership from control
discount rate	

VI.   QUESTIONS

A.   Completion

1.   Production cannot occur without _____.

2.   _____ production involves the production of capital goods.

3.   Interest rates are positive because consumers have a _____.

4.   _____ is the reward for forgoing present consumption.

5.   The _____ equals the market interest rate when the firm is investing optimally.

6.   _____ is the current value of a payment to be received in the future.

7. The _____ refers to the relationship between the interest rate and the duration of the loan.

8. The interest rate used for _____, or expressing the value of future dollars in terms of current dollars, is called the _____.

9. A(n) _____ is a sum of money received each year for a given number of years.

10. The owners of _____ are liable for debts of the firm only to the extent of their investment in the firm.

11. Reinvested profits are called _____.

12. A _____ is a debt security, a firm's promise to pay the holder a fixed sum of money on a designated _____ date.

13. The concern that managers of large corporations do not serve the best interests of the stockholders arises from the _____.

14. The initial sale of stock to the public is known as an _____.

15. The manager of a mutual fund is also known as an _____.

B. True/False

_____ 1. Roundabout production is an important source of the greater labor productivity in industrialized nations.

_____ 2. The greater the current level of investment in an economy, the less current consumption there is.

_____ 3. Present consumption is valued more than future consumption.

_____ 4. The greater the interest rate, the greater the opportunity cost of future consumption in terms of present consumption.

_____ 5. The marginal revenue product curve for capital falls because of the law of diminishing marginal returns.

_____ 6. Because capital differs from other inputs, the rules for the optimal use of capital differ from those for other inputs.

_____ 7. In the simple model in the textbook, the greater the marginal resource cost of capital, the greater the marginal rate of return on investment.

_____ 8. An increase in the demand for loans will increase the interest rate.

_____ 9. Since human capital involves people, the tools used to analyze investment decisions cannot be used to analyze human capital decisions.

_____ 10. Human capital investments tend to be risky, but physical capital investments are not.

_____ 11. Other things equal, larger loans have greater interest rates.

_____ 12. Interest rates tend to increase as the duration of the loan increases.

_____ 13. The greater the interest rate, the greater the present value of a dollar in the future.

_____ 14. The present value of a perpetuity of $100 a year is greater than the present value of a 20-year annuity of $100 a year.

_____ 15. If a corporation purchases new equipment with retained earnings, other things constant, stockholder dividends will be less.

_____ 16. Investors consider bonds to be less risky than stocks.

_____ 17. Capital markets allocate funds to more successful firms more readily than to firms in financial difficulty.

_____ 18. Managers of large corporations may be concerned with their own interests more than with maximizing profits for shareholders.

_____ 19. Managers' compensation packages are often tied to the performance of the firm to encourage managers to pursue profits rather than other goals.

_____ 20. Evidence collected by researchers indicates that stockholders of firms involved in take-overs lose wealth.

C. Multiple Choice

1. Roundabout production requires
   a. savings.
   b. time.
   c. capital equipment.
   d. All of the above.
   e. a and b only.

2. Which of the following does not indicate that consumers value current consumption more than future consumption?
   a. The interest rate is greater than zero.
   b. Hardback books cost more than paperback books.
   c. Overnight film developing costs more than two-day developing.
   d. College graduates earn more than high school graduates.
   e. A family stores cash in a cookie jar for emergencies.

3. If an individual is willing to give up $50 today for $53.50 a year from now, the interest rate is
   a. 3.5 percent.
   b. 5.0 percent.
   c. 107 percent.
   d. 7 percent.
   e. None of the above.

4. Direct production requires
   a. time.
   b. savings.
   c. capital equipment.
   d. All of the above.
   e. a and b.

5. Roundabout production
   a. is generally more efficient than producing goods directly.
   b. is less efficient than producing goods directly because it takes longer.
   c. increases productivity on farms but not in factories.
   d. requires less saving than producing goods directly.
   e. b and c.

6. In a modern economy, a producer does not have to save in order to produce because
   a. the capital goods are already produced.
   b. time is not as important in manufacturing as it is in farming.
   c. a producer can use his or her own money to finance production.
   d. money is not a factor of production.
   e. producers can borrow money in the market for loanable funds.

7. When buying capital, a producer should purchase additional capital until
   a. total product is at a maximum.
   b. the marginal revenue product equals the marginal resource cost.
   c. the average revenue product equals the average resource cost.
   d. the marginal rate of return on investment equals the market rate of interest.
   e. the marginal revenue product equals the market rate of interest.

8. Which of the following would cause the marginal rate of return on investment to increase?
   a. The price of capital increases.
   b. The marginal product of capital increases.
   c. The price of the good produced increases.
   d. The price of capital decreases.
   e. b, c, and d

9. Which of the following could cause the demand for loanable funds to increase?
   a. The marginal product of capital increases.
   b. The interest rate falls.
   c. The rate of saving increases.
   d. The marginal rate of return on investment decreases.
   e. All of the above.

10. An increase in the interest rate can be caused by
    a. a decrease in the demand for loanable funds.
    b. an increase in the demand for loanable funds.
    c. a decrease in the supply of loanable funds.
    d. an increase in the supply of loanable funds.
    e. both b and c.

11. Interest rates are higher
    a. the longer the duration of a loan.
    b. the greater the reliability of the borrower.
    c. the larger the size of the loan.
    d. the lower the expected rate of inflation.
    e. None of the above.

12. The present value of $100 to be received in the future is greater
    a. the shorter the time before the $100 is received.
    b. the longer the time before the $100 is received.
    c. the lower the interest rate.
    d. b and c.
    e. a and c.

13. The present value of a $1,000 perpetuity at a 5 percent interest rate is
    a. infinite.
    b. $10,000.
    c. $5,000.
    d. $20,000.
    e. $50,000.

14. The present value of a given payment in the future will
    a. get smaller the further in the future the payment is to be received.
    b. get smaller the greater the interest rate.
    c. get larger the greater the interest rate.
    d. get larger if the expected inflation rate increases over time.
    e. a and b only.

15. A corporation may do all of the following except
    a. vote.
    b. own property.
    c. sue someone.
    d. incur debt.
    e. None of the above.

16. Corporations acquire funds by
    a. issuing stock.
    b. selling bonds.
    c. retaining part of their profit.
    d. receiving dividends.
    e. a, b, and c only.

17. The existence of securities markets makes the allocation of capital more efficient by
    a. providing a market for corporations to sell new stock issues.
    b. enhancing the liquidity of the securities once they are issued and sold.
    c. providing information about the value of the corporation.
    d. regulating the investments of the managers of the corporation.
    e. b and c.

18. The issue of the separation of ownership from control is about which of the following problems?
    a. whether managers operate firms so as to make monopoly profits
    b. whether managers operate firms in the best interests of the stockholders
    c. whether managers operate firms in the best interests of society
    d. whether managers of firms get together to collude and maximize joint profits
    e. a and d.

19. Which of the following reduce the likelihood that managers will behave in ways detrimental to stockholders?
    a. stock options for executives
    b. the rigors of competition
    c. stockholder voting
    d. the threat of a takeover
    e. All of the above.

20. The market for corporate control will work well when
    a. the incumbent managers fight takeover vigorously.
    b. the value of the assets of a firm is easily determined by outsiders.
    c. the government prohibits takeovers.
    d. All of the above.
    e. None of the above.

D.   Discussion Questions

1. "Time is important in roundabout production but not in direct production." Is this statement true or false? Explain.

2. Explain why producers must rely on their own or another's savings to produce.

Exhibit 1

Units of Capital	Total Product	Marginal Product	Total Resource Cost	Marginal Resource Cost	Marginal Revenue Product	Marginal Rate of Return on Investment
0	0	____	$0	____	____	____
1	500	____	____	____	____	____
2	950	____	____	____	____	____
3	1,350	____	____	____	____	____
4	1,700	____	____	____	____	____
5	2,000	____	____	____	____	____
6	2,250	____	____	____	____	____
7	2,450	____	____	____	____	____
8	2,600	____	____	____	____	____

3. a. A unit of capital costs $15,000, the interest rate is 10 percent, and the price of output is $5. Assume that the capital is expected to last indefinitely and operating costs are negligible. Fill in the blanks in Exhibit 1.
    b. How many units of capital will the producer buy? How do you know?
    c. If the interest rate increased to 15 percent, how many units would the producer buy?

Exhibit 2

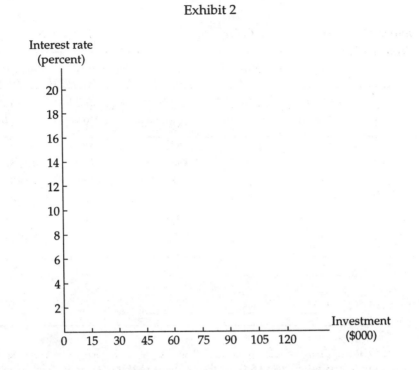

4. In Exhibit 2, draw the marginal rate of return on investment curve. Indicate the optimal amount of investment if the market rate of interest is 10 percent.

5. Explain why the supply curve for loanable funds slopes upward.

6. Many private schools in the country cost three to four times more than many state universities. Why would a rational student choose to go to an expensive school?

7. Explain why there is more than one interest rate in a market economy.

Exhibit 3

Number of Years from Today	Project A		Project B	
	Payments	*Receipts*	*Payments*	*Receipts*
0	$10,000	$0	$6,000	$0
1	10,000	2,000	0	0
2	0	5,000	0	0
3	0	5,000	0	4,000
4	0	10,000	0	4,000
5	0	10,000	0	4,000
6	0	5,000	0	4,000
7	0	0	0	1,000

8. Exhibit 3 shows the income and payment schedules of two research projects. If the interest rate is 10 percent, what is the present value of each?

9. Suppose a third project will cost $20,000 today and yield a return of $2,500 a year indefinitely. What is the present value of the project? What is the present value if the interest rate increases to 20 percent?

10. Suppose an entrepreneur starts and runs a new firm. The firm generates $50,000 in revenues in excess of payments to other resource owners. The entrepreneur supplies $50,000 worth of capital that could be leased for $5,000 a year and manages the firm instead of hiring a manager for $25,000 a year. What is the economic profit? How much is the reward to the entrepreneur for supplying entrepreneurial ability?

11. Suppose the firm in question 10 is expected to perform at that level forever. If the interest rate is 10 percent, how much could the entrepreneur sell the firm for?

12. Explain how security exchanges affect the allocation of investment funds even though only secondhand securities are sold on the exchanges.

13. Explain how the market for corporate control is supposed to work. What factors might cause this market to work inefficiently?

14. Who are institutional investors? What impact are they having on the market for corporate control?

15. How is the model of corporate finance developed in the second part of the chapter related to the model developed in the first part of the chapter concerning roundabout production and the market for loanable funds?

VII. ANSWERS

A. Completion

1. saving
2. Roundabout
3. positive rate of time preference
4. Interest
5. marginal rate of return on investment
6. Present value
7. term structure of interest rates
8. discounting; discount rate
9. annuity
10. corporations
11. retained earnings
12. bond; maturity
13. separation of ownership and control
14. initial public offering
15. institutional investor

B. True/False

1. True
2. True
3. True
4. False. The greater the interest rate, the greater the opportunity cost of *present* consumption.
5. True
6. False
7. False
8. True
9. False
10. False
11. False
12. True
13. False
14. True
15. True
16. True
17. True
18. True
19. True
20. False

C. Multiple Choice

1. d
2. e
3. d
4. e
5. a
6. e
7. d
8. e
9. a. Answers b and c are not correct because they cause an increase in the quantity demanded. The demand curve does not shift.
10. e
11. a
12. e
13. d
14. e
15. a
16. e
17. e
18. b
19. e
20. b

D. Discussion Questions

1. False. Time is also important in direct production. All production involves time, not just roundabout production. A seed planted by hand takes as much time to grow as a seed planted with capital equipment like tractors and tillers.

2. Production takes time, so producers must have access to savings in order to produce. The producer must be able to compensate owners of resources used in production before the goods are sold. Further, capital equipment reduces current consumption, so savings must exist before capital goods can be produced.

3. a.

Units of Capital	Total Product	Marginal Product	Total Resource Cost	Marginal Resource Cost	Marginal Revenue Product	Marginal Rate of Return on Investment
0	0	---	$ 0	---	---	---
1	500	500	15,000	$15,000	$2,500	16.67%
2	950	450	30,000	15,000	2,250	15
3	1,350	400	45,000	15,000	2,000	13.33
4	1,700	350	60,000	15,000	1,750	11.67
5	2,000	300	75,000	15,000	1,500	10
6	2,250	250	90,000	15,000	1,250	8.33
7	2,450	200	105,000	15,000	1,000	6.67
8	2,600	150	120,000	15,000	750	5

  b. 5 units of capital, because at that point the marginal rate of return on investment equals the market rate of interest
  c. 2 units

4.

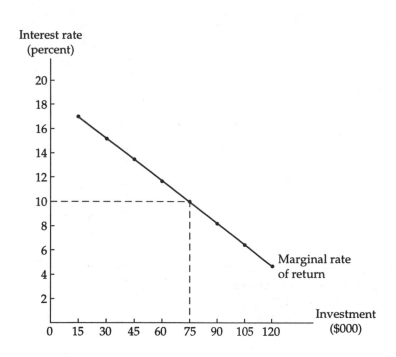

5. The supply curve of loanable funds slopes upward because present consumption is valued more than future consumption. Consequently, people must be compensated to save, and the interest rate determines their compensation. The greater the interest rate, the greater one's claim on future resources, the greater the opportunity cost of present consumption, and therefore, the greater the amount saved.

6. The extra cost of the private schools can be thought of as a higher marginal resource cost. If everyone faces the same interest rate, then all will invest in school until the marginal rate of return on investment equals the interest rate. The marginal rate of return on investment equals the marginal revenue product divided by the marginal resource cost. If the marginal revenue product of the private schools is at least three to four times greater than the marginal revenue product of the state universities, then it is rational to attend the more expensive schools.

7. The main reason there is more than one interest rate is that loans differ in riskiness. Less reliable borrowers are riskier to lend to, so lenders require a higher interest rate. The longer the duration of the loan the greater the risk of higher-than-expected inflation, so the higher the interest rate. The dollar cost of processing a loan tends to be the same regardless of the size of the loan, so small loans have a higher relative cost and require higher interest rates. Finally, lenders are interested in their after-tax rate of return, so loans made to organizations that are not taxable will carry lower interest rates.

8. Present value of Project A

$$= -\$10,000 - \frac{8,000}{(1.1)^1} + \frac{5,000}{(1.1)^2} + \frac{5,000}{(1.1)^3} + \frac{10,000}{(1.1)^4} + \frac{10,000}{(1.1)^5} + \frac{5,000}{(1.1)^6}$$

$$= -\$10,000 - 7,272.73 + 4,132.23 + 3,756.57 + 6,830.13 + 6,209.21 + 2,822.3$$

$$= \$6,477.78$$

Present value of Project B

$$= -\$6,000 + \frac{4,000}{(1.1)^3} + \frac{4,000}{(1.1)^4} + \frac{4,000}{(1.1)^5} + \frac{4,000}{(1.1)^6} + \frac{1,000}{(1.1)^7}$$

$$= -\$6,000 + 3,005.26 + 2,732.05 + 2,483.69 + 2,257.90 + 513.16$$

$$= \$4,992.06$$

9. At an interest rate of 10 percent, the present value of the third project =

$$\frac{\$2,500}{0.10} - 20,000 = \$25,000 - 20,000 = \$5,000$$

If the interest rate rises to 20 percent, the project's present value =

$$\frac{\$2,500}{0.20} - \$20,000 = 12,500 - 20,000 = -\$7,500$$

10. $5,000 should be counted as the return to those supplying capital and $25,000 as the return to the entrepreneur for managing the firm. Economic profit is then $50,000 − $5,000 − $25,000 = $20,000. The return to the entrepreneur for supplying entrepreneurial ability is also $20,000, the economic profit.

11. $$\frac{\$20,000}{0.10} = \$200,000$$

12. The prices of securities on the exchanges reflect the profitability of the firms. The price of the stock of a company whose performance declines will fall. The lower price makes it more difficult for the firm to raise new financial capital because it will have to sell more shares of stock to receive a certain level of funds. Successful firms will receive a higher price for their new issues and will find it easier to raise the investment funds they want. Thus, the information provided by the security exchanges affects the allocation of capital.

13. The market for corporate control works by lowering stock prices for a company that is not efficiently run so that the firm's assets are undervalued. Outsiders can see the low stock price, buy large numbers of shares to gain control of the company, and replace the inefficient management. This process will not work efficiently if outsiders have a difficult time evaluating the true value of the firm or if management can take actions that reduce the gains from taking over the firm.

14. Institutional investors are professional money managers who invest funds for others and include insurance companies and mutual funds. They invest heavily and are very knowledgeable about firms and markets, and are able to monitor and control managers of corporations better than small stockholders can.

15. Corporations raise funds for investing by selling stock, selling bonds, or investing retained earnings. The determination of whether profitable investment opportunites exist will utilize the ideas developed in the first part of the chapter—calculating the marginal rate of return on the projects and comparing that with the interest rate. Once the investment projects are identified, the firm has to finance them. It can either use retained earnings to do so or enter the capital markets, what was called earlier in the chapter the *market for loanable funds*. It can borrow (sell bonds) or it can raise equity capital (sell shares of stock). If the firm does not have enough investment projects that it expects to be profitable, it could also lend some of its retained earnings in the market for loanable funds.

CHAPTER 27

Transaction Costs, Imperfect Information, and Market Behavior

I. INTRODUCTION

In this chapter, we examine more closely the effects of imperfect information on the behavior of firms and consumers. We will investigate why firms exist and discuss the factors that affect the internal structure of firms. Since consumers do not have all the information needed to make the best decisions, we will examine how imperfect information affects their decisions. Finally, the chapter briefly discusses some market responses to the problems of imperfect information.

II. OUTLINE

1. Rationale for the Firm and Its Scope of Operation. The model of perfect competition assumes that all participants in the market possess all the information they need about prices, technology, inputs, and the like. If perfect information, frictionless exchange, and perfect competition actually existed, entrepreneurs would not be needed and production would not be performed by firms.

    1.1 Firms Reduce Transaction Costs
        a. In the 1930s, Ronald Coase recognized that the firm may often be more efficient than market exchange because production requires the coordination of many resource owners.
        b. The costs of organizing production through market transactions often exceed the costs of undertaking production within the firm.
        c. There are costs involved in using markets to make transactions:
            (1) Costs of determining what resources are needed
            (2) Costs of negotiating separate contracts with each resource owner
        d. When the transaction costs of using the market are relatively high, households buy from a firm rather than directly hire the inputs.

    1.2 The Bounds of the Firm
        a. Firms are a way to minimize the sum of the transaction costs and the production costs of economic activity.
        b. *Vertical integration* is expansion of a firm into earlier or later stages of production. Other things equal, firms should buy an input in the market when the cost of doing so is lower than it would be if the input were produced internally.
        c. Internal production and markets are alternative ways of organizing transactions.
        d. Firms use specific criteria to determine whether to purchase a particular component or whether to produce it.

(1) Bounded rationality of managers: a manager can understand only a limited amount of information.

(2) Minimum efficient scale: the larger the minimum efficient scale of producing a component, the more likely a firm is to buy it from another firm that specializes in producing the component.

(3) Easily observable quality: when an input is well defined and quality is easily determined, the firm is more likely to purchase the input.

(4) Number of suppliers: the more suppliers there are, the more likely the firm is to purchase an input.

1.3 *CASE STUDY:* The Trend toward Outsourcing

1.4 Economies of Scope
   a. If it is cheaper to produce two or more product lines at the same time than to produce them separately, the firm is more likely to do so.
   b. Per-unit production costs fall as the firm produces additional types of products when there are economies of scope.

2. Market Behavior with Imperfect Information

2.1 Optimal Search with Imperfect Information
   a. People often obtain information about a product before they purchase it.
   b. The primary cost of gathering information is the opportunity cost of a consumer's time.
   c. The marginal cost of search increases as the search for information widens.
   d. The marginal benefit from obtaining additional information decreases as the search for information widens.
   e. Optimal search occurs when the marginal benefit of searching for additional information exactly equals the marginal cost of search for additional information.
   f. Search costs generate price dispersion and quality differences across sellers.

2.2 The Winner's Curse
   a. The "winner's curse" refers to a situation in which the winner in a bidding contest for an asset loses money by winning the bid.
   b. The winner's curse can occur when the true value of the asset is unknown and the most optimistic bidder wins. Sometimes the winner was too optimistic.

3. Asymmetric Information in Product Markets
   a. There is *asymmetric information* in a situation when one participant in a transaction has more reliable information than the other participant.
   b. Characteristics of a product may be hidden from one of the participants, or actions taken by one party may be hidden from the other.

3.1 Hidden Characteristics: Adverse Selection
   a. The seller of a product often knows more about the characteristics of the product than the potential buyer.
   b. When buyers know that the quality of a product varies across units and are unable to judge the quality before buying the good, the maximum price they will pay is below the price that sellers of the higher-quality units must receive to induce them to sell.

     c.   Owners of higher-quality units will pull their units off the market, so the only units still for sale in the market are the lowest-quality units.

     d.   The end result can be that only the "lemons" end up for sale in the market.

     e.   *Adverse selection* occurs when those on the informed side of the market can self-select in a way harmful to those on the uninformed side of the market.

   3.2   Hidden Actions: Principal-Agent Problem

     a.   A *principal-agent* contractual relationship exists when one person (the *agent*) acts on behalf of another person (the *principal*).

     b.   If the agent's goals are incompatible with the principal's goals, the agent can pursue hidden actions that are costly to the principal.

   3.3   Asymmetric Information in Insurance Markets

     a.   Adverse selection creates problems in insurance markets because those who are more likely to use the insurance benefits are more likely to purchase insurance; this causes insurance rates to increase and drive out those who are less likely to use the insurance benefits.

     b.   In insurance markets, people with insurance coverage may alter their behavior in ways that make it more likely the event insured against will occur. This is the moral hazard problem.

     c.   Moral hazard arises on the part of the person who can engage in hidden actions.

   3.4   Coping with Asymmetric Information. Ways of reducing the costs of asymmetric information have been found in many markets.

4.   Asymmetric Information in Labor Markets. It is more difficult to relate compensation to the marginal productivity of workers when labor is heterogeneous and production requires the coordinated efforts of several workers.

   4.1   Adverse Selection Problems in Labor Markets

     a.   Before a worker is hired, the worker's true abilities are hidden from the employer.

     b.   A given advertised wage tends to reflect the average marginal revenue product of all workers in the market and thus to attract the least-productive workers in the pool.

     c.   Employers must often rely on proxy information, such as education, to determine the most qualified applicant.

     d.   Sometimes employers pay a higher wage, called *efficiency wages*, to attract higher-quality workers into the labor pool.

   4.2   Signaling and Screening

     a.   A *signal* is a proxy measure of the unobservable characteristics of a potential employee.

     b.   Education is often used as a signal.

     c.   Employers often use a screening device to determine who is more likely to be a productive worker.

   4.3   *CASE STUDY:* The Reputation of a Big Mac

III. DISCUSSION

Rationale for the Firm and Its Scope of Operation

Previous chapters assumed that the firm exists in order to transform inputs into outputs. In a world of perfect competition and frictionless exchange, there would be no reason for firms to exist, however. Ronald Coase argued that firms exist because market transactions are costly. Economic activity can be carried on by firms or by markets. When the marginal cost of a transaction using direct managerial controls in a firm is less than the marginal cost of using the price system to allocate resources, then a firm will carry out the transaction. As the cost of using firms to organize economic activities falls, firms get larger.

The extent of the firm's activities will be determined by comparing the costs of using markets with the costs of internal production and coordination. The scope of the firm is determined by considering factors such as the point where the *bounded rationality* of managers creates diseconomies, the minimum efficient scale for producing inputs, how easily the quality of inputs can be determined, and the number of suppliers of inputs there are. Some firms realize *economies of scope*, which make it cheaper to combine two or more product lines in one firm than to produce them separately.

Market Behavior with Imperfect Information

Information is a scarce good that is costly to acquire. This is true for both consumers and producers. A consumer will collect information about a product before making the purchase. This information may include data about the characteristics of various brands and makes, the prices at different stores, warranty information, reliability, and so on. The more extensive the search for information, the greater the costs of the search. The costs include explicit costs such as purchase of magazines that provide information and gasoline used to drive to several stores. The major cost usually is the opportunity cost of the consumer's time spent in search activity. The marginal cost of search for additional information increases as the search process continues. The marginal benefits from acquiring additional information include the lower prices discovered during the search process and the higher-quality obtained by the additional search. The marginal benefit will eventually decline as the search process continues. The optimal search occurs where the marginal costs of additional search for information exactly equal the marginal benefits from additional search for information. Search costs generate price dispersion and quality differences for the same product.

Imperfect information can cause another problem in the case of bidding on assets when the true value of the asset is unknown. Examples of such assets would include off-shore oil leases, movie rights to a book, and broadcast rights to sporting events. Since the true value of the asset is unknown, people have to estimate the value and base their bids on their estimates. The highest bid obtains the asset. It is possible that the highest bidder will have overestimated the true value of the asset, in which case the winner will actually suffer losses on the asset. This phenomenon is referred to as the *winner's curse*.

Asymmetric Information in Product Markets

Another problem that can develop in some markets is the problem of asymmetric information—the situation when one side of a transaction has better information than the other side. There are two types of information that a market participant may lack: information about the characteristics of the product and information about the actions of the other participant in the market activity.

The problem of the hidden characteristics of a product is sometimes referred to as the "lemon" problem. Keep in mind the conditions that are necessary for this to be a problem. The product's quality must vary across units and important characteristics of the product must be hidden from the potential buyer. Potential buyers would then make an estimate of the expected or average quality of the units and would be willing to pay a price no higher than the price of the average quality of the product. But when the owners know the true quality of the units they have, they will not offer for sale their higher-quality units because what the price buyers will pay is too low. Hence, only lower-quality units, or lemons, appear on the market. As buyers realize this, they lower their offer prices accordingly until the lemons have driven all the higher-quality units out of the market.

The problem of the lemon can show up in many different market contexts. In insurance markets, the buyer often has better information about the likelihood of actually using the insurance benefits than the insurance company. Suppose the insurance company sets rates based on the average medical expenses of families in the country. Those families that expected to generate medical costs equal to or greater than this average would definitely buy the insurance, whereas those that knew they would generate medical costs below this would not. That is, the people self-select on the basis of their better information. If this occurs, the actual premiums received by the insurance company will not cover the medical costs generated by policyholders. If the insurance company increases rates, more people leave the system. In insurance markets, this behavior is referred to as *adverse selection*. It is easy to see that adverse selection is another form of the lemon problem.

Market participants have developed some methods of reducing the costs associated with asymmetric information. Warranties and guarantees are used to alleviate the hidden characteristics problem in many product markets; the development of a reputation for quality has been used in other markets. Insurance companies try to obtain health histories of people in order to assess the riskiness of individuals and families and set a range of prices that depend on these estimates of risk. These practices do not eliminate the costs associated with adverse selection and lemons, but they do reduce these costs.

The second type of asymmetric information problem is due to hidden actions, or the *principal-agent problem*. Again, this problem occurs in many market settings. A *principal* is one party in a contractual relationship who obtains the services of another party, known as the *agent*. The agent is to act on the behalf of the principal and has some discretion in doing so. For example, business managers represent athletes or entertainers; the managers of a firm (agents) act on behalf of the owners of the corporation (principals); employees carry out the wishes of employers; auto mechanics act in a sense as agents for the car owners; and doctors act on behalf of patients. The problem develops when the interests of the agent are not the same as the interests of the principal. An extreme case would be a business manager who embezzled funds from his or her principal. A more benign case occurs when a worker takes a longer coffee break than company rules allow.

There is a similar phenomenon, known as *moral hazard*, in insurance markets. Suppose a family purchases fire insurance for their home that will compensate them fully for a fire (including all "psychic" costs). The likelihood of a fire is dependent, at least to some degree, on the behavior of the members of the family. With the insurance, they may not be as cautious as they would otherwise be, which increases the probability of a fire. Insurance companies respond to this possibility by refusing to insure many activities fully. Instead, they have deductibles so the insured bear a part of the cost of a loss. In this way, the insured have an incentive to behave in a way that minimizes the likelihood that the event insured against will occur.

Asymmetric Information in Labor Markets

Adverse selection can occur in labor markets too. A firm advertises for workers at a certain wage. Workers who know that the value of their marginal product exceeds the wage will not apply for the job. The people who apply are those whose value of marginal product is less than or equal to the announced wage. Firms sometimes offer higher wages than necessary in order to attract higher-quality workers. Further, potential employers screen applicants, and workers may offer signals, such as education, to provide evidence of their productivity.

Other solutions to asymmetric information problems is signaling and screening. Signaling is an attempt by the informed side of the market to communicate information to the other side. Education is an example. Screening is an attempt by the uninformed side to obtain better information.

IV. LAGNIAPPE

Size of Firms

Corporations became important phenomena in the late 19th century. As firms grew larger, their capital requirements became so large that a few individuals could no longer provide all of the necessary capital. Firms also became larger because of changes in the fields of communication and transportation. Railroads made it possible for goods to be shipped over longer distances, which expanded markets and enabled individual plants to be made larger. Telegraphs and then telephones made it possible for firms to have offices in various parts of the country. Improvements in communication and information also lowered the marginal cost of carrying out an activity within the firm relative to using the marketplace.

Other factors also encouraged the expansion of firms. Inflation raises the cost of using markets by making it more difficult to determine the real price of a good or service. Price controls also raise the cost of using markets, encouraging firms to handle additional activities internally.

Question to Think About: How might tax policy encourage expansion of firms?

Using Up a Reputation

The idea that a reputation for quality can be a "hostage" that ensures quality has become widely used in economics. It is helpful in explaining market behavior concerning franchising, advertising, and finance. However, there is always one problem that must be dealt with: the problem of the final period. Once a reputation for quality has been established, it may be profitable to cheat and produce products or services of lesser quality than you have in the past. The incentive to do so is especially great if you will not be around in the future. That is, if there is a last period to the life of a firm, there is a strong incentive to consume the "reputation capital" in the last period. Given that potential consumers know this, they will not believe that you will produce the higher-quality in the last period and will not pay the higher price for higher-quality goods in the last period. If this is so, then the next-to-last period becomes just like the last period. The logic of the last-period problem eventually leads to the conclusion that the firm will never provide the higher-quality good. What often prevents this type of behavior from actually taking place is that for most business firms, especially corporations, the last period is unknown. Hence, the firms always have a future to be concerned with and thus have an incentive to maintain their reputations.

Question to Think About: Could a similar problem apply to workers as they approach retirement age?

V. KEY TERMS

vertical integration
bounded rationality
outsourcing
economies of scope
winner's curse
asymmetric information
hidden characteristics
hidden actions

adverse selection
principal-agent problem
principal
agent
moral hazard
efficiency wage theory
signaling
screening

VI. QUESTIONS

A. Completion

1. Ronald Coase argues that economic activity is best understood in terms of the _____ costs involved in exchange.

2. Firms exist because entrepreneurs are trying to reduce _____.

3. The expansion of a firm into earlier or later stages of production is called _____.

4. Internal production and _____ are alternative ways of organizing transactions.

5. Management has _____ because it can comprehend only a limited amount of information.

6. _____ exist when it is cheaper to combine two or more product lines within one firm than it is for separate firms to produce them.

7. In real-world markets, reliable information is _____ for consumers and producers.

8. Price dispersion is the result of _____ costs.

9. The _____ often afflicts those who offer the highest bid on assets of unknown value.

10. When one side of a transaction has more reliable information than the other, the situation involves _____.

11. In the doctor-patient relationship, the doctor is known as the _____ and the patient is the _____.

12. The problem of hidden characteristics in insurance markets generates the problem of _____.

13. _____ occurs when the behavior of one party to a transaction affects the likelihood of an unfavorable outcome.

14. A proxy measure, which is an observable indicator of a hidden characteristic, is called a(n) _____.

15. An attempt by an employer to obtain information about the hidden characteristics of a potential employee is called _____.

B. True/False

_____ 1. Firms would not exist in a world of perfect competition, perfect information, and frictionless exchange.

_____ 2. According to Coase, firms exist to economize on transaction costs.

_____ 3. The exchange relationship between individuals using markets is contractual in nature, but relationships within a firm are not contractual.

_____ 4. Resources are allocated by prices within a firm.

_____ 5. Firms minimize the sum of production and transaction costs.

_____ 6. When exchange is characterized by incomplete contracts, firms often produce a good directly rather than buy it from another firm.

_____ 7. The easier it is to determine the quality of an input, the more likely the firm that uses the input is to produce the input itself.

_____ 8. Economies of scope are another name for economies of scale.

_____ 9. In market activities, reliable information is more costly for consumers than for producers.

_____ 10. The primary cost of search for information is the opportunity cost of the person's time.

_____ 11. A rational person will search more when buying a car than when buying tires.

_____ 12. Optimal search occurs when the difference between the marginal benefit of additional search and the marginal cost of additional search is at a maximum.

_____ 13. Search costs associated with buying a product will be greater for a couple when both spouses work outside the home than when only one of the spouses works outside the home.

_____ 14. The winner's curse applies to all cases of bidding.

_____ 15. In a market characterized by asymmetric information about the characteristics of a good, buyers usually pay more for lower-quality goods than the goods are worth.

_____ 16. The principal-agent problem is an example of adverse selection.

_____ 17. Health insurance is affected more by adverse selection problems than moral hazard problems.

_____ 18. Moral hazard arises on the part of the agent.

_____ 19. Firms sometimes pay higher wages to improve the productivity of their workforce.

_____ 20. A signal that can be acquired easily by all workers does not make a good signaling device.

C. Multiple Choice

1. Firms exist because of
   a. greed.
   b. transaction costs.
   c. perfect information.
   d. diminishing marginal returns.
   e. All of the above.

2. Transactions that are carried on within the hierarchy of the firm are often more efficient than transactions carried out through markets because
   a. production is costly.
   b. production often requires the coordination of many transactions among many resource owners.
   c. markets generally allocate resources inefficiently.
   d. production involves many stages, and it is always better to perform all stages at one location.
   e. b, c, and d.

3. Which of the following statements is correct?
   a. Firms arise because transaction costs are greater than production costs.
   b. The choice between using internal production and using markets is determined by government regulation.
   c. Incomplete contracts are problems for firms so markets generally are used in such cases.
   d. Where inputs are easily measured, priced, and hired, production tends to be carried out by firms.
   e. One advantage of market transactions is that they do not require as much conscious effort as direct controls in a firm.

4. Which of the following would be an example of vertical integration?
   a. A steel company buys an interest in a coal company.
   b. A steel company buys an interest in an automobile manufacturer.
   c. Two competing steel companies merge.
   d. All of the above.
   e. a and b only

5. The costs of organizing an additional transaction within the firm increase as the size of the firm increases because
   a. it gets more difficult to determine the quality of inputs.
   b. communication within the firm gets more difficult.
   c. the transactions get more complex.
   d. All of the above.
   e. None of the above. The costs do not increase as the firm gets larger.

6. Suppose that research done by an R&D lab can improve two different products. This would be an example of
   a. economies of scope.
   b. vertical integration.
   c. economies of scale.
   d. increasing returns to scale.
   e. a and b only.

7. Based on the information in question 6, can we conclude that the firm will produce both product lines?
   a. No, because the economies of scope could be small relative to other production or transaction costs that would make it more costly to produce both products in one firm.
   b. No, because it will be cheaper for the R&D lab to be separate from the firm that produces the product lines.
   c. Yes, because the economies of scope will lower the costs of producing the two product lines when they are produced within the same firm.
   d. Yes, because vertical integration between the firm producing the goods and the R&D lab will generate lower costs of production.
   e. Yes, but we cannot tell without more information whether c or d provides the best reason.

8. The primary cost of searching for information on a product is
   a. the cost of advertising the product.
   b. the opportunity cost of the consumer's time.
   c. the wear and tear on the consumer's automobile.
   d. the price of magazines and reports that provide information about the product.
   e. the psychic costs associated with making the wrong decision.

9. Optimal search for information occurs when
   a. the consumer has the same amount of information as there would be if information were perfect.
   b. the marginal benefit from additional search equals zero.
   c. the costs of search are minimized.
   d. the marginal benefit of additional search equals the marginal cost of additional search.
   e. the total benefits of additional search equal the total costs of additional search.

10. An implication of Stigler's search model is that
    a. more information will be gathered by consumers on homogeneous products than on heterogeneous products.
    b. consumers' search for information will be more extensive as levels of education increase.
    c. the price dispersion of high-priced items will be less than the price dispersion of low-priced goods.
    d. the price dispersion of a good will be less, the less time people spend searching for information about the good.
    e. the marginal cost of additional search is less for lower-priced goods than for higher-priced goods.

11. Which of the following would be an example of the winner's curse?
    a. CBS wins the rights to the World Series and the teams end up in St. Louis and Milwaukee.
    b. A publishing company outbids other companies to publish a new textbook written by a young economist.
    c. A businessperson outbids all others for a Van Gogh sold by a Dutch museum.
    d. All of the above. are possible examples of the winner's curse.
    e. Only a and b are possible examples of the winner's curse.

12. Asymmetric information is associated with
    a. any product for which certain characteristics are hidden.
    b. products for which some characteristics are hidden from the buyer but known by the seller.
    c. products of variable quality.
    d. all insurance markets.
    e. All of the above.

13. Suppose 20 percent of the cars produced are lemons. The value of a high-quality car after a year is $10,000, and the value of the lemon after a year is $4,000. The probable price for a year-old used car is
    a. $10,000 for good cars and $4,000 for lemons.
    b. $10,000.
    c. $8,800.
    d. $7,000.
    e. $4,000.

14. The principal-agent problem arises whenever
    a. one person acts on the behalf of another.
    b. the goals of the principal and the agent are incompatible.
    c. the actions of the agent can be hidden from the principal.
    d. All of the above.
    e. b and c only.

15. Adverse selection will not be a problem in the insurance industry when
    a. the event insured against is equally likely to affect anyone.
    b. the insurance company cannot charge different customers different prices.
    c. the insurance company cannot inquire into the characteristics of the customers.
    d. the insurance pool is small.
    e. None of the above.

16. Moral hazard affects all of the following except
    a. fire insurance.
    b. theft insurance.
    c. auto insurance.
    d. flight insurance.
    e. health insurance.

17. Insurance companies require the insured to pay a portion of a loss to reduce the problem of
    a. adverse selection.
    b. moral hazard.
    c. screening.
    d. hidden characteristics.
    e. a, b, and d.

18. If a proxy measure is to be a good signal for some hidden characteristic, it must be
    a. valuable in its own right.
    b. easily obtained by the one wanting to give the signal.
    c. difficult to obtain by those not having the hidden characteristics.
    d. perfectly correlated with the hidden characteristic.
    e. All of the above.

19. Adverse selection in labor markets leads to
    a. signaling.
    b. employers screening applicants.
    c. both signaling and screening.
    d. using reputation as a hostage.
    e. moral hazard.

20. Suppose a firm has built up a reputation for high quality and then reduces quality to increase profits. The cost to the firm of doing this is
    a. lost profits in the future after consumers realize the actual quality level.
    b. lower profits right away because people instantaneously realize that the quality is lower.
    c. higher screening costs in the future.
    d. increased moral hazard on the part of consumers.
    e. zero. The firm can always increase quality later and regain its reputation.

D.   Discussion Questions

1. Explain why production would not have to be carried out by firms if the marginal product of all inputs could be measured without cost, if prices for all inputs could be identified without cost, and if transactions were without cost.

2. Describe Coase's theory of the firm.

3. What is vertical integration?

4. What determines the extent of vertical integration in a firm?

5. If market transactions are costly, why isn't all production carried on by one giant firm?

6. Firms often produce some of the inputs they use and buy other inputs. What characteristics of the inputs are important in determining whether the firm will make the input itself or purchase it from a supplier?

7. What are economies of scope? How do they differ from economies of scale?

8. Explain why the marginal cost of search for information increases as search activity increases.

9. Apply the model of optimal search to the search for a college to attend. Can the model also be applied to the search for a job?

10. What economic differences are there between the effects of imperfect information and asymmetric information?

11. Explain why the correct answer to multiple choice Question 13 is e.

12. How is the lemon problem related to insurance markets? What are some things insurance companies can do to reduce the costs of the problem?

13. Owners of firms usually raise some financial capital by borrowing. Lenders generally require the owner to have some of his or her own money in the company to prevent moral hazard. How could moral hazard be a problem if the owner used debt exclusively to finance the company?

14. Is adverse selection likely to be a greater problem when hiring a welder or when hiring a personnel manager? Why?

15. What must be true if signaling is to solve the adverse selection problem?

16. Based on information in this chapter, can you offer an economic justification for trademarks and brand names?

17. Can the problems of imperfect and asymmetric information be used to enrich Coase's theory of the firm? How?

VII. ANSWERS

A. Completion

1.	transaction	9.	winner's curse
2.	transaction costs	10.	asymmetric information
3.	vertical integration	11.	agent; principal
4.	markets	12.	adverse selection
5.	bounded rationality	13.	Moral hazard
6.	Economies of scope	14.	signal
7.	costly	15.	screening
8.	search		

B. True/False

1.	True	13.	True
2.	True	14.	False. The winner's curse applies only when the actual value of the asset is unknown.
3.	False		
4.	False		
5.	True	15.	False
6.	True	16.	True
7.	False	17.	False
8.	False	18.	False. It can arise on the part of either the agent or the principal, depending on circumstances.
9.	False		
10.	True		
11.	True	19.	True
12.	False	20.	True

C. Multiple Choice

1.	b	11.	e
2.	b	12.	b
3.	e	13.	e
4.	e	14.	e
5.	b	15.	a
6.	a	16.	d
7.	a	17.	b
8.	b	18.	c
9.	d	19.	c
10.	c	20.	a

D. Discussion Questions

1. Markets transmit information quickly and efficiently. Firms are used when there are costs to using markets. If there were no costs to using markets, then firms would not be needed. Each input owner would contract directly with anyone who wanted to use the input. If the price of each input were known by all and the marginal product of each input were also known, market transactions would be used to produce all goods.

2. Coase points out that there are costs to using markets. The prices and productivity of all inputs are not known with certainty. When the costs of discovering prices and productivity and contracting with resource owners are high, consumers will purchase from firms rather than contracting with all input owners. Firms will take on activities as long as the additional cost of performing each activity within the firm is less than the cost of using the market.

3. Vertical integration is the expansion of a firm into stages of production earlier or later than those in which the firm has specialized.

4. The firm will expand production into an earlier or later stage of production if its combined costs are less than if it carried on the extra transactions by using markets.

5. There are also costs to carrying on activities within the firm and coordinating transactions by managers. The amount of information managers have is often limited, as are their abilities to assimilate the information, and communication among members of the firm gets more difficult the larger the firm becomes.

6. The easier it is to determine the quality of an input by examining it, the more likely the firm will be to purchase the input from a supplier rather than produce it itself. The more suppliers of the input there are, the more likely the firm will be to purchase the input because the firm can be less concerned with interruptions in delivery of the input.

7. Economies of scope exist when it is cheaper to combine two or more products in the same firm than to produce them in separate firms. Generally, economies of scope rely on the sharing of some activities of the firm such as advertising or research and development. Economies of scale differ in that they are cost savings associated with producing more of one product.

8. As search expands, the consumer travels farther or has to search longer for additional information. The easiest places to obtain information will be searched first, more difficult places later. Since the opportunity cost of time can be thought of as constant, the increasing additions of time needed to expand search imply the marginal costs of search increase.

9. The benefits of additional search include the probability of finding a school that matches your interests more closely or finding a school that is cheaper. When searching for a college, you can use guidebooks and high school counselors to obtain a lot of information at a relatively low cost. To get more information about schools requires further effort: trips to the campus; interviews with students, faculty, and alumni; careful examination of the library; and so on. The marginal benefits of additional search soon begin to diminish and the marginal costs increase, so the optimal stopping point is when the marginal cost of additional information equals the marginal benefit.

   The model can also be applied to the search for employment, where the benefit of additional search is the possibility of finding a better job. Again, marginal benefits of additional search will diminish and the marginal costs will increase, so an optimal stopping point exists.

10. Imperfect information requires people to search for more information. Asymmetric information adds the possibility of undesirable behavior on the part of other participants in the market. The price of an asset whose value is not known to anyone at the time of the sale will be around the expected value of the asset, whereas the price of an asset when the seller has better information than the buyer will tend to be near the price of the lowest quality units of the good. In insurance markets, a price based on probabilities of an undesirable event occurring will prevail when the event is truly random but will not be an equilibrium price if the actions of those insured can affect the probability of the undesired event happening.

11. $4,000 is the value of the lowest-quality cars. Potential buyers know that if they pay more than $4,000 for a used car, the only cars that will be offered for sale are those whose true value is equal to or less than the offered price. Hence, the buyers know that it is likely they will end up paying more than the car is worth. They will not do this, though, so only the lowest-valued cars will end up in the market and people will not pay more than $4,000 for a used car. The lower-quality cars have driven the higher-quality cars out of the market.

12. The lemon problem is called adverse selection in insurance markets. For a given price for insurance coverage, customers will self-select on the basis of their risk characteristics. Customers who are good risks are less likely to buy the insurance. Customers who are poor risks are more likely to buy the insurance. If the less-risky customers do not buy, then the price for the insurance will not generate enough revenues to pay the claims of the poorer risks who did buy the insurance. If the company raises premiums, it drives out the better risks that had bought insurance. In the extreme, the company can be left with only high-risk customers. The adverse selection problem is handled by offering different premiums on the basis of the riskiness of the customer. To determine the riskiness, insurance companies have to collect information about the customers that is related the riskiness of the client. People often have to obtain a physical from a physician before obtaining life or medical insurance; similarly, a person's driving record and other characteristics that are statistically related to the likelihood of an accident (age, gender, education) are used to set rates for auto insurance.

13. The owner of the firm is the residual claimant. If the owner uses debt to finance the entire investment, then the owner has a greater incentive to undertake very risky projects. These projects have a very high return if they succeed, which implies that the owner will receive a very large residual. If the projects fail, the lenders lose and the owner ends up with zero, which is where the owner started. That is, the downside risk is borne by the lenders in this case, but the upside gains are reaped by the owner. Lenders are aware of the moral hazard problem, so they require the owner to have a sizable investment of his or her own in the firm to reduce the incentive to undertake risky projects.

14. Adverse selection would be more of a problem when selecting a personnel manager. It is easier to observe whether an individual has the qualities desired in a welder than it is to see whether the person would be a good personnel manager.

15. It must be more difficult for the less productive group to acquire the signal than for the more productive group to do so.

16. Trademarks and brand names symbolize a firm's reputation for quality, which can be used by customers as a hostage to encourage the firm to maintain its quality standards. For reputation to be effective as an incentive to maintain quality, customers must know what firm is producing the goods they buy so they can reward the high-quality firms with repeat business and punish firms that do not provide the quality they promised by boycotting them in the future.

17. Yes. The material on asymmetric information and principal-agent problems demonstrates the costs of carrying on transactions within the firm. The greater the problems within the firm of either adverse selection or moral hazard, the more likely it is that the transaction will be carried on by means of markets rather than within the firm.

CHAPTER 28

Economic Regulation and Antitrust Activity

I. INTRODUCTION

In this chapter we will apply what we have learned about market structure to some real-world phenomena. If firms seek to maximize profits, then they are likely to attempt to collude or use some other method to make monopoly profits. Government policies sometimes aid and sometimes hinder collusive behavior. This chapter examines government regulation and antitrust policies, both of which have changed considerably in recent years.

II. OUTLINE

1. Business Behavior and Public Policy. *Market power* is the ability to maintain a price above the competitive level. The exercise of market power causes a misallocation of resources.

    1.1 Government Regulation of Business
       a. *Social regulation* consists of government controls related to health and safety.
       b. *Economic regulation* controls price, output, and entry in industries where monopoly is inevitable or desirable.
       c. *Antitrust activity* includes measures designed to curb monopoly and to promote competition.

2. Regulating Natural Monopolies

    2.1 Unregulated Profit Maximization
       a. With a natural monopoly, the lowest average total cost is achieved if one firm serves the entire market.
       b. Because price exceeds marginal cost, there is an underallocation of resources to pro-duction of the good.
       c. Government has four options for dealing with natural monopoly:
          (1) Do nothing and let the unregulated price stand.
          (2) Sell monopoly rights in the market.
          (3) Own and operate the monopoly itself.
          (4) Regulate the privately owned natural monopoly.
       d. Regulated natural monopolies are known as *public utilities*.

    2.2 Setting Price Equal to Marginal Cost
       a. The government can set price equal to marginal cost if it wants to achieve allocative efficiency.
       b. If the government sets price equal to marginal cost, the utility will suffer losses and go out of business in the long run.

2.3 Subsidizing the Natural Monopolist. Government can subsidize the utility and make it charge marginal cost.

2.4 Setting Price Equal to Average Cost. Government can set price equal to average cost, and the utility will make a normal profit.

2.5 The Regulatory Dilemma. The regulatory dilemma is whether to set the allocatively efficient price (marginal cost) or to set price equal to average cost.

3. Alternative Theories of Economic Regulation. Economic regulation is in the public interest, according to some. Economic regulation is in the special interest of producers, according to many economists.

3.1 Producers Have a Special Interest in Economic Regulation
   a. Producers have a strong interest in matters that affect their income.
   b. Consumers buy many goods and services and have no special interest in legislation that affects one good or service.
   c. Producer interests in matters relating to regulation tend to be stronger than consumer interests.
   d. There are two variants of the special-interest theory:
      (1) Capture theory: over time the regulating machinery acts more in accord with producer interests.
      (2) Interest groups compete for favorable regulations.

3.2 *CASE STUDY*: Airline Regulation and Deregulation
   a. The Civil Aeronautics Board (CAB) controlled entry and prices beginning in 1938.
   b. No new entry was allowed by the CAB for 40 years.
   c. Nonprice competition was used extensively in the industry.
   d. Deregulation began in the late 1970s.
   e. Prices have fallen, as have wages in the industry.
   f. Air travel has increased substantially, but airport capacity has not increased, which has retarded competition to some extent.

4. Antitrust Law and Enforcement. Antitrust laws attempt to promote a market structure that encourages competition. Antitrust laws attempt to eliminate anticompetitive behavior.

4.1 Origins of Antitrust Policy
   a. In the second half of the 19th century, technological change led to larger firms in many U.S. industries.
   b. The growth of railroads lowered the costs of transportation, extending markets and allowing firms to grow.
   c. Depressions caused concern among manufacturing firms, with the result that many of them began colluding and forming trusts.
   d. Antitrust legislation was passed in response to these developments. The important U.S. laws:
      (1) The Sherman Antitrust Act of 1890, which prohibits collusion and monopolization
      (2) The Clayton Act of 1914, which outlawed certain anticompetitive practices

          (3)   The Federal Trade Commission Act of 1914, which established the Federal Trade Commission

          (4)   The 1950 Celler-Kefauver Anti-Merger Act, which prevents one firm from buying the assets of another if the effect is to reduce competition

4.2   Antitrust Law Enforcement

    a.   Government agencies often initiate action against a firm because of a complaint from a customer or competitor.

    b.   A firm can sign a consent decree whereby it agrees to discontinue the alleged offense without admitting guilt.

    c.   If the case goes to trial and the firm loses, it can pay fines totaling three times the amount of the damages.

4.3   Per Se Illegality and the Rule of Reason

    a.   Some practices are illegal *per se*, which means that no economic rationale can be used to justify the practice.

    b.   Other practices fall under a *rule of reason*, which means that the aim or the effect of the practice must be unreasonable for the firm to be guilty.

4.4   Mergers and Public Policy

    a.   In looking at the possible harm of a merger, the Justice Department examines the concentration of the industry.

    b.   To measure concentration, the Justice Department uses the Herfindahl index.

    c.   The *Herfindahl index* is the sum of the squared percentage market shares of all firms in the market.

    d.   The Justice Department's guidelines on mergers distinguish between horizontal mergers and non-horizontal mergers.

4.5   Merger Movements. There have been four major merger waves in the last 100 years.

    a.   The first wave involved mostly horizontal mergers and took place from 1887 to 1904.

    b.   The second wave was from 1916 to 1929 and involved primarily vertical mergers.

    c.   The third wave, from 1948 to 1969, involved mostly conglomerate mergers.

    d.   The fourth wave began in the 1980s and is still going on.

5.   Competitive Trends in the U.S. Economy

5.1   Market Competition over Time

    a.   A recent study concludes that there was an increase in the competitiveness of the U.S. economy from 1958 to 1988.

    b.   Reasons for the growth of competition:

          (1)   Increased imports from abroad

          (2)   Deregulation

          (3)   Antitrust activity

5.2   Recent Competitive Trends

    a.   International competition has intensified.

    b.   Antitrust activity is picking up again.

5.3   Problems with Antitrust Legislation

    a.   Many cases take years to settle.

b. There is too much reliance on the model of perfect competition.

c. Treble damage suits may be anticompetitive.

d. International competition is becoming more important and is often overlooked in evaluating the domestic market.

5.4 CASE STUDY: Windows 98 Sold with Microsoft Browser

III. DISCUSSION

Business Behavior and Public Policy

Market power is the ability to raise price and maintain it above the competitive level. The market structure of an industry affects the conduct of firms in the industry. The fewer firms in an industry, the easier it is for them to collude and raise prices above the competitive level. If this occurs, economists say the firms are performing poorly because production is not allocated efficiently.

Regulating Natural Monopolies

A natural monopoly has a downward-sloping long-run average cost curve throughout the entire range of market demand. Regulators do not want the natural monopoly to set the monopoly price. The socially optimal price is found by setting price equal to marginal cost. Unfortunately, if the regulatory agency sets this price, the firm loses money and goes out of business in the long run because marginal cost is less than average cost. The government could require marginal cost pricing and then subsidize the utility so it would not lose money. Generally, this is not done. Instead, regulators typically set price equal to average cost. Average cost pricing is a compromise between the more efficient marginal cost pricing and monopoly pricing.

Alternative Theories of Economic Regulation

Economic regulation involves the control of price, output, entry and exit, and the quality of services in an industry. Ideally, economic regulation is designed to promote social welfare by controlling natural monopolies and promoting competition in some industries. In reality, however, economic regulation often creates what amounts to a government-enforced cartel.

Economists tend to view regulation as the result of competition among interest groups. Interest groups seek favors from the government in the form of subsidies, tariffs, or regulation. Government officials provide the favors, depending on the effectiveness of the lobbying efforts of the interest groups and the likely effects of the officials' actions on the probability of reelection. Within this framework, it is often likely that producer interests will be expressed more forcefully than consumer interests. The producers that are able to gain control of the regulatory process are often able to earn monopoly profits as the government restricts entry into the industry.

The Interstate Commerce Commission (ICC) and the Civil Aeronautics Board (CAB) are two examples of regulatory agencies that have shaped U.S. industries so that they resemble government-sponsored cartels. The ICC restricted entry into the trucking industry, and the CAB restricted entry into the airline industry. For forty years, the CAB permitted no entry into the interstate airline industry. Prices were set to allow profits, although the firms did not always earn monopoly profits for two reasons. First, nonprice competition often eroded the profits. For example, in the airline industry, firms competed by offering more flights, roomier seats, and complimentary food or drinks. Second, the regulatory agencies often required firms to maintain unprofitable routes along with the profitable ones.

Deregulation of the U.S. railroad, trucking, and airline industries occurred during the 1980s. Consequently, rates have fallen as entry and output have expanded. Some carriers that had been able to survive in the protected, regulated environment have gone bankrupt. Wages have fallen in these industries as competition has increased. Economic efficiency has increased as a result of deregulation, but producers and employees who have been negatively affected by these changes are still lobbying for a return to regulation.

Antitrust Law and Enforcement

Antitrust laws attempt to promote competition in the marketplace. The Sherman Antitrust Act makes it illegal for firms to conspire to restrict trade and to attempt to monopolize an industry. The Clayton Act prohibits certain practices associated with monopoly or monopolization if they substantially lessen competition: price discrimination, *tying contracts*, *exclusive dealing*, and *interlocking directorates*. The Federal Trade Commission was established in 1914 to prevent unfair methods of competition.

The courts have used two criteria in interpreting the antitrust laws. Some activities—price fixing, for example—are illegal per se. If the government can show that a firm committed the forbidden act, then the firm is found guilty. Depending on the view of the Supreme Court, other activities fall under the *rule of reason*. Under the rule of reason, not only must a complainant show that the firm committed the practice, it must also prove that the effects of the practice were harmful.

There have been four merger waves in the past 100 years, the last of which is still taking place.

Competitive Trends in the U.S. Economy

A recent study indicates that the U.S. economy is more competitive today than it was 20 or even 40 years ago. This increased competitiveness has been attributed to growing competition from abroad, deregulation, and antitrust activity.

IV. LAGNIAPPE

A Riot in Ephesus

The text states that producer groups seeking favorable legislation usually claim that the legislation is to aid consumers or society. Such claims are not new. An interesting incident is recorded in the book of Acts in the Bible. A silversmith named Demetrius called other silversmiths together for a meeting. The city they lived in, Ephesus, was the site of a temple to the goddess Artemis (Diana), and the silversmiths made and sold silver shrines of Artemis. The Christian missionary Paul had been preaching in the area with such success that many were converting to

Christianity. The converts no longer bought silver shrines of Artemis. The silversmiths were upset because of the loss of business and started a riot. When pressing their case before others, however, they argued that Artemis and the city of Ephesus were being discredited by Paul's preaching. (See Acts 19:23–41.)

Question to Think About: Can you think of groups today that use public interest arguments when lobbying for special favors from the government?

Does Antitrust Legislation Protect Competition or Competitors?

Many economists claim that the antitrust laws have often reduced competition by protecting smaller competitors from their larger rivals. In 1911, the Standard Oil Company was found guilty of violating the Sherman Act because it competed unfairly. A few years later, U.S. Steel was found not guilty because competitors had not been harmed by the giant steel company. U.S. Steel had been charging a high price, which encouraged other steel companies to expand. All steel producers profited by U.S. Steel's actions, although consumers of steel paid higher prices than necessary. In 1945, the Aluminum Company of America (Alcoa) was found guilty of violating the Sherman Act because it sought to meet a growing demand with increased capacity and sought to take advantage of new opportunities. If Alcoa had merely charged a higher, monopoly price and allowed other firms to enter and grow, it might have been found not guilty. The result of these cases was to encourage large firms to charge high prices rather than to compete vigorously with rivals.

Question to Think About: Would you rather have been a customer of U.S. Steel or Standard Oil?

V.   KEY TERMS

market power
social regulation
economic regulation
antitrust activity
tying contract
exclusive dealing
interlocking directorate
horizontal merger

vertical merger
consent decree
per se illegal
rule of reason
predatory pricing
Herfindahl index
conglomerate merger

VI. QUESTIONS

A. *Completion*

1. A firm that possesses _____ is able to maintain price above the competitive level.

2. _____ regulation is concerned with health and safety.

3. _____ regulation is concerned with price and output.

4. _____ tries to prohibit monopolization and collusion.

5. A _____ exists when the long-run average cost curve slopes downward over the entire range of market demand.

6. A public utility that is forced by regulation to set price equal to marginal cost will earn economic _____.

7. When a public utility is not subsidized, regulators often try to get the utility to set price equal to _____.

8. According to the _____ theory, regulation tends to benefit producers.

9. Airfares were set by the CAB but _____ competition was abundant.

10. A(n) _____ exists when the seller of one good requires buyers to purchase another good as well.

11. A(n) _____ exists when the same individual sits on the boards of directors of competing companies.

12. In antitrust cases, a _____ ruling simply requires evidence that a certain practice was carried on; in using a _____, a court requires additional evidence that the effects of the practice are harmful.

13. The U.S. Justice Department's merger guidelines use the _____ in determining whether to challenge a proposed merger.

14. A _____ merger involves two unrelated firms.

15. Joseph Schumpeter argued that competition should be thought of as a _____ process.

B. *True/False*

_____ 1. Market power exists when a firm can maintain price above the competitive level.

_____ 2. The Environmental Protection Agency is an example of economic regulation.

_____ 3. Regulation of electric utilities is an example of economic regulation.

_____ 4. The government seeks to control the price and output of an industry when it uses antitrust policy.

_____ 5. Under natural monopoly, the average costs of production are lower if one firm produces the good than if more than one firm produces the good.

_____ 6. If the government sets price equal to marginal cost for a natural monopoly, the monopoly most likely will go out of business in the long run unless it is subsidized.

_____ 7. Regulating agencies usually try to set the price that allocates resources efficiently.

_____ 8. According to the special-interest theory of regulation, consumers exert a lot of influence on regulatory agencies.

_____ 9. Legislation favoring producer groups usually is described as an advancement of consumer interests.

_____ 10. According to the capture theory of regulation, regulation is operated for the producers' benefit.

_____ 11. One consequence of deregulation in the airline industry is that airline pilots and other workers receive lower wages.

_____ 12. Deregulation of airlines has made air travel less safe.

_____ 13. Competing firms may want to form trusts to stabilize markets during turbulent economic times.

_____ 14. Price fixing is illegal per se in the United States.

_____ 15. A horizontal merger involves firms in the same market.

_____ 16. The Supreme Court has consistently used market conduct instead of market structure as the test of legality.

_____ 17. The merger wave in the 1950s and 1960s involved mostly horizontal mergers.

_____ 18. Since World War II, the largest U.S. firms have increased their share of the country's manufacturing assets.

_____ 19. The U.S. economy is less competitive today than it was at the start of World War II.

_____ 20. Where markets are open to foreign competition, antitrust enforcement that focuses solely on domestic production doesn't make good economic sense.

C.   Multiple Choice

1. The term *market power* refers to the ability of a firm to
    a. force consumers to buy its product.
    b. make long-run profits.
    c. induce the government to grant special favors to the firm.
    d. maintain price above the competitive level.
    e. All of the above.

2. Which of the following is an example of social regulation?
    a. Interstate Commerce Commision
    b. National Highway Traffic and Safety Administration
    c. Civil Aeronautics Board
    d. Federal Trade Commission
    e. All of the above.

3. Economic regulation is usually carried out by regulatory bodies at the
    a. local government level.
    b. state government level.
    c. federal government level.
    d. All of the above.
    e. b and c only.

4. The fundamental dilemma in regulating public utilities is
    a. whether to subsidize a monopoly that is charging a price equal to its average cost.
    b. whether to subsidize a monopoly that is charging the socially optimal price or let the firm charge a higher price.
    c. that a firm can charge the socially optimal price only if it is a natural monopoly, which most are not.
    d. that the socially optimal price is higher than consumers ought to pay.
    e. None of the above.

5. Regulation of a natural monopoly can increase social welfare by
    a. bringing price closer to marginal cost.
    b. increasing consumer surplus.
    c. reducing economic profits of the monopoly.
    d. All of the above.
    e. a and b only.

6. Some argue that business regulations often favor producer interests over consumer interests because
    a. there are more producers than consumers.
    b. producers are richer than consumers.
    c. producers have more interest in matters that affect their income than consumers have in matters that affect the prices they pay.
    d. the regulations are needed to promote the public interest.
    e. a, b, and c.

7. Which of the following is difficult to explain using the capture theory of regulation?
   a. The legislation establishing regulation was sponsored by public-minded reformers.
   b. The firms that were to be regulated opposed the legislation establishing the regulatory agency.
   c. Regulation appears to benefit producers more than consumers.
   d. All of the above.
   e. None of the above.

8. Which of the following statements is true?
   a. The capture theory says that consumer interest groups usually influence regulators more than producer interest groups.
   b. Interest groups have less influence today than 30 years ago.
   c. Legislation favoring producer groups is usually introduced under the guise of advancing consumer interests.
   d. All of the above.
   e. a and b only

9. Which of the following was not a form of competition within the airline industry under CAB regulation?
   a. frequent flights
   b. roomy seats
   c. price
   d. advertising
   e. quality of meals

10. A factor that has restricted competition in the airline industry after deregulation has been
    a. safety regulation imposed by the Federal Aviation Administration (FAA).
    b. high oil prices.
    c. bankruptcies of some airlines.
    d. the failure of airport capacity to increase.
    e. All of the above.

11. Developments that led to the passage of the Sherman Antitrust Act included
    a. an increase in the cost of transporting manufactured goods.
    b. growth of firms, leading to diseconomies of scale.
    c. technological change, leading to more extensive use of capital and greater economies of scale.
    d. business booms that led to rapidly increasing prices.
    e. All of the above.

12. The Clayton Act prohibits which of the following if it substantially lessens competition?
    a. price discrimination
    b. tying contracts
    c. interlocking directorates
    d. exclusive dealing
    e. All of the above.

13. The Clayton Act prohibits
    a. monopolization
    b. all price discrimination
    c. price discimination that leads to monopoly.
    d. monopoly.
    e. All of the above.

14. Mergers accomplished by acquiring assets of another company were restricted by
    a. the Clayton Act.
    b. the Robinson-Patman Act.
    c. the Sherman Act.
    d. the Wheeler-Lea Act.
    e. the Celler-Kefauver Act.

15. A firm found guilty of breaking the antitrust laws and of causing harm to another firm equal to $1 million will have to pay damages to that firm equal to
    a. zero. The officers of the firm will go to jail.
    b. $100,000.
    c. $1 million.
    d. $3 million.
    e. $10 million.

16. In 1920, the Supreme Court ruled that U.S. Steel
    a. had no monopoly power.
    b. possessed monopoly power.
    c. had not used its monopoly power in unreasonable ways.
    d. had engaged in predatory pricing.
    e. b and c

17. In the Alcoa case, the courts ruled
    a. in Alcoa's favor.
    b. that Alcoa was guilty because of its large share of the market.
    c. that Alcoa was guilty because the firm's actions were unreasonable.
    d. that Alcoa had to pay its rivals $15 million in damages.
    e. c and d

18. The merger guidelines used by the Justice Department
    a. no longer use the Herfindahl index.
    b. treat vertical mergers differently from all other types of mergers.
    c. treat horizontal mergers differently from all other types of mergers.
    d. allow all mergers to occur.
    e. a and b

19. The merger between Daimler Benz and Chrysler is an example of a
    a. horizontal merger.
    b. vertical merger.
    c. conglomerate merger.
    d. All of the above.
    e. None of the above because Daimler Benz is a foreign firm.

20. Foreign imports increase U.S. competitiveness by
   a. providing cheaply made, low-quality substitutes for U.S. products.
   b. penetrating domestic oligopolistic markets with lower-priced products.
   c. taking jobs from Americans.
   d. getting around tariff barriers, which keep prices high.
   e. None of the above.

D. Discussion Questions

1. Explain why answers a, b, and c are not correct in multiple choice question 1.

2. What is market power and what are its effects?

3. How does social regulation differ from economic regulation?

4. What options are available to the government for dealing with a natural monopoly? Which one tends to be used in the United States?

5. What dilemma faces regulators trying to regulate natural monopolies?

6. How does the public interest theory of economic regulation differ from the special-interest theory? How are the capture theory and the special interest theory alike and how are they different?

7. Why do economists argue that producer interests will be stronger than consumer interests when it comes to influencing regulators?

8. CAB regulations generated higher prices and revenues for producers, but producers did not receive all the profits. What happened to the profits the producers did not capture?

9. What hampered enforcement of the Sherman Act?

10. Why does the Clayton Act prohibit interlocking directorates?

11. Explain the difference between per se illegality and the rule of reason. Which would you prefer to use if you were prosecuting a case for the Justice Department?

12. "Tariffs are the friend of monopoly." Is this statement true or false? Explain.

13. Using the data in Exhibit 1, calculate the Herfindahl index.

Exhibit 1

Firm	Market Share (Percent)
A	20%
B	20
C	15
D	15
E	10
F	6
G	5
H	4
I	3
J	2

14. According to William Shepherd, what factors have contributed to the increased competitiveness of the U.S. economy?

15. Explain why the answer to true/false question 20 is true.

VII. ANSWERS

A. Completion

1. market power
2. Social
3. Economic
4. Antitrust activity
5. natural monopoly
6. losses
7. average cost
8. special interest
9. nonprice
10. tying contract
11. interlocking directorate
12. per se; rule of reason
13. Herfindahl index
14. conglomerate
15. dynamic

B. True/False
1. True
2. False
3. True
4. False. Controlling price and output is part of economic regulation.
5. True
6. True
7. False
8. False
9. True
10. True
11. True
12. False
13. True
14. True
15. True
16. False
17. False
18. True
19. False
20. True

C. Multiple Choice

1.	d	6.	c	11.	c	16.	e
2.	b	7.	e	12.	e	17.	b
3.	d	8.	c	13.	c	18.	c
4.	b	9.	c	14.	e	19.	a
5.	e	10.	d	15.	d	20.	b

D. Discussion Questions

1. Market power is the ability to raise price by restricting output. People can choose not to buy the good at all, so answer a is incorrect. It is possible that there is no price that will permit the firm to make economic profits, so answer b is incorrect. A firm can possess market power without being able to influence public policy, and firms (or other economic actors) without market power are able to influence public policy in some situations (e.g., farmers), so answer c is incorrect.

2. Market power is the ability to raise price and maintain it above the competitive level. Under perfect competition, price equals marginal cost. The effect of market power is to raise price above marginal cost, which causes inefficiency. Market power creates a misallocation of resources and a transfer of wealth from consumers to producers.

3. Social regulation is concerned with health and safety issues while economic regulation is concerned with price, output, entry of new firms, and quality of service in industries that have monopoly power.

4. The government can do nothing, or it can sell rights to monopoly, or it can own and operate the monopoly itself, or it can regulate the privately owned monopoly. The last option is usually taken, but there are situations in which one of the others is used.

5. The optimal policy from the point of view of economic efficiency is to set price equal to marginal cost. But if the firm is a natural monopoly, marginal cost will lie below average cost, so if price is set equal to marginal cost, the firm will suffer economic losses and go out of business in the long run. The dilemma, then, is whether to seek the efficient price and subsidize the monopoly or to allow for a normal profit by setting price equal to average cost.

6. The public-interest theory is that economic regulation is designed to promote the public interest by controlling natural monopolies when production by one firm seems most efficient and encouraging competition in some industries when it is economically desirable. The special-interest theory says that regulation benefits special-interest groups—in particular producers. According to the latter theory, regulation prevents entry into the market or prevents competition among existing firms, enabling them to charge a price above the competitive level. Both the special-interest theory and the capture theory hold that producers benefit from regulation. They differ in that the special-interest theory says that regulation is designed to benefit producers; the capture theory says that the intent of the legislation may be to benefit consumers but that over time the producers exert more influence on the regulatory agency and "capture" it.

7. Producers are affected more by regulations that affect the price of the good than consumers are. Hence, producers have more at stake when regulators are considering policy. Producers can be expected to work harder to influence policy than consumers will work to generate lower prices.

8. Employees captured some of the profits in the form of higher wages. Consumers in smaller cities captured some, in that service was provided to these areas at prices below cost. Some of the profits were lost through nonprice competition.

9. The law prohibited the creation of trusts, restraint of trade, and monopolization but didn't define what constituted these activities.

10. Interlocking directorates occur when one person serves on the board of directors of competing firms. This would make collusion between the firms easier, so it is illegal.

11. If per se illegality applies, all a prosecutor must show is that a firm actually committed an illegal practice. The rule of reason requires that a prosecutor also show that the effects of the practice were harmful. Hence, a prosecutor would prefer to be able to use a per se approach than to have to satisfy the rule of reason.

12. True. Tariffs raise the prices of imported goods, which shields domestic firms from foreign competition and permits higher prices and profits.

13. The Herfindahl index is $400 + 400 + 225 + 225 + 100 + 36 + 25 + 16 + 9 + 4 = 1,440$.

14. Increasing foreign competition, deregulation, and antitrust activity.

15. The answer turns on the issue of market definition. If the Antitrust Division computes a Herfindahl Index based on domestic market shares, it may find a specific market to be highly concentrated. (Think about the U. S. Automobile industry.) But it may be that foreign competitors have a significant share of that domestic market. (Again, think of automobiles.) In that case, the market may be much less concentrated than the Herfindahl Index suggests.

CHAPTER 29

Public Goods and Public Choice

I.   INTRODUCTION

This chapter examines the role of government more closely. Until now, the government has been treated as an economic agent that makes optimal decisions when it steps in to correct deficiencies in the marketplace. Now we examine problems with the decision-making process used in government as well as the distortions the government can introduce into the economy.

II.   OUTLINE

1.   Optional Provision of Public Goods

      1.1   Private Goods, Public Goods, and In Between
          a.   Public goods are nonrival in consumption.
          b.   Once a public good is produced, it is impossible to exclude those who refuse to pay for it.
          c.   Because public goods are nonrival and nonexclusive, private firms cannot sell them profitably.
          d.   Some goods are nonrival but exclusive, and are called quasi-public goods.
          e.   Some goods are rival but nonexclusive, and are called open-access goods.

      1.2   Optimal Provision of Public Goods
          a.   The market demand curve for a public good is the vertical sum of each consumer's demand for the good.
          b.   The efficient level of a public good is where the market demand curve intersects the marginal cost curve.

2.   Public Choice in a Representative Democracy

      2.1   Median Voter Model
          a.   Under certain conditions, majority rule delegates the choice to the person whose preference is the median of the group.
          b.   Only the median voter receives his or her most preferred amount of a good or most preferred policy decision.

      2.2   Goals of the Participants
          a.   Elected officials may try to maximize their political support.
          b.   Elected officials may cater to special interests rather than common interests because of the asymmetry between special interests and the common interest.

2.3   Rational Ignorance
  a.   The individual voter or consumer is unlikely to have an effect on public choice.
  b.   The benefits to the individual voter or consumer of a change in public policy are likely
       to be small.
  c.   Hence, the rational voter or consumer is unlikely to spend resources to acquire in-
       formation concerning proposed changes in public policy.

2.4   Distribution of Costs and Benefits
  a.   The costs and benefits of a policy change or legislative measure may be either widely
       or narrowly distributed.
  b.   The more widely distributed the costs or benefits, the less incentive an individual has
       to try to influence the public choice.
  c.   *Special-interest legislation* involves cases in which benefits are concentrated and costs
       are widely distributed.
  d.   *Competing-interest legislation* involves cases in which both benefits and costs are
       concentrated.

2.5   *CASE STUDY:* Farm Subsidies

2.6   Rent Seeking
  a.   *Rent seeking* involves activities that interest groups undertake to elicit special favors
       from government.
  b.   To the extent that special-interest groups engage in rent-seeking activities, resources
       are diverted from wealth-creating activities to activities that transfer wealth, which
       usually results in a reduction of wealth.

2.7   *CASE STUDY:* Campaign Finance Reform

3.   The Underground Economy. The *underground economy* refers to market activity that goes
     unreported to the government in an attempt to avoid taxes. Tax avoidance is the legal attempt to
     arrange one's economic affairs so as to minimize taxes. Tax evasion involves fraudulent or illegal
     behavior.

4.   Bureaucracy and Representative Democracy. The task of implementing legislation passed by
     elected representatives is typically left to government bureaus.

   4.1   Ownership and Funding of Bureaus
     a.   Bureaus have different incentives than business firms.
     b.   Ownership in a government jurisdiction does not include the right to transfer
          ownership to others in the way stockholders can.
     c.   Bureaus are typically financed by a budget appropriation from the legislature rather
          than by the sale of output.

   4.2   Ownership and Organizational Behavior
     a.   Bureaus receive less information concerning the customers' desired quantity and
          quality of output.
     b.   There is less incentive for workers in bureaus to respond to the wishes of consumers
          than is the case in business firms.
     c.   Government bureaus tend to be less concerned with minimizing costs than are private
          firms.

4.3 Bureaucratic Objectives
   a. One theory of bureaucratic behavior assumes that bureaus attempt to maximize their budgets.
   b. Budget maximization results in a larger budget than that desired by the median voter.

4.4 Private versus Public Production. Governments sometimes contract with private firms to provide services to a community.

III. DISCUSSION

Optimal Provision of Public Goods

Public goods are characterized by nonrival consumption and nonexclusion. Nonrival consumption is when one person's consumption of a good doesn't reduce the amount available to others. Nonexclusion refers to a situation in which no one can be excluded from consuming a good once it is produced. Examples of public goods include national defense and flood control. A quasi-public good is a good characterized by nonrival consumption but exclusion is possible. Cable television is an example. A good that is rival but nonexclusive is an open-access good.

Recall that the market demand curve for a private good is found by summing horizontally the demand curves of the consumers. That is, the quantities demanded of each consumer are added at a price to determine the market quantity demanded at that price. The market demand curve for a public good is found by summing vertically the demand curves of the consumers. That is, for a given quantity, the price each consumer is willing to pay is summed for all consumers. The efficient level of provision of a public good is where the sum of the marginal valuations equals the marginal cost. Review Exhibit 2 in the textbook to ensure you understand this process.

Public Choice in a Representative Democracy

Majority rule is often used to decide public choices. Often this means that the *median voter* actually chooses the public policy. Exhibit 1 illustrates how this happens. The line represents possible approaches to public funding of education. At point *a*, the policy is that no government funds are used to support education; at *e*, 100 percent of the spending on education comes from the government. Suppose one voter favors each point on the line. (Note that this means that there are 101 voters, as we are including 0 percent as a choice.) We assume that people prefer a point closer to their ideal than one that is further away. That is, a person who favors point *b* (10 percent of the cost of education to be provided by the government) would prefer point *a* (0 percent government funding) over point *d* (90 percent government funding) since *b* is closer to *a* than it is to *d*.

Exhibit 1

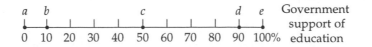

Based on the median voter model, we predict that point *c* will be chosen. Compare point *c* with any other point on the line. Any point to the left of *c* will generate fewer votes than *c* because all voters to the right of *c* will vote for *c*. So if the choice is between, say, 10 percent government funding of education (point *b*) and 50 percent funding (point *c*), *c* will garner at least 51 votes—that is, those who prefer more funding to less funding will vote for *c*. Obviously, the same is true for any point to the right of *c*: if the choice is between point *c* and point *d*, all voters to the left of the median voter will join with *c*. The preference of the median voter prevails even though 100 of the 101 voters have a different first choice.

It is very unusual for direct democracy to be used to make public decisions. Instead, representatives are usually elected to make the decisions. Representatives presumably make decisions on the basis of self-interest. Since they face reelection, they are interested in increasing their political support. Such support includes votes as well as campaign contributions.

Special-interest groups are often successful in obtaining favorable legislation that generates transfers of wealth to their members. This can occur even if, or perhaps because, the group is relatively small in number. Such a group may not provide a lot of votes to a representative but may contribute financially in a substantial way. As long as the transfer of wealth does not cause the larger group of taxpayers who pay for the transfer to vote against the representative, the representative gains by supporting the transfer. But why would the taxpayers not punish the legislator for the higher taxes? Because they might not be aware of the higher taxes or of the transfer. Since the taxes to pay for the transfer are spread out over a very large number of taxpayers, the additional tax paid by an individual taxpayer is not very large. Consequently, it is not worth the individual taxpayer's time to monitor all the activities of the legislator. Whenever the benefits of a change in policy are distributed over a relatively small group and the costs are borne by a relatively large group, there is a good chance that the special-interest group will be able to receive the transfer it seeks.

Recall that a resource owner receives economic rent whenever the payment received exceeds the opportunity cost of the resource. This is why monopoly profits are often called *monopoly rents*. Special-interest groups may try to obtain legislation that will allow them to earn rents. The activity undertaken to elicit such rents is called *rent seeking*. Generally, rent-seeking activity diverts resources from productive activities to unproductive activities. That is, the competition for rents is generally a negative-sum game.

The Underground Economy

Market activity often goes unreported to the government to avoid taxes or because the activity is illegal. One effect of a tax on an activity is the increasing use of the underground economy.

Bureaucracy and Representative Democracy

Although legislatures pass legislation, they seldom implement the legislation. Implementation is the responsibility of government *bureaus*. Just as some are concerned with whether managers of corporations act in the best interests of the shareholders, others express concern that bureaucrats may not always act in the best interests of the citizens or of the representatives who passed the legislation. The incentives that help keep corporate managers in line, such as stock options and fears of takeovers, are not applicable to government bureaucrats. Consequently, there is real concern over whether bureaucrats implement legislation in an optimal manner.

IV. LAGNIAPPE

Change at the New York Stock Exchange

For over 175 years, the New York Stock Exchange (NYSE) established fixed brokerage rates. The NYSE limits the number of members and regulates the business practices of its members. The Securities and Exchange Commission (SEC), which is the government agency established to regulate the exchanges, helped enforce the fixed prices established by the NYSE until 1975. In 1975, the SEC outlawed the fixed brokerage rates. Such a policy change does not seem to be consistent with the discussion in this chapter concerning the political power of special-interest groups. However, beginning in the 1960s, institutional buyers became a larger part of the total market. Institutional buyers include insurance companies and other financial institutions that handle large blocks of stock for pension funds, college endowments, and the like. As the institutional buyers became more numerous and important, they were able to exert influence on the SEC to get lower rates. In earlier years, the costs of the high fixed rates had been spread over a large group, but as institutions became more important, the costs were borne by a smaller group. Eventually, this smaller group was able to get the fixed rates eliminated, and brokerage rates fell by approximately 25 percent.

Question to Think About: Could forces similar to those that brought changes in brokerage rules have led to deregulation of airlines?

Rent Seeking and the Line-Item Veto

Many Republican presidents have tried to get the line-item veto power as a way of lowering government spending. Finally, the Republican Congress passed a line-item veto bill, and President Clinton used it to eliminate some specific spending programs. However, the law was challenged in the courts and found to be unconstitutional.

An argument for the line-item veto is that the president is less susceptible to the rent-seeking lobbying of special-interest groups than Congress is. If so, Congress is likely to pass specific programs to benefit specific special-interest groups, which a more independent president can excise from the budget with a line-item veto.

Question to Think About: Would a line-item veto actually lead to less spending for special interests than the status quo?

V. KEY TERMS

quasi-public good
open-access good
median voter model
rational ignorance

special-interest legislation
competing-interest legislation
underground economy
bureaus

VI. QUESTIONS

A. *Completion*

1. If the amount of a good consumed by one individual is not available for others to consume, then the good is characterized by _____ consumption.

2. If a firm is unable to exclude those households that haven't paid for a good, then the good is characterized by _____ consumption.

3. Quasi-public goods are characterized by _____ and _____ consumption.

4. The whales in the ocean are an example of _____ goods.

5. The market demand curve for a public good is found by _____ summing the individual consumers' demand curves.

6. The government can solve the problems caused by non-exclusion by producing a public good and paying for it with_____

7. When a single issue is under consideration, the policy selected is likely to reflect the preferences of the _____

8. We assume that elected officials seek to _____ their political support.

9. Taxpayers may choose to remain _____ of a change in policy when the costs to an individual taxpayer are very low.

10. Political candidates who want to please the median voter take _____ positions.

11. _____ legislation involves concentrated benefits and concentrated costs.

12. Special-interest groups engage in _____ activity when they attempt to obtain special favors from the government.

13. The _____ consists of market activities that are not reported to the government in order to avoid taxation.

14. Tax _____ is illegal.

15. Niskanen argues that bureaus attempt to maximize their _____.

B. True/False

____ 1. A good that is nonrival is a public good.

____ 2. Government can solve the market failure associated with a public good by providing the good and paying for it through enforced taxation.

____ 3. Once congestion sets in, quasi-public goods become actual public goods.

____ 4. Private goods are usually provided by private firms.

____ 5. In a society, everyone consumes the same amount of a public good.

____ 6. The market demand curve for a public good is the horizontal summation of the individual consumers' demand curves for the good.

____ 7. The median voter model says that the policy that is the first choice of most people will be selected.

____ 8. There will be few differences among candidates if all the candidates attempt to appeal to the median voter.

____ 9. There are likely to be many dissatisfied voters under majority rule.

____ 10. There is a greater chance that representative democracy will represent the choice of special interests than is the case with direct democracy.

____ 11. When the cost of acquiring and acting on the information needed to affect legislation exceeds the expected benefits, rational citizens ignore what is going on in Congress.

____ 12. A public policy that transfers income from a small group to a very large group will probably pass Congress.

____ 13. Competing-interest legislation often involves concentrated costs and concentrated benefits.

_____ 14. The total costs generally exceed the total benefits of legislation that caters to special-interest groups.

_____ 15. Rent seeking is an important type of productive activity.

_____ 16. The underground economy would be much smaller if there were no taxes.

_____ 17. An important portion of the underground economy results from tax avoidance.

_____ 18. Managers of government bureaus face the same incentives as managers of private corporations.

_____ 19. Government bureaus tend to produce goods or services at higher cost than private firms do.

_____ 20. All goods financed by the government are produced by government agencies.

C. Multiple Choice

1. Private goods are
   a. quasi-public goods produced by the government.
   b. always produced by private firms.
   c. rival but nonexclusive.
   d. exclusive but nonrival.
   e. both rival and exclusive.

2. Goods that are nonexclusive and rival are
   a. private goods.
   b. public goods.
   c. quasi-public goods.
   d. open-access goods.
   e. None of the above.

3. An example of a public good is
   a. cable TV.
   b. flood control.
   c. a crowded swimming pool.
   d. Yellowstone National Park.
   e. the fish in the ocean.

4. Fred values a specific quantity of national defense at $1,000, Sandy values it at $200, George values it at $500, Joan at -$200, Archie at $1,500, and Bill at zero. The social value of the national defense is
   a. $0.
   b. $500.
   c. $1,500.
   d. $3,000.
   e. can't tell without more information

5. The decisions concerning what public goods should be produced, in what quantities, and who should pay are decided
    a. by consumer sovereignty.
    b. by equating the sum of the total valuations with the total cost of producing the public goods.
    c. optimally when each resident pays a tax equal to his or her marginal valuation.
    d. optimally when each resident can tell the government how much he or she values the public good.
    e. by public choice.

6. Public choices are those choices that are
    a. best.
    b. fair.
    c. made collectively by all voters directly.
    d. made collectively by representatives.
    e. both c and d.

7. Majority voting often amounts to delegating the choice to the
    a. mean voter.
    b. median voter.
    c. richest voter.
    d. most important special-interest group.
    e. most committed voter.

8. Under majority rule,
    a. there are usually many dissatisfied voters.
    b. there is always a clear choice.
    c. the first choice of the majority of people is chosen.
    d. All of the above.
    e. None of the above.

9. In a representative democracy, there is a good chance that public choice will serve special interests rather than the interests of the majority because
    a. representatives tend to be corrupt.
    b. the median voter tends to be a member of a special-interest group.
    c. special interests have more votes.
    d. there is an asymmetry between special interests and majority interests in terms of potential individual gains and losses.
    e. All of the above.

10. Rational voters often remain ignorant of the costs and benefits of many proposals because
    a. the costs of acquiring and acting on the required information exceed the expected benefits.
    b. they take democracy for granted.
    c. they know that they cannot influence politicians.
    d. they trust their representatives.
    e. they know they are not intelligent enough to understand the policies.

11. Special-interest legislation involves issues in which
    a. both the benefits and the costs are widely dispersed.
    b. the benefits are concentrated and the costs are widely dispersed.
    c. the costs are concentrated and the benefits are widely dispersed.
    d. both the benefits and costs are concentrated.
    e. either b or d.

Exhibit 2

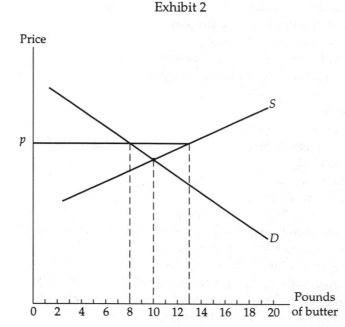

12. Exhibit 2 illustrates a system of price supports for butter. How many pounds of butter will the government buy?
    a. 0
    b. 2
    c. 3
    d. 5
    e. There is not enough information to be able to tell.

13. In Exhibit 2, the higher price for butter benefits
    a. all dairy farmers.
    b. dairy farmers who enter the industry after the subsidy is introduced.
    c. owners of resources specialized to dairy farming.
    d. consumers.
    e. The question cannot be answered without more information.

14. Which of the following is an example of rent seeking?
    a. steel companies seeking tariffs on steel
    b. dairy farmers trying to get an increase in price supports for milk
    c. accountants trying to make the CPA exam more difficult
    d. homeowners lobbying for zoning laws that restrict the number of new homes that can be built in a community
    e. All of the above.

15. Resources employed in trying to get the government to redistribute income
    a. tend to create income.
    b. are used by people to help the poor.
    c. make society more productive.
    d. have little effect on government policy.
    e. generally make society less productive.

16. People use barter more when
    a. they do not have good jobs.
    b. they are unemployed.
    c. tax rates fall.
    d. tax rates increase.
    e. None of the above.

17. Which of the following is **not** a part of the underground economy?
    a. A cab driver doesn't report all his income to the IRS.
    b. A drug dealer buys a large quantity of cocaine.
    c. A woman operates an unregulated taxi in New York City.
    d. A family buys a tax-exempt municipal bond to avoid taxes.
    e. All of the above. are examples of underground economic activity.

18. The residual claimants of bureaus are
    a. the residents of the jurisdiction.
    b. the heads of the bureaus.
    c. the head of the executive branch of the government.
    d. the stockholders of the bureaus.
    e. None of the above. There are no residual claimants.

19. Which of the following is the source of differences between bureaus and business firms?
    a. Ownership in a firm is transferable, but ownership in a bureau is not.
    b. Firms have greater feedback from customers than bureaus do.
    c. Workers in bureaus are lazier than workers in business firms.
    d. both a and b
    e. a, b, and c

20. Legislatures often prefer dealing with bureaus to dealing with private firms because
    a. bureaus are always more efficient at spending taxpayers' money.
    b. firms tend to be too greedy.
    c. bureaus may provide legislators more opportunities to reward friends with jobs.
    d. contracts with firms are sometimes difficult to specify completely.
    e. both c and d.

D. Discussion Questions

1. Distinguish among private goods, public goods, quasi-public goods, and open-access goods.

2. Police services generally are provided by government. Are police services a public good? Explain.

Exhibit 3

Marginal Valuation

Quantity	Alice	Bill	Cindy	Dave	Ernie	Linda
1	$10	$25	$50	$10	$12	$25
2	8	22	30	5	10	20
3	6	18	10	0	8	15
4	4	14	1	0	4	10
5	2	10	0	0	0	5
6	0	5	−50	0	0	0

3. Use Exhibit 3. If the good is a private good, what would be the quantity demanded at $10? What is the market demand schedule if the good is a public good?

4. If the good in Exhibit 3 is a public good, how much should be produced if the marginal cost of producing the good is always $95? When should zero units be produced?

5. a. Suppose seven people are trying to decide whether to get a pizza with pepperoni, a pizza with sausage and pepperoni, or a pizza with everything on it. Four people want everything, one wants pepperoni and sausage, and two want pepperoni only. Assume that each person prefers a pizza closer to his or her first choice to a pizza that is unlike the first choice. What is the preference of the median voter? Which pizza will be selected if the majority rules?

    b. Suppose that three people favor pizza with everything, three favor pizza with pepperoni only, and one favors pizza with pepperoni and sausage. Assume that each person prefers a pizza closer to his or her first choice to a pizza that is unlike the first choice. What is the preference of the median voter? Which pizza will be selected if the majority rules?

6. Why are there likely to be many dissatisfied voters under majority rule?

7. How does representative democracy differ from direct democracy? What differences are there in the policies chosen under the different systems?

8. Explain why it is often rational for taxpayers to remain ignorant about the effects of some policies.

9. What is the difference between special-interest legislation and competing-interest legislation?

10. What is rent seeking? How does rent seeking affect efficiency? Why do legislatures permit such activities?

11. Accountants who pass the CPA exam are considered to be of high quality and earn more than other accountants. Some believe that in order to keep the number of CPAs relatively low, the CPA exam is made more difficult than is necessary. Why would CPAs want to do this? Will someone who passes the exam earn rents? Explain.

12. How is the size of the underground economy related to tax rates?

13. Political corruption is relatively great in Russia today. What effect does this have on the Russian economy?

14. Distinguish between tax avoidance and tax evasion.

15. Compare and contrast bureaus and business firms.

VII. ANSWERS

A. Completion

1. rival
2. nonexclusive
3. nonrival; exclusive
4. open-access
5. vertically
6. taxes
7. median voter
8. maximize
9. rationally ignorant
10. similar
11. Competing-interest
12. rent-seeking
13. underground economy
14. evasion
15. budgets

B. True/False

1. False. Public good is also nonexclusive.
2. True
3. False
4. True
5. True
6. False
7. False. The policy preferred by the median voter will be selected.
8. True
9. True
10. True
11. True
12. False
13. True
14. True
15. False
16. True
17. False. Tax avoidance is legal.
18. False
19. True
20. False

C. Multiple Choice

1.	e	6.	e	11.	b	16.	d
2.	d	7.	b	12.	d	17.	d
3.	b	8.	a	13.	c	18.	a
4.	d	9.	d	14.	e	19.	d
5.	e	10.	a	15.	e	20.	e

D. Discussion Questions

1. Private goods are rival and exclusive, public goods are nonrival and nonexclusive, quasi-public goods are nonrival but exclusive, and open-access goods are rival but nonexclusive. Private goods usually are produced by private firms, and public goods by the government. Quasi-public goods can be produced by the private or the public sector. Open-access goods generally are regulated by government.

2. Police services are not a pure public good, but have some of the characteristics of a public good. To the extent the level of police services benefit everyone in a city, it is nonrival. But, the more police there are in one part of town the less police are available for another part of town. Further, there are private firms that provide police services to specific neighborhoods, so they can be considered exclusive. Probably it is best to consider police services a quasi-public good.

3. The quantity demanded at \$10 is $1 + 5 + 3 + 1 + 2 + 4 = 16$ units. If the good is a public good, the market demand schedule is:

Quantity	Sum of Marginal Variations
1	\$132
2	95
3	57
4	33
5	17
6	–45

4. Marginal cost equals the sum of the marginal valuations at 2 units. Zero units should be produced when the marginal cost of producing the first unit exceeds \$132.

5. a. The median voter will prefer a pizza with everything, because three people want some other kind of pizza and four want pizza with everything. The group will choose to get a pizza with everything on it.
   b. The preference of the median voter is for pizza with pepperoni and sausage. This is the choice that will be made, even though only one person actually wants this kind of pizza. In each choice between two kinds of pizza, three people will join with the single individual because her preference is as close as they can get to their own preference.

6. There will be many dissatisfied voters because only the median voters will get exactly what they most prefer.

7. In a direct democracy, people make choices by voting directly on every issue. The median voter often determines public choices in a direct democracy. In a representative democracy, people elect representatives to make public choices. Representatives must then try to respond to the various wishes of the people in their constituencies. Special-interest groups have more influence under representative democracy than under direct democracy because of the asymmetry between special interests and the common interest; individual voters concentrate on private choice rather than attempting to influence public choices.

8. The cost to a single taxpayer of a given policy is likely to be low. Further, the taxpayer is unlikely to have an effect on policy unless he or she organizes many other taxpayers. This will involve a lot of time and money. The expected benefit from getting involved is generally less than the cost of the policy that favors a special-interest group.

9. Special-interest legislation refers to legislation that generates concentrated benefits, but the costs are borne by many people. Competing-interest legislation involves concentrated costs and concentrated benefits. It is usually easier to get legislation through when the costs are widespread than when the costs are concentrated.

10. Rent seeking is activity undertaken by special-interest groups to persuade Congress to give them some special market advantage or transfer payments. Such activity shifts resources from the production of output to efforts to transfer income and thus tends to reduce the total output of society from what it would be if there were no rent seeking. Congress and state legislatures do not legislate against the activity because it provides political support and campaign funds to individual legislators.

11. Current CPAs want to make the tests hard so that fewer people can become CPAs. This keeps their salaries higher. Someone who passes the exam will earn rent, but the rent will not be as large as those of CPAs already in the profession. This is because people tend to invest in courses to help them pass the CPA exam. Such expenditures raise the costs of becoming a CPA. Further, the high income of CPAs may attract able people from other fields who would have earned high salaries in the other fields. That is, the opportunity cost of those who actually become CPAs may be relatively high, so their rents will not be as great as those of current CPAs.

12. Part of the underground economy exists to avoid taxes. The larger marginal tax rates are, the greater the incentive to hide income and participate in the underground economy.

13. The underground economy tends to expand when there is political corruption. One effect is to reduce the taxes collected by the government. The size of the overall economy generally is smaller the greater the political corruption.

14. Tax avoidance is legal activity designed to reduce one's tax burden. Examples include giving to charities, buying tax-free municipal bonds, and investing in tax-deferred IRAs. Tax evasion is illegal and involves either failing to file a return or understating one's income or overstating one's deductions.

15. Bureaus are government agencies designed to implement some legislation. Their revenues generally come from taxes allocated by the legislature. Residents in the jurisdiction are the residual claimants. Unlike stockholders, they cannot sell their ownership in the bureau if they are unhappy with the performance of the bureau. It is also more difficult for the customers of the bureau to provide the bureau with information concerning their level of satisfaction with the service the bureau provides than is the case with customers of business firms. Consequently, bureaucrats have less incentive to minimize costs or operate efficiently than do managers of business firms.

CHAPTER 30

Externalities and the Environment

I. INTRODUCTION

Our implicit assumption throughout most of the text has been that property rights are well defined and easily enforced. Under such conditions, we expect that market prices will allocate resources to their highest-valued use and the economy will operate efficiently. There are many situations in which property rights are not well defined, however, and society ends up using a resource inefficiently. This chapter explores some of these situations.

II. OUTLINE

1. Externalities and the Common-Pool Problem.

    1.1 Renewable Resources
       a. A resource is exhaustible if it is available in a finite amount and cannot be renewed.
       b. A resource is *renewable* if periodic use of it can continue indefinitely.
       c. Biological resources such as fish, timber, and grasslands are renewable resources if they are husbanded properly.
       d. Some renewable resources are *open-access resources*, which means that it is costly to exclude people from using the resource.
       e. Open-access resources are often subject to the common-pool problem.
       f. *Negative externalities* arise when there are no enforceable property rights to commonly owned resources and the market prices fail to reflect the cost to society of the externalities.
       g. Property rights allow individuals the right to control the use of certain resources.
       h. Not all resources are owned as private property because defining and enforcing property rights on some resources is very costly.
       i. Pollution arises because private property rights to some open-access resources are not practical.

    1.2 Resolving the Common-Pool Problem
       a. Open-access resources tend to be overused or overharvested.
       b. The common-pool problem can be reduced if some central authority imposes restrictions on resource use.
       c. Government regulations can improve allocative efficiency when imposing and enforcing private property rights would be too costly.

2. Optimal Level of Pollution

    2.1 External Costs with Fixed Technology
       a. When the only way to reduce a negative externality is to reduce output, the negative externality occurs with a fixed-production technology.

b. The marginal external cost of a negative externality is the extra cost to society that is not reflected in the market price of a good or service.

c. The marginal social cost includes both the marginal private cost and the marginal external cost.

d. Since market participants ignore the marginal external cost, equilibrium occurs at a greater rate of output than is optimal. The equilibrium generates a market failure.

e. The efficient rate of output occurs where the demand curve (reflecting marginal benefits) and the marginal social cost curve intersect.

f. A tax equal to marginal external cost would induce industry to generate the optimal rate of output.

2.2 External Costs with Variable Technology
a. In the long run, firms can change their resource mix to reduce negative externalities.

b. The marginal social cost curve of pollution abatement slopes upward; the marginal social benefit curve of pollution control slopes downward.

c. The optimal level of pollution abatement occurs where the marginal social cost of further abatement equals the marginal social benefit of that abatement.

d. Pollution should be abated only as long as the marginal benefit of additional abatement exceeds its marginal cost.

2.3 *CASE STUDY:* Destruction of the Tropical Rain Forest

2.4 The Coase Analysis of Externalities
a. Ronald Coase points out that external costs can arise when the activities of two parties are incompatible.

b. The efficient solution to the problem of externalities depends on which party can avoid the problem at lower cost.

c. With a private property rights arrangement, the two parties could agree on the efficient outcome.

d. The *Coase theorem* states that an efficient solution to the problem of externalities will be achieved regardless of which party is assigned property rights as long as bargaining costs are small.

2.5 A Market for Pollution Rights
a. One solution to the problem of pollution is to sell the right to pollute.

b. The price per unit of discharge is often called an *effluent fee*.

c. Only those who value the pollution rights the most will buy the rights, so an efficient method of reducing pollution is achieved.

d. A problem is that legislation dealing with pollution suffers from rent-seeking activities as do other public policy questions in a representative democracy.

3. Environmental Protection

3.1 Air Pollution
a. The Clean Air Act of 1970 set national standards for the amount of pollution that can be emitted.

b. Average pollution levels are down from the 1970s.

c. A tentative accord was reached in Kyoto, Japan, in 1997 to improve air quality on a global scale.

3.2 *CASE STUDY:* City in the Clouds

3.3 Water Pollution
   a. The major sources of water pollution are sewage and chemicals.
   b. Most of the money of the Environmental Protection Agency has gone to constructing sewage treatment plants.
   c. Most chemical pollution results from runoff of pesticides and fertilizers used in agriculture.

3.4 Hazardous Waste and the Superfund
   a. The Comprehensive Environmental Response, Compensation, and Liability Act of 1980, or Superfund law, requires that anyone generating, storing, or transporting hazardous waste must pay to clean it up.
   b. Superfund administrators have often reacted to political pressure in addressing pollution rather than tackling the most widespread or long-term problems first.

3.5 Solid Waste: "Paper or Plastic?"
   a. The country is running out of landfills.
   b. In the United States, only a small percentage of solid waste is recycled.

4. Positive Externalities
   a. The benefits of consuming some goods accrue to people other than the consumer.
   b. Marginal social benefits include both the marginal private benefits and the positive externalities.
   c. An individual consumer making decisions on the basis of marginal private benefits and marginal private costs will underconsume a good that generates positive externalities.
   d. The government often encourages the consumption of goods with positive externalities by subsidizing consumption of the good.

III. DISCUSSION

Externalities and the Common-Pool Problem

A resource is renewable if periodic use of it can continue indefinitely. Most biological resources, such as fish, forests, and grasslands are renewable. A renewable resource that is also an open-access good is subject to the common-pool problem. Such goods tend to be overused or over harvested. With an open-access good, each person may make decisions concerning the use of the resource without taking into consideration the effects of this use on the other owners.

Suppose a community sets aside a pasture where all members can graze their cows. The land will accommodate only a certain number of cows, and any more than this number will lead to overgrazing and diminish the quality of the pasture. A person's marginal private benefit of placing a cow in the pasture is the value of the milk the person gets from the cow. The marginal cost is the price of keeping the cow and the cost of the deterioration in the pasture caused by an extra cow's grazing in it. This latter cost, though, is borne by the community as a whole, so each individual bears only a small portion of this cost. That is, the marginal social cost of the extra cow is greater than the marginal private cost of the extra cow. Consequently, an individual is likely to add an additional cow to the pasture even though the result may be overuse of the land. If everybody adds extra cows to the pasture, the collective result is a serious overuse of the land. In such cases, rational decision making on the part of each individual leads to decisions that are harmful for the group as a whole.

The efficiency of markets is directly related to the existence of a system of *private property rights*. Resource owners with easily enforceable private property rights have an incentive to devote their resources to their highest-valued use because they maximize their own return by doing so. This is an example of Adam Smith's "invisible hand" at work—resources are used efficiently when people act in their own self-interest.

Negative externalities are unpriced by-products of consumption or production that impose costs on other consumer firms. Pollution is the best-known example of a negative externality, but it is certainly not the only example. A homeowner who fails to maintain his home or property imposes negative externalities on his neighbors; a teenager who plays a radio at high volume imposes negative externalities on those nearby; a diner with very bad table manners imposes negative externalities on other patrons of a restaurant. Pollution and other negative externalities arise when there are no practical enforceable private property rights to open-access resources.

The *common-pool problem* applies to many situations: air and water pollution, the hunting of whales today or buffalo in the last century, and fishing for lobsters in New England or for redfish in Louisiana. Eventually, the overuse of a resource results in a change in property rights, government action, or depletion of the resource. One solution is to convert property held in common to private property. This solution has often been used and offers the best chance of the resource's being used efficiently. However, it is not possible to assign private property rights to some resources—the air or whales, for example. Another solution is for the government to take action and restrict the use of the resource. Hunting and fishing seasons and limits on takes, a ban on killing buffalo, and restrictions on air pollution are examples of this response. One difficulty with this approach is that there is not a world government that can enforce a ban in all nations. As a result, some common-pool problems are difficult to solve. For example, the over-harvesting of whales is not as easy to stop as was the over-harvesting of buffalo.

Optimal Level of Pollution

Negative externalities generate *marginal social costs* that are greater than marginal private costs. The individual equates marginal private benefits and marginal private costs instead of equating marginal private benefits and marginal social costs. Since marginal social costs are greater than marginal private costs, the individual selects a rate of output that exceeds the optimal rate. (In this case, we are assuming that marginal private benefits and *marginal social benefits* are the same.)

Most people agree that the less pollution there is, the better. However, zero pollution is not optimal because there are substantial costs to reducing pollution. The level of pollution can be reduced only by increasing the costs of production that generate the pollution (e.g., by installing pollution abatement equipment in factories) or by reducing the production that generates the pollution. Thus, one consequence of reducing pollution is to reduce the quantity of consumer goods and services available. Of course, there are also benefits to reducing pollution, such as improved health and increased attractiveness of the environment. The total benefits of pollution abatement will increase with additional abatement, but the marginal benefits will decline; the marginal costs of pollution abatement will increase with additional abatement. The optimal quantity of abatement is determined at the point where marginal social benefits and marginal social costs are equal. Study Exhibit 2 in the text carefully to be sure that you understand this.

The Coase Analysis of Externalities

Ronald Coase offers a different way of treating the question of externalities. If a factory emits pollution that bothers the residents in its vicinity, it is creating a negative externality. But why does the externality exist? The traditional response is that the externality exists simply because the factory emits pollution. Coase argues that this is incorrect—the externality exists because the pollution from the factory disturbs the people living in the vicinity. If the factory is removed, the externality no longer is a problem; the same is true if the residents are removed. That is, an externality is not the fault of one party but is the result of the incompatible activities of both parties. It takes at least two to have an externality.

Coase also points out that people have an incentive to alter the situation when there is a negative externality. Suppose the factory could reduce the pollution for a cost of $1,000, and that the pollution is imposing costs on the local residents (in the form of health problems and lower property values) that total $2,000. In this situation, society is better off if the pollution is reduced, for the savings to the residents ($2,000) exceed the cost to the factory ($1,000). Will the pollution be curtailed? According to Coase, it will be if property rights are assigned and bargaining costs are low. The parties involved will negotiate an agreement that produces this result. Suppose that the law allows the residents to force the factory to spend the $1,000 to reduce the pollution. Then obviously they will force the factory to do so. But what if the factory has the legal right to pollute? It will still reduce its level of pollution because the residents will agree to pay the factory to do so. That is, the residents would be willing to pay the $1,000 to have the pollution reduced because the cost of the pollution is greater than the cost of reducing it. The negotiated solution will reduce the pollution. But what if the cost to the residents is only $500? In this case, the factory will continue to pollute. If the factory is liable for damages, it will pay the $500 in damages because this is less than the $1,000 it takes to clean up the pollution. If the factory is not liable, then the residents will be unable to pay the factory to reduce the pollution level because the most they will offer is $500. Hence, the efficient outcome is achieved via negotiations when property rights are assigned and negotiating costs are minimal.

What happens when negotiating is very costly? Then there is no reason to think that the outcome will be efficient. In this situation, the courts or the government may have to step in. Coase argues that if this happens, the liability should be determined on the basis of which party can avoid the costly interaction (the negative externality) at the lowest cost. In this way, the combined private and external costs of production are minimized.

The optimal level of pollution can be achieved in some situations by selling pollution rights. Under such a system, firms would pay for the right to pollute—for example, to dispose of a given level of effluents into a commonly owned resource, a river. The optimal level of pollution can be achieved by this method when polluters can be easily identified and monitored. The price per unit of discharge is called an effluent fee.

Environmental Protection

The federal government has attempted to reduce pollution by imposing environmental standards on industry. The Clean Air Act of 1970 established national standards for the amount of pollution that can be emitted into the atmosphere. The government has also established standards for water pollution. Two pollution problems that have not been addressed adequately as yet are solid waste and hazardous materials.

Positive Externalities

Positive externalities arise when the unpriced by-product of consumption or production benefits other consumers or firms. When positive externalities arise, people do not produce or consume as much of the good as is optimal from society's viewpoint. Education is an example of a good that generates positive externalities. If all schools were private, then individuals would face higher prices for education and would consume less education. Each person would calculate the expected marginal private benefits of additional units of education and purchase additional education until the marginal private benefit equaled the marginal private cost. However, education benefits not only the individual but also others. The educated person is less likely to commit crimes, to be on welfare, or to be a burden on other members of society. The marginal social benefit of education thus is greater than the marginal private benefit. Usually people do not take into account these benefits that spill over onto others when deciding how much education to purchase. If they took these external benefits into consideration, people would purchase more education. To encourage people to purchase more education, the government subsidizes education in this country.

IV. LAGNIAPPE

Exporting Pollution

Pollution abatement requirements imposed on industry by the federal government generate higher production costs for many products. This is especially true for products that generate serious pollution, such as steel. Since firms' costs increase because of the pollution abatement efforts, U.S. firms find it more difficult to compete with producers from other countries. Consequently, their production levels decrease and imports increase. The increase in imports increases production of these pollution-causing products by other countries. In a sense, the United States is exporting pollution to other countries that are producing more of the goods and selling them to the United States.

Question to Think About: Why do the governments of other countries allow the increased production of such products if it also causes increased pollution?

Rationality in Los Angeles

It is well known that Los Angeles has a smog problem, and that pollution from automobiles is a major source of the smog. Consequently, California has the strictest pollution-control requirements for autos of any state in the country. But the pollution abatement equipment on a car imposes costs on the car owner above and beyond the higher sticker price for the car. The equipment makes a car less fuel efficient and reduces the performance of the engine. These costs are borne by the individual car owner, and the owner can benefit by removing the pollution abatement equipment. However, if the owner removes the equipment, the amount of pollution in Los Angeles increases.

Why would a car owner remove the equipment? The owner realizes that the total amount of pollution in Los Angeles is not affected in any meaningful way if he or she removes the pollution abatement equipment on one car. That is, the extra costs to society are virtually zero, whereas the benefits to the car owner are positive. So a car owner who removes the pollution abatement equipment benefits, and nobody is really hurt. This is true for an individual. The problem is that when one million people reach the same conclusion and also remove pollution abatement equipment from their cars, the combined effects of the extra pollution are significant. Note that people who do not remove the pollution abatement equipment from their cars cannot bring about a noticeable improvement in air quality because it is true that the extra pollution from one more car is minuscule.

Question to Think About: Why would a person not remove the pollution abatement equipment from a car under these circumstances?

V. KEY TERMS

exhaustible resource
renewable resource
common-pool problem
private property rights
fixed-production technology

marginal social cost
variable technology
marginal social benefit
Coase theorem
recycling

VI. QUESTIONS

A. Completion

1. _____ property rights allow individuals to control the use of certain resources now and in the future.

2. A resource is _____ if it is in a finite quantity and cannot be renewed.

3. A _____ resource is one that can be used at a certain rate indefinitely because the amount that is used can be replaced.

4. Open-access resources are often subject to _____ problems.

5. A resource that is owned in common tends to be _____.

6. If the only way to reduce pollution from the production of a good is to reduce the amount of the good produced, the technology used to produce the good is called a _____ technology.

7. The marginal social cost of production includes the marginal private cost of production and the marginal _____ cost of production.

8. _____ reduces the quality of air because there are fewer trees to convert carbon dioxide into oxygen.

9. The _____ states that the efficient solution to the problem of externalities will be achieved by bargaining if property rights are assigned and bargaining costs are low.

10. One way of keeping pollution to an optimal level is for government to sell _____.

11. _____ pollution refers to water pollution from factories; _____ pollution refers to water pollution from the runoff of pesticides and fertilizers from agricultural land.

12. Prior to 1970, control of pesticides was handled by the U.S. _____.

13. The _____ gives the federal government authority over hazardous waste sites.

14. Most solid waste in the United States is disposed of by using _____.

15. _____ is the process of converting waste products into reusable material.

B. True/False

_____ 1. A resource is renewable if you can take as much as you want every year and still have some in the future.

_____ 2. The common-pool problem refers to the overuse of goods used by some large corporations.

_____ 3. Open-access resources are often overused.

_____ 4. Negative externalities are more likely to arise when a resource is privately owned than if the resource is an open-access resource.

_____ 5. The way to establish ownership of a fish in the ocean is to catch it.

_____ 6. The government can use a tax to force competitive firms to use a resource at the optimal rate.

_____ 7. Private property rights are usually easy to establish on open-access resources.

_____ 8. An individual's demand curve for a good is the good's marginal social benefit curve.

_____ 9. Pollution arises because there are no enforceable property rights to some commonly owned resources.

_____ 10. With fixed technology, the only way to reduce pollution is to reduce output.

_____ 11. Unlike the production of other goods, the production of cleaner air is not subject to diminishing marginal returns.

_____ 12. The optimal level of pollution is zero.

_____ 13. The world's rain forests tend to be located in countries that are relatively poor.

_____ 14. According to Ronald Coase, it is always possible to find out who is at fault when there is an externality.

_____ 15. The efficient solution to an externality problem depends on which party can avoid the problem at the lowest cost.

_____ 16. Selling permits to pollute can reduce pollution, but it is an inefficient solution to the problem.

_____ 17. Positive externalities tend to be overproduced by competitive firms.

_____ 18. Over 80 percent of air pollution in the United States comes from industry.

_____ 19. The United States and Japan rely on incineration of solid waste to the same extent.

_____ 20. Most of the Superfund budget is spent on costs associated with litigation.

C. *Multiple Choice*

1. Which of the following is an example of a renewable resource?
   a. oil
   b. agricultural soil
   c. silver
   d. bauxite
   e. None of the above.

2. Resources that are not privately owned often are
   a. overused.
   b. exhaustible.
   c. nonappropriable.
   d. All of the above.
   e. a and c only.

3. Open-access resources tend to be
   a. used until the net marginal value of additional use is less than zero.
   b. used until the marginal private cost and marginal social cost are equalized.
   c. resources in abundant supply and thus have no price.
   d. overharvested, because everyone uses the resource until the net marginal value of additional use is zero.
   e. owned by the military.

4. Which of the following is an example of an open-access resource?
   a. air
   b. oceans
   c. a military base
   d. All of the above.
   e. a and b

5. Private property differs from open-access property in that
   a. private property involves consumer goods and open-access property involves productive resources.
   b. private property refers to things owned by individuals and open-access property refers to things owned by governments.
   c. private property is owned by specific individuals whereas open-access property is owned by everyone.
   d. private property involves goods that are scarce and open-access property involves goods that are not scarce.
   e. private property is owned by individuals and open-access property is owned by corporations.

6. Pollution exists because
   a. people do not realize that their actions cause pollution.
   b. the government does not subsidize production of goods characterized by negative externalities to the optimal degree.
   c. people have bounded rationality and are not able to calculate their marginal private benefits and marginal private costs.
   d. people only care about consumer goods and not about the quality of the environment.
   e. there are no enforceable property rights in the case of commonly owned resources.

7. The efficient level of output of a good with negative externalities is where
   a. marginal private benefits equal marginal private costs.
   b. marginal private benefits equal marginal social costs.
   c. total private benefits equal total private costs.
   d. total private benefits equal total social costs.
   e. the pollution tax equals marginal private costs.

8. The marginal social benefit of pollution abatement
   a. increases at an increasing rate with the quantity of pollution abated.
   b. increases at a decreasing rate with the quantity of pollution abated.
   c. decreases in direct relation to the quantity of pollution abated.
   d. is constant as the quantity of pollution abated increases.
   e. can be increasing, decreasing, or constant relative to the quantity of pollution abated, depending upon the type of pollution under consideration.

9. An increase in the costs of pollution abatement would
   a. cause the optimal quantity of abatement to increase.
   b. cause the optimal quantity of abatement to decrease.
   c. have no effect on the optimal quantity of abatement.
   d. have no effect on the optimal quantity of abatement unless the benefits of abatement changed also.
   e. The question cannot be answered without more information.

10. Improving air quality benefits society as long as
    a. any air pollution exists.
    b. the marginal benefit of cleaner air is positive.
    c. the marginal cost of cleaner air is more than the marginal benefit of cleaner air.
    d. the marginal cost of cleaner air is less than the marginal benefit of cleaner air.
    e. there are any social costs to pollution.

11. Which of the following could reduce the effects of a negative externality to the socially optimal level?
    a. converting an open-access resource to a privately owned resource
    b. converting a privately owned resource to a government-owned resource
    c. setting a tax equal to the marginal private cost of the externality
    d. prohibiting production of the good
    e. None of the above.

12. Deforestation is the result of
    a. growing world demand for lumber.
    b. clearing of land for farming.
    c. lack of private property rights on most of the world's rain forests.
    d. All of the above.
    e. a and b only.

13. Coase argued that the efficient resolution of an externality problem will be achieved as long as
    a. the government assigns property rights to one of the parties and bargaining costs are low.
    b. the government imposes a tax on the party generating the negative externality.
    c. the government assigns property rights to the party that is able to avoid the problem at the lowest cost.
    d. the parties do not act selfishly.
    e. None of the above. He argued that an efficient outcome will not be achieved.

14. According to the Coase theorem, the solution to an externality problem is likely to be inefficient if
    a. transaction costs are very high.
    b. property rights are not assigned to one of the parties.
    c. it is difficult to determine who is at fault.
    d. All of the above.
    e. a and b.

15. Suppose the government has sold pollution permits that set a maximum total allowable level of pollution that can be discharged into a certain river. If a new firm wants to set up a factory along the river and wants to discharge effluents into the river,
    a. it will be unable to do so.
    b. it will be given a permit to pollute because it is new.
    c. it will buy a permit from another firm so long as it values the discharge rights more than the firm currently holding the permit.
    d. it will sue and receive another firm's permit if it can prove it values the permit more than the firm that currently holds the permit.
    e. None of the above.

16. Which of the following is true of water pollution in the United States that is caused by chemicals?
    a. The majority of the pollution is point pollution, which is pollution from factories.
    b. The majority of the pollution is nonpoint pollution, which is pollution from factories.
    c. The majority of the pollution is nonpoint pollution, which is runoff of pesticides and fertilizers from agriculture.
    d. The majority of the pollution is caused by sewage.
    e. The EPA has spent most of its money on cleaning up water that has been polluted by chemicals.

17. According to the Superfund law, the cleanup of hazardous waste is to be paid for by
    a. those who generate the waste.
    b. those who store the waste.
    c. those who transport the waste.
    d. All of the above.
    e. a and b.

18. In the absence of government intervention, a person who consumes a good that is characterized by positive externalities
    a. overconsumes the good because the good is usually commonly owned.
    b. underconsumes the good because he or she does not take into consideration the benefits of consumption that accrue to others.
    c. underconsumes the good because he or she does not realize how much private benefit the good really provides.
    d. overconsumes the good because he or she does not bear the full cost of the consumption.
    e. None of the above.

Exhibit 1

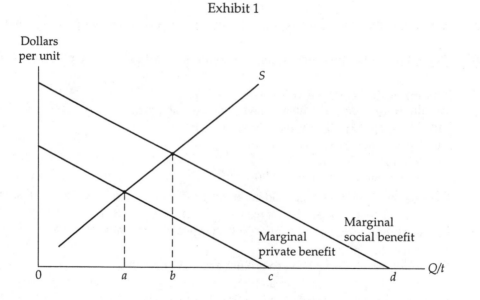

19. Exhibit 1 illustrates supply and demand for a good that generates a positive externality. In the absence of government intervention, the output that will be selected by an individual is _____; the optimal output is _____.
    a. *c; d*
    b. *b; d*
    c. *a; c*
    d. *a; b*
    e. *b; a*

20. The optimal amount of the good in Exhibit 1 can be achieved if the government
    a. imposes a tax on the good.
    b. provides a subsidy equal to the amount *a-b*.
    c. provides a subsidy equal to the amount *c-d*.
    d. provides a subsidy equal to the vertical distance between the marginal social benefit curve and the marginal private benefit curve.
    e. None of the above.

D. Discussion Questions

1. Explain how property rights and negative externalities are related.

2. Why are open-access resources often overused?

3. If easily enforceable private property rights allow the most efficient use of resources, why are people not assigned property rights to all resources?

4. What is the difference between fixed-production technology and variable technology when it comes to pollution reduction?

5. How can a tax be used to correct a problem of negative externalities?

6. Explain why the optimal level of pollution is not zero.

7. Suppose there are four factories along a river and each dumps the same amount of pollution into the river. The government determines that the amount of pollution should be cut in half. The only way the pollution can be reduced is if one or more of the firms closes down and moves elsewhere. The firms' costs of moving are as follows: firm 1, $5,000; firm 2, $10,000; firm 3, $4,000; and firm 4, $7,500. If the government sells two permits to pollute, which firms will buy them and how much will they pay? Which firms will move? Why is this solution optimal?

8. Explain how the deforestation of tropical rain forests is related to the greenhouse effect.

9. According to Coase, what causes a negative externality?

10. Suppose a factory is next door to a laundry, and the smoke emitted by the factory increases the costs of operating the laundry. The laundry's extra cost is $500; the cost of eliminating pollution by shutting down the factory is $600.
    a. If transaction costs are zero, what will happen if the laundry has the legal right to receive compensation for pollution damages? What will happen if the factory has the legal right to pollute?
    b. Suppose a scrubber that eliminates pollution can be installed at the factory for $550. Transaction costs are zero. What will be the result? What if the cost of the scrubber is $250?
    c. Suppose that the costs of negotiating and bargaining are very great, so no bargaining takes place. What will happen if the laundry has the legal right to operate free of pollution from the factory? if the factory has the legal right to generate pollution?

Externalities and the Environment

11. Suppose there are three firms along a river. Each discharges 1,000 units of effluent into the river. The government determines that 2,000 units of effluent is the maximum that should go into the river, and the government will sell two permits to the highest bidder. A device that eliminates the effluent can be installed by any firm. It would cost firm A $10,000, firm B $15,000, and firm C $20,000 to install the device. Which firms will buy the permits and at what price? If a fourth firm enters and the cleaning device costs it $25,000, what will happen?

12. According to a recent EPA study, the health hazards of Superfund sites have been greatly exaggerated and air pollution tends to be a bigger health hazard than toxic waste dumps. Why is more attention focused on toxic waste dumps than on air pollution?

13. Explain why the Japanese use landfills for disposal of solid waste much less than we do in the United States. Why might the United States start behaving more like the Japanese in the future?

14. Suppose a freak of nature caused the Los Angeles area to be free of air pollution forever. How might this affect the residents of Los Angeles?

15. Explain why goods characterized by positive externalities tend to be consumed in quantities that are less than optimal.

VII. ANSWERS

A. Completion

1.	Private	9.	Coase theorem
2.	exhaustible	10.	pollution rights
3.	renewable	11.	Point; nonpoint
4.	common-pool	12.	Department of Agriculture
5.	overutilized	13.	Superfund law
6.	fixed production	14.	landfills
7.	external	15.	Recycling
8.	Deforestation		

B. True/False

1. False. A resource is renewable only if it is allowed to replenish itself; you cannot take as much as you want each year because the resource will be used up faster than it can be replenished.
2. False
3. True
4. False
5. True
6. True
7. False
8. False
9. True
10. True
11. False
12. False. The optimal level occurs where the marginal social cost of abatement equals the marginal social benefit of abatement.
13. True
14. False
15. True
16. False
17. Falsc
18. False
19. False
20. True

C. Multiple Choice

1.	b	6.	e	11.	a	16.	c
2.	e	7.	b	12.	d	17.	d
3.	d	8.	c	13.	a	18.	b
4.	e	9.	b	14.	e	19.	d
5.	c	10.	d	15.	c	20.	d

D. Discussion Questions

1. Negative externalities may arise when a resource is owned in common by the members of a community. Each individual has an incentive to use the resource more intensively than it would be used if it were owned privately. Everybody ignores the effects of their actions on the other members of the community. The combined actions of everyone in the community result in overuse of the resource.

2. Anyone can use an open-access resource, but the full costs of using the resource are not borne by the person using it. Hence, each uses the resource more than is optimal.

3. It is impossible to define and enforce private property rights for some resources; the air and the oceans are obvious examples.

4. The only way to reduce pollution associated with a good produced with fixed-production technology is to reduce production of the good. With variable technology, there are ways of reducing pollution without reducing output of the good.

5. When production of a good generates a negative externality, some costs associated with the production are borne by people other than the producers of the good. The producers take into consideration only their own marginal private costs of production. A tax is a way to make the producers bear the full cost of their actions; it induces them to produce less of the good that is generating the negative externality.

6. Cleaning up pollution is costly, both in terms of resources devoted to cleanup efforts and in terms of a reduction in the quantity of consumer goods available to society. The marginal social cost of cleanup will increase and the marginal social benefit of cleanup will fall as cleanup efforts increase. The optimum level of cleanup is the level at which the marginal benefit of cleanup equals the marginal cost of cleanup. As long as costs are positive, the optimal level of pollution will be greater than zero.

7. Firms 2 and 4 will buy the permits at a price of $7,500 each, as this is the most that firm 4 will pay for a permit. Neither of the other two firms would be willing to pay that much because it is cheaper for them to move. This result is optimal because the problem is solved at the lowest cost: the pollution created by the two firms with the cheapest moving costs is eliminated; total pollution is cut in half.

8. The greenhouse effect results from an increase in carbon dioxide in the atmosphere. Forests convert carbon dioxide into oxygen, so the depletion of tropical rain forests retards the rate at which carbon dioxide is being converted to oxygen.

9. A negative externality is caused by incompatible activities of two parties. If bargaining costs are relatively high, the two parties will not necessarily negotiate an efficient solution.

10. a. If the laundry is entitled to compensation for pollution damages, the factory will pay the laundry $500 in damages and continue to emit pollution, since the cost of paying damages is less than the cost of eliminating pollution. If the factory has the legal right to pollute, it will continue to operate (and to pollute). That is, the factory continues to pollute in either case. However, when the factory has pollution rights, it does not pay the laundry $500.

    b. The scrubber will not be installed regardless of the parties' compensation or pollution rights, because at $550 the cost of the scrubber is more than the cost of the pollution. If the scrubber costs $250, it will be installed. If the laundry has compensation rights, then the factory will install the scrubber because the $250 for the scrubber is less than the $500 it would have to pay in damages. If the factory has pollution rights, then the laundry will pay the factory to install the scrubber.

    c. If the laundry has the right to operate free of pollution, the factory will be forced to stop polluting even if its costs of doing so are larger than the laundry's costs. If the factory has pollution rights, it will continue to produce and impose pollution costs on the laundry. The outcome depends on who is assigned the property rights.

11. Firms B and C will buy pollution permits for $10,000 each as firm A will drop out of the bidding at that price. Firm A will buy the pollution control device. If the new firm entered, it would buy a pollution permit from firm B for a price between $15,000 and $20,000, and then firm B would buy a pollution control device.

12. Those who are near a toxic waste dump know it and exert political pressure to close it down; those who are affected by air pollution are less likely to be aware of the danger and are less likely to apply political pressure.

13. Land is much more abundant in the United States than it is in Japan, which makes it less costly in the United States to use land for landfills than it is in Japan. As U.S. landfills close down, however, and it becomes more costly to open new ones, the cost of using landfills for solid waste will rise. Consequently, Americans will probably use landfills less in the future and turn more to burning and recycling.

14. The effects of such an event on residents of Los Angeles would be many and varied. On the positive side, clean air would mean fewer health risks, greater ability to enjoy the beauty of the area, lower costs for washing cars and painting houses, and the like. There would also be some negative effects, however. The improved air quality would probably lead to an influx of people into the area, which would cause greater congestion, crime, water pollution, and so forth.

15. People make decisions on the basis of the marginal private benefits and marginal private costs they face. A positive externality implies that people other than the decision maker are receiving benefits from the consumption of the good. These benefits are not considered by the decision maker, who only equates marginal private benefits and marginal private costs in determining what quantity to consume. Since the good is being undervalued from society's perspective, too little is being consumed.

CHAPTER 31

Income Distribution and Poverty

I. INTRODUCTION

A family's income is determined by the resources it owns and the prices of those resources. Families that own few resources or whose resources command a very low price will earn less than families that own more resources or more valuable resources. The result is that the distribution of income is not equal. Some families have very large incomes; others live in poverty. In this chapter, we will examine how the distribution of income is measured and determined, and describe government programs designed to reduce the level of poverty in this country.

II. OUTLINE

1. The Distribution of Household Income

    1.1 Income Distribution by Quintiles
        a. The share of income going to the top quintile of households has increased and the share going to the bottom quintile has decreased slightly in recent years.
        b. An important reason for the growing share of income to the highest group is the growth of two-earner households in the top group and single-parent households in the lowest group.

    1.2 A College Education Pays Relatively More
        a. Between 1980 and 1996, the real median wage for those with only a high school education declined 6 percent, while the real median wage for college graduates increased 12 percent.
        b. More educated workers have done better because
            (1) demand for knowledge workers has increased;
            (2) industry deregulation, declining unionization, and greater international trade have reduced the demand for unskilled workers; and
            (3) immigration has caused the supply of unskilled workers to increase.

    1.3 Problems with Distributional Benchmarks
        a. There is no objective standard for evaluating them.
        b. Accounting for taxes and transfer payments reduces income inequality.
        c. Income distribution estimates include only reported income.

    1.4 Why Do Household Incomes Differ?
        a. The number of family members who work differs.
        b. There are differences in education, training, and ability.
        c. The age of the family head affects income.

2. Poverty and the Poor

    2.1   Official Poverty Level
        a.   To derive the official poverty level, the U.S. government estimates the cost of minimum food consumption for each family size.
        b.   This number is multiplied by three to calculate the official poverty level for each family size.
        c.   The number of people below the poverty line fell from 1959 to 1973 but has fluctuated since. The most recent rate was higher than the rate in 1973.

    2.2   Programs to Help the Poor
        a.   The U.S. social insurance system is designed to help those who have worked but are now retired, temporarily unemployed, or unable to work because of total disability.
        b.   U.S. income assistance programs provide money and in-kind assistance to the poor, even those who have not worked or contributed to the program.
            (1)   Income assistance programs are *means tested* (i.e., the programs require that a household's income and/or assets fall below a certain level before the household members can qualify).
            (2)   People who qualify are entitled to receive the benefits of the program, so these programs are also called *entitlement programs*.
        c.   There are two primary cash transfer programs:
            (1)   Temporary Assistance to Needy Families (TANF) provides cash to poor households with children.
            (2)   Supplemental Security Income (SSI) provides cash to the indigent elderly and the totally disabled.
        d.   There are several in-kind transfer programs, including food stamps, Medicaid, and housing assistance programs.

3. Who Are the Poor?

    3.1   Poverty and Age
        a.   The U.S. poverty rate is highest in families in which the head of the household is under 25 years old, and the poverty rate for this group has grown substantially since 1968.
        b.   The poverty rate for the elderly has fallen dramatically over the last 40 years because of increases in Social Security and Medicare transfers.

    3.2   Poverty and Public Choice. The elderly are a powerful interest group who have been successful in lobbying Congress for greater Social Security benefits.

    3.3   The Feminization of Poverty
        a.   Married couples have poverty rates only one-third that of female householders.
        b.   The poverty rate among black families is about twice as great as the poverty rate among white families.
        c.   The highest U.S. poverty rate is among black families headed by women.
        d.   Households headed by women have become an increasingly large proportion of households in poverty.
        e.   The growth in the number of poor families since 1969 resulted primarily from the growth in the number of female householders.

3.4 Poverty and Discrimination
  a. Blacks earn less than whites on average.
  b. When factors such as education, age, and job experience are considered, the gap between blacks and whites narrows. Differences in education and job experience could themselves reflect past discrimination.

3.5 Affirmative Action
  a. The federal government requires firms that do business with the government to meet numerical hiring, training, and promotion goals for minorities.
  b. The constitutionality of some affirmative action plans has been questioned in recent years.

4. Unintended Consequences of Income Assistance

4.1 Work Disincentives. Families that do earn income see transfers reduced sharply as a result, which discourages them from working.

4.2 Does Welfare Cause Dependency?
  a. Most recipients receive welfare benefits for only a short time.
  b. There is a correlation between people's income levels and the income levels of their parents.

5. Welfare Reform

5.1 Recent Reforms
  a. Many states require welfare recipients to seek work or participate in training programs.
  b. The Personal Responsibility and Work Reconciliation Act of 1996 was the biggest reform in the welfare system in the last 60 years.
    (1) The act replaced AFDC with Temporary Assistance for Needy Families (TANF).
    (2) TANF offers a block grant to states to run their welfare programs.
    (3) States are granted wide latitude to run their own welfare programs.
    (4) The act imposes a lifetime limit of five years a recipient can be on welfare.
    (5) Benefits are limited for non citizens and for teenage mothers not living at home.
    (6) The act tightens eligibility requirements for disabled children receiving Supplemental Security Income.
  c. States have an incentive to constrain the growth of welfare rolls.

5.2 *CASE STUDY:* Is Welfare-to-Work Working?

5.3 *CASE STUDY:* Oregon's Program of "Tough Love"

III. DISCUSSION

The Distribution of Household Income

If all families earned the same income, there would be an equal distribution of income. This is not the case in the United States, which has an unequal distribution of income. There are many ways to measure the distribution of income. One way is to assign families to equal-sized groups so that the lowest-income families are grouped together. The next group consists of the next-lowest-income families, and so on. Exhibit 1 shows two hypothetical distributions using five equal-sized groups, or quintiles, in each case. Income distribution B is more unequal than A.

Exhibit 1

Income Distribution

	Lowest Fifth	Second-Lowest Fifth	Middle Fifth	Second-Highest Fifth	Highest Fifth
A	15%	18%	20%	22%	25%
B	2%	8%	18%	22%	50%

Exhibit 1 in the textbook provides actual quintiles for the United States for 1967, 1977, 1987, and 1997. The top quintile has increased slightly, the bottom three quintiles have decreased slightly, and the second highest quintile has been relatively unchanged. The poorest 20 percent of families receive less than 5 percent of aggregate household income, while the richest 20 percent of households receive over 45 percent of aggregate household income. It appears the rich have gotten richer and the poor poorer. Is this accurate?

Yes and no. Other things in the economy have changed as well. Several factors contribute to the rising inequality. First, the premium paid college graduates has increased since 1980. The information age puts greater emphasis on education, while the demand for unskilled labor has fallen. Further, the supply of unskilled labor has increased. Household incomes differ because the number of household members who work differs. Differentiation incomes also reflect differences in age and work experience.

Poverty and the Poor

Poverty is a relative term, and what is considered poverty in one country or in one historic period may be considered a more-than-adequate living standard in another country or time. The U.S. federal government has been calculating an official poverty level since 1955. It is based on the cost of minimum food consumption for each family size. This figure is then multiplied by three on the grounds that poor families spend one-third of their income on food. The percentage of the U.S. population below the official poverty line fell during the 1960s, fluctuated during the 1970s, rose slightly between 1979 and 1983, declined between 1983 and 1989, rose until 1993, and fell slightly by 1997. The lowest poverty rate occurred in 1973.

The two primary types of U.S. government programs to help the poor are social insurance programs and income assistance programs. The most important social insurance program is Social

Security. The two most important income assistance cash transfer programs are Temporary Assistance for Needy Families (TANF) and Supplemental Security Income (SSI). There are also in-kind assistance programs, such as Medicaid and food stamps. Medicaid is by far the largest welfare program. Most of the government expenditures to these programs are for social insurance programs; welfare spending amounted to only about 4 percent of GDP in 1995.

Who Are the Poor?

Poverty in the United States is greater among families headed by relatively young people, among families headed by women, and among black families. The number of poor in households headed by women has increased significantly in the last 30 years, mostly because the number of households headed by women has increased as more children have been born to unwed mothers and divorce rates have risen. The growth in the number of poor families since 1969 has resulted mainly from the growth in the number of female householders. Poverty among the elderly has fallen substantially—from 30 percent in 1959 to 10.5 percent in 1997. This is in part because the elderly have become a very effective lobbying force in Congress.

Because there is a greater incidence of poverty among blacks than among whites on average, it is appropriate to examine whether this situation is due to discrimination or to other factors. Income depends on the productivity of workers, which depends on such factors as age, experience, and education. Once these factors are controlled for, the difference between incomes of whites and blacks narrows. In fact, the wages of young black males with college degrees are greater than those of their white counterparts. However, the fact that there are more blacks living in poverty could be accounted for by the fact that the unemployment rate of blacks is greater than that of whites, or by the fact that the percentage of blacks with college degrees is significantly smaller than the percentage of whites with college degrees. Such differences in education levels and experience may themselves be results of discrimination.

Unintended Consequences of Income Assistance

The goal of programs for the poor is to reduce the number of people living in poverty. The programs have other consequences that are not intended yet are often very important. First, welfare may create disincentives to work. Two things happen when a member of a household that is receiving welfare obtains a job. The first is that the income from the job is taxed (if it is high enough), so the after-tax income is less than the pretax income. (This applies to all income earners, whether they are on welfare or not.) The second thing that happens is that welfare payments decrease. The combination of the effects of these events is equivalent to increasing the tax rate on the income of the worker. If the welfare payment falls dollar for dollar, then the effective tax rate can be more than 100 percent. Unless the income from the job is significantly greater than the welfare payments, many people rationally choose not to work.

Some observers fear that a second unintended consequence of antipoverty programs is that welfare causes dependency on the welfare system. There is very little evidence to suggest that this is the case, but it is true that almost half of the young adults who grew up in the lowest income group are themselves in the lowest group when they form their own households.

To some extent, the pattern of poverty is a result of public choice. The bulk of government expenditures for the poor are for social insurance programs rather than for welfare. This means that most of the expenditures are directed to the elderly. As noted, in recent years the elderly have become a powerful interest group that has received a great deal of attention in Congress. Even though the poverty rate of the elderly is very low, the government has been more likely to reduce welfare benefits to the poor than to reduce Social Security benefits.

Welfare Reform

States have been trying to reform welfare programs to reduce their cost and increase their effectiveness. Many states now require a "workfare" component for welfare recipients. Federal welfare reform includes the Personal Responsibility and Work Reconciliation Act of 1996. This act replaced AFDC with TANF, provided block grants to states, and set limits on how long people can receive welfare.

IV. LAGNIAPPE

Private Charity

Historically, governments did not provide for the poor. Instead, the poor were the concern of private charity. An important source of income for the poor in such situations was begging. Beggars usually had a disability of one sort or another, although disabilities might be faked to generate increased sympathy and gifts. Arthur Conan Doyle wrote a story about a man who quit his job as a reporter because he made more money begging. (See "The Man with the Twisted Lip," in *The Complete Sherlock Holmes*. Garden City, NY: Doubleday & Company, Inc., 1960.)

Many societies established customs to help the poor. In ancient Israel, the Mosaic Law contained numerous instructions on the care of the poor. These included exhortations to be charitable, rules concerning gleaning, and even provisions for the return of land to the original owners every so often.

In the United States today we rely much more on government than on private charity. As society becomes more complex and urbanized, the poor become more anonymous; it is easy to forget their problems and even their existence. As both the group of potential recipients and the group of potential donors increase in size, the free-rider problem increases—that is, people assume that someone else will deal with the problem—and per capita giving decreases. Note, too, that much of what are classified as charitable donations have little to do with helping the poor. Charitable donations to medical research may have important future benefits but do not help the poor today. Donations to churches are called charitable donations, but the money may be used for the operations of the church rather than to help the poor.

Question to Think About: Would people give more to help the poor if the government did not operate welfare programs?

Age and Earnings

We must be careful in comparing average earnings of various racial and ethnic groups because there can be variations that have nothing to do with discrimination. Blacks, Puerto Ricans, and Mexicans are groups that earn, on average, significantly less than the U.S. national average; Japanese, Chinese, and Jews earn significantly more than the U.S. national average. Since all six groups have been targets of discrimination in this country, the income differences among them may not be due to discrimination. An important difference is the average age of the groups. The average age of members of the first three groups is less than 20, whereas the average age of members of the latter three groups is over 35. Since 35-year-olds generally earn more than 20-year-olds, part of the difference in average incomes is due to differences in demographic characteristics.

Question to Think About: What other differences among the groups would help account for differences in average earnings?

V. KEY TERMS

median income
U. S. official poverty level
Social Security
Medicare
income assistance programs
means-tested program

Temporary Assistance for
    Needy Families (TANF)
Supplemental Security Income (SSI)
Medicaid
food stamps

VI. QUESTIONS

A. Completion

1.   The distribution of income in all societies is _____.

2.   The _____ income is the middle income when incomes are ranked from lowest to highest.

3.   The Census Bureau includes only _____ transfers in the definition of income.

4.   Differences in earnings based on age and education reflect the _____ pattern of income.

5.   The growth in the number of poor families since 1969 has resulted from the growth in the number of _____ households.

6.   Temporary Assistance to Needy Families (TANF) is an example of an _____ program.

7.   A _____ program requires that a household's income and/or assets fall below a certain level before the family can qualify for benefits; those families that do qualify are _____ to the program.

8.   Food stamps are an example of a(n) _____ program.

9.   A problem with some welfare programs is that they create work _____.

10.   Some states have implemented _____, which is a requirement that welfare recipients participate in training programs or search for work.

_____	1.	The share of total income received by 20 percent of families in the highest U.S. income group has decreased steadily since 1929.

_____	2.	One reason incomes differ across families is that the number of family members who are working varies.

_____	3.	The average income of all households is also known as the median income.

_____	4.	The cost of housing is the basis on which the U.S. official poverty level is calculated.

_____	5.	Benefits in most social insurance programs depend on a prior record of employment.

_____	6.	People must have worked and contributed to an entitlement program to be entitled to the benefits of the program.

_____	7.	Social insurance programs account for a larger share of total U.S. government expenditures than entitlement programs.

_____	8.	Poverty rates for U.S. families headed by someone under 25 are greater than the rates for all U.S. families.

_____	9.	The poverty rate for the elderly is lower than that of any other age group in the United States.

_____	10.	The black poverty rate in the United States is about three times the white poverty rate.

_____	11.	Any difference in average earnings between whites and blacks is due to discrimination.

_____	12.	The distribution of income among black families is more even than for the population as a whole.

_____	13.	Differences in earnings between blacks and whites that can be attributed to differences in experience and differences in quality of education cannot be due to racial discrimination.

_____	14.	Current welfare programs create work disincentives.

_____	15.	TANF is designed to limit federal welfare costs.

C.   Multiple Choice

1.   Since the end of World War II, the distribution of income in the United States has been
  a.   increasingly more unequal.
  b.   increasingly more equal.
  c.   relatively stable.
  d.   fluctuating considerably, becoming more unequal at times and more equal at other times.
  e.   very different from the distribution of income in other industrialized countries.

2.   Differences in family incomes arise from differences in
  a.   the age of the head of the household.
  b.   education.
  c.   ability.
  d.   the number of people in the household who are working.
  e.   All of the above.

3.   A high-income household usually consists of
  a.   people who were in low-income households when children.
  b.   well-educated couples who both are employed.
  c.   female-headed households.
  d.   single males who have no children.
  e.   both a and b only.

4.   The percentage of the U.S. population below the official poverty level
  a.   has declined steadily since 1960.
  b.   declined during the 1960s, fluctuated during the 1970s, increased from 1979 to 1983, and decreased slightly since 1983.
  c.   declined during the 1960s, rose during the 1970s, fluctuated in the early 1980s, and fell in the latter 1980s.
  d.   has been unaffected by any government policies since 1960.
  e.   declined steadily from 1960 to 1975 and has risen steadily since 1975.

5.   Which of the following is not an example of a social insurance program?
  a.   Social Security
  b.   Medicare
  c.   Worker's compensation
  d.   Unemployment insurance
  e.   Supplemental Security Income

6.   Which of the following is not an example of an in-kind transfer program?
  a.   school lunches
  b.   low-income housing
  c.   TANF
  d.   food stamps
  e.   Medicaid

7. Which of the following has the greatest effect on reducing poverty?
   a. increased spending on social insurance programs
   b. a strong economy that creates a lot of new jobs
   c. excluding in-kind transfers from the definition of income
   d. raising the benefits associated with in-kind transfers
   e. All of the above. reduce the number of citizens who are below the official poverty line.

8. The number of households below the poverty line that are headed by women has been increasing because
   a. female-headed households have become more common in the population as a whole.
   b. discrimination against women has increased.
   c. women have been moving out of the labor force.
   d. the service sector has been growing faster than the manufacturing sector.
   e. All of the above.

9. For any given age group,
   a. black workers are likely to have less job experience than white workers.
   b. black workers earn a lower wage rate than white workers even after the data are adjusted for experience, education, marital status, and geographic location.
   c. black workers earn the same wage as white workers when experience, education, marital status, and geographic location are taken into consideration.
   d. a and b.
   e. a and c.

10. The work disincentives associated with welfare are due to
    a. the fact that welfare recipients are lazy.
    b. the requirement that welfare recipients not work.
    c. the fact that most welfare programs involve in-kind rather than cash transfers.
    d. the sharp decline in benefits received as earned income increases.
    e. All of the above.

11. A University of Michigan study found that if a young adult's parents were in the lowest fifth of all families in terms of income, the young adult was most likely to be in which segment of the population?
    a. lowest fifth
    b. second-lowest fifth
    c. middle fifth
    d. second-highest fifth
    e. highest fifth

12. One concern with recent welfare reform is that
    a. states may be tempted to offer relatively low levels of benefits.
    b. the costs to the federal government may skyrocket.
    c. the reforms may cause a recession.
    d. All of the above.
    e. None of the above.

D. Discussion Questions

1. Exhibit 2 contains data on four distributions of income. Which is the most equal distribution? Which is the most unequal? Explain.

Exhibit 2

Distribution	Lowest Fifth	Second-Lowest Fifth	Middle Fifth	Second-Highest Fifth	Highest Fifth
A	2%	5%	8%	15%	70%
B	12	15	20	23	30
C	5	10	25	26	34
D	10	14	16	20	40

2. Why do family incomes differ?

3. Why is private charity not enough to care for the poor?

4. What are the differences between social insurance programs and income assistance programs?

5. What has caused the feminization of poverty?

6. Discuss the factors that cause the average income of blacks to be lower than the average income of whites.

7. Explain how differences in earnings between blacks and whites can be a result of racial discrimination.

8. Explain how welfare creates work disincentives.

9. What has caused the recent poverty rate among the elderly to be lower than that of any other group in the United States?

10. Explain the changes in welfare caused by the Personal Responsibility and Work Reconciliation Act of 1996.

VII. ANSWERS

A. Completion

1. unequal
2. median
3. money
4. life cycle
5. female

6. entitlement (or income assistance)
7. means-tested; entitled
8. in-kind
9. disincentives
10. workfare

B. True/False

1. False
2. True
3. False
4. False. The official poverty level is based on the cost of food.
5. True
6. False
7. True

8. True
9. True
10. True
11. False
12. False
13. False
14. True
15. True

C. Multiple Choice

1. c
2. e
3. b

4. b
5. e
6. c

7. b
8. a
9. a

10. d
11. a
12. a

D. Discussion Questions

1. Distribution B is the most equal because the bottom quintile's share of household income is the greatest of the four distributions, and the top quintile's share of household income is the lowest of the four distributions. For opposite reasons, A is the least equal. It is difficult to compare distributions C and D since their middle quintiles differ.

2. Family incomes differ because of differences in the number of members who work; differences in education, ability, and training; and racial and gender discrimination.

3. Each person realizes that the plight of the poor will not be materially affected if he or she provides assistance, so the amount of help individuals provide is limited. Each person has little incentive to help and counts on others to do it instead. Consequently, private charity is likely to be insufficient to alleviate the problems of the poor.

4. Social insurance programs are designed for people who have worked and contributed to their own support. Income assistance programs are provided to people in need, whether they have ever worked or not.

5. The main reason is that the number of female householders has increased.

6. Discrimination is one factor that causes average incomes to differ between the two groups. Related factors include differences in education levels, differences in quality of education, and differences in job experience.

7. Differences in quality of education and job experience may be the result of discrimination, so any differences in income that are due to these factors are, by extension, caused by racial discrimination.

8. Welfare creates work disincentives because benefits are reduced if the recipient earns income. The extra income from a low-paying or part-time job may not be sufficient to overcome the loss of benefits. Consequently, there is less incentive to work.

9. The elderly have become a powerful interest group and have successfully lobbied Congress for increases in benefits, especially in Social Security benefits.

10. The act replaced AFDC with TANF, which provides block grants to states to run their welfare programs. States are given more latitude to run their own welfare programs. The act tries to limit welfare dependency by imposing a lifetime limit of 5 years a recipient can be on welfare. The act also tightens eligibility requirements for disabled children and limits benefits of non-citizens and teenage mothers who do not live at home.

CHAPTER 32

International Trade

I.   INTRODUCTION

This chapter examines trade among nations. Given the growing importance of international trade, you should understand the forces that determine patterns of trade.

II.   OUTLINE

1.   The Gains from Trade

   1.1   A Profile of Imports and Exports
      a.   Countries' levels of involvement in international trade differ.
      b.   U.S. exports are about 14 percent of GDP.
      c.   The main exports of the United States are high-technology manufactured products, industrial supplies and materials, agricultural products, and entertainment products.
      d.   The main imports of the United States are manufactured consumer goods and capital goods.
      e.   U.S. imports equal about 16 percent of GDP.

   1.2   Production Possibilities without Trade
      a.   In the absence of trade, a country's consumption possibilities are determined by its production possibilities.
      b.   A country's possible production combinations can be portrayed graphically.

   1.3   Consumption Possibilities Based on Comparative Advantage
      a.   Each country specializes in the product for which its opportunity cost is lowest relative to other countries.
      b.   Two countries can each consume more by trading than they could before trading when the terms of trade are based on the two countries' opportunity costs.
      c.   Total world production of each good increases if each country specializes in producing the good for which it has a comparative advantage.
      d.   The exchange of goods between two countries yields a surplus to both consumers and producers.

   1.4   Reasons for International Specialization
      a.   People expect to benefit when they engage in trade.
      b.   Exchange can benefit those involved when
         (1)   there are differences in resource endowments;
         (2)   there are economies of scale; and
         (3)   there are differences in tastes.

2. Trade Restrictions

    2.1   Consumer and Producer Surplus
- a. Market exchange usually yields a surplus, or a bonus, to both producers and consumers.
- b. Consumer surplus and producer surplus are affected by international trade.

    2.2   Tariffs
- a. A *tariff* is a tax on imports or exports.
  - (1) A *specific tariff* is a lump-sum tariff per unit of a good.
  - (2) An *ad valorem tariff* is a percentage of the cost of the imports at the port of entry.
- b. Tariffs generate higher prices for domestic producers of goods that compete with imports.
- c. Consumers are harmed by tariffs; domestic producers whose products compete with imports benefit from tariffs.
- d. The loss in consumer surplus from tariffs is greater than the increase in producer surplus and government revenue from tariffs.
- e. Tariffs redistribute income from consumers to producers and government.

    2.3   Import Quotas
- a. An *import quota* is a legal limit on the quantity of a particular commodity that can be imported per year.
- b. Tariffs and effective quotas have similar effects.
- c. An effective quota limits imports and raises domestic price.
- d. If a tariff and an effective quota have the same effect on price, then they result in the same quantity demanded, the same loss in consumer surplus, and the same increase in producer surplus for domestic firms.

    2.4   Quotas in Practice
- a. The quota system creates two groups that want to secure and maintain the quotas—domestic producers and foreign producers with the right to sell goods to the United States.
- b. An important difference between a quota and a tariff is that the government obtains revenue with tariffs, whereas those with the right to export gain revenues with quotas.

    2.5   Other Trade Restrictions
- a. Free trade is restricted by government subsidies to export firms and low-interest loans to foreign buyers.
- b. Other rules and regulations, such as domestic content requirements, can be used to discriminate against foreign producers.

    2.6   Freer Trade by Multilateral Agreement
- a. The General Agreement on Tariffs and Trade (GATT) is an international treaty to reduce trade barriers.
- b. Tariffs have fallen sharply since World War II as a result of GATT.

    2.7   *CASE STUDY:* The World Trade Organization

    2.8   Common Markets. Some countries join together into common markets in order to take advantage of free trade with other countries.

3. Arguments for Trade Restrictions

    3.1 National Defense Argument
        a. Certain industries are essential in wartime so they must be kept viable.
        b. Many industries try to use this argument even though their military application is often nebulous.
        c. Government subsidies to domestic producers would be more efficient than import restrictions.

    3.2 Infant Industry Argument
        a. Emerging domestic industries need temporary protection so they can compete with mature industries in other countries until they can exploit economies of scale.
        b. Among the problems with this rationale are the fact that it is difficult to identify industries with the potential to become competitive and the fact that it is possible that protection itself will foster inefficiencies so that protected industries will not mature.

    3.3 Antidumping Argument
        a. *Dumping* is the sale of a commodity abroad for less than its domestic price.
        b. Predatory dumping by foreign firms may deter domestic firms from entering an industry.

    3.4 Jobs and Income Argument
        a. Some foreign countries are able to compete because of low wages.
        b. The high wages in the United States reflect the greater productivity of U.S. labor.

    3.5 Declining Industries Argument
        a. Tariffs can be used to ease the transition of domestic industries that are in decline.
        b. If tariffs are imposed for this reason, care must be taken to ensure that the protection is not so great as to encourage new investment in the industry.
        c. Wage subsidies or special tax breaks can be used instead of import restrictions.

    3.6 Problems with Protection
        a. Protecting one industry often leads to protecting other industries because of the need to counteract the effects of higher prices in the protected industry on the other industries.
        b. Costs of rent seeking also are associated with protection.
        c. Policing protective arrangements can be costly.

    3.7 *CASE STUDY:* Enforcing Trade Restrictions

4. Conclusion. Trade allows people to use their scarce resources more efficiently. Yet trade restrictions are common. Losers from trade restrictions include consumers, exporting industries, and businesses that use the same resources as the protected industries. Winners from trade restrictions include the domestic producers of goods that compete with imports and, in the case of quotas, those who have secured rights to import a good.

III. DISCUSSION

The Gains from Trade

People exchange goods with those in other nations for the same reasons they exchange goods with other people in their own nation—because they believe they will be better off as a result. Individuals gain by specializing in the production of one thing, selling their output for money, and using the money to buy the goods and services they want. Similarly, nations specialize in production and sell the goods they specialize in for goods in which they do not specialize. There is one difference between individuals who specialize and nations that specialize. Individuals often specialize completely and produce none of the goods they buy; nations often produce some of almost all goods but not enough to satisfy domestic demand for some goods.

Suppose a worker in the United States can produce either 10 units of wheat or 5 units of cloth per day, and a worker in Britain can produce either 5 units of wheat or 3 units of cloth per day. The U.S. worker is more productive than the British worker in either case, so the United States has an absolute advantage in producing both commodities. However, trade is based on comparative, not absolute, advantage. The opportunity cost of a unit of wheat in the United States is $1/2$ unit of cloth, and the opportunity cost of a unit of cloth is 2 units of wheat. In Britain, the opportunity cost of a unit of wheat is $3/5$ unit of cloth, and the opportunity cost of a unit of cloth is $5/3$ units of wheat. Hence, the opportunity cost of wheat is lower in the United States than in Britain ($1/2 < 3/5$), and the opportunity cost of cloth is lower in Britain than in the United States ($5/3 < 2$). The United States has a comparative advantage in wheat and Britain has a comparative advantage in cloth.

The different opportunity costs in the two countries mean that world production of wheat and cloth can increase if each country specializes in the commodity that it can produce more cheaply. If the United States produces 1 less unit of cloth, it can produce 2 additional units of wheat. If Britain produces 1 less unit of wheat, it can produce $5/3$ additional units of cloth. So the United States produces 1 less unit of cloth, Britain produces an additional $5/3$ units of cloth, and, on net, there is $2/3$ unit of cloth more than before. Similarly, Britain produces 1 less unit of wheat, but the United States has produced 2 additional units of wheat. On net, the world now has 1 additional unit of wheat and $2/3$ additional unit of cloth.

Since world production is greater when each country specializes, it is possible for residents of each country to consume more with trade than without. Suppose each country has 100 workers (and consumers). Exhibit 1 presents the production possibilities schedule for each country, and Exhibit 2 illustrates the production possibilities frontier (PPF) of each. The PPF for the United States is line *AB*, with a slope equal to the opportunity cost of cloth in the United States, and the PPF for Britain is line *CD*, with a slope equal to the opportunity cost of cloth in Britain. The price of a unit of cloth in the United States is 2 units of wheat, but the price of cloth in England is $5/3$ units of wheat. Trade is beneficial to both as long as they trade cloth at a price that is between the domestic prices without trade. That is, both can benefit if wheat can be exchanged for cloth at a rate that is more than 1.67 ($5/3$) but less than 2.

Exhibit 1

Production Possibilities Schedules

United States

Wheat	1,000	800	600	400	200	0
Cloth	0	100	200	300	400	500

Britain

Wheat	500	400	300	200	100	0
Cloth	0	60	120	180	240	300

Exhibit 2

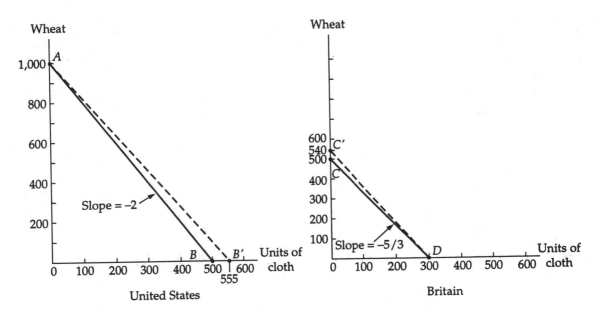

Suppose the exchange ratio, or *terms of trade*, is 1.8 units of wheat per unit of cloth. Without trade, in the United States 2 units of wheat had to be given up to get a unit of cloth. Now the United States can completely specialize and produce 1,000 units of wheat, and exchange wheat for cloth at a rate of 1.8 instead of 2. Exhibit 3 presents the consumption possibilities schedules when the rate of exchange is 1.8 units of wheat for 1 unit of cloth and the United States produces wheat while Britain produces cloth. Exhibit 2 also shows the consumption possibilities frontiers: *AB′* in the United States and *C′D* in Britain. Each country is able to consume more of both commodities than it could when it did not trade.

Exhibit 3

Consumption Possibilities Schedules
(Terms of trade = 1.8 units of wheat for 1 unit of cloth)

United States

Wheat	1,000	800	600	400	200	0	
Cloth	0	111	222	333	444	555	

Britain

Wheat	540	450	360	270	180	90	0
Cloth	0	50	100	150	200	250	300

Exchange between nations can be beneficial when the nations involved differ in resource endowments. Resources are not equally distributed among countries. Some countries have more oil than others; other countries have more skilled labor. Countries with a relatively large supply of skilled labor have a comparative advantage in producing goods that require skilled labor. Exchange can also be beneficial if there are differences in tastes among nations. Further, exchange can occur if there are economies of scale so that specialization generates lower production costs.

Trade Restrictions

Even though the gains from trade exceed the losses from trade, restrictions on trade are ubiquitous. The two major types of trade restrictions are import *tariffs* and import *quotas*. Both have the effect of raising price in the domestic economy above the world price. A tariff raises price directly, since an import tariff is a tax on imports. Import quotas raise prices indirectly by restricting the quantity of imports. Their effects are almost identical to those of a tariff.

Exhibit 4 illustrates the effects on imports of tariffs and effective quotas. Domestic demand and supply of cloth are represented by D and S, respectively. The world price, $5, is below the domestic equilibrium price, so in the absence of trade restrictions the relevant supply curve is mnS_w. It intersects the demand curve at point v, so domestic quantity demanded is 6,000 units, and 2,000 units is the quantity supplied by U.S. cloth producers. The United States imports 4,000 units of cloth. A specific tariff adds $1 to the world price, so the new domestic price is $6, and the new supply curve is $mn\acute{}S\acute{}_w$. Quantity demanded falls to 5,000 units, the amount of cloth produced by domestic firms increases to 3,000 units, and imports fall to 2,000 units. Instead of a tariff, the government could have imposed a quota and achieved the same result. A quota equal to 2,000 units of cloth causes the supply curve to shift to $mnrS\acute{}$. In other words, the supply curve shifts out by the quota limit at the world price of $5. It intersects domestic demand at f, which implies a price of $6. Domestic production increases from 2,000 to 3,000 units, and domestic consumption falls from 6,000 to 5,000 units.

Exhibit 4

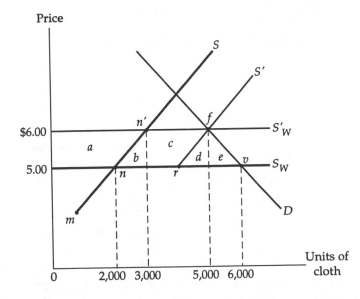

The increase in price as a result of the tariff (or quota) makes consumers worse off. Consumer surplus falls by areas *a*, *b*, *c*, *d*, and *e*. Some of the loss to consumers is transferred to other members of society, but the rest of the loss to consumers represents a deadweight loss to society. In Exhibit 4, area *a* represents a transfer of surplus from consumers to domestic producers and areas *c* and *d* represent revenue received by the government as the result of a tariff. (In the case of a quota, areas *c* and *d* represent a transfer from domestic consumers to those who obtain the right to import cloth.) The remaining areas, *b* and *e*, represent deadweight losses to society of the tariff (or quota). Clearly, the losses from the trade restrictions exceed the gains from the restrictions.

Arguments for Trade Restrictions

Arguments for trade restrictions are generally expressed in terms of national welfare. Proponents of trade restrictions justify them by using national defense, infant industry, and antidumping arguments. In recent years, proponents in the United States have argued that restrictions are needed to protect U.S. labor from cheap foreign labor. Wages in the United States are considerably higher than wages in many less developed nations, and those in favor of trade restrictions fear that U.S. labor cannot compete with the foreign labor. However, this argument ignores the reason for the higher U.S. wages: labor in the United States is more productive than labor in less developed nations. Thus, many goods can still be produced at lower cost in the United States.

IV. LAGNIAPPE

The Cost of Automobile Quotas

Robert Crandall attempted to estimate the cost to U.S. consumers of import quotas on Japanese autos. He calculated the difference between the average price of autos with the quotas and the average price without the quotas. He found that the quotas added approximately $235 to the price of a car in 1981 and 1982, and $829 in 1983. He also estimated the number of jobs saved in the U.S. auto industry because of quotas and concluded that the cost to consumers per job saved was nearly $160,000 per year.

(See Robert W. Crandall, "Import Quotas and the Automobile Industry: The Costs of Protection," *The Brookings Review*, Summer 1984: 8–16.)

Question to Think About: Can you think of ways to help auto workers that might be less expensive than using import quotas?

Economists, Tariffs, and Influence

George Stigler, a winner of the Nobel Prize in economics, has argued that the continued use of tariffs is proof that economists have no influence on policy. Since virtually all economists believe that free trade is preferable to protection and since all countries decide to protect a large portion of their economies, politicians must not be paying attention to economists.

Given that tariffs and quotas do more harm than good, why do they continue to be used? Free trade does not benefit all members of society. In particular, it harms those who work in industries that compete with lower-priced foreign goods. The owners and workers in the industries that face considerable competition from abroad lobby their representatives for help. Those who are harmed tend to be harmed a great deal, even though the number of people harmed may not be large relative to the total population. Consumers are major beneficiaries of free trade. However, each individual consumer receives relatively small benefits from free trade in any particular industry. Consumers are unlikely to lobby their representatives concerning tariff legislation. Consequently, the industry groups lobby harder than consumers, and the tariff legislation passes.

Question to Think About: Are there groups that might lobby effectively against tariffs?

V. KEY TERMS

Autarky

Terms of trade

World price

General Agreement on Tariffs and Trade (GATT)

Dumping

World Trade Organization (WTO)

VI. QUESTIONS

A. Completion

1. The two main types of imports to the United States are _____ and _____.

2. In the absence of trade, a country's production possibilities schedule is also its _____ possibilities schedule.

3. National self-sufficiency is called _____.

4. Trade is based on _____ advantage rather than on _____ advantage because gains can be made from specialization and trade whenever relative production costs of two goods in two countries differ.

5. The _____ must lie between the no-trade equilibrium prices in two countries.

6. The only constraint on trade is that, for each good, total world _____ must equal total world _____.

7. _____ is the difference between the actual sum producers receive for the quantity traded and the minimum sum they would accept for the quantity traded.

8. Countries can benefit from trade when there are differences in _____ or differences in tastes.

9. Countries can gain from trade if production is subject to _____ so that the per-unit cost of production falls as a country specializes in a good.

10. A tariff on oil of $10 a barrel is a(n) _____ tariff.

11. A(n) _____ is a legal limit on the quantity of a commodity that can be imported into a country.

12. Tariff reductions granted to one country must be granted to all other trading members of the World Trade Organization under the _____ clause.

13. Domestic firms may not find entry into an industry attractive if foreign producers are _____.

14. The _____ argument for trade restrictions views the restrictions as a temporary device for allowing domestic firms to achieve sufficient economies of scale.

15. The cost of protection includes the deadweight loss arising from the higher domestic prices and the cost of _____.

B. True/False

_____ 1. Foreign trade is more important to the United States than to most of the countries in western Europe.

_____ 2. The majority of U.S. imports are manufactured consumer goods.

_____ 3. Under autarky, each country can concentrate on producing those goods and services that involve the least opportunity costs.

_____ 4. A country can have a comparative advantage in all goods.

_____ 5. If wheat and cloth are the only goods under consideration and the production costs of wheat in terms of cloth are less in the United States than in mythical Izodia, then the production costs of cloth are less in Izodia than in the United States.

_____ 6. All countries can benefit if countries specialize in producing the goods for which they are the least-cost producers.

_____ 7. Market exchange usually benefits one country at the expense of the other country.

_____ 8. Differences in resource endowments generate differences in costs of production, which lead to trade.

_____ 9. A country will import a good for which the world price is above the domestic equilibrium price.

_____ 10. The gains from trade to an importing nation tend just to offset the losses from trade to an exporting nation, so the world is neither better nor worse off.

_____ 11. A tariff raises the price of the good to consumers, but a quota does not.

_____ 12. Tariff revenue represents a net loss to a society.

_____ 13. Each member of the World Trade Organization has agreed to treat all other member nations equally with respect to trade.

_____ 14. The effect of an import quota is to redistribute income from consumers to producers and to impose losses on consumers that are not transferred to anyone.

_____ 15. Consumers who are also taxpayers do better if government imposes a tariff than if it imposes an equivalent quota.

_____ 16. Regional trading blocs like NAFTA and the European Community are permitted by the rules of the World Trade Organization.

_____ 17. The infant industry argument for tariffs is an argument for temporary tariffs.

_____ 18. The Trade Agreement Act of 1979 prohibits only predatory dumping.

_____ 19. Using tariffs to protect domestic jobs often reduces trade and the gains from trade.

_____ 20. A tariff on steel likely will lead to pressure for a tariff on autos.

C.   Multiple Choice

1. The largest trading partner of the United States is
   a. Japan.
   b. Germany.
   c. Canada.
   d. Mexico.
   e. Great Britain.

Consider the following information in answering questions 2 through 7. A worker in the United States can produce either 8 computers or 6 motorcycles in a day; a worker in Japan can produce either 12 computers or 9 motorcycles in a day.

2. If there are 100 million workers in the United States, then the autarkic equilibrium will be
   a. 800 million computers and 600 million motorcycles produced and consumed.
   b. 400 million computers and 300 million motorcycles produced and consumed.
   c. 400 million computers and 600 million motorcycles produced and consumed.
   d. 800 million computers and 300 million motorcycles produced and consumed.
   e. The question cannot be answered without more information.

3. Which of the following is true?
   a. Japan has an absolute advantage in both goods and a comparative advantage in computers.
   b. Japan has an absolute advantage in both goods and a comparative advantage in neither good.
   c. Japan has an absolute advantage in both goods and a comparative advantage in motorcycles.
   d. Japan has an absolute and a comparative advantage in both goods.
   e. The United States has an absolute advantage in computers and a comparative advantage in motorcycles.

4. Which of the following is true?
   a. Japan will specialize in motorcycles because its opportunity cost of producing motor-cycles is less than the opportunity cost of producing motorcycles in the United States.
   b. Japan will specialize in computers because its opportunity cost of computers is less than the opportunity cost of computers in the United States.
   c. The opportunity cost of computers is the same in both countries, so there will be no specialization in trade.
   d. Japan will specialize in both computers and motorcycles because the cost of each is less in Japan than in the United States.
   e. none of the above

5. Suppose the conditions change so that a worker in Japan can now produce 15 motorcycles in a day. Under these conditions,
   a. Japan has a comparative advantage in computers.
   b. the opportunity cost of motorcycles in Japan is less than the opportunity cost of motorcycles in the United States.
   c. the United States has a comparative advantage in motorcycles.
   d. the cost of a motorcycle in Japan is 1.25 computers.
   e. a, c, and d

6. Given the change described in question 5,
   a. Japan has an absolute advantage in motorcycles but a comparative advantage in computers.
   b. Japan will export motorcycles and import computers.
   c. Japan will export computers and import motorcycles.
   d. there will be no trade.
   e. The question cannot be answered without more information.

7. Given the information in question 5, suppose the terms of trade are 1 computer in exchange for 0.8 motorcycle. We know that
    a. Japan's consumption possibilities frontier shifts farther out from its production possibilities frontier than does that of the United States.
    b. The United States' consumption possibilities frontier shifts farther out from its production possibilities frontier than does that of Japan.
    c. the consumption possibilities frontiers shift out by the same amount in both countries.
    d. both countries share equally in the gains from trade.
    e. both c and d

8. If all countries had an equal endowment of all resources,
    a. there would be no trade.
    b. trade would arise only from differences in taste or economies of scale.
    c. trade would depend on absolute advantage rather than comparative advantage.
    d. trade flows would be larger than they currently are.
    e. none of the above

9. Moving from autarky to free trade will generate
    a. increases in consumer surplus for consumers of the imported good.
    b. decreases in consumer surplus for consumers of the exported good.
    c. increases in producer surplus for the producers of the exported good.
    d. decreases in producer surplus for the producers of the imported good.
    e. all of the above.

10. If the domestic equilibrium price of wheat in the United States is $4 a bushel, then
    a. the United States will export wheat at any world price below $4.
    b. the United States will export wheat at any world price above $4.
    c. there will be an excess demand for wheat at any world price above $4, and this excess demand will be met by imports.
    d. a and c.
    e. none of the above. More information is necessary to answer the question.

Exhibit 5

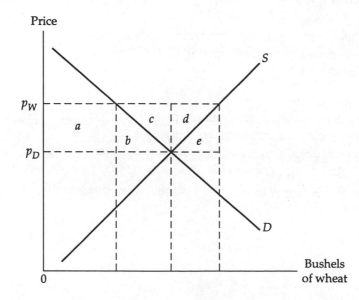

11. The world price for wheat in Exhibit 5 is p_W and the price in the United States is p_D. The loss to domestic consumers if trade occurs in the wheat market is represented by area(s)
   a.   *a.*
   b.   *a* and *b.*
   c.   *b.*
   d.   *b* and *c.*
   e.   *a, b,* and *c.*

12. The gain to domestic producers from trade is represented in Exhibit 5 by area(s)
   a.   *c.*
   b.   *d.*
   c.   *c* and *d.*
   d.   *a, b, c,* and *d.*
   e.   *e.*

13. In Exhibit 5, if the United States imposes a tariff equal to $p_W - p_D$,
   a.   trade will stop.
   b.   domestic producers will be harmed and domestic consumers will benefit.
   c.   domestic consumers will be harmed and domestic producers will benefit.
   d.   a and b
   e.   none of the above. The tariff will have no effect since the United States is exporting wheat.

14. In Exhibit 5, if the trading partner imposed a prohibitive tariff on wheat from the United States,
   a.   the gain to U.S. consumers of wheat would be greater than the loss to U.S. producers of wheat.
   b.   the gain to U.S. consumers of wheat would be less than the loss to U.S. producers of wheat.
   c.   the gain to U.S. consumers of wheat would exactly offset the losses to U.S. producers of wheat.
   d.   the gain to U.S. consumers of wheat would exactly offset the loss to U.S. consumers of whatever good had been imported from the trading partner.
   e.   The question cannot be answered without more information.

15. The net social loss of a tariff is greater,
   a.   the steeper the domestic supply curve.
   b.   the flatter the domestic demand curve.
   c.   the steeper the domestic demand curve.
   d.   the larger the tariff revenue the government receives.
   e.   all of the above except c

16. An import quota differs from a tariff in that
   a.   a quota does not affect the domestic price of a commodity.
   b.   a quota does not harm consumers the way a tariff does.
   c.   a quota encourages increased domestic production more than a tariff does.
   d.   a tariff generates revenue to the government but a quota does not.
   e.   a tariff harms all consumers of the commodity; a quota harms only those who cannot obtain as much of the commodity as they would like.

17. Japanese auto producers would prefer
    a. a tariff on their cars rather than a quota because tariffs tend to be removed before quotas.
    b. a tariff on their cars rather than a quota because tariffs do not cost the exporter as much.
    c. a quota on their cars rather than a tariff because quotas generate extra profits for the exporter.
    d. a quota on their cars rather than a tariff because quotas tend to be reversed faster.
    e. none of the above.

18. Suppose it costs a U.S. steel company $20 a ton to produce steel, it costs a Japanese firm $15 a ton, the domestic price of steel in Japan is $18, and the domestic price in the United States is $22. Japanese firms would be dumping if they charged U.S. firms
    a. any price below $22.
    b. any price below $20.
    c. any price below $18.
    d. any price below $15.
    e. none of the above.

19. Low wages in developing countries indicate that
    a. U.S. workers cannot compete with workers in developing countries.
    b. the United States cannot have a comparative advantage in any product produced by developing countries.
    c. the standard of living of U.S. workers must fall in order for them to compete with workers from developing countries.
    d. all of the above
    e. none of the above

20. One problem with trade restrictions is that
    a. policing and enforcing restrictions is costly.
    b. they do not last long enough to have the beneficial effects they are designed to provide.
    c. they tend to be imposed in inefficient ways (i.e., tariffs tend to be used instead of more efficient quotas).
    d. the national defense argument is not used for some industries vital to the defense of the country.
    e. all of the above

D. Discussion Questions

1. What additional information is needed to answer multiple choice question 2?

2. How can two countries both be better off as a result of trade?

3. Suppose that a worker in Brazil can produce 10 units of coffee and 6 units of cloth per day, and a worker in the United States can produce 5 units of coffee and 5 units of cloth. Brazil has 500 workers; the United States has 1,000 workers.
   a. What is the opportunity cost of cloth in Brazil? in the United States?
   b. What is the opportunity cost of coffee in Brazil? in the United States?
   c. Which country has a comparative advantage in producing coffee? in producing cloth?
   d. Draw production possibilities frontiers for both Brazil and the United States, with cloth on the horizontal axis. What is the slope of Brazil's production possibilities frontier? What is the slope of the production possibilities frontier for the United States?
   e. If the United States and Brazil trade, which country will export coffee and which will export cloth? At what rate will trade take place?
   f. Show on your graph the gains from trade for both countries for one set of prices that would lead to trade.

4. If the terms of trade in question 3 are 1.01 units of coffee for 1 unit of cloth, which country receives a larger share of the gains from trade? How do you know?

5. The United States both imports and exports autos. Which of the explanations for international specialization explains this?

6. Why do differences in resource endowments lead to trade?

7. How does an ad valorem tariff differ from a specific tariff?

8. Suppose a $10 shirt is subject to a $1 specific tariff and a $10 blouse is subject to a 10 percent ad valorem tariff. If the prices of both goods double, what happens to the tariff on each good?

9. What is an import tariff? What are the effects of a tariff? Use a graph to illustrate your answers.

10. What is an import quota? What are the effects of an effective quota? Use the same graph you used for question 10 to illustrate your answers to this question.

11. How can tariffs protect U.S. jobs? Do tariffs lead to a net increase in jobs? Explain.

12. Explain why true/false question 16 is false.

13. What are some of the problems associated with trade restrictions?

14. Explain why true/false question 20 is true.

15. Who are the winners and losers from trade restrictions? Given that trade restrictions impose losses on an economy, why are trade restrictions so common?

VII. ANSWERS

A. Completion

1. manufactured consumer goods; capital goods
2. consumption
3. autarky
4. comparative; absolute
5. terms of trade
6. production; consumption
7. Producer surplus
8. resource endowments
9. economies of scale
10. specific
11. import quota
12. most-favored-nation
13. dumping
14. infant industry
15. rent seeking

B. True/False

1. False. Trade as a percent of GDP is less for the United States than for the western European countries.
2. True
3. False
4. False
5. True
6. True
7. False
8. True
9. False. The country will export goods whose world price exceeds the domestic equilibrium price.
10. False
11. False
12. False
13. True
14. True
15. True
16. False
17. True
18. False
19. True
20. True

C. Multiple Choice

1. c
2. e
3. b
4. c
5. b
6. b
7. a
8. b
9. e
10. b
11. b
12. d
13. e
14. b
15. b
16. d
17. c
18. c
19. e
20. a

D. Discussion Questions

1. Information concerning the tastes of the citizens is needed in order to determine which part of the production possibilities frontier the autarkic equilibrium will lie on.

2. Two countries can be better off as a result of trade if their opportunity costs of producing the goods being traded differ. Different opportunity costs imply that relative prices in the two countries are different, which means that each country can gain if it produces the good for which its opportunity cost is lowest and buys the other good from the other country.

3. a. $^{10}/_6$, or $1^2/_3$, units of coffee; 1 unit of coffee
    b. 0. 6 units of cloth; 1 unit of cloth
    c. Brazil has a comparative advantage in producing coffee and the United States in producing cloth. That is, the opportunity cost of coffee is lower in Brazil than it is in the United States, and the opportunity cost of cloth is lower in the United States than it is in Brazil.
    d. The slope of Brazil's PPF is $-^{10}/_6$ (or $^5/_3$) and the slope of the United States' PPF is -1. (See the exhibit.)

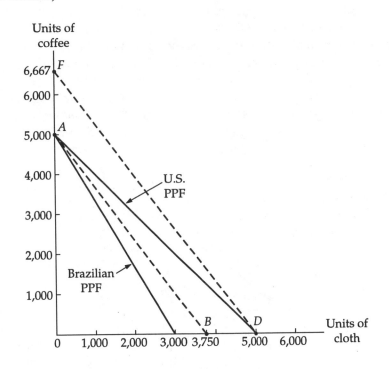

    e. Brazil will export coffee and the United States will export cloth. The rate at which trade will take place lies between 1 and $^{10}/_6$ units of coffee for 1 unit of cloth.
    f. Refer again to the graph. At a rate of exchange of 4 units of coffee for 3 units of cloth, each country's consumption possibilities frontier is farther from the origin than its PPF. (Brazil's consumption possibilities curve is line *AB* and the United States' is line *DF*, assuming Brazil specializes in the production of coffee and the United States specializes in the production of cloth.)

4. Brazil will receive larger gains from trade. The terms of trade imply a very large shift of Brazil's consumption possibilities frontier, whereas the consumption possibilities frontier for the United States lies very close to its production possibilities frontier.

5. A combination of economies of scale and different tastes help explain this. If most people in the United States want larger cars and most people in Japan want smaller cars, then it makes sense for U.S. auto firms to make large cars to satisfy their domestic market and for Japanese firms to make small cars. Those Japanese who want large cars then can import them from the United States.

6. Differences in endowments of resources lead to differences in opportunity costs of production, which lead to trade.

7. A specific tariff is an amount per unit of the good; an ad valorem tariff is a percent of the price.

8. At the initial prices, the tariffs are equivalent. If prices double, the ad valorem tariff doubles because it is based on the price of the good. The specific tariff remains $1, so the price of the shirt is now $21, whereas the price of the blouse is $22.

9. A tariff is a tax on imports. A tariff raises the domestic price of an imported good. The graph shows that 245 units of a good are purchased when the world price is p_W; of these, 30 are produced domestically. Hence, imports are 215 units. A tariff of T per unit raises the domestic price to $p_W + T$. At this price, quantity demanded drops to 200 units, domestic producers supply 85 of them, and imports fall to 115 units (200 – 85). Area a represents a transfer of surplus from consumers to producers, areas c plus d represent the revenue raised by the tariff, and areas b and e represent net social losses from the tariff.

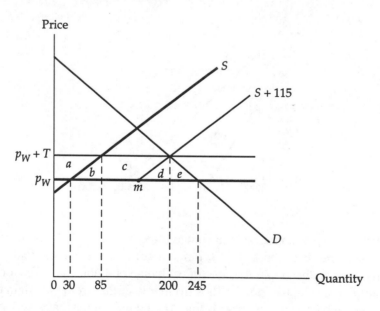

10.   An import quota is a limit on the number of units of a good that can enter a country. A quota of 115 units generates the same results as the tariff of T. The relevant supply curve is $S + 115$ (see the graph in answer 10). With a quota, price increases from p_W to $p_W + T$, and imports are at 115 units. The revenue shown by areas c plus d no longer flows to the government but instead is a transfer from consumers to firms that obtain the right to import the good.

11.   In the graph in answer 10, the tariff was shown to increase domestic production of the good from 30 to 85 units. This increase in production creates jobs for people in the industry. However, the tariff does not necessarily create a net increase in jobs. If we buy fewer imports we usually sell fewer exports, so some people may lose their jobs in the export industries.

12.   Trading blocs violate the World Trade Organization provision that requires all members treat all the other members equally with respect to trade. Trade blocs require an exemption from the rules.

13.   Protecting one industry often requires protecting other industries. For example, protecting the textile industry raises the price of textiles for the clothing industry, which may in turn require protection because of its higher costs. Since protection creates higher profits for domestic firms, firms may lobby for protection; the resources expended on lobbying are also lost to the economy. Further, it is often difficult to police and enforce trade restrictions.

14.   The higher price of steel raises costs to U.S. auto makers, which will lead to a higher price for domestic autos and more imports. This may lead the auto makers to lobby for a tariff or quota on autos.

15.   The winners are the domestic producers of goods that compete with imports (and their employees), who receive higher prices as a result of trade restrictions. With an import quota, those to whom the quota is allocated are also winners. The losers are consumers, domestic producers who use imported intermediate goods, and producers (and their employees) in export industries, especially if other countries respond to tariffs by instituting tariffs of their own. Firms facing stiff competition from trade are obviously harmed a great deal by the competition, so they have a strong incentive to lobby Congress for protection. Consumers are harmed by protection, but no single consumer is harmed enough to make it worth his or her while to lobby against a tariff bill. Hence, Congress is likely to pass a given trade restriction bill.

CHAPTER 33

International Finance

I. INTRODUCTION

Exchange between people in different countries usually requires at least one of the traders to use the currency of the other country. International finance deals with the markets for the currencies of countries and the arrangements involving international payments. This chapter examines the payment mechanism that is currently in use as well as some mechanisms that were used in the past. We will also discuss the balance of payments accounts.

II. OUTLINE

1. Balance of Payments. A *balance of payments* is a summary statement reflecting all economic transactions that occur during a year between residents of one country and residents of all other countries.

    1.1 International Economic Transactions
        a. The *balance of payments* measures the volume of transactions that occur during a particular period of time; it is a flow measure.
        b. Some transactions do not involve payments of money but are still included in the balance of payments.
        c. Balance-of-payments accounts are maintained according to the principles of double-entry bookkeeping.

    1.2 Merchandise Trade Balance
        a. The *merchandise trade balance* measures the difference in the value of a country's exports of merchandise and its imports of merchandise.
        b. The United States had a merchandise trade deficit throughout the 1980s and 1990s.
        c. When the economy expands, spending on all goods, including imports, increases.

    1.3 Balance on Goods and Services
        a. *Services* are intangible goods, such as banking, insurance services, and tourism.
        b. The *balance on goods and services* measures the difference in the value of a country's exports of goods and services and its imports of goods and services.

    1.4 Unilateral Transfers
        a. Transfers and gifts to foreigners from domestic residents or from the government are called *unilateral transfers*.
        b. The *balance on current account* equals net unilateral transfers plus exports of goods and services minus imports of goods and services.

1.5   Capital Account
   a.   The *capital account* records transactions involving the purchase or sale of financial assets.
   b.   U.S. capital inflows reflect foreign purchases of U.S. assets, and U.S. capital outflows reflect purchases of foreign assets by Americans.
   c.   The U.S. capital account is in surplus if U.S. residents sell more assets to foreigners than they buy from foreigners.
   d.   The United States was a net capital exporter in the past but is now a net capital importer.
   e.   The *official reserve transactions* account shows the net amount of international reserves that must be shifted among central banks to settle international transactions.

1.6   Statistical Discrepancy
   a.   Some international transactions go unreported, so the total of debits often does not equal the total of credits.
   b.   The account called the *statistical discrepancy* is used to equalize the total of debits and the total of credits.

1.7   Deficits and Surpluses
   a.   A deficit in a country's current account means that its foreign exchange earnings from its exports are less than the foreign exchange it needs to pay for its imports plus net unilateral transfers.
   b.   Any surplus or deficit in the current account must be offset by other changes in the balance-of-payments account.
   c.   When all transactions are considered, the balance of payments must balance.

2.   Foreign Exchange Rates and Markets

2.1   Foreign Exchange
   a.   The *exchange rate* is the price of one country's currency in terms of another country's currency.
   b.   *Foreign exchange* is the currency of another country needed to carry out international transactions.
   c.   The foreign exchange incorporates all the arrangements used to buy and sell foreign exchange. It is always open since some trading center is always open somewhere in the world.
   d.   An increase in the number of dollars needed to purchase a unit of currency of another country indicates a depreciation of the dollar, and a decrease in the number of dollars needed indicates an appreciation of the dollar.

2.2   Demand for Foreign Exchange
   a.   People must have foreign currency to buy goods or services from foreign countries, to purchase foreign assets, and the like.
   b.   The demand for foreign exchange is related to the demand for foreign goods and services.
   c.   The demand curve for foreign exchange slopes downward. A decrease in the exchange rate decreases the price of foreign goods for domestic residents, which in turn increases the quantity of foreign goods demanded.

2.3   Supply of Foreign Exchange
       a.   The supply of foreign exchange to the market defined in terms of dollars is generated by the desire of foreign residents to buy dollars.
       b.   An increase in the dollar-per-foreign-currency exchange rate makes U.S. products cheaper to foreigners, so the foreigners increase the quantity demanded of U.S. goods and services.
       c.   The increased demand for U.S. goods and services usually means an increase in the quantity supplied of foreign exchange, so the supply curve for foreign exchange slopes up.

2.4   Determining the Exchange Rate
       a.   The exchange rate is determined at the intersection of the demand curve for foreign exchange and the supply curve for foreign exchange.
       b.   In an international monetary system based on flexible exchange rates, the exchange rate will vary with changes in domestic or foreign income levels, expected inflation rates, price levels, interest rates, and consumer preferences.

2.5   Arbitrageurs and Speculators
       a.   An *arbitrageur* buys a currency in markets where the price is low and immediately sells it in markets where the price is higher.
       b.   Arbitrage assures that any discrepancies between exchange rates across markets will be eliminated quickly.
       c.   *Speculators* buy and sell foreign exchange at the current exchange rate in hopes of profiting by buying or selling it at a different exchange rate later.

2.6   Purchasing Power Parity
       a.   The *purchasing power parity theory* predicts that under free trade and floating exchange rates, exchange rates between two nations will adjust to reflect differences in the price levels of the two nations.
       b.   The purchasing power parity theory is a theory of the long-run relationship between the price level and the exchange rate.

2.7   *CASE STUDY:* The Big Mac Price Index

2.8   Flexible Exchange Rates
       a.   *Flexible*, or *floating*, *exchange rates* adjust to the forces that affect the foreign exchange market.
       b.   Wild swings in exchange rates have forced policymakers to consider alternatives.

2.9   Fixed Exchange Rates
       a.   *Fixed exchange rates* are rates that are set at some specific level by government.
       b.   Government central banks must intervene in foreign exchange markets to maintain the fixed exchange rate.

3. Development of the International Monetary System. The gold standard prevailed from 1879 to 1914. The gold standard provided a stable exchange rate but generated inflation or deflation whenever gold production varied substantially.

   3.1 The Bretton Woods Agreement
      a. The Bretton Woods Agreement established a system of fixed exchange rates that lasted from 1945 to 1971.
      b. The U.S. dollar was the key reserve currency, and all other exchange rates were fixed in terms of the dollar.
      c. The United States was ready to convert dollars to gold or gold to dollars at a fixed rate.
      d. The Bretton Woods Agreement created the International Monetary Fund and the World Bank.

   3.2 Demise of the Bretton Woods System
      a. In the late 1960s, the dollar was overvalued and foreigners were demanding gold from the United States.
      b. In 1971, the United States refused to exchange gold for dollars, and the dollar was devalued. The Bretton Woods system ended in 1973 when West Germany stopped defending the dollar.

   3.3 The Current System: Managed Float
      a. The current system involves floating exchange rates among the world's major currencies but allows substantial intervention by the central banks of many countries.
      b. Some countries try to tie their currencies together. Many smaller countries continue to peg their exchange rates.
      c. Criticisms of flexible exchange rates:
         (1) They are inflationary.
         (2) They are often very volatile.

   3.4 *CASE STUDY:* The Asian Contagion

III. DISCUSSION

Balance of Payments

A country's *balance of payments* is a summary statement that reflects all economic transactions between residents of that country and residents of the rest of the world. Balance-of-payments accounts use double-entry bookkeeping, which means that one side of the ledger reflects assets and the other liabilities. Further, the total of all liabilities must equal the total of all assets. Thus, the balance of payments is always in balance. An outflow of payments is entered as a debit, and an inflow of payments is entered as a credit.

Exhibit 1 provides balance of payments data for the United States for 1998. Total debits equal total credits, so the overall balance is zero. However, the total of debits at any point above the "bottom line" may exceed or fall short of the total of credits. That is, portions of the balance of payments may be in deficit and other portions in surplus during any particular year. In 1998, the *merchandise trade balance* was in deficit (merchandise exports – merchandise imports = 671.0 – 919.0 = –248.0), but the service account was in surplus (service exports – service imports = 503.0 – 446.6 = 56.4). The *balance on goods and services* ran a deficit of $191.6 billion. The *balance on current account* was also in deficit. Given the nature of double-entry bookkeeping, a deficit in the current account plus a debit entry in the statistical discrepancy implies that private plus government capital inflows must exceed private plus government capital outflows. In 1998, this was the case because foreign purchases of U.S. assets exceeded U.S. purchases of foreign assets by almost $226.8 billion.

Exhibit 1

U.S. Balance of Payments, 1998
(billions of dollars)

Item	
Current Account	
1. Merchandise exports	671.0
2. Merchandise imports	−919.0
3. Trade balance (1 + 2)	−248.0
4. Service exports	503.0
5. Service imports	−446.6
6. Goods and services balance (3 + 4 + 5)	−191.6
7. Net unilateral transfers	−41.9
8. Current account balance (6 + 7)	−233.5
Capital Account	
9. Outflow of U.S. capital	−297.8
10. Inflow of foreign capital	546.6
11. Capital account balance (9 + 10)	266.8
Official Reserve Transactions Account	
12. Change in U.S. official assets abroad	−7.6
13. Change in foreign official assets in U.S.	−22.1
14. Official reserve balance (12 + 13)	−29.7
15. Statistical Discrepancy	−3.6
TOTAL (8 + 11 + 14 + 15)	**0.0**

Source: *Survey of Current Business*, U.S. Department of Commerce, April 1999.

Foreign Exchange Rates and Markets

Foreign exchange is the currency of another country needed to carry out international transactions. Foreign exchange can be bought in foreign exchange markets. The price is called the *exchange rate* and can be expressed in two ways. First, the exchange rate can be expressed as the domestic currency price for a unit of the foreign currency. Second, the exchange rate can be expressed as the foreign currency price for a unit of the domestic currency. The two exchange rates are reciprocals. That is, if the U.S. dollar price of one French franc is $1.50, then the French franc price of a dollar is 1/1.50, or 0.67 franc.

The foreign exchange market includes the whole world. It consists of a network of telephone and other communication systems that connect large banks in all the major cities. If the exchange rate between the dollar and the franc in Tokyo differs from the exchange rate between the two currencies in New York, then *arbitrageurs* will buy the currency that is relatively cheap in Tokyo and sell it in New York. Because of arbitrage, exchange rates tend to be the same all over the world.

Consider the market for German marks in terms of U.S. dollars. Americans do not desire marks, or other foreign exchange, for the currencies themselves. Instead, they demand foreign exchange because they wish to buy goods or services from foreign countries. Residents of a foreign country want to be paid in their own currency rather than in dollars. Thus, Americans wishing to buy products from Germany must obtain German marks, and Germans who wish to buy U.S. products must obtain dollars. An increase in demand for foreign goods and services causes a greater demand for foreign exchange. The demand curve for foreign exchange slopes down because at lower exchange rates, other things constant, the dollar price of foreign goods and services falls, Americans buy more goods and services from foreigners, and the quantity of foreign exchange demanded rises. When Americans are demanding foreign exchange, they are also supplying dollars to foreign exchange markets. Hence, in general, the supply of foreign exchange is determined by foreigners wishing to buy dollars. The quantity of foreign exchange supplied to foreign exchange markets usually increases as the exchange rate (defined in dollars) increases. The exchange rate is determined by the intersection of the demand curve for foreign exchange and the supply curve of foreign exchange. The curves are drawn holding other things constant, including domestic and foreign income levels, price levels, interest rates, and expected inflation rates.

Exchange rates are flexible when the exchange rate is determined by supply and demand in the marketplace. Exchange rates are fixed when they are set by the government, and central banks intervene in markets to keep rates fixed. Central banks must have a supply of other currencies, especially reserve currencies, to sell in order to keep the exchange rate fixed when the quantity demanded of the foreign currency exceeds the quantity supplied at the fixed rate.

Development of the International Monetary System

The international monetary system operated on a *gold standard* from 1879 to 1914. The currencies of all countries were defined in terms of gold, and each country agreed to buy or sell gold at fixed rates. The gold system meant that exchange rates were fixed, but each country's money supply was determined by the flow of gold between countries. World War I and the Great Depression brought about the end of the gold standard.

After World War II, the international monetary system operated under the Bretton Woods Agreement. The U.S. dollar was defined in terms of gold, and all other currencies were defined in terms of the dollar. The United States agreed to buy or sell gold at the predetermined rate; countries in the rest of the world used dollars as their reserve currency. For example, under the Bretton Woods system, the French central bank could send British pounds to the Bank of England and receive dollars. In the late 1960s, the dollar became overvalued, and many countries were turning dollars in for gold. The United States stopped converting dollars to gold in 1971. The Bretton Woods system collapsed in 1973, and major world economies moved to a managed float system, which allows for occasional central bank intervention to moderate fluctuations in floating exchange rates.

IV. LAGNIAPPE

Exchange Rate Changes and Prices

Suppose the U.S. dollar price of a euro is $1.05 and that a German automobile costs 20,000 euros. The dollar price of the car is thus $21,000. Now, if the dollar depreciates against the euro so that the dollar price of a euro rises to $1.155, the price of the car rises to $23,100. On the other hand, if the dollar appreciates and the price of the euro moves to $0.945, the price of the car will be $18,900. A 10 percent change in the exchange rate, other things constant, leads to a 10 percent change in the dollar price of German goods. When the price of the euro falls, German goods are cheaper for Americans, but if the price of the euro rises, German goods are more expensive.

Question to Think About: What happens to the price of U.S. goods in Germany when the price of a mark rises or falls?

The Gold Standard

The gold standard is appealing to some people because it gives politicians no discretionary authority in determining monetary policy. Advocates of a gold standard argue that the current system tends to be inflationary. For a gold standard to be effective, all major nations must use the system and define their currencies in terms of gold. Suppose the United States defines $1 to be equal to $1/35$th ounce of gold, and Germany defines the mark as $1/70$th ounce of gold. Then an ounce of gold costs either $35 or 70 marks, which means that $1 equals two marks. If Americans increase their purchases of German goods, dollars go to Germany. The Germans can then turn the dollars in to the Federal Reserve System in exchange for gold. Since the U.S. money stock is tied to the quantity of gold held by the Fed, the money stock falls. In the long run, the lower money stock implies lower prices. If U.S. prices fall relative to German prices, U.S. products should be relatively more attractive. The gold standard provides an automatic adjustment mechanism.

Question to Think About: If we return to the gold standard, what should the price of gold be in dollars?

V. KEY TERMS

Balance on goods and services
Net unilateral transfers
Balance on current account
Capital account
Official reserve transactions account
Exchange rate
Currency depreciation
Currency appreciation
Arbitrageur

Speculator
Purchasing power parity (PPP) theory
Flexible exchange rates
Fixed exchange rates
Currency devaluation
Currency revaluation
Gold standard
International Monetary Fund
Managed float system

VI. QUESTIONS

A. Completion

1. Because the balance of payments measures the volume of transactions over a particular time period, it measures a _____.

2. Balance of payments accounts utilize the principles of _____ bookkeeping.

3. The _____ trade balance involves trade in tangible products.

4. A trade _____ exists when the value of merchandise exports exceeds the value of merchandise imports.

5. The demand for imports usually _____ when the economy is expanding.

6. A gift to a friend living abroad is a(n) _____.

7. A nation has a _____ when its outflow of payments exceeds its inflow of receipts for transactions in currently produced goods and services plus net unilateral transfers.

8. An initial debit entry in a country's current account will generate some sort of offsetting _____ entry in the balance of payments.

9. International investments and borrowing are _____ transfers.

10. The currency of another country needed to carry out international transactions is known as _____.

11. A currency undergoes _____ when more units of the currency are needed to buy foreign exchange.

12. Exchange rates are almost always equal at different places around the country because of _____.

13. _____ are people who buy and sell foreign exchange in hopes of profiting from fluctuations over time in exchange rates.

14. The International Monetary Fund was created by the _____.

15. The current international monetary system is known as a _____.

B. True/False

_____ 1. In balance of payments terminology, "residents" refers to individuals and families only.

_____ 2. To be included in balance-of-payments accounts, a payment must be made in money.

_____ 3. Balance-of-payments accounting requires that the total of debits equal the total of credits.

_____ 4. The trade deficit tends to increase when the economy expands.

_____ 5. The merchandise trade balance includes unilateral transfers.

_____ 6. The hotel bill of an English tourist in San Francisco is listed as a credit in the U.S. balance of payments and a debit in the United Kingdom's balance of payments.

_____ 7. The capital account records transactions involving purchases or sales of assets.

_____ 8. A trade deficit indicates that the value of merchandise imports exceeds the value of merchandise exports.

_____ 9. The United States is the world's largest debtor nation.

10. The rate of exchange between the U.S. dollar and the German mark can be expressed as either the number of dollars per mark or the number of marks per dollar.

_____ 11. The foreign exchange market is located in New York City.

_____ 12. Appreciation of the dollar occurs when fewer dollars are needed to buy foreign exchange.

_____ 13. Exchange rates tend to change in all markets by the same amount simultaneously.

_____ 14. An appreciation of the dollar can cause the quantity demanded of foreign exchange to increase.

_____ 15. The supply of foreign exchange in the United States is generated by the desire of foreign residents to buy dollars.

_____ 16. An increase in the demand by U.S. residents for foreign exchange leads to a depreciation of the dollar, other things constant.

_____ 17. In the long run, economic theory predicts that exchange rates between two national currencies will reflect the price level differences in the two countries.

_____ 18. Monetary authorities maintain fixed exchange rates by fixing the supply of money.

_____ 19. Under the Bretton Woods Agreement, the U.S. dollar was the key reserve currency in the international monetary system.

_____ 20. Central banks do not intervene in foreign exchange markets today.

C. Multiple Choice

1. Which of the following represent international economic transactions that must be included in the balance of payments?
   a. A family that recently immigrated sends money to other family members in its home country.
   b. A corporate executive flies to London on a French airline.
   c. The U.S. government gives wheat to India.
   d. all of the above
   e. a and b only

2. The balance of payments accounts use double-entry bookkeeping, which implies that
   a. a country cannot run a perpetual deficit in its balance of merchandise trade.
   b. balance of payments figures cannot be used to tell anything about the economic strength of a nation.
   c. each account must be in balance every year.
   d. changes in exchange rates cannot affect balance-of-payments accounts.
   e. the total must always be in balance, but different accounts can be in deficit or surplus.

3. Which of the following transactions would not be included in the merchandise trade balance?
   a. IBM sells $10 million worth of computers to Mexico.
   b. GM buys spark plugs from a Canadian firm.
   c. The CEO of a German firm flies on an American airline to New York.
   d. An American subscribes to the German magazine *Die Zeit*.
   e. All would be included in the merchandise trade balance.

4. Which of the following would generate a credit in the U.S. balance of payments?
   a. An American tourist in London buys a cup of coffee.
   b. A Mexican citizen working in Texas sends money to her family in Mexico.
   c. An American buys a Toyota.
   d. all of the above
   e. none of the above

5. A U.S. capital outflow results when
   a. Americans purchase foreign assets.
   b. Americans sell foreign assets.
   c. Americans sell capital goods to foreigners.
   d. foreigners buy U.S. assets.
   e. none of the above

6. Which of the following is not part of official reserves?
   a. gold
   b. dollars
   c. yen
   d. special drawing rights
   e. none of the above. All are part of official reserves.

7. If the United States is running a current account deficit, it can acquire additional reserves by
   a. Americans' buying foreign bonds.
   b. Americans' buying foreign stocks.
   c. borrowing from foreigners.
   d. all of the above.
   e. a and b only.

8. In the U.S. balance of payments in recent years,
   a. the net outflow of capital has offset the deficit in the current account.
   b. the current account has had a smaller deficit than the capital account.
   c. there is evidence that the United States has been a less attractive place to invest than many other countries.
   d. the net inflow of capital has offset the deficit in the current account.
   e. the net inflow of capital has increased the deficit in the balance of goods and services.

9. In order to reduce foreign claims on U.S. assets, it is necessary to
   a. increase the sale of U.S. assets to foreigners.
   b. increase imports of foreign goods and services.
   c. increase net exports of goods and services.
   d. increase the gold stock held by the Fed.
   e. none of the above

10. If the price of one British pound is $3, the price of one dollar is
    a. 3 pounds.
    b. 2 pounds.
    c. 0.5 pound.
    d. 0.33 pound.
    e. The question cannot be answered without more information.

11. Which of the following might demand foreign exchange?
    a. consumers
    b. investors
    c. speculators
    d. arbitrageurs
    e. all of the above

12. The demand for British pounds would decrease when
    a. the pound depreciated.
    b. the pound appreciated.
    c. the demand for imports increased in Britain.
    d. the foreign demand for British goods decreased.
    e. the supply of pounds increased.

13. The supply of U.S. dollars in the foreign exchange market comes from
    a. foreigners who want gold.
    b. foreigners who want to purchase U.S. goods.
    c. foreigners who want dollars.
    d. Americans who demand foreign exchange.
    e. none of the above.

14. Under flexible exchange rates, an increase in the demand for marks by Americans will
    a. also cause an increase in the supply of dollars.
    b. cause the price of marks to increase.
    c. cause the mark price of the dollar to fall.
    d. cause the mark to appreciate.
    e. all of the above

15. Under fixed exchange rates, an increase in the demand for marks by Americans will
    a. cause the Fed to buy marks.
    b. cause the German central bank to buy marks.
    c. cause the dollar to appreciate.
    d. cause the Fed to buy dollars.
    e. b and d

16. If the price of one pound is $3.00 in New York and $3.10 in London, arbitrageurs will
    a. buy dollars in New York and sell them in London.
    b. buy pounds in New York and sell them in London.
    c. simultaneously buy pounds in both New York and London.
    d. not do anything, because the difference is only 10 cents.
    e. speculate by buying pounds and holding them.

17. If the German mark and the French franc are in long-run equilibrium at DM = 1 Fr and then French domestic prices increase by 50 percent while German prices remain constant, the new long-run equilibrium exchange rate will be
   a. 1 DM = 1 Fr.
   b. 1 DM = 2 Fr.
   c. 1 DM = 0.5 Fr.
   d. 1 Fr = 0.2 DM.
   e. both b and d.

18. Under a gold standard, a balance-of-payments deficit in a given country would ultimately lead to
   a. a change in the price of gold in the country.
   b. an inflow of gold.
   c. a fall in the price level in the country.
   d. a deficit in the country's capital account.
   e. none of the above.

19. Special Drawing Rights are a substitute for
   a. gold.
   b. dollars.
   c. pounds.
   d. yen.
   e. long-term bonds.

20. The current international monetary system is characterized by
   a. fixed exchange rates.
   b. freely fluctuating exchange rates.
   c. a gold exchange standard.
   d. both floating and managed exchange rates.
   e. a commodity standard.

D. Discussion Questions

1. If merchandise exports equal $50, merchandise imports equal $50, net unilateral transfers equal –$10, and both the capital account and the statistical discrepancy are zero, what is the balance on goods and services?

2. If the balance on goods and services is –$40, net unilateral transfers are –$5, official reserve transactions are zero, and the statistical discrepancy is zero, what is the current account balance and what is the capital account balance?

3. Why can't all the balance of payments accounts be in surplus?

4. Would relatively high interest rates in the United States cause a U.S. capital inflow or a U.S. capital outflow? Why?

5. Suppose the exchange rate between the British pound and the U.S. dollar is $1.64 per pound and the exchange rate between the dollar and the German mark is $0.55.
    a. What would be the dollar price of a German camera that sells for 650 marks?
    b. What would be the price in pounds of a U.S.-made personal computer that sells for $2,200?
    c. What would be the pound price of the German camera?

6. Suppose the exchange rate between the U.S. dollar and the mark is $0.55 in New York and $0.57 in Frankfurt. How would arbitrageurs profit by this difference?

7. What factors determine the demand for marks in foreign exchange markets?

8. What determines the supply of marks in foreign exchange markets?

9. How are exchange rates determined under a flexible exchange rate system?

10. What does the purchasing power parity theory predict about equilibrium exchange rates?

11. Suppose a fixed exchange rate is in effect, and the exchange rate between the dollar and the mark is $0.55, with a two-cent margin on either side permitted. What actions will authorities take to maintain the exchange rate if the demand for marks increases? if the demand for dollars increases?

12. Suppose a fixed exchange rate is in effect. What problem is likely to develop if the equilibrium exchange rate continually remains above the pegged rate? How can the government eliminate the disequilibrium at the pegged rate?

13. How did the Bretton Woods system operate? What caused its collapse?

14. The fixed exchange rate system under the Bretton Woods Agreement had an asymmetry that forced deficit countries to respond to a disequilibrium faster than surplus countries. Can you explain why this was so? (*Hint*: What is used to pay for a deficit?)

15. Explain why the correct answer to multiple choice question 18 is c.

VII. ANSWERS

A. Completion

1.	flow	9.	capital
2.	double-entry	10.	foreign exchange
3.	merchandise	11.	depreciation
4.	surplus	12.	arbitrage
5.	increases	13.	Speculators
6.	unilateral transfer	14.	Bretton Woods Agreement
7.	current account deficit	15.	managed float system
8.	credit		

B. True/False

1. False
2. False
3. True
4. True
5. False. Unilateral transfers are included in the current account.
6. True
7. True
8. True
9. True
10. True
11. False
12. True
13. True
14. True
15. True
16. True
17. True
18. False
19. True
20. False

C. Multiple Choice

1. d
2. e
3. c
4. e
5. a
6. e
7. c
8. d
9. c
10. d
11. e
12. d
13. d
14. e
15. d
16. b
17. b
18. c
19. a
20. d

D. Discussion Questions

1. The merchandise trade balance, the current account, and the capital account are all in balance. Since the net unilateral transfers equal –$10, imports of services must be $10 less than exports of services, so the balance of goods and services has a $10 surplus.

2. The current account balance equals the balance on goods and services plus net unilateral transfers; thus, the current account balance is –$45. The capital account balance must offset the current account balance, so it must equal $45.

3. If all accounts were in surplus, the total would have to be in surplus too. This cannot happen under a double-entry bookkeeping system.

4. High interest rates in the United States would cause a capital inflow. Foreign investors would seek the high return in the United States and buy U.S. financial instruments. (This assumes the high interest rates are not due to expected higher inflation rates in the United States.)

5. a. 650 marks x $0.55/mark = $357.50
   b. $2,200/1.64 = 1,341.46 pounds
   c. $357.50 x 0.61 pound/dollar = 218.08 pounds

6. An arbitrageur could use $1,000 to buy 1,818.18 marks in New York and then immediately sell the 1,818.18 marks in Frankfurt and receive $1,036.36, making a profit of $36.36 for every $1,000.00. These actions would help equalize the exchange rates in the two cities.

7. The demand for marks is determined by the foreign demand for German products by producers and consumers (including Americans who travel to Germany), the foreign demand for German assets, cash gifts from foreign residents to German residents, and the like. Demand is also determined by speculators who hope to profit by exchange-rate changes in the future and arbitrageurs who hope to profit from differences in exchange rates across markets.

8. The supply of marks is determined by the demand for foreign exchange, such as dollars, in Germany. That is, it is determined by the German demand for foreign goods and services, foreign assets, and the like.

9. Exchange rates are determined by the interaction of supply and demand for foreign exchange. The demand for foreign exchange depends on the demand for imports and the demand for financial securities denominated in other currencies. The supply of foreign exchange depends on the demand of foreigners for U.S. export goods and services.

10. According to the purchasing power parity theory, as long as trade across borders is unrestricted and exchange rates are allowed to adjust freely, exchange rates between two currencies should adjust in the long run to reflect the price level differences in the two countries. For example, if a given basket of traded commodities costs $1,000 in the United States and 2,000 marks in Germany, the long-run equilibrium exchange rate between the United States and Germany should be $0.50 per mark.

11. An increase in the demand for marks will cause the exchange rate to increase. If the equilibrium rate now exceeds its upper limit of $0.57, the Fed will have to sell marks at the rate of $0.57 to maintain the exchange rate. An increase in the demand for dollars will cause the exchange rate to decrease. If the equilibrium rate falls below its lower limit of $0.53, the German central bank will have to sell dollars at the $0.53 rate to maintain the exchange rate.

12. If the equilibrium exchange rate continually remains above the pegged rate, the central bank is likely to run out of foreign exchange reserves to sell in order to maintain the pegged rate. There are several ways to eliminate the disequilibrium at the pegged rate: (1) the pegged exchange rate can be increased (a devaluation of the domestic currency); (2) the government can impose restrictions on imports or capital outflows in order to reduce demand for foreign exchange directly; or (3) the government can adopt contractionary fiscal or monetary policies in order to reduce domestic income, interest rates, or inflation and indirectly reduce the demand for foreign exchange.

13. The Bretton Woods Agreement established a reserve currency standard by which the U.S. dollar was defined in terms of gold, and all other currencies were defined in terms of the dollar. Exchange rates were fixed, and both gold and dollars served as international reserves. Central banks of other countries could turn in dollars to the United States in exchange for gold. Inflation in the United States in the 1960s induced other countries to try to turn more dollars in for gold. The dollar became overvalued and, as confidence in the dollar fell, so did the exchange rate system.

14. Deficit countries had to meet the deficit with official reserves. Eventually, the reserves would run out. Surplus countries were receiving reserves and could do so forever.

15. The deficit would be financed by gold. The country's money supply is determined by the supply of gold in the country, so an outflow of gold would mean the money supply would decrease, which would cause the price level to fall.

CHAPTER 34

Developing and Transitional Economies

I. INTRODUCTION

This chapter discusses the economic situation of the majority of the world's population. The majority of people are poor and live in less-developed countries. The chapter contrasts the characteristics of developing and developed countries and discusses some causes of the problems of the developing countries. In the last section, the transitions currently going on in countries that used central planning to organize production is discussed. The material in this chapter is more descriptive than analytical.

II. OUTLINE

1. Worlds Apart

    1.1 Developing and Industrial Economies
        a. *Developing countries* are those with high rates of illiteracy, unemployment, and population growth, and exports consisting of agricultural products and raw materials.
        b. Developing countries tend to be rural and the people tend to be very poor.
        c. The World Bank divides countries that report income data into three major groups: low-income economies, middle-income economies, and high-income economies.
        d. Another group of countries does not provide data to the World Bank. Most of these are the socialist countries such as Cuba and North Korea.
        e. The World Bank uses GNP per capita to classify countries as low-income economies, middle-income economies, and high-income economies.

    1.2 Health and Nutrition
        a. Life expectancy is lower in developing countries.
        b. Infant mortality rates are much higher in the developing countries than in the developed countries.
        c. People in the poorest countries tend to have insufficient food to maintain good health; they consume half the calories of those in high-income countries.
        d. The population per physician is about 12 times greater in low-income nations than in high-income nations.

    1.3 High Birth Rates
        a. Birth rates are much greater in developing countries than in developed countries.
        b. Aid from developed nations has often come in the form of medical assistance, which has increased life expectancy and added to the growing populations.

    1.4 Women in Developing Countries. Poverty is greater among women than among men.

2.   Productivity: Key to Development

    2.1   Low Labor Productivity
        a.   Labor productivity is lower in developing countries because there is less physical and human capital to combine with labor.
        b.   Capital formation requires saving, but savings tend to be low because people are so poor.

    2.2   Technology and Education
        a.   Education tends to be linked to economic growth.
        b.   Literacy rates remain low in most developing countries, and only 1 percent of those aged 20 to 24 are enrolled in postsecondary education in low-income countries.

    2.3   Inefficient Use of Labor
        a.   Unemployment, especially in urban areas, tends to be high in developing countries. Underemployment tends to be high in rural areas.
        b.   Agricultural productivity is low because of the large number of farmers relative to the amount of land farmed and a lack of other inputs such as capital and fertilizer.
        c.   Low productivity results in low incomes, but low incomes also result in lower productivity.

    2.4   Natural Resources. Some developing countries are hampered by a lack of natural resources.

    2.5   Financial Institutions. A good financial system is needed as a source of investment funds for development. Banks in many developing countries do not function well as financial intermediaries.

    2.6   Capital Infrastructure. Many developing countries have severe deficiencies in their infrastructure of transportation and communication networks.

    2.7   Entrepreneurial Ability. A country needs entrepreneurs to bring together the resources and take the risks of starting new enterprises. The colonial system offered local populations little opportunity to develop entrepreneurial skills.

    2.8   Government Monopolies. Government monopolies often hinder development.

    2.9   *CASE STUDY*: Crony Capitalism in Indonesia—All in the Family

3.   International Trade and Development. Developing countries need to trade with developed countries in order to obtain capital and technology. Developing countries export mainly primary products.

    3.1   Import Substitution versus Export Promotion
        a.   An *import substitution* policy protects domestic industries by restricting imports.
        b.   *Export promotion* is a strategy that concentrates on developing export markets.
        c.   Export promotion has been a more successful strategy than import substitution.

    3.2   Migration and the Brain Drain
        a.   Migration can provide a safety valve on population growth.
        b.   Often the ones who migrate are the educated and skilled.

3.3   Trade Liberalization and Special Interests
- a.   Free trade harms some special interests in developing countries.
- b.   Governments that cater to special interests tend to generate low rates of economic growth.

4.   Foreign Aid and Economic Development

4.1   Foreign Aid
- a.   *Foreign aid* is an international transfer on concessional terms made for the purpose of promoting economic development.
- b.   Several international agencies exist to provide multilateral assistance to developing countries.

4.2   Does Foreign Aid Promote Economic Development?
- a.   It is unclear whether foreign aid supplements or substitutes for domestic saving.
- b.   A donor's motives may often be geopolitical or commercial rather than humanitarian.

5.   Transitional Economies. The attempt to replace central planning with markets in once socialist economies is a tremendous economic experiment.

5.1   Types of Economic Systems
- a.   Economic systems can be classified based on the ownership of resources, the way resources are allocated, and the incentive structure.
- b.   In capitalist systems, resources are owned by individuals and allocated through markets.
- c.   In socialist economies, resources (except labor) are owned by the state.

5.2   Enterprises and Soft Budget Constraints
- a.   Enterprises that earned a "profit" had the profit taken by the state; those that experienced losses received a subsidy to cover the loss.
- b.   Shortages in many products developed because the planning system was often inefficient.

5.3   *CASE STUDY:* Ownership and Resource Use

6.   Markets and Institutions. Institutions are the incentives and constraints that structure political, economic, and social interaction. A reliable system of property rights and enforceable contracts are necessary for creating incentives that support a healthy market economy.

6.1   Institutions and Economic Development
- a.   Political decisions can change the formal rules of society, but the informal constraints are more difficult to change.
- b.   Centrally planned economies often experience widespread corruption.
- c.   The exchange relation is impersonal in market economies but more personal in centrally planned economies.

6.2   The Big Bang versus Gradualism
- a.   Some economists advocate a gradual approach to the transformation to a market economy.
- b.   A big bang approach depends on a very short transition.
- c.   China is experimenting with gradualism in transforming parts of its economy.

6.3   Privatization
   a.   *Privatization* is the turning of public enterprises into private enterprises.
   b.   Privatization requires the development of modern accounting and other information systems.

6.4   Transparent Finances
   a.   Prospective buyers of enterprises need reliable information about the enterprise's finances.
   b.   A firm's finances should be transparent so that someone looking at the accounting books can tell what is going on.

6.5   Institutional Requirements of Efficient Markets
   a.   To shift from central planning to markets requires the development of supporting institutions.
   b.   No one really understands the institutional requirements of efficient markets.

III. DISCUSSION

Worlds Apart

Standards of living vary widely across countries. The World Bank divides countries into three major groups: low-income economies, middle-income economies, and high-income economies.

The text discusses several societal characteristics that reflect differences in development among countries. These include health and nutrition, birth rates, and the role of women. The distribution of income is shown to be more skewed in most developing countries than in the developed economies.

Productivity: Key to Development

One reason that standards of living tend to be low in developing countries is that labor productivity tends to be low as a result of the lack of physical and human capital for labor to work with. Developing countries are also characterized by low levels of education, poor use of labor, a lack of well-developed financial markets and infrastructure, low savings rates, and other obstacles to development. Make sure you are familiar with the factors that contribute to the level of productivity in developing countries.

International Trade and Development

Developing countries need to trade with developed countries in order to acquire capital goods and technology. Developing countries trade mainly primary products. Prices of primary products tend to fluctuate, and developing countries have a hard time generating foreign exchange to buy capital goods. Special interests in developing counties are often able to get protection from foreign competition; this makes the country worse off as a whole.

Foreign Aid and Economic Development

Developing countries must often rely on foreign capital to finance the investment needed to en-courage economic growth. Several international agencies and institutions exist to provide the capital. The World Bank provides loans to support activities that are viewed as prerequisites for development. Some countries do not qualify for loans from the World Bank because they are perceived as poor credit risks. The International Development Association was formed to provide financing for poor credit risks. The International Finance Corporation makes loans directly to private enterprises in developing nations instead of to governments. It is unclear whether foreign aid fosters development. A stable political climate with well-defined property rights and a good system of education appear to be the important prerequisites for development.

Transitional Economies

Capitalism refers to the private ownership of all resources and *socialism* to the state ownership of all resources except labor. All societies must find ways to coordinate the economic activities of their members. Under capitalism, coordination is achieved by individuals' responding to market forces and trying to maximize utility or profits. Under planned socialism, coordination is achieved by bureaucratic control. Central planners determine what is to be produced, and other planners determine how it is to be produced. To some extent, the distribution of the output is determined by individual choice.

Enterprises had soft budget constraints. An enterprise that generated a residual ("profit") found that the central government took it. Enterprises that generated losses received subsidies. Under such a system, plant managers had little incentive to be efficient.

Markets and Institutions

Societies develop institutions that support their political and economic arrangements. A market economy requires property rights, contract law, and other institutions that are often taken for granted in capitalist countries. Political decisions can introduce some of these formal institutions, but many informal constraints still exist that may be incompatible with a market economy. No unified and generally accepted theory of the formation of institutions has been developed, so it is difficult for anyone to advise the Russian government with confidence. Economists will have the opportunity to learn a lot from the attempts of the countries shifting from central planning to markets.

IV. LAGNIAPPE

The Economics of Being Poor

Theodore W. Schultz, in his Nobel lecture, discussed the general results of research on economic development he and others conducted over the course of 40 years. He concluded that the poor are just as concerned about improving their position as other people are, but that wealthier people have a difficult time understanding the choices the poor make. Schultz argues that economists have made two errors in their approach to the problems of economic development. The first error is to assume that standard economic analysis does not apply to poor countries. The second error, Schultz argues, is that economists tend to neglect economic history. Since all developed nations were developing nations at one time, an understanding of the way developed nations actually developed can help our understanding of the problems faced by developing nations today.

Schultz also argued that land is often overrated and the quality of human beings is underrated in assessing the prospects of poor nations. Japan has poor land and yet is highly developed, whereas India has good land and is poor. Schultz pointed out that labor productivity can increase when the population becomes healthier and better educated. Further, he argued that the policies of many developing nations encourage industrialization, which encourages migration to urban areas and neglects the agricultural sector. The result is reduced agricultural production, which makes it more difficult to feed the population. He urged an approach that does not distort the incentives that farmers have to grow more food. (See Theodore W. Schultz, "The Economics of Being Poor," *Journal of Political Economy* 88, August 1979: 639–651.)

Question to Think About: What effect would longer life expectancies have on decisions concerning the number of years spent in obtaining an education?

What Is the Optimal Speed of Adjustment?

There is a great deal of uncertainty about the optimal speed of adjustment to a market economy. Alfred Kahn was head of the U.S. Civil Aeronautics Board when the government deregulated the airlines. Initially, Kahn favored a policy of gradualism, but later he changed his views and advocated a very short transition. The main reason for his change in views was that the long transition created some perverse incentives that made the adjustment more difficult. Does this imply that Russia and other formerly socialist countries should aim for a rapid transition? Not necessarily. There are many important differences between deregulating one industry and deregulating an entire economy. One important difference is that the institutions associated with capitalism were in place in the United States and the deregulation only involved one segment of the economy. Just because a rapid transition involving one industry in the United States is optimal does not imply that a rapid transition to a market economy is optimal for an entire economy.

Question to Think About: Would a gradual transition to a market economy likely create perverse incentives that would make the transition more difficult?

V.　KEY TERMS

Developing countries
Industrial market countries
Import substitution
Export promotion
Foreign aid

Soft budget constraint
Gradualism
Big bang theory
Privatization
Transparent finances

VI. QUESTIONS

A. Completion

1. France is an example of an _____ nation, and Peru is an example of a _____ nation.

2. _____ are countries with high rates of illiteracy, rapid population growth, and primarily agricultural production.

3. The _____ is an economic development institution affiliated with the United Nations.

4. Countries with low life expectancies usually also have high _____ rates.

5. _____ is a primary or contributing factor in the majority of deaths among children under the age of five in low-income countries.

6. The number of _____ in a country is used as a measure of the availability of health care.

7. _____ are lower when women have better employment opportunities.

8. Poor nutrition may generate low labor _____, resulting in low income.

9. Other resources may be used inefficiently if _____ is insufficient.

10. Constraints that structure economic interactions such as property rights are _____.

11. The imposition of tariffs to insulate domestic industries is part of a policy of _____.

12. An international transfer made on concessional terms to promote economic development is called _____.

13. Under market coordination, transactions occur because each party expects to benefit, so exchange is _____.

14. The idea that a firm's financial records should clearly indicate the economic health of the company is called _____.

15. The process of turning public enterprises into private enterprises is called _____.

B. True/False

_____ 1. Differences in the level of economic development are greater among developing countries than among developed industrial countries.

_____ 2. The gross national product of the United States is greater than the combined gross national products of all developing countries.

_____ 3. Per capita GNP figures for developing countries tend to overstate the quantity of goods and services consumed by citizens in the country.

_____ 4. More than half the population of most developing countries is employed in agriculture.

_____ 5. Countries with high life expectancy rates tend to have low infant mortality rates.

_____ 6. Developing countries have significantly higher birth rates than developed countries.

_____ 7. Poverty is greater among men than women in most developing countries.

_____ 8. In developing countries, income is low, so saving tends to be low and thus investment is low.

_____ 9. Low income and low productivity reinforce each other.

_____ 10. Some development economists believe that the single most important ingredient in economic development is the political organization of a country and the administrative competence of its government.

_____ 11. A country's institutions can be an obstacle to development.

_____ 12. Primary products make up the bulk of developing countries' imports.

_____ 13. Import substitution helps a country by capitalizing on comparative advantage.

_____ 14. An export promotion strategy forces firms in developing countries to be more efficient because they are in competition with firms in other countries.

_____ 15. Many developing countries have a shortage of entrepreneurs.

_____ 16. The prices of the primary goods produced by developing nations tend to fluctuate more than the prices of the manufactured goods produced by the industrialized nations.

_____ 17. The law of demand does not apply in a centrally planned economy.

_____ 18. The soft budget constraint faced by enterprises permitted directors to be inefficient, because a state subsidy would always be available to bail them out of trouble.

_____ 19. People in the Soviet Union tended to treat public property with more care than Americans do.

_____ 20. The accounting systems of socialist firms are valueless in a market economy.

C. *Multiple Choice*

1. Which of these developed countries were developing countries at one time?
    a. Japan
    b. Germany
    c. United States
    d. Canada
    e. all of the above

2. Developing countries tend to be characterized by all of the following except
    a. low unemployment.
    b. high rates of illiteracy.
    c. rapid population growth.
    d. exports consisting mainly of agricultural and primary products.
    e. low farm productivity.

3. Which of the following is a new industrialized country?
    a. Canada
    b. France
    c. South Korea
    d. India
    e. all of the above

4. Infant mortality rates are
    a. slightly higher in the less-developed countries than in the industrial countries.
    b. significantly higher in the developing countries than in the industrial countries.
    c. higher in the industrial countries than in the developing countries because of pollution.
    d. lower in countries with lower life expectancies.
    e. none of the above

5. Families tend to be larger in developing countries because
    a. government policies are designed to encourage high birth rates.
    b. international aid has made medical care a low priority.
    c. infant mortality rates are low.
    d. children are a source of labor on farms.
    e. a and b

6. Fertility rates decline when
    a. infant mortality rates increase.
    b. health care availability increases.
    c. employment opportunities for women get better.
    d. income falls.
    e. none of the above

7. Which of the following is a true statement about developing countries?
   a. Poverty is greater among women even though women are better educated.
   b. Women have fewer opportunities for employment than men in rural areas but not in urban areas.
   c. Poverty is greater among women, and women have fewer educational opportunities.
   d. Women are not covered by minimum wage laws whereas men are.
   e. b, c, and d only

8. Women in developing countries tend to
   a. work more outside of the home than women in developed countries.
   b. be better educated relative to men than women in developed countries.
   c. head up fewer households than women in developed countries.
   d. have more employment opportunities than men.
   e. none of the above

9. Labor productivity tends to be lower in developing countries because
   a. there is less capital for labor to work with than in industrial nations.
   b. technological breakthroughs tend to occur in developed nations.
   c. education levels are lower than in developed countries.
   d. all of the above
   e. a and c

10. More educational achievement benefits developing countries by
    a. increasing the productivity of labor.
    b. increasing the productivity of other resources.
    c. making people more receptive to new ideas and technology.
    d. increasing productivity of farmers in the economy.
    e. all of the above.

11. Poverty can result in
    a. low saving.
    b. low capital formation.
    c. malnutrition.
    d. low productivity.
    e. all of the above.

12. To have a sound market economy, a country needs
    a. a reliable system of property rights.
    b. a highly educated labor force.
    c. extensive government involvement in the economy.
    d. protection from foreign competition.
    e. all of the above.

13. Developing countries need foreign exchange to import capital and technology, and the foreign exchange is obtained by
    a. producing exports.
    b. receiving foreign aid.
    c. soliciting private investment from abroad.
    d. all of the above.
    e. a and b only.

14. One advantage to a developing country of an import substitution policy is that
    a. it reduces competition faced by domestic firms.
    b. it requires less bureaucratic intrusion.
    c. demand already exists for the products protected by the tariffs.
    d. all of the above
    e. a and b only

15. Which of the following countries has relied primarily on an export promotion strategy?
    a. Argentina
    b. Peru
    c. India
    d. Hong Kong
    e. Somalia

16. The governments of developing countries often hinder development by
    a. failing to obtain foreign aid.
    b. creating state enterprises and granting them monopoly status.
    c. relying too much on private entrepreneurs to develop new industry.
    d. keeping taxes too low.
    e. all of the above.

17. Which of the following is an example of foreign aid?
    a. a grant that never has to be repaid
    b. a loan at market interest rates
    c. a shipment of wheat
    d. concessional loans
    e. all of the above except b

18. A problem with foreign aid is that
    a. it comes from international agencies rather than the United States.
    b. loans are not made to countries that are credit risks.
    c. it focuses too much on education and agriculture and not enough on manufacturing.
    d. there is no attempt to promote self-sufficiency.
    e. it sometimes distorts domestic prices and discourages domestic agriculture.

19. One problem facing Russia in its attempt at privatization is that
    a. people prefer enterprises that are publicly owned.
    b. many of the enterprises have been so inefficient no one wants to buy them.
    c. falling prices make investing in the firms unattractive.
    d. the government is unwilling to sell the most important enterprises.
    e. all of the above

20. Russia's move to a market economy has been hampered by
    a. the lack of some institutions needed in a capitalist economy.
    b. a constitution that prevents privatization in key industries.
    c. a refusal by Russian leaders to follow well-known paths of institutional development.
    d. all of the above.
    e. a and c only.

D. Discussion Questions

1. What are some characteristics of developing countries?

2. What problems arise when trying to compare per capita GNP figures across countries?

3. The text describes several characteristics of developing countries. Discuss how these characteristics are interrelated.

4. What factors can reduce fertility rates?

5. The text says that improved health does little to avert poverty. Why not?

6. What factors contribute to low labor productivity in the developing countries?

7. How are education and development related?

8. How are institutions and development related?

9. How can international trade help a developing country?

10. What obstacles may prevent international trade from being a source of economic growth?

11. Why do economists tend to favor export promotion policies rather than import substitution policies?

12. The text cited a number of factors that contribute to the productivity and growth of a developing country. Which of these factors can be enhanced by foreign aid? What are some of the reasons that foreign aid might not foster development?

13. Why might you expect market coordination to be more efficient than bureaucratic coordination?

14. Why might the Soviet people take better care of their personal property than people in capitalist countries?

15. What is privatization? How effective has privatization been in Russia?

16. Discuss the role of institutions in a market system. Should Russia pursue a fast transition or should it pursue gradualism?

VII. ANSWERS

A. Completion

1. industrial market; developing
2. Developing countries
3. World Bank
4. infant mortality (birth rates is also an answer here)
5. Malnutrition
6. physicians
7. Fertility (or birth) rates
8, productivity
9. knowledge
10. institutions
11. import substitution
12. foreign aid
13, voluntary
14. transparent finances
15. privatization

B. True/False

1. True
2. True
3. False. Per capita GNP figures tend to understate consumption.
4. True
5. True
6. True
7. False
8. True
9. True
10. True
11. True
12. False
13. False
14. True
15. True
16. True
17. False
18. True
19. False
20. True

C. Multiple Choice

1. e
2. a
3. c
4. b
5. d
6. c
7. c
8. e
9. d
10. e
11. e
12. a
13. d
14. c
15. d
16. b
17. e
18. e
19. b
20. a

D. Discussion Questions

1. Developing countries are characterized by high illiteracy rates, high unemployment, high infant mortality rates, poor nutrition, short life expectancy, few physicians per capita, high birth rates, and a heavy reliance on agriculture.

2. Countries use different national income accounting procedures, exchange rates are often inappropriate, and the proportion of output sold on markets varies across countries.

3. Several of the characteristics of developing countries are interrelated. The high infant mortality rates and the short life expectancy rates are obviously related. Malnutrition is related to both because it makes people more susceptible to disease. All of these also lower the productivity of labor in a country, which contributes to low income and thus to low savings and investment.

4. Fertility rates tend to fall as incomes rise, as education levels of women increase, and as employment opportunities for women increase.

5. Better health generates longer life spans, which increase the size of the population and the stress on resources. There is usually a lag before it also reduces fertility rates.

6. Productivity is low because labor does not have much capital to work with and the quality of the existing capital is poor. Education levels tend to be low, which makes it difficult for industry to take advantage of technological change. The labor force tends to be under-utilized, which also reduces productivity.

7. Increased education levels in a country improve the efficiency with which all resources, including labor, are used. Education also makes people more receptive to new ideas and technology, which helps stimulate economic growth.

8. Institutions affect the incentives people have to invest and to produce. A reliable system of property rights can aid development. Some institutions may hinder development. For example, restrictions on the activities women can participate in may reduce output.

9. Trade can help a country develop by providing foreign exchange to purchase capital, a market for products produced by the country, an opportunity for technology transfer that will increase labor productivity, and competition to force greater efficiencies in the economy.

10. It is possible that international trade will not be a source of economic growth. First, developing countries tend to export primary products, whose prices fluctuate more widely than the prices of manufactured goods. Therefore, exports may not provide a stable source of foreign exchange. Second, many industrial countries impose trade restrictions that hinder trade in primary products. Finally, government policies within the developing countries themselves sometimes obstruct exports.

11. Import substitution policies tend to reduce welfare, retard efficiency, and prevent gains from trade. Export promotion policies do not close markets to trade and rely on the discipline of markets to encourage firms to be efficient. Firms are more likely to adopt new technology when they face competition from other firms. Finally, the evidence suggests that export promotion has been more effective in encouraging development than has import substitution.

12. Foreign aid can help a developing country develop its natural resources. It can also help provide technological know-how and the capital necessary to build the infrastructure that will contribute to growth. Foreign aid will not foster development if it simply substitutes for domestic saving, thus increasing consumption rather than investment. Further, much foreign aid is motivated by geopolitical and commercial concerns or is ill-conceived, so it leads to a misallocation of the country's resources. Finally, development aid often insulates the country's leaders from the consequences of the country's problems, thus reducing incentives to implement appropriate government policies.

13. Market coordination relies on voluntary exchange, in which all participants are seeking their own best deal. Consequently, they have the incentive to produce efficiently. Under bureaucratic control, the people making the decisions often do not have all the information they need and also lack the incentive to act in an efficient way.

14. Since durable goods were hard to obtain and expensive, and since repair parts were also hard to obtain, the Soviet people had incentives to take very good care of the durable goods they did buy.

15. Privatization is the transfer of enterprises owned by the government to private owners. So far, the efforts at privatization in Russia have met with limited success. Many of the formerly publicly owned plants had been very inefficient, which did not make them desirable purchases by private citizens. The overall state of the economy has also hampered the transition to a privately owned system.

16. A market economy requires certain institutions to be able to function. For example, a legal system that recognizes and enforces contracts and a system of private property rights are usually associated with market economies. The planned socialism that existed for decades in the Soviet Union did not rely on these institutions, so they did not exist when the government changed and the policies changed. The transition has been a difficult one. Whether you believe the transition should be rapid or not is up to you, but you should be able to support your point of view by reference to the issues raised in the latter portions of the chapter.